D0605174

Oxford University Press

Oxford   New York
Athens Auckland Bangkok Bogotá Buenos Aires Calcutta
Cape Town Chennai Dar es Salaam Delhi Florence Hong Kong Istanbul
Karachi Kuala Lumpur Madrid Melbourne Mexico City Mumbai
Nairobi Paris São Paulo Singapore Taipei Tokyo Toronto Warsaw

and associated companies in
Berlin Ibadan

Published by Oxford University Press, Inc.
198 Madison Avenue, New York, New York 10016
http://www.oup-usa.org

Library of Congress Cataloging-in-Publication Data

Huang, Han-Way
   Using the MCS-51 microcontroller / by Han-Way Huang.
      p.   cm.
   Includes bibliographical references.
   ISBN-13 978-0-19-512513-9
   ISBN 0-19-512513-4 (cloth)
      1. Programmable controllers.   2. Intel microprocessors.   I. Title.
TJ233.P76 H83   1999
629.8'95416—dc21   99-35427
                                                                  CIP

Printing (last digit) 9 8 7 6 5

Printed in the United States of America
on acid-free paper

To my wife Su-Jane and my sons Craig and Derek

CONTENTS

Chapter 7   Timer Function   261

PREFACE

Using the MCS-51 Microcontroller is a textbook intended to be used for an introductory course on microprocessors or microcontrollers. It can be used in a one-semester course or a two-quarter sequence on microprocessors. The prerequisite for this course includes basic logic design and some experience programming in any language. Since the book includes extensive program and interfacing examples, it should also be suitable for practicing engineers who want to learn the MCS-51 microcontroller. The book starts with the programming model and memory organization of the MCS-51 family microcontrollers. It then progresses into the details of the MCS-51 instruction set and the techniques on assembly programming. After these, all the peripheral I/O functions and subsystems are covered in depth. Specific peripheral I/O functions are discussed in terms of the fundamental concept and then the design techniques. Many examples are used in exploring the applications and design alternatives.

This book covers most of the I/O functions available in an 8-bit microcontroller:

- Parallel I/O ports. The concepts of I/O synchronization, I/O addressing, and I/O pin latch structure are presented. Interfacing examples include DIP switches, LEDs, seven-segment displays, LCDs, keypads, D/A converters, centronic printers, and the Intel parallel interface chip i8255.

- Timer functions. The operation modes of Timer 0, 1, and 2 and the programmable counter array (PCA) are illustrated. Applications including the creation of time delay, the measurement of pulse width, period, frequency, phase difference, and duty cycle, the generation of digital waveform, pulse width modulation, and the control of stepper motors and DC motors are covered.

- Serial communication port. The EIA-232-E standard is presented in addition to the serial communication port. Applications that interface with Xicor serial SRAM, EIA-232 serial port, and null modem connection are provided.

- A/D converter. The method of A/D conversion and voltage shifting and scaling are presented. The 8-bit A/D converter in the 87C51GB microcontroller is discussed. Applications in the measurement of barometric pressure, temperature, and humidity are detailed.

- Serial expansion port (SEP). The principle of a serial expansion port is presented. Numerous examples of using the SEP to interface with I/O devices are covered.

Chapter 1 discusses basic computer concepts, semiconductor memory technologies, the MCS-51 memory organization, addressing modes, a sample of MCS-51 instructions, and the procedure for disassembling machine instruction into assembly instructions.

Chapter 2 provides an introduction to assembly language programming for the MCS-51 microcontrollers. It starts with a discussion of assembler directives. Instructions are presented by categories along with their applications. Numerous examples are provided to demonstrate the implementation of multiprecision arithmetic, program loops, multiway branch, and time delay creation. An overview of software development tools and hardware evaluation boards is provided at the end of the chapter. The software tools and evaluation board marketed by Keil Software are chosen to develop and test the programs and perform experiments for this book. The MCB520 evaluation board from Keil Software is moderately priced and the demo versions of software tools are easy to use.

Chapter 3 presents advanced techniques in assembly programming. Issues in subroutine calls are explored. Stacks, strings, arrays, and matrices processing techniques are illustrated in many examples.

Chapter 4 introduces the concept of system bus, read and write bus cycles, and timing diagrams. It then discusses the issues involved in memory system design: memory space assignments, address decoder design, and timing verification. Examples are used to verify all the timing requirements in an MCS-51-based memory system.

Chapter 5 introduces the concepts of interrupt, interrupt processing, interrupt vectors, and interrupt service routine. It then details the interrupt structure of the MCS-51. A few examples are used to demonstrate the interrupt programming.

Chapter 6 introduces the concepts of I/O addressing, I/O synchronization, and peripheral chips. DIP switches and keypads are used to illustrate interfacing with input devices. Key bouncing problem is discussed in detail and alternatives to solve the problem are explored. LEDs, seven-segment displays, LCDs, and D/A converters are used to illustrate the interfacing with output devices. Centronics printer interface is presented and the output handshake process is illustrated in this example.

Chapter 7 discusses timer functions including Timer 0, Timer 1, Timer 2, and the programmable counter array (PCA). Examples are provided to illustrate how to use these functions to create time delays and digital waveforms, how to measure pulse width, frequency, period, duty cycle, and phase shift. The mechanism of a watchdog timer, a special function of timer system, is explained and its application in detecting system failure is also illustrated. This chapter also includes extensive hardware interfacing and programming examples to the stepper motors and DC motors.

Chapter 8 is about analog-to-digital (A/D) converters. Microcontrollers have been used in data acquisition extensively. The key components to this application include transducers and A/D converters. The transducer converts the nonelectric quantity into electric volt. The A/D converter then does the A/D conversion so that the microcontroller can perform further processing. Examples on barometric pressure, humidity, and temperature measurements are illustrated.

Chapter 9 introduces the EIA-232-E interface standard. The EIA-232-E standard has been used in asynchronous serial data communication since 1960s. All computers have included one or more serial communication ports that conform to this interface standard. Application examples on interfacing with Xicor serial memory chip X24C44 and serial port I/O programming are included.

Chapter 10 deals with the greatest limitation of 8-bit microcontrollers—limited I/O pins. The Intel serial expansion port (SEP) is introduced in this chapter. Using the SEP, the 8XC51GB and 8XC1452JX series microcontrollers can interface to many peripheral chips with serial interface. Examples have been included to illustrate the use of SEP to interface with the MC14489 seven-segment driver chip, shift registers (74HC589 and 74HC595) with serial interface, the Xicor X24165 SRAM, AD7303 serial D/A converter, and ADC1303 A/D converter.

Numerous exercise problems are included at the end of each chapter. Laboratory projects, assignments, and exercises are also provided in eight chapters. These materials are very important to the learning of the MCS-51 microcontrollers. You will learn the MCS-51 microcontroller only after working through many of these exercises and projects.

The evaluation board is the key to learning microcontroller hardware. Based on its functionality, moderate price, and the user-friendliness of its software and documentation, I have chosen the MCB520 marketed by Keil Software. The MCB520 evaluation board has neither the PCA nor the A/D converter. These functions are available in the Intel 87C51FX target board or the HTE SBC552 evaluation board. The evaluation software included in this text also works with most of these boards.

A tutorial is included in Chapter 2 on how to use the Keil evaluation software to debug programs on the MCB520 evaluation board. Since the Dallas 87C520 microcontroller is used in the board, we also include the specifics of this microcontroller in appropriate chapters.

Acknowledgments

This book would not have been possible without the help of a number of people. I would like to thank my colleagues at the Department of Electrical Engineering and Electronic Engineering Technology at Minnesota State University, Mankato, for their support. I would like to thank my electronic engineering technology students who let me test the manuscript and provided useful feedback. Many thanks to my editor Peter Gordon and his assistant Jasmine Urmeneta for their enthusiastic support during the preparation of this book. I also appreciate the outstanding work of the production staff at Oxford University Press. I would also like to express my thanks for the many useful comments and suggestions of my colleagues who reviewed this text during the course of its development, especially Wayne Loucks, University of Waterloo, Canada; Albert O. Richardson, California State University at Chico; and Oleg Bouianov, Espoo-Vantaa Institute of Technology, Finland. Finally, I am grateful to my wife, Su-Jane, and my sons, Craig and Derek, for their encouragement and support during the entire preparation of this book.

Han-Way Huang

1

INTRODUCTION TO
THE INTEL MCS-51

1.1 OBJECTIVES

After you have completed this chapter, you should be able to

- define or explain the following terms: computer, processor, microprocessor, microcomputer, microcontroller, hardware, software, cross assembler, cross compiler, RAM, SRAM, DRAM, ROM, EPROM, EEPROM, byte, nibble, bus, KB, MB, mnemonic, opcode, and operand
- explain the memory organization of the MCS-51 microcontroller
- explain the differences among the register inherent, direct, immediate, indirect, indexed, relative, absolute, long, bit inherent, and bit direct addressing modes
- disassemble machine code into mnemonic assembly language instructions
- explain the Intel MCS-51 instruction execution cycles
- find out MCS-51 instruction execution time

1.2 WHAT IS A COMPUTER?

A computer is made up of hardware and software. The computer hardware consists of four main components: (1) a processor, which serves as the computer's "brain," (2) an input unit, through which programs and data can be entered into the computer, (3) an output unit, from which the results of computation can be displayed or viewed, and (4) memory, in which the computer software programs and data are stored. Figure 1.1 shows a simple block diagram of a computer. The processor communicates with memory and input/output devices through a set of signal lines referred to as a *bus*. The common bus actually consists of three buses: a *data* bus, an *address* bus, and a *control* bus.

1.2.1 The Processor

The processor, which is also called the central processing unit (CPU), can be further divided into two major parts:

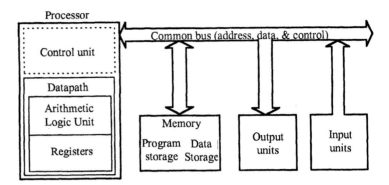

Figure 1.1 Computer organization.

Datapath. The datapath consists of a *register file* and an *arithmetic logic unit*. The register file consists of one or more registers. A register is a storage location in the CPU. It is used to hold data and/or a memory address during execution of an instruction. Because of its small size and closeness to the arithmetic logic unit, access to data in registers is much faster than access to data in memory. Registers play an essential role in the efficient execution of programs. The number of registers varies greatly from computer to computer. The arithmetic logic unit (ALU) is the computer's numerical calculator and logical operation evaluator. The ALU receives data from main memory and/or registers, performs a computation, and, if necessary, writes the result back to main memory or registers.

Control unit. The control unit contains the hardware instruction logic. It decodes and monitors the execution of instructions and also acts as an arbiter as various portions of the computer system compete for the resources of the CPU. The system clock synchronizes the activities of the CPU. All CPU activities are measured by clock cycles. The clock rates of modern microprocessors can be as high as several hundred MHz, where

$$1 \text{ MHz } = 1 \text{ million ticks (or cycles) per second}$$

(for example, the Alpha 21164 microprocessor from DEC runs at 500 MHz and higher). The period of a 1-MHz clock signal is 1 μs (10^{-6}s). The control unit also maintains a register called the *program counter* (PC), which controls the memory address of the next instruction to be executed. During the execution of an instruction, the presence of overflow, an addition carry, a subtraction borrow, and so forth, is flagged by the system and stored in another register called a *status register*. The resultant flags are then used by programmers for program control and decision making.

What Is a Microprocessor?

The processor in a very large computer is built from a number of integrated circuits. A *microprocessor* is a processor fabricated in a single integrated circuit. A *microcomputer* is a computer that uses a microprocessor as its CPU. Early microcomputers were quite simple and slow. However, many of today's desktop microcomputers have become very sophisticated and are even faster than many large computers only a few years ago.

Microprocessors come in 4-bit, 8-bit, 16-bit, 32-bit, and 64-bit models. The number of bits refers to the number of binary digits that the microprocessor can manipulate in one operation. A 4-bit microprocessor, for example, is capable of manipulating 4 bits of information in one operation. Four-bit microprocessors are used for the electric controls of relatively simple machines. Some pocket calculators, for example, contain 4-bit microprocessors.

Many 32-bit and 64-bit microprocessors also contain on-chip memory to enhance performance. Because microprocessors and input/output devices have different characteristics and speeds, peripheral chips are required to interface input/output (I/O) devices with the microprocessor. For example, the integrated circuit Intel i8255 is often used to interface a parallel device such as a printer or seven-segment displays with the Intel 8-bit microprocessor MCS-85.

Microprocessors have been widely used since their invention. It is not an exaggeration to say that the invention of microprocessors has revolutionized the electronic industry. However, the following limitations of microprocessors led to the invention of microcontrollers:

- A microprocessor requires external memory to execute programs.
- A microprocessor cannot directly interface with I/O devices. Peripheral chips are needed.
- Glue logic (such as address decoders and buffers) is needed to interconnect external memory and peripheral interface chips with the microprocessor.

Because of these limitations, a microprocessor-based design cannot be made as small as might be desired. The invention of microcontrollers not only eliminated most of these problems but also simplified the hardware design of microprocessor-based products.

What Is a Microcontroller?

A microcontroller is a computer implemented on a single very large-scale integration (VLSI) chip. A microcontroller contains everything a microprocessor contains and also one or more of the following components:

- memory
- timer
- analog-to-digital (A/D) converter
- digital-to-analog (D/A) converter
- direct memory access (DMA) controller
- parallel I/O interface (often called parallel port)
- serial I/O interface
- memory component interface circuitry

Introduced in 1980, the 8051 is the original member of the MCS-51 family and is the core for all MCS-51 devices. The MCS-51 microcontroller family has more than 50 members and the number is still increasing. Members in this family differ mainly in the amount of on-chip memories and I/O capabilities. The characteristics of different memory technologies will be discussed shortly. The features (shown in Figure 1.2) of the 8051 core are

- 8-bit CPU
- extensive Boolean processing (single bit logic) capabilities
- 64-KB program memory address space
- 64-KB data memory address space
- 4 KB of on-chip program memory
- 128 bytes of on-chip data random access memory
- 32 bidirectional and individually addressable I/O lines
- two 16-bit timers/counters
- full duplex universal asynchronous receiver transmitter (UART)
- six-source/five-vector interrupt structure with two priority levels
- on-chip clock oscillator

The 4-KB read-only memory (ROM) is used to hold the startup program that will be executed whenever the MCS-51 is powered up. The 128-byte internal static random access memory (SRAM) is used as storage space for temporary variables when a program is running. The block labeled as BUS CONTROL generates the control signals needed

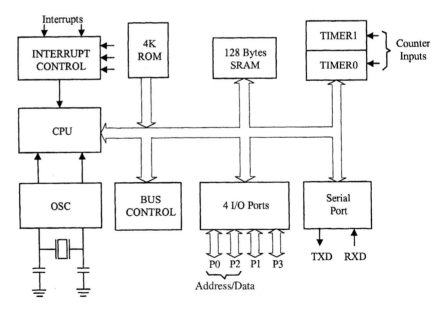

Figure 1.2 Block diagram of 8051 core.

when the CPU is performing external memory accesses. The four I/O ports allow us to interface I/O devices such as light-emitting diode (LED) display, keyboard, A/D converter, D/A converter, etc. Timer 0 and 1 allow us to create a time delay, and measure the period, frequency, and pulse width of an unknown signal. The serial port allows the MCS-51 to communicate with a PC. The block labeled as INTERRUPT CONTROL prioritizes the pending interrupts and enables the CPU to provide appropriate service for interrupts. The OSC block converts the sinusoidal waveform generated by the external crystal oscillator into a square waveform so that it can be used as the clock input for memory components (flip-flops, latches, registers, counters, etc.) in the microcontroller. The CPU block contains an ALU, a register file, a program counter, and a status register.

Applications of Microcontrollers

Since their introduction, microcontrollers have been used in every imaginable application. They are used as controllers of displays, printers, keyboards, modems, charge card phones, and home appliances such as refrigerators, washing machines, and microwave ovens. They are also used to control the operation of automobile engines and the operation of machines in factories. Today, most homes have one or more microcontroller-controlled appliances.

1.2.2 Memory

Memory is the place where software programs and data are stored. A computer may contain semiconductor, magnetic, and/or optical memory. Only semiconductor memory will be discussed in this chapter. The semiconductor memory can be further classified into two major types: *random access memory,* or RAM, and *read-only memory*, or ROM.

Random Access Memory

Random access memory is *volatile* in the sense that it cannot retain data in the absence of power. RAM is also called *read/write memory* because it allows the processor to read from and write into it. The microprocessor can temporarily store or write data into RAM, and later read those data back. Reading memory is nondestructive to the contents of the memory location. Writing memory is destructive. When the microprocessor writes data to memory, the old data are written over and destroyed.

There are two types of RAM technology: dynamic RAM (DRAM) and static RAM (SRAM). *Dynamic memories* are memory devices that require periodic refresh of the stored information. *Refresh* is the process of restoring binary data stored in a particular memory location. The dynamic RAM uses one transistor and one capacitor to store one bit of information. The information is stored in the capacitor in the form of electric charges. The charges stored in the capacitor will leak away over time, so periodic refresh operation is needed to maintain the contents in the DRAM. The time interval over which each memory location of a DRAM chip must be refreshed at least once in order to maintain its contents is called its *refresh period.* Refresh periods typically range from a few milliseconds to over a hundred milliseconds for today's high-density DRAMs.

Static memories are designed to store binary information without needing periodic refreshes and require the use of more complicated circuitry for each bit. Four to six transistors are needed to store one bit of information. As long as power is stable, the information stored in the SRAM will not be degraded.

RAM is mainly used to store *dynamic* programs or data. A computer user often wants to run different programs on the same computer, and these programs usually operate on different sets of data. The programs and data must therefore be loaded into RAM from the hard disk or other secondary storage, and for this reason they are called dynamic.

Read-Only Memory

ROM is nonvolatile. When power is removed from ROM and then reapplied, the original data will still be there. However, as its name implies, ROM data can only be read. If the processor attempts to write data to a ROM location, ROM will not accept the data, and the data in the addressed ROM memory location will not be changed.

Mask-programmed read-only memory (MROM) is a type of ROM that is programmed when it is manufactured. The semiconductor manufacturer places binary data in the memory according to the request of the customer. To be cost effective, many thousands of MROM memory units, each consisting of a copy of the same data (or program), must be sold. MROM is the major memory technology used to hold microcontroller application programs and constant data. Most people simply refer to MROM as ROM.

Programmable read-only memory (PROM) is a type of read-only memory that can be programmed in the field (often by the end user) using a device called PROM programmer or PROM "burner." PROM is also called one-time programmable ROM (OTP ROM) by some companies. Fused-based PROM technology is no longer popular today.

Erasable programmable read-only memory (EPROM) is a type of programmable read-only memory that can be erased by subjecting it to strong ultraviolet light. It can then be reprogrammed. A quartz window on top of the EPROM integrated circuit permits ultraviolet light to be shone directly on the silicon chip inside. Once the chip is programmed, the window can be covered with dark tape to prevent gradual erasure of the contents of an individual location. The EPROM is often used in prototype computers, where the software may be revised many times until it is perfected. The EPROM does not allow the erasure of the contents of an individual location. The only way to make change is to erase the entire EPROM chip and reprogram it. The EPROM can be manufactured without providing the window. This type of EPROM is one-time programmable only. Some members of the MCS-51 microcontroller family incorporate a small amount of EPROM as internal program memory.

Electrically erasable programmable read-only memory (EEPROM) is a type of non-volatile memory that can be erased by electrical signals and reprogrammed. EEPROM allows the user to selectively erase a single location, a row, or the whole chip. This feature requires a complicated programming circuitry. Because of this, the EEPROM cannot achieve the density of the EPROM technology. Intel does not use EEPROM in its MCS-51 microcontrollers.

Flash memory was invented to incorporate the advantages and avoid the drawbacks of EPROM and EEPROM technologies. The flash memory can be erased and reprogrammed in the system without using a dedicated programmer. It achieves the density of EPROM, but it does not require a window for erasure. Like EEPROM, flash memory can be programmed and erased electrically. However, it does not allow individual locations to be erased—the user can only erase the whole chip. Today, the monitor programs [also called basic I/O system (BIOS)] of many high-performance PCs are stored in flash memory. Many MCS-51 microcontroller variants use flash memory as their internal program memory.

Parallel and Serial Memory

A parallel memory has all the address pins needed for addressing each memory location and multiple data pins to carry all the information contained in one memory location. In contrast, a *serial memory* system does not have multiple data pins and, in most cases, no address inputs. A serial memory has a data pin and a clock input pin. Data to be written into and read from are transferred via this single data pin. Address signals are also sent to the serial memory via this single data pin. The clock signal is provided to synchronize data transfer between the processor and the serial memory system. We can find serial SRAM, EPROM, EEPROM, flash memory, etc. Xicor is one of the major vendors of serial memory components. The major advantage of serial memory is its small size. Serial memory interface will be discussed in Chapters 9 and 10.

1.3 THE COMPUTER'S SOFTWARE

A computer is useful because it can execute programs. Programs are known as *software*. A program is a set of instructions that the computer hardware can execute. The program is stored in the computer's memory in the form of binary numbers called *machine instructions*. For example,

> The binary number *00000100* increments accumulator A by 1.
>
> The binary number *00010100* decrements accumulator A by 1.

It is difficult and not productive to program a computer in machine instructions. Assembly language was then invented to simplify the programming job. An assembly program consists of assembly instructions. An assembly instruction is the mnemonic representation of a machine instruction. For example, in the MCS-51

> ADD   A,#53H stands for "add the hexadecimal value 53 to accumulator A." The corresponding machine instruction is 0010010001010011 (in binary).
>
> INC   A stands for "increment the contents of accumulator A by 1." The corresponding machine instruction is 00000100 (in binary).

Address and data values are represented in binary format inside the computer. However, it is not easy for human beings to deal with a large binary number so decimal and hexadecimal formats are often used instead. In this text, we will use a notation that adds a suffix to a number to indicate the base used in the number representation. The suffixes for binary, decimal, and hexadecimal numbers are given in Table 1.1. This method is also used in Intel microcontroller and microprocessor manuals.

TABLE 1.1
Suffixes for Number Representations

Base	Suffix
Binary	B
Hexadecimal	H
Decimal	(Nothing)

For example,

10101011B

specifies the binary number 10101011_2.

A097H

refers to the hexadecimal number $A097_{16}$.

3467

is a decimal number.

From now on, we will use **hex** as the shorthand for hexadecimal.

A *text editor* is used to develop a program using a computer. A text editor allows the user to type, modify, and save the program statements in a text file. The assembly program that a programmer enters is called the *source program* or *source code*. A software program called an *assembler* is then invoked to translate the program written in assembly language into machine instructions. The output of the assembly process is called *object code*. It is a common practice to use a *cross assembler* to assemble assembly programs. A cross assembler is an assembler that runs on one computer but generates machine instructions that will be executed by another computer that has a different instruction set. In contrast, a *native assembler* runs on a computer and generates machine instructions to be executed by machines of the same instruction set. Most people are using a cross assembler that runs on a PC to develop assembly programs for the MCS-51.

There are several drawbacks of programming in assembly language:

- The programmer must be very familiar with the hardware organization of the computer in which the program is to be executed.
- A program, especially a long one, written in assembly language is extremely difficult to understand for anyone other than the author of the program. Even the author of the program may lose track of the program logic if the program is very long.
- Programming productivity is not satisfactory for large programming projects.

For these reasons, high-level languages such as FORTRAN, PASCAL, C, and C++ were invented to avoid the problems of assembly language programming. A program written in a high-level language is also called a source program, and it requires a software program called a *compiler* to translate it into machine instructions. A compiler translates a program into object code. Just as there are cross assemblers, there are *cross compilers* that runs on one computer but translate programs into machine instructions to be executed on a computer with a different instruction set.

High-level languages are not perfect either. One of the major problems with high-level languages is that the machine code compiled from a program in a high-level language cannot run as fast as its equivalent in assembly language. For this reason, many time-critical programs are still written in assembly language. However, the user still needs to be fairly familiar with the microcontroller hardware in order to write a program in high-level language.

In the following, we will discuss the register file and addressing modes and examine a subset of the MCS-51 instructions. Since the MCS-51 system memory organization is closely related to the addressing modes, it will be presented first.

1.4 THE MCS-51 MEMORY ORGANIZATION

All MCS-51 devices have separate address spaces for program and data memory, as shown in Figure 1.3. The data memory can be accessed by either an 8-bit or a 16-bit address. Program memory can only be read, not written into.

When the MCS-51 is first started, the CPU begins execution from location 0 of the program memory. Depending on the version of the microcontroller, a portion of the program memory may be located inside the microcontroller chip. The program memory that is located on the microcontroller chip is called *internal program memory*; the program memory that is located outside the microcontroller chip is called *external program memory*. The internal

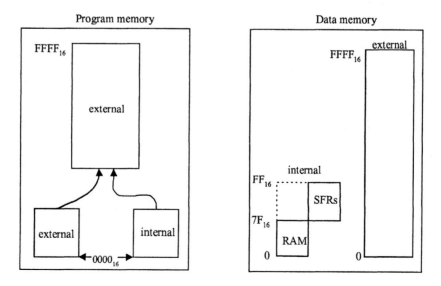

Figure 1.3 MCS-51 memory structure. SFR, special function register.

program memory of the MCS-51 microcontroller is often implemented using ROM or EPROM or flash memory technology.

A small portion of the data memory is on the MCS-51 chip, but most of the data memory is outside the microcontroller chip. Internal data memory addresses are always 1 byte wide, which implies a size of 256 bytes. External data memory address can be either 1 or 2 bytes wide. One-byte addresses are often used in conjunction with one or more I/O lines to page the data memory. We will return to this subject in Chapter 4.

Internal data memory is RAM. The lower 128 bytes of RAM are present in all MCS-51 devices as mapped in Figure 1.4. The lowest 32 bytes are grouped into four banks of eight registers. Program instructions call out these registers as R0 through R7. Two bits in the program status word (PSW) select which register bank is in use. These registers are similar to the general-purpose registers of some other microprocessors/microcontrollers.

The next 16 bytes above the register bank form a block of bit-addressable memory space. The MCS-51 instruction set includes a wide selection of single-bit instructions, and the 128 bits in this area can be directly addressed by these instructions. The bit addresses in this area are from 0 to 127_{10}.

1.5 THE MCS-51 REGISTERS

The MCS-51 microcontroller has many registers as listed in Table 1.2. These registers are called special function registers (SFRs) and they occupy the data memory space from 128 to 255. A few of them are mainly used in ALU operations while the remaining registers are used in I/O operation. The improved variants of the MCS-51 such as MCS-52 have many more special function registers and will be discussed in later chapters.

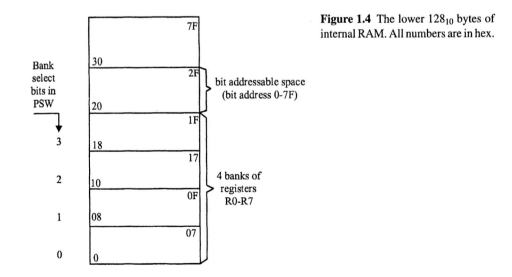

Figure 1.4 The lower 128_{10} bytes of internal RAM. All numbers are in hex.

TABLE 1.2
MCS-51 Special Function Registers

Symbol[2]	Name	Address (Hexidecimal)
*ACC	Accumulator	E0
*B	B register	F0
*PSW	Program status word	D0
SP	Stack pointer	81
DPTR	Data pointer 2 Bytes	
DPL	Low byte	82
DPH	High byte	83
*P0	Port 0	80
*P1	Port 1	90
*P2	Port 2	A0
*P3	Port 3	B0
*IP	Interrupt priority control	B8
*IE	Interrupt enable control	A8
TMOD	Timer/counter mode control	89
*TCON	Timer/counter control	88
*+TCON2	Timer/counter 2 control	C8
TH0	Timer/counter 0 high byte	8C
TL0	Timer/counter 0 low byte	8A
TH1	Timer/counter 1 high byte	8B
TL1	Timer/counter 1 low byte	8D
+TH2	Timer/counter 2 high byte	CD
+TL2	Timer/counter 2 low byte	CC
+RCAP2H	T/C 2 capture register high byte	CB
+RCAP2L	T/C 2 capture register low byte	CA
*SCON	Serial control	98
SBUF	Serial data buffer	99
PCON	Power control	87

[a] *, Bit addressable; + 8052 only.

The following registers are related to the ALU operations:

Accumulator ACC.   Accumulator ACC is 8 bit and is referred to by A. Most arithmetic logic functions are performed in A. A is bit addressable.

B register.   The B register is used with ACC for multiplication and division operations. The B register can be treated as a general-purpose scratch-pad register and is also bit addressable.

Stack pointer SP.   A stack is a first-in–first-out data structure. The MCS-51 has an 8-bit stack pointer. It contains the address of the data item on the top of the stack. The operations and instructions associated with stack will be discussed in detail in Chapter 3.

Data Pointer DPTR.   The DPTR register consists of two 8-bit registers, DPH and DPL, that are used to furnish address information for internal and external code and data accesses. There are three major applications for the DPTR register:

1. Perform table lookup in the program memory space (using the MOVC A,@A+DPTR instruction).
2. Implement multiway jump (using the JMP @A+DPTR instruction).
3. Access external data memory (using the MOVX A,@DPTR or MOVX @DPTR,A instruction).

Program Counter PC.   The address of the next instruction to be executed is specified by the 16-bit program counter. The MCS-51 fetches the instruction one byte at a time and increments the PC by 1 after fetching each instruction byte. After a reset, the PC value will be forced to 0 and the MCS-51 CPU will start executing the first instruction stored at program memory location 0.

Program Status Word PSW.   This 8-bit register is used to keep track of the program execution status and control the program execution. Situations such as overflow on adding two 8-bit numbers and carry (or borrow for subtraction) generated during an addition are recorded in this register. The contents of the PSW are shown in Figure 1.5. The carry flag CY may be used to make decisions or as an operand for an ADD or SUBTRACT instruction.

1.6 MEMORY ADDRESSING

Memory consists of a sequence of directly addressable "locations." In this book a location will be referred to as an *information unit*. The term is deliberately generic to emphasize that the contents of a location can hold data, instructions, the status of peripheral devices, and so on. As shown in Figure 1.6, an information unit has two components: its *address* and its *contents*.

7	6	5	4	3	2	1	0
CY	AC	F0	RS1	RS0	OV	--	P

CY: Carry flag
AC: Auxiliary carry flag
F0:   Flag 0 available to the user for general purpose
RS1:   Register bank select bit 1
RS0:   Register bank select bit 0

RS1	RS0	
0	0	Select register bank 0
0	1	Select register bank 1
1	0	Select register bank 2
1	1	Select register bank 3

OV: Overflow flag
--:   Undefined flag
P: Parity flag. Set/cleared by hardware in each instruction cycle to indicate an odd/even number of "1" bits in the accumulator.

Figure 1.5 Program status word (PSW).

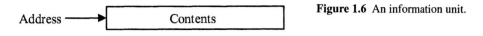

Figure 1.6 An information unit.

By supplying the address, the contents of each location in memory can be accessed. All memory chips have decoder in them that will select one and only one memory location to be accessed with any address input. The CPU communicates with memory by applying the location's address on the address bus. The data are transferred between memory and the CPU through the data bus (see Figure 1.7). The number of bits that can be transferred on the data bus at one time is called the *data bus width* of the processor.

The MCS-51 has an 8-bit data bus and can access only one memory byte at a time. The MCS-51 has an address bus of 16 signal lines and can address up to 2^{16} (65,536) different memory locations. The range of accessible memory addresses is from 0000_{16} to $FFFF_{16}$.

The size of memory is measured in bytes. Each byte has 8 bits. The 4-bit quantity is called a *nibble*. According to Intel, two bytes are called a *word* and four bytes are called a *double word*. The reader must know that some other companies define four bytes as a word and 8 bytes as a double word. To simplify the measurement, the unit kilobyte (KB) is often used. K is given in the following formula:

$$K = 2^{10} = 1024$$

Using powers of 2, the size of memory can be computed in decimal and hexadecimal format. For example,

$$64 \text{ KB} = 2^6 \times 2^{10} \text{ bytes} = 2^{16} \text{ bytes} = 65,536 \text{ bytes}$$

Another frequently used unit is *megabyte* (MB), which is given by the following formula:

$$M = K^2 = 1024 \times 1024 = 1,048,576$$

1.7 THE MCS-51 ADDRESSING MODES

A MCS-51 instruction has 1 byte of opcode and 0 to 2 bytes of operand information. The opcode byte specifies the operation to be performed and may also specify some of the operands.

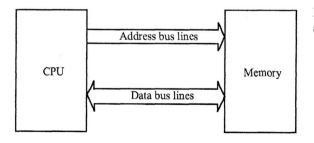

Figure 1.7 Transferring data/in-struction between CPU and memory.

Addressing modes are used to specify the operands needed in an instruction. Ten addressing modes are provided in the MCS-51: *register inherent, direct, immediate, indirect, indexed, relative, absolute, long, bit inherent,* and *bit direct.*

There is some difficulty in differentiating the register inherent mode from the direct mode because all registers except the program counter have an address in the data memory space. For convenience, we will use the register inherent mode for those registers that do not need an extra byte to specify and we will use the direct mode for those registers that require an extra byte to specify.

The following sections describe each of the addressing modes.

1.7.1 Register Inherent

The lowest 32 bytes of the MCS-51 internal RAM are organized as four banks of eight registers. Only one bank is active at a time. Any active register can be accessed by using the symbolic name R0 through R7. The lowest three bits of the opcode byte of the instruction that involve Ri (i = 0...7) select the register to be operated on. The following instructions illustrate the register inherent mode:

    MOV   R0,#20

places the decimal value 20 in register R0.

    INC   R1

increments the contents of register R1 by 1.

The active register bank can be set by programming the bits 3 and 4 of the PSW register. For example, the instruction

    MOV   PSW,#00010000B

selects bank 2 as the active register bank.

Specifying one of the following registers as one of the operands in an instruction is done by the opcode and does not need an extra byte:

- accumulator A
- data pointer DPTR
- program status word PSW
- stack pointer SP
- program counter PC

1.7.2 Direct

The direct addressing mode is provided to allow us to access internal SRAM. The direct mode uses an 8-bit value to specify the address and hence can specify an address only in the range from 0 to 255.

In direct addressing, a byte is appended to the instruction opcode. An on-chip variable or hardware register can be specified by this addressing mode. Depending on the most significant bit of the direct address, one of the two on-chip memory spaces is selected. When bit 7 = 0, the lower 128 on-chip RAM bytes are selected. When bit 7 = 1, one of the special function registers is referenced. The following instructions illustrate the direct addressing mode:

        MOV   20H,A

copies the contents of accumulator A into the memory location at 20H (hex address).

        ADD   A,30H

adds the value stored at memory location 30H (hex address) to accumulator A.

The programmer can use direct address to specify a special function register. However, the resultant assembly programs will not be very readable. In addition, it will be very easy to make mistakes. All Intel MCS-51 assemblers allow the user to use symbolic names to specify special function registers. For example, to output the contents of accumulator A to port 1, the instruction

        MOV   90H,A

can be used. However, the following instruction will make much more sense to the user:

        MOV   P1,A

The MCS-51 assembler will translate all symbolic names into their corresponding addresses during the assembly process.

1.7.3 Immediate

In some applications, we want to provide an initial value to a variable or a register so that the computation can start from there. Examples include the following:

1. Program loop index: A program loop is a sequence of instruction to be repeated many times. The loop index, which keeps track of the number of times that the loop needs to be repeated, has to be initialized to some value.
2. Dynamic variables: A dynamic variable is a variable that needs to be updated when a program is being executed. Examples include the sum of an array and the frequency to be measured. A dynamic variable must be initialized.

Sometimes it is necessary to specify a value as an operand to perform an arithmetic or logic operation or to make a decision on whether a jump should be taken based on the relationship between a register and a value. Immediate addressing mode allows us to specify *that* value. Immediate mode specifies a value to be computed on. It does not specify a memory location. The immediate mode can specify either an 8-bit or a 16-bit value. A

16-bit immediate value can be used only with the DPTR register. An 8-bit immediate value must be used for all other registers.

In the immediate addressing mode, the actual argument is contained in the byte or bytes immediately following the instruction opcode. In assembly language syntax, an immediate value is preceded by a "#" character. The following instructions illustrate the immediate addressing mode:

    MOV   A,#11

loads the decimal value 11 into accumulator A.

    ADD   A,#10

adds the decimal value 10 to accumulator A.

    MOV   DPTR,#2000H

loads the hex value 2000 into the data pointer DPTR.

1.7.4 Indirect

There are situations in which it is necessary to process all or most elements of an array in sequential order. It will be extremely inconvenient to compute the addresses of elements that we need to process. A more efficient method is to place the starting (or base) address of the array (or vector) into a register. After that, we simply increment the register to make it point to the next sequential element. We then use the contents of the register as the address to access the variable. By doing this, we do not need to specify the exact address of every element that we want to manipulate. Indirect addressing mode makes this possible.

The indirect addressing mode uses a register to hold the actual address that will be used in data movement. Registers R0, R1, and DPTR are the only registers that can be used as the "data pointer." Both internal and external RAM can be indirectly addressed. Both R0 and R1 can hold only 8-bit addresses whereas DPTR can hold a 16-bit address. The following instructions illustrate the indirect addressing mode:

    ADD   A,@R0

adds the contents of the memory location pointed to by R0, i.e., R0 contains the address of the memory location, to accumulator A.

    MOV   @R1,A

stores the contents of accumulator A into the memory location pointed to by R1.

    MOVX   A,@DPTR

copies the contents of the external data memory location pointed to by DPTR into accumulator A.

The DPTR register actually consists of two 8-bit registers, i.e, DPH and DPL. DPH is the upper byte and DPL is the lower byte of DPTR. There are situations in which we want to decrement the value of DPTR by 1. However, there is no instruction for this. We must use an instruction sequence to do it. One example is as follows:

```
MOV    A,DPL        ; start the subtraction from the lower byte of DPTR
DEC    A
MOV    DPL,A        ; place the result back to DPL
MOV    A,DPH
SUBB   A,#0         ; subtract the borrow from A
MOV    DPH,A        ; place the result back to DPH
```

1.7.5 Indexed

There are situations in assembly programming in which it is necessary to manipulate the array or vector elements and look up a table in a random manner. We know the starting address of the array or table and also the relative position of the element in the array or table. It would be very inefficient to compute the addresses of array elements when we need to process an array randomly. Indexed addressing mode allows us to access an array or table in a random manner without computing the address.

The indexed addressing mode uses a base register (either the program counter or the data pointer) and an offset (in accumulator A) in forming the memory address for a JMP or a MOVC instruction. Indexed addressing mode is ideal for implementing jump tables and lookup tables. Only program memory can be accessed with the indexed addressing mode. The following instructions illustrate the indexed addressing mode:

```
JMP   @A+DPTR
```

sets the program counter to the value equal to the sum of accumulator A and the data pointer DPTR and instruction execution will be continued from there.

```
MOVC   A,@A+DPTR
```

loads the contents of the memory location pointed to by the sum of the contents of accumulator A and the data pointer DPTR into accumulator A.

```
MOVC   A,@A+PC
```

loads the contents of the memory location pointed to by the sum of the contents of accumulator A and the program counter PC into accumulator A.

The functions of a subset of memory addressing modes are illustrated in Figure 1.8.

1.7.6 Relative

Programs need to make decisions. At a decision point, the program flow will follow one of two paths if the decision variable satisfies the specified condition, and will follow the

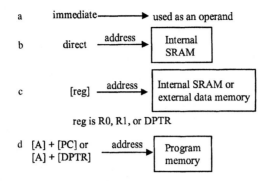

Figure 1.8 Illustration of memory addressing modes for instruction operands. (a) Immediate addressing mode. (b) Direct addressing mode. (c) Indirect addressing mode. (d) Indexed addressing mode.

other path when the variable does not. Program decision is implemented by conditional jump (or called branch) instructions. A conditional jump instruction needs to specify the destination of the jump. The direction of jump may be forward or backward. The distance of jump is measured in reference to the first byte after the jump instruction as shown in Figure 1.9.

Relative addressing is used only with conditional jump instructions. The jump offset is 8 bit, and hence has a range of −128 to +127 bytes. Jump is also called *branch*. When a jump is taken, the offset is added to the program counter to form the jump address. The jump destination is usually specified using a label and the assembler calculates the jump offset accordingly. The following instructions illustrate the relative addressing mode:

    JZ   equal

will jump to the instruction with the label *equal* if the value of accumulator A is zero.

    JNC   larger

will jump to the instruction with the label *larger* if the carry flag of PSW is zero.

1.7.7 Absolute

Absolute addressing is used with the ACALL and AJMP instructions. These are 2-byte instructions. The absolute addressing mode specifies the lowest 11 bits of the destination instruction. The upper 5 bits of the destination address are the upper 5 bits of the current program counter. Because of that, absolute addressing allows branching only within the current 2-KB page of the program memory. The upper 3 bits (A10–A8) of the absolute address are the upper 3 bits of the opcode byte and the lower 8 bits (A7–A0) are the second byte of the instruction. The absolute address is usually specified using a label and the assembler will generate the absolute address accordingly. The following instructions illustrate the absolute addressing mode:

    ACALL   quicksort

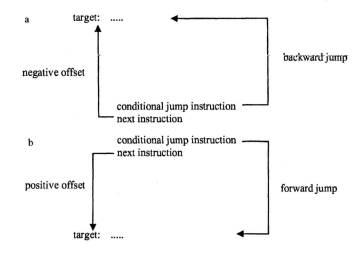

Figure 1.9 Conditional jump instruction. (a) A backward conditional jump. (b) A forward conditional jump.

calls the subroutine that is started at the label *quicksort*. Subroutine calls will be explored in Chapter 3.

    AJMP   loop

causes the instruction with the label *loop* to be executed after the current instruction.

1.7.8 Long

Long addressing is used to specify the destination for the LCALL and LJMP instructions. These are 3-byte instructions. The long addressing mode specifies a 16-bit address for the jump destination. The long address is usually specified using a label and the assembler will generate the long address accordingly. The following instructions illustrate the long addressing mode:

    LCALL   binsearch

calls the subroutine that is started at the label *binsearch*.

    LJMP   loop

causes the instruction with the label *loop* to be executed after the current instruction.

The MCS-51 provides a set of instructions (often called *Boolean instructions*) that can operate on bit operands. These instructions are suitable for representing Boolean variables. As shown in the Figure 1.4, the address range of 20H to 2FH of the internal data RAM is bit addressable. In addition, many special function registers are also bit addressable. There are two different methods for specifying bit operands.

1.7.9 Bit Inherent

Instructions that operate on the carry flag do not need an extra byte to specify the carry flag. The opcode bytes of these instructions have implied carry flag as an operand. The following instructions illustrate the bit inherent addressing:

    SETB   C

sets the carry flag (in PSW) to 1.

    CLR   C

clears the carry flag to 0.

    CPL   C

complements the carry flag.

1.7.10 Bit Direct

The byte following the opcode byte of a Boolean instruction specifies the bit to be operated on. Though this format potentially allows 256 directly addressable bit operands, not all of them are implemented in the MCS-51 family. The RAM space 20H to 2FH and most of the special function registers are bit addressable as shown in Figure 1.10.

The addressing of RAM bits is different from that of the bits of special function registers. Bit address values between 0 and 127 defines the bits of the on-chip RAM. They are numbered consecutively from the lowest order byte's least significant bit through the highest order byte's most significant bit. Bit addresses between 128 and 255 correspond to bits in a number of special function registers, mostly used for I/O or peripheral control. These numbers are numbered with a different scheme than RAM: the five high-order address bits match those of the register's own address, whereas the three low-order bits identify the bit position within that register.

The MCS-51 assembly language specifies a bit address in one of three ways:

1. by a number or expression corresponding to the direct address (0–255)
2. by the name or address of the register containing the bit, the dot operator symbol (a period: "."), and the bit's position in the register (7–0)
3. by the predefined assembler symbols listed in Table 1.3 (in the case of control and status registers). The meaning of each bit of these control and status registers will be explained in later chapters.

The bit operand specified in these three formats will be translated into the appropriate bit direct address by the assembler. The following instructions illustrate the bit direct addressing:

CLR   PSW.7

clears the bit 7 (carry flag) of the program status word.

SETB   TR0

sets the bit 4 of the TCON register to 1.

SETB   10H

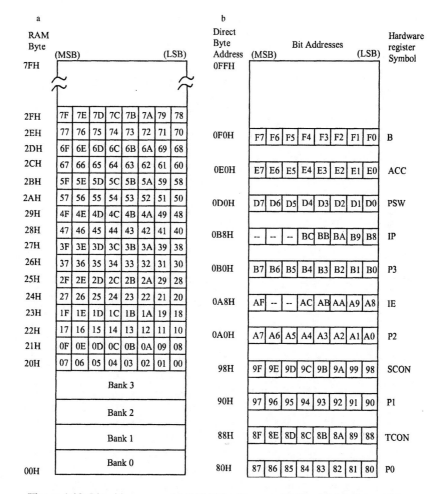

Figure 1.10 Bit address map. (a) RAM bit addresses. (b) Special function registers.

TABLE 1.3
Assembly Language Symbols for Control and Status Registers Bits

Register Name	Bit Position							
	7	6	5	4	3	2	1	0
PSW	CY	AC	F0	RS1	RS0	OV	—	P
P3	RD	WR	T1	T0	INT1	INT0	TXD	RXD
TCON	TF1	TR1	TF0	TR0	IE1	IT1	IE0	IT0
SCON	SM0	SM1	SM2	REN	TB8	RB8	TI	RI
IE	EA	—	—	ES	ET1	EX1	ET0	EX0
IP	—	—	—	PS	PT1	PX1	PT0	PX0

sets the bit 0 of the internal RAM location at 22H to 1.

> JNB   P1.3,not_equ

will jump to the instruction with the label "not_equ" if the bit 3 of port 1 is not equal to 1.

1.8 THE MCS-51 MEMORY SPACES

The term *memory space* refers to the range of addresses and size of a type of memory that the CPU can access. Physically, the MCS-51 has only two memory spaces: the *program memory space* and the *data memory space*. Each memory space is 64 KB. However, to facilitate the accesses of operands, the data memory space is further divided into four subspaces: external data memory, internal data memory, special function registers, and bit memory.

The external data memory resides outside the MCS-51 chip. This memory space contains all the variables, buffers, and data structures that cannot fit on chip. It is principally addressed by the 16-bit data pointer (DPTR), although the first two general purpose registers (R0, R1) of the currently selected bank can access a 256-byte page of external data memory. External data memory can be accessed using only the indirect addressing mode with the DPTR, R0, or R1.

The internal data memory is functionally the most important data memory space. In it reside four banks of general-purpose registers, the program stack, 128 bits of the 256-bit memory, and all the variables and data structures that are operated on directly by the program. The maximum size of the internal data memory is 256 bytes. However, different 8051 family members integrate different amounts of this memory space on chip. The lower 128 bytes of this space can be accessed by both direct and indirect addressing modes and the upper 128 bytes can be accessed using only the indirect addressing mode.

The special function register space contains all the on-chip peripheral I/O registers as well as particular registers (ACC, B, SP, and PSW) that our programs need to access. The maximum number of special function registers (SFRs) is 128, though the actual number on a particular MCS-51 family member depends on the number and type of peripheral functions integrated on chip. All of the SFRs have addresses greater than 127 and overlap the address space of the upper 128 bytes of the internal data memory space. Addressing mode differentiates the two memory spaces. The SFRs can be accessed only using the direct addressing mode whereas the upper 128 bytes of the internal data memory can be accessed using only the indirect addressing mode.

The Bit Memory space is used for storing bit variables and flags. There are specific instructions in the MCS-51 that operate only in the bit memory space. The maximum size of the bit memory space is 256 bits. The lower 128 bits overlap with the 16 bytes of the internal memory space and the upper 128 bits overlap with 16 special function registers. Bits can be accessed using only the bit instructions and the bit direct addressing mode.

1.9 A SAMPLE OF MCS-51 INSTRUCTIONS

An MCS-51 instruction consists of 1 byte of opcode and 0 to 2 bytes of operand information. The opcode specifies the operation to be performed. An MCS-51 instruction may have from one to three operands. For most instructions, one of the operands is used both as a source and as the destination of the operation. The operand information is represented by one of the addressing modes.

1.9.1 The MOVE Instruction

MOVE is the generic name of a group of instructions that places a value or copies the contents of a memory location into a register or a memory location. Most MCS-51 arithmetic and logical instructions include a register as one of the operands. Before a meaningful operation can be performed, a value must be placed in the register. The MOVE instructions can be used to place a value or copy the contents of a memory location into a register. The MCS-51 has MOVE instructions for loading a value into accumulator A, register B, registers R7–R0, stack pointer SP, data pointer DPTR, and a RAM location. For example,

    MOV   A,#10H

loads the hex value 10 into accumulator A:

    MOV   A,10H

copies the contents of the memory location at 10H into accumulator A. A complete list of MOVE instructions is given in Table 1.4.

Example 1.1 Write an instruction to place the starting address 2000H of a table into the data pointer DPTR.

Solution: The instruction "MOV DPTR,#2000H" will place the hex value 2000H into the data pointer DPTR.

The binary representation of the hex value 2000H is 0010000000000000_2. After the execution of this instruction, the contents of the 16-bit register DPTR are as shown in Figure 1.11.

15	14	13	12	11	10	9	8	7	6	5	4	3	2	1	0
0	0	1	0	0	0	0	0	0	0	0	0	0	0	0	0

Figure 1.11 The contents of DPTR after the instruction execution.

To unify the representation, we will use the following notations throughout this book:

DEFINITION

[reg]: The contents of the register *reg. reg* can be any one of the following:

   R0-R7, PC, SFRs

[addr]: The contents of the memory location at address *addr.*
Mem[addr]: The memory location at address *addr*.

For example,

   [R0]   refers to the contents of register R0.

   [A]   refers to the contents of accumulator A.

   [1000H]   refers to the contents of memory location at 1000H.

   Mem[1000H] ← [A]   means "store the contents of accumulator A in memory location at 1000H."

Example 1.2 There is an array with 100 8-bit integers. The array is stored in program memory starting at the address 1000H. Write an instruction sequence to load the tenth element into accumulator A.

   Solution: This problem can be solved in three steps:

STEP 1   Place the starting address 1000H in DPTR.

STEP 2   Place 10 in accumulator A

STEP 3   Use the indexed addressing mode to place the contents of the tenth element in A.

```
MOV    DPTR,#1000H
MOV    A,#10
MOVC   A,@A+DPTR
```

TABLE 1.4
MCS-51 MOVE Instructions[a]

Instruction		Meaning
MOV	A,Rn	Copy the contents of register Rn to A
MOV	A,direct	Copy the contents of direct address to A
MOV	A,@Ri	Copy the contents of the memory location pointed to by Ri to A
MOV	A,#data	Load the immediate value "data" into A
MOV	Rn,A	Copy the contents of A into register Rn
MOV	Rn,direct	Copy the contents of direct byte to register Rn
MOV	Rn,#data	Load the immediate value "data" into register Rn
MOV	direct,A	Copy the contents of A to direct address
MOV	direct,Rn	Copy the contents of register Rn to direct address
MOV	direct1,direct2	Copy the contents of the memory location at address "direct2" to location at "direct1"
MOV	direct,@Ri	Copy the contents of the memory location pointed to by Ri to direct address
MOV	direct,#data	Load the immediate value "data" into direct address
MOV	@Ri,A	Copy the contents of A to the memory location pointed to by Ri
MOV	@Ri,direct	Copy the contents at address "direct" to the memory location pointed to by Ri
MOV	@Ri,#data	Load the immediate value "data" into the memory location pointed to by Ri
MOV	DPTR,#16bitdata	Load the immediate value "16bitdata" into the data pointer DPTR
MOVC	A,@A+DPTR	Copy the contents of the program memory location pointed to by the sum of A and DPTR to A
MOVC	A,@A+PC	Copy the contents of the program memory location pointed to by the sum of A and PC to A
MOVX	A,@Ri	Copy the contents of the external data memory location pointed to by register Ri to A
MOVX	A,@DPTR	Copy the contents of the external data memory location pointed to by DPTR to A
MOVX	@Ri,A	Copy the contents of A to the external data memory location pointed to by Ri
MOVX	@DPTR,A	Copy the contents of A to the external data memory location pointed to by DPTR

[a] Rn refers to R1–R7; Ri refers to R0 or R1; "direct" can be the address of an internal memory location or a special function register.

Example 1.3 Write an instruction sequence to swap the contents of two memory locations at 50H and 60H, respectively.

Solution: This problem can be solved as follows:

STEP 1   Load the contents of the memory location at 50H into A.

STEP 2   Load the contents of the memory location at 60H into B.

STEP 3   Store the contents of A into memory location at 60H.

STEP 4   Store the contents of B into memory location at 50H.

The appropriate instructions are

```
MOV   A,50H
MOV   B,60H
MOV   60H,A
MOV   50H,B
```

1.9.2 The ADD Instruction

ADD is the generic name of a group of instructions that performs the addition operation. The ADD instruction, which is one of the most important arithmetic instructions in the MCS-51, has either two or three operands. In a three-operand ADD instruction, the C flag of the program status word register is always included as one of the source operands. Three-operand ADD instructions are mainly used in multiprecision arithmetic, which will be discussed in Chapter 2. The ADD instruction has the following constraints:

- The ADD instruction can specify at most one memory location as a source operand. The memory operand can be specified only in *direct* or *8-bit indirect* addressing mode.
- The memory operand can be used only as a source operand.
- The destination operand must be accumulator A.
- Accumulator A is also used as a source operand.

For example,

```
ADD   A,#10
```

adds the decimal value 10 to the contents of A and places the result in accumulator A.

```
ADD   A,50H
```

adds the contents of the memory location at 50H to the contents of accumulator A and places the result in A.

```
ADDC   A,50H
```

adds the carry bit (in the PSW register) and the contents of the memory location at 50H to accumulator A and places the result in accumulator A.

A complete list of ADD instructions is given in Table 1.5.

Example 1.4 Write an instruction sequence to add the contents of memory locations at 40H and 50H and leave the sum in accumulator A.

Solution: This problem can be solved in two steps:

STEP 1   Load the contents of the memory location at 40H into accumulator A.

STEP 2   Add the contents of the memory location at 50H to accumulator A.

The appropriate instructions are

```
MOV   A,40H
ADD   A,50H
```

1.9.3 The SUB Instruction

SUB is the generic name of a group of instructions that performs the subtract operation. Unlike the ADD instruction, the SUB instruction must have three operands. The CY flag in the PSW register is included as one of the source operands. The SUB instruction has the following constraints:

- The SUB instruction can specify at most one memory location as a source operand.
- The memory operand can be specified using only either the *direct* or the *8-bit indirect* addressing mode.
- The destination operand must be accumulator A.
- Accumulator A is both the destination operand and one of the source operands.

For example,

```
SUBB   A,#30
```

subtracts the decimal value 30 and the carry flag CY from accumulator A and stores the difference in accumulator A.

```
SUBB   A,40H
```

TABLE 1.5
A Sample of ADD Instructions[a]

Instruction		Meaning
ADD	A,Rn	Add register Rn to accumulator A and store the result in A
ADD	A,direct	Add the contents of the direct memory to A and store the sum in A
ADD	A,@Ri	Add the contents of the memory location pointed to by Ri to A and store the sum in A
ADD	A,#data	Add the immediate value "data" to A and store the sum in A
ADDC	A,Rn	Add the contents of Rn and the carry flag CY in PSW to A and store the sum in A
ADDC	A,direct	Add the contents at address "direct" and the carry flag CY in PSW to A and store the sum in A
ADDC	A,@Ri	Add the contents of the memory location pointed to by Ri and the carry flag CY in PSW to A and store the sum in A
ADDC	A,#data	Add the immediate value "data" and the carry flag CY in PSW to A and store the sum in A

[a] SFR, special function register. Rn refers to R7 . . . R0; Ri refers to R0 or R1.

subtracts the contents of the memory location at 40H and the carry flag CY from accumulator A and leaves the difference in accumulator A.

Example 1.5 Write an instruction sequence to subtract the value of the memory location at 50H and the carry flag from that of the memory location at 40H and store the result in accumulator A.

Solution: This problem can be solved in two steps:

STEP 1   Load the contents of the memory location at 40H into accumulator A.

STEP 2   Subtract the contents of the memory location at 50H and the carry flag CY from A.

The appropriate instructions are

    MOV   A,40H
    SUBB   A,50H

A complete list of SUB instructions is given in Table 1.6.

1.10 THE MCS-51 MACHINE CODE

We have learned that each MCS-51 instruction consists of one byte of opcode and 0 to 2 bytes of operand information. In this section, we will look at the machine code of a sample of MCS-51 instructions, the disassembly of machine instructions, and the instruction execution time.

1.10.1 A Machine-Code Sequence

Basic instructions can be sequenced to perform calculations. We have seen several examples before. Consider the following high-level language statements:

TABLE 1.6
A Sample of Subtract Instructions[a]

Instruction	Meaning
SUBB A,Rn	Subtract the contents of register Rn and the carry flag CY from accumulator A and leave the result in A
SUBB A,direct	Subtract the contents at the address "direct" and the carry flag CY from the accumulator A and store the result in A
SUBB A,@Ri	Subtract the contents of the memory location pointed to by Ri and the carry flag CY from accumulator A and leave the result in A
SUBB A,#data	Subtract the immediate value "data" and the carry flag CY from accumulator A and leave the result in A

[a] Rn refers to R7 . . . R0. Ri refers to R1 or R0.

$$W := 100$$

$$X := W + Y$$

Assume that the variables W, X, and Y refer to memory locations 40H, 41H, and 42H, respectively. The first statement assigns the decimal value 100 to variable W, and the second statement assigns the sum of variables W and Y to variable X. The high-level language statements are translated into the equivalent assembly language and machine instructions shown in Table 1.7.

The decimal number 100 is equivalent to hex value 64H. Assume these four instructions are stored at memory locations starting from 1000H; the contents of memory locations from 1000H to 1007H are then shown in Table 1.8.

If the memory location at 42H contains 14H, then the memory location at 41H is assigned the value 64H + 14H = 78H. Table 1.9 shows the changes in the values stored in memory locations and in accumulator A when the instructions are executed. (These values are represented in hex format.)

1.10.2 Decoding Machine Language Instructions

The process of decoding (disassembling) a machine language instruction is more difficult than assembling it. The opcode is the first byte of an instruction. By decomposing its bit pattern, the assembly instruction mnemonic and the addressing mode of the operand can be identified.

TABLE 1.7
Equivalent Assembly and Machine Instructions

Assembly Instructions	Machine Instructions (in hex Format)
MOV A,#100	74 64
MOV 40H,A	F5 40
ADD A,42H	25 42
MOV 41H,A	F5 41

TABLE 1.8
Machine Codes in Memory Locations

Address	Machine Code
1000H	74
1001H	64
1002H	F5
1003H	40
1004H	25
1005H	42
1006H	F5
1007H	41

TABLE 1.9
Changes in the Contents of Memory Locations and Accumulator A after Program Execution

Address	Before Program Execution	After Program Execution
40H	???	64
41H	???	78
42H	14	14
A	???	78

Example 1.6 A segment of machine code program contains the following opcode and addressing information:

E5 30 24 0F F5 30 E5 31 24 06 F5 31 E5 32 94 0A F5 32

Given the machine opcode and their corresponding assembly instructions in Table 1.10, decode the given machine code into assembly instructions.

Solution: The process of decoding a machine language instruction begins with the opcode byte E5.

TABLE 1.10
Machine Codes and Their Corresponding Assembly Instructions [a]

Machine Code	Assembly Instruction Format	
00	NOP	
24	ADD	A,#data
25	ADD	A,direct
94	SUBB	A,#data
95	SUBB	A,direct
74	MOV	A,#data
E5	MOV	A,direct
F5	MOV	direct,A
A8	MOV	R0,direct
A9	MOV	R1,direct
AA	MOV	R2,direct
AB	MOV	R3,direct
AC	MOV	R4,direct
AD	MOV	R5,direct
AE	MOV	R6,direct
AF	MOV	R7,direct

[a] All numbers are in hex format.

1. The opcode byte E5 corresponds to the following MOV instruction format:

MOV   A,direct

To complete the decoding of this instruction, the byte (that is, 30) that immediately follows E5 should be included. Therefore, the machine code of the first instruction is E5 30. The corresponding assembly instruction is MOV A,30H.

2. The opcode of the second instruction is 24 and corresponds to the following ADD instruction format:

ADD   A,#data

To decode this instruction completely, the byte (0F) that immediately follows 24 should be included. The machine code of the second instruction is thus 24 0F. The corresponding assembly instruction is ADD A,#0FH.

3. The opcode of the third instruction is F5, which corresponds to the following MOV instruction format:

MOV   direct,A

Including the byte that immediately follows F5 (that is, 30), we see that the machine code of the third instruction is F5 30. The corresponding assembly instruction is MOV 30H,A.

Continuing this manner, we can decode the remaining machine code bytes into the following assembly instructions:

    MOV   A,31H
    ADD   A,#06
    MOV   31H,A
    MOV   A,32H
    SUBB   A,#0A
    MOV   32H,A

A program that can disassemble machine code into assembly instructions is called a *disassembler*. A disassembler can be used to translate the machine code in RAM or ROM into assembly instructions. Most microprocessor/microcontroller evaluation boards include disassemblers so they can be used to view the assembly instructions in memory.

1.10.3 The Instruction Execution Cycle

To execute a program, the microprocessor or microcontroller must access memory to fetch instructions or operands. The process of accessing a memory location is called a *read cycle*, the process of storing a value in a memory location is called a *write cycle*, and the process of executing an instruction is called an *instruction execution cycle*.

When executing an instruction, the MCS-51 performs a combination of the following operations:

- A read cycle (or a sequence of read cycles) to fetch the instruction opcode byte and addressing information.
- A read cycle required to fetch the memory operand (optional).
- The operation specified by the opcode.
- A write cycle to write back the result either to a register or to a memory location (optional).

We will illustrate the instruction execution cycle using the MOV, ADD, and SUB instructions shown in Table 1.11. The details of data transfer on the buses are included to illustrate the read/write cycles. Assume the program counter PC is set at 1000H, the starting address for the machine instructions. The contents of data memory locations at 40H, 50H, and 60H are 10H, 33H, and 20H, respectively. The carry flag CY is 0.

TABLE 1.11
A Segment of Instructions

Assembly Language Instructions	Program Memory Address	Machine Code
MOV A,40H	1000H	E5 40
ADD A,50H	1002H	25 50
SUBB A,60H	1004H	95 60
MOV 40H,A	1006H	F5 40

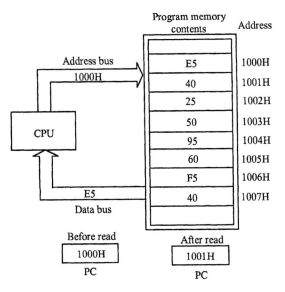

Figure 1.12 Instruction 1—opcode read cycle.

Instruction 1 MOV A,40H

Execution of this instruction involves the following steps:

STEP 1   The value in PC (1000H) is placed on the address bus with a request to "read" the contents of that location.

STEP 2   The 8-bit value at the location 1000H is the instruction opcode E5H. This value is placed on the data bus by the program memory hardware and passed to the processor, where the control unit begins interpretation of the instruction. In the read cycle, the control unit causes the PC to be incremented by 1, and it now points to location 1001H. Figure 1.12 shows the opcode read cycle.

STEP 3   The control unit recognizes that the MOVE instruction requires a byte value for the operand address. This is found in the byte immediately following the opcode byte (at location 1001H). Another read cycle is executed. The value of the PC is incremented by 1. The PC has a final value of 1002H and the address 40H is stored in an internal register (invisible to the programmer) inside the CPU. Figure 1.13 shows the address byte read cycle.

STEP 4   The actual execution of the MOVE instruction requires an additional read cycle. The address 40H is put on the address bus with a "read" request. The contents of memory location 40H are placed on the data bus and stored in accumulator A, as shown in Figure 1.14.

Instruction 2 ADD A,50H

The PC initially has the value 1002H. Two read cycles are required to fetch the second instruction from memory. The execution cycle for this instruction involves the following steps:

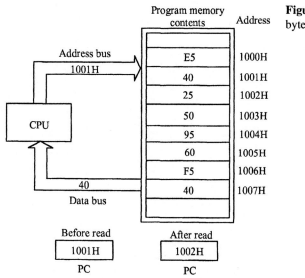

Figure 1.13 Instruction 1—address byte read cycle

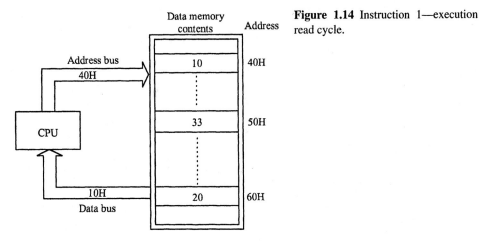

Figure 1.14 Instruction 1—execution read cycle.

STEP 1   Fetch the opcode byte at location 1002H. At the end of this read cycle, the PC is incremented to 1003H. The opcode byte 25H is fetched. Control unit recognizes that this version of ADD instruction requires one read cycle to fetch the direct address. This read cycle is performed in the next step.

STEP 2   Fetch the address byte (50H) from the memory location at 1003H. The PC is then incremented to 1004H.

STEP 3   Execution of this instruction requires an additional read cycle to read in the operand at location 50H. The control unit places the value 50H on the address bus to fetch the contents of the memory location at 50H.

STEP 4   The returned value 33H is added to accumulator A. Accumulator A now has the value 43H (10H + 33H = 43H).

Instruction 3 SUBB A,60H

As was the case for the previous two instructions, two read cycles are required to fetch this instruction from memory. The PC initially has the value 1004H. The execution cycle for this instruction involves the following steps:

STEP 1   Fetch the opcode at 1004H. At the end of this read cycle, the PC is incremented to 1005H. The opcode byte 95H is fetched. Control unit recognizes that this version of SUB instruction requires one read cycle to fetch the direct address. This read cycle is performed in the next step.

STEP 2   Fetch the address byte (60H) from the memory location at 1005H. The PC is then incremented to 1006H.

STEP 3   Execution of this instruction requires an additional read cycle to read in the operand at location 60H. The control unit places the value 60H on the address bus to fetch the contents of the data memory location at 60H.

STEP 4 The returned value 20H and the carry flag CY are subtracted from accumulator A. The accumulator A now has the value 23H (43H − 20H = 23H).

Instruction 4 MOV 40H,A

As was the case for the previous three instructions, two read cycles are required to fetch this instruction from the program memory. The PC initially has the value 1006H. The execution cycle of this instruction involves the following steps:

STEP 1 Fetch the opcode byte at the location 1006H. At the end of the read cycle, the PC is incremented to 1007H and the opcode byte F5 is fetched. The control unit recognizes that this version of MOVE instruction requires another read cycle to fetch the direct address.

STEP 2 Fetch the direct address byte (40H) from the memory location at 1007H. The PC is then incremented to 1008H.

STEP 3 The purpose of this instruction is to store the contents of accumulator A in data memory, so the control unit places the direct address 40H on the address bus, and the value in accumulator A (23H) is written into the memory location at 40H. Figure 1.15 shows the execution write cycle.

1.10.4 Instruction Timing

The MCS-51 internal operations and external read/write cycles are controlled by the oscillator clock input signal. Every 12 oscillator periods are defined as a *machine cycle*. According to the Intel literature, a machine cycle consists of a sequence of six states, numbered S1 through S6, and each state lasts for two oscillator periods. As shown in Figure 1.16, each state is divided into *phase 1 half* (P1) and *phase 2 half* (P2). The control logic of the MCS-51 is implemented in a finite state machine (FSM) and each state lasts for two oscillator periods. An MCS-51 instruction takes from one to four machine cycles to execute. The MCS-51 instruction execution time is listed in Appendix A.

Example 1.7 Suppose a member of the MCS-51 microcomputer family is operating with an oscillator running at 12 MHz. Find the execution time in machine cycles, in oscillator cycles, and in midroseconds for the following three instructions:

   1. ADD   A,35H
   2. MOV   DPTR,#3000H
   3. MOVX   A,@DPTR

Solution: Since the oscillator frequency is 12 MHz, one machine cycle corresponds to

$$12 \times 1 \div 12\,\text{MHz} = 1\,\mu\text{s}$$

The execution times of the given three instructions can be found in Appendix A as shown in Table 1.12.

TABLE 1.12
Instruction Execution Time of a Sample of Instructions

Instruction		Execution Time in Oscillator Cycles	Execution Time in Machine Cycles	Execution Time (μs)
ADD	A,35H	12	1	1
MOV	DPTR,#3000H	24	2	2
MOVX	A,@DPTR	24	2	2

1.11 SUMMARY

A computer system consists of hardware and software. The hardware consists of four components: a processor, an input unit, an output unit, and memory. The processor can be further divided into the datapath and the control unit. The datapath consists of a register file and an arithmetic logic unit (ALU). The processor communicates with memory and input/output devices through a set of signal lines referred to as a bus.

The processor of a large computer is built from a number of integrated circuits. A microprocessor is a processor fabricated in a single integrated circuit. A microcomputer is

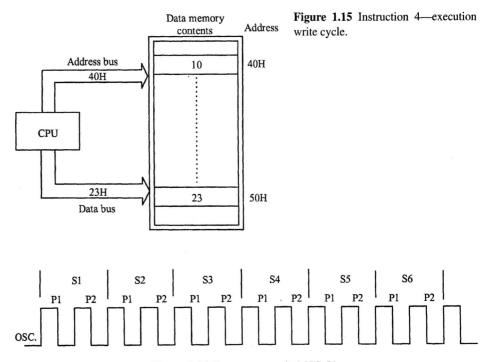

Figure 1.15 Instruction 4—execution write cycle.

Figure 1.16 State sequence in MCS-51.

a computer that uses a microprocessor as its CPU. Microprocessors come in 4-bit, 8-bit, 16-bit, 32-bit, and 64-bit models. The number of bits refers to the number of binary digits that the microprocessor can manipulate in one operation.

Many 32-bit and 64-bit microprocessors also contain on-chip memory to enhance the performance. Microprocessors and input/output devices have different characteristics and speeds. Peripheral chips are required to interface I/O devices to the microprocessors. Because of this requirement, a microprocessor-based design cannot be made as small as might be desired. This drawback led to the invention of microcontrollers.

A microcontroller is a computer implemented on a single very large-scale integration (VLSI) chip. A microcontroller contains everything in a microprocessor and also peripheral functions such as memory, timers, A/D converter, D/A converter, parallel I/O ports, and serial I/O interface. Since their introduction in the 1970s, microcontrollers have been used in almost every electronic product that we can imagine.

Introduced in 1980, the 8051 is the original member of the Intel MCS-51 family and is the core for all MCS-51 variants. In addition to Intel, there are many other companies producing 8051-compatible microcontrollers. These devices can execute the same instruction set and support the same addressing modes.

Memory is where software programs and data are stored. A computer may contain semiconductor, magnetic, and optical memory. The semiconductor memory can be classified according to its characteristics: read/writeable and read-only, volatile and nonvolatile, dynamic and static, serial and parallel. There are five major ROMs: MROM, PROM, EPROM, EEPROM, and flash memory.

Computer programs are known as software. A program consists of a set of instructions that the hardware can execute. The program is stored in the computer's memory in the form of binary numbers called *machine instructions.* The earliest computer programs were written directly in machine language. Writing programs in machine language is unproductive and error prone. Assembly language was invented to overcome the drawbacks of machine language. An assembly program consists of assembly instructions that are the mnemonic representation of machine instructions. Writing programs in assembly language is still not very productive and the resultant programs are hard to understand. High-level languages such as Fortran, Pascal, C, C++, and Java were invented to improve programming productivity. Programs written in assembly and high-level languages are called *source code*; they require a translator to translate them into machine instructions before they can be executed. An assembler is executed to translate programs written in assembly language. A compiler is run to translate programs written in high-level languages.

All MCS-51 devices have separate address spaces for program and data memories. The data memory can be accessed by either 8-bit or 16-bit address. Program memory can only be read, not written into. A portion of the data/program memory is located inside the MCS-51 microcontroller chip. The lowest 32 bytes of the internal data memory are grouped into four banks of eight registers. Program instructions call out these registers as R0 through R7. Two bits in the program status word select which register bank is in use. The MCS-51 has many registers. Registers related to ALU operations include ACC, B, SP, DPTR, PSW, and PC.

Memory consists of a sequence of directly addressable locations. A location is also referred to as an information unit. An information unit has two components: its address and its contents. An instruction uses address to specify the memory location that it wants to access. The address information is sent to the memory on the address bus while the data are transferred between the memory and the CPU on the data bus. The MCS-51 has an 8-bit data bus and a 16-bit address bus. Instructions operate on operand(s). Operands are specified by addressing modes. The MCS-51 implements the following addressing modes: register inherent, direct, immediate, indirect, indexed, relative, absolute, long, bit inherent, and bit direct.

The MCS-51 instructions can be classified into five categories: arithmetic operation, logical operation, data transfer, Boolean variable manipulation, and program branching.

An instruction may consist of from 1 to 3 bytes and may take from 1 to 4 machine cycles to execute. A machine cycle consists of 12 oscillator periods. We may occasionally need to decode machine language instructions into assembly instructions. The translation process includes three steps:

1. Decompose the opcode byte to identify the assembly instruction mnemonic and the addressing mode.
2. Fetch the appropriate (optional) operand (address) byte(s).
3. Assemble the opcode byte and the optional operand byte(s) into an assembly instruction.

When executing an instruction, the MCS-51 (and any other microcontroller) performs a combination of the following operations:

1. A read cycle (or a sequence of read cycle) to fetch the instruction opcode byte and addressing information.
2. A read cycle required for fetching the memory operand (optional).
3. The operation specified by the opcode.
4. A write cycle to write back the result either to a register or to a memory location (optional).

1.12 EXERCISES

1.1 What is a processor? What sections of a computer make up a processor?

1.2 What makes a microprocessor different from the processor of a large-scale computer?

1.3 What makes a microcontroller different from the microprocessor used in personal computers?

1.4 How many bits of data are stored in each memory location of a microcontroller trainer built around the MCS-51 microcontroller?

1.5 How many different memory locations can the MCS-51 microcontroller address?

1.6 Why must every computer have some nonvolatile memory?

1.7 What are the differences among MROM, PROM, EPROM, EEPROM, and Flash memory? For what type of application is each most suitable?

1.8 What is the difference between source code and object code?

1.9 What register is used to keep track of the address of the next instruction to be executed?

1.10 How many on-chip register banks are there in the MCS-51? How is a bank set to be active?

1.11 Convert 30K into decimal representation.

1.12 What special function registers are bit addressable? What are not?

1.13 Write instructions to swap the contents of data memory locations at 50H and 60H.

1.14 Write instructions to subtract 4 from data memory locations 30H to 35H.

1.15 Write an instruction sequence to translate the following high-level language statements into MCS-51 assembly instructions:

$$X := 15$$
$$Y := 35$$
$$Z := Y - X$$

Assume variables X, Y, and Z are located at internal data memory locations 60H, 62H, and 64H, respectively.

1.16 Translate the following assembly instructions into machine instructions using Table 1.10.

```
MOV   A,#30H
ADD   A,40H
MOV   40H,A
```

1.17 Translate the following assembly instructions into machine instructions using Table 1.10.

```
MOV   A,40H
MOV   50H,A
MOV   A,60H
MOV   40H,A
```

1.18 Disassemble the following machine code into MCS-51 assembly instructions using Table 1.10.

74 50 24 30 F5 40 A8 40

1.19 Disassemble the following machine code into MCS-51 assembly instructions using Table 1.10.

74 10 F5 70 24 40 F5 50 A9 50

1.20 Disassemble the following machine code into MCS-51 assembly instructions using Table 1.10.

74 01 F5 20 24 10 F5 30 24 10 F5 10

1.21 What are the contents of memory locations at 30H, 31H, and 32H after the execution of the following instruction sequence, given that [30H] = 01, [31H] = 02, and [32H] = 03?

MOV   40H,30H
MOV   30H,31H
MOV   31H,32H
MOV   32H,40H

1.22 Write down the contents of the data memory locations at 50H, 51H, and 52H after the execution of the following instruction sequence, given that [50H] = 3, [51H] = 5, and [52H] = 8.

MOV   A,50H
ADD   A,#3
MOV   R1,A
MOV   A,51H
DEC   A
MOV   50H,A
MOV   A,52H
INC   A
MOV   51H,A
MOV   52H,R1

1.23 Find the execution time (in machine cycles) of the following instructions by referring to Appendix A.

a. MOV A,#0
b. MOV DPTR,#1000H
c. MOVX @DPTR,A
d. ADD A,#2
e. INC DPTR
f. MOVX @DPTR,A

1.24 Suppose the MCS-51 is operating under the control of an external crystal oscillator running at 24 MHz.

1. What is the period of the oscillator clock signal?
2. How much time (in machine cycles) does it take to execute the following four instructions once?
loop: NOP
      NOP
      NOP
      DJNZ R2,loop
3. How many times must this instruction sequence be executed to create a delay of 10 ms.

2

MCS-51 ASSEMBLY PROGRAMMING

2.1 OBJECTIVES

After completing this chapter, you should be able to

- explain the structure of an assembly language program
- use assembler directives to allocate memory blocks, define constants, etc.
- write assembly programs to perform simple arithmetic operations
- write program loops to perform repetitive operations
- use a flowchart to describe program flow
- create delays of any length using program loops

2.2 ASSEMBLY LANGUAGE PROGRAM STRUCTURE

An assembly language program consists of a sequence of statements that tells the computer to perform the desired operations. From a global view, an MCS-51 assembly program consists of four sections. In some cases these sections can be mixed to provide better algorithm design.

- Assembler directives: Assembler directives instruct the assembler how to process subsequent assembly language instructions. Directives also provide a way to define program constants and reserve space for dynamic variables. Some directives may also set a location counter for the active segment. The meaning of *segment* will be explained later.
- Assembly language instructions: These instructions are MCS-51 instructions; some are defined with labels.
- The END directive: This is the last statement in an MCS-51 assembly language source code, and it causes termination of the assembly process.
- Comments: There are two types of comments in an assembly program. The first type is used to explain the function of a single instruction or directive. The second type explains the function of a group of instructions or directives or a whole routine. Adding comments makes a program more readable.

41

Each line of an MCS-51 assembly program, excluding certain special constructs, is comprised of four distinct fields. Some of the fields may be empty. The order of these fields is

1. Label
2. Operation
3. Operand (0 to 3)
4. Comment

Most assemblers are not case sensitive. You can use uppercase or lowercase letters or even mix the use of cases to represent each of the four fields. Some assemblers do provide the option to be case sensitive.

The Label Field

Labels are symbols defined by the user to identify memory locations in the program or data areas of the assembly module. For most instructions and directives, the label is optional. The following rules are used to form a label:

- A label name must begin with a letter (A–Z, a–z) and the letter can be followed by letters, decimal digits (0–9), and special characters. Some assemblers allow the use of some special characters (for example, underscore "_" and question mark "?").
- Most assemblers restrict the number of characters in a label name. The Keil Software's A51 cross assembler allows 31 characters in a label or symbol.
- A label that represents a memory location must be terminated by a colon whereas a symbol that does not represent a memory location must not.
- Only one label can be defined on a line.

The reader must be aware that a label is a symbol that refers to a memory location. When a symbol represents a constant or a register instead of a memory location, we do not terminate it with a colon. For example, the following symbols are not terminated with a colon:

```
loop_cnt    SET    R2
true        EQU    1
false       EQU    0
```

The directives SET and EQU will be explained shortly.

Example 2.1 Valid and invalid labels.

The following instructions contain valid labels:

```
a. begin:    ADD      A,#10
b. print:    LCALL    hexout
```

The following instructions contain invalid labels:

c. to be: SUBB A,#10   ; a blank is included in the label
d. loop   ADD   A,R0   ; the label is not terminated with a colon

The Operation Field

This field contains the mnemonic names for machine instructions or assembler directives. If a label is present, the opcode or directive must be separated from the label field by at least one space. If there is no label, the operation field must be at least one space from the left margin.

Example 2.2 Examples of operation fields:

```
        DEC   R1        ; DEC is the operation field
        ADD   A,#10     ; ADD is the operation field
zero    EQU   0         ; the assembler directive EQU is the
                        ; operation field
```

The Operand Field

If an operand field is present, it follows the operation field and is separated from the operation field by at least one space. The operand field may contain operands for instructions or arguments for assembler directives. The following examples include operand fields:

```
        MOVX  A,@DPTR   ; A and @DPTR are operands
loop:   JNC   loop      ; loop is the operand
```

The Comment Field

The comment field is optional and is added for documentation purpose. The comment field starts with the semicolon ";" and is ignored by the assembler. Two types of comments are illustrated in the following examples:

a.   DEC   30H   ; decrement the contents at location 30H
b.   ; The whole line is a comment

Example 2.3 Identify the four fields in the following source statements:

```
start:    INC  R0     ; increment the loop counter by 1
```

Solution: The four fields in the above source statement are as follows:

a. *start* is a label.
b. *INC* is an instruction mnemonic.
c. *R0* is the operand
d. *; increment the loop counter by 1* is a comment.

2.3 ASSEMBLER DIRECTIVES

Assembler directives look just like instructions in an assembly language program, but they tell the assembler to do something other than create the machine code for an instruction. Assembler directives provide the assembly programmer with a means to instruct the assembler how to process subsequent assembly language instructions. Directives also provide a way to define program constants and reserve space for dynamic variables. Each assembler uses various directives and the ones described here correspond to ones used in version 5.1 of Keil Software's A51 cross assembler. The A51 assembler directives are listed in Table 2.1.

2.3.1 Segment Control Directives

A segment is a block of code or data memory created by the assembler from code or data in an 8051 assembly source file. How you use segments depends on the complexity of your application. Only one segment is active at a time. There are two types of segments: *generic* and *absolute*.

Location Counter

A51 assembler maintains a location counter for each segment. The location counter is a pointer to the address space of the active segment and represents an offset for generic segments or the actual address for absolute segments. When a segment is first activated, its associated location counter is set to 0. The location counter is changed after each instruction by the length of the instruction. The memory initialization and reservation directives (i.e., DS, DB, DW, or DBIT) change the value of the location counter as these directives allocate

TABLE 2.1
Assembler Directives of A51

Category	Directives
Segment control	SEGMENT, RSEG, CSEG, DSEG, BSEG, ISEG, XSEG
Symbol definition	EQU, SET, BIT, CODE, DATA, IDATA, XDATA
Memory initialization	DB, DW
Memory reservation	DBIT, DS
Program linkage	PUBLIC, EXTERN, NAME
Address control	ORG, USING
Others	END

memory. The ORG directive sets a new value for the location counter. If we change the active segment and later return to that segment, the location counter is restored to its previous value. Whenever the assembler encounters a label it assigns the current value of the location counter and the type of the current segment to that label.

The dollar sign ($) indicates the value of the location counter in the active segment. When using the $ symbol, keep in mind that its value changes with each instruction, but only after that instruction has been completely evaluated. If you use $ as an operand of an instruction or directive, it represents the address of the first byte of that instruction.

Generic Segments

Generic segments, which are created using the **SEGMENT** directive, have a name and a class as well as other attributes. We must specify the name of the segment, the segment class, and an optional relocation type and alignment type when we create a relocatable segment. A segment is relocatable if its address is not fixed when it is defined. For example,

    myprog   SEGMENT CODE

defines a segment named **myprog** with a memory class of **CODE**. This means that data in the **myprog** segment will be located in the code or program area of the MCS-51.

Once we have defined a relocatable segment name, we must select that segment using the **RSEG** directive. When RSEG is used to select a segment, that segment becomes the active segment that A51 uses for subsequent code and data until the segment is changed with RSEG or with an absolute segment directive. For example,

    RSEG   myprog

selects the *myprog* segment that is defined above as the current active segment.

Absolute Segments

Absolute segments reside in a fixed memory location. They are created using the **BSEG, CSEG, DSEG, ISEG,** and **XSEG** directives, which allow us to locate code and data or reserve memory space in a fixed location. By default, A51 selects CODE segment as the active segment and initializes its location counter to 0000H.

SEGMENT

The SEGMENT directive is used to declare a generic segment. A relocation type and an allocation type may be specified in the segment declaration. The format of this directive is as follows:

    Segment   SEGMENT *class reloctype alloctype*

where

   Segment   The symbol name to be assigned to the segment.

Class   The memory class to use for the specified segment. The class specifies the memory space for the segment. There are five memory classes: BIT, CODE, DATA, IDATA, and XDATA

Reloctype   Defines the relocation operation that may be performed by the Linker/Locator. The valid relocation types are listed in Table 2.2.

Alloctype   Defines the allocation operation that may be performed by the *Linker/Locator* is the only valid allocation type for A51 is PAGE. The allocation type **PAGE** specifies a segment whose starting address must be on a 256-byte page boundary.

For example,

DDS   SEGMENT DATA

defines a segment with the name DDS and the memory class DATA.

MYSEG   SEGMENT CODE AT 2000H

defines a segment with the name **MYSEG** and the memory class CODE that will be located at address 2000H.

XDS   SEGMENT XDATA PAGE

defines a segment with the name **XDS** and the memory class XDATA. The segment is page aligned, which means it starts on a 256-byte page boundary.

BSEG, CSEG, DSEG, ISEG, and XSEG

Each of the BSEG, CSEG, DSEG, ISEG, or XSEG directives selects an absolute segment, which becomes the active segment. These directives use the following formats:

```
BSEG   AT      address    ; defines an absolute BIT segment
CSEG   AT      address    ; defines an absolute CODE segment
```

TABLE 2.2
Relocation Types

Relocation Type	Description
AT *address*	Specifies an absolute segment; the segment will be placed at the specified address
Bitaddressable	Specifies a segment that will be located within the bitaddressable memory area (20H to 2FH in DATA space); bitaddressable is allowed only for segments with the class DATA that do not exceed 16 bytes in length
Inblock	Specifies a segment that must be contained in a 2048-byte block; this relocation type is valid only for segments with the class CODE
Inpage	Specifies a segment that must be contained in a 256-byte page
Overlayable	Specifies that the segment can share memory with other segments; segments declared with this relocation type can be overlaid with other segments that are also declared with the overlayable relocation type

DSEG	AT	address	; defines an absolute DATA segment
ISEG	AT	address	; defines an absolute IDATA segment
XSEG	AT	address	; defines an absolute XDATA segment

where *address* is an optional base address at which the segment begins. The address may not contain any forward reference and must be an expression that can be evaluated to a valid address. The term *forward reference* refers to the reference made to a symbol that has not been defined at the time of the assembly process. For example,

BSEG   AT 30H

selects absolute BIT segment and sets its location counter to 30H.

CSEG   AT 1000H

selects absolute CODE segment and sets its location counter to 1000H.

2.3.2 Symbol Definition Directives

The symbol definition directives allow you to create symbols that can be used to represent registers, numbers, and addresses. Symbols defined by these directives may not have been previously defined and may not be redefined. The **SET** directive is the only exception to this. There are two advantages in using symbols to represent values or registers. First, the readability of the program is improved because using symbols to refer to registers or values makes the meaning and purpose of each instruction more understandable. Second, the program becomes easier to maintain. We need to change the values of the constants defined by these directives in only one place for all the statements that make reference to those symbols to be updated.

EQU, SET

The EQU and SET directives assign a numeric value or register symbol to the specified symbol name. Symbols defined with EQU may not have been previously defined and may not be redefined by any means. The SET directive allows later redefinition of symbols. The formats of these two directives are as follows:

symbol	EQU	*expression*
symbol	EQU	*register*
symbol	SET	*expression*
symbol	SET	*register*

where

symbol   is the name of the symbol to be defined. The expression or register specified in the EQU or SET directive will be substituted for each occurrence of *symbol* that is used in your assembly program.

expression   is a numeric expression that contains no forward references, or a simple relocatable expression that does not contain absolute or fixed addresses.

register   is one of the following register names: A, R0, R1, R2, R3, R4, R5, R6, or R7.

The following are examples of using EQU and SET directives:

wd_ptr	SET	R0	; use R0 as wd_ptr
true	EQU	1	; use true to represent 1
arr_cnt	EQU	R3	; use R3 as arr_cnt (array counter)

BIT, CODE, DATA, IDATA, and XDATA

The BIT, CODE, DATA, IDATA, and XDATA directives assign an address value to the specified symbol. Symbols defined with the BIT, CODE, DATA, IDATA, and XDATA directives may not be changed or redefined. The formats of these directives are

symbol	BIT	*bit_address*	; defines a BIT symbol
symbol	CODE	*code_address*	; defines a CODE symbol
symbol	DATA	*data_address*	; defines a DATA symbol
symbol	IDATA	*idata_address*	; defines an IDATA symbol
symbol	XDATA	*xdata_address*	; defines an XDATA symbol

where

bit_address   is the address of a bit in internal data memory. Bit address cannot be greater than 255.

code_address   is a code address in the range from 0000H to 0FFFFH.

data_address   is a DATA memory address in the range from 0 to 127 or a special function register (SFR) address in the range from 128 to 255.

idata_address   is an IDATA memory address in the range from 0 to 255.

xdata_address   is a XDATA memory address in the range from 0000H to 0FFFFH

Examples of using these directives follow:

ena_flg	BIT	60H	; use bit location at 60H as ena_flg
PORT1	DATA	90H	; a special function register
buffer	IDATA	60H	; use a location at IDATA as buffer
time	XDATA	1000H	; use external data memory location 1000H ; as variable *time*
restart	CODE	00H	; make restart to be identical to CODE ; memory location 00H

2.3.3 Memory Initialization Directives

The memory initialization directives are used to initialize code space in either byte or word unit. The memory image starts at the point indicated by the current value of the location counter in the currently active segment.

DB

The DB directive initializes program memory with 8-bit byte values. It can be used only when CSEG is the active segment. The DB directive has the following format:

> *label:*   DB expression, expression, . . .

where

> *label*   is the symbol that is given the address of the initialized memory location.
> *expression*   is a byte value. Each *expression* may be a symbol, a character string, or a numeric expression.

Examples of using the DB directive follow. If an optional label is used, its value will point to the first byte constant listed.

Prompt:	DB	'Hello, how are you!' ; ASCII literal
segment:	DB	7EH,60H,6DH,79H,33H,5BH,5FH,70H,7FH,7BH
mixed:	DB	2*3,'cnn news',2*8 ; can mix literals and numbers

DW

The DW directive initializes the program (code) memory with 16-bit constants. It can be used only when CSEG is the active segment. The DW directive has the following format:

> *label:*   DW *expression, expression, . . .*

The following examples illustrate the use of this directive:

jump_tab:	DW	Sunday,Monday,Tuesday,Wednesday,Thursday,Friday,Saturday
misc:	DW	'D',1020H ; first byte contains 0
		; second byte contains 44H
		; third byte contains 10H
		; fourth byte contains 20H

The symbols "Sunday", "Monday", . . . , "Saturday" are labels of some instructions in your program.

2.3.4 Memory Reservation Directives

The memory reservation directives are used to reserve space in bit, byte, or word units. The space reserved starts at the point indicated by the current value of the location counter in the currently active segment.

DBIT

The DBIT directive is used to reserve bits within the BIT segment. The location counter of the segment is advanced by the value of the directive. Care should be taken to ensure that the location counter does not advance beyond the limit of the segment. The format of the DBIT directive is

label: DBIT *expression*

The following are examples of using the DBIT directive:

```
            DBIT   10        ; reserve 10 bits
status:     DBIT   5         ; reserve 5 bits to keep track of program
                             ; status
```

DS

The DS directive is used to reserve space in the currently selected segment in byte units. It can be used only when ISEG, DSEG, or XSEG is the currently active segment. The location counter of the segment is advanced by the value of the directive. Care should be taken to ensure that the location counter does not advance beyond the limit of the segment.

The format of the DS directive is as follows:

label: DS *expression*

The following are examples of using the DS directive in the external data segment.

```
            XDATA            ; select the external data segment
            DS     20        ; reserve 20 bytes (label is optional)
io_buf:     DS     40        ; reserve 40 bytes for I/O
```

Sometimes, it is desirable to tell the assembler where to reserve a block of memory. The programmer can combine the use of AT and DS directives. For example, the following directives reserve 100 bytes starting from the address 2000H:

```
XDATA   AT 2000H     ; reserve memory block starting from the
                     ; address 2000H
DS      100          ; reserve 100 bytes
```

Another example that shows the use of the storage reservation directives is as follows:

```
            BSEG   AT 20H                    ; absolute bit segment at 20H
dec_flag:   DBIT   1                         ; absolute bit
inc_flag:   DBIT   1
            CSEG   AT 100H                   ; absolute code segment at 100H
seg7_tab:   DB     7EH,30H,6DH,79H           ; seven-segment display patterns
                                             ; for 0-9
            DB     33H,5BH,5FH,70H,7FH,7BH
            DSEG   AT 40H                     ; absolute data segment at 40H
i:          DS     1                         ; reserve one byte for variable i
```

j:	DS	1	
sum:	DS	2	; reserve two bytes used for sum
	ISEG	AT D0H	; absolute indirect data segment ; at D0H
ptr_1:	DS	2	
ptr_2:	DS	2	
	XSEG	AT 2000H	; absolute external data segment at ; 2000H
string1:	DS	100	
string2:	DS	100	
in_buf:	DS	80	

2.3.5 Program Linkage Directives

A large software project is usually worked on by more than one person. Each software engineer creates his or her programs in separate files. A program may need to access variables that reside in different files or call subroutines in different files to perform its intended computations. To make this type of cross-reference possible, we need to use assembler directives to tell the assembler that some variables referenced in this program or some subroutines called by this program reside in different files. We also need to inform the assembler of those variables and subroutines (or procedures) that will be accessed by programs in different files. At some point, these programs (created by different people) must be combined into a single executable module—this job is done by a linker. One of the functions of a linker is to resolve this type of cross-reference issue.

Program linkage directives allow the separately assembled program modules (files) to communicate by permitting intermodule references and naming of modules. A module may consist of one file or multiple files.

PUBLIC

The PUBLIC directive lists symbols that may be used in other object modules. A symbol declared PUBLIC must be defined in the current module. Declaring it PUBLIC allows it to be referenced in another module. The following example illustrates the use of this directive:

        PUBLIC   inchar, outchar, globesum, quicksort

EXTRN

The EXTRN directive informs the assembler of a list of symbols to be referenced in the current module but that are defined in other modules. The list of external symbols must have a segment associated with each symbol in the list. The segment type can be CODE, XDATA, DATA, IDATA, BIT, or NUMBER. NUMBER is a typeless symbol defined by EQU. The segment type indicates the way a symbol may be used. The format of this directive is as follows:

EXTERN   *class (symbol, symbol, . . .)*

where

class   is the memory class where the symbol has been defined and may be one of the following: BIT, CODE, DATA, IDATA, XDATA, or NUMBER.

symbol   is an external symbol name

The PUBLIC and EXTRN directives work together. When one symbol is declared EXTRN in one module, it must be declared as PUBLIC in another module as illustrated in the following example:

In module main.a51:

EXTRN CODE(quicksort, binsearch)
.
.
.

LCALL quicksort
.
.
.

In module second.a51:

PUBLIC quicksort, binsearch
.
.

quicksort: (begin of subroutine)
.
.
.

RET

binsearch: (begin of subroutine)
.
.
.

RET

NAME

For very large programs, NAME facilitates the program development by partitioning the problem in modules, where each module may be comprised of several files. The NAME directive specifies the name to be used for the object module generated for the current program. The file name for the object file is not the object module name. The object module name is embedded within the object file. The format for the NAME directive is

NAME   module_name

2.3.6 Address Control Directives

The following directives allow the control of the address location counter or the control of absolute register symbols.

ORG

The ORG directive is used to specify a value for the currently active segment's location counter. It can be used only when the location counter needs to be changed. Care should be taken to ensure that the location counter does not advance beyond the limit of the selected segment.

The format for the ORG directive is as follows:

    ORG *expression*

The following examples illustrate the use of this directive:

ORG	1000H	; set active location counter to 4096
ORG	RESET	; RESET is a previously defined symbol
ORG	jump_tab+200H	; arithmetic expression

Using

Some 8051 instructions (i.e., PUSH/POP) allow only absolute register addresses to be used. It is a common practice to save registers during subroutine calls (to be discussed in Chapter 3). The A51 assembler uses symbols AR0–AR7 to represent absolute data addresses of R0 through R7 in the current register bank. The absolute addresses for these registers will change depending on the register bank that is currently selected. The **USING** directive enables the register bank selection. By combining the use of the USING directive with the symbols AR0–AR7, we can specify the address of any register in these four register banks. It should be noted that the USING directive selects the register bank but does not do the actual register bank switching; this must still be done in the code. For example,

MOV	PSW,#00	; switch to register bank 0
MOV	AR5,#11H	; place the value 11H into the location 05H
USING	2	; select the register bank 2
PUSH	AR2	; push the memory location 12H into the stack
MOV	R5,#22H	; place the value 22H in memory location 05H

This directive simplifies the direct addressing of a specified register bank.

2.3.7 Other Directives

END

The END directive signals the end of the assembly module. Any text in the assembly file that appears after the END directive is ignored. The END directive is needed in every assembly source file; if the END statement is missing, the A51 assembler will generate an error message.

2.3.8 Macro Definition Directives

A macro is a name that we assign to one or more assembly statements. There are situations in which we need to include the same sequence of instructions in several places. This sequence of instructions may operate on different parameters. By placing this sequence of instructions in a macro we need to type the sequence of instructions only once. The macro capability not only makes us more productive but also makes the program more readable.

MACRO

The MACRO directive is used to define the start of a macro. A macro is a segment of instructions that is enclosed between the directives MACRO and ENDM. The format of a macro is as follows:

```
macro_name:        macro arg1, . . . ,argn ; comment
                     .
                     .
                     .
                   endm
```

ENDM

This directive terminates a macro definition. Assume we have the following macro definition:

```
aver:      macro  arg1,arg2,arg3       ; a macro that computes the average of arg1,
           mov    A,arg1               ; arg2, and arg3 and places the result in A
           add    A,arg2
           add    A,arg3
           mov    B,#3
           div    AB                   ; divide B into A and A gets the average
           endm                        ; terminate the macro definition
```

To invoke this macro, simply enter the macro name and its parameters. The statement

```
aver   R1,R2,R3
```

will enable the assembler to generate the following instructions starting from the current location counter:

```
mov   A,R1
add   A,R2
```

```
add    A,R3
mov    B,#3
div    AB
```

If a macro is invoked *n* times in a program, then there will be *n* copies of the instructions enclosed in the macro definition to be duplicated in the program.

2.4 FLOWCHARTS

In the real world, a programming project is often done by a team rather than a single person. To facilitate communication among the team, program documentation becomes very important. Without the documentation, it will be extremely hard for other people to read your programs. Adding comments is one form of documentation. Flowcharting is another type of documentation. A *flowchart* is a diagram that shows the structure of a program. The flowchart symbols used in this book are shown in Figure 2.1.

The terminal symbol is used at the beginning and end of each program. When it is used at the beginning of a program, the word *Start* is written inside it. When it is used at the end of a program, it contains the word *Stop*.

The *process box* indicates what must be done at this point in the program execution. The operation specified by the process box could be shifting accumulator A to the right by one place, decrementing the index register by 1, etc.

The *input/output box* is used to represent data that are either read or displayed by the computer.

The *decision box* contains a question that can be answered either yes or no. A decision box has two exits, also marked yes and no. The computer will take one action if the answer is yes and will take a different action if the answer is no.

The *on-page connector* indicates that the flowchart continues elsewhere on the same page. The place where it is continued will have the same label as the on-page connector. The

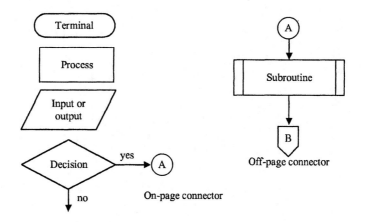

Figure 2.1 Flowchart symbols used in this book.

off-page connector indicates that the flowchart continues on another page. To determine where the flowchart continues, you need to look at the following pages of the flowchart to find the matching off-page connector.

Normal flow on a flowchart is from top to bottom and from left to right. Any line that does not follow this normal flow should have an arrowhead on it.

2.5 WRITING PROGRAMS TO DO ARITHMETIC

In this section, we will use short programs that perform simple calculations to demonstrate how a program is written.

Example 2.4 Write a program to add the values of three memory locations (40H, 41H, and 42H) and save the sum at 43H.

Solution: The procedure for solving this problem is illustrated in the flowchart shown in Figure 2.2. The program is as follows:

```
MOV   A,40H      ; load the contents of the memory location at 40H into A
ADD   A,41H      ; add the contents of the memory location at 41H to A
ADD   A,42H      ; add the contents of the memory location at 42H to A
MOV   43H,A      ; save the sum at 43H
END
```

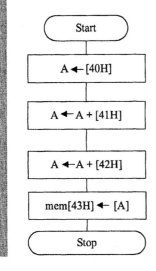

Figure 2.2 Flowchart for adding the contents of three memory locations.

Example 2.5 Write a program to subtract 5 from three 8-bit numbers stored at 50H, 51H, and 52H.

Solution: We must be aware of the limitations of the subtract instruction of the MCS-51:

1. A memory location cannot be the destination.

2. The carry is included as one of the source operands.

Therefore, four steps must be followed to subtract a number from a memory location:

STEP 1   Load the memory contents into accumulator A.

STEP 2   Clear the carry flag.

STEP 3   Subtract 5 from accumulator A

STEP 4   Store the contents of accumulator A in the same memory location.

The program is as follows:

```
MOV    A,50H        ; load the first number into A
CLR    C            ; clear the borrow
SUBB   A,#5         ; subtract 5 from the first number
MOV    50H,A        ; store the result at 50H
MOV    A,51H
CLR    C
SUBB   A,#5
MOV    51H,A
MOV    A,52H
CLR    C
SUBB   A,#5
MOV    52H,A
```

2.5.1 The Carry/Borrow Flag

So far we have been working with one-byte hex numbers because these are the largest numbers that can fit into accumulator A. However, programs can be written to add and subtract numbers that contain two or more bytes. Arithmetic performed in an 8-bit microcontroller on numbers that are larger than 1 byte is called *multiprecision arithmetic*. Multiprecision arithmetic makes use of the carry flag in the program status word (PSW).

Bit 7 of the PSW register is the carry (CY) flag. It can be thought of as a temporary ninth bit that is appended to any 8-bit register. The CY flag enables the programmer to write programs to add and subtract hex numbers that are larger than 1 byte. For example, consider the following instructions:

```
MOV    A,#89H
ADD    A,#8AH
```

These two instructions add the numbers 89H and 8AH and store the result in A.

$$
\begin{array}{r}
89\text{H} \\
+\ 8\text{AH} \\
\hline
113\text{H}
\end{array}
$$

The result is 113H, a 9-bit number, which is too large to fit into the 8-bit accumulator A. When the MCS-51 executes these two instructions, the lower 8 bits of the answer, 13H are placed in accumulator A. This part of the answer is called the *sum*. The ninth bit is called a *carry*. A carry of 1 following an addition instruction sets the CY flag of the PSW register to 1. A carry of 0 following an addition instruction clears the CY flag to 0. For example, execution of the following two instructions

```
MOV   A,#40H
ADD   A,#36H
```

will clear the CY flag to 0 because the carry resulting from this addition is 0. In summary,

- If the addition produces a carry of binary 1, the carry flag is set to 1.
- If the addition produces a carry of binary 0, the carry flag is cleared to 0.

2.5.2 Multiprecision Addition

Multiprecision addition is the addition of numbers that are larger than 1 byte in an 8-bit computer. The numbers 35C8H and 45B4H are both 2-byte numbers. To find their sum using the MCS-51 microcontroller, we have to write a program that uses multiprecision addition. If we add these two numbers on paper from the right to the left, we get the following:

STEP 1   Add 8H and 4H, which gives the sum CH (or decimal 12).

STEP 2   Add CH and BH, which gives a result of 17H, or a sum of 7H and a carry of 1. The carry is written above the column of numbers on the immediate left. This transfers the carry from the low byte of the number to its high byte.

STEP 3   Add 5H and 5H and the carry 1H, which gives a sum of BH (decimal 11).

STEP 4   Add 3H and 4H, which gives a sum of 7.

$$
\begin{array}{r}
1 \quad \leftarrow \text{carry from the low byte to high byte} \\
35\text{C8H} \\
+45\text{B4H} \\
\hline
7\text{B7CH}
\end{array}
$$

The important point is that the carry had to be transferred from the low byte of the sum to its high byte. The following program can add these 2-byte numbers and store the high byte of the sum at 40H and the low byte at 41H:

```
MOV   A,#C8H        ; load the low byte of the first number into A
ADD   A,#B4H        ; add the low byte of the second number to A
```

```
MOV     40H,A         ; save the low byte of the sum
MOV     A,#35H        ; load the high byte of the first number into A
ADDC    A,#45H        ; add the high byte of the second number and the carry to A
MOV     41H,A         ; save the high byte of the sum
END
```

Note that the MOV instructions do not affect the value of the CY flag (otherwise, the program would not work).

Example 2.6 Write a program to add two 3-byte numbers stored at 41H–43H and 51H–53H, respectively. Save the sum at 61H–63H. Assume the most significant to least significant bytes are stored from low address to high address.

Solution: The addition should start from the least significant byte, then proceed to the second significant byte, and then to the most significant byte. The program is as follows:

```
MOV     A,43H         ; load the low byte of the first number into A
ADD     A,53H         ; add the low byte of the second number to A
MOV     63H,A         ; save the low byte of the sum
MOV     A,42H         ; load the middle byte of the first number into A
ADDC    A,52H         ; add the middle byte of the second number and the carry to A
MOV     62H,A         ; save the middle byte of the sum
MOV     A,41H         ; load the high byte of the first number into A
ADDC    A,51H         ; add the high byte of the second number and the carry to A
MOV     61H,A         ; save the high byte of the sum
END
```

2.5.3 Subtraction and the CY Flag

The CY flag also enables the MCS-51 to borrow from the high byte to the low byte during a multiprecision subtraction. Consider the following problem:

```
 3CH
−4AH
```

We are attempting to subtract a larger number from a smaller number. Subtracting AH from CH is not a problem:

```
 3CH
−4AH
   2
```

Now we need to subtract 4H from 3H. To do this, we need to borrow from somewhere. The MCS-51 borrows from the CY flag, thus setting the CY flag. When we borrow from the next higher digit of a hex number, the borrow has a value of decimal 16. After borrowing from the CY flag, the problem can be completed:

```
  3CH
−4AH
  F2H
```

When the MCS-51 executes a subtract instruction, it always borrows from the CY flag. The borrow is either a 1 or a 0. The CY flag operates as follows during a subtraction:

- If the MCS-51 borrows a 1 from the CY flag during a subtraction, the CY flag is set to 1.
- If the MCS-51 borrows a 0 from the CY flag during a subtraction, the carry flag is cleared to 0.

2.5.4 Multiprecision Subtraction

Multiprecision subtraction is the subtraction of numbers that are larger than 1 byte. To subtract the hex number 3394H from 653BH, the MCS-51 has to perform a multiprecision subtraction:

```
  653BH
−3394H
```

Like a multiprecision addition, a multiprecision subtraction is performed one byte at a time, beginning with the low byte. Because the borrow flag (CY in PSW) is involved in all of the MCS-51 subtraction instructions, it must be cleared to zero when the subtraction is performed on the low bytes. The following three instructions can be used to subtract the low bytes:

```
CLR   C           ; clear the CY flag
MOV   A,#3BH       ; place the low byte of the first number in A
SUBB  A,#94H       ; subtract the low byte of the second number from A
```

Because a larger number is subtracted from a smaller one, a 1 is borrowed from the CY flag, causing it to be set to 1. The contents of accumulator A should be saved before the high bytes are subtracted. Let us save the low-byte result at 41H:

```
MOV   41H,A
```

When the high bytes are subtracted, the borrow of 1 has to be subtracted from the high-byte result. The MCS-51 subtract instructions do exactly that. The instructions to subtract the high bytes are

```
MOV   A,#65H
SUBB  A,#33H
```

We also need to save the high byte of the result with the following instruction:

MOV   40H,A

The complete program with comments is as follows:

```
CLR    C            ; clear the CY flag
MOV    A,#3BH       ; place the low byte of the first number in A
SUBB   A,#94H       ; subtract the low byte of the second number from A
MOV    41H,A        ; save the low byte of the result
MOV    A,#65H       ; place the high byte of the first number in A
SUBB   A,#33H       ; subtract the high byte of the second number and borrow
                    ; from A
MOV    40H,A        ; save the high byte of the difference
END
```

Example 2.7 Write a program to subtract the 3-byte number stored at 41H–43H from the 3-byte number stored at 51H–53H and save the difference at 61H–63H.

Solution: Subtraction proceeds from the least significant byte to the most significant byte:

```
CLR    C            ; clear the carry (borrow) flag to 0
MOV    A,53H        ; place the low byte of the first number in A
SUBB   A,43H        ; subtract the low byte of the second number from A
MOV    63H,A        ; save the low byte of the difference
MOV    A,52H        ; place the middle byte of the first number in A
SUBB   A,42H        ; subtract the middle byte of the second number and borrow
                    ; from A
MOV    62H,A        ; save the middle byte of the difference
MOV    A,51H        ; place the high byte of the first number in A
SUBB   A,41H        ; subtract the high byte of the second number and borrow
                    ; from A
MOV    61H,A        ; save the high byte of the difference
END
```

2.5.5 Binary-Coded Decimal Addition

Although virtually all digital systems are binary in the sense that all signals within the systems can take on only two values, some perform arithmetic in the decimal system. In some circumstances, the identity of decimal numbers is retained to the extent that each decimal digit is individually represented by a binary code. There are 10 decimal digits, so four binary bits are required for each code element. The most obvious choice is to use binary numbers 0000 through 1001 to represent the decimal digits 0 through 9. This form of representation is known as the binary-coded decimal (BCD) *representation* or *code*. The binary numbers 1010 through 1111 do not represent decimal digits, and they are therefore illegal BCD code.

Keyboard inputs, screen displays, and printer outputs in decimal system are most convenient for human users. On input, the decimal numbers are converted into some binary form for processing, and this conversion is reversed on output. In a "straight binary" computer, a decimal number is converted into its binary equivalent; for example, the decimal number 54 is converted to 110110. In a computer using the BCD system, 54 would be converted into 0101 0100. If the BCD format is used, it must be preserved during arithmetic processing.

The principal advantage of the BCD system is the simplicity of input/output conversion; its principal disadvantage is the complexity of arithmetic processing. The choice (between binary and BCD) depends on the type of problems the system will handle.

The MCS-51 microcontroller can add only binary numbers—not decimal numbers. The following program appears to cause the MCS-51 to add the decimal numbers 23 + 41 and store the sum in the memory location at 40H:

```
MOV   A,#23H
ADD   A,#41H
MOV   40H,A
END
```

The program performs the following addition:

$$
\begin{array}{r}
23H \\
+41H \\
\hline
64H
\end{array}
$$

When the MCS-51 executes this program, it adds the numbers according to the rules of hex addition and produces the sum 64H. This is the correct BCD answer, because the result represents the decimal sum of 23 + 41. In this example, the MCS-51 gives the appearance of performing decimal addition. However, a problem occurs when the MCS-51 adds two BCD digits and gets a sum digit greater than 9. The sum is incorrect in the decimal system, as the following three examples illustrate:

$$
\begin{array}{ccc}
23H & 35H & 18H \\
+07H & +47H & +68H \\
\hline
2A & 7CH & 80H
\end{array}
$$

The answers to the first two problems are obviously erroneous in the decimal number system because the hex digits A and C are not between 0 and 9. The answer to the third example appears to contain valid BCD digits, but in the decimal system 18 plus 68 equals 86, not 80; this example involves a carry from the low nibble to the high nibble.

In summary, a sum in the BCD format is incorrect if a sum digit is greater than 9 or if there is a carry to the next higher nibble. Incorrect BCD sums can be adjusted by adding 6 to them. To correct the examples,

1. Add 6H to every sum digit greater than 9.
2. Add 6H to every sum digit that had a carry of 1 to the next higher digit.

Here are the problems with their sums adjusted:

23H	35H	18H
+07H	+47H	+68H
2AH	7CH	80H
+ 6H	+ 6H	+ 8H
30H	82H	86H

The sixth bit of the program status word register is the *auxiliary carry*, or AC flag. A carry from the low nibble to the high nibble during addition is an auxiliary carry. An auxiliary carry of 1 during addition sets the AC flag to 1, and an auxiliary carry of 0 during addition clears it to 0. If there is a carry from the high nibble during addition, the C flag is set to 1, which indicates the high nibble is incorrect. The rules for adjusting the result of BCD addition are as follows:

- If the accumulator bits 3–0 are greater than 9 (xxxx1010–xxxx1111), or the AC flag is one, six is added to the accumulator to produce the proper BCD digit in the low-order nibble.

- If the carry flag is now set, or if the four high-order bits in the accumulator now exceed 9 (1010xxxx–1111xxxx), these high-order bits are incremented by six, producing the proper BCD digit in the high-order nibble.

The MCS-51 provides the instruction **DA A** to implement the BCD addition adjustment operation. The DA A instruction does not apply to decimal subtraction and it must be used immediately after one of the eight addition instructions. Of course, the numbers added must be legal BCD numbers.

Example 2.8 Write a program to add the BCD numbers stored at memory locations 40H and 41H and save the sum at 42H.

Solution:

```
MOV   A,40H      ; load the first BCD number into A
ADD   A,41H      ; add the second BCD number to A
DA    A          ; decimal adjustment of the sum in A
MOV   42H,A      ; save the sum
END
```

Execution of the DA A instruction may set the CY flag, allowing the user to implement multiprecision BCD addition.

2.5.6 Multiplication and Division

The MCS-51 provides only one multiplication instruction and one division instruction. The **MUL AB** instruction multiplies the unsigned 8-bit integers in accumulator A and register B. The low-order byte of the 16-bit product is left in accumulator A, and the high-order byte in B. If the product is greater than 65535 (0FFFFH) the overflow flag is set; otherwise it is cleared. The carry flag is always cleared.

Example 2.9 Multiply the integers stored at 41H and 42H and save the product at 51H–52H. Place the upper and lower bytes in 51H and 52H, respectively.

Solution: We need to place two integers in A and B before the multiplication.

```
MOV   A,41H     ; place the first integer in A
MOV   B,42H     ; place the second integer in B
MUL   AB        ; perform multiplication
MOV   51H,B     ; save the upper byte of the product
MOV   52H,A     ; save the lower byte of the product
END
```

The unsigned multiply procedure also allows multiprecision operations. In multiprecision multiplication, the multiplier and the multiplicand must be broken down into 8-bit chunks, and several 8-bit by 8-bit multiplications must be performed. Assume we want to multiply a 16-bit hexadecimal number M by another hexadecimal 16-bit number N. To illustrate the procedure, we will break M and N down as follows:

$$M = M_H M_L$$

$$N = N_H N_L$$

where M_H, M_L, N_H, and N_L are the upper, and lower 8 bits of M and N, respectively. Four 8-bit by 8-bit multiplications must be performed, and then the partial products are added together as shown in Figure 2.3. The procedure to add these four partial products is as follows:

STEP 1   Allocate 4 bytes to hold the product. Assume these 4 bytes are located at P, P + 1, P + 2, and P + 3.

STEP 2   Generate the partial product $M_L N_L$ and save it at locations P + 2 and P + 3.

STEP 3   Generate the partial product $M_H N_H$ and save it at locations P and P + 1.

STEP 4   Generate the partial product $M_H N_L$ and add it to locations P + 1 and P + 2. A multiprecision addition is performed. This addition may set the carry flag to 1. Add the carry flag to location P.

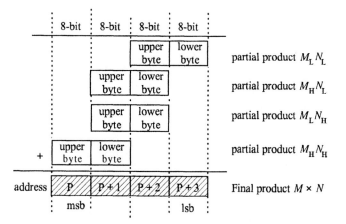

Figure 2.3 16-bit by 16-bit multiplication. msb, most significant byte; lsb, least significant byte.

STEP 5   Generate the partial product $M_L N_H$ and add it to locations P + 1 and P + 2. A multiprecision addition is performed. This addition may set the carry flag to 1. Add the carry flag to location P.

Example 2.10 Assume there are two unsigned 16-bit integers stored at 30H–31H and 40H–41H, respectively. Write a program to compute their product and store the result at 50H–53H.

Solution: The most significant to least significant bytes of the product are to be stored from 50H to 53H, respectively.

MOV	A,31H	; place M_L in A
MOV	B,41H	; place N_L in B
MUL	AB	; compute $M_L N_L$
MOV	53H,A	; save the lower byte of $M_L N_L$
MOV	52H,B	; save the upper byte of $M_L N_L$
MOV	A,30H	; place M_H in A
MOV	B,40H	; place N_H in B
MUL	AB	; compute $M_H N_H$
MOV	51H,A	; save the lower byte of $M_H N_H$
MOV	50H,B	; save the upper byte of $M_H N_H$
MOV	A,30H	; place M_H in A
MOV	B,41H	; place N_L in B
MUL	AB	; compute $M_H N_L$
ADD	A,52H	; add the lower byte of $M_H N_L$ to memory location P + 2
MOV	52H,A	; "

```
MOV    A,B       ; add the carry and the upper byte of M_H N_L to location P + 1
ADDC   A,51H     ; "
MOV    51H,A     ; "
MOV    A,50H     ; add the carry to memory location P
ADDC   A,#0      ; "
MOV    50H,A     ; "
MOV    A,31H     ; place M_L in A
MOV    B,40H     ; place N_H in B
MUL    AB        ; compute M_L N_H
ADD    A,52H     ; add the lower byte of M_L N_H to location P + 2
MOV    52H,A     ; "
MOV    A,B       ; add the upper byte of M_L N_H and carry to location P + 1
ADDC   A,51H     ; "
MOV    51H,A     ; "
MOV    A,50H     ; add the carry to memory location P
ADDC   A,#0      ; "
MOV    50H,A     ; "
END
```

In some applications, the user may need to multiply two numbers longer than 16 bits or even two numbers of different numbers of bits. A more general multiprecision multiplication program can be written using the same method. This problem is left as an exercise.

The **DIV AB** instruction divides the unsigned 8-bit integer in accumulator A by the unsigned 8-bit integer in register B. Accumulator A receives the integer part of the quotient; register B receives the integer remainder. The carry and OV flags will be cleared. However, if B originally contains 00H, the values returned in accumulator A and register B will be undefined and the overflow flag will be set to 1.

Example 2.11 Write a program to convert the binary number stored in accumulator A to a decimal number and save the result at the memory location 40H. Assume the binary number in A is no larger than decimal 99.

Solution: Divide the binary number in accumulator A by 10, then the quotient is the tens digit and the remainder is the ones digit. The procedure is as follows:

STEP 1   Place decimal 10 in register B.

STEP 2   Divide accumulator A by register B.

STEP 3   Store register B at the memory location 40H. This will clear the upper 4 bits of this memory location because the remainder is no larger than 9.

STEP 4   Place decimal 16 in register B and multiply accumulator A and register B. This will shift the contents of accumulator A to the left by four places.

STEP 5   Add the contents of the memory location at 40H to accumulator A and store the result back to the same location. This will combine the tens and ones digits together.

The program is as follows:

```
MOV   B,#10        ; place decimal 10 in register B
DIV   AB           ; divide A by B
MOV   40H,B        ; save the ones digit in memory location
MOV   B,#10H       ; place decimal 16 in B
MUL   AB           ; shift A to the left by four places
ADD   A,40H        ; combine the tens and ones digits
MOV   40H,A        ; "
```

2.6 PROGRAM LOOPS

Performing repetitive operations is the strength of a computer. For a computer to perform repetitive operations, program loops must be written to tell the computer to repeat the same sequence of instructions many times. A *finite loop* is a program loop that will be executed only a finite number of times while an *infinite loop* is one in which the computer stays forever.

There are four major variants of the looping mechanism:

• DO statement S forever

This is an infinite loop in which statement S is repeated forever. In some applications, the programmers might add the statement *IF C then EXIT* to leave the infinite loop. An infinite loop is shown in Figure 2.4.

• FOR $I = i_1$ to i_2 DO S or FOR $I = i_2$ down to i_1 DO S

Here, the variable I is the loop counter, which keeps track of the number of remaining times statement S is to be executed. The loop number can be incremented (in the first case) or decremented (in the second case). Statement S is repeated $i_2 - i_1 + 1$ times. The value of i_2 is assumed to be no smaller than i_1. If there is concern that the relationship $i_1 \leq i_2$ may not hold, then it must be checked at the beginning of the loop. Five steps are required to implement a FOR loop:

STEP 1   Initialize the loop counter.

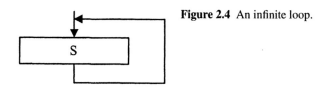

Figure 2.4 An infinite loop.

STEP 2   Perform the specified operations and increment (or decrement) the loop counter.

STEP 3   Compare the counter with the limit.

STEP 4   Exit if the value of the loop counter is greater (or less) than the upper (lower) limit.

STEP 5   Return to Step 2.

A FOR loop is shown in Figure 2.5.

• WHILE C DO S

Whenever a WHILE construct is executed, the logical expression C is evaluated first. If it yields a false value, statement S will not be executed. The action of a WHILE construct is illustrated in Figure 2.6. Four steps are required to implement a WHILE loop:

STEP 1   Initialize the logical expression C.

STEP 2   Evaluate the logical expression C.

STEP 3   Perform the specified operations if the logical expression C evaluates to true. Update the logical expression C and go to Step 2.

STEP 4   Exit the loop.

• REPEAT S UNTIL C

Statement S is first executed then the logical expression C is evaluated. If C is false, the next statement will be executed. Otherwise, statement S will be executed again. The action of this construct is illustrated in Figure 2.7. Statement S will be executed at least once. Three steps are required to implement this construct:

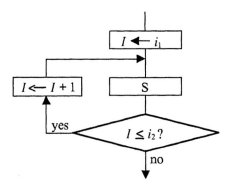

Figure 2.5 For $I = i_1$ to i_2 DO S.

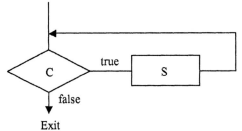

Figure 2.6 The WHILE . . . DO construct.

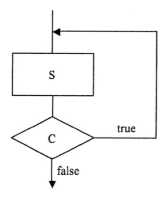

Figure 2.7 The REPEAT . . . UNTIL construct.

STEP 1   Initialize the logical expression.

STEP 2   Execute statement S.

STEP 3   Go to Step 2 if the logical expression C evaluates to true. Otherwise, exit.

To implement a finite loop in the MCS-51 assembly language, the programmer must use one of the *conditional jump* (other microcontrollers may refer to conditional jump as *conditional branch* instead) instructions. When executing a conditional jump instruction, the MCS-51 decides whether the jump should be taken by

- checking the values of condition flags or
- checking a memory bit or
- comparing the contents of accumulator A with zero or
- comparing the contents of accumulator A with a direct byte or an immediate byte or
- comparing the contents of a register with an immediate value or
- comparing the contents of a memory location with an immediate value

2.6.1 Jump Instructions

A jump instruction is required to implement a program loop. The MCS-51 jump instructions are listed in Table 2.3.

The MCS-51 provides conditional jump instructions that determine if two operands are equal or not equal. There are applications in which we want to implement the conditional jump based on the following conditions:

- greater than
- greater than or equal to
- less than
- less than or equal to
- higher than

TABLE 2.3
MCS-51 Jump Instructions

Mnemonic		Description
JC	rel	Jump if carry is set
JNC	rel	Jump if carry is not set
JB	bit,rel	Jump if direct bit is set
JNB	bit,rel	Jump if direct bit is not set
JBC	bit,rel	Jump if direct bit is set and clear bit
AJMP	addr11	Absolute jump (jump distance is 11 bits)
LJMP	addr16	Long jump (jump with 16-bit destination)
SJMP	rel	Short jump (relative)
JMP	@A+DPTR	Jump indirect relative to the DPTR
JZ	rel	Jump if accumulator A is zero
JNZ	rel	Jump if accumulator A is not zero
CJNE	A,direct,rel	Compare direct byte to accumulator A and jump if not equal
CJNE	A,#data,rel	Compare immediate data to accumulator A and jump if not equal
CJNE	Rn,#data,rel	Compare immediate data to register and jump if not equal
CJNE	@Ri,#data,rel	Compare immediate data to indirect byte and jump if not equal
DJNZ	Rn,rel	Decrement register and jump if not zero
DJNZ	direct,rel	Decrement direct byte and jump if not zero

- higher than or the same as
- lower than
- lower than or the same as
- etc.

These conditional jump operations must be synthesized.

The comparison of two operands can be signed or unsigned. The conditions of *greater than*, *greater than or equal to*, *smaller than*, and *smaller than or equal to* require a signed comparison. The remaining conditions require an unsigned comparison.

In an unsigned comparison, two operands are treated as unsigned (i.e., positive) numbers. The second operand (say operand2) is subtracted from the first operand (say operand1). The first operand is higher than or equal to the second operand if the carry bit is 0 after the subtraction. Since the MCS-51 provides only subtract instructions that include carry bit, it must be cleared before subtraction is performed. For example, the instruction sequence

```
CLR    C
SUBB   A,R0
JNC    somewhere       ; jump if A is larger than or equal to R0
```

will cause the jump to be taken if the value in A is higher than or equal to that in R0. The instruction sequence

```
CLR    C
SUBB   A,R0
```

	JC	fallthru	; A is smaller
	JNZ	higher	; A is higher if C = 0 and A ≠ 0
fallthru:	.		
	.		
	.		
	.		
higher:	.		
	.		
	.		
	.		

will cause the program control to be switched to the instruction with the label "higher" if the value in A is higher than that in R0.

The signs of operands must be checked when a signed comparison is to be performed. Signed numbers are represented in two's complement number system. The procedure to test if operand1 is greater than operand2 is as follows:

STEP 1   If the most significant bit of operand1 is 0 (operand1 is positive) and bit 7 of operand2 is 1 (operand2 is negative), then operand1 is greater (or larger).

STEP 2   If most significant bits of both operand1 and operand2 are 0s (both operands are positive), subtract operand2 from operand1. If carry bit is 0 and the result is nonzero, then operand1 is greater than operand2.

STEP 3   If most significant bits of both operand1 and operand2 are 1s (both operands are negative), then complement both operands. This operation computes the magnitude of two operands. Subtract the magnitude of operand2 from that of operand1. If carry bit is 1, then operand1 is greater than operand2.

STEP 4   Operand1 is not greater than operand2 for all the other conditions.

Example 2.12 Write an instruction sequence to implement *jump if accumulator A is greater than memory location 20H*. Memory location at 20H is bit addressable.

Solution: Translate the previous algorithm directly into MCS-51 instructions:

	MOV	R0,A	; save a copy of A in R0
	JB	ACC.7,op1_neg	; A is negative if its bit 7 is 1
	JB	07,greater	; A is nonnegative and [20H] is
			; negative so A is greater
	CLR	C	; both operands are nonnegative
	SUBB	A,20H	; subtract [20H] from A
	JC	le	; A is smaller
	JNZ	greater	; A is greater
	JMP	le	; A is equal to [20H]
op1_neg:	JNB	07,le	; [20H] is nonnegative so A is smaller
	CPL	A	; compute the 1's complement of A
	ADD	A,#1	; add 1 to A to get the magnitude of A

```
                 XCH   A,20H              ; exchange the magnitude of A with [20H]
                 CPL   A                  ; compute the 1's complement of [20H]
                 ADD   A,#1               ; add 1 and get the magnitude of [20H]
                 CLR   C                  ; clear the C bit
                 SUBB  A,20H              ; perform a reverse subtraction
                 JC    le                 ; A is greater
                 JNZ   greater
le:              .
                 .
                 .
greater:         .
                 .
                 .
```

Other conditions can be tested in a similar way and will be left as exercise problems.

The JMP @A+DPTR instruction supports case jumps. The destination address is computed as the sum of the 16-bit DPTR register and accumulator A when the instruction is executed. Typically, DPTR is loaded with the base address of a jump table, and accumulator A is given the index to the table. In an eight-way branch, for example, an integer 0 through 7 is loaded into accumulator A. The code to be executed might be as follows:

```
MOV   DPTR,#jump_tab
MOV   A,index_no
RL    A                      ; multiply the index by 2
JMP   @A+DPTR
```

The "RL A" instruction converts the index number (0 through 7) to an even number in the range from 0 to 14 because each entry in the jump table is 2 bytes long:

```
jump_tab:     AJMP case_0
              AJMP case_1
              AJMP case_2
              AJMP case_3
              AJMP case_4
              AJMP case_5
              AJMP case_6
              AJMP case_7
```

2.6.2 Decrement and Increment Instructions

A program loop requires a counter, often called the *loop count*, to keep track of the number of times remaining for the loop to be executed. The loop count can be either incremented or decremented by 1. The following instructions decrement a register or a memory location:

- DEC A: subtract one from the contents of accumulator A
- DEC direct: subtract one from the contents of an internal memory byte or register
- DEC Rn: subtract one from the contents of register Rn
- DEC @Ri: subtract one from an indirect byte

These instructions increment a register or a memory location:

- INC A: add one to the contents of accumulator A
- INC Rn: add one to the contents of the register Rn
- INC direct: add one to the contents of a direct byte
- INC @Ri: add one to the contents of an indirect byte
- INC DPTR: add one to the contents of the data pointer DPTR

2.6.3 Instructions for Variable Initialization

When writing a program, we often need to provide an initial value to a variable. In addition to using the MOV instruction to place an immediate value to a register or to a memory location, the following instructions can be used to initialize a variable to 0 or 1:

- CLR   A   ; clear accumulator A to 0
- CLR   C   ; clear the carry flag to 0
- CLR   bit   ; clear a memory bit to 0
- SETB C   ; set the carry flag to 1
- SETB bit   ; set a memory bit to 1

Example 2.13 Write a program to convert a string of letters into uppercase. The string is stored at locations starting from 40H and is terminated with a NULL character. The ASCII code of the NULL character is 0. Assume the string contains no special characters other than a NULL and spaces.

Solution: The flowchart of the program is illustrated in Figure 2.8. Register R0 is used as the string pointer. The program checks each character and takes different actions depending on whether the character is a letter or the NULL character:

- Letter: the program clears the bit 5 by ANDing the letter with DFH.
- NULL character: stop.

The program is as follows:

```
str_ptr    SET    R0
NULL       EQU    0
space      EQU    20H
```

```
            MOV   str_ptr,#40H
again:      MOV   A,@str_ptr          ; place the current character in A
            CJNE  A,#NULL,check
            JMP   exit                ; stop at the end of the string
check:      CJNE  A,#space,clear
            ajmp  next                ; don't touch space character
clear:      ANL   A,#DFH              ; clear bit 5
            MOV   @str_ptr,A          ; store it back to memory
next:       INC   str_ptr             ; increment the string pointer
            JMP   again               ; check next character
exit:       NOP
            END
```

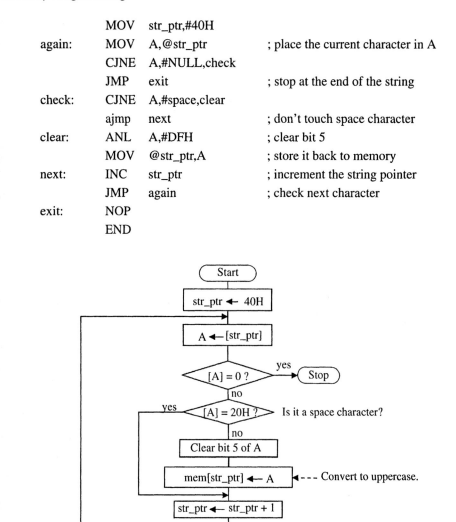

Figure 2.8 Program flowchart for converting letters of a string to uppercases.

Example 2.14 Write a program to compute $1 + 2 + 3 \cdots + N$ (say 20) and save the sum at 40H.

Solution: The procedure for computing the sum of the integers from 1 to 20 is illustrated in Figure 2.9. We will use register R0 as the loop count i and accumulator A as the variable *sum*. The assembly program that implements this algorithm is as follows:

```
N       equ   20                ; loop count limit
i       set   R0                ; use R0 for loop count i
```

```
             MOV    i,#0
             CLR    A              ; initialize sum to 0
again:       INC    i
             ADD    A,i
             CJNE   i,#N,again     ; branch if i is not equal to N yet
             MOV    40H,A          ; save sum in memory
             END
```

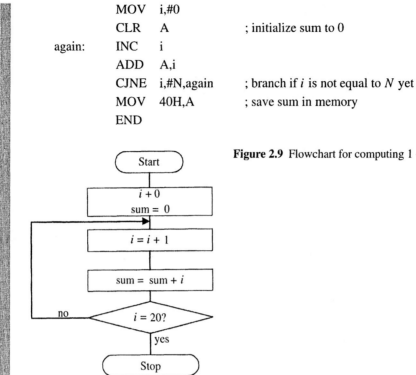

Figure 2.9 Flowchart for computing $1 + 2 + \cdots + 20$.

Example 2.15 Write a program to find the smallest element of an array of N integers. The starting address of the array is at 1000H (in external memory). Leave the result in register R1.

Solution: Since the array is stored in external memory, the data pointer register DPTR must be used as a pointer to the array. The program logic flowchart is shown in Figure 2.10. Register R1 will be used to hold the smallest element of the array. Register R2 will be used as the loop count. The program is as follows:

```
N        EQU    20                ; array count
i        SET    R2                ; loop count
arr_min  SET    R1                ; smallest element of the array
         USING  0                 ; specify register bank 0
         MOV    i,#1              ; initialize i to 1
         MOV    DPTR,#1000H       ; place the starting address of the array
                                  ; in DPTR
         MOVX   A,@DPTR           ; set A[0] as the array_min at the
                                  ; beginning
```

```
                MOV       arr_min,A        ; "
again:    INC       DPTR             ; increment loop index
          MOVX      A,@DPTR          ; get the next array element
          MOV       R3,A             ; save the current array element
          CLR       C                ; clear the borrow before subtraction
          SUBB      A,arr_min        ; compare array_min with A[i]
          JNC       next_i           ; If A[i] is larger then check the next elemen
; the instruction format "MOV Rn,Rm" is illegal and so use AR1 to
; specify the direct address of R1
          MOV       AR1,R3           ; make A[i] the current array_min
next_i:   CJNE      i,#N,next        ; if i is smaller than array count then
                                     ; continue
          JMP       exit             ; otherwise stop
next:     INC       i                ; increment the loop count
          JMP       again            ; and continue
exit:     END
```

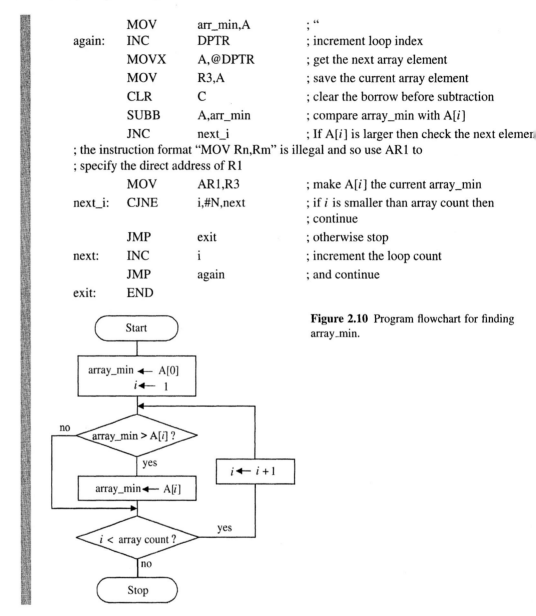

Figure 2.10 Program flowchart for finding array_min.

2.7 LOGICAL OPERATIONS

Logical instructions allow the MCS-51 to manipulate bit patterns. The user may selectively

- clear a few bits in a byte to 0s
- set a few bits in a byte to 1s

- complement the values of a few bits in a byte
- etc.

For example,

    ANL   A,#0FH

clears the upper four bits of accumulator A to 0s.

    ORL   A,#11H

sets the bit 4 and bit 0 of accumulator A to 1s.

    XRL   A,#F0H

complements the upper four bits of accumulator A.

Logical operations are very useful in input/output operations. The MCS-51 logical instructions are listed in Table 2.4.

2.8 ROTATE INSTRUCTIONS

Rotate instructions are useful in bit field manipulation. Using them properly may also improve the performance of some multiplication and division operations. The MCS-51 provides four rotate instructions, listed in Table 2.5, which all operate on accumulator A.

TABLE 2.4
MCS-51 Logical Instructions

Mnemonic		Description
ANL	A,Rn	AND register to accumulator A
ANL	A,direct	AND direct byte to accumulator A
ANL	A,@Ri	AND indirect RAM to accumulator A
ANL	A,#data	AND immediate data to accumulator A
ANL	direct,A	AND accumulator A to direct byte
ANL	direct,#data	AND immediate data to direct byte
ORL	A,Rn	OR register to accumulator A
ORL	A,direct	OR direct byte to accumulator A
ORL	A,@Ri	OR indirect RAM to accumulator A
ORL	A,#data	OR immediate data to accumulator A
ORL	direct,A	OR accumulator A to direct byte
ORL	direct,#data	OR immediate data to direct byte
XRL	A,Rn	Exclusive-OR register to accumulator A
XRL	A,direct	Exclusive-OR direct byte to accumulator A
XRL	A,@Ri	Exclusive-OR indirect RAM to accumulator A
XRL	A,#data	Exclusive-OR immediate data to accumulator A
XRL	direct,A	Exclusive-OR accumulator A to direct byte
XRL	direct,#data	Exclusive-OR immediate data to direct byte
CPL	A	Complement accumulator A
SWAP	A	Swap the upper and lower nibbles of accumulator A

TABLE 2.5
MCS-51 Rotate Instructions

Mnemonic	Description
RL A	Rotate accumulator A left one place
RLC A	Rotate accumulator A left one place through the carry
RR A	Rotate accumulator A right one place
RRC A	Rotate accumulator A right one place through the carry

Example 2.16 Compute the new value of accumulator A after executing the *RL A* instruction. Assume that A contains 47H before the operation.

Solution: The operation of this instruction is shown in Figure 2.11.

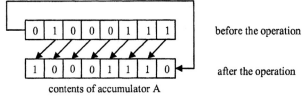

Figure 2.11 Result of execution of the instruction *RL A*.

contents of accumulator A

Example 2.17 Compute the new values of accumulator A and carry flag after execution of the instruction *RLC A*. Assume that the original value of accumulator A is 39H and the carry flag is 1.

Solution: The operation of this instruction is shown in Figure 2.12.

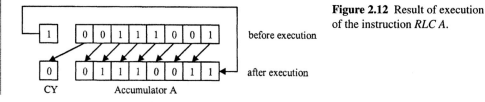

Figure 2.12 Result of execution of the instruction *RLC A*.

CY   Accumulator A

Example 2.18 Compute the new value of accumulator A after executing the *RR A* instruction. Assume that A contains 57H before the operation.

Solution: The operation of this instruction is shown in Figure 2.13.

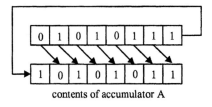

Figure 2.13 Result of execution of the instruction *RR A*.

contents of accumulator A

Example 2.19 Compute the new values of accumulator A and carry flag after the execution of the instruction *RRC A*. Assume that the original value of accumulator A is 63H and the carry flag is 0.

Solution: The operation of this instruction is shown in Figure 2.14.

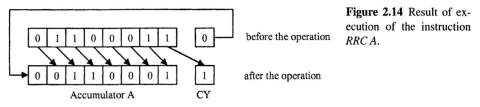

before the operation

after the operation

Accumulator A   CY

Figure 2.14 Result of execution of the instruction *RRC A*.

The MCS-51 does not provide instructions for *logical shift left*, *logical shift right*, *arithmetic shift left,* and *arithmetic shift right*. However, these operations can be synthesized by appropriate MCS-51 instructions.

Example 2.20 Write an instruction sequence to perform *logical shift left operation* on accumulator A. After this operation, every bit of accumulator A will be shifted to the left by one place and a zero will be shifted in to the least significant bit of A.

Solution: Logical shift left operation can be implemented by clearing the carry to 0 and then executing the *RLC A* instruction.

    CLR   C
    RLC   A

This instruction sequence multiplies the contents of A by 2 and is faster than the *MUL AB* instruction.

Example 2.21 Write an instruction sequence to perform *logical shift right operation* on accumulator A. After this operation, every bit of accumulator A will be shifted to the right by one place and a zero will be shifted in to the most significant bit of A.

Solution: Logical shift right operation can be implemented by clearing the carry to 0 and then executing the *RRC A* instruction.

    CLR   C
    RRC   A

This instruction sequence performs an unsigned divide-by-2 operation on accumulator A and is faster than the *DIV AB* instruction.

Example 2.22 Write an instruction sequence to perform *arithmetic shift right operation* on accumulator A. After this operation, every bit of accumulator A will be shifted to the right by one place and the most significant bit will remain the same as before the operation.

Solution: Arithmetic shift right operation can be implemented by

- clearing the carry flag to 0
- testing the sign of accumulator A
- executing the *RRC A* instruction

```
          JB      ACC.7,set_cy
          CLR     C
          SJMP    rotate
set_cy:   SETB    C                    ; the involved number is negative
rotate:   RRC     A
```

This instruction sequence performs a signed divide-by-2 operation on accumulator A. The sign of accumulator A is maintained after the division operation.

In some applications, the user may need to shift a number larger than 8 bits, but the MCS-51 does not have such an instruction. This issue can be dealt with as follows: Assume that the number has k bytes (or $8k$ bits) and the most significant byte is located at *loc*. The remaining $k - 1$ bytes are located at loc + 1, loc + 2, . . ., loc +k − 1, as shown in Figure 2.15a. The shift-one-bit-to-the-right operation is illustrated in Figure 2.15b. As shown in Figure 2.15b,

- Bit 7 of each byte will receive bit 0 of the byte on its immediate left, with the exception of the most significant byte, which will receive a zero.
- Each byte will be shifted to the right by one bit logically. Bit 0 of the least significant byte will be shifted out and lost.

This operation can therefore be implemented as follows:

STEP 1   Clear the carry flag to 0.

STEP 2   Rotate the byte at *loc* through carry to the right one place (using the RRC A instruction).

STEP 3   Repeat Step 2 for the remaining bytes.

By repeating this procedure, the given number can be shifted to the right as many places as desired.

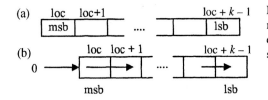

Figure 2.15 (a) A multiple byte number in memory. (b) A multiple byte shift right operation. msb, most significant byte; lsb, least significant byte.

Example 2.23 Write a program to shift the 32-bit number stored at 40H–43H to the right logically four places.

Solution: The most significant bytes (msb) to the least significant bytes (lsb) of this number are stored at 40H~43H, respectively. The following instruction sequence will shift the given number to the right logically four places.

```
          MOV     R0,#4       ; set up loop count to 4
again:    MOV     A,40H       ; place the number in A before it can be shifted
          CLR     C           ; shift msb to the right one place logically
          RRC     A           ; "
          MOV     40H,A       ; "
          MOV     A,41H       ; rotate the second byte to the right one place
          RRC     A           ; "
          MOV     41H,A       ; "
          MOV     A,42H       ; rotate the third byte to the right one place
          RRC     A           ; "
          MOV     42H,A       ; "
          MOV     A,43H       ; rotate the lsb to the right one place
          RRC     A           ; "
          MOV     43H,A       ; "
          DJNZ    R0,again    ; not done yet?
          END
```

2.9 BOOLEAN VARIABLE MANIPULATION INSTRUCTIONS

The MCS-51 devices contain a complete Boolean (single-bit) processor. The internal RAM contains 128 addressable bits, and the SFR space supports up to 128 other addressable bits. All of the I/O port lines are bit addressable, and each line can be treated as a separate single-bit port. The MCS-51 provides instructions that move, set, clear, complement, OR, and AND these bits and also conditional jump instructions that access these bits. The instruction set for the Boolean processor is shown in Table 2.6.

Addressable RAM bits can be used as software flags or to store program variables. For example, in the following instruction sequence

```
MOV   C,flag
MOV   P1.0,C
```

flag is the name of any addressable bit in the lower 128-byte RAM or SFR space. An I/O line (the least significant bit of port 1, in this case) is set or cleared depending on whether the flag is 1 or 0.

The carry flag in the PSW is used as the single-bit accumulator of the Boolean processor. Bit manipulation instructions refer to the carry bit as C (for example, CLR C). The carry

TABLE 2.6
MCS-51 Boolean Instructions

Mnemonic		Operation
ANL	C,bit	C = C AND bit
ANL	C,/bit	C = C AND NOT bit
ORL	C,bit	C = C OR bit
ORL	C,/bit	C = C OR NOT bit
MOV	C,bit	C = bit
MOV	bit,C	bit = C
CLR	C	C = 0
CLR	bit	bit = 0
SETB	C	C = 1
SETB	bit	bit = 1
CPL	C	C = NOT C
CPL	bit	bit = NOT bit
JC	rel	Jump if C = 1
JNC	rel	Jump if C = 0
JB	bit,rel	Jump if bit = 1
JNB	bit,rel	Jump if bit = 0
JBC	bit,rel	Jump if bit = 1; CLR bit

bit also has a direct address, since it resides in the PSW register, which is bit addressable. Note that the Boolean instruction set includes ANL and ORL operations, but not the XRL (Exclusive OR) operation. An XRL operation can be implemented in software. Suppose, for example, it is required to form the Exclusive OR of two bits:

$$C = bit1 \; XRL \; bit2$$

This operation can be implemented as follows:

```
          MOV   C,bit1
          JNB   bit2,over
          CPL   C
over:      .
           .
           .
```

First, bit1 is moved to the carry. If bit2 = 0, then C already contains the correct result. That is, bit1 XRL bit2 = bit1 if bit2 = 0. On the other hand, if bit2 = 1 then C contains the complement of the correct result. We need only to invert CY flag (CPL C) to complete the operation. In the above case, bit2 is tested. If bit2 = 0 the CPL C instruction is jumped over.

JBC executes the jump if the addressed bit is set, and also clears the bit. Thus a flag can be tested and cleared in one operation. All the PSW bits are directly addressable and are available to the bit-test instructions.

2.10 PROGRAM EXECUTION TIME

The MCS-51 instruction execution time can be found in Appendix A. It is indicated in either the number of machine cycles or the oscillator periods. A machine cycle is equal to 12 oscillator cycles. As long as the oscillator frequency is known, the instruction execution time can be figured out quickly. Knowing the execution time of each instruction allows a time delay of any length to be created.

Example 2.24 Write a program to create a time delay of 5 ms. Assume the oscillator frequency is 12 MHz.

Solution: Since the oscillator frequency is 12 MHz, the oscillator period is $1/12$ μs. Each machine cycle lasts for 1 μs. A time delay can be created by executing a program loop. Let τ be the execution time of the program loop, and let T be the desired delay. Then the number of times N that the program loop needs to be executed can be computed from the following equation:

$$N = T \div \tau$$

For example, the execution time of the following instruction sequence is 20 μs:

```
again:   PUSH  ACC          ; 2 machine cycles
         POP   ACC          ; 2 machine cycles
         PUSH  ACC          ; 2 machine cycles
         POP   ACC          ; 2 machine cycles
         PUSH  ACC          ; 2 machine cycles
         POP   ACC          ; 2 machine cycles
         PUSH  ACC          ; 2 machine cycles
         POP   ACC          ; 2 machine cycles
         NOP                ; 1 machine cycles
         NOP                ; 1 machine cycles
         DJNZ  R0,again     ; 2 machine cycles
```

To create a delay of 5 ms, this loop must be executed 250 times:

$$5 \text{ ms} \div 20 \text{ } \mu s = 250$$

A delay of 5 ms can be created by the following program loop:

```
         MOV   R0,#250      ; R0 is used as the loop count
again:   PUSH  ACC          ; 2 machine cycles
         POP   ACC          ; 2 machine cycles
         PUSH  ACC          ; 2 machine cycles
         POP   ACC          ; 2 machine cycles
         PUSH  ACC          ; 2 machine cycles
```

	POP	ACC	; 2 machine cycles
	PUSH	ACC	; 2 machine cycles
	POP	ACC	; 2 machine cycles
	NOP		; 1 machine cycles
	NOP		; 1 machine cycles
	DJNZ	R0,again	; 2 machine cycles

The actual execution time is two machine cycles more than 5 ms because the instruction "MOV R0,#250" takes two machine cycles to execute. This instruction is the overhead for setting up the delay loop.

Using nested program loops can create a longer delay.

Example 2.25 Write a program to create a time delay of 1 s. Assume the oscillator frequency is 12 MHz.

Solution: By repeating the previous program loop 200 times, a time delay of 1 s can be created:

$$1 \text{ s} \div 5 \text{ ms} = 1000 \text{ ms} \div 5 \text{ ms} = 200$$

The program is as follows:

(1)		MOV	R1,#200	; outer loop count is 200 (2 machine cycles)
(2)L1:		MOV	R0,#250	; inner loop count is 250 (2 machine cycles)
(3)L2:		PUSH	ACC	; 2 machine cycles
(4)		POP	ACC	; 2 machine cycles
(5)		PUSH	ACC	; 2 machine cycles
(6)		POP	ACC	; 2 machine cycles
(7)		PUSH	ACC	; 2 machine cycles
(8)		POP	ACC	; 2 machine cycles
(9)		PUSH	ACC	; 2 machine cycles
(10)		POP	ACC	; 2 machine cycles
(11)		NOP		; 1 machine cycle
(12)		NOP		; 1 machine cycle
(13)		DJNZ	R0,L2	; 2 machine cycles
(14)		DJNZ	R1,L1	; 2 machine cycles
(15)		END		

This program also has overhead that makes the delay slightly longer than 1 s. As explained earlier, it takes 20 μs to execute instruction (3) to (13). These 11 instructions must be repeated 50,000 times to create a delay of 1 s. However, as you have learned, program loops repeat a sequence of instructions, while certain other instructions are needed to set up the program loops. Those instructions are often not included in the calculation of execution time just for simplicity—they are the overhead of creating program loops. The overhead in this example is created by the instructions listed in Table 2.7. Therefore, the total overhead is 802 μs. To create an exact delay, these instructions must be taken into account when setting up the program loop. Using timer functions, which will be discussed in Chapter 7, we can create more accurate delays.

TABLE 2.7
Execution Time of a Sample of Instructions

Instruction	Execution Time (Machine Cycles)	Execution Time (μs)
MOV R1,#200	2	2
MOV R0,#250	2	400
DJNZ R1,L1	2	400

2.11 MCS-51 DEVELOPMENT TOOLS

Development tools for microprocessors/microcontrollers can be classified into two categories: software and hardware. Software tools include programmer's editors, assemblers, compilers, simulators, debuggers, and integrated software. Hardware tools include evaluation boards, logic analyzers, microprocessor/microcontroller emulators, oscilloscopes, logic probes, etc.

Discussing all of these tools is beyond the scope of this book. However, we will give an overview of four evaluation boards and software tools in this section.

2.11.1 Software Tools

Text Editors

The text editor is a program that allows us to enter and edit programs and any text files. Editors range from very primitive to very sophisticated. A simple editor like the EDIT bundled with DOS and Windows 98/NT provides simple edit functions in four different categories: *file, edit, search,* and *option.* The functions provided in these four categories are listed in Table 2.8.

To invoke EDIT, enter **edit filename** at the DOS command prompt.

The notepad program bundled with the Windows 98/NT is another simple editor that we can use to enter our programs.

A programmer's editor provides many functions that can improve productivity. The **ED** editor from Lahey is an example of a programmer's editor. ED provides automatic keyword completion, syntax checking, parenthesis matching, etc. All of these functions can speed up the program entering process. A serious programmer should consider using a programmer's editor.

TABLE 2.8
EDIT Functions

Category	Command	Functions
File	New	Allows the user to enter and edit a new file
	Open	Allows the user to edit an existing file
	Save	Saves the file being edited using the same name
	Save as	Saves the current file in a different name
	Exit	Leaves the editor
Edit	Cut	Cuts a block of text and puts it in a buffer
	Copy	Copies a block of text
	Paste	Pastes the text in the buffer to the cursor position
	Clear	Deletes the character at the cursor position
Search	Find	Searches the specified word
	Repeat last find	Repeats the previous search
	Change	Searches for a word and replaces it with another word
Option	Display	Allows the user to set the monitor screen foreground and background colors, display scroll bars, and set tab positions
	Path	Allows the user to select a different location (path) for the editor help file (edit.hlp)

Intel Hex Format

All Intel cross assemblers and C compilers generate outputs in Intel HEX format. Intel HEX format is a format acceptable to all EPROM programmers and MCS-51 simulators. The Intel HEX format was defined in the mid-1970s to promote the tool compatibility of Intel's microprocessors. An executable code file is divided into lines (or records) of absolute code in HEX format. A line of Intel HEX code example is as follows:

:0B00A00066726F6D20556172743100B4

A line in Intel HEX format consists of the following fields:

1. A *colon* character.
2. *Length*: two digits (0B in this example) that specify the length of the absolute code.
3. *Starting address* of the location (00A0 in this example) where the code in this line should be stored.
4. *Type of code* (00 in this example)—00 for absolute code and 01 for an end-of-file record.
5. *Actual code* (66726F6D20556172743100 in this example).
6. *Checksum* (B4 in this example). For each line of HEX values, add all two-character HEX values in modulo 256 with the checksum; the total for an uncorrupted block is 0. For example, $(66 + 72 + 6F + 6D + 20 + 55 + 61 + 72 + 74 + 31 + 00 + B4)$ modulo 256 = 00.

Cross Assemblers and Cross Compilers

Cross assemblers and cross compilers generate executable code to be placed in ROM, EPROM, EEPROM, or flash memory of an MCS-51-based product. Cross assemblers and cross compilers vary significantly in many areas; readers should refer to the vendors' reference manuals.

There are several free assemblers (or demo versions of some commercial assemblers) available for the MCS-51. They can be downloaded from several ftp sites:

1. Metalink's ML-ASM51.ZIP. This assembler is available at *ftp.pppl.gov:/pub/8051/ signetics-bbs* and *ftp.funet.fi:/pub/microprocs/MCS-51/signetics-bbs.*
2. PseudoSam's A51.ZIP is available at *ftp.pppl.gov:/pub/8051/signetics-bbs.*
3. CAS 8051 assembler by Mark Hopkins is available at *ftp.pppl.gov:/pub/8051/assem* and *ftp.funet.fi:/pub/microprocs/MCS-51/csd4-archive/assem.*

Many commercial vendors provide cross assemblers for the MCS-51 microcontroller. A partial list of vendors for cross assemblers, cross C compilers, simulators, and debuggers is in Appendix E. The evaluation board from Keil Software includes a demo version of its cross assembler.

There are several companies that provide C language compiler for the MCS-51. Some of them make the demo version of their products available for evaluation. This text includes a demo version of the C language compiler from Keil Software. Compilers for other languages such as Forth, Basic, PL/M, and Pascal are also available.

Simulator

Simulator allows us to run an MCS-51 program without having the actual hardware. A simulator is normally menu driven. The contents of registers, internal memory, external memory, and the program are displayed in separate windows. The user can set breakpoints to the program and examine the program execution results. The simulator allows the user to step through the program to identify the problem spots in the program.

Source-Level Debugger

The source-level debugger is a program that allows you to find problems in your code at the high-level (such as C) or assembly language level. A debugger may have the option to run your program on the evaluation board or simulator. Like a simulator, a debugger can display the contents of registers, internal memory, external memory, and program code in separate windows. With a debugger, all debugging activities are done at the source level. You can see the value of a variable after a statement has been executed. You can set a breakpoint at a statement in a high-level language. A source-level debugger requires a lot of computation. A debugger may run slowly if it needs to simulate the MCS-51 instruction set instead of using the actual hardware to run the program.

A source-level debugger needs to communicate with the monitor program on the evaluation board in order to display the contents of CPU registers and memory locations, set or eliminate breakpoints, trace program execution, etc. Since the monitor programs on different evaluation boards may not be the same, a source-level debugger may be used with only one type of evaluation board.

Integrated Development Software

An integrated development software includes everything that you need to enter, assemble or compile, link, and debug your program. It includes every software tool mentioned earlier. A tool is invoked by clicking at the icon of the corresponding tool. A demo version of Integrated Development Tool from Keil Software is included in this text.

2.11.2 Hardware Development Tools

Evaluation boards may be the most important hardware development tools for the development of a microcontroller-based product. Logic analyzers, emulators, oscilloscopes, and logic probes are also important. It is beyond the scope of this text to discuss all the hardware development tools. In this text, we will discuss the MCB520 evaluation board from Keil Software in detail. The MCB520 is based on Dallas Semiconductor's DS87C520 microcontroller.

2.11.3 MCB520 Evaluation Board

Keil Software markets the MCB520 evaluation board. The following are the most important features of the MCB520:

1. A 33-MHz Dallas DS87C520 microcontroller. The DS87C520 is a high-speed derivative of the MCS-51 microcontroller. Each machine cycle on the DS87C520 takes four clock cycles instead of 12 cycles for the standard MCS-51/52.
2. Two 9-pin serial port connectors that interface with the serial communication port 0 and port 1 of the DS87C520. User programs should be downloaded into the MCB520 via serial port 1.
3. 32-KB EPROM in which the monitor program resided.
4. 128-KB SRAM to hold dynamic programs and data.
5. 8 LEDs driven by port 1.
6. On-board flash memory programming capability.
7. A small prototyping area.

Figure 2.16 is a photograph of the MCB520.

MCB520 Operation

The 87C520 on the MCB520 begins instruction execution at address 0000H after reset. The MCB520 is shipped with the Keil 8051 monitor programmed into the EPROM. This EPROM is relocated to 8000H immediately following reset. Therefore, our programs can begin execution starting at 0000H. The memory space assignment on the MCB520 is as follows:

• External EPROM from 8000H to FFFFH is program space (MON51 resides here).

Figure 2.16 MCB520 evaluation board. (Reprinted with permission of Keil Software.)

- External SRAM from 0000H to 7FFFH is a shared external data and external program space (user programs can be downloaded into this area).
- External SRAM from 8000H to FFFFH is external data space.

A demo version of μVision-51 (can also be downloaded from Keil Software's web page *www.keil.com*) is shipped with the MCB520 evaluation board. The μVision-51 consists of the following tools:

- A51 macro assembler
- C51 optimizing C compiler for the MCS-51 microcontroller
- BL51 code banking linker/locator
- OC51 banked object file converter
- OH51 object code to HEX format converter
- tScope-51 target debugger
- Monitor-51 ROM monitor and terminal program MON51
- Integrated development environment
- RTX-51 tiny real-time operating system

Depending on the hardware resources available, we can choose two different approaches to execute and debug our programs on the MCB520 evaluation board:

1. Use the combination of the MON51 terminal program and the on-board monitor monitor-51 to download our program (in HEX format) into the MCB520 for execution. This approach requires us to have at least a cross assembler to assemble the program. Fortunately, any vendor's cross assembler (or compiler) can be used.

2. Use the μVision-51 integrated development environment to enter, assemble (or compile), link, and download the generated code into the MCB520 for execution. The μVision-51 provides a debugger that allows us to debug our programs at the source level.

These two approaches are illustrated in the following sections.

Using the MON51 Terminal Program

MON51 is a program to be run under Microsoft Disk Operating System (DOS). After making sure that the MON51 is at the DOS search path, enter **mon51** at the DOS prompt and the following message will appear:

MS-DOS MON51 V1.09

COPYRIGHT KEIL ELECTRONIK GmbH 1991–1996

INSTALLED FOR PC/XT/AT (COM LINE 1) USING HARDWARE INTERRUPT SERVICE

BAUDRATE: 9600 (DEFAULT)

*** MONITOR ***

#

The "#" character is the monitor-51 prompt. The on-board monitor supports an extensive set of commands as shown in Table 2.9. Every command must be followed by an **enter** key.

Using the Monitor-51 Commands

After the monitor-51 prompt appears on the monitor screen, we can enter commands to request the monitor-51 to perform the desired operation. The command

DD   [range]

displays the contents of the directly addressable internal memory at the specified range. A range is specified by **address1, address2.** Other display commands allows us to display the contents of bit memory, program memory, indirectly addressable internal memory, and external data memory at the specified range. If we do not specify the range, the monitor-51 will display the contents of four rows of memory locations starting from the address of the previous display command. If we only specify one address, the monitor will display the contents of four rows of memory locations starting from the given address. One row has 16 locations.

Commands starting with the letter **E** allow us to change the value of a memory location. A command that starts with the word **FILL** allows us to fill the memory locations at the specified range with the given value. A FILL command allows us to initialize a block of memory locations before running a program.

TABLE 2.9
Monitor-51 Commands[a]

Command	Description
DB range	Display bit memory contents in the specified range
DC range	Display code memory contents in the specified range
DD range	Display directly addressable internal data memory contents in the specified range
DI range	Display indirectly addressable internal data memory in the specified range
DX range	Display external data memory contents in the specified range
EB address	Change the value of the bit memory at the specified address
EC address	Change the contents of the code memory at the specified address
ED address	Change the contents of the directly addressable internal data memory at the specified address
EI address	Change the contents of the indirectly addressable internal data memory at the specified address
EX address	Change the contents of the external data memory at the specified address
FILLB range value	Fill bit memory at the specified range with the specified value
FILLC range value	Fill code memory at the specified range with the specified value
FILLD range value	Fill directly addressable internal memory at the specified range with the specified value
FILLI range value	Fill indirectly addressable internal memory at the specified range with the specified value
FILLX range value	Fill external data memory at the specified range with the specified value
A address	Assemble (enter) instruction at the specified address
U range	Disassemble machine code at the specified range into assembly instructions
X [register]	Examine a register (optional) and display
BS address	Set a breakpoint at the specified address
BD bp	Disable the specified breakpoint
BE bp	Enable the specified breakpoint
BK bp	Kill (delete) the specified breakpoint
BL	List all the breakpoints
LOAD file	Load a program in HEX or binary format
SAVE file range	Save program in the specified range in a file in HEX format
LS file	Load the specified symbol file
G [address]	Start the program at the optionally specified address
T [count]	Trace the specified number of instructions
P [count]	Procedure trace
Help	List all available commands

[a] A range is specified by address1, address2. A breakpoint **bp** is specified by the ordinal number when it is set (starting from 0) instead of the address. All numbers are considered to be in hex.

Example 2.26 Use monitor-51 commands to fill the external data memory locations starting from 0000H to 003FH with the value FF and then display them.

Solution: At the monitor-51 prompt type the command "FILLX 0000,003F FF." Wait until the next monitor prompt appears, and then enter the command DX 00,003F. You should see the following information on your screen (the commands that you typed are in boldface):

#FILLX 00,003F FF

#DX 00,003F

X:0000: FF FF FF FF FF FF FF FF FF FF FF FF FF FF FF FF : . . . .

X:0010: FF FF FF FF FF FF FF FF FF FF FF FF FF FF FF FF : . . . .

X:0020: FF FF FF FF FF FF FF FF FF FF FF FF FF FF FF FF : . . . .

X:0030: FF FF FF FF FF FF FF FF FF FF FF FF FF FF FF FF : . . . .

Example 2.27 Use a monitor-51 command to set the contents of the internal data memory at 80H to 0 and verify this operation.

Solution: The internal data memory locations from 80H to FFH are indirectly addressable. At the monitor-51 prompt type the command "EI 80H." You will see the current contents of the memory location at 80H displayed on the screen. After seeing the current contents of the memory location, enter the new value 0 followed by the **enter** key. The contents of the next location (81H) will be displayed. Type the period "." character or ctrl-C to get out. To display the new value of the location 80H, enter the command "DI 80,80." You should see the following information on the screen (the commands that you typed are in boldface):

#EI 80

I:80: xx **0**

I:81: yy .

#DI 80,80

I:80: 00

#

where,

    xx is the current value of the memory location at 80H

    yy is the current value of the memory location at 81H

Sometimes we need to enter a few instructions into the program memory for testing or debugging purpose. The command "A address" is useful. After entering a few instructions, we can use the command "U range" to verify.

Example 2.28 Enter the following instructions into the program memory starting at 1000H and verify them:

    mov   A,#69H

    clr   C

    rrc   A

    mov   30H,A

Solution: At the monitor-51 prompt, type "A 1000." The current instruction at the memory location 1000H will be displayed and you can enter the instruction "mov

A,#69H" followed by an **enter** key. The next instruction will be displayed and you can enter the second instruction. After entering these four instructions, enter a period or ctrl-C to terminate the process. The monitor-51 prompt will reappear and we can use the command "u 1000,1004" to verify our effort. You should see the following information on the screen (the commands that you typed are in boldface):

```
#A   1000
1000H   NOP            mov A,#69H
1002H   NOP            clr C
1003H   NOP            rrc A
1004H   NOP            mov 30H,A
1006H   NOP            .
#u   1000,1004
1000H   MOV A,#69H
1002H   CLR C
1003H   RRC A
1004H   MOV 30H,A
#
```

In this example, we assume that the program memory locations 1000H to 1006H contain seven NOP (00H) instructions. This may not be true in your MCB520 evaluation board.

Sometimes we need to examine and change the contents of registers. Entering the letter "X" without any argument will display the contents of all CPU registers.

Example 2.29 Use monitor-51 commands to set the values of accumulators A and B, and registers R0 and R1 to 1, 2, 3, 4, respectively, and verify. Assume all CPU registers contain the value FFH.

Solution: Use the command "X reg" four times. The monitor-51 displays the current value of the specified register and wait for the new value to be entered. At the end of the session, you should see the following information on the screen:

```
#x ra
D:E0: 00 1
#x rb
D:F0: 00 2
#x r0
D:00: 00 3
#x r1
D:01: 00 4
#x
```

RA RB R0 R1 R2 R3 R4 R5 R6 R7 PSW	DPTR	SP	PC
01 02 03 04 00 00 00 00 00 00 - - -R0- - -	0000	07	0000

In the above, accumulators A and B are represented as RA and RB, respectively.

Debugging is a very important step during the program development process. Breakpoints allow us to examine the program execution results wherever we suspect there is a problem. A *breakpoint* is a memory location where instruction execution will be stopped. When a breakpoint is reached, the monitor program displays the contents of CPU registers. We can optionally display the contents of some memory locations to examine the program execution results, which may help us identify the problem.

The monitor-51 allows us to set, disable, enable, list, and kill (eliminate) breakpoints. When setting a breakpoint, we specify its address. Breakpoints are ordered: the first breakpoint is referred to as breakpoint 0, the second one is referred to as breakpoint 1, etc.

Example 2.30 Use monitor-51 commands to perform the following operations:

- Set a breakpoint at 1000H, 1020H, 2000H, and 3000H.
- Disable the breakpoint at 1020H and 2000H.
- List all the breakpoints.
- Kill the breakpoint at 1000H
- List all the breakpoints.

Solution: Use appropriate monitor-51 commands to perform the specified operations and you will see the following information displayed on the screen (the commands that you typed are in boldface):

#BS 1000

#BS 1020

#BS 2000

#BS 3000

#BD 1

#BD 2

#BL

0: (ena) 1000

1: (dis) 1020

2: (dis) 2000

3: (ena) 3000

#BK 0

#BL

1: (dis) 1020

2: (dis) 2000

3: (ena) 3000

There are two methods to enter our program into the MCB520 evaluation board for execution:

1. Use the command "A address": This method is good only for very short programs because only very primitive editing functions are available in this method.
2. This method consists of five steps: (1) enter the program using an editor, (2) assemble the program using a cross assembler, (3) link the program, (4) convert the linked file into HEX format, and (5) download the HEX code into the MCB520 board. Depending on the cross assembler, Steps 2–4 may be done in one step.

Example 2.31 Assume that you have already entered an assembly program in a file called *oddsum.a51*. Describe the procedure to download the HEX version to the MCB520 evaluation board for execution.

Solution: Here we assume that A51 cross assembler from Keil Software is being used. We need to run the cross assembler, linker, binary to hex converter in a DOS command window. Here is the procedure:

STEP 1   Assemble the program. Enter the following command at the DOS prompt:

A51   oddsum.a51

The object file of oddsum.a51 will be created. The filename of the object file is oddsum.obj.

STEP 2   Link the program by entering the following command:

BL51   oddsum.obj

STEP 3   Convert the executable code into HEX format.

OH51   oddsum

The executable program will be converted into HEX format and this new file's name is **oddsum.hex**.

STEP 4   Start the terminal program MON51 by entering the following command at the DOS command prompt:

mon51

After this command, the MON51 will talk to the monitor-51 program and the monitor prompt # will appear on the screen.

STEP 5   Use the monitor-51 command "*LOAD file*" to download the program **odd-sum.hex** into the MCB520 evaluation board for execution. You will see the following information on the screen:

#load oddsum.hex

#

The file name extension **.hex** is optional.

After Step 5, the program *oddsum* is ready for execution. We need to know the starting address of the program before we execute it. In assembly language, we can use the assembler directive **org address** to specify the starting address of our program. Suppose the program *oddsum* starts at address 0000H and ends at 0017H, we can use the following command to execute it and return the CPU control to the monitor-51:

g   00,0017H

Another method to run the program is to specify the starting address and let the program execute until a breakpoint is reached.

There are situations in which we want to examine the execution results of every instruction in order to identify the program bug. The *trace* command enables us to do that. We can specify the number of instructions to be traced. A *procedure trace* command is identical to a regular trace command if there is no procedure call in our program. When there is a procedure call, the processor will execute

1. all the instructions before the first procedure call instruction (either ACALL or LCALL),
2. the first procedure call instruction, and
3. $n - 1$ instructions after the first procedure call instruction (n is the trace count) and stop.

2.11.4 Using the μVision

The demo version of the μVision software is bundled with the MCB520 evaluation board. You can also request it from or download it from Keil Software's web page. The μVision software can be started by clicking on its icon in Windows 3.1 or Windows 98.

Creating the oddsum.a51 Source File

After μVision is started, select the **New** command from the **File** menu and μVision will open a new text window in which you may create the *oddsum.a51* program. Enter the oddsum.a51 program and your screen should look something like Figure 2.17. You should save the oddsum.a51 program after you enter it. Select the **Save As . . .** command from the **File** menu and μVision will display the **Save As** dialog box for you to enter the file name and the directory to store the program. Enter **oddsum.a51** as the file name and specify an appropriate directory to hold it.

```
N        equ      20
         org      00H
         jmp      main

main:    mov      DPTR,#array
         mov      R2,#20          ; use R2 to hold the loop count
         mov      R3,#0           ; use R3 to hold the sum
again:   mov      A,#0
         movc     A,@A+DPTR
         clr      C
         rrc      A
         jnc      next
         rlc      A               ; restore the number
         add      A,R3            ; accumulate the odd sum
         mov      R3,A            ; update the sum
next:    inc      DPTR
         djnz     R2,again
         ajmp     $               ; stay in a do nothing infinite loop
array:   db       1,2,3,4,5,6,7,8,9,10,11,12,13,14,15,16,17,18,19,20
         end
```

Figure 2.17 The assembly program oddsum.a51.

Creating the Oddsum Project File

After the program oddsum.a51 is saved, you should create an **ODDSUM** project file. A project file contains a list of all the source files in your project as well as the options to use for the *compiler*, *assembler*, *linker*, and *make*. Additionally, the project manager helps you assemble (or compile), link, and test your target program.

To create a project file for ODDSUM, select the **New Project . . .** command from the **Project** menu. μVision will display the dialog box shown in Figure 2.18. Enter the name for the project in the File Name text box. This example uses **oddsum.prj**.

Including oddsum.a51 in the Project

After the project file is created, μVision will display the Project manager dialog box. Here, you select the source files to be included in your project. Click the **Add** button and choose the *oddsum.a51* file from the file list. Click the **Save** button to close the file selection dialog box. Then, click the **Save** button to save changes to the project file. This session is shown in Figure 2.19.

To return to the Project Manager dialog box, select the **Edit Project . . .** command from the project menu.

When you have created a project file and inserted the source files into the project, you are ready to set options for the compiler, assembler, linker, and other tools.

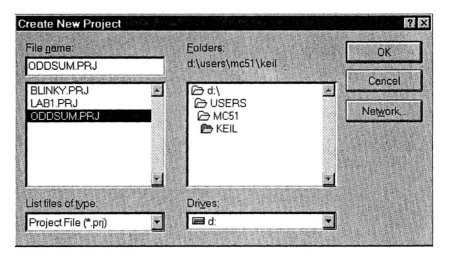

Figure 2.18 A dialog for new project.

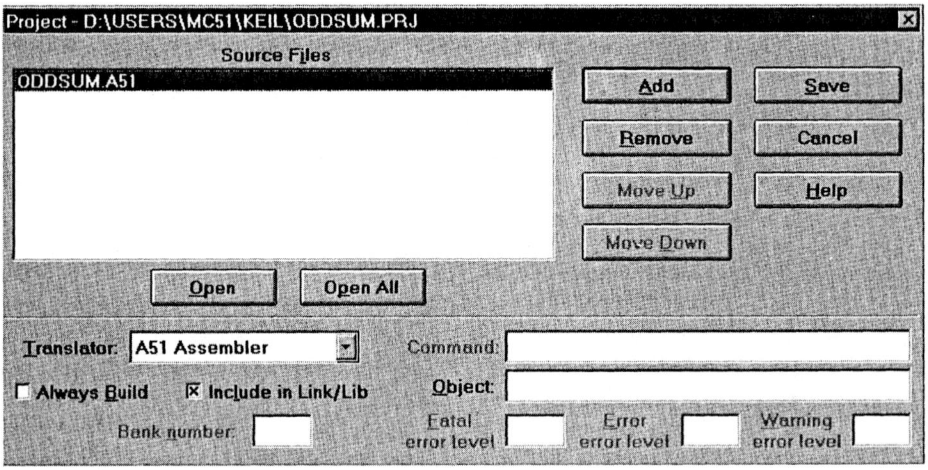

Figure 2.19 Adding oddsum.a51 to the project.

Setting the A51 Assembler Options for the Project

To set the A51 assembler options, select the **A51 Assembler . . .** command from the **Options** menu and μVision will display the A51 Assembler Options dialog box as shown in Figure 2.20. Then follow these steps:

- Click the Default button. This restores the default command line settings for the assembler. Accept the default setting for Listing.

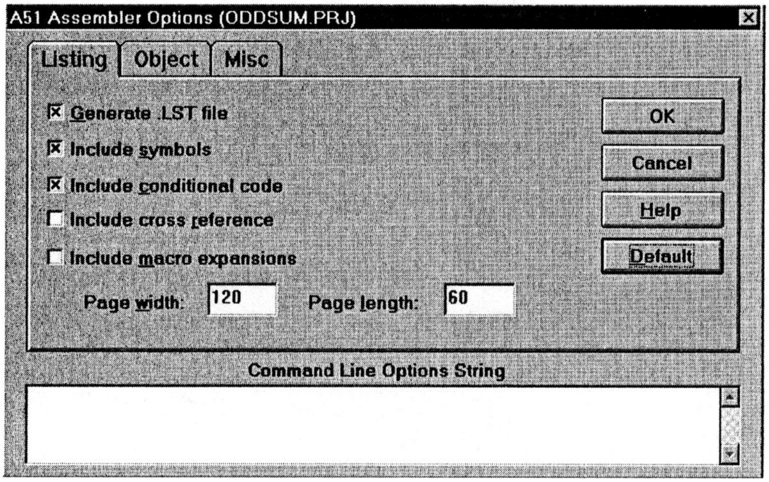

Figure 2.20 Setting assembler options.

- Click on the Object button. Make sure that the following features are selected:
  1. Include debug information
  2. Define 8051SFRs
  3. Register bank used—check 0
  4. Macro processor—standard

Click OK to close the Assembler Options window.

Setting the BL51 Linker Options for the Project

To set the BL51 linker options, select the **BL51 Code Banking Linker . . .** command from the **Options** menu and μVision will display the BL51 Linker Options dialog box. Then, follow these steps:

- Click the Default button. This restores the default command line settings for the linker.
- Click on the Size/Location tab at the top of the dialog box.
- Set the RAM Size to 256. This tells the linker that 256 bytes of internal data memory are available on the 87C520.

Then click the OK button to close the Linker Options window. This session is shown in Figure 2.21.

Setting the Path Specifications for the 8051 Tools

You may want to specify the paths to the 8051 tools directly in μVision rather than rely on the settings in the AUTOEXEC.BAT file. You may do this in the **Environment Pathspecs**

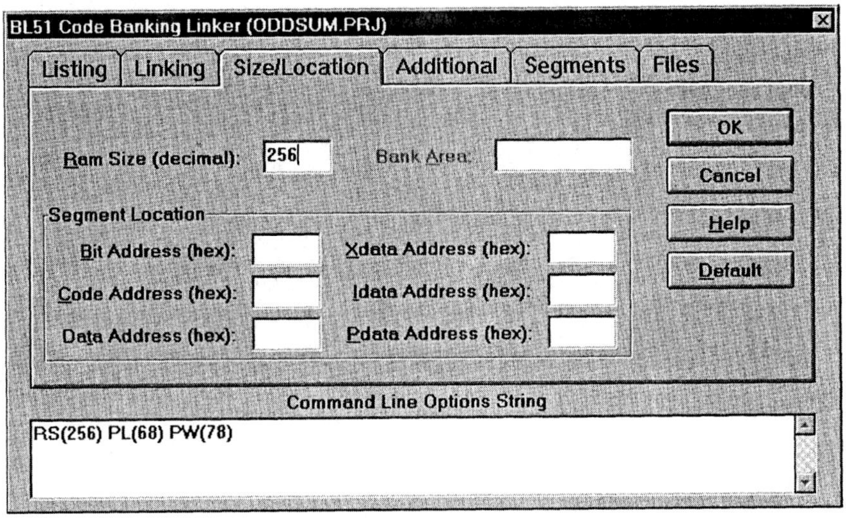

Figure 2.21 Linker options window.

dialog box. Open this dialog box using the **Environment Pathspecs . . .** command in the Options menu. This session is shown in Figure 2.22.

You may specify the paths to BIN directory, the INC directory, and the LIB directory. Additionally, you may specify a temporary directory for the assembler (or compiler) and linker to use when assembling (or compiling) and linking.

Setting the Make Options for the Project

"Make" is a utility originated from UNIX operating system environment. A *make file* must be created to be processed by the make utility. A make file describes the steps used to compile (or assemble) source files, link object files, delete temporary files, update library,

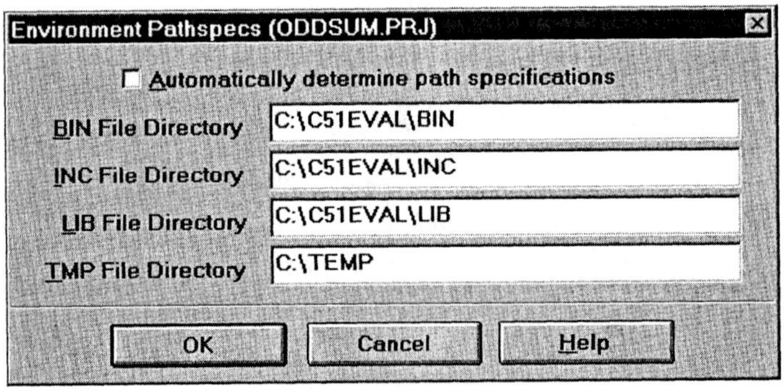

Figure 2.22 Path specification window.

convert executable file into HEX, etc. When the make utility is running, it will compile (or assemble) a source file only if it has been modified. A make file is automatically created by μVision when a new project is created.

Open the **Make Options** dialog box by selecting the **Make . . .** command in the Options menu and click the Default button. This restores the default make options that work perfectly for most applications. Click OK to close the make options window. This session is illustrated in Figure 2.23.

Building the Project

Now you are ready to build the ODDSUM project. Select the **Make: Build Project** command from the **Project** menu to begin assembling and linking. μVision responds by assembling the ODDSUM.A51 source file and creating the HEX file. The Make utility may need to link the object files to appropriate library files for other projects in this step. This step is called *making* the project. While the make utility is running, μVision displays the status as shown in Figure 2.24.

If errors occur during the *make* process, a message window will appear. If there are warnings or errors in your source file, you may interactively select an error and see the corresponding line in your source file. When *make* completes successfully, you are ready to begin debugging the ODDSUM program.

Using dScope to Debug the ODDSUM Program

To download the ODDSUM program into the MCB520 evaluation board using dScope, you need to perform the following steps:

- Load the MON51.DLL CPU driver.
- Configure the CPU driver for the appropriate COM port and baud rate.
- Configure the CPU driver for serial break.

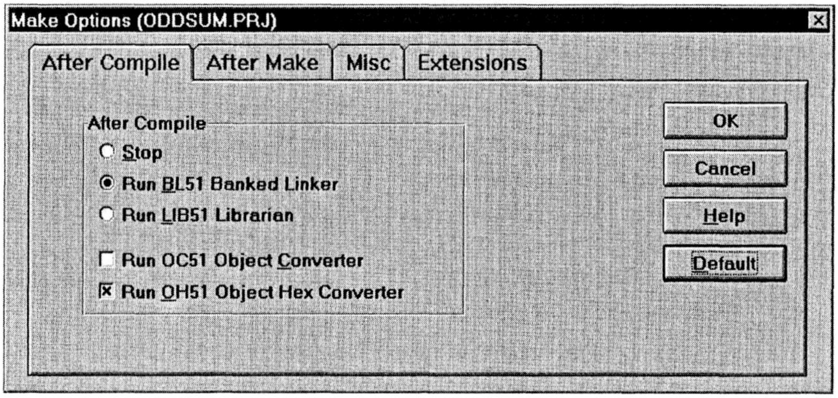

Figure 2.23 Make options window.

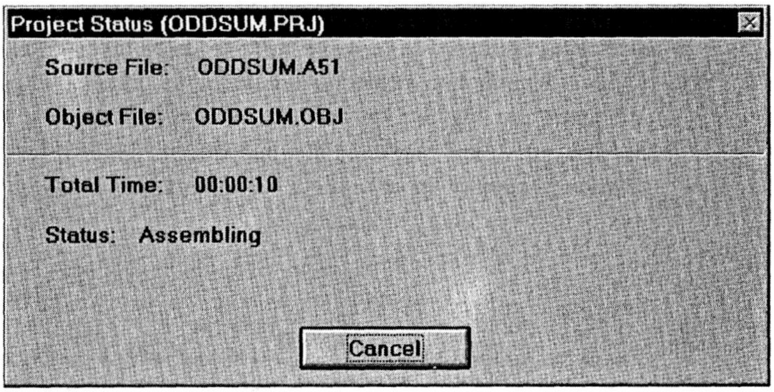

Figure 2.24 Make project window.

- Load the ODDSUM program.
- Step through the ODDSUM program.

Each of these steps is described in detail below.

Starting dScope

Start dScope by selecting the **dScope Debugger . . .** command from the **Run** menu in μVision. This loads dScope and sets the current path to the path in which your project file is saved. After dScope is started, a screen similar to that in Figure 2.25 is displayed.
   In Figure 2.25,

- The debug window (with the title **Module: <none>**) displays your program.
- The register window displays the current values of CPU registers (excluding PC).
- The command window allows us to enter commands.
- The watch window displays (not shown in Figure 2.25) the values of scalars, structures, unions, and arrays.
- The serial window emulates a serial terminal connected to 8051 special function registers. All keyboard inputs are passed to the user program using serial interface.
- The memory window displays the contents of a range of memory locations. We can specify the range of memory locations to be displayed in the command window.

To load the MON51.DLL CPU driver, type **load mon51.dll** (shown in Figure 2.26) in the command window.
   Typically, the first time you load the CPU driver for the 8051 monitor, you must set the COM port and the baud rate. If dScope cannot determine the COM port and the baud rate automatically, a dialog box that indicates NO TARGET SYSTEM FOUND! will appear. Click the Quit button and configure the CPU driver to enable serial breaks. To do

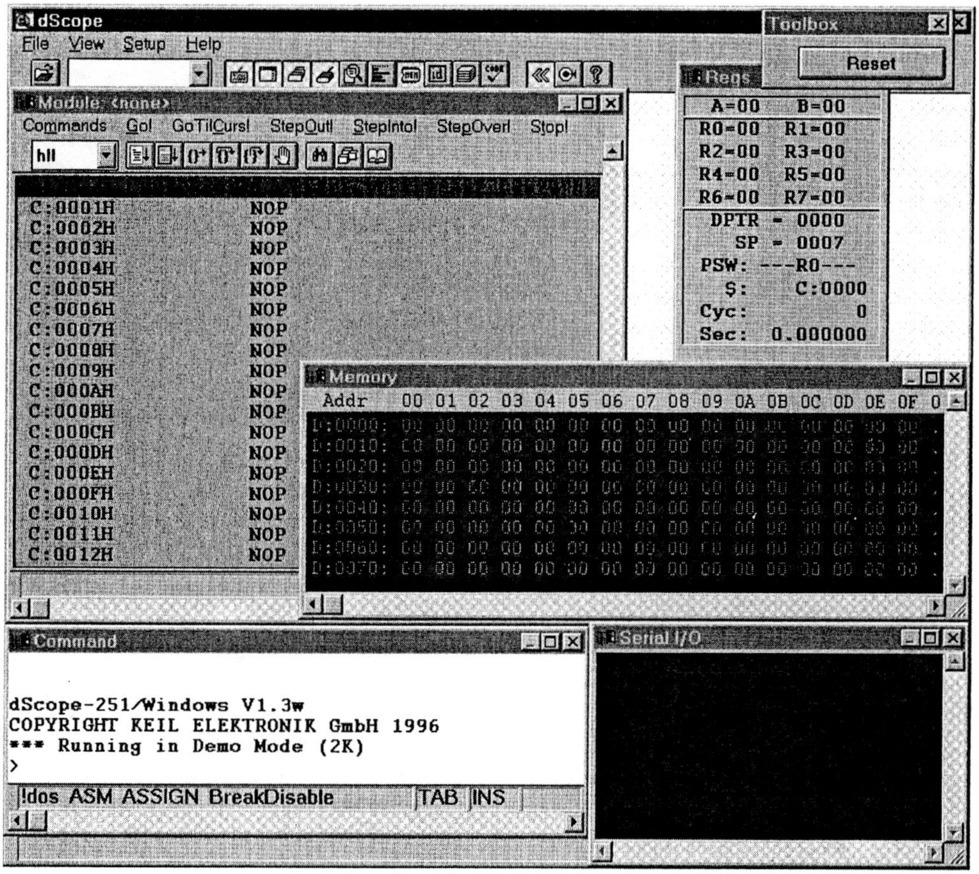

Figure 2.25 dScope debugger screen.

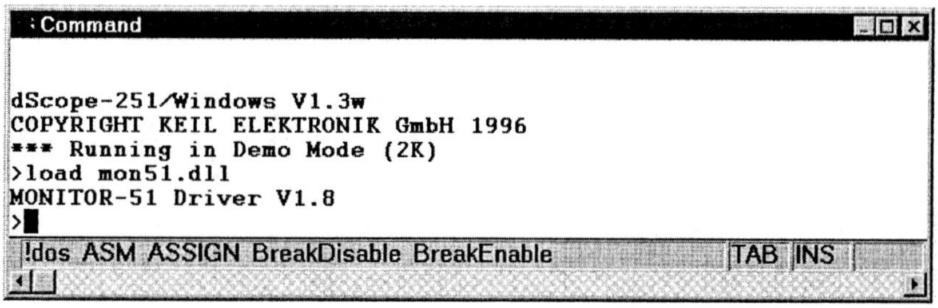

Figure 2.26 Load the MON52.DLL CPU driver.

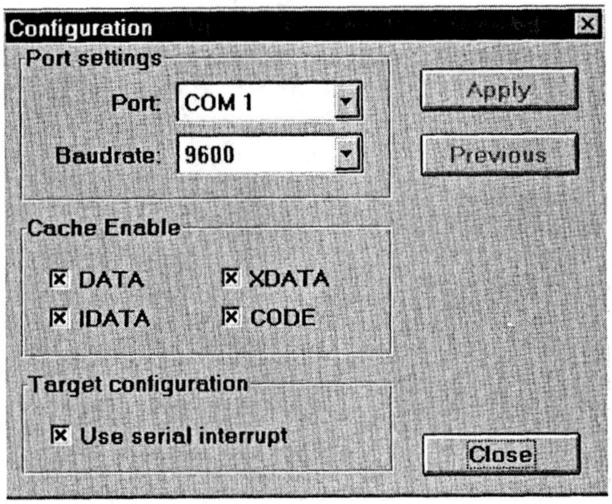

Figure 2.27 Configure CPU driver.

this, select the **Configuration** command from the **Peripherals** menu. dScope displays the Configuration dialog box as shown in Figure 2.27.

Finally, you are ready to load the ODDSUM program. To do so, type the following command in the command window:

```
load oddsum      /* this loads the oddsum program */
g,main           /* this steps over the startup code */
                 /* and stops on the first line of main */
```

Once ODDSUM is loaded, the debug window will display the ODDSUM program as shown in Figure 2.28.

You may now start to execute the ODDSUM program. The operations most commonly performed during the program debugging process are as follows:

1. *Setting the values of registers.* This can be done by using an assignment statement in the command window. For example,

A = 30H, R0 = 01H, R4 = 02H

sets the registers A, R0, and R4's value to 30H, 01H, and 02H, respectively.

2. *Displaying memory contents.* This is done by the D command. The general syntax of D command is

D   x:range

where x can be B (bit memory), C (code memory), D (directly addressable internal data memory), I (indirectly addressable internal data memory), and X (external memory).

3. *Setting and eliminating breakpoints.* dScope allows us to set up to 40 breakpoints. Setting a breakpoint is done by double-clicking the instruction (or a high-level language

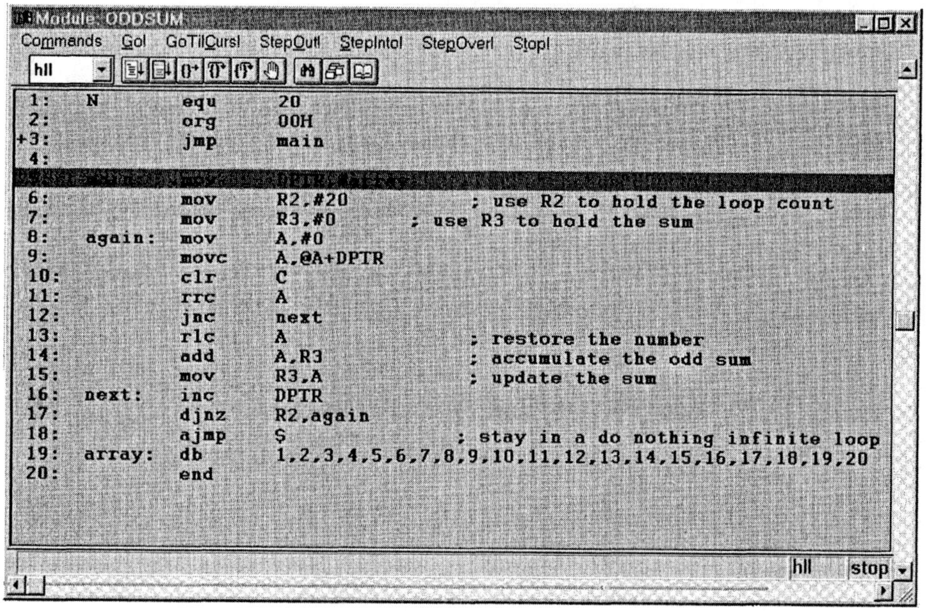

```
Module: ODDSUM                                                    _ □ ×
Commands  Go|  GoTilCurs|  StepOut|  StepInto|  StepOver|  Stop|

hll    ▼

  1:     N         equ      20
  2:               org      00H
 +3:               jmp      main
  4:

  6:               mov      R2,#20              ; use R2 to hold the loop count
  7:               mov      R3,#0       ; use R3 to hold the sum
  8:     again:    mov      A,#0
  9:               movc     A,@A+DPTR
 10:               clr      C
 11:               rrc      A
 12:               jnc      next
 13:               rlc      A                   ; restore the number
 14:               add      A,R3                ; accumulate the odd sum
 15:               mov      R3,A                ; update the sum
 16:     next:     inc      DPTR
 17:               djnz     R2,again
 18:               ajmp     $                   ; stay in a do nothing infinite loop
 19:     array:    db       1,2,3,4,5,6,7,8,9,10,11,12,13,14,15,16,17,18,19,20
 20:               end

                                                                 hll    stop ▼
```

Figure 2.28 Debug window.

statement) where we want program execution to stop. Double-clicking a breakpoint will eliminate it. The instruction (or statement) at the breakpoint is highlighted in yellow.

4. *Program execution.* To control the program execution, we may use a GO command or a TRACE command. The syntax for a GO command is **G [address]** whereas the syntax for a TRACE command is **T [count].** The parameter within the brackets is optional.

Now, set a breakpoint at the instruction **ajmp $** and click on the **go** button. The dScope will run until the breakpoint and stop. You will see that the content of register R3 has been changed to 64H.

2.11.5 Other Evaluation Boards

There are many evaluation boards available from different vendors. The features of three other boards that I have tested follow.

Intel 8XC51FX Target Board

The Intel 8XC51FX target board includes the following:

- An Intel 87C51FB microcontroller
- 32-KB SRAM
- A 50-pin connector (all 87C51FB signals are available from this connector)

- A 9-pin serial communication port connector (can communicate with a PC)
- 10 LEDs

The ApBUILDER package is bundled with this board. The ApBUILDER is essentially a collection of demo software from several vendors. The most important software is the COMPASS/51 IDE software from Production Language Inc. The COMPASS/51 IDE is an integrated development environment that includes an editor, an assembler, a C compiler, and a debugger. The COMPASS/51 IDE is similar to Keil Software's integrated development environment μVision. Unlike the MCB520, the 8XC51FX target board does not have an on-board debug monitor. Universities can contact Intel's University Support Program to acquire this board.

Systronix HSM/KISS Evaluation Board

The HSM/KISS evaluation board includes the following:

- A Dallas Semiconductor's 25-MHz or 33-MHz 80C320 microcontroller
- Loader PROM
- 128-KB external NVRAM with battery backup (can hold data for 1 week)
- Two 9-pin serial communication port (COM0 and COM1) connectors
- A prototyping area
- Two rows of pins that bring out all microcontroller signals

We need to run a terminal emulation program to communicate with the HAM/KISS board. The HyperTerminal program in Windows 98 (or NT) can be used. The HSM/KISS board has two operation modes: LOAD mode and RUN mode. In the LOAD mode, users can download their program from a PC via the COM1 serial port into the HSM/KISS board. After the program has been downloaded into the SRAM, the user needs to move the serial cable to the COM0 serial port and press the reset button to run the program. A cross assembler is included with this board. No debug monitor is included. For debugging purpose, the user program must output the contents of memory locations or registers through the serial port to the PC monitor screen. An assembly program on how to perform serial port output is provided. The HSM/KISS is inexpensive.

HTE SBC552 Development Board

The HTE SBC552 development board is marketed by HiTech Equipment Corporation. This board includes the following:

- An 80C552 microcontroller from Philips/Signetics running at 11.059 MHz
- Two 9-pin serial communication port connectors
- Four JEDEC 28-pin sockets: (1) Monitor program EPROM, (2) 32-KB user data and program SRAM, (3) 32-KB user SRAM, and (4) 8-KB SRAM for Monitor parameters
- A battery-backed real-time clock

- Serial 512-byte external EEPROM
- An interrupt encoder in a Generic Array Logic (GAL) chip
- An Intel 8255 chip for expanding parallel I/O ports

The 80C552 microcontroller has an 8-input, 10-bit A/D converter that allows us to perform data acquisition without an external A/D chip. The on-chip timer function of the 80C552 is comparable to that of the 8XC51FX.

The HTE SBC552 development board has an on-board monitor that provides commands and functions similar to those of the MCB520 monitor-51. The user of this board needs a PC and a terminal emulation program such as Procomm, Crosstalk, or hyper terminal in Windows 98/NT etc. to communicate with the on-board monitor. There is no integrated development software dedicated to this board.

2.12 SUMMARY

An assembly language program consists of four major parts: assembler directives, assembly language instructions, the END directive, and comments. Assembler directives do not generate machine code. Comments and flowcharts provide program documentation.

The MCS-51 can perform only 8-bit arithmetic. Numbers longer than 8 bit must be manipulated using the multiprecision arithmetic. The MCS-51 instruction set provides several ADD and SUB instructions that include CY flag as one of the operands. These instructions can be used to implement multiprecision arithmetic. In some applications, we may want to represent numbers in decimal format (BCD). Some adjustment must be made after we perform an arithmetic operation on decimal numbers. The MCS-51 provides the *DA A* instruction for this purpose. The MCS-51 provides only 8-bit multiplication and division instructions. If we want to perform multiplication and division on numbers longer than 8 bits, we need to synthesize them. Both are based on the pen-and-paper method that we have been familiar with in our daily life. To perform multiprecision multiplication, we generate *partial products*, align partial products properly, and add them together. Multiprecision division is discussed in Chapter 3.

Performing repetitive operations is the strength of a computer. For a computer to perform repetitive operations, program loops must be written to tell the computer to repeat the same sequence of instructions many times. A program loop may be executed a finite or infinite number of times. The implementation of program loops requires the use of a jump (either conditional or unconditional) instruction. The MCS-51 provides several versions of jump instruction for this purpose. The implementation of program loops also requires the initialization and maintenance of loop indices and some other variables. Instructions that increment, decrement, clear, and set a variable (bit or byte version) may be used for this purpose.

The MCS-51 instruction set includes many logical instructions, which may be useful for implementing control and I/O applications.

Rotate instructions are useful for bit field manipulations and multiplying or dividing a variable by a power of 2. All rotate instructions operate on 8-bit operands only. We can write a sequence of instructions to rotate a number longer than 8 bits. Shift instructions are useful for some applications but are not provided in the MCS-51 instruction set. Therefore, they must be synthesized by using one of the rotate instructions and some other instructions.

All instructions take some amount of time to execute. A time delay of some length can be created and can be implemented by repeating a sequence of instructions for some number of times. A longer time delay may require the use of nested program loops. All program loops involve some overhead on initialization and maintenance of loop indices and hence it is difficult to create a delay equal to the exact desired length.

2.13 EXERCISES

For the following exercise problems the most significant digit of a multiprecision number is stored at the lowest address; the least significant digit is stored at the highest address.

2.1 Find the valid and invalid labels in the following assembly statements, and explain why the invalid labels are not valid.

```
1.  start:      CLR    A              ; initialize A to 0
2.  NB C:       MOV    R0,#20
3.    me_too:   DEC    A
4.  lo+hi       INC    R0
5.  CBS         DJNZ   R0,greater
6.  again       SUBB   A,lp_cnt       ; check loop count
```

2.2 Identify the four fields of the following instructions:

```
a.          MOV    A,#30H     ; initilaize A to 30H
b. loop:    JNZ    contine    ; branch if not zero yet
```

2.3 Write assembler directives to reserve 10 bytes starting from program memory location 1000H and initialize them to 0.

2.4 Write assembler directives to construct a table of the ASCII code of lowercase letters. The table should be stored in program memory from 30H to 49H.

2.5 Write assembler directives to store the following message in program memory locations starting from 30H: Welcome to Intel program builder kit!

2.6 Write a program to add the 16-bit numbers stored at internal data memory 30H–31H and 40H–41H, respectively, and save the sum at 50H–51H.

2.7 Write a program to add the 4-byte numbers stored at internal data memory 30H–33H and 34H–37H, respectively, and store the sum at 38H–3BH.

2.8 Write a program to subtract the 16-bit number stored at internal data memory 40H–41H from the 16-bit number stored at 50H–51H and store the difference at 60H–61H.

2.9 Write a program to subtract the 32-bit number stored at internal data memory 30H–33H from the 32-bit number stored at 40H–43H and save the difference at 50H–53H.

2.10 Write a program to multiply two 32-bit numbers stored at internal data memory 30H–33H and 34H–37H and save the product at 40H–47H.

2.11 Write a program to divide the 8-bit number stored at internal data memory 30H into the 8-bit number stored at 32H and store the quotient at 34H.

2.12 Write a program to compute the average of an array of 16 unsigned 8-bit numbers stored at internal data memory 30H–3FH and store the average at 40H. Use right shift operation to implement divide-by-16.

2.13 Find the values of A and B after the execution of the *MUL AB* instruction if they originally contain the following values:

a. 34H and 79H, respectively
b. 6BH and 66H, respectively

2.14 Write a program to swap the last element of an array with the first element, the next-to-last element with the second element, etc. Assume that the array has 20 8-bit numbers and the array starts at 30H (stored at internal data memory).

2.15 Write a program to compute the sum of the positive numbers of an array with 30 8-bit numbers. Store the sum at internal data memory 30H–31H. The array starts at 40H in internal data memory. The array may contain negative numbers.

2.16 Generate the machine code of the following conditional jump instructions, if each of the instructions occurs at location A100H. Let alpha be the address A092H and let beta be the address A150H.

a. JNZ   alpha
b. JZ   beta

2.17 What will be the value of the carry flag after the execution of each of the following instructions? Assume accumulator A contains 59H and the carry flag is 0 before the execution of each instruction.

a. ADD   A, #30H
b. ADD   A, #66H
c. SUBB   A, #49H
d. SUBB   A, #7FH

2.18 Determine the jump instructions and the jump distances relative to the PC from the following machine code.

a. 40 44   **d.** 50 80
b. 60 E0   **e.** 70 50
c. B4 20 59   **f.** D8 50

2.19 Write a program to compute the average of the square of each element of an array with 32 8-bit numbers. The array is stored at internal data memory 30H–4FH. The average should be stored at 50H–51H. *Hint*: use arithmetic shift right five places to implement divide-by-32.

2.20 Write a program to find the number of elements that are divisible by 8 from an array of 40 8-bit numbers. The array starts at 30H (internal data memory).

2.21 Determine the number of times the following loop will be executed.

```
           MOV   A,#64
repeat:    CLR   C
           RRC   A
           DEC   A
           JNZ   repeat
```

2.22 Write a small program to shift the 32-bit number stored at internal data memory 30H–33H four places to the right.

2.14 LAB EXERCISES AND ASSIGNMENTS

2.1 Turn on the PC and start the MON51 program to connect to the evaluation board. Then perform the following operations:

a. Enter a command to display the contents of memory locations 00H~30H.
b. Set the contents of the above memory locations to 01H.
c. Display the contents of the above memory locations to verify the previous operation.

2.2 Enter monitor commands to perform the following operations:

1. Set breakpoints at 1000H, 1200H, 1300H, 1400H, and 1500H.
2. Display all the breakpoints.
3. Disable the breakpoints at 1000H and 1400H.
4. Display all the breakpoints.
5. Enable the breakpoint at 1400H.
6. Display all the breakpoints.
7. Delete all the breakpoints.
8. Display all the breakpoints.

2.3 Enter monitor commands to set the contents of accumulator A and B to 20H and 30H, respectively.

2.4 Invoke the one-line assembler to enter the following instructions to the evaluation board, starting from address 100H, and trace through the program:

```
mov   A,#12
mov   B,#20
mul   AB
mov   30H,A
mov   31H,B
```

2.5 Exit the MON51 program and invoke an editor to enter the following program as a file with the file name *prog1.a51:*

```
                org    00H              ; choose an available address
                ljmp   main
main:           mov    DPTR,#array      ; use DPTR as the pointer
                mov    R2,#20           ; initialize the loop count to 20
                mov    20H,#00H         ; initialize the sum to 0
                mov    R3,#0            ; use R3 as loop count
again:          mov    A,R3
                movc   A,@A+DPTR        ; get a copy of the current element
                clr    C                ; clear the carry
                rrc    A                ; shift the least significant bit to C
                jc     chend            ; test the end of the loop
                rlc    A                ; restore the array element
                add    A,20H
                mov    20H,A            ; update the sum
chend:          inc    R3               ; increment the array index
                djnz   R2,again
                nop
array:          db     1, 2, 3, 4,5,6,7,8,9,10,11,12,13,14,15,16,17,18,19,20
                end
```

After entering the program, do the following:

a. Assemble and link the program. Convert the executable file into HEX format.
b. Start the MON51 program.
c. Download the program into the MCB520 evaluation board.
d. Display the contents of the program memory locations from 00H to 30H.
e. Execute the program.
f. Display the contents of the direct data memory location at 20H.

Note: This program adds all the even numbers in the given array and stores the sum at 20H.

2.6 Exit the MON51 terminal program and return to the DOS command window. Invoke an editor to enter the following program (call it reg_bank.a51):

```
1.        org    00H
2.        ajmp   start
3.        start: mov SP,#80H           ; set the stack pointer to 80H
4.        mov    PSW,#00H              ; select register bank 0
5.        mov    R0,#00
6.        mov    R1,#01
7.        mov    R2,#02
8.        mov    R3,#03
```

9.	push	AR0	; push register R0 into the stack
10.	push	AR1	
11.	push	AR2	
12.	push	AR3	
13.	mov	PSW,#18H	; select register bank 3
14.	pop	AR3	
15.	pop	AR2	
16.	pop	AR1	
17.	pop	AR0	
18.	nop		
	end		

Assemble and link the program reg_bank.a51. Convert it into HEX format. Start the MON51 terminal program. Do the following operations:

1. Set a breakpoint at instruction 9.
2. Start executing the program until the breakpoint.
3. Display all the CPU registers (use the X command).
4. Display the internal data memory from 00H to 2FH.
5. Set a breakpoint at instruction 13 and 18.
6. Reexecute the program until the second breakpoint is reached.
7. Display internal memory locations from 80H to 8FH (in stack area).
8. Reexecute the program until the third breakpoint is reached.
9. Display the contents of CPU registers.
10. Display internal data memory locations 00H–1FH.

You can use the **U range** command to display the program that you downloaded into the MCB520 board.

2.7 Write a program to compute the sum of even numbers from 0 to 100 and save the sum at internal data memory locations 10H and 11H. Store the most significant byte of the sum at 10H.

2.8 Write a program to determine the number of elements in an array that are divisible by 8. The array has 20 8-bit elements and is stored immediately after the program. Leave the result in B.

3

ADVANCED ASSEMBLY PROGRAMMING

3.1 OBJECTIVES

After completing this chapter you should be able to

- access stack elements and manipulate the stack data structure
- manipulate array, matrix, and string data structures
- write subroutines
- make subroutine calls

3.2 INTRODUCTION

The main function of a computer is to execute programs that manipulate information and data. A program consists of two major parts: one is *data structure*, which deals with how data are organized; the other is *algorithm*, which deals with the steps for data manipulation. To manipulate information and data efficiently, we need to study data structures to learn how information and data are organized and how elements of particular structures can be manipulated. There are many data structures being used. However, we will discuss only stacks, vectors, matrices, and strings in this book.

3.3 STACK

Conceptually, a stack is a list of data items whose elements can be accessed from only one end. A stack data structure has a top and a bottom. The operation that adds a new item to the top is called *push*. The top element can be removed by performing an operation called *pop* or *pull*. Physically, a stack is often a reserved area in main memory where programs agree to perform only push and pop operations. The structure of a stack is shown in Figure 3.1. A stack has a stack pointer that points to the top element.

The MCS-51 has an 8-bit stack pointer SP. Whenever a byte of data is pushed onto the stack, it is pushed into the location with address equal to [SP] + 1. Whenever a byte

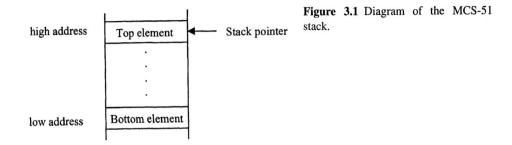

Figure 3.1 Diagram of the MCS-51 stack.

is popped, it is popped from the memory location pointed to by SP. Since SP is 8 bit, it can access only the internal data RAM. The stack grows from low addresses toward high addresses. The MCS-51 provides two instructions to facilitate the implementation of the stack data structure:

```
PUSH   direct      ; push direct byte into stack
POP    direct      ; pop direct byte from stack
```

The PUSH instruction increments SP by 1 and then copies the data at direct address to the location pointed to by SP. The POP instruction copies the data from the location pointed to by SP to the direct address and then decrements SP by 1. The SP register must be initialized properly before the stack can be used. The SP register is set to 07H when the MCS-51 is reset, which is the same direct address in internal RAM as register R7 in bank 0. Without changing SP, the first PUSH operation will write data to R0 of bank 1. SP should be initialized to point to an internal RAM address above the highest address likely to be used by the program. The MCS-51 members have only 128 bytes of internal SRAM and can all be used as stack space. The MCS-52 members have 256 bytes of internal SRAM. The lower 128 bytes can be accessed using direct or indirect addressing mode while the upper 128 bytes can be accessed only using the indirect addressing mode. All internal SRAM can be used as stack area.

Example 3.1 Write down an instruction to initialize the stack pointer to 3FH.

Solution: The following instruction will initialize the stack pointer to 3FH.

```
MOV   SP,#3FH
```

Example 3.2 Initially, the stack pointer points to memory location 4FH and the contents of the memory locations at 20H, 21H, and 22H are 11H, 12H, and 13H, respectively. Illustrate the stack contents after the execution of each of the following instructions:

```
PUSH   20H
PUSH   21H
PUSH   22H
```

Solution: The solution is shown in Figure 3.2.

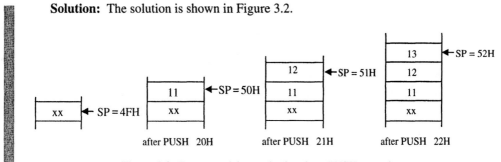

Figure 3.2 Contents of the stack after three PUSH operations.

3.4 INDEXABLE DATA STRUCTURES

The elements of a vector can be ordered as the zeroth element, the first element, the second element, etc. The elements of a matrix can be ordered as the (0, 0)th element, the (0,1)th element, . . . , the $(M - 1, N - 1)$th element, where the first and second number enclosed by the parentheses are the row and column numbers of the matrix element, and M and N represent the number of rows and columns of the matrix, respectively. For this reason, vectors and matrices are called *indexable* data structures. A vector consists of a sequence of elements in which each element is associated with an index i that can be used to access it. All of the elements of a vector are of the same size. To facilitate address calculation, the first element is associated with the index 0 and each successive element with the next integer, but you can change the index origin of the vector to 1 or other number if you are willing to modify the address calculation method. A vector can be defined by using the assembler directives DB (or DW, depending on the length of the element). For example, the following assembler directives define a vector of elements 2, 3, 5, 7, 11, and 13 starting at memory location E000H in program memory space:

```
        CSEG   AT E000H
vector:  DB    2,3,5,7,11,13
```

The first element, which is 2, is referred to as vector(0). To access the ith element, use the following instructions:

```
MOV   DPTR,#E000H
MOV   A,#i
MOVC  A,@A+DPTR
```

An array is also a vector data structure.

Example 3.3 Write a program to perform a *binary search* on an array that is sorted in ascending order. The sorted array is located at ARR and has *n* 8-bit integers. The key for searching is stored at KEY. The program leaves the address of the element that matches the key in DPTR or FFFFH in DPTR if no element matches the key. The key is stored in internal memory and the array is stored in external memory.

Solution: The idea of a binary search algorithm is to divide the sorted array into three parts:

- The portion of the array with indices range from $N/2 + 1$ to $N - 1$. This portion is the upper half of the array.
- The middle element.
- The portion of the array with indices range from 0 to $N/2 - 1$. This portion is the lower half of the array.

The binary search algorithm compares the key with the middle element and does the following based on the comparison result:

- If the key equals the middle element then stop.
- If the key is larger than the middle element, then the key can be found only in the portion of the array with higher indices. The search will be continued in the upper half.
- If the key is smaller than the middle element, then the key can be found only in the portion of the array with lower indices. The search will be continued in the lower half.

The binary search algorithm is as follows:

STEP 1   Use *max* and *min* as the upper and lower indices of the array for searching and initialize *max* and *min* to be $n - 1$ and 0, respectively.

STEP 2   If *max* < *min*, then exit. No element matches the key.

STEP 3   Let *mean* = (*min* + *max*)/2.

STEP 4   If *key* = ARR(*mean*), key is found, exit.

STEP 5   If *key* < ARR(*mean*), then set *max* to *mean* − *1* and go to Step 2.

STEP 6   If *key* > ARR(*mean*), then set *min* to *mean* + *1* and go to Step 2.

The program that implements the binary search algorithm is as follows:

```
min         set     R1
max         set     R2
mean        set     R3
key         set     R4
n           equ     xxH                 ; array count
            org     xxxxH               ; starting address of the program
```

```
                    MOV     DPTR,#ARR
                    MOV     min,#0
                    MOV     max,#n-1
        repeat:     CLR     C                   ; check the stop condition
                    MOV     A,max               ; "
                    SUBB    A,min               ; "
                    JC      nomatch             ; exit if min is larger than max
                    MOV     A,min               ; place low index in A
                    ADD     A,max               ; compute (max + min)
                    CLR     C                   ; compute the index mean
                    RRC     A                   ; "
                    MOV     mean,A              ; save it in mean
                    ADD     A,DPL               ; compute the address of ARR[mean]
                    MOV     DPL,A               ; and leave it in DPTR
                    MOV     A,DPH               ; "
                    ADDC    A,#0                ; "
                    MOV     DPH,A               ; "
                    MOVX    A,@DPTR             ; load ARR(mean) in A
        ; compare the key with ARR(mean)
                    CLR     C
                    SUBB    A,KEY
                    JZ      exit
                    JNC     go_low              ; the key is smaller
        ; prepare to go to upper half
                    MOV     A,mean
                    INC     A
                    MOV     min,A               ; set min to mean + 1
                    AJMP    repeat              ; continue
        go_low:     MOV     A,mean              ; set max to mean − 1
                    DEC     A                   ; "
                    MOV     max,A               ; "
                    AJMP    repeat              ; continue
        nomatch:    MOV     DPTR,#FFFFH         ;
        exit:       NOP
                    END
```

Example 3.4 Write a program to compute the sum of odd elements of an array of 8-bit integers. The array is stored in external memory and is located at *arr1*. The array has n elements. Store the sum at registers R2 and R3.

Solution: The least significant bit of an odd number is 1. By rotating the number to the right through carry flag and then checking the carry flag, we can decide if a number is odd.

N	EQU	xx	; *n* is an 8-bit number
sum1	SET	R2	; upper byte of sum
sum0	SET	R3	; lower byte of sum
I	SET	R4	; loop index
	ORG	00H	; starting address of the program
	MOV	sum1,#0	; initialize sum to 0
	MOV	sum0,#0	; "
	MOV	I,#0	; initialize the loop index to 0
repeat:	MOV	A,I	;
	MOV	DPTR,#arr1	; compute the address of arr[I] and leave it
	ADD	A,DPL	; in DPTR
	MOV	DPL,A	; "
	MOV	A,DPH	; "
	ADDC	A,#0	; "
	MOV	DPH,A	; "
	MOVX	A,@DPTR	; copy the *i*th element
	RRC	A	; check if the number is odd
	JNC	next	; skip the even number
	RLC	A	; restore the original number
	ADD	A,sum0	; add the odd number to sum
	MOV	sum0,A	; update the lower byte of sum
	MOV	A,sum1	; place the upper half of sum in A
	ADDC	A,#0	; add carry to the upper 8 bits of sum
	MOV	sum1,A	; update the upper byte of sum
next:	INC	I	
	CJNE	I,#N, repeat	; if *I* is not equal to *N*, then repeat
	END		

A *matrix* is a vector whose elements are vectors of the same length. We normally think of a matrix as a two-dimensional pattern as follows:

$$\text{matrix} = \begin{array}{ccccc} 11 & 12 & 13 & 14 & 15 \\ 21 & 22 & 23 & 24 & 25 \\ 31 & 32 & 33 & 34 & 35 \\ 41 & 42 & 43 & 44 & 45 \\ 51 & 52 & 53 & 54 & 55 \end{array}$$

A matrix can be stored in *row major* order, as shown in the following example:

```
matrix_1:      DB    11,12,13,14,15
               DB    21,22,23,24,25
               DB    31,32,33,34,35
               DB    41,42,43,44,45
               DB    51,52,53,54,55
```

or it can be stored in *column major* order, which is created as follows:

```
matrix_2:      DB    11,21,31,41,51
               DB    12,22,32,42,52
               DB    13,23,33,43,53
               DB    14,24,34,44,54
               DB    15,25,35,45,55
```

In the following discussion, matrices are assumed to have N rows and M columns, and the notation (i, j)th is used to refer to the matrix element located at the intersection of the ith row and the jth column. To facilitate address calculation, the first element in a row or a column is associated with the index 0. The address of the (i,j)th matrix element can be computed by using a polynomial equation that depends on which order is used. For example, in a row major order matrix *matrix_1* where each element is 1 byte, the address of the (i, j)th element is

$$\text{address of the } (i, j)\text{th element} = (i \times M) + j + \text{ address of matrix\_1}(0,0)$$

For a similar matrix *matrix_2* defined in column major order, the address of the (i,j)th element is

$$\text{address of the } (i,j)\text{th element} = (j \times N) + i + \text{ address of matrix\_2}(0,0)$$

For example, suppose registers R2 and R3 contain the row and column indices, respectively. The following instruction sequence computes the address of the element matrix_1(i,j) and leaves the address in the data pointer DPTR:

```
i      SET    R2                      ; row index
j      SET    R3                      ; column index
       MOV    A,i
       MOV    B,#M
       MUL    AB                      ; compute i × M
       ADD    A,j                     ; compute (i × M) + j
       MOV    DPL,A                   ; "
       MOV    A,B                     ; "
       ADDC   A,#0                    ; "
       MOV    B,A                     ; transfer the upper 8 bits of (i × M) + j to B
       MOV    A,DPL                   ; save the lower 8 bits of (i × M) + j in A
```

```
          MOV    DPTR,#matrix_1    ; place the address of matrix_1(0,0) in DPTR
          ADD    A,DPL             ; compute (i × M) + j + address of
                                   ; matrix_1(0,0)
          MOV    DPL,A             ; "
          MOV    A,DPH             ; "
          ADDC   A,B               ; "
          MOV    DPH,A             ; "
```

Example 3.5 Compute the addresses of the (2,3)th, the (5,8)th, and the (7,9)th elements of a 10 × 10 matrix of 8-bit integers. The given matrix is stored in column major order at E000H~E063H.

Solution: Apply the previous equation to compute the addresses of these matrix elements as follows:

The   (2,3)th element is located at $3 \times 0AH + 2 + E000H = E020H$

The   (5,8)th element is located at $8 \times 0AH + 5 + E000H = E054H$

The   (7,9)th element is located at $9 \times 0AH + 7 + E000H = E061H$

Example 3.6 Write a program to swap the last row of a matrix with the first row of the matrix, swap the second row with the second-to-last row, and so on. The matrix is N by M and is stored in row major order. Assume that the matrix is stored at **mat_x** in external data memory.

Solution: To swap rows of the matrix, the row index will run from 0 to $N/2 - 1$ and the column index will run from 0 to $M - 1$. The algorithm for matrix swapping is illustrated in Figure 3.3. The macro facility will be used to compute the matrix element address. Macro is defined in Section 2.3.

The following program performs the matrix row swapping:

```
N                EQU    xx                ; number of rows
M                EQU    yy                ; number of columns
i                SET    R0                ; row index
j                SET    R1                ; column index
ptr_hi           SET    R2                ; upper 8 bits of the matrix
                                          ; element address
ptr_lo           SET    R3                ; lower 8 bits of the matrix
                                          ; element address
temp1            SET    R4                ; to hold matrix element
temp2            SET    R5                ; to hold row number N−i−1
;The following macro computes the address of matrix(i,j) and places the address in
; DPTR
mat_addr         macro    n,i,j,matrix
```

```
                    MOV     A,i
                    MOV     B,#n
                    MUL     AB              ; compute i × n
                    ADD     A,j             ; compute (i × n) + j
                    MOV     DPL,A           ; "
                    MOV     A,B             ; "
                    ADDC    A,#0            ; "
                    MOV     B,A             ; transfer the upper 8 bits of
                                            ; (i × n) + j to B
                    MOV     A,DPL           ; save the lower 8 bits of
                                            ; (i × n) + j in A
                    MOV     DPTR,#matrix    ; place the address of matrix(0,0)
                                            ; in DPTR
                    ADD     A,DPL           ; compute (i × n) + j + address
                                            ;  of matrix(0,0)
                    MOV     DPL,A           ; "
                    MOV     A,DPH           ; "
                    ADDC    A,B             ; "
                    MOV     DPH,A           ; "
                    ENDM                    ; end of macro definition
                    ORG     00H
start:              MOV     i,#0            ; start from row 0
next_row:           MOV     j,#0            ; start from column 0
next_col:           mat_addr M,i,j,mat_x   ; compute the address of mat_x(i,j)
                    MOV     ptr_hi,DPH      ; save the matrix address
                    MOV     ptr_lo,DPL      ; "
                    MOVX    A,@DPTR         ; read the value of mat_x(i,j)
                    MOV     temp1,A         ; save the matrix element
                    MOV     A,#N-1          ; compute the row number to be
                                            ; swapped
                    CLR     C
                    SUBB    A,i             ; compute the value of N−i−1
                    MOV     temp2,A
                    mat_addr N,temp2,j,mat_x ; compute the address of
                                            ; mat_x(N−i−1,j)
                    MOVX    A,@DPTR         ; load the value of
                                            ; mat_x(N−i−1,j)
                    XCH     A,temp1         ; get the matrix element to be
                                            ; swapped
                    MOVX    @DPTR,A         ; store mat_x(i,j) at the address of
                                            ; mat_x(N−i−1,j)
```

MOV	DPH,ptr_hi	; transfer the address of ; *mat_x(i,j)* to DPTR
MOV	DPL,ptr_lo	; "
XCH	A,temp1	; move the value of ; *mat_x(N−i−1,j)* to A
MOVX	@DPTR,A	; store *mat_x(N−i−1,j)* at ; the address of *mat_x(i,j)*
CJNE	j,#M-1,next_col	; not done with the current ; row yet?
CJNE	i,#N/2-1,next_row	; not done with all the rows yet?
END		

Figure 3.3 Flowchart for matrix row swapping.

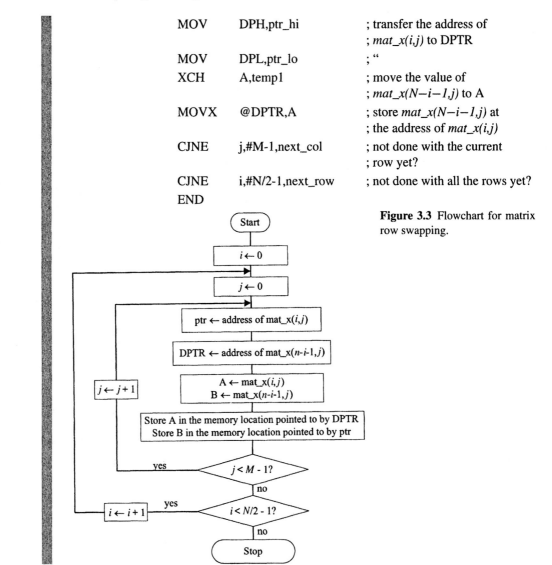

3.5 STRINGS

A string is a sequence of characters terminated by a null (ASCII code 00H) or other special characters such as EOT (ASCII code 04H). In this book, we will use the null character to terminate strings. Common operations applied to strings include concatenation, insertion, deletion, character and word counting, word matching, and so on.

In this book, we will use the external data memory of the MCS-51/52 to perform most of the string operations for the following reasons:

- A string may have more than several hundred characters.
- The MCS-51/52 internal memory is small—128 bytes for the MCS-51 family and 256 bytes for the MCS-52 family.

Example 3.7 Write a program to insert a word (or string) into another string.

Solution: To perform this operation, we need to know the insertion point. To make room for the word or string to be inserted, all of the characters after the insertion point must be moved by the number of characters contained in the word or string to be inserted. Let the number of characters contained in the word, the number of characters in the string after the insertion point, and the insertion point be represented by *char_cnt*, *char_moved*, *ins_pos*. Each character in the string starting from the insertion point should be moved by the distance of *char_cnt*. The main steps of the algorithm (also illustrated in Figure 3.4) are as follows:

1. Count the number of characters that need to be moved (the null character is included because the resultant new string must be terminated by a null character).
2. Count the characters in the word to be inserted (excluding the null character).
3. Move the characters in the string starting from the insertion point until the end of the string (move the last character first).
4. Insert the word (the first character of the word is inserted first).

The detailed program flow for solving this problem is illustrated in Figure 3.5. The program that implements the algorithm is as follows:

wd_ptrh	SET	R0	; high byte of word pointer
wd_ptrl	SET	R1	; low byte of word pointer
ptr2_h	SET	R2	; high byte of pointer 2
ptr2_l	SET	R3	; low byte of pointer 2

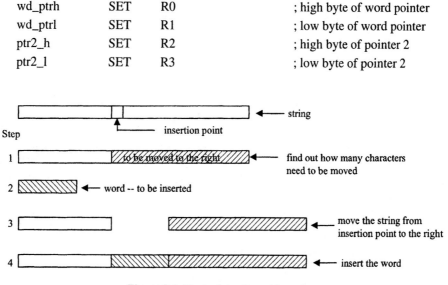

Figure 3.4 Illustration of word insertion.

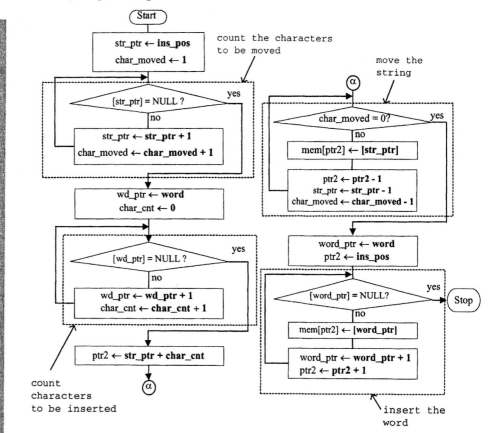

Figure 3.5 Algorithm for inserting a word to a string.

ch_moved	SET	R4	; number of characters to ; be moved
char_cnt	SET	R5	; number of characters in ; the word to be inserted
buf	SET	R6	; buffer to hold a character
	XSEG	at ppppH	; starting address of the word ; to be inserted
word:	DS	100	; buffer that holds the word ; to be inserted
string:	DS	1024	; buffer that holds the string
offset	EQU	zz	; offset of the insertion point ; from the start of the string
ins_pos	EQU	string+offset	; address for word insertion

```
                CSEG      at qqqqH                ; starting address of the
                                                  ; program
```

; The following 7 instructions count the number of characters to be moved

```
                MOV       ch_moved,#1            ; initialize ch_moved to 1
                MOV       DPTR,#ins_pos          ; set DPTR to insertion point
cnt_moved:      MOVX      A,@DPTR                ; check the current character
                JZ        cnt_chars              ; when done count the
                                                 ; characters in word
                INC       DPTR                   ; move the pointer
                INC       ch_moved
                SJMP      cnt_moved              ; not done and continue
cnt_chars:      MOV       ptr2_h,DPH             ; save the address of the end
                                                 ; of the string
                MOV       ptr2_l,DPL             ; "
```

; The following 7 instructions count the number of characters to be inserted

```
                CLR       char_cnt               ; initialize character count
                                                 ; to 0
                MOV       DPTR,#word             ; set DPTR to point to the
                                                 ; word to be inserted
wd_loop:        MOVX      A,@DPTR                ; check the current character
                JZ        move_to                ; prepare to move the string
                                                 ; from insertion point
                INC       char_cnt
                INC       DPTR
                SJMP      wd_loop
move_to:
                MOV       DPL,ptr2_l             ; get the address of the
                                                 ; character to be moved
                MOV       DPH,ptr2_h             ; "
                MOVX      A,@DPTR                ; get the character to be
                                                 ; moved
                MOV       buf,A                  ; put it in a buffer
                MOV       A,DPL                  ; compute the address to be
                                                 ; moved to
                ADD       A,char_cnt             ; "
                MOV       DPL,A                  ; "
                MOV       A,DPH                  ; "
                ADDC      A,#0                   ; "
                MOV       DPH,A                  ; "
```

```
                        MOV    A,buf              ; get back the character to be
                                                  ; moved
                        MOVX   @DPTR,A            ; move the character
                        MOV    A,ptr2_l           ;
                        CLR    C                  ; clear the carry
                        SUBB   A,#1               ; decrement the string
                                                  ; pointer by 1
                        MOV    ptr2_l,A           ; "
                        MOV    A,ptr2_h           ; "
                        SUBB   A,#0               ; "
                        MOV    ptr2_h,A           ; "
                        DJNZ   ch_moved,move_to   ; continue if not done yet
            insert:     MOV    DPTR,#word         ; prepare to insert
                        MOV    wd_ptrh,DPH        ; save a copy of the word
                                                  ; pointer
                        MOV    wd_ptrl,DPL        ; "
                        MOVX   A,@DPTR            ; get a character from the
                                                  ; word
                        MOV    DPTR,#ins_pos      ; get the address for insertion
            check_ch:   JZ     exit               ; is this the end of the word
                                                  ; to be inserted?
                        MOVX   @DPTR,A            ; insert the character
                        INC    DPTR               ; move to the next insertion
                                                  ; point
                        MOV    ptr2_h,DPH         ; save the value so that
                                                  ; DPTR can be reused
                        MOV    ptr2_l,DPL         ; "
                        MOV    DPH,wd_ptrh
                        MOV    DPL,wd_ptrl
                        INC    DPTR               ; compute the address of the
                                                  ; next character to be
                                                  ; inserted
                        MOV    wd_ptrh,DPH        ; update the word pointer
                        MOV    wd_ptrl,DPL        ; "
                        MOVX   A,@DPTR            ; get the next character
                        MOV    DPH,ptr2_h         ; get the address for insertion
                        MOV    DPL,ptr2_l         ; "
                        SJMP   check_ch
            exit:       NOP
                        END
```

Example 3.8 Write a program to delete a substring from a given string.

Solution: The starting address and the ending address of the substring to be deleted are known. The basic plan is to copy (or concatenate) the substring after the ending address to the starting address. The program is as follows:

```
                XSEG    at xxxxH          ; starting address of the string to
                                          ; be manipulated
string_X:       DS      1024              ; buffer that holds the string
off_1           EQU     yy
off_2           EQU     zz
del_begin       EQU     string_X+off_1    ; starting address for deletion
del_end         EQU     string_X+off_2    ; ending address for deletion
ptr1_h          SET     R0                ; upper byte of the pointer 1
ptr1_l          SET     R1                ; lower byte of the pointer 1
ptr2_h          SET     R2                ; upper byte of the pointer 2
ptr2_l          SET     R3                ; lower byte of the pointer 2
                CSEG    at ppppH          ; starting address of the program
                MOV     DPTR,#del_begin
                MOV     ptr2_h,DPH        ; initialize the destination
                                          ; address for copy
                MOV     ptr2_l,DPL        ; "
                MOV     DPTR,#del_end
next:           INC     DPTR              ; get the address of the next
                                          ; character to be copied
                MOV     ptr1_h,DPH        ; save the source address for
                                          ; copy
                MOV     ptr1_l,DPL        ; "
                MOVX    A,@DPTR           ; get a byte
                MOV     DPH,ptr2_h        ; place the destination address
                                          ; for copy in DPTR
                MOV     DPL,ptr2_l        ; "
                MOVX    @DPTR,A           ; copy the character
                JZ      exit              ; is this the end of the string?
                INC     DPTR              ; move the destination address
                                          ; for copying
                MOV     ptr2_h,DPH        ; save and update the
                                          ; destination pointer
                MOV     ptr2_l,DPL        ; "
                MOV     DPH,ptr1_h
                MOV     DPL,ptr1_l
                SJMP    next
```

```
exit:        NOP
             END
```

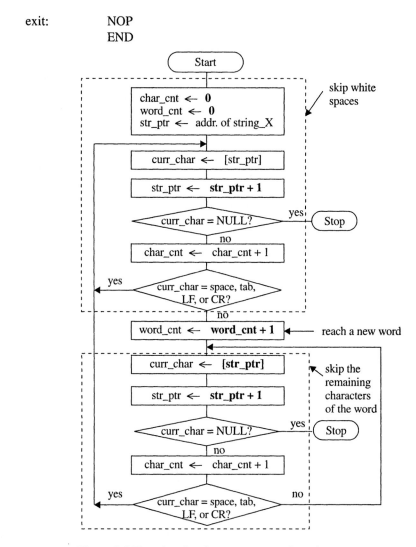

Figure 3.6 Flowchart for character count and word count program.

Example 3.9 Write a program to count the numbers of characters and words contained in a given string. Two adjacent words are separated by one or more white spaces—space, tab, carriage return, and line-feed characters are considered white spaces. A word may consist of only one character. White spaces are included in the character count.

Solution: To count the numbers of characters and words contained in a string, we need to scan through the whole string. A pointer will be used to point to the string. The pointer points to the first character at the beginning. Let the character count, word count, and current character (the one pointed to by the character pointer) be represented by *char_cnt,* *word_cnt,* and *curr_char,* respectively. The starting address of the string to be processed is at string_X. The string pointer is placed in the DPTR register. An empty string consists of a null character.

The algorithm of this program is illustrated in Figure 3.6. The algorithm is based on the following plan:

- Every character that the program encounters should cause the character count to be incremented by 1.
- The first nonspace character to the right of one or more white spaces is the beginning of a new word and should increment the word count by 1.
- A white space character that may be a space, a line feed, a character return, or a null character terminates a word.

The following program implements this algorithm:

```
tab         EQU     09H             ; ASCII code for horizontal tab
sp          EQU     20H             ; ASCII code for space character
CR          EQU     0DH             ; ASCII code for carriage return
LF          EQU     0AH             ; ASCII code for line feed
char_cnt    SET     R0              ; use R0 as the character count
word_cnt    SET     R1              ; use R1 as the word count
            XSEG    at 1000H
string_X:   DS      255             ; buffer that holds the string to be
                                    ; scanned

            CSEG    at 2000H        ; starting address of the program
            MOV     DPTR,#string_X  ; place the string pointer in DPTR
            MOV     char_cnt,#0     ; initialize character count to 0
            MOV     word_cnt,#0     ; initialize word count to 0
repeat:     MOVX    A,@DPTR         ; read the current character
            JZ      exit            ; is this a NULL character?
            INC     char_cnt
            INC     DPTR            ; move to the next character
            CJNE    A,#sp,check_tab ; is this a space character?
            SJMP    repeat          ; the current character is a space
check_tab:  CJNE    A,#tab,check_cr ; is this a tab character?
            SJMP    repeat          ; the current character is a tab
check_cr:   CJNE    A,#CR,check_lf  ; is this a carriage return
                                    ; character?
            SJMP    repeat          ; the current character is a
                                    ; carriage return
check_lf:   CJNE    A,#LF,new_word  ; reach a new word?
            SJMP    repeat          ; the current character is a line
                                    ; feed
```

```
new_word:    INC     word_cnt        ; a nonspace character is the
                                      ; beginning of a word
wd_loop:     MOVX    A,@DPTR
             JZ      exit            ; is this a NULL character?
             INC     DPTR            ; move the character pointer
             INC     char_cnt
; The following instructions check the end of a word
             CJNE    A,#sp,ch_tab    ; is it a space?
             LJMP    repeat          ; it is a space so check next word
ch_tab:      CJNE    A,#tab,ch_cr    ; is it a tab?
             LJMP    repeat          ; it is a tab so check next word
ch_cr:       CJNE    A,#CR,ch_lf     ; is it a carriage return?
             LJMP    repeat          ; it is a CR so check next word
ch_lf:       CJNE    A,#LF,wd_loop   ; is it a line feed?
             LJMP    repeat          ; it is a LF so check next word
exit:        END
```

Example 3.10 Write a program to search for a word from a string.

Solution: Assume the string and the word are stored at string_X and word_X, respectively, in external data memory. The basic plan of this program is to identify the beginning of each new word and compare the new word with the given word. If they are equal, then stop. Otherwise, continue until the end of the string. The bit memory location *found* will be set to 1 if the word is found; otherwise, it will be cleared to 0. The given word must be matched character by character, and the comparison must continue one character beyond the last non-white-space character of the given word if the word occurs in the given string.

There are three possible outcomes for the matched word:

CASE 1   The matched word is not the last word in the string. Comparison of the last characters will yield "not equal."

CASE 2   The matched word is the last word in the given string, but there is one or a few white spaces between the last word and the null character. Comparison of the last characters will again give the result "not equal."

CASE 3   The matched word is the last word of the given string, and it is followed by the null character. In this case, the comparison result for the last character is "equal."

The major steps of the algorithm are as follows:

STEP 1   Skip white spaces to look for the next word in the string.

STEP 2   Compare the current word of the string with the word to be matched. If they match, then stop.

STEP 3   If the end of the string is reached then stop. Otherwise, go to Step 1.

A detailed flowchart of the algorithm is shown in Figure 3.7.
The program is as follows:

tab	EQU	09H	; ASCII code for tab character
sp	EQU	20H	; ASCII code for space
CR	EQU	0DH	; ASCII code for carriage return
LF	EQU	0AH	; ASCII code for line feed
NULL	EQU	0	; ASCII code for null character
match_flag	BIT	0	; flag to indicate if the word is ; found in the string
str_ptrh	SET	R1	; high byte of the string pointer ; holder
str_ptrl	SET	R2	; low byte of the string pointer ; holder

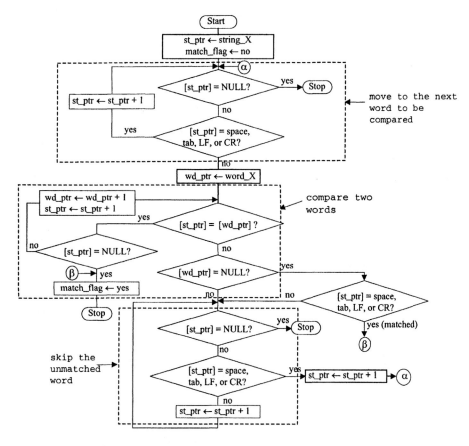

Figure 3.7 Flowchart for searching for a word in a string.

```
wd_ptrh      SET    R3           ; high byte of the word pointer
                                 ; holder
wd_ptrl      SET    R4           ; low byte of the word pointer
                                 ; holder
             XSEG   zzzzH        ; external data memory starting
                                 ; address
word_X:      DS     100          ; buffer that holds the word to be
                                 ; matched
string_X:    DS     1024         ; buffer that holds the string to be
                                 ; searched
             CSEG   kkkkH        ; starting address of the program
             CLR    match_flag   ; initialize the match flag
             MOV    DPTR,#string_X ; place the starting address of the
                                 ; string in DPTR
loop:        MOVX   A,@DPTR      ; get a character from the string
             JZ     exit         ; done with the search?
             CJNE   A,#sp,ch_CR  ; compare with space
             SJMP   skip         ; it is sp and skip it
ch_CR:       CJNE   A,#CR,ch_LF  ; compare with CR
             SJMP   skip         ; it is CR and skip it
ch_LF:       CJNE   A,#LF,ch_tab ; compare with LF
             SJMP   skip         ; it is LF and skip it
ch_tab:      CJNE   A,#tab,compare ; compare with tab
skip:        INC    DPTR
             LJMP   loop         ; continue to skip white spaces
compare:     MOV    B,A          ; put the current string character
                                 ; in register B
             INC    DPTR         ; move the string pointer
             MOV    st_ptrh,DPH  ; save the string pointer
             MOV    st_ptrl,DPL  ; "
             MOV    DPTR,#word_X ; place the address of word in
                                 ; DPTR
             MOVX   A,@DPTR      ; get the first character of word_X
             INC    DPTR         ; move the word pointer
             MOV    wd_ptrh,DPH  ; save the word pointer
             MOV    wd_ptrl,DPL  ; "
next_ch:     CJNE   A,B,end_of_wd ; compare two characters
             JZ     matched      ; if the current char is NULL, then
                                 ; matched
             MOVX   A,@DPTR      ; get the next character from the
                                 ; word
```

```
            MOV    B,A                ; put it in B
            INC    DPTR               ; move the word pointer
            MOV    wd_ptrh,DPH        ; save the word pointer
            MOV    wd_ptrl,DPL        ; "
            MOV    DPH,st_ptrh        ; place the string pointer in DPTR
            MOV    DPL,st_ptrl        ; "
            MOVX   A,@DPTR            ; get the next character from the
                                      ; string
            INC    DPTR               ; move the string pointer
            MOV    st_ptrh,DPH        ; save the string pointer
            MOV    st_ptrl,DPL        ; "
            XCH    A,B                ; exchange A and B so that A
                                      ; contains the character
                                      ; from the word
            MOV    DPH,wd_ptrh        ; place word pointer in DPTR
            MOV    DPL,wd_ptrl        ; "
            LJMP   next_ch            ; prepare to compare next
                                      ; characters
end_of_wd:  CJNE   A,#0,next_wd       ; is it the end of the word?
            CJNE   B,#CR,chek_LF      ;
            SJMP   matched            ; the word is found in the string
chek_LF:    LF:    CJNE B,#LF,chek_tab
            SJMP   matched            ; the word is found in the string

chek_tab:   CJNE   B,#tab,chek_sp
            SJMP   matched
chek_sp:    CJNE   B,#sp,next_wd      ; not matched, need continue?
            SJMP   matched
; The following instructions skip the unmatched word
next_wd:    MOV    DPH,st_ptrh        ; place the string pointer in DPTR
            MOV    DPL,st_ptrl        ; "
            MOVX   A,@DPTR            ; get the next character from the
                                      ; string
            INC    DPTR               ; move the string pointer
            MOV    st_ptrh,DPH        ; save the string pointer
            MOV    st_ptrl,DPL        ; save the string pointer
            JZ     exit               ; is this the end of the string?
            CJNE   A,#sp,chk_CR       ; is it a space?
            LJMP   loop               ; repeat the process
chk_CR:     CJNE   A,#CR,chk_LF       ; is it a CR?
```

```
                    LJMP    loop              ; repeat the process
chk_LF:             CJNE    A,#LF,chk_tab     ; is it an LF?
                    LJMP    loop              ; repeat the process
chk_tab:            CJNE    A,#tab,next_wd    ; need to continue?
                    LJMP    loop              ; repeat the process
matched:            SETB    match_flag        ; set the matched flag
exit:               END
```

3.6 SUBROUTINES

Good program design is based on the concept of modularity—the partitioning of a large program into subroutines. A main program contains the logical structure of the algorithm, while smaller program units execute many of the details.

The principles of program design in high-level languages apply even more to the design of assembly language programs. Begin with a simple main program whose steps clearly outline the logical flow of the algorithm, and then assign the execution details to subroutines. Of course, subroutines may themselves call other subroutines. The structure of a program is illustrated in Figure 3.8.

A subroutine is a sequence of instructions stored in memory at a specified address. The subroutine can be called from various places in the program. When a subroutine is called, the address (called *return address*) of the instruction immediately following the subroutine call instruction (ACALL or LCALL) is saved and the program control is passed to the called subroutine. The subroutine is then executed. The subroutine terminates with a return

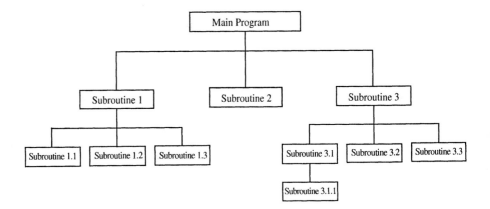

Figure 3.8 A structured program.

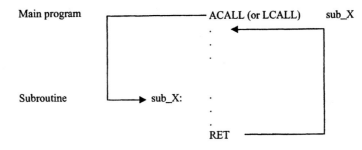

Figure 3.9 Subroutine processing.

instruction (RET) that directs the program control back to the instruction following the one that called the subroutine. Figure 3.9 illustrates this process.

Subroutine call is often used in the following situations:

- There are several places in a program that require the same computation to be performed with different parameters. Using subroutine calls can shorten the program.
- The program is complex. If the programmer can divide a large problem into smaller ones and solve each smaller problem using a subroutine, the problem will be easier to manage and understand, and it will also be easier to maintain.

The MCS-51 provides two instructions for calling subroutines:

[<label>] ACALL addr11 [<comment>]
[<label>] LCALL addr16 [<comment>]

where

- *addr11* is the lower 11 bits of the subroutine address. The upper 5 bits of the subroutine address are identical to those of the current program counter. The subroutine called must be within the same 2K-byte page of the program memory as the first byte of the instruction after the ACALL instruction.
- *addr16* is the whole 16 bits of the destination of the subroutine. The subroutine called may be anywhere within the 64K-byte program memory address space.
- Both the label and comment fields are optional.

These two instructions push the return address into the system stack. The return address is the address of the instruction that follows the subroutine call.

The last instruction to be executed in a subroutine is the RET instruction. RET pops the high-order and low-order bytes of the PC successively from the stack, decrementing the stack pointer by two. Program execution continues at the resultant address, generally the instruction immediately following an ACALL or LCALL.

3.7 ISSUES IN SUBROUTINE CALLS

The program or routine that makes the subroutine call is referred to as *caller* and the subroutine called by other program is designated as *callee*. A subroutine is *entered* when it is being executed. There are three important issues involved in subroutine calls:

- *Parameter passing.* The caller of the subroutine usually wants the subroutine to perform computation using the parameters passed to it. There are several methods available for passing parameters to the subroutine:
  1. *Use registers.* In this method, the parameters are placed in registers before a subroutine is called. This method is very convenient when there are only a few parameters to be passed to the callee.
  2. *Use the stack.* The parameters are pushed into the stack before the subroutine is called. The stack must be cleaned up after the computation is completed. This can be done by the caller or the callee.
  3. *Use global memory.* Global memory is accessible to both the caller and the callee. The caller simply places the parameters in global memory, and the callee will be able to access them.

- *Result returning.* The result of a computation can be returned by three methods:
  1. *Use registers.* This method is most convenient when there are only a few bytes of values to be returned. When this method is used, the caller may need to save registers before making the subroutine call.
  2. *Use the stack.* The caller creates a hole in the stack by incrementing the stack pointer before making a subroutine call. The callee saves the computational result in the hole before returning to the caller.
  3. *Use global memory.* The callee simply places the result in global memory and the caller can access it.

- *Allocation of local variables.* In addition to the parameters passed to it, a subroutine may need memory locations to hold temporary variables and results. Temporary variables are useful only during the execution of the subroutine and are called local variables because they are local to the subroutine. Local variables are always allocated in the stack so that they are not accessible to any other subroutine. There are two methods for allocating local variables:
  1. Use as many *INC SP* instructions as needed if fewer than 4 bytes are needed. This approach takes less time if no more than 3 bytes are needed for local variables.
  2. Use the following instruction sequence if more than 3 bytes are needed:

; the following three instructions perform the operation of $SP \leftarrow [SP] + N$

```
MOV    A,SP
ADD    A,#N        ; allocate N bytes
MOV    SP,A        ; move the stack pointer up by N bytes
```

It takes three machine cycles to allocate 3 bytes using the *INC SP* instruction, while the instruction sequence for the second method takes three machine cycles for any number of bytes no more than 255 − [old SP]. Since the above instruction sequence destroys the value in accumulator A, it must be saved in the stack. Saving registers is often done at the entrance of the subroutine.

The space allocated to local variables must be deallocated before the subroutine returns to the caller. There are two corresponding methods for deallocating local variables:

1. Use as many *DEC SP* instructions as needed if no more than 4 bytes are to be deallocated. This approach takes less time if no more than 4 bytes are to be deallocated.
2. Use the following instruction sequence if there are more than 4 bytes to be deallocated:

```
MOV   A,SP
CLR   C
SUBB  A,#N
MOV   SP,A      ; move down the stack pointer by N bytes
```

It takes four machine cycles to deallocate 4 bytes from the stack using the DEC SP instruction, while it takes only four machine cycles to deallocate any number (to be more accurate, we can deallocate only up to the current value of SP) of bytes using this instruction sequence.

3.8 THE STACK FRAME

The stack is heavily used during a subroutine call: the caller may need to save registers and allocate local variables in the stack. If the subroutine needs to call another routine, it may place outgoing parameters in the stack. The region that holds incoming parameters, the subroutine return address, saved registers, local variables, and outgoing parameters is referred to as *stack frame*. Since the stack frame is created during a subroutine call, it is also called the *activation record* of the subroutine. An example of a stack frame is shown in Figure 3.10. The portion for outgoing parameters does not exist for a subroutine that does not call other routines.

During the execution of a subroutine, parameters in the stack frame may need to be accessed. One way of accessing parameters in the stack frame is as follows:

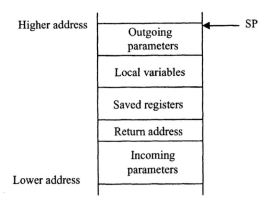

Figure 3.10 A stack frame.

STEP 1   Place the current stack pointer in accumulator A.

STEP 2   Subtract the offset of the parameter from the top of the stack and place the result in either R0 or R1.

STEP 3   Access the parameter using indirect addressing mode.

Example 3.11   You are given a stack frame as shown in Figure 3.11. Write an instruction sequence to access the parameter arr_cnt and place it in accumulator A.

Solution: The size of the stack frame is 16 bytes and the parameter arr_cnt is 13 bytes below the top of the stack. The following instruction sequence will place the value arr_cnt into accumulator A:

```
MOV      A,SP
CLR      C
SUBB     A,#13        ; compute the address of arr_cnt
MOV      R0,A
MOV      A,@R0        ; fetch arr_cnt
```

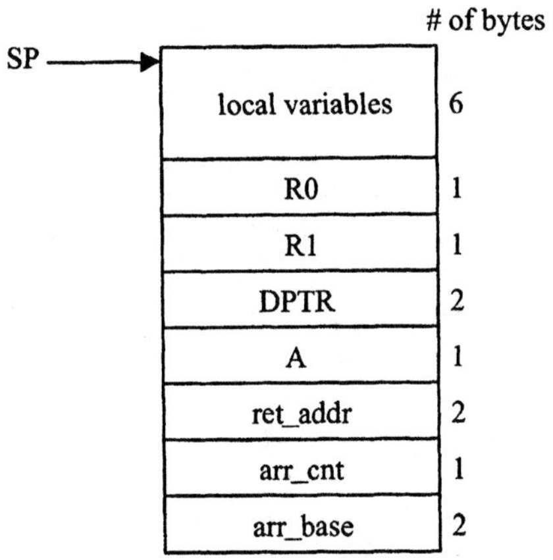

Figure 3.11 A stack frame example.

	# of bytes
SP →	
local variables	6
R0	1
R1	1
DPTR	2
A	1
ret_addr	2
arr_cnt	1
arr_base	2

3.9 EXAMPLES OF SUBROUTINE CALLS

The examples in this section illustrate parameter passing, result returning, and local variable allocation.

3.9.1 Multiprecision Division

The MCS-51 instruction set includes only one division instruction that divides the 8-bit register B into the 8-bit accumulator A. Any division that involves numbers that cannot be

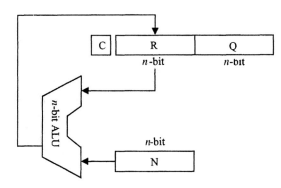

Figure 3.12 Division hardware.

represented in 8 bits must be synthesized using other instructions. One of the most famous division algorithms is the *paper-and-pencil* method.

To divide an unsigned n-bit number into another unsigned n-bit number using the paper-and-pencil method, three n-bit registers and a carry flag are required. The hardware connection is shown in Figure 3.12. Initially, registers R, Q, and N hold 0, the dividend, and the divisor, respectively. At the end of the division operation, registers R and Q hold the remainder and quotient, respectively. The carry flag C is used to indicate whether the subtraction result is negative. The n-bit ALU can perform n-bit unsigned addition and subtraction operations. The paper-and-pencil division method consists of n division steps. Each division step consists of four parts:

1. Shift the register pair (R, Q) one bit left.
2. Subtract register N from register R, put the result back to R.
3. If the result of Step 2 is negative then set the least significant bit of Q to 0. Otherwise, set the least significant bit of Q to 1.
4. If the result of Step 2 is negative then restore the old value of R by adding the contents of register N back into R.

The restoring step (Step 4) can be eliminated by modifying Step 2 to

> *Subtract the contents of N from register R, put the result back into R only if the result is positive.*

After repeating this division step n times, the quotient is in Q and the remainder is in R. Before the division steps are performed, the dividend and divisor must be loaded into register Q and register N, respectively.

The MCS-51 CPU can perform only 8-bit subtraction. As long as n is larger than 8, the technique described in Chapter 2 must be used to perform the subtraction. The sign of the result can be determined by checking the carry flag. The result is positive when the carry flag is 0. Otherwise, the result is negative.

Example 3.12 Write a subroutine that divides an unsigned 16-bit integer into another unsigned 16-bit integer. Parameters are passed to this subroutine in registers and the quotient and remainder are also returned to the caller in registers.

Solution: Suppose register pairs R2...R3, R4...R5, and R6...R7 are used in Figure 3.12 as the registers R, Q, and N, respectively. The caller of this subroutine uses the following instruction sequence to make the subroutine call:

```
MOV      R4,#dividend_h      ; place the upper byte of the dividend in R4
MOV      R5,#dividend_l      ; place the lower byte of the dividend in R5
MOV      R6,#divisor_h       ; place the upper byte of the divisor in R6
MOV      R7,#divisor_l       ; place the lower byte of the divisor in R7
LCALL    div16u              ; call the 16-bit unsigned divide subroutine
```

The register B will be used as the loop count to keep track of the number of iterations remaining to be performed. The subroutine is as follows:

```
temp      SET    R1
div16u:   push   B
          MOV    B,#0           ; initialize the loop count to 0
          MOV    R2,#0
          MOV    R3,#0
repeat:   INC    B
```
; The following instructions shift registers R and Q to the left one place
```
          MOV    A,R5
          CLR    C
          RLC    A
          MOV    R5,A
          MOV    A,R4
          RLC    A
          MOV    R4,A
          MOV    A,R3
          RLC    A
          MOV    R3,A
          MOV    A,R2
          RLC    A
          MOV    R2,A
```
; The following instructions perform a division step by carrying subtract operations
```
          CLR    C
          MOV    A,R3
          SUBB   A,R7           ; subtract the lower bytes of two numbers
          MOV    temp,A         ; save the difference in the temporary
                                ; register
          MOV    A,R2
          SUBB   A,R6           ; subtract the upper bytes of the 16-bit
                                ; numbers
          JC     less           ; the minuend (R) is smaller
```

	MOV	R2,A	; store the difference back to the minuend
	MOV	A,R5	
	ORL	A,#01H	; set the lsb of Q to 1
	MOV	R5,A	; "
	MOV	R3,temp	; also store the lower byte of the ; difference back to the minuend
	AJMP	checkend	
less:	MOV	A,R5	
	ANL	A,#FEH	; set the lsb of Q to 0
	MOV	R5,A	; "
checkend:	CJNE	B,#16,repeat	
exit:	pop	B	; restore B
	RET		

Signed division can be implemented by modifying this subroutine and will be left as an exercise problem.

3.9.2 Average of Array

There are two parameters to be passed to the subroutine that computes the average of an array:

- *ar_cnt*: array count
- *ar_base*: starting address of the array

Assume the array is stored in external memory. The algorithm for computing the array average is illustrated in Figure 3.13.

This algorithm checks the array count before performing the computation. If the array count is less than 1, then the error flag is set to 1.

Example 3.13 Write a subroutine to compute the average of an array of 8-bit elements.

Solution: The caller will include the following instruction sequence before calling this subroutine:

CLR	error	; clear the error flag
MOV	B,#ar_cnt	; place the array count in register B
MOV	DPTR,#ar_base	; place the array base in DPTR
LCALL	array_av	; make the subroutine call

where the error flag is defined by the following assembler directive:

error	BIT	0	; the bit of address 0 is used as an error flag

Since both the array count and array elements are 8 bit, the array average will also be 8 bit and hence can be placed in an 8-bit register. This subroutine calls the 16-bit division subroutine in Example 3.12 to compute the array average. Register pair R4 and R5 will be used to accumulate the array sum. Before calling the 16-bit division subroutine, array count will be placed in register R7 and register R6 will be cleared to 0.

```
array_av:    CJNE    B,#0,check_1      ; is array count equal to 0?
             SETB    error             ; set the error flag
             AJMP    exit              ; prepare to return
check_1:     CJNE    B,#1,normal       ; does array have only one
                                       ; element?
             MOVX    A,@DPTR           ; fetch array[0]
             AJMP    exit              ; prepare to return
normal:      MOV     R7,B              ; save the array count in register
                                       ; N (R6...R7)
             MOV     R6,#0             ; place the divisor in register
                                       ; N (R6&R7)
             MOV     R4,#0             ; initialize array sum to 0
             MOV     R5,#0             ; "
again:       MOVX    A,@DPTR           ; place array[i] in A (i starts
                                       ; from 0)
             INC     DPTR              ; move to the next array element
             ADD     A,R5              ; compute sum + array[I]
             MOV     R5,A              ; "
             MOV     A,R4              ; "
             ADDC    A,#0              ; "
             MOV     R4,A              ; "
             DJNZ    B,again           ; is this the end of the loop?
             LCALL   div16_u           ; compute sum ÷ ar_cnt and
                                       ; leave quotient in
                                       ; R5
             MOV     A,R5              ; transfer quotient to A
exit:        RET                       ; return to the caller
```

3.9.3 Bubble Sort

Sorting is among the most common ingredients of programming and there are many sorting methods being used. Bubble sort is a widely known sorting method.

The basic idea underlying the bubble sort is to go through the array or file sequentially several times. Each iteration consists of comparing each element in the array or file with its successor ($x[i]$ with $x[i+1]$) and interchanging the two elements if they are not in proper order (either ascending or descending). Consider the following array:

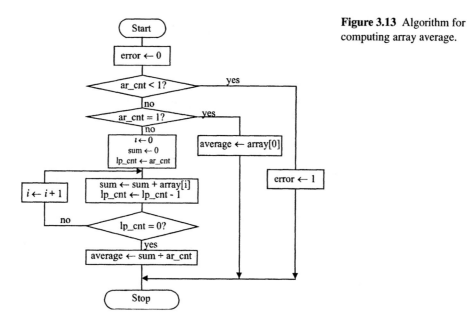

Figure 3.13 Algorithm for computing array average.

23 50 49 39 14 99 82 31

Suppose we want to sort this array in ascending order. The following comparisons are made in the first iteration:

x[0]   with x[1] (23 with 50) no interchange
x[1]   with x[2] (50 with 49) interchange
x[2]   with x[3] (50 with 39) interchange
x[3]   with x[4] (50 with 14) interchange
x[4]   with x[5] (50 with 99) no interchange
x[5]   with x[6] (99 with 82) interchange
x[6]   with x[7] (99 with 31) interchange

Thus, after the first iteration, the array is in the order

23 49 39 14 50 82 31 99

Notice that after this first iteration, the largest element (in this case 99) is in its proper position within the array. In general, $x[n - i]$ will be in its proper position after iteration i. The method is called the bubble sort because each number slowly bubbles up to its proper position. After the second iteration the array is

23 39 14 49 50 31 82 99

Notice that 82 is now in the second highest position. Since each iteration places a new element into its proper position, an array or a file of n elements requires no more than $n - 1$ iterations.

The complete set of iterations is the following:

iteration	0 (original array)	23 50 49 39 14 99 82 31
iteration	1	23 49 39 14 50 82 31 99
iteration	2	23 39 14 49 50 31 82 99
iteration	3	23 14 39 49 31 50 82 99
iteration	4	14 23 39 31 49 50 82 99
iteration	5	14 23 31 39 49 50 82 99
iteration	6	14 23 31 39 49 50 82 99
iteration	7	14 23 31 39 49 50 82 99

There are some obvious improvements to the foregoing method.

First, since all elements in positions greater than or equal to $n - i$ are already in proper position after iteration i, they need not be considered in succeeding iterations. Thus in the first iteration $n - 1$ comparisons are made, on the second iteration $n - 2$ comparisons, and on the $(n - 1)$th iteration only one comparison is made (between $x[0]$ and $x[1]$). Therefore the process is sped up as it proceeds through successive iterations.

Second, although we have shown that $n - 1$ iterations are sufficient to sort an array or a file of size n, in the preceding sample array of eight elements, the array was sorted after five iterations, making the last two iterations unnecessary. To eliminate unnecessary iterations we must be able to detect the fact that the array is already sorted. An array is sorted if no interchanges are made in any iteration. By keeping a record of whether any interchanges are made in a given iteration it can be determined whether any further iterations are necessary. The program logic flow of bubble sort is shown in Figure 3.14. The following example implements the bubble sort subroutine in MCS-51/52 assembly language.

Example 3.14 Write a subroutine to sort an array of 8-bit elements using the bubble sort method, and write an instruction sequence to call this routine. The starting address of the array is passed in DPTR and the array count is passed in register B.

Solution: The caller would use the following instruction sequence to call the bubble subroutine:

```
        .
        .
        MOV       DPTR,#ar_bas      ; place array base address in DPTR
        MOV       B,#ar_cnt         ; place array count in register B
        LCALL     bubble
        <next instruction>
```

In the program, we will use the values of [DPTR] and [DPTR]+1 as addresses to access array[i] and array[i+1], respectively.

The bubble sort subroutine is as follows:

```
arptr_H    SET    R0        ; upper byte of array pointer
arptr_L    SET    R1        ; lower byte of array pointer
arbas_H    SET    R2        ; the upper byte of the array base
                            ; address
arbas_L    SET    R3        ; the lower byte of the array base
                            ; address
iteration  SET    R4        ; iteration index
inner      SET    R5        ; loop index in each iteration
buffer     SET    R6        ; buffer for swapping array
                            ; elements
in_order   SET    R7        ; array in order flag
bubble:    PUSH   A
           MOV    arbas_H,DPH  ; save the upper byte of the DPTR
                            ; register
           MOV    arbas_L,DPL  ; save the lower byte of the DPTR
                            ; register
           DEC    B         ;
           MOV    iteration,B  ; initialize iteration number to
                            ; ar_cnt − 1
ploop:     MOV    in_order,#1  ; set the array in-order flag to true
           MOV    DPH,arbas_H  ; get the array base for the next
                            ; iteration
           MOV    DPL,arbas_L  ; "
           MOV    inner,iteration  ; initialize the inner loop count
cloop:     MOVX   A,@DPTR   ; get one array element
           MOV    B,A       ; save the array element
           MOV    arptr_H,DPH  ; save the array pointer
           MOV    arptr_L,DPL  ; "
           INC    DPTR      ; move to the next array element
           MOVX   A,@DPTR   ; get the next array element
           MOV    buffer,A  ; save it
           CLR    C         ; compare X[i] with X[i+1]
           SUBB   A,B       ; "
           JC     swap      ; C will be set to 1 when
                            ; X[i+1] < X[i]
           AJMP   lptest
swap:      MOV    A,buffer  ; place X[i+1] back to A
           XCH    A,B       ; place X[i] in A and X[i+1] in B
           MOVX   @DPTR,A   ; place X[i] at the location of
```

```
                                                        ; X[i+1]
                MOV     DPH,arptr_H         ; place the address of X[i] in DPTR
                MOV     DPL,arptr_L         ; "
                XCH     A,B                 ; place X[i+1] in A again
                MOVX    @DPTR,A             ; place X[i+1] at the location of
                                            ; X[i]
                CLR     in_order            ; clear the in-order flag to 0
                INC     DPTR                ; restore the DPTR register to point to X[i-
lptest:         DJNZ    inner,cloop         ; is this the end of an iteration?
                CJNE    in_order,#0,exit    ; is the array already in order?
                DJNZ    iteration,ploop     ; have we completed all iterations?
exit:           POP     A                   ; restore A
                RET
```

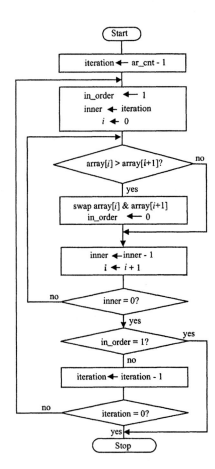

Figure 3.14 Logic flow of bubble sort.

3.9.4 Calculating the Root-Mean-Square Value

The magnitude of a signal is often represented by its root-mean-square (RMS) value. The root-mean-square value of an AC signal is defined as

$$V_{RMS} = \sqrt{\frac{1}{T} \int_0^T V^2(t)\, dt} \tag{3.1}$$

Since the MCS-51/52 cannot compute the integral, the following equation will be used to approximate the RMS value:

$$V_{RMS} \approx \sqrt{\frac{1}{N} \sum_{i=0}^{N-1} V_i^2} \tag{3.2}$$

To make Equation 3.2 a good approximation of the real RMS value, samples of the signal must be taken as equally spaced in time (in a period) as possible. It is obvious that the more samples taken the better the result will be.

The MCS-51/52 has no instruction to compute the square root of a value. However, we can use integer arithmetic to perform the computation for square root value. The technique is based on the following equation:

$$\sum_{i=0}^{n-1} i = \frac{n(n-1)}{2} \tag{3.3}$$

This equation can be transformed into

$$n^2 = \sum_{i=0}^{n-1} (2i + 1) \tag{3.4}$$

Equation 3.4 provides a clue about how to compute the square root of a value. The square root of a value p can be found by the following procedure:

STEP 1   Set temporary *sum* and index i to 0.

STEP 2 $sum = sum + (2i + 1)$

STEP 3 $i = i + 1$

STEP 4   If $sum < p$ then go to Step 2.

STEP 5   If $i^2 = p$ then i is the real square root of p. Stop.

STEP 6   If $(i^2 - p) < p - (i - 1)^2$, then i is chosen as an approximate value of the square root of p. Otherwise, $i - 1$ is chosen as the square root.

The algorithm stops when the accumulating *sum* is equal to or larger than p. If *sum* is equal to p then p has an integer square root. If i is larger than the square root of p, we need to choose either i or $i - 1$ as the square root depending on whichever is closer to p. The purpose of Step 6 is to choose the number closer to the square root of p.

Example 3.15 Write a subroutine to compute the square root of a 16-bit value. Use stack to pass parameters and allocate local variables. Return the result in accumulator A.

Solution: Assume the value p (located at internal memory) is pushed into the stack by the caller as follows:

```
push   p_l          ; push the lower byte of p into the stack
push   p_h          ; push the upper byte of p into the stack
acall  sq_root
       .
       .
```

The subroutine sq_root saves R0~R6 in the stack and allocates local variables i, sum in the stack. The stack frame of the subroutine sq_root is shown in Figure 3.15.

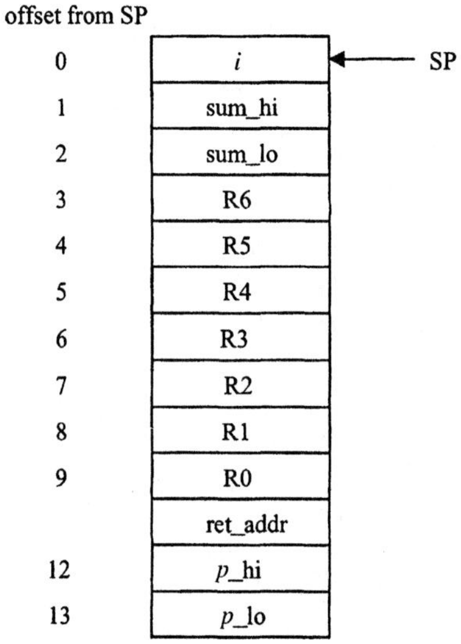

offset from SP

Figure 3.15 Stack frame of the subroutine sq_root.

offset	
0	i ← SP
1	sum_hi
2	sum_lo
3	R6
4	R5
5	R4
6	R3
7	R2
8	R1
9	R0
	ret_addr
12	p_hi
13	p_lo

The subroutine sq_root is as follows:

```
; The following macro computes the address of the element located offset bytes below the
; top of the stack and leaves the result in register RR
fram_ptr        macro       offset,RR
                mov         A,SP
                clr         C
                subb        A,#offset
                mov         RR,A
                endm
sum_lo          EQU         1           ; distance of sum_lo from top of stack
sum_hi          EQU         2           ; distance of sum_hi from top of stack
p_lo            EQU         13          ; distance of p_lo from top of stack
p_hi            EQU         12          ; distance of p_hi from top of stack
```

```
tmp1_lo         SET       R3
tmp1_hi         SET       R4
tmp2_lo         SET       R5
tmp2_hi         SET       R6
                USING     0               ; assume register bank 0 is being
                                          ; selected
sq_root:        PUSH      AR0             ; save registers R0–R6
                PUSH      AR1             ; "
                PUSH      AR2             ; "
                PUSH      AR3             ; "
                PUSH      AR4             ; "
                PUSH      AR5             ; "
                PUSH      AR6             ; "
                INC       SP              ; make room for local variables
                INC       SP              ; "
                INC       SP              ; "
                fram_ptr  sum_lo,R0       ; place the address of the low byte of
                                          ; sum in R0
                MOV       @R0,#0          ; clear sum to 0
                INC       R0              ; "
                MOV       @R0,#0          ; "
                MOV       R1,SP
                MOV       @R1,#0          ; initialize i to 0
; the following loop accumulates sum until it is equal to or larger than p
loop:           fram_ptr  sum_lo,R0
                MOV       A,@R0           ; add 1 to sum
                ADD       A,#1            ; "
                MOV       @R0,A           ; "
                INC       R0              ; "
                MOV       A,@R0           ; " (R0 points to the high byte of sum)
                ADDC      A,#0            ; "
                MOV       @R0,A
                MOV       A,@R1           ; put i in A
                CLR       C
                RLC       A               ; compute 2i + 1 and the msb of A goes
                                          ; into C
                MOV       R2,A            ; save 2i in R2
                DEC       R0              ; compute the address of the low byte of
                                          ; sum
                MOV       A,@R0           ; place sum_lo in A
```

```
                    ADD     A,R2          ; add 2i to sum
                    MOV     @R0,A         ; "
                    INC     R0            ; "
                    MOV     A,@R0         ; "
                    ADDC    A,#0          ; "
                    MOV     @R0,A         ; "
                    INC     @R1           ; increment i (Step 3 of the algorithm)
; The following instructions compare sum with p
                    MOV     R2,A          ; save the high byte of sum in R2
                    fram_ptr p_hi,R0      ; compute the address of p and place it
                                          ; in R0
                    MOV     A,R2          ; put sum back to A
                    CLR     C
                    SUBB    A,@R0         ; compare the high bytes of sum and p
                    JZ      check_lo      ; are high bytes equal?
                    JNC     select_hl     ; is sum larger than p?
                    AJMP    loop          ; not done yet
check_lo:           DEC     R0            ; compute the address of p_lo
                    MOV     R2,@R0        ; place p_lo in R2
                    fram_ptr sum_lo,R0    ; compute the address of sum_lo
                    MOV     A,@R0         ; place sum_lo in A
                    CLR     C
                    SUBB    A,R2          ; compare sum_lo and p_lo
                    JZ      choose_n      ; found the square root
                    JNC     select_hl     ; select i or i − 1
                    AJMP    loop          ; need to continue
select_hl:
                    MOV     A,@R1         ; place the last i value in A
                    MOV     B,@R1         ; place the last i value in B
                    MUL     AB            ; compute i²
                    MOV     R2,A          ; save the low byte of i² in R2
                    fram_ptr p_lo,R0      ; compute the address of p
; compute i² − p
                    MOV     A,R2          ; put the low byte of i² in A
                    CLR     C
                    SUBB    A,@R0
                    MOV     tmp1_lo,A     ; place the low byte of i² − p in tmp1_lo
                    INC     R0            ; R0 points to p_hi now
                    MOV     A,B
```

	SUBB	A,@R0	; compute the high byte of $i^2 - p$
	MOV	tmp1_hi,A	; save the high byte of $i^2 - p$ in tmp1_hi
; compute $p - (i - 1)^2$			
	MOV	A,@R1	; place i in A
	DEC	A	
	MOV	B,A	
	MUL	AB	; compute $(i - 1)^2$
	MOV	tmp2_lo,A	; save in tmp2_lo and tmp2_hi
	MOV	tmp2_hi,B	; "
	DEC	R0	; compute the address of p_lo
	MOV	A,@R0	; put the low byte of p in A
	CLR	C	
	SUBB	A,tmp2_lo	; compute the low byte of $p - (i - 1)^2$
	MOV	tmp2_lo,A	; "
	INC	R0	; compute the address of p_hi
	MOV	A,@R0	; place p_hi in A
	SUBB	A,tmp2_hi	; compute the high byte of $p - (i - 1)^2$
	MOV	tmp2_hi,A	; "
; compare $i^2 - p$ with $p - (i - 1)^2$			
	MOV	A,tmp1_lo	; place the low byte of $i^2 - p$ in A
	CLR	C	
	SUBB	A,tmp2_lo	
	MOV	A,tmp1_hi	; place the high byte of $i^2 - p$ in A
	SUBB	A,tmp2_hi	; compare the high byte of $i^2 - p$ with ; that of $p - (i - 1)^2$
	JC	choose_n	; choose i if it is smaller
	DEC	@R1	; choose $i - 1$ as the square root
choose_n:	MOV	A,@R1	; place the square root in A
	DEC	SP	; deallocate i and sum
	DEC	SP	; "
	DEC	SP	; "
	POP	AR6	; restore R0 to R6
	POP	AR5	; "
	POP	AR4	; "
	POP	AR3	; "
	POP	AR2	; "
	POP	AR1	; "
	POP	AR0	; "
	RET		

The MCS-51/52 microcontroller needs to execute up to five instructions to access one stack element because it has no addressing modes to facilitate the accessing of stack elements.

However, the stack will be useful for passing parameters and results, and allocating local variables in the following conditions:

- The level of subroutine calls is deep
- Implementing recursive procedure calls
- Writing location independent (reentrant) subroutines

We will not discuss how to write recursive subroutine calls and reentrant subroutines in this book.

3.10 DUAL DATA POINTERS OF THE DS87C520 MICROCONTROLLER

The microcontrollers (listed in Table 3.1) from Dallas Semiconductor implement dual data pointers (DPTR and DPTR1) to speed up block data transfer. In the DS87C520, the standard data pointer is DPTR and is located at SFR addresses 82H and 83H. These are the standard locations. No modification of standard code is needed to use DPTR. The new DPTR is located at SFR addresses 84H and 85H and is called DPTR1. The DPTR Select bit (DPS) chooses the active pointer and is located at the LSB of the SFR location 86H. No other bits in register 86H have any effect and are set to 0. The user switches between data pointers by toggling the LSB of register 86H. The increment (INC) instruction is the fastest way to accomplish this. All DPTR-related instructions use the currently selected DPTR for any activity. Therefore only one instruction is required to switch from a source to a destination address. Using the Dual Data Pointer saves code from needing to save source and destination addresses when doing a block move. Once loaded, the software simply switches between DPTR0 and DPTR1. The relevant register locations are as follows:

DPL	82H	Low byte of the original DPTR
DPH	83H	High byte of the original DPTR
DPL1	84H	Low byte of DPTR1
DPH1	85H	High byte of DPTR1
DPS	86H	DPTR Select (LSB)

Assume that SL, SH, DL, and DH are the low bytes and high bytes of the source and destination addresses, respectively. The following code performs a 100-byte block move.

```
DPS     EQU     #86H
        MOV     R2,#100         ; number of bytes to move
        MOV     DPTR,#DHDL      ; load destination address
        INC     DPS             ; change active DPTR
```

TABLE 3.1
Features of Dallas Semiconductor Microcontrollers

Feature	DS80C310	DS80C320	DS80C323	DS83C520	DS87C520	DS83C530
Internal program ROM	0 byte	0 byte	0 byte	16-KB mask ROM	16-KB EPROM	16-KB EPROM
Internal SRAM	256 bytes	256 bytes	256 bytes	256 bytes	256 bytes	256 bytes
Internal MOVX SRAM[a]	0 byte	0 byte	0 byte	1 KB	1 KB	1 KB
Serial ports	1	2	2	2	2	2
External interrupts	6	6	6	6	6	6
16-bit timers	3	3	3	3	3	3
Watchdog timer	No	Yes	Yes	Yes	Yes	Yes
Power-fail/precision reset	No	Yes	Yes	Yes	Yes	Yes
Power-fail/interrupt	No	Yes	Yes	Yes	Yes	Yes
Data pointers	2	2	2	2	2	2
Power management modes	No	No	No	Yes	Yes	Yes
Ring oscillator	No	Yes	Yes	Yes	Yes	Yes
EMI reduction mode	No	No	No	Yes	Yes	Yes
Real-time clock	No	No	No	No	No	Yes
Nonvolatile SRAM	No	No	No	No	No	Yes
Operating voltage	4.5–5.5 V	4.5–5.5 V	2.7–5.5 V	4.5–5.5 V	4.5–5.5 V	4.5–5.5 V

[a] We can use the MOVX instruction to access this special internal SRAM.

```
              MOV    DPTR,#SHSL      ; load source address
move:         MOVX   A,@DPTR         ; read source byte
              INC    DPTR            ; move to the next byte
              INC    DPS             ; switch DPTRs
              MOVX   @DPTR,A         ; store data to destination
              INC    DPTR
              INC    DPS             ; switch DPTRs
              DJNZ   R2,move         ; finish with the block move?
```

3.11 SUMMARY

A program consists of two major parts: one is data structure, which deals with how data are organized; the other is algorithm, which deals with the steps for data manipulation. This chapter discusses the array, stack, matrix, and string data structures.

A stack is a *last-in–first-out* data structure. The most common operations on a stack include push and pop (or called pull). A stack pointer is required for the stack operation. The stack can grow from low to high addresses (Intel MCS-51) or from high to low addresses (Motorola 68HC11). The MCS-51 has an 8-bit stack pointer and also the PUSH and POP instructions for implementing the stack data structure. The stack data structure is normally implemented using the internal SRAM. It is possible to implement the stack using external RAM. However, it will be inefficient for the MCS-51.

Vectors and matrices are indexable data structures. A vector is a one-dimensional data structure whose first element is associated with the index 0 to facilitate the address calculation. Indirect addressing mode is often used to access elements in a vector. A matrix can be stored in memory in row major order or column major order. The matrix element at the intersection of ith row and jth column is specified by the notation (i, j). The address of the (i, j)th element of a matrix can be calculated by using a first-order polynomial equation. A matrix is often used to store large amount of data.

A string is a sequence of characters terminated by a null or other special characters such as EOT (ASCII code 04H). The most common operations on a string include concatenation, insertion, deletion, character and word counting, word matching, etc.

A good programming style is based on modularity—partitioning code into subroutines. A main program contains the logical structure of the algorithm, while smaller program units execute many of the details. The MCS-51/52 provides instructions ACALL, LCALL, and RET to implement subroutine calls. When a subroutine is called, the address of the next instruction is saved in the stack and the program control is passed to the called subroutine, which then executes its instructions. The subroutine terminates with a return instruction (RET) that directs program control back to the instruction following the one that called the subroutine.

There are three issues involved in subroutine calls: parameter passing, result returning, and allocation of local variables. The caller can use registers, the stack, and the global memory to pass parameters to the subroutine (callee). Local variables are created when the subroutine is entered and are invisible to the caller. Local variables are allocated in the stack. When a subroutine is entered, a data structure called *stack frame* is created. The stack frame consists of saved registers, return address, incoming parameters, outgoing parameters, and local variables. A subroutine will need to access parameters and local variables in the stack. Most people will use registers to pass parameters and return results.

Multiprecision division is implemented by using repetitive subtraction and shifting. Sorting is among the most important algorithms used in programming. Bubble sort is a widely known sorting algorithm. It goes through the array or file sequentially many times when performing the comparison. The magnitude of a signal is often represented by its root-mean-square (RMS) value. The computation of RMS value involves (1) computing the sum of the square of every sample and (2) computing the square root of the sum. The computation of the square root is based on an iterative method.

3.12 EXERCISES

3.1 Write instructions to set up the top five bytes of the stack as follows:

Figure 3E.1 Stack contents of Exercise 3.1.

31H ◄──── SP
32H
33H
34H
35H

3.2 Write an instruction sequence to load the ninth element of an array into accumulator A. The base address of the array is ARRAY. The first element is associated with index 0. The array is stored in external memory. The array has 8-bit elements.

3.3 Compute the addresses of the (2, 3)th, (4, 5)th, and (7, 2)th elements of a matrix with eight rows and nine columns. The address of the (0, 0)th element is 3000H. The matrix has 8-bit elements.

3.4 You are given a matrix with nine rows and nine columns. The starting address of the matrix is 4000H. Write a program to set all diagonal elements to 1, divide all upper right elements by 2, and multiply all lower left elements by 2. The matrix has 8-bit elements.

3.5 Write a program to transpose an $M \times N$ matrix. In mathematics, the transpose M^T of a matrix M is the matrix obtained by writing the rows of M as the columns of M^T. To obtain the transpose of a matrix, the (i, j)th element must be swapped with the (j, i)th element for each i and j. The matrix has 8-bit elements.

3.6 How many comparisons need to be performed in the worst case when applying the binary search method to an array of n elements, which have been in sorted order.

3.7 Write a subroutine to compare two strings. The starting addresses of these two strings are passed in register pairs R2...R3 and R4...R5. Return a 1 in accumulator A if these two strings are equal. Otherwise, return a 0 in A.

3.8 Write a subroutine to compute the greatest common factor (or divisor) of two 16-bit integers. These two integers are passed to this subroutine in register pairs R2...R3 and R4...R5. Return the result in R6...R7.

3.9 Convert the program in Example 3.9 to a subroutine. The starting address of the string is passed in register pair R2...R3 and the character count and word count are returned in register R4 and R5, respectively.

3.10 Modify the subroutine in Example 3.12 so that it can perform a signed 16-bit integer division. Use bit memory to indicate the signs of two operands.

3.11 Use the stack to allocate local variables and pass parameters. Rewrite the bubble sort subroutine. Delineate the stack frame for this subroutine.

3.12 Modify the subroutine in Example 3.12 so that it can divide an unsigned 32-bit integer into another unsigned 32-bit integer. Use internal memory to pass parameters.

3.13 LAB EXERCISES AND ASSIGNMENTS

Please note that the space of the external SRAM from 0000H to 7FFFH in the MCB520 is shared by XDATA and CODE memory space. Therefore, you can use the DB (or DW) directive to define an array, matrix, or string and manipulate them. Although the DS87C520 has 1-KB of internal SRAM that can be accessed using the MOVX instruction, it is disabled after reset.

3.1 Write a program to swap the first element of an 8-bit array with the last element, swap the second element with the second-to-last element, and so on. The array has N 8-bit elements and is stored in external memory (use the DB directive to define the array).

3.2 Write a main program and a subroutine with the following characteristics:

1. The subroutine tests to see if the number passed to it via accumulator A is a prime. If the number is a prime, then the carry flag will be set to 1.
2. The main program places the number to be tested in A and calls the subroutine 100 times. The number to be tested starts from 0 until 99. If a number is a prime, it will be stored in an external memory location. Use the external memory locations starting from 400H to store the result.
3. Convert the integer from HEX to BCD so that it is easier to read before storing it in external memory.

You may need to write a subroutine to perform hex to BCD conversion.

3.3 Write a subroutine to implement *selection sort* and write a main program to test it. The selection sort method works like this:

1. Suppose we have an array of integer values. Search through the array, find the largest value, and exchange it with the value stored in the first array location. Next, find the second largest value in the array and exchange it with the value stored in the second array location. Repeat the same process until we reach the end of the array.
2. Store the array in internal memory locations starting from 30H. The main program passes the starting address of the array and array count in registers R0 and R2.

4

BUS CYCLES AND MEMORY
EXPANSION

4.1 OBJECTIVES

After completing this chapter, you should be able to

- define or explain the following terms: bus, types of bus, pull-up resistor, pull-up transistor, bus driver, bus receiver, bus transceiver, bus transaction, memory organization, and memory capacity
- make memory space assignments and design an address decoder
- read the memory cycle timing diagrams
- perform timing analysis for a memory system

4.2 INTRODUCTION

Adding memory components and I/O devices is very common for a microprocessor-based design. In this chapter we are going to learn the basic concepts of bus, bus transactions, bus cycle timing diagrams, memory technologies, memory design issues, and adding memory to an MCS-51/52 microcontroller.

The discussion on bus is not comprehensive. We will not discuss standard buses such as VMEbus, Nubus, Multibus II, STD bus, etc. The discussion of these bus standards is beyond the scope of this book. Interested readers should refer to the book *Digital Bus Handbook* edited by Di Giacomo.

Among all of the memory technologies, DRAM has the lowest per-bit cost. However, DRAM memory requires periodic refresh to maintain its contents. Because of that, the interfacing of DRAM with a microprocessor or microcontroller is more complicated than other memory technologies. It is not economical to use DRAM in 8-bit microprocessor applications. In this text, we will discuss only how to interface SRAM, EPROM, and EEPROM with the 8-bit microcontroller. DRAM is suitable for those applications that require large amount of external memories.

4.3 BASICS OF BUS

An electrical device is *active* if it can amplify either its output current or voltage and is *passive* if it can amplify neither its output voltage nor its output current. Resistors, capacitors, and inductors are considered passive devices whereas transistors and operation amplifiers are considered active devices.

A bus is a set of conducting wires interconnecting the CPU, memory, and I/O devices. A bus can be *active* or *passive*. An active bus has pull-up devices to pull the bus voltage to high whereas an inactive bus does not. As shown in Figure 4.1, a pull-up device can be a simple resistor or a transistor. A bus is usually in the form of conductors on top of a printed circuit board. Each bus conductor and the ground plane of the printed circuit board form a capacitor. The pull-up device of a real microcontroller may consist of several transistors. The driving current determines the pull-up speed. If the pull-up transistor(s) can supply a large pull-up current, the bus is referred to as strongly pulled up. Otherwise, the bus is weakly pulled up.

For an active bus, the bus voltage will be low only when one or more devices attached to the bus apply a low voltage to the bus. When no device drives the bus, the bus voltage will be pulled up to high (V_{CC}). The equivalent circuit of an undriven bus is like an RC circuit connected to a battery as shown in Figure 4.2. The time constant for the bus to be pulled up to 63% of V_{CC} is $R_P C_{BUS}$. The $R_P C_{BUS}$ constant of the bus determines the propagation delay of the pull-up bus.

An open-collector bipolar transistor or an open-drain MOS transistor can be used to drive a pull-up bus. When the open-drain MOS transistor is turned on, its drain terminal will pull the bus line to the ground level. Otherwise, the bus line will be pulled up to V_{CC}. When the output transistor of a device with open-drain output is turned off, the device is essentially disconnected from the bus. This property allows many devices with open-driven output transistors to be connected to an active bus.

A passive bus requires the devices attached to the bus to drive the bus to high or low.

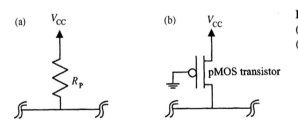

Figure 4.1 Examples of an active bus.
(a) Active bus with pull-up resistor.
(b) Active bus with pull-up transistor.

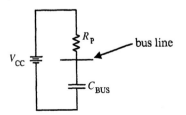

Figure 4.2 Equivalent circuit for an undriven bus.

To drive the bus, a *bus driver* is needed. To receive data from the bus, a *bus receiver* is needed. The bus driver and bus receiver can be combined to form a *bus transceiver*. A bus driver is simply a *transmit buffer* and a bus receiver is simply a *receive buffer* as shown in Figure 4.3. In Figure 4.3, bus driver and receiver enable signals are active low.

A passive bus should be driven by no more than one device at any time. Otherwise, *bus contention* will occur. When bus contention occurs, the devices that are involved in bus contention could be damaged.

As shown in Figure 4.3, a device is disconnected from the bus when the driver-enable and receiver-enable signals are deasserted. When the enable signal is deasserted, the output of the driver or the receiver is in a high-impedance state in which no current flows into or out of the device involved.

A group of bus lines can be multiplexed, that is, they serve multiple functions. Address and data signals are often multiplexed to share the same bus lines in 8-bit microprocessors and microcontrollers.

4.4 WAVEFORMS OF BUS SIGNALS

The waveform of a typical digital signal is shown in Figure 4.4. It takes time for a signal to go from low to high and from high to low. The time needed for a signal to rise from 10% of the power supply voltage to 90% of the power supply voltage is called the *rise time* (t_r). The time needed for a signal to drop from 90% of the power supply voltage to 10% of the power supply voltage is called the *fall time* (t_f).

A single signal is represented as a set of line segments (for example, see Figure 4.5). The horizontal axis and vertical axis represent the time and the magnitude (in volts) of the signal, respectively. Multiple signals of the same nature, such as address and data, are often grouped together and represented as parallel lines with crossovers, as illustrated in Figure 4.6. A crossover represents the point at which one or multiple signals change value.

Sometimes a signal value is unknown because the signal is changing. Hatched areas in the timing diagram, as shown in Figure 4.7, represent single and multiple unknown

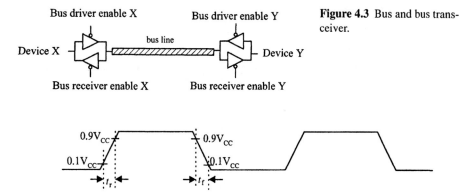

Figure 4.3 Bus and bus transceiver.

Figure 4.4 A typical digital waveform.

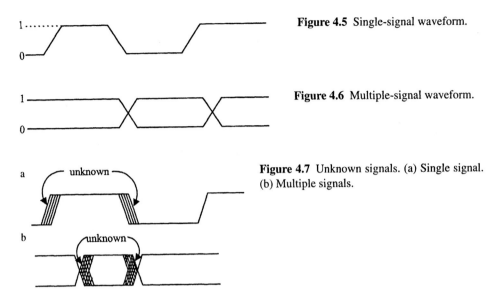

Figure 4.5 Single-signal waveform.

Figure 4.6 Multiple-signal waveform.

Figure 4.7 Unknown signals. (a) Single signal. (b) Multiple signals.

signals. Sometimes one or multiple signals are not driven (because their drivers are in a high impedance state) and hence cannot be received. An undriven signal is said to be *floating*.

Single or multiple floating signals are represented by a value between high and low, as shown in Figure 4.8. A floating signal is in *high-impedance* state.

In a microprocessor or microcontroller system, a bus signal falls into one of the following three categories: address, data, and control.

4.5 BUS TRANSACTIONS

A bus transaction includes two parts: sending the address and receiving or sending the data. Bus transactions are usually defined by what they do to memory: a *read* transaction transfers data from memory (to either the CPU or I/O device), and a *write* transaction writes data to memory. In a read transaction, the address is first sent down the bus to the memory, together with the appropriate control signals indicating a read. In Figure 4.9, this means pulling read signal to low. The memory responds by returning the data on the bus with the appropriate control signals, in this case deasserting the wait signal. Depending on the microcontroller,

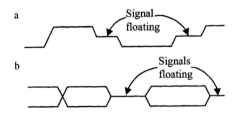

Figure 4.8 Floating signals. (a) Single signal. (b) Multiple signals.

the wait signal may not be provided. In this situation, the microcontroller expects the data to be returned from memory no later than the allowed time.

In Figure 4.9, a bus transaction takes one clock cycle to complete. The wait signal allows the bus transaction to extend to more than one clock cycle and hence can accommodate slower memory components. All 32-bit and wider microprocessors from Intel and Motorola and other companies have this feature. A write transaction requires that the CPU or I/O device sends both address and data and requires no return of data.

In a bus transaction, there must be a device that can initiate a read or a write transaction. The device that can initiate a bus transaction is called a *bus master*. A microcontroller or microprocessor is always a bus master. A device such as a memory chip that cannot initiate a bus transaction is called a *bus slave*.

In a bus transaction, some kind of signal is needed to synchronize the data transfer. When a common clock signal is used, the bus is *synchronous*. In a synchronous bus, a fixed protocol for address and data relative to the clock is followed.

An asynchronous bus, on the other hand, is not clocked. Instead, self-timed, handshaking protocols are used between the bus sender and receiver. Figure 4.10 shows the steps of a master performing a write on an asynchronous bus.

A synchronous bus is often used between the CPU and the memory system whereas an asynchronous bus is often used to handle more different types of devices. If a synchronous bus can be used, it is usually faster than an asynchronous bus because it avoids the overhead of synchronizing the bus for each transaction.

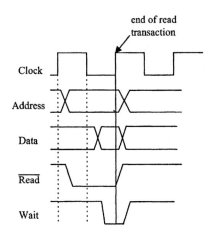

Figure 4.9 A typical bus read transaction.

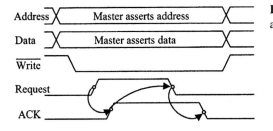

Figure 4.10 Asynchronous write bus transaction.

4.6 BUS TRANSACTION TIMING DIAGRAM

To make a bus transaction successful, timing requirements must be satisfied. Timing requirements are expressed in the form of timing parameters. In a synchronous bus, most timing parameters are measured relative to the clock edge (either the rising or the falling edge).

A simplified read transaction timing diagram is shown in Figure 4.11. This timing diagram tells us that the read bus transaction takes exactly one clock cycle to complete. The processor requires the data to become valid at least t_{DS} s before the next rising edge of the CLK signal. Also, the data must remain valid at least t_{DH} s after CLK goes high. The signal $\overline{RD}$ indicates that the processor is performing a read access to memory or I/O device. The processor guarantees that the $\overline{RD}$ signal will remain valid for t_{RLRH} s during a read cycle.

The meaning of each timing parameter is as follows:

DEFINITION t_{CH}: *Clock high time*. The interval that the CLK signal is high.

DEFINITION t_{CL}: *Clock low time*. The interval that the CLK signal is low.

DEFINITION t_{CW}: *Clock width*. Clock period. This parameter puts an upper limit to the amount of time available for accessing memory.

DEFINITION t_{AV}: *Clock high to address valid*. This parameter tells us the delay from the moment that the clock goes high until the moment that the address signals become valid. This delay and the clock period dictate the amount of time available for the processor to perform read access to external memory.

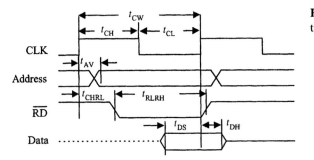

Figure 4.11 A simplified read bus transaction timing diagram.

DEFINITION t_{CHRL}: *Clock high to $\overline{RD}$ low*. This is the delay from the rising edge of CLK to the falling edge of the $\overline{RD}$ signal. A memory device normally requires the $\overline{RD}$ signal to determine the type of operation the processor is requesting.

DEFINITION t_{RLRH}: *$\overline{RD}$ low to $\overline{RD}$ high*. This parameter specifies the length of the interval during which the $\overline{RD}$ signal is low.

DEFINITION t_{DS}: *Data setup time*. This parameter specifies the amount of time that the processor requires for the data to become valid before the processor latches the data (on the rising edge of CLK).

DEFINITION t_{DH}: *Data hold time*. This parameter specifies the amount of time that the memory or I/O device must hold the data valid after the rising edge of the CLK signal.

A real microprocessor's bus cycle timing diagram has many more timing parameters than those shown in this example. In the following sections, we will learn the timing parameters of the MCS-51FX microcontroller.

4.7 A SUMMARY OF THE MCS-51/52 SIGNAL PINS

A typical 40-pin MCS-51/52 microcontroller—the Intel 8XC51FX for example—has 32 programmable I/O lines that are divided into four 8-bit I/O ports. Most of the I/O pins serve multiple functions. A block diagram of the Intel 8XC51FX is shown in Figure 4.12. The Intel 8XC51FX is a series of microcontrollers that consists of the members listed in Table 4.1. All four I/O ports (0...3) are 8-bit, bidirectional. They all require a 1 to be written into a pin before it can be used as input. Port 0 has open-drain output whereas other ports have internal pull-ups. A more detailed examination of I/O buffer structure is found in Chapter 6.

The low-order address signals (A7–A0) and data bus (D7–D0) are multiplexed on port 0 during accesses to external program and data memory. In this application it uses strong internal pull-ups when emitting 1s, and can source and sink several low-power Schottky transistor-transistor logic (LS TTL) inputs. Port 0 pins that have 1s written to them float, and in that state can be used as inputs.

The port 1 output buffers could drive LS TTL inputs. Port 1 pins serve alternate functions as shown in Table 4.2. These alternate functions will be explored in Chapter 7.

Port 2 output buffers could drive LS TTL loads. Port 2 sends out high-order address byte during instruction fetch from external program memory and during accesses to external

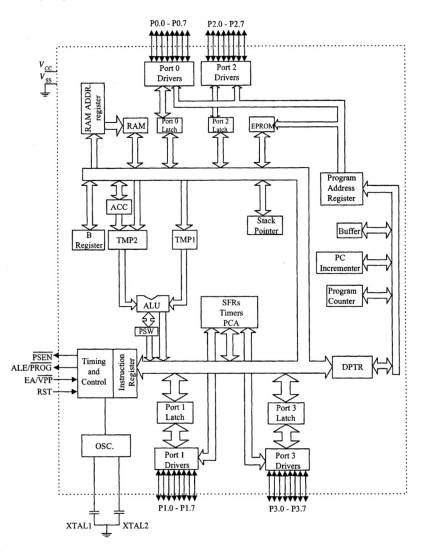

Figure 4.12 8XC51FX block diagram. (Redrawn with pemission of Intel.)

TABLE 4.1

The 8XC51FX Subfamily Members

ROM Device	EPROM Device	ROMless Device	ROM/EPROM (bytes)	RAM (bytes)
83C51FA	87C51FA	80C51FA	8K	256
83C51FB	87C51FB	80C51FA	16K	256
83C51FC	87C51FC	80C51FA	32K	256

TABLE 4.2
Port 1 Pin Alternate Functions

Port Pin	Alternate Function
P1.0	T2 (external count input to timer/counter 2, clock out)
P1.1	T2EX (timer/counter 2 capture/reload trigger and direction control)
P1.2	ECI [external count input to the programmable counter array (PCA)]
P1.3	CEX0 (external I/O for compare/capture module 0)
P1.4	CEX1 (external I/O for compare/capture module 1)
P1.5	CEX2 (external I/O for compare/capture module 2)
P1.6	CEX3 (external I/O for compare/capture module 3)
P1.7	CEX4 (external I/O for compare/capture module 4)

data memory that use 16-bit addresses (MOVX @DPTR,A). During accesses to external data memory that use 8-bit addresses (MOVX @Ri,A), port 2 emits the contents of the P2 special function register.

In addition to being a bidirectional I/O port, port 3 also serves various alternate functions of the MCS-51/52 family, as listed in Table 4.3. These alternate functions will be discussed in this chapter and in Chapters 5, 7, and 9.

The RST input is the reset input. A high voltage applied on this pin for two machine cycles while the oscillator is running resets the device. The reset function will be discussed in detail in Chapter 5.

The ALE output is the address latch enable signal for latching the lower byte of the address during accesses to external memory. This pin (ALE/PROG) is also the program pulse input during EPROM programming for the 87C51FX. In normal operation ALE is emitted at a constant rate of one-sixth the oscillator frequency, and may be used for external timing or clocking purposes. Note, however, that one ALE pulse is skipped during each access to external data memory. Therefore, an external data memory access takes 2 machine cycles. If desired, setting bit 0 of special function register (SFR) location 8EH can disable the ALE operation. With this bit set, the pin is weakly pulled high. However, the ALE-disable feature will be suspended during an MOVX or MOVC instruction, idle mode, power down

TABLE 4.3
Port 3 Pin Alternate Functions

Port Pin	Alternate Function
P3.0	RXD (serial input port)
P3.1	TXD (serial output port)
P3.2	INT0 (external interrupt 0)
P3.3	INT1 (external interrupt 1)
P3.4	T0 (timer 0 external input)
P3.5	T1 (timer 1 external input)
P3.6	WR (external data memory write strobe)
P3.7	RD (external data memory read strobe)

mode, and ICE mode. The ALE-disable feature will be terminated by reset. Setting the ALE-disable bit has no effect if the microcontroller is in external execution mode.

The PSEN output is the program store enable signal that is the read enable signal to the external program memory. When the 8XC51FX is executing code from external program memory, PSEN is activated twice each machine cycle. The PSEN signal is not activated when the 8XC51FX accesses external data memory.

The EA input is the external access enable signal. EA must be strapped to V_{SS} to enable the device to fetch instructions from external program memory locations 0000H to 0FFFH. EA should be strapped to V_{CC} for internal program executions. This pin receives the programming supply voltage (V_{PP}) during EPROM programming.

The XTAL1 pin is input to the inverting oscillator amplifier. The XTAL2 pin is output from the inverting oscillator amplifier.

4.8 THE 8XC51FX BUS CYCLE TIMING DIAGRAM

The 8XC51FX external bus cycle is controlled by the ALE signal. There are 16 address signals and 8 data signals. Each read or write bus cycle takes one ALE cycle. A read bus cycle to the external program memory is shown in Figure 4.13 and the corresponding timing parameters are shown in Table 4.4. Table 4.4 contains all the timing parameters shown in Figure 4.13 and those of external data memory read (shown in Figure 4.15) and write (Figure 4.16) bus cycles. The lower eight address signals and the data signals are time multiplexed. ALE is emitted at a constant rate of one-sixth the oscillator frequency.

The ALE signal has a periodic waveform and is used by the 8XC51FX microcontroller as the clock signal for synchronizing external memory access cycles. During the first half of the ALE cycle, the lower eight address signals appear on port 0 pins. During the second half of the ALE cycle, instruction is driven on the same port 0 pins by external memory devices.

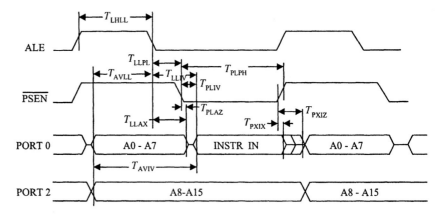

Figure 4.13 External program memory read cycle. (Redrawn with permission of Intel.)

TABLE 4.4
External Memory Access Characteristics

Symbol	Parameter	Oscillator								Unit
		12 MHz		24 MHz		33 MHz		Variable		
		Min	Max	Min	Max	Min	Max	Min	Max	
$1/T_{CLCL}$	Oscillator frequency									
	8XC51FX							3.5	12	
	8XC51FX-1							3.5	16	
	8XC51FX-2							0.5	12	MHz
	8XC51FX-24							3.5	24	
	8XC51FX-33							3.5	33	
T_{LHLL}	ALE pulse width	127		43		21		$2T_{CLCL} - 40$		ns
T_{AVLL}	Address valid to ALE low									
	8XC51FX	43						$T_{CLCL} - 40$		ns
	8XC51FX-24			12				$T_{CLCL} - 30$		ns
	8XC51FX-33					5		$T_{CLCL} - 25$		ns
T_{LLAX}	Address hold after ALE low									
	8XC51FX/-24	53		12				$T_{CLCL} - 30$		ns
	8XC51FX-33					5		$T_{CLCL} - 25$		ns
T_{LLIV}	Address low to valid instr in									
	8XC51FX		234						$4T_{CLCL} - 100$	ns
	8XC51FX-24				91				$4T_{CLCL} - 75$	ns
	8XC51FX-33						56		$4T_{CLCL} - 65$	ns
T_{LLPL}	ALE low to $\overline{PSEN}$ low									
	8XC51FX/-24	53		12				$T_{CLCL} - 30$		ns
	8XC51FX-33					5		$T_{CLCL} - 25$		ns
T_{PLPH}	$\overline{PSEN}$ pulse width	205		80		46		$3T_{CLCL} - 45$		ns
T_{PLIV}	$\overline{PSEN}$ low to valid instr in									
	8XC51FX		145						$3T_{CLCL} - 105$	ns
	8XC51FX-24				35				$3T_{CLCL} - 90$	ns
	8XC51FX-33						35		$3T_{CLCL} - 55$	ns
T_{PXIX}	Input instr hold after $\overline{PSEN}$	0		0		0		0		ns
T_{PXIZ}	Input instr float after $\overline{PSEN}$									
	8XC51FX		59						$T_{CLCL} - 25$	ns
	8XC51FX-24				21				$T_{CLCL} - 20$	ns
	8XC51FX-33						5		$T_{CLCL} - 25$	ns
T_{AVIV}	Address to valid instr in									
	8XC51FX/-24		312		103				$5T_{CLCL} - 105$	ns
	8XC51FX-33						71		$5T_{CLCL} - 80$	ns
T_{PLAZ}	$\overline{PSEN}$ low to address float		10		10		10		10	ns
T_{RLRH}	$\overline{RD}$ pulse width	400		150		82		$6T_{CLCL} - 100$		ns
T_{WLWH}	$\overline{WR}$ pulse width	400		150		82		$6T_{CLCL} - 100$		ns
T_{RLDV}	$\overline{RD}$ low to valid data in									
	8XC51FX		252						$5T_{CLCL} - 165$	ns
	8XC51FX-24				113				$5T_{CLCL} - 95$	ns
	8XC51FX-33						61		$5T_{CLCL} - 90$	ns

Continued

TABLE 4.4
Continued

Symbol	Parameter	12 MHz Min	12 MHz Max	24 MHz Min	24 MHz Max	33 MHz Min	33 MHz Max	Variable Min	Variable Max	Unit
T_{RHDX}	Data hold after $\overline{RD}$	0		0		0		0		ns
T_{RHDZ}	Data float after $\overline{RD}$									
	8XC51FX/-24		107		23				$2T_{CLCL}-60$	ns
	8XC51FX-33						35		$2T_{CLCL}-25$	ns
T_{LLDV}	ALE low to valid data in									
	8XC51FX		517						$8T_{CLCL}-150$	ns
	8XC51FX-24/33				243		150		$8T_{CLCL}-90$	ns
T_{AVDV}	Address to valid data in									
	8XC51FX		585						$9T_{CLCL}-165$	ns
	8XC51FX-24/33				285		180		$9T_{CLCL}-90$	ns
T_{LLWL}	ALE low to $\overline{RD}$ or $\overline{WR}$ low	200	300	75	175	41	140	$3T_{CLCL}-50$	$3T_{CLCL}+50$	ns
T_{AVWL}	Address to $\overline{RD}$ or $\overline{WR}$ low									
	8XC51FX	203						$4T_{CLCL}-130$		ns
	8XC51FX-24			77				$4T_{CLCL}-90$		ns
	8XC51FX-33					46		$4T_{CLCL}-75$		ns
T_{QVWX}	Data valid to $\overline{WR}$ transition									
	8XC51FX	33						$T_{CLCL}-50$		ns
	8XC51FX-24/33			12		0		$T_{CLCL}-30$		ns
T_{WHQX}	Data hold after $\overline{WR}$									
	8XC51FX	33						$T_{CLCL}-50$		ns
	8XC51FX-24			7				$T_{CLCL}-35$		ns
	8XC51FX-33					3		$T_{CLCL}-27$		ns
T_{QVWH}	Data valid to $\overline{WR}$ high									
	8XC51FX	433						$7T_{CLCL}-150$		ns
	8XC51FX-24/33			222		142		$7T_{CLCL}-70$		ns
T_{RLAZ}	$\overline{RD}$ low to address float		0		0		0		0	ns
T_{WHLH}	$\overline{RD}$ or $\overline{WR}$ high to ALE high									
	8XC51FX	43	123					$T_{CLCL}-40$	$T_{CLCL}+40$	ns
	8XC51FX-24			12	71			$T_{CLCL}-30$	$T_{CLCL}+30$	ns
	8XC51FX-33					5	55	$T_{CLCL}-25$	$T_{CLCL}+25$	ns

Reprinted with permission of Intel.

Most memory chips require address signals to remain stable during the complete read/write bus cycle. However, the 8XC51FX drives the lower eight address signals only part of a read bus cycle. The solution to this problem is to put the lower address signals in latches so that they are stable throughout the whole bus transaction cycle. External devices can use the ALE signal to latch the lower eight address signals. Address signals should be latched by the falling edge of the ALE signal because they are not valid on the rising edge, as shown in the timing diagram. The low address signals become valid T_{AVLL} ns before the falling edge of the ALE signal and remain valid for T_{LLAX} ns after the falling edge of the ALE signal.

A circuit that uses the falling edge of ALE to load the lower address signals A7–A0 into an address latch is shown in Figure 4.14. The 74F373 has high impedance output, which must be enabled by the OE signal (this signal is grounded permanently in Figure 4.14).

For convenience, the Intel 8XC51FX measures all timing parameters using 20 and 70% of the power supply voltage (V_{CC}) as the reference points. Many timing parameters are measured with reference to the rising and falling edges of the ALE signal. For example, the delay from the moment that the ALE signal falls to 20% of V_{CC} until the moment that the instruction becomes valid is T_{LLIV} ns.

The $\overline{\text{PSEN}}$ signal allows the 8XC51FX to access external program memory. This signal is asserted T_{LLPL} ns after the falling edge of the ALE signal and will be asserted for at least T_{PLPH} ns. The instruction must be valid T_{PLIV} ns after the falling edge of the $\overline{\text{PSEN}}$ signal and T_{AVIV} ns after the upper address signals A15 ~ A8 become valid (both must be satisfied). To be latched correctly, the external instruction must remain valid for T_{PXIX} ns. The external instruction will be floated no more than T_{PXIZ} ns after the rising edge of the $\overline{\text{PSEN}}$ signal.

The external data read timing diagram is shown in Figure 4.15. In an external data memory read cycle, the read signal $\overline{\text{RD}}$ must be asserted (low) during the second half of the cycle. In Figure 4.15,

- The $\overline{\text{RD}}$ signal is asserted T_{LLWL} ns after the falling edge of ALE (measured from the point that the magnitude of the ALE is 20% of V_{CC}).

- The $\overline{\text{RD}}$ signal has a pulse width of T_{RLRH} ns and will rise to 70% of V_{CC} no later than T_{WHLH} ns before the rising edge of ALE.

- The 8XC51FX requires external data to be valid no later than T_{LLDV} ns after the falling edge of ALE, no later than T_{RLDV} ns after the falling edge of the $\overline{\text{RD}}$ signal, and no later than T_{AVDV} ns after the upper address signals A15~A8 become valid.

- The 8XC51FX requires external data to remain valid for T_{RHDX} ns after the rising edge of the $\overline{\text{RD}}$ signal (relative to the moment when $\overline{\text{RD}}$ has risen to 70% of V_{CC}).

- The 8XC51FX requires that external data become floating T_{RHDZ} ns after the rising edge of the $\overline{\text{RD}}$ signal so that they will not conflict with the lower address signals of the next bus cycle.

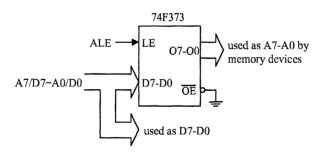

Figure 4.14 Circuit to latch A7–A0 into a latch.

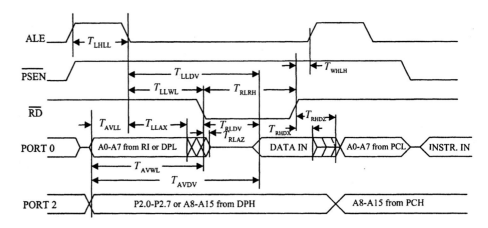

Figure 4.15 External data memory read cycle timing. (Redrawn with permission of Intel.)

The timing diagram of the external data memory write bus cycle is illustrated in Figure 4.16. This diagram is similar to that in Figure 4.15 with two exceptions: the signal $\overline{WR}$ instead of $\overline{RD}$ is asserted and the data are driven by the 8XC51FX.

4.9 MEMORY TERMINOLOGY AND SRAM

Memory chips are major components of many digital systems. Thus it is very important for a digital system designer to understand the characteristics of memory chips and know how to interface them with a microprocessor and a microcontroller.

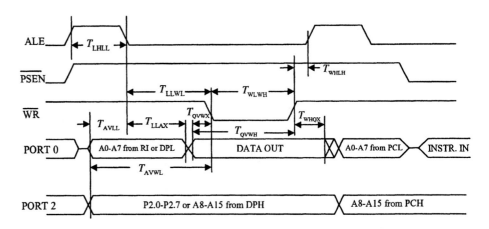

Figure 4.16 External data memory write cycle timing. (Redrawn with permission of Intel.)

4.9.1 Memory Capacity and Organization

Memory devices are often labeled with shorthand notations, such as $1M \times 1$, $4M \times 1$, $1M \times 8$, etc., that indicate their storage capacities and organizations. It is necessary to understand these notations to select the appropriate size and type of memory chip.

Memory Capacity

The capacity of a memory device is the total amount of information that the device can store. The capacity of semiconductor memories is often referred to as their *memory density*. Since addresses are binary in nature, semiconductor memories are always manufactured in powers of 2. For example, a 64-Kbit memory chip has 2^{16} memory cells of storage, for a total of 65,536 bits. A 4-Mbit memory chip has 2^{22} or 4,194,304 total memory bits of storage.

Memory Organization

Information in a single memory chip can be retrieved (read) or stored (written) one bit at a time or several bits at a time. The term memory organization describes the number of bits that can be written into or read from a memory chip during an input or an output operation. For example, if only one bit can be stored or retrieved at a time, the organization is "by one," written as $\times 1$. If eight bits can be read or written at a time, the organization is "by eight," written as $\times 8$. Another common organization is by 4, which is referred to as a nibble-organized memory. A memory chip that is labeled $m \times n$ has m locations and each location has n bits. For example, a $256K \times 8$ SRAM chip has $256K$ different locations and each location has 8 bits.

Example 4.1 Using the following memory chips, how many SRAM chips will be needed to build a 256-KB, 16-bit memory system for a 16-bit microprocessor? The memory is to be designed so that 16-bit data can be accessed in one read/write operation.

    a. $256K \times 1$ SRAM
    b. $64K \times 4$ SRAM
    c. $64K \times 8$ SRAM
    d. $256K \times 4$ SRAM

Solution:

    a. If we use $\times 1$ organization memory chips, 16 chips will be needed to build a 16-bit-wide memory system. Sixteen $256K \times 1$ SRAM chips will be needed. However, 16 $256K \times 1$ SRAM chips have the capacity of 512 KB. Therefore, half of the memory capacity is wasted for this design.

    b. With $\times 4$ organization memory chips, four chips are needed to construct a 16-bit-wide memory system. Four $64K \times 4$ SRAM chips are 128 KB. Therefore, eight $64K \times 4$ SRAM chips are needed.

c. With × 8 organization memory chips, two chips are needed to construct a 16-bit-wide memory system. Two 64K × 8 SRAM chips have the capacity of 128 KB. Therefore, we need four 64K × 8 SRAM chips to build a 256-KB 16-bit memory system.

d. With × 4 organization memory chips, four chips are needed to construct a 16-bit-wide memory system. Four 256K × 4 SRAM chips have the capacity of 512 KB. Again, half of the memory capacity is wasted for this design.

4.9.2 Memory Expansion Issues

To add memory or peripheral devices to a microprocessor involves the following issues:

- Memory space assignment
- Address decoder design
- Timing

Memory Space Assignment

It is a common practice to allocate memory space in blocks of equal size, with each block comprising contiguous memory locations. The number of memory locations contained in a memory chip is a power of 2; the address decoder can be simplified if all the memory chips have the same capacity. Since the 8XC51FX has two independent 64-KB-memory spaces, memory space assignments must be done separately.

Example 4.2 Assign the data memory space of the 8XC51FX using a block size of 8KB.

Solution: The 64-KB data memory space can be divided into eight 8-KB blocks. The address range of each block is given in Table 4.5.

TABLE 4.5
Example of Memory Space Assignment

Block Number	Address Range
0	0000H~1FFFH
1	2000H~3FFFH
2	4000H~5FFFH
3	6000H~7FFFH
4	8000H~9FFFH
5	A000H~BFFFH
6	C000H~DFFFH
7	E000H~FFFFH

If a microcontroller- or microprocessor-based system has many I/O devices along with a few memory components, you may want to consider some other alternatives in making the memory space assignment. Because an I/O device normally has very few registers to be addressed (this will be discussed in Chapter 6), it does not need a large memory space. We can further divide a block in Table 4.5 into several subblocks and assign the space of each subblock to one I/O device. This method is called *two-level assignment*.

Decoder

As shown in Figure 4.17, a decoder has n address inputs and 2^n outputs. For each address value, one and only one of the 2^n outputs is asserted. This feature can be utilized to select one and only one device in a microcontroller-based system to respond to the CPU bus request and to avoid the bus contention problem.

A decoder may have one or multiple enable signals to control its operation. When all of the enable signals are not asserted then none of the decoder outputs will be asserted. The 74138 and 74139 are two common decoders. The 74138 is a 3-to-8 decoder and the 74139 is a dual 2-to-4 decoder. These two chips are often used as an address decoder in a microprocessor-based system. The pin layouts of these two chips are shown in Figure 4.18. In Figure 4.18,

- O0–O7, 1Y0–1Y3, 2Y0–2Y3 are active low decoder outputs.
- E1, E2, and E3 are decoder enable inputs. E1 and E2 are active low and E3 is active high.
- A2–A0, A1–A0, and B1–B0 are addresses or select inputs. They are all active high.

Address Decoder Design

A microprocessor or microcontroller can use either the *full address-decoding* or the *partial address-decoding* scheme. A memory device is said to be fully decoded if each of its

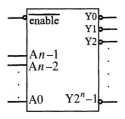

Figure 4.17 An n-to-2^n decoder.

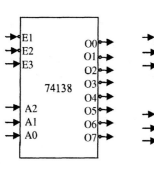
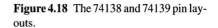

Figure 4.18 The 74138 and 74139 pin layouts.

addressable memory locations responds to only one address value on the system bus. A memory device is said to be *partially decoded* when each of its addressable locations responds to more than one address on the system bus.

Example 4.3 Use a full decoding scheme to design an address decoder for a computer that has the following address assignments:

SRAM1:   0000H~1FFFH

I/O1:   2000H~3FFFH

EPROM1: E000H~FFFFH

Solution: The full decoding scheme can be used in this example because each memory module or I/O device is 8 KB. A 3-to-8 decoder 74138 can be used. The three highest address bits of each module are used to select the memory modules or I/O device:

SRAM1:   000

I/O1:   001

EPROM1: 111

As shown in Figure 4.19, the ALE signal is used as the E1 and E2 signals because address inputs are valid when ALE is low. E3 is pulled up to high to enable the decoder operation.

Figure 4.19 Address decoder for Example 4.3.

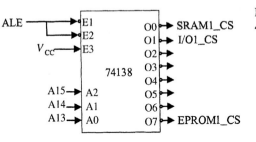

Output signals O0, O1, and O7 are used as the chip-select signals of SRAM1, I/O1, and EPROM1, respectively.

Example 4.4 Assume you are designing an 8-bit microcontroller-based system (with 64-KB memory space) with two external 8-KB SRAM chips, two 8-KB EPROM chips, one 8-KB EEPROM chip, and six I/O devices. Make the space assignment and design the address decoder. The address 0000H must reside in one of the EPROM chips.

Solution: Since there are 11 devices to be decoded, a single 3-to-8 decoder is not adequate. We are going to use a two-level space assignment and use two 74138 decoders to do the address decoding. The address space assignment is shown in Table 4.6 and the decoder circuit is shown in Figure 4.20.

TABLE 4.6
Space Assignment for Example 4.4

Block Number	Address Range	Assigned to
	Level-One Memory	
0	0000H~1FFFH	EPROM1
1	2000H~3FFFH	EPROM2
2	4000H~5FFFH	EEPROM
3	6000H~7FFFH	I/Os
4	8000H~9FFFH	SRAM1
5	A000H~BFFFH	SRAM2
6	C000H~DFFFH	Not assigned
7	E000H~FFFFH	Not assigned
	Level-Two Memory	
0	6000H~63FFH	I/O 1
1	6400H~67FFH	I/O 2
2	6800H~6BFFH	I/O 3
3	6C00H~6FFFH	I/O 4
4	7000H~73FFH	I/O 5
5	7400H~77FFH	I/O 6
6	7800H~7BFFH	Not assigned
7	7C00H~7FFFH	Not assigned

Apply the address signals A15...A13 to the address inputs of the first-level decoder and apply address signals A12...A10 to the address inputs of the second-level decoder. Connect the O3 output to the $\overline{\text{E2}}$ input of the second 74138 decoder. The second decoder can operate only when the O3 output of the first 74138 is asserted (low). Most memory devices have chip-enable ($\overline{\text{CE}}$) or chip-select ($\overline{\text{CS}}$) inputs to control their operation. The decoder outputs will be connected to these inputs to enable/disable the memory chips.

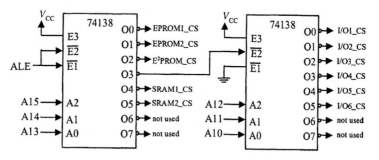

Figure 4.20 An example of two-level decoding.

4.9.3 The MSM5165AL SRAM

The pin layout of the OKI 8KB MSM5165AL is shown in Figure 4.21. The MSM5165AL has 13 address lines to address each of the 8192 locations on the chip, and it uses × 8

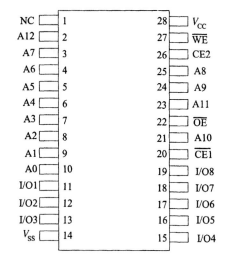

Figure 4.21 OKI MSM5165AL SRAM pin assignment.

NC	1	28	V_{CC}
A12	2	27	$\overline{WE}$
A7	3	26	CE2
A6	4	25	A8
A5	5	24	A9
A4	6	23	A11
A3	7	22	$\overline{OE}$
A2	8	21	A10
A1	9	20	$\overline{CE1}$
A0	10	19	I/O8
I/O1	11	18	I/O7
I/O2	12	17	I/O6
I/O3	13	16	I/O5
V_{SS}	14	15	I/O4

organization, i.e., each location has 8 bits. There are two chip-enable signals: $\overline{CE1}$ is active low and CE2 is active high. The active low *write-enable* ($\overline{WE}$) and active low *output-enable* ($\overline{OE}$) signals control the data in and out of the chip. Data cannot be written into the SRAM if the $\overline{WE}$ signal is not asserted (low) and the data output pins will be in a high-impedance state if the output enable ($\overline{OE}$) signal is not asserted.

The read cycle timing diagram is shown in Figure 4.22. The MSM5165AL comes in three versions, which can be classified according to access time: one version (MSM5165AL-10) has a 100-ns access time, the second (MSM5165AL-12) has a 120-ns access time, and the third (MSM5165AL-15) has a 150-ns access time. The read cycle timing parameters for the MSM5165AL are shown in Table 4.7.

Read cycle time is the shortest separation allowed between two consecutive memory read accesses. A read access takes at least as long as the *read cycle time* (t_{RC}). For SRAM, the read cycle time is as long as the *read access time*. There are three kinds of read access time in the MSM5165AL:

Address access time (t_{AC}):   the access time from the moment that the address becomes valid until data become available at the data pins (I/O8–I/O1), if all other control signals ($\overline{CE1}$, CE2, and $\overline{OE}$) are active.

Chip-enable access time (t_{CO}):   the access time from the moment that $\overline{CE1}$ (or CE2) becomes valid until valid data become available at the data pins, if all other control signals are active and a valid address is applied at the address pins.

Output-enable access time (t_{OE}):   the access time from the moment that $\overline{OE}$ becomes valid until valid data appear at the data pins, if all other control signals are asserted and a valid address is applied at the address pins.

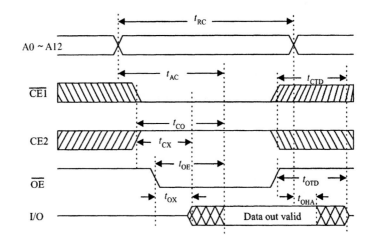

Figure 4.22 MSM5165AL read cycle timing diagram.

TABLE 4.7
MSM5165AL Read Cycle Timing Parameters[a]

Parameter	Symbol	MSM5165AL-10 Min	MSM5165AL-10 Max	MSM5165AL-12 Min	MSM5165AL-12 Max	MSM5165AL-15 Min	MSM5165AL-15 Max
Read cycle time	t_{RC}	100	—	120	—	150	—
Address access time	t_{AC}	—	100	—	120	—	150
Chip-enable access time	t_{CO}	—	100	—	120	—	150
Output enable to output valid	t_{OE}	—	50	—	60	—	70
Output hold from address change	t_{OHA}	10	—	10	—	15	—
Chip selection to output active	t_{CX}	10	—	10	—	10	—
Output enable to output active	t_{OX}	5	—	5	—	5	—
Output 3-state from chip deselection	t_{CTD}	0	50	0	60	0	70
Output 3-state from output disable	t_{OTD}	0	35	0	40	0	50

[a] All times are in nanoseconds.

The *output hold time from address change* (t_{OHA}) is the length of time that data from the I/O8–I/O1 pins stay valid after the address changes. The *output 3-state from output-disable time* (t_{OTD}) is the amount of time that output data remain in a low-impedance state after $\overline{OE}$ goes high. Another timing parameter of interest to the memory system designer is *output 3-state from chip deselection* (t_{CTD}), which is the amount of time that output data remain in a low impedance state after the chip is deselected.

A write cycle occurs during the overlap of a low $\overline{CE1}$, a high CE2, and a low $\overline{WE}$. The output-enable signal $\overline{OE}$ may be either high or low in a write cycle. The timing diagram of

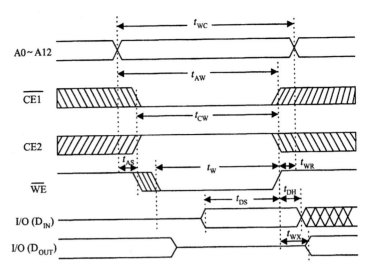

Figure 4.23 MSM5165AL write cycle timing diagram.

TABLE 4.8
MSM5165AL Write Cycle Timing Parameters[a]

Parameter	Symbol	MSM5165AL-10		MSM5165AL-12		MSM5165AL-15	
		Min	Max	Min	Max	Min	Max
Write cycle time	t_{WC}	100	—	120	—	150	—
Chip select to end of write	t_{CW}	80	—	100	—	120	—
Address setup time	t_{AS}	0	—	0	—	0	—
Address valid to end of write	t_{AW}	80	—	100	—	120	—
Write time	t_W	60	—	70	—	90	—
Data setup time	t_{DS}	40	—	50	—	60	—
Data hold from write time	t_{DH}	0	—	0	—	0	—
Output 3-state from write	t_{OTW}	0	35	0	40	0	50
Output active from end of write	t_{WX}	5	—	5	—	5	—
Write recovery time	t_{WR}	15	—	15	—	15	—

[a] All times are in nanoseconds.

a write cycle is shown in Figure 4.23, and the corresponding timing parameters are given in Table 4.8. The MSM5165AL requires the write data to be valid at least t_{DS} ns before the $\overline{WE}$ signal goes to high and to remain valid at least t_{DH} ns after the rising edge of the $\overline{WE}$ signal. The write pulse width (t_W) must be long enough for data to be written into the memory chip correctly. A write cycle takes at least t_{WC} ns.

4.10 MEMORY SYSTEM DESIGN FOR MCS-51/52

Since the Intel MCS-51/52 microcontroller has separate memory spaces for program and data, the memory designer has many design alternatives from which to choose:

- *Internal program memory and external data memory.* This configuration is suitable for applications that will be produced in large quantities and need more data memory than can be satisfied by the internal one.

- *External program and data memories.* This configuration is suitable for any application that is still in prototype phase or building evaluation boards for the microcontroller. The external program will use EPROM because the program may need to be revised many times. An evaluation board may also use SRAM for external program memory so that dynamic programs can be downloaded for execution. Program memory must start from address 0000H because the MCS-51/52 begins program execution from address 0000H after reset.

- *Internal program memory and external program and data memories.* This configuration probably will be used only in microcontroller evaluation boards in which the monitor program resides in the internal EPROM and the user program needs to be downloaded into external program memory for execution. The external program and data memories can be combined.

- *Internal program and data memories.* This configuration will be the ideal choice if the program and data storage requirements can be satisfied by internal program and data memories. This configuration will have the smallest size among all possible memory configurations.

When the MCS-51/52 needs to access external memory, port 0 and port 2 cannot be used for I/O purposes. Two port 3 pins (P3.7 and P3.6) must be used as read ($\overline{RD}$) and write ($\overline{WR}$) control signals and hence are not available for I/O purposes. Adding external parallel interface chips such as the Intel 8255 or choosing an MCS-51/52 member with more I/O pins may be necessary if there are other I/O devices that need to be interfaced. I/O peripheral chips may need to occupy part of the data memory space. The Intel 8255 will be discussed in Chapter 6.

Example 4.5 Add an 8-KB MSM5165AL-10 to the 12-MHz 87C51FB (with 16-KB internal EPROM program memory) as data memory. Include an address decoder so that other peripheral chips can also be added later. Assign the address space 0000H~1FFFH to this SRAM chip.

Solution: Since the low address signals A7~A0 and data signals D7~D0 are time multiplexed, an address latch such as 74F373 is needed to hold A7~A0 valid throughout the whole instruction/data access cycle. An address decoder is needed to enable one and only one external device (memory or peripheral chip) to respond to the access request from the 87C51FB. We will use the 74F138 3-to-8 decoder. Since the address is not valid most of the time when the ALE signal is high, the ALE signal is used to qualify the address decoder. The circuit connection is shown in Figure 4.24.

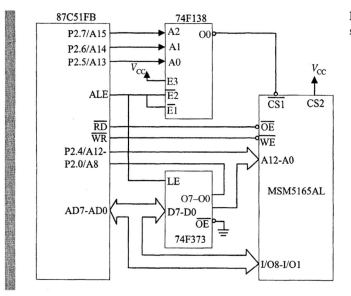

Figure 4.24 An example 87C51FB system circuit diagram.

The upper three address signals A15–A13 are decoded by the 74F138 3-to-8 decoder, which has a propagation delay of 8 ns at room temperature. The lower address signals are connected to the corresponding address signals of the MSM5165AL chip. A user program may accidentally access a nonexistent memory location. The access of a nonexistent memory location is called a *bus error*. When a bus error occurs, a program cannot execute correctly. The design of 87C51FB does not allow it to detect a bus error because each bus cycle takes exactly one ALE cycle, even if the bus cycle is accessing a nonexistent memory location. If we OR those decoder outputs that map to nonexistent memory locations and connect the result to either the INT0 or the INT1 input of the 87C51FB, the microcontroller will be interrupted when a nonexistent location is accessed. The user can then identify the problem from the external interrupt signal. Interrupts will be discussed in Chapter 5.

The $\overline{RD}$ signal is connected to the $\overline{OE}$ signal of the SRAM that will enable the SRAM to output only when $\overline{OE}$ is low. The $\overline{WR}$ signal is connected to the $\overline{WE}$ signal so that data can be written into the SRAM only when $\overline{WR}$ is low.

Example 4.6 Verify that the read access timing parameters are satisfied in the circuit diagram of Figure 4.24.

Solution: The timing analysis is performed as follows:

1. *Address latch timing requirement.* The address latch 74F373 requires that data inputs D7–D0 (connected to AD7–AD0 from 87C51FB) be valid 2.0 ns before the LE signal goes low and remain valid for 3.0 ns after it goes low. The 87C51FB drives A7–A0 43 ns before the falling edge of the ALE signal (connected to LE) and holds them valid for 53 ns after ALE falls. Therefore, both the data input setup and hold time requirements for the address latch are satisfied. The propagation delay of the address latch is 11.5 ns.

Therefore, the low address signals A7–A0 will become valid 11.5 ns after the falling edge of the ALE signal.

2. *Read access timing requirement.* The 87C51FB requires that the read data be valid no more than 517 ns (T_{LLDV}) after the signal ALE goes low. The read data must remain valid 0 ns (T_{RHDX}) after the $\overline{RD}$ signal goes high.

The MSM5165AL data output timing is determined by the following signals:

- $\overline{CE1}$. This signal is connected to the O0 output of the 74F138 decoder. Since A2–A0 are valid long before the ALE goes low, the signal $\overline{CE1}$ will become valid 8 ns after the falling edge of ALE.
- CE2. This signal is tied to high permanently and hence does not affect the timing.
- A12–A0. A12–A8 are valid 43 ns before the falling edge of ALE whereas A7–A0 become valid 11.5 ns after the falling edge of ALE (due to the fact that these signals are latched into 74F373 by ALE). Therefore, this group is valid 11.5 ns after the falling edge of ALE.
- RD. This signal becomes valid between 200 and 300 ns after the falling edge of the ALE signal.

Since the signal $\overline{RD}$, being used as the $\overline{OE}$ input for the SRAM, is the latest signal to become valid, it determines the actual read access time. Data output from the MSM5165AL will become valid 250~350 ns ($T_{LLWL} + t_{OE}$) after the falling edge of ALE and hence the read data setup time requirement is satisfied. There are several read cycle timing parameters that need to be satisfied and are verified in the following:

ALE Low to Valid Data In (T_{LLDV}) requirement. According to the previous analysis, $\overline{RD}$ is the latest signal that is asserted and hence determines when data from SRAM become valid. Since $\overline{RD}$ becomes valid 200~300 ns after the falling edge of ALE and the MSM5165AL-10 has a data access time t_{OE} that equals 50 ns, the actual value of T_{LLDV} is 250~350 ns and is smaller than the required value 517 ns (worst case). The timing calculation of this parameter is illustrated in Figure 4.25.

RD Low to Valid Data In (T_{RLDV}) Requirement. The 12-MHz 87C51FB requires external data to be valid no later than 252 ns after the falling edge of $\overline{RD}$. The actual value is 50 ns shown in Figure 4.26 and satisfies the requirement.

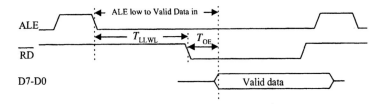

Figure 4.25 ALE low to valid data in calculation.

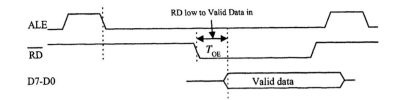

Figure 4.26 $\overline{RD}$ low to valid data in calculation.

Address to Valid Data In (T_{AVDV}) Requirement. This parameter is equal to the sum of T_{AVLL} and T_{LLDV}. Since T_{AVLL} is 43 ns, the actual value of T_{AVDV} will be 293~393 ns. The 12-MHz 8XC51FX requires T_{AVDV} to be no larger than 585 ns and hence this requirement is satisfied. The calculation of this parameter is shown in Figure 4.27.

Data Hold After RD (T_{RHDX}) Requirement. The 12-MHz 87C51FB requires external data to hold for 0 ns after $\overline{OE}$ ($\overline{RD}$) becomes invalid. The data output from MSM5165AL will become invalid 35 ns after $\overline{OE}$ goes high. Therefore, read data hold time requirement is satisfied. Figure 4.28 illustrates this.

A summary of read timing parameter verification is shown in Table 4.9.

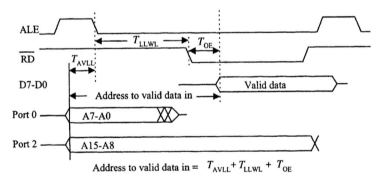

Figure 4.27 Address to valid data in calculation.

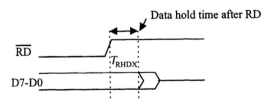

Figure 4.28 Data hold time after $\overline{RD}$ goes high.

TABLE 4.9
A Summary of Read Cycle Timing Requirement Verification

Timing Parameter	Required Value (ns)	Actual Value (ns)
T_{RHDX}	0 (min)	35
T_{LLDV}	517 (max)	250~350
T_{RLDV}	252 (max)	50
T_{AVDV}	585 (max)	293~393

Example 4.7 Verify that all write timing requirements are satisfied in the circuit diagram of Figure 4.24.

Solution: The following SRAM timing parameters must be satisfied:

- Write cycle time (t_{WC})
- Chip-select to end of write (t_{CW})
- Address setup time (t_{AS})
- Write time (t_W)
- Address valid to end of write (t_{AW})
- Data setup time (t_{DS})
- Data hold time (t_{DH})
- Write recovery time (t_{WR})

Write Cycle Time (t_{WC}) Requirement. The write cycle time is defined as the period in a write access during which the address inputs are valid. The higher address inputs to the MSM5165AL remain valid for 84 ns ($127 - 43$) after the ALE signal rises to high. The address inputs A7–A0 will remain valid until new values are latched into the 74F373. Therefore, the actual write cycle time is calculated as follows and is shown in Figure 4.29:

$$\text{Write cycle time} = T_{LLWL} + T_{WLWH} - \text{delay of 74F373} + T_{WHLH}$$
$$+ \text{ the width of ALE} - T_{AVLL}$$
$$= 200\text{~}300 \text{ ns} + 400 \text{ ns} - 11.5 \text{ ns} + 43\text{~}123 \text{ ns} + 127 \text{ ns} - 43 \text{ ns}$$
$$= 770\text{~}950 \text{ ns} - 54.5 \text{ ns}$$
$$= 715.5\text{~}895.5 \text{ ns} > 100 \text{ ns (required by SRAM)}$$

Chip-Select to End of Write (t_{CW}) Requirement. This parameter is measured from the falling edge of the $\overline{CE1}$ (or CE2) signal to the rising edge of the $\overline{WE}$ signal. Since the CE2 signal is tied to V_{CC} permanently, only $\overline{CE1}$ needs to be considered. According to the analysis in Example 4.5, the $\overline{CE1}$ signal goes to low 8 ns after the falling edge of ALE. The $\overline{WR}$ signal from the microcontroller stays low for 400 ns (T_{WLWH}). Therefore, the actual chip-select to end of write time is computed by the following formula:

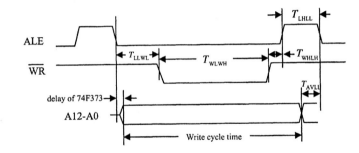

Figure 4.29 Calculation of write cycle time.

$$\text{Chip-select to end of write time} = T_{\text{LLWL}} + T_{\text{WLWH}} - \text{address decoder delay}$$
$$= 200\text{~}300 \text{ ns} + 400 \text{ ns} - 8 \text{ ns} = 592\text{~}692 \text{ ns}$$

The MSM5165AL requires the actual t_{CW} to be at least 80 ns and is satisfied. The calculation of this parameter is illustrated in Figure 4.30.

Address Setup Time (t_{AS}) Requirement. This parameter is measured from the moment that all address inputs to the MSM5165AL become valid until the moment that the WE signal falls. Upper address signals A12–A8 are valid before the ALE signal falls whereas the lower address signals A7–A0 are valid 11.5 ns after the falling edge of ALE. The actual value is computed as follows:

$$\text{Actual address setup time} = \text{smallest } T_{\text{LLWL}} - 11.5 \text{ ns} = 200 \text{ ns} - 11.5 \text{ ns}$$
$$= 188.5 \text{ ns}$$

The MSM5165AL requires a 0 ns address setup time and hence is satisfied. The calculation of the address setup time is illustrated in Figure 4.31.

Write Time (t_{W}) Requirement. The MSM5165AL requires that the write pulse width be at least 60 ns. The $\overline{\text{WR}}$ signal from the microcontroller is asserted (low) for 400 ns and hence this requirement is satisfied.

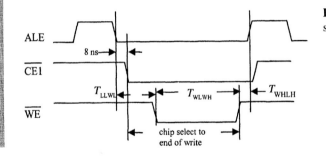

Figure 4.30 Computation of chip select to end of write.

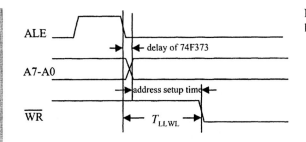

Figure 4.31 Address setup time calculation.

Address Valid to End of Write (t_{AW}) Requirement. This parameter is measured from the moment that all address inputs to the SRAM become valid until the moment that the $\overline{WE}$ signal rises to high. The actual value for this parameter is computed as follows:

Actual time for address valid to end of write

$$= T_{LLWL} + T_{WLWH} - \text{address valid delay relative to the falling edge of ALE}$$

$$= 200\text{~}300 \text{ ns} + 400 \text{ ns} - 11.5 \text{ ns} = 588.5\text{~}688.5 \text{ ns}$$

The MSM5165AL requires this value to be at least 80 ns and hence this requirement is satisfied. The calculation is depicted in Figure 4.32.

Data Setup Time (t_{DS}) Requirement. The MSM5165AL requires that the write data be valid at least 40 ns before the rising edge of the WE input. The 87C51FB drives the write data 433 ns before the rising edge of the $\overline{WR}$ signal and hence this requirement is satisfied.

Data Hold Time (t_{DH}) Requirement. The MSM5165AL requires that the write data remain valid at least 0 ns after the rising edge of the WE input. The 87C51FB drives write data for 33 ns after the write signal $\overline{WR}$ goes high.

Write Recovery Time (t_{WR}) Requirement. Write recovery time is the time delay from the moment that the write-enable signal ($\overline{WE}$) becomes invalid until the moment that the address signals become invalid. A 15 ns write recovery time is required by the MSM5165AL. Because the 74F373 latches the lower address signals A7–A0, they do not change until 127 ns after the rising edge of ALE. Higher address signals A12–A8 stay valid until 84 ns before the next falling edge of the ALE signal ($T_{LHLL} - T_{AVLL}$). The $\overline{WR}$ signal goes to high 43 ns (latest time) before ALE goes high. The actual write recovery time is calculated as follows:

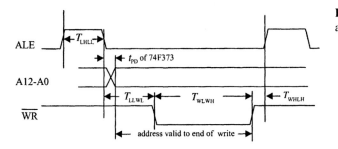

Figure 4.32 The calculation of address valid to end of write.

$$\text{Actual write recovery time} = T_{\text{WHLH}} + T_{\text{LHLL}} - T_{\text{AVLL}}$$
$$= 43 \text{ ns} + 127 \text{ ns} - 84 \text{ ns} = 86 \text{ ns}$$

The calculation of *write recovery time* is illustrated in Figure 4.33. A summary of the write timing analysis is shown in Table 4.10.

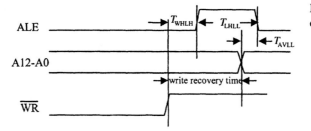

Figure 4.33 Calculation of write recovery time.

TABLE 4.10
A Summary of Write Timing Analysis

Parameter	Required Value (ns)	Actual Value (ns)
Write cycle time (t_{WC})	100	715.5~895.5
Chip select to end of write (t_{CW})	80	592~692
Address setup time (t_{AS})	0	188.5
Address valid to end of write (t_{AW})	80	588.5~688.5
Write time (t_{W})	60	400
Data setup time (t_{DS})	40	433
Write data hold time (t_{DH})	0	33
Write recovery time (t_{WR})	15	86

Example 4.8 Design an 87C51FB-based single board computer so that both user programs and data can be downloaded into the external memory. The monitor program resides in the internal program EPROM. Let the external program and data memories share the same memory component so that the size of the printed circuit board can be reduced. An 8-KB SRAM such as MSM5165AL is adequate for this purpose. Assign the address space 4000H~5FFFH to this memory chip.

Solution: One of the important design considerations is that the $\overline{\text{OE}}$ signal must be asserted when the microcontroller fetches instructions or accesses data items in the given address range. The $\overline{\text{PSEN}}$ signal will be asserted whenever the microcontroller fetches the external instruction memory. By ANDing the $\overline{\text{RD}}$ and $\overline{\text{PSEN}}$ signals, the $\overline{\text{OE}}$ signal will be asserted (low) whenever the microcontroller fetches instructions or accesses data in the given address range. The resultant circuit is shown in Figure 4.34. To select the address range in 4000H~5FFFH, the O2 output is used to select the SRAM chip. Although the instruction fetch cycle timing is not the same as external data read cycle, the timing analysis of this memory system is similar to that in the previous example and hence will be left as an exercise problem.

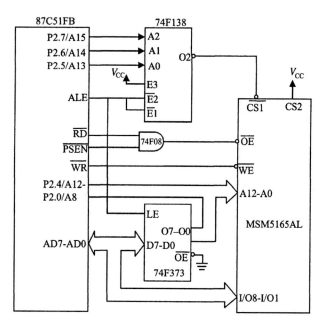

Figure 4.34 An example of shared external program and data memory.

4.11 SUMMARY

A bus is a set of wires that interconnects the CPU, memory, and I/O devices together. A bus with pull-up devices is an active bus and a bus without a pull-up device is a passive bus. A pull-up device can be either a resistor or a transistor. An open-collector bipolar or an open-drain MOS transistor can drive an active bus. A passive bus must be driven by a bus driver and received by a bus receiver. A bus transaction includes two parts: the sending of address and the transmission or receiving of data. A read bus transaction transfers data from memory to the processor or an I/O device and a write bus transaction transfers data from the processor or an I/O device to memory.

A successful bus transaction requires the timing parameters to be satisfied. A synchronous bus provides a clock signal to synchronize the sender and receiver of data. An asynchronous bus does not have a clock signal to synchronize the sender and receiver of data. Instead, handshaking signals are needed to do the synchronization. An asynchronous bus has the advantage of being able to accommodate devices of different speeds. However, it has more overhead than the synchronous bus. The timing parameters involved in a real microprocessor's bus transaction can be overwhelming.

Many different types of memory technologies are available for microprocessor applications. PROM, EPROM, EEPROM, and flash memories are often used for those programs that will be executed whenever the power is turned on and need not be changed. DRAMs and SRAMs are used to load dynamic programs and data.

Memory components are often labeled with shorthand notations, such as 64K × 1, or 64K × 8, etc., that indicate their storage capacity and organizations. The capacity of a memory chip is the total amount of information that the device can store. Memory organization describes the number of bits that can be read from or written into a memory chip during an input or output operation. A "by one" (written as × 1) chip allows us to access 1 bit in one access operation whereas a "by eight" (written as × 8) chip allows us to access 8 bits in one access operation.

Memory expansion involves address space assignment, address decoder design, and timing verification. Address space is often assigned in blocks of equal size. However, it can also be assigned in multiple levels.

Address decoder design is closely related to address space assignment. One and only one of the decoder outputs will be active at any time so that no more than one device is allowed to respond to the bus transfer request from the CPU. A microcontroller can use either the full address-decoding or partial address-decoding scheme. A memory is said to be fully decoded if each of its addressable memory locations responds to only one address value on the system bus. A memory device is said to be partially decoded when each of its addressable locations responds to more than one address on the system bus. When there are many memory-mapped I/O devices being used in a system, a two-level or even three-level decoder design may be needed. A single 3-to-8 decoder is usually adequate in many microprocessor applications.

SRAM is often the choice if our design requires only a small amount of RAM. The read cycle timing diagram of SRAM specifies three access times: the access time relative to address input, the access time relative to chip-select (or enable) signal, and the access time relative to output-enable signal. The latest of these access times is the actual access time of SRAM in a system. The read cycle timing diagram also specifies the read cycle time, which represents the shortest separation between two accesses. In a write cycle, write data must satisfy the write data setup and hold time requirements. Address signals must remain stable throughout the whole access cycle.

Since the MCS-51/52 has separate program and data memory spaces, we have many design alternatives to choose from: internal program memory and external data memory, external program and data memories, internal program memory and external program and data memories, and internal program and data memories. When the MCS-51/52 is accessing the external memory, port 0 and 2 and two port 3 pins (P3.6 and P3.7) are not available for I/O purposes.

Timing verification is a very important step in memory system design. All timing parameters must be satisfied to guarantee correct operations of a memory system.

4.12 EXERCISES

4.1 How many memory chips are required to build a 1-MB, 32-bit-wide memory system using the following SRAM chips?

   a. 256K × 1 SRAM chips
   b. 256K × 4 SRAM chips

c. 64K × 8 SRAM chips

d. 128K × 16 SRAM chips

4.2 Refer to Figure 4.18. Suppose the 2-to-4 decoder 74139 A1 and A0 inputs are connected to A15 and A14, respectively, and A13–A12 are used neither in address decoding nor as address inputs of the memory chips. What is the address range selected by the 1Y0~1Y3 outputs, respectively?

4.3 Design an address decoder for an 80C51FA-based product containing the following memory modules:

EPROM: 8 KB (used to hold monitor program)

SRAM1:   8 KB (used to hold data)

8255:   8 KB (parallel interface chip)

The reset handling routine is stored in the EPROM. Assign the address space so that the EPROM covers address 0000H.

4.4 Add an 8-KB external data memory to an 87C51FB that runs at 24 MHz and select a SRAM chip that meets the speed requirement. Perform a timing analysis to verify that the chip that you choose satisfies all timing requirements.

4.5 Suppose that the address inputs A2–A0 of the 74138 decoder are connected in order to the address outputs of A15–A13 of the 87C51FB and that the E3 input is connected to A12. E1 and E2 are grounded permanently. Determine the address range controlled by each of the O7–O0 outputs.

4.6 Can an MSM5165AL-15 be used in the design shown in Figure 4.24? Verify your answer by performing a timing analysis.

4.7 Design a control circuitry to interface the OKI MSM2764A 8K × 8 bit EPROM with the 12-MHz 80C51FA. The pin assignment of this chip is shown in Figure 4E.1, and the normal read access-timing diagram and timing parameters are given in Figure 4E.2 and Table 4E.1, respectively. Choose the MSM2764A-12, which has a 120-ns access time. Perform read access-timing analysis to verify that all timing requirements are satisfied.

TABLE 4E.1
MSM2764A Read Timing Parameters

Parameter	Symbol	2764A-12		2764A-15		2764A-20	
		Min	Max	Min	Max	Min	Max
Address access time	t_{ACC}	—	120	—	150	—	200
$\overline{CE}$ access time	t_{CE}	—	120	—	150	—	200
$\overline{OE}$ access time	t_{OE}	—	50	—	60	—	70
Output disable time	t_{DF}	0	40	0	50	0	55

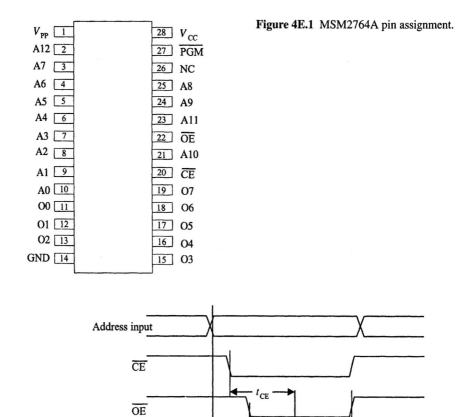

Figure 4E.1 MSM2764A pin assignment.

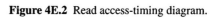

Figure 4E.2 Read access-timing diagram.

5

INTERRUPTS, RESETS, AND
EXCEPTION PROCESSING

5.1 OBJECTIVES

After completing this chapter, you should be able to

- explain interrupts and resets
- describe the handling procedures for interrupts and resets
- enable and disable maskable interrupts
- use the low-power mode to reduce power consumption
- set up interrupt vector tables

5.2 BASICS OF INTERRUPTS

Interrupt is a mechanism provided by a microprocessor or a computer system to synchronize I/O operations, handle error conditions and emergency events, coordinate the use of shared resources, and so on. Without the interrupt mechanism, many of these operations become either impossible or very difficult to implement.

5.2.1 What Is an Interrupt?

An interrupt is an unusual event that requires the CPU to stop normal program execution and perform some service related to the unusual event. An interrupt can be generated internally (inside the chip) or externally (outside the chip). An external interrupt is generated when external circuitry asserts an interrupt signal to the CPU. An internal interrupt can be generated by the hardware circuitry inside the chip or by software errors. In some microcontrollers, for example, the Intel MCS-51/52 and the Motorola 68HC11 family microcontrollers, timers, I/O interface functions, and the CPU are incorporated on the same chip, and these subsystems can generate interrupts to the CPU. Abnormal situations that occur during program execution, such as illegal opcodes, overflow, divided-by-zero, and underflow, are called *software interrupts*. The terms *traps* and *exceptions* are both used to refer to software interrupts.

5.2.2 Why Interrupts?

Interrupts are useful in many applications, such as

- *Coordinating I/O activities and preventing the CPU from being tied up during the data transfer process.* The CPU needs to know if the I/O device is ready before it can proceed. Without the interrupt capability, the CPU will need to check the status of the I/O device periodically. The interrupt mechanism is often used by the I/O device to inform the CPU that it is ready for data transfer. CPU time can thus be utilized more efficiently because of the interrupt mechanism. Interrupt-driven I/O operations will be explained in more detail in later chapters.

- *Time-critical applications.* Many emergent events, for example, power failure and process control, require the CPU to take action immediately. The interrupt mechanism provides a way to force the CPU to divert from normal program execution and take immediate actions.

- *Providing a graceful way to exit from application when a software error occurs.* The service routine for a software interrupt may also output some useful information about the error so that it can be corrected.

- *Reminding the CPU to perform routine tasks.* There are many microprocessor applications that require the CPU to perform routine work, for example:
  1. Keeping the time of day. Without the timer interrupt, the CPU will need to use program loops to update the current time. The CPU cannot do anything else in this application. The periodic timer interrupts prevent the CPU from being tied up.
  2. Switching CPU control in a multitasking operating system. In modern computer operating systems, multiple user programs are resident in the main memory and the CPU time is divided into slots of about 10 to 20 ms. The operating system assigns a program to be executed for one time slot. At the end of a time slot or when a program is waiting for the completion of an I/O operation, the operating system takes over and assigns another program to be executed. This technique is called *multitasking*. Multitasking can dramatically improve the utilization of the CPU and is implemented by using periodic timer interrupts.

5.2.3 Interrupt Maskability

Depending on the situation and application, some interrupts may not be desired and should be prevented from interrupting the CPU. Most microprocessors and microcontrollers have the option to ignore these interrupts. These types of interrupts are called *maskable interrupts*. Other types of interrupts, which the CPU cannot ignore to which it must take immediate action, are called *nonmaskable interrupts*. A program can request the CPU to service or ignore a maskable interrupt by setting or clearing an *enable bit*. When an interrupt is enabled, the CPU will service it. When an interrupt is disabled, the CPU will ignore it. An interrupt is said to be *pending* when it is active but not yet serviced by the CPU. A pending interrupt may or may not be serviced by the CPU depending on whether or not it is enabled.

5.2.4 Interrupt Priority

It is very common for a computer system to have multiple pending interrupts at the same time. In this situation the CPU has to decide which interrupt should receive service first. The solution is to prioritize all interrupt sources. An interrupt with higher priority always receives service before interrupts at lower priorities. In most microprocessors and microcontrollers, interrupt priorities are not programmable.

5.2.5 Interrupt Service

The CPU provides service to an interrupt by executing a program called the *interrupt service routine*. After providing service to an interrupt, the CPU must resume normal program execution. How does the CPU stop the execution of a program and resume it later? It does this by saving the program counter and the CPU status information before executing the interrupt service routine and then restoring the saved program counter and CPU status before exiting the interrupt service routine. The complete interrupt service cycle is as follows:

1. Save the program counter value when an interrupt occurs.
2. Save the CPU status (including the CPU status register and some other registers) in the stack. This step is optional for some microcontrollers and microprocessors. The MCS-51 does not save the CPU status.
3. Identify the cause of the interrupt.
4. Resolve the starting address of the corresponding interrupt service routine.
5. Execute the interrupt service routine.
6. Restore the CPU status from the stack (not needed in MCS-51).
7. Restore the program counter from the stack.
8. Restart the interrupted program.

Another issue is related to the time when the CPU begins to service an interrupt. For all maskable hardware interrupts, the microprocessor starts to provide service when it completes the execution of the current instruction. For some nonmaskable interrupts, the CPU may start the service without completing the current instruction. Many software interrupts are caused by an error in instruction execution that prevents the instruction from being completed. The service to this type of interrupt is simply to output an error message and abort the program.

5.2.6 Interrupt Vector

The term *interrupt vector* refers to the starting address of the interrupt service routine. In general, interrupt vectors are stored in a table called an *interrupt vector table*. The interrupt vector table may be fixed or relocateable depending on the microprocessor.

The CPU needs to determine the interrupt vector before it can provide service. The interrupt vector can be determined by one of the following methods:

1. *Predefined.* In this method, the starting address of the service routine is predefined when the microcontroller is designed. The processor uses a table to store all the

interrupt service routines. The MCS-51/52 uses this approach. Each interrupt is allocated the same number of bytes to hold its service routine. The MCS-51 allocates 8 bytes to each interrupt service routine. When the service routine requires more than 8 bytes, the solution is to place a jump instruction (AJMP or LJMP) in the predefined location to jump to the actual service routine. For example, the INT0 service routine may look like the following:

```
                    org    03H
                    ljmp   INT0_ISR
                    . . .
INT0_ISR:           . . .              ; actual INT0 service routine is longer than
                                       ; 8 bytes

                    . . .
                    reti
```

2. *Fetch the vector from a predefined memory location.* For most microprocessors and microcontrollers, the interrupt vector of each interrupt source is stored at a predefined location in the interrupt vector table, where the microprocessor can get it directly. The Motorola 68HC11 uses this approach.

3. *Execute an interrupt acknowledge cycle to fetch a vector number to locate the interrupt vector.* During the interrupt acknowledge cycle, the microprocessor performs a read bus cycle and the external I/O device that requested the interrupt places a number on the data bus to identify itself. This number is called *interrupt vector number*. The address of the memory location that stores the interrupt vector is usually a multiple (2 and 4 are most common) of the vector number. The CPU needs to perform a read cycle to obtain it.

5.2.7 Interrupt Programming

There are three steps in interrupt programming:

STEP 1   *Write the service routine.* An interrupt service routine is similar to a subroutine—the only difference is the last instruction. An interrupt service routine uses the *return from interrupt* (RETI) instruction instead of *return* (RET) to return to the interrupted program. A simple interrupt service routine is as follows:

```
cnt_lo      set    R1
cnt_hi      set    R2
            .
            .
            .
ti_ISR:     mov    A,cnt_lo
            inc    A              ; add 1 to the lower byte
            mov    cnt_lo,A       ; "
            mov    A,cnt_hi       ; add carry to the upper byte
```

```
addc    A,#0        ; "
mov     cnt_hi,A    ; "
reti                ; return from interrupt
```

The above interrupt service routine simply increments a 16-bit counter and returns to the interrupted program.

The interrupt service routine may or may not return to the interrupted program depending on the cause of the interrupt. It makes no sense to return to the interrupted program if the interrupt is caused by a software error such as divided-by-zero or overflow, because the program is unlikely to generate correct results under these circumstances. In such cases the service routine would return to the monitor program or the operating system instead. Returning to a program other than the interrupted program can be achieved by changing the saved program counter (in the stack) to the desired value. Execution of the RETI instruction will then return CPU control to the new address.

STEP 2 *Initialize the interrupt vector table* (that is, place the starting address of each interrupt service routine in the table). This can be done by using the assembler directive ORG (or its equivalent):

```
ORG    xxxxH
DW     hndler_1
DW     hndler_2
    .
    .
    .
```

where, *hndler_i* is the starting address of the service routine for interrupt source i. The Intel MCS-51/52 interrupt service routines are stored in fixed locations and hence this step is not necessary.

STEP 3 *Enable interrupts to be serviced.* Setting the corresponding enable bit in the *interrupt enable* (IE) *register* can enable an MCS-51/52 interrupt. It is a common mistake to forget enabling interrupts. The contents of the IE register are shown in Figure 5.1.

5.2.8 Interrupt Overhead

Interrupt mechanism involves some overhead. The overhead is due to the saving and restoring of the program counter and other registers. The default interrupt overhead of the MCS-51/52 is relatively light because the MCS-51/52 saves and restores only the program counter. Other microcontrollers may save and restore many other registers during an interrupt. For example, the Motorola 68HC11 saves six registers (9 bytes) on an interrupt.

5.3 RESETS

The initial values of some CPU registers, flip-flops, and control registers in I/O interface chips must be established before the computer can operate properly. Computers provide a reset mechanism to establish initial conditions.

| EA | EC | ET2 | ES | ET1 | EX1 | ET0 | EX0 |

Enable Bit = 1 enables the interrupt
Enable Bit = 0 disables the interrupt

Symbol Function

EA: **Enable all interrupts.** If EA = 0, no interrupt will be
      acknowledged. If EA = 1, each interrupt source is
      individually enabled or disabled by setting or clearing
      its enable bit.
EC: PCA interrupt enable bit (existed in 8XC51FX & 8XC51GB only).
ET2: Timer 2 interrupt enable bit (not available in MCS-51).
ES: Serial port interrupt enable bit.
ET1: Timer 1 interrupt enable bit.
EX1: External interrupt 1 enable bit.
ET0: Timer 0 interrupt enable bit.
EX0: External interrupt 0 enable bit.

Figure 5.1 IE: Interrupt enable register.

There are at least two types of reset in each microprocessor: the *power-on reset* and
the *manual reset*. A power-on reset allows the microprocessor to establish the initial
values of registers and flip-flops and to initialize all I/O interface chips when power to
the microprocessor is turned on. A manual reset without power-down allows the computer
to get out of most error conditions (if the hardware has not failed) and reestablish the initial
conditions. The computer *reboots* itself after a reset.

The reset service routine has a fixed starting address and is stored in the read-only
memory of all microprocessors. At the end of the service routine, control should be returned
to either the monitor program or the operating system. An easy way to do that is to push
the starting address of the monitor program or the operating system into the stack and then
execute a return from interrupt instruction.

Like nonmaskable interrupts, resets are unmaskable. However, resets are different from
nonmaskable interrupts in that no register is saved by resets because resets establish the
values of registers.

5.4 MCS-51 INTERRUPTS

The Intel MCS-51 has five interrupt sources; the MCS-52 has six. They are listed in Table 5.1.

The external interrupts INT0 and INT1 can each be either level sensitive or edge
sensitive, depending on bits IT0 and IT1 in timer control register TCON. When the bit ITx
($x = 0$ or 1) = 0, the external interrupt INTx ($x = 0$ or 1) is low-level sensitive. Otherwise,
it is falling-edge sensitive. The contents of the TCON register are shown in Figure 5.2.

When an external interrupt (INT0 or INT1) occurs, the corresponding flag (IE0 or IE1)
in the TCON register will be set. If the external interrupt is edge triggered, the associated
interrupt flag will be cleared when its service routine is vectored to.

Timer 0 (or Timer 1) interrupt will be generated if the following two conditions are
satisfied:

TABLE 5.1
MCS-51 and MCS-52 Interrupt Sources

Source	Comment
INT0 external interrupt	Available in both
INT1 external interrupt	Available in both
Timer 0 overflow interrupt	Available in both
Timer 1 overflow interrupt	Available in both
Serial port interrupt	Available in both
Timer 2 overflow interrupt	Available only in MCS-52

7	6	5	4	3	2	1	0
TF1	TR1	TF0	TR0	IE1	IT1	IE0	IT0

Symbol	Significance
TF1:	*Timer 1 overflow flag*. Set by hardware on timer/counter overflow. Cleared by hardware when processor vectors to interrupt routine.
TR1:	*Timer 1 run control bit*. Set/cleared by software to turn timer/counter on/off.
TF0:	*Timer 0 overflow flag*. Set by hardware on timer/counter overflow. Cleared by hardware when processor vectors to interrupt routine.
TR0:	*Timer 0 run control bit*. Set/cleared by software to turn timer/counter on/off.
IE1:	*Interrupt 1 edge flag*. Set by hardware when external interrupt edge detected. Cleared when interrupt processed.
IT1:	*Interrupt 1 type control bit*. Set/cleared by software to specify falling edge/low level triggered external interrupts.
IE0:	*Interrupt 0 edge flag*. Set by hardware when external interrupt edge detected. Cleared when interrupt processed.
IT0:	*Interrupt 0 type control bit*. Set/cleared by software to specify falling edge/low level triggered external interrupts.

Figure 5.2 Contents of timer/counter control register (TCON).

- The Timer 0 (or Timer 1) interrupt is enabled.
- The timer/counter overflow occurs.

The interrupt flag associated with Timer 0 (or Timer 1) will be cleared by the hardware when its service routine is vectored to.

Timer 2 interrupt is available only in the MCS-52. The interrupt flags associated with Timer 2 must be cleared by the software and this is often done in the Timer 2 interrupt service routine. If the service routine did not clear the interrupt, then another Timer 2 interrupt will be requested immediately after the service routine is exited.

There are two interrupt flags (RI and TI) associated with serial port interrupt: one is associated with reception and the other is associated with transmission. Both of these flags must be cleared by the software.

5.4.1 The MCS-51/52 Interrupt Priority Structure

Each interrupt source can also be individually programmed to one of two priority levels by setting or clearing a bit in special function register IP. A low-priority interrupt can itself be interrupted by a high-priority interrupt, but not by another low-priority interrupt. A high-priority interrupt can not be interrupted by any other interrupt sources. The contents of the IP register are shown in Figure 5.3.

If two requests of different priority levels are received simultaneously, the request of higher priority level is serviced. If requests of the same priority level are received simultaneously, an internal polling sequence determines which request is serviced. Thus within each priority level there is a second priority structure determined by the polling sequence (implemented by a priority decoder) as shown in Table 5.2.

5.4.2 How Interrupts Are Handled

As explained in Chapter 1, a machine cycle has six states (S1ellipsisS6) and each state has two phases: P1 and P2. The MCS-51/52 samples interrupt flags at S5P2 of every machine

7	6	5	4	3	2	1	0
—	—	PT2	PS	PT1	PX1	PT0	PX0

Priority bit = 1 assigns high priority
Priority bit = 0 assigns low priority

Symbol	Function
—:	reserved
PT2:	Timer 2 interrupt priority bit
PS:	Serial port interrupt priority bit
PT1:	Timer 1 interrupt priority bit
PX1:	External interrupt 1 priority bit
PT0:	Timer 0 interrupt priority bit
PX0:	External interrupt 0 priority bit

Figure 5.3 IP: interrupt priority register.

TABLE 5.2
MCS-51/52 Interrupt Priority within Each Level

Source	Priority Within Level
External interrupt 0	(highest)
Timer 0 interrupt	▲
External interrupt 1	
Timer 1 interrupt	
Serial port interrupt	
Timer 2 interrupt	(lowest)

cycle and polls them during the following machine cycle. The interrupt timing is illustrated in Figure 5.4. If an interrupt flag is found to be set and none of the following three conditions exists, then the interrupt system will generate an LCALL to the appropriate service routine:

1. An interrupt of equal or higher priority level is already in progress.
2. The current cycle is not the final cycle in the execution of the instruction in progress.
3. The instruction in progress is RETI or any write to the IE or IP registers.

Any of these three conditions will block the generation of the LCALL to the interrupt service routine. Condition 2 ensures that the instruction in progress will be completed before vectoring to any service routine. Condition 3 ensures that if the instruction in progress is RETI or any access to IE or IP, at least one more instruction will be executed before any interrupt service routine is executed.

The hardware generated LCALL pushes the contents of the program counter into the stack (but it does not save the PSW) and reloads the PC with the starting address of the interrupt service routine. Instruction execution proceeds from that location until the RETI instruction is encountered. The RETI instruction informs the processor that this interrupt routine is no longer in progress, then pops the top two bytes from the stack and reloads the program counter. Execution of the interrupted program continues from where it left off. The MCS-51/52 interrupt service routines are shown in Table 5.3.

Note that a simple RET instruction might also have returned execution to the interrupted program, but it would have misinformed the interrupt control system that an interrupt was still in progress.

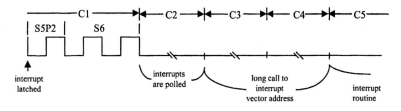

Figure 5.4 Interrupt response timing diagram.

TABLE 5.3
The MCS-51/52 Interrupt Service Routines

Interrupt Source	Vector Address
External interrupt 0	0003H
Timer 0 interrupt	000BH
External interrupt 1	0013H
Timer 1 interrupt	001BH
Serial port interrupt	0023H
Timer 2 interrupt	002BH

5.4.3 External Interrupts

The external interrupt sources (INT0 and INT1) can be programmed to be edge sensitive or level sensitive. Since the external interrupt pins are sampled once in each machine cycle, an input high or low should hold for at least 12 oscillator periods to ensure sampling. If the external interrupt is edge sensitive, the external source has to hold the request pin high for at least one machine cycle, and then hold it low for at least one machine cycle to ensure that the transition is seen so that the external interrupt flag (IE0 or IE1) can be set.

If the external interrupt is level sensitive, the external source has to hold the request active until the requested interrupt is actually generated. Then it has to deactivate the request before the interrupt service routine is completed, or else another interrupt (from the same source) will be generated.

5.4.4 Single-Step Operation

During the software development process, we may use the single-step operation technique to debug our programs. Using this technique, one instruction in the user program is executed at a time. After one instruction is executed, the contents of related registers and memory locations are displayed. With this operation, the program bug may be identified.

The MCS-51/52 interrupt structure allows single-step execution with very little software overhead. As previously noted, an interrupt request will not be responded to while an interrupt of equal priority level is still in progress, nor will it be responded to after RETI until at least one other instruction has been executed. Thus, once an interrupt routine has been entered, it cannot be reentered until at least one instruction of the interrupted program is executed. This feature can be utilized to single step through a program.

One way to use this feature of single-step operation is to program one of the external interrupts (say INT0) to be level sensitive. The service routine for the interrupt will terminate with the following three instructions:

```
JNB     P3.2,$      ; wait here till INT0 goes high
JB      P3.2,$      ; now wait here till it goes low
RETI                ; go back and execute one instruction
```

Now if the INT0 pin, which is also the P3.2 pin, is held normally low, the CPU will go right into the service routine of the external interrupt 0 and stay there until INT0 is pulsed (from low to high to low). Then it will execute RETI, go back to the user program, execute one instruction, and immediately reenter the interrupt service routine to await the next pulsing of P3.2. One step of the user program is executed each time P3.2 is pulsed.

5.5 THE MCS-51/52 RESET

The RST pin is the reset input. A reset is accomplished by holding the RST pin high for at least two machine cycles (24 oscillator periods) while the oscillator is running. The external reset signal is asynchronous with the internal clock. The RST pin is sampled during the State 5 Phase 2 of every machine cycle. The port pins will maintain their current activities for 19 oscillator periods after a logic 1 has been sampled at the RST pin, that is, for 19 to 31 oscillator periods after the external reset signal has been applied to the RST pin.

While the RST pin is high, ALE and PSEN pins are weakly pulled high. After RST is pulled low, it will take one to two machine cycles for ALE and PSEN to start clocking. For this reason, other devices cannot be synchronized with the internal timings of the MCS-51/52. Driving the ALE and PSEN pins to 0 while reset is active could cause the device to go into an indeterminate state.

The internal reset algorithm writes 0s to all the SFRs except the port latches, the Stack Pointer, and SBUF. The port latches are initialized to FFH, the Stack Pointer to 07H, and SBUF is indeterminate. Table 5.4 lists the SFRs and their reset values. The internal RAM is not affected by reset. On power up the RAM contents are indeterminate.

5.5.1 Power-On Reset

For HMOS devices when V_{CC} is turned on an automatic reset can be obtained by connecting the RST pin to V_{CC} through a 10-μF capacitor and to V_{SS} through an 8.2-kΩ resistor as shown in Figure 5.5. For CHMOS devices the external resistor can be removed because

TABLE 5.4
Reset Values of the SFRs

SFR	Reset Value[a]
PC	0000H
ACC	00H
B	00H
PSW	00H
SP	07H
DPTR	0000H
P0-P3	FFH
IP(8051)	xxx00000B
IP(8052)	xx000000B
IE(8051)	0xx00000B
IE(8052)	0x000000B
TMOD	00H
TCON	00H
TH0	00H
TL0	00H
TH1	00H
TL1	00H
TH2(8052)	00H
TL2(8052)	00H
RCAP2H(8052)	00H
RCAP2L(8052)	00H
SCON	00H
SBUF	Indeterminate
PCON(HMOS)	0xxxxxxxB
PCON(CHMOS)	0xxx0000B

[a] x, unknown.

they have an internal pulldown resistor on the RST pin. The capacitor value could then be reduced to 1 μF.

When power is turned on, the circuit holds the RST pin high for an amount of time that depends on the capacitor value and the rate at which it charges. To ensure a valid reset the RST pin must be held high long enough to allow the oscillator to start up plus two machine cycles.

On power up, V_{CC} should rise within approximately 10 ms. The oscillator start up time will depend on the oscillator frequency. For a 10-MHz crystal, the start-up time is typically 1 ms. For a 1-MHz crystal, the start up time is typically 10 ms. With the given circuit, reducing V_{CC} quickly to 0 causes the RST pin voltage momentarily fall below 0 V. However, this voltage is internally limited and will not harm the device.

Powering up the device without a valid reset could cause the CPU to start executing instructions from an indeterminate location. This is because the SFRs, specifically the program counter, may not get properly initialized.

5.6 POWER-SAVING MODES OF OPERATION

For applications in which power consumption is critical the 8XC51FX provides power-reduced modes of operation as standard features. The 8XC51FX has two power-reduced modes, *Idle* and *Power-Down*. The input through which backup power is supplied during these operations is V_{CC}. Figure 5.6 shows the internal circuitry that implements these features. In the Idle mode, the oscillator continues to run and the interrupt, serial port, and timer blocks continue to be clocked, but the clock signal is gated off to the CPU. In the Power-Down mode, the oscillator is frozen. Setting bits in special function register PCON activates the Idle and Power-Down modes. The address of this register is 87H. The contents of PCON are shown in Figure 5.7.

5.6.1 Idle Mode

The user's software can invoke the Idle mode by setting bit 0 of the PCON register. When the microcontroller is in this mode, power consumption is reduced. The special function

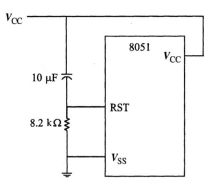

Figure 5.5 Power-on reset circuit.

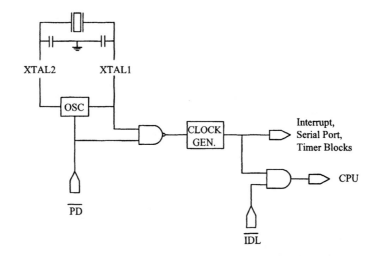

Figure 5.6 Idle and power-down hardware. PD and IDL are bits in the PCON register (shown in Figure 5.7).

7	6	5	4	3	2	1	0
SMOD	—	—	—	GF1	GF0	PD	IDL

Symbol	Name and Function
SMOD:	***Baud rate doubler enable bit***. When set to 1, baud rate is double that defined by baud rate generation equation
----- :	reserved
GF1:	***General-purpose flag bit***.
GF0:	***General-purpose flag bit***.
PD:	***Power-down bit***. Setting this bit activates power-down operation
IDL:	***Idle mode bit***. Setting this bit activates Idle mode operation

Figure 5.7 Contents of the PCON register. If 1s are written to PD and IDL at the same time, PD takes precedence.

registers and the on-chip RAM retain their values during Idle, but the processor stops executing instructions. Idle mode will be exited if the chip is reset or if an enabled interrupt occurs. The programmable counter array (PCA) timer/counter can optionally be left running or paused during Idle mode.

The flag bits GF0 and GF1 can be used to indicate whether an interrupt occurred during normal operation or when the CPU is idle. For example, an instruction that activates Idle mode can also set one or both flag bits. When Idle mode is terminated by an interrupt, the interrupt service routine can examine the flag bits.

5.6.2 Power-Down Mode

To save even more power, a Power-Down mode can be invoked by software. In this mode, the oscillator is stopped and the instruction that invoked Power Down is the last instruction executed. The on-chip RAM and SFRs retain their values until the Power-Down mode is terminated.

Either hardware reset or external interrupt can terminate the Power-Down mode. Reset redefines all the SFRs but does not change the on-chip RAM. An external interrupt allows both the SFRs and the on-chip RAM to retain their values.

To properly terminate Power Down the reset or external interrupt should not be executed before V_{CC} is restored to its normal operating level and must be held active long enough for the oscillator to restart and stabilize (normally less than 10 ms).

For an external interrupt, INT0 and INT1 must be enabled and configured as level sensitive. Holding the pin low restarts the oscillator but bringing the pin back to high completes the exit. Once the interrupt is serviced, the next instruction to be executed after RETI will be the one following the instruction that put the microcontroller into Power Down.

5.7 MCS-51/52 INTERRUPT PROGRAMMING

As shown in Table 5.3, the MCS-51/52 allocates only 8 bytes to each interrupt service routine. For many applications, 8 bytes are enough. If 8 bytes are not enough, the user can use a jump instruction to jump to the appropriate interrupt service routine.

There are two steps in the MCS-51/52 interrupt programming:

STEP 1   Write the interrupt service routine.

STEP 2   Set the appropriate interrupt enable bits.

An interrupt service routine should have the following form:

```
hndler:      .

             .

             .

          reti
```

where *hndler* is the label of the first instruction in the interrupt service routine.

Example 5.1 Write an instruction sequence to set external interrupt 1 to high priority level and all other interrupt sources to low priority.

Solution: To set external interrupt 1 to high priority and all other interrupt sources to low priority, store the binary value 00000100_2 to the IP register. This can be done by using the following instruction:

```
mov   IP,#04H
```

Example 5.2 Write an instruction sequence to set the external interrupt INT1 to high priority, enable it, initialize the variable *int_cnt* to 100, and also write an interrupt service routine for INT1. The service routine will simply decrement the variable int_cnt by 1 and return. The main program will stay in a loop until the variable int_cnt is decremented to 0 and then disable the INT1 interrupt.

Solution: We will assume that the INT1 input signal satisfies the timing requirements so that it can be recognized by the MCS-51/52.

```
int_cnt       set     R2
              org     00H                 ; starting address of the main program
              ljmp    start_up
                . . .
              org     0013H               ; starting address of INT1 service routine
int1_hnd:     dec     int_cnt
              reti
start_up:     mov     int_cnt,#100
              mov     IP,#04H             ; set INT1 to high priority, other interrupts
                                          ; to low priority
              mov     IE,#84H             ; enable INT1 interrupt
loop:         mov     A,int_cnt           ; wait until int_cnt is decremented to 0
              jnz     loop                ; "
              mov     IE,#80H             ; disable INT1 interrupt
              .
              .
              end
```

The handling of timer interrupts will be discussed in Chapter 7.

5.8 SUMMARY

Interrupt is a mechanism provided by a microprocessor or a computer system to synchronize I/O operations, handle error conditions and emergency events, coordinate the use of shared resources, and so on. Interrupts that can be ignored by the processor are called maskable interrupts. Interrupts that cannot be ignored by the processor are called nonmaskable interrupts. The processor provides service to the interrupt by executing a program called interrupt service routine. The last instruction of the interrupt service routine is the RETI instruction. When there are more multiple active interrupts, the processor uses the priority assigned to each interrupt source to choose one of the pending interrupt requests to service. The active interrupt with the highest priority will receive service first.

The term interrupt vector refers to the starting address of the interrupt service routine. In general, interrupt vectors are stored in a table called an interrupt vector table. The interrupt vectors of the MCS-51/52 are predefined and need not be stored in a table. The MCS-51/52 series microcontrollers have five or six interrupt sources whereas the 8XC51FX and

8XC51GB series microcontrollers have seven interrupt sources. Each of these interrupts can be programmed to one of two priority levels by setting or clearing a bit in the IP register. The polling sequence within each priority determines the priority structure within each level.

The interrupt mechanism involves some overhead. The handling of an interrupt requires the processor to save the program counter and other registers before executing the interrupt service routine and restore them when the service routine is done. The MCS-51/52 has very light interrupt overhead because it does not save any register other than the PC.

The MCS-51/52 has two external interrupt pins: INT0 and INT1. Both can be programmed to be falling edge or level triggered. Setting or clearing a bit in the TCON register does this.

There are two steps in the MCS-51 interrupt programming:

STEP 1   Write the interrupt service routine.

STEP 2   Set the appropriate interrupt enable bits.

The MCS-51 allocates 8 bytes to each interrupt in the interrupt service routine table. However, some interrupt service routines are longer than 8 bytes. In this situation, the first instruction in the corresponding interrupt service routine will be an appropriate jump instruction that jumps to the actual service routine in another place.

There are at least two types of resets in each microprocessor: power-on reset and manual reset. A power-on reset allows the microprocessor to establish the initial values of registers and flip-flops and to initialize all I/O interface chips when power to the microprocessor is turned on. A manual reset without power-down allows the computer to get out of most error conditions (if the hardware does not fail) and reestablish the initial conditions. The computer reboots itself after a reset. The reset service routine has a fixed starting address and is stored in the read-only memory of all microprocessors. After executing the reset service routine, processor control should be returned to either the monitor program or the operating system. No register is saved during a reset.

The MCS-51/52 has a reset input pin. The reset signal provides all the registers with default values so that the user program can start from there.

The MCS-51/52 has two power saving modes: Idle and Power-Down. The oscillator is not stopped in the Idle mode but is stopped in the Power-Down mode. Power consumption is reduced significantly in these two modes. The Power-Down mode saves more power than the Idle mode.

5.9 EXERCISES

5.1 What is the name given to a routine that is executed in response to an interrupt?

5.2 What are the advantages of using interrupts to handle data inputs and outputs?

5.3 What is the last instruction in most interrupt service routines? What does this instruction do?

5.4 Is the MCS-51/52 interrupt priority programmable?

5.5 Does the MCS-51/52 need a table to hold interrupt vectors?

5.6 How does the MCS-51/52 determine which interrupt to service when there are several simultaneous pending interrupts?

5.7 Write an instruction sequence to enable all except serial port interrupts.

5.8 Write an instruction sequence to set Timer 0 and Timer 1 to high priority and set other interrupt sources to low priority.

5.9 Write an instruction sequence and an interrupt service routine. The instruction sequence does the following:

    1. Initialize the variable int_cnt to 0.
    2. Set INT0 to high priority level and set other interrupts to low priority.
    3. Enable INT0 interrupt.
    4. Stay in a loop while the variable int_cnt is less than 3.

The interrupt service routine does the following:

- Increment the variable int_cnt by 1.
- Call the subroutine *prompt*.
- Return from interrupt.

5.10 LAB EXERCISE AND ASSIGNMENT

5.1 *INT0 and INT1 interrupt experiments.* Connect debounced pulse sources to the INT0 and INT1 pins, respectively. Write a main program and interrupt service routines for INT0 and INT1. The main program initializes the variable *intcnt_0* and *intcnt_1* to 3 and 5, respectively, enables both interrupt sources, and stays in a loop until both *intcnt_0* and *intcnt_1* have been decremented to zero. The main program disables INT0 interrupt when intcnt_0 is decremented to 0 and disables INT1 interrupt when intcnt_1 is decremented to 0. The interrupt service routines for INT0 interrupt decrements the variable *intcnt_0* by 1. The interrupt service routine for INT1 interrupt decrements the variable *intcnt_1* by 1. Set up the hardware properly. Download the program into the MCB520 evaluation board for execution. Apply pulses to INT0 and INT1 pins accordingly until the monitor-51 prompt reappears.

6

PARALLEL I/O PORTS

6.1 OBJECTIVES

After completing this chapter, you should be able to

- define I/O addressing methods
- explain the data transfer synchronization methods between the CPU and I/O interface chip
- explain the data transfer synchronization methods between the I/O interface chip and the I/O device
- explain input and output handshake protocols
- input data from simple switches
- explain keyboard scanning and debouncing
- output data to light-emitting diodes (LED) and liquid-crystal displays (LCD)
- use the D/A converter
- explain the operation of the Centronics printer interface
- do I/O programming
- add parallel interface chip i8255 to the MCS-51/52
- perform the i8255 programming

6.2 BASIC I/O CONCEPTS

Peripheral devices (also called I/O devices) are pieces of equipment that exchange data with a computer. Examples of peripheral devices include switches, light-emitting diodes, cathode-ray tube (CRT) screens, printers, modems, keyboards, liquid-crystal displays, magnetic tapes, hard disks, optical disks, and so on. The speeds and characteristics of these devices are very different from that of the microprocessor, so they cannot be connected to the microprocessor directly. Interface chips are needed to resolve the difference between the microprocessor and peripheral devices.

The main function of an interface chip is to synchronize data transfer between the CPU and an I/O device. An interface chip consists of one or more of the following devices:

- control registers
- data register
- status register
- latches
- control circuitry

In an input operation, the input device places data in the data register of the interface chip, which holds data until the microprocessor reads it. In an output operation, the microprocessor writes data into the data register in the interface chip, and the data register holds data until the output device fetches it.

An interface chip has data pins that are connected to the microprocessor data bus and I/O port pins that are connected to the I/O device. Since a computer may have multiple I/O devices, the microprocessor data bus can be connected to the data buses of multiple interface chips. An address decoder is used to select one and only one device to respond to the microprocessor I/O request. An interface chip may have one or more *chip-enable* (or equivalent) inputs. When the chip-enable signal is asserted, the interface chip is allowed to react to the data transfer request from the CPU. Otherwise, the data pins of the interface chip are isolated from the microprocessor data bus.

Data transfer between the I/O device and the interface chip can proceed bit by bit (serial) or in multiple bits (parallel). Data are transferred serially to low-speed devices such as modems and low-speed printers. High-speed I/O devices mainly use parallel data transfer. We will discuss only parallel I/O in this chapter. Serial I/O will be discussed in Chapters 9 and 10.

6.3 I/O ADDRESSING

An interface chip normally has several registers. Each of these registers must be assigned a separate address to be accessed. It is possible to have two or more registers share the same address, but in this case some other control signals, such as the $R/\overline{W}$ signal, must then be used to select one of these registers. This approach is very common in the interface chips designed for 8-bit microprocessors.

Different microprocessors deal with I/O devices differently. Some microprocessors have dedicated instructions for performing input and output operations—this approach is called *isolated I/O*. In this method, an input instruction, such as IN 2, reads from the input device. This instruction inputs a word from input device 2 into the accumulator. Similarly, the output instruction OUT 3 outputs a word from the accumulator to the third output device. In the isolated I/O method, I/O devices have their own address space, which is separated from the main memory address space.

Other microprocessors use the same instructions for reading from memory and reading from input devices, as well as writing data into memory and writing data into output devices. This approach is called *memory-mapped I/O*. In this method, an I/O address such as 1000H is considered a byte in memory space. Assume the value 1000H has been placed in the DPTR register. A move instruction like *movx A, @DPTR* is then an input instruction, and a move instruction like *movx @DPTR,A* is an output instruction.

Traditionally, Intel microprocessors use the isolated I/O method, whereas Motorola microprocessors use the memory-mapped I/O method. The MCS-51/52 microcontroller has no separate I/O instructions and uses memory-mapped I/O exclusively.

6.4 I/O TRANSFER SYNCHRONIZATION

The role of an interface chip is illustrated in Figure 6.1. The circuit in the I/O device converts electrical signals into mechanical actions or vice versa. But the microprocessor interacts with the interface chip instead of dealing with the I/O device directly.

When input, the microprocessor reads data from the interface chip instead of from the input device. There must be a mechanism to make sure that there are valid data in the interface chip when the microprocessor reads them. When output, the microprocessor writes data into the interface chip. Again, the microprocessor must make sure that the interface chip is ready to accept new data. There are two aspects of the I/O synchronization process— synchronization between the interface chip and the microprocessor and synchronization between the interface chip and the I/O device circuits. The interface chip function is implemented on the microcontroller chip.

6.4.1 Synchronizing the Microprocessor and the Interface Chip

To input valid data from an input device, the microprocessor must make sure that the interface chip has correctly latched the data from the input device. There are two ways to do this:

1. *The polling method.* The interface chip uses a status bit to indicate if it has valid data for the microprocessor. The microprocessor knows that the interface chip has valid data when the status bit is set to 1. The microprocessor keeps checking the status register until the status bit is set to 1, and then it reads data from the data register. When it is reading the data the CPU is tied up and cannot do anything else. This method is simple and is mainly used when the CPU has nothing else to do when waiting for the completion of input operation.

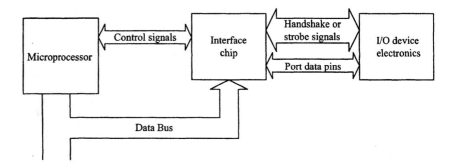

Figure 6.1 The role of an interface chip.

2. *The interrupt-driven method.* In this method, the interface chip asserts an interrupt signal to the microprocessor when it has new data in the data register. The microprocessor then executes the interrupt service routine associated with the interrupt to read the data.

To output data, the microprocessor must make sure that the output device is not busy and can accept more data. There are two ways to do this:

1. *The polling method.* The interface chip has a data register that holds data that is to be output to the output device. The microprocessor should send new data to the interface chip only when the data register is empty. In this method, the interface chip uses a status bit to indicate if the output data register is empty. The microprocessor keeps checking the status bit until it indicates that the output data register is empty and then writes new data into it.

2. *The interrupt-driven method.* The interface chip activates an interrupt signal to the microprocessor when the output data register is empty and can accept more data. The microprocessor then executes the interrupt service routine associated with the interrupt and outputs the data.

6.4.2 Synchronizing the Interface Chip and the I/O Devices

The interface chip is responsible for making sure that data are properly transferred to and from I/O devices. The following methods have been used to synchronize data transfer between the interface chip and the I/O devices:

1. The brute-force method. Nothing special is done in this method. For input, the interface chip returns the voltage levels on the input port pins to the microprocessor. For output, the interface chip makes the data written by the microprocessor directly available on output port pins. This method is useful in situations in which the timing of data is unimportant. It can be used to test the voltage level of a signal, set the voltage of an output pin to high or low, or drive LEDs. All I/O ports of the MCS-51/52 can perform brute-force I/O.

2. *The strobe method.* This method uses strobe signals to indicate that data are stable on input or output port pins. During input, the input device activates a strobe signal when the data are stable on the input port pins. The interface chip latches data into the data register using the strobe signal. For output, the interface chip first places the output data on the output port pins. When the data become stable, the interface chip activates a strobe signal to inform the output device to latch the data on the output port pins. This method can be used if the interface chip and the I/O device can keep up with each other. None of the MCS-51/52 I/O ports supports the strobe I/O method.

3. *The handshake method.* The previous two methods cannot guarantee correct data transfer between an interface chip and an I/O device when the timing of data is critical. For example, it takes a much longer time to print a character than it does to send a character to the printer circuit, so data should not be sent to the printer if it is still printing. The solution is to use a handshake protocol between the interface chip and the printer circuit. There are two handshake methods: the *interlocked handshake* and the *pulse-mode handshake*. Whichever handshake protocol is used, two handshake signals are needed—one (call it H1) is asserted by the interface chip and the other (call it H2) is asserted by the I/O device. The handshake signal transactions for input and output are described in the following subsections. Note that the handshake operations of some interface chips may differ slightly from what we describe here. The MCS-51/52 microcontroller does not support handshake protocol.

Input Handshake Protocol

The signal transaction of the input handshake protocol is illustrated in Figure 6.2.

STEP 1   The interface chip asserts (or pulses) H1 to indicate its intention to input a byte.

STEP 2   The input device puts valid data on the data pins and also asserts (or pulses) the handshake signal H2.

STEP 3   The interface chip latches the data and deasserts the H1 signal. After some delay, the input device also deasserts the H2 signal. This action completes the input handshake cycle.

The whole process will be repeated if the microprocessor wants more data.

Output Handshake Protocol

The signal transaction for output handshaking is shown in Figure 6.3. It also takes place in three steps:

STEP 1   The interface chip places data on the data pins and asserts (or pulses) H1 to indicate that it has data to be output.

STEP 2   The output device latches the data and asserts (or pulses) H2 to acknowledge the receipt of data.

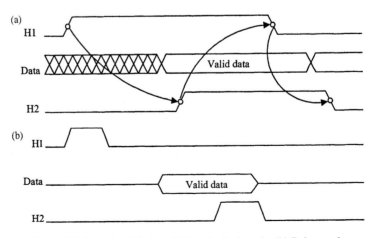

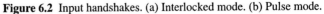

Figure 6.2 Input handshakes. (a) Interlocked mode. (b) Pulse mode.

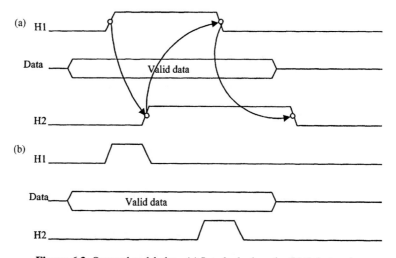

Figure 6.3 Output handshakes. (a) Interlocked mode. (b) Pulse mode.

STEP 3   The interface chip deasserts H1 following the assertion of H2. The output device then deasserts H2.

The whole process will be repeated if the microprocessor has more data to output.

6.5 MCS-51/52 PARALLEL I/O OVERVIEW

This section discusses the MCS-51/52 port structure and operation, I/O configuration, reading and writing, and port loading and interfacing.

6.5.1 Port Structures and Operation

The MCS-51/52 has 32 I/O pins that are further divided into four ports. All four ports are bidirectional. Each pin consists of a latch, an output driver, and an input buffer. The output drivers of port 0 and 2 and the input buffers of port 0 are used in accesses to external memory. In this application, port 0 outputs the lower byte of the external memory address, which is time multiplexed with the byte being written or read. Port 2 outputs the upper byte of the external memory address when the address is 16-bit wide. Otherwise the port 2 pins continue to emit the contents of the P2 special function register.

   All the port 3 pins and (in the MCS-52) two port 1 pins are multifunctional. They are not only port pins, but also serve the functions of various special features as listed in Tables 4.1–4.3. The alternate functions can be activated only if the corresponding bit latch in the port special function register contains a 1. Otherwise the port pin is stuck at 0.

6.5.2 I/O Configurations

Figure 6.4 shows a functional diagram of a typical bit latch and I/O buffer in each of the four ports. The bit latch (one bit in the port special function register) is represented as a type D flip-flop, which will clock in a value from the internal bus in response to a "write to latch" signal from the CPU. The Q output of the flip-flop is placed on the internal bus in response to a "read latch" signal from the CPU. The level of the port pin itself is placed on the internal bus in response to a "read pin" signal from the CPU. Some instructions that read a port activate the "read latch" signal, and others activate the "read pin" signal.

The instructions that read the latch rather than the pin are the ones that read a value, possibly change it, and then rewrite it to the latch. These are called *"read-modify-write"* instructions. The instructions listed in Table 6.1 are read-modify-write instructions.

The reason that read-modify-write instructions are directed to the latch rather than the pin is to avoid a possible misinterpretation of the voltage level at the pin. For example, a port bit might be used to drive the base of a transistor. When a 1 is written to the bit, the transistor is turned on. If the CPU then reads the same port bit at the pin rather than the latch, it will read the base voltage of the transistor and interpret it as a 0. Reading the latch rather than the pin will return the correct value of 1.

As shown in Figure 6.4, the output drivers of ports 0 and 2 are switchable to an internal ADDR/DATA and ADDR bus by an internal CONTROL signal for use in external memory accesses. During external memory accesses, the P2 special function register remains unchanged, but the P0 special function register gets 1s written to it.

Figure 6.4 also shows that if a P3 bit latch contains a 1, the output level is controlled by the signal labeled "alternate output function." The actual P3.X pin level is always available to the pin's alternate input function, if any.

Ports 1, 2, and 3 have internal pull-ups. Port 0 has open drain outputs. Each I/O line can be independently used as input or output. To be used as input, the port bit latch must contain a 1, which turns off the output driver FET. Then, for ports 1, 2, and 3, each pin is pulled high by the internal pull-up, but can be pulled low by an external source.

Port 0 differs in not having internal pull-ups. The pull-up FET in the P0 output driver

TABLE 6.1
MCS-51 Read-Modify-Write Instructions

Mnemonic	Function	Example
ANL	Logical AND	ANL P1,A
ORL	Logical OR	ORL P2,A
XRL	Logical XOR	XRL P3,A
JBC	Jump if bit = 1 and clear bit	JBC P1.1,label
CPL	Complement bit	CPL P3,0
INC	Increment	INC P2
DEC	Decrement	DEC P2
DJNZ	Decrement and jump if not 0	DNJZ P3,label
MOV PX,Y,C	Move carry bit to bit Y or port X	
CLR PX,Y	Clear bit Y of port X	
SETB PX,Y	Set bit Y of port X	

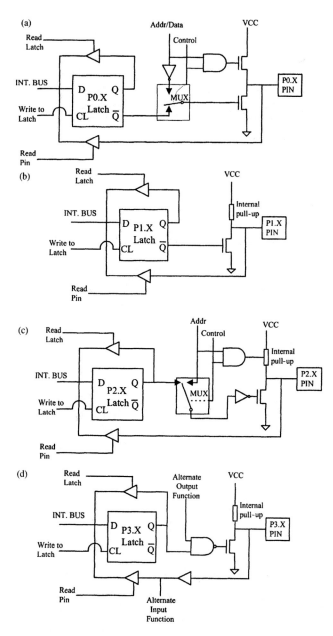

Figure 6.4 8XC51FX port bit latches and I/O buffers. (a) Port 0 bit. (b) Port 1 bit. (c) Port 2 bit. (d) Port 3 bit. (Redrawn with permission of Intel.)

is used only when the port is emitting 1s during external memory accesses. Otherwise the pull-up FET is off. Consequently P0 lines that are being used as output port lines are open drains. Writing a 1 to the bit latch leaves both output FETs off, so the pin floats. In that condition it can be used as a high-impedance input.

Because ports 1, 2, and 3 have fixed internal pull-ups they are sometimes called "quasibidirectional" ports. When configured as inputs they will pull high and will source current when they are externally pulled low. Port 0, on the other hand, is considered "true" bidirectional, because when configured as an input it floats.

All the port latches in the MCS-51/52 have 1s written to them by the reset function. If a 0 is subsequently written to a port latch, it can be reconfigured as input by writing a 1 to it. For the 8XC51FX, port 1 bit latches and I/O buffers are identical to those of port 3.

6.6 SIMPLE INPUT DEVICES

An input device is any device that can send a binary number to the microprocessor. Examples of input devices include switches, analog-to-digital converters, and keyboards. A set of eight dual line package (DIP) switches is probably the simplest input device that we can find. Such switches can be connected directly to an I/O port of the MCS-51, as shown in Figure 6.5. When a switch is closed, the associated port 0 pin is 0. Otherwise, the associated port 0 pin has an input of 1. Each port 0 pin is pulled up to high via a 10-kΩ resistor when the associated switch is open.

Example 6.1 Write a sequence of instructions to read the values from a set of eight DIP switches connected to port 1 of the MCS-51/52.

Solution:

```
mov   P1,#FFH      ; configure port 1 as input
mov   A,P1         ; read a byte from port 1.
      .
      .
      .
```

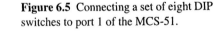

Figure 6.5 Connecting a set of eight DIP switches to port 1 of the MCS-51.

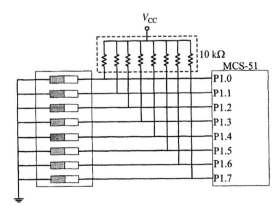

Inputting data to the computer usually requires interaction with the user. The procedure is as follows:

STEP 1   Output a message to prompt the user to enter a value.

STEP 2   Set a new value to the eight DIP switches.

STEP 3   Use interrupt or other methods to inform the user program to read the value.

Repeat Steps 1 to 3 as many times as needed.

6.7 INTERFACING PARALLEL PORTS WITH THE KEYBOARD

A keyboard or keypad is often organized as a matrix of switches, which can be mechanical, membrane, capacitive, or Hall-effect in construction. In mechanical switches, two metal contacts are brought together to complete an electrical circuit. The drawback of a mechanical keyboard is its size. In membrane switches, a plastic or rubber membrane presses one conductor onto another; this type of switch can be made very thin, and as a sealed unit. Capacitive switches internally are comprised of two plates of a parallel plate capacitor; pressing the key cap effectively increases the capacitance between the two plates. Special circuitry is needed to detect this change in capacitance, but the advantage of this type of switch is that it does not use mechanical contacts (which can become dirty and corroded over time). In a *Hall-effect* key switch, the motion of the magnetic lines of a permanent magnet perpendicular to a crystal induces a voltage between the two faces of the crystal—it is this voltage that registers a switch closure. These four switch types are shown in Figure 6.6.

Because of their construction, mechanical switches have a problem called *contact bounce*. Instead of producing a single, clean pulse output, pressing a mechanical switch generates a series of pulses because the switch contacts do not come to rest immediately. This phenomenon is illustrated in Figure 6.7, where it can be seen that a single physical press of the button results in multiple electrical signals being generated and sent to the computer. Because the microprocessor is much faster than the pressing of the keyboard, a single key press will be registered as multiple key presses, as the key bounces. A debouncing scheme

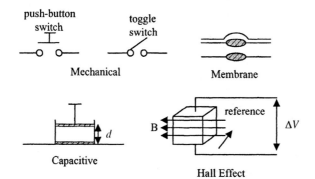

Figure 6.6 Switch types.

is called for. Debouncing may be accomplished in hardware or in software. A keyboard-input program can be divided into three stages, which will be discussed in the following subsections:

1. Keyboard scanning to find out which key has been pressed.
2. Key debouncing to make sure a key was indeed pressed.
3. Table lookup to find the ASCII code of the key that was pressed.

6.7.1 Keypad Scanning Techniques

A keypad with more than a few keys is often arranged as a matrix of switches that uses two decoding and/or selecting devices to determine which key was pressed by coincident recognition of the row and column of the key.

As shown in Figure 6.8, a 16-key keypad is interfaced with the port 1 of the MCS-51/52. Pins P1.7–P1.4 select the rows, and pins P1.3–P1.0 select the columns. The row selection of the 16-key keypad is shown in Table 6.2. When a key is pressed, the corresponding row and column are shorted together. For example, the P1.4 output should be set to low to detect whether key 0, 1, 2, or 3 is pressed. If key 3 was pressed, the P1.3 input would be a low value.

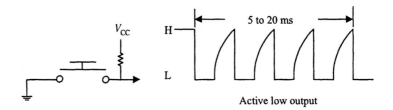

Figure 6.7 Contact bounce.

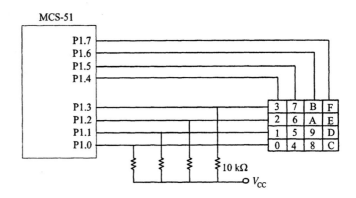

Figure 6.8 Sixteen-key keypad connected to MCS-51.

TABLE 6.2
Sixteen-Key Keypad Row Selections

P1.7	P1.6	P1.5	P1.4	Selected Keys
1	1	1	0	0, 1, 2, and 3
1	1	0	1	4, 5, 6, and 7
1	0	1	1	8, 9, A, and B
0	1	1	1	C, D, E, and F

The keypad scanning logic flow is illustrated in Figure 6.9. The instruction sequence for keyboard scanning is as follows:

```
scan:       mov   P1,#EFH      ; set lower 4 bits of P1 as input and set P1.4 to 0
            jnb   P1.0,dbt_0   ; debounce key 0 if it is pressed
scan_1:     jnb   P1.1,dbt_1   ; debounce key 1 if it is pressed
scan_2:     jnb   P1.2,dbt_2   ; debounce key 2 if it is pressed
scan_3:     jnb   P1.3,dbt_3   ; debounce key 3 if it is pressed
scan_4:     mov   P1,#DFH      ; prepare to scan the row containing keys 4–7
            jnb   P1.0,dbt_4   ; debounce key 4 if it is pressed
scan_5:     jnb   P1.1,dbt_5   ; debounce key 5 if it is pressed
scan_6:     jnb   P1.2,dbt_6   ; debounce key 6 if it is pressed
scan_7:     jnb   P1.3,dbt_7   ; debounce key 7 if it is pressed
scan_8:     mov   P1,#BFH      ; prepare to scan the row containing keys 8–B
            jnb   P1.0,dbt_8   ; debounce key 8 if it is pressed
scan_9:     jnb   P1.1,dbt_9   ; debounce key 9 if it is pressed
scan_A:     jnb   P1.2,dbt_A   ; debounce key A if it is pressed
scan_B:     jnb   P1.3,dbt_B   ; debounce key B if it is pressed
scan_C:     mov   P1,#7FH      ; prepare to scan the row containing keys C–F
            jnb   P1.0,dbt_C   ; debounce key C if it is pressed
scan_D:     jnb   P1.1,dbt_D   ; debounce key D if it is pressed
scan_E:     jnb   P1.2,dbt_E   ; debounce key E if it is pressed
scan_F:     jnb   P1.3,dbt_F   ; debounce key F if it is pressed
            ljmp  scan         ; continue to scan
dbt_0:      ljmp  db_0
dbt_1:      ljmp  db_1
dbt_2:      ljmp  db_2
dbt_3:      ljmp  db_3
dbt_4:      ljmp  db_4
dbt_5:      ljmp  db_5
dbt_6:      ljmp  db_6
```

dbt_7:	ljmp	db_7
dbt_8:	ljmp	db_8
dbt_9:	ljmp	db_9
dbt_A:	ljmp	db_A
dbt_B:	ljmp	db_B
dbt_C:	ljmp	db_C
dbt_D:	ljmp	db_D
dbt_E:	ljmp	db_E
dbt_F:	ljmp	db_F

6.7.2 Keyboard Debouncing

Contact bounce is due to the dynamics of a closing contact. The signal falls and rises a few times within a period of about 5 ms as the contact bounces. Since a human being cannot press and release a switch in less than 20 ms, a debouncer will recognize that the switch is closed after the voltage is low for about 10 ms and will recognize that the switch is open after the voltage is high for about 10 ms.

Both hardware and software solutions to the key bounce problem are available. Using a good switch can reduce keyboard bouncing. A mercury switch is much faster and optical and Hall-effect switches are free of bounce. Hardware solutions to contact bounce include an analog circuit that uses a resistor and a capacitor to smooth the voltage and two digital solutions that use set–reset flip-flops or CMOS buffers and double-throw switches.

In practice, hardware and software debouncing techniques are both used (but not at the same time). Dedicated hardware scanner chips are also available—typical ones are the National Semiconductor 74C922 and 74C923. These two chips perform both keyboard scanning and debouncing.

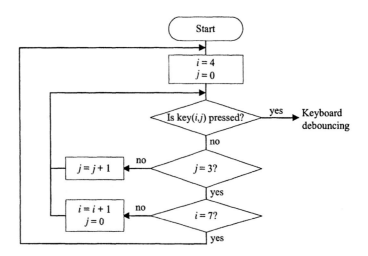

Figure 6.9 Flowchart of keypad scanning of the circuit in Figure 6.8.

Hardware Debouncing Techniques

- *Set–reset flip-flops.* Before being pressed, the key is touching either the set or reset input. When pressed, the key moves to the other position. When the key bounces, it will not return to its original position. Both the set and reset inputs are pulled up to high, and hence the output Q will not change. Since the flip-flop has memory, the key will be recognized as closed. This solution guarantees that the flip-flop changes value only once when the key plate moves from one side to the other. This solution is illustrated in Figure 6.10a.

- *Noninverting CMOS gates with high-input impedance.* This is shown in Figure 6.10b. The gate output is high or low when it is on the top or bottom plate. When the key switch moves, the resistor tends to hold the input where it was. On the first bounce, the output changes, and it remains at that level as the switch leaves the plate, because of the resistor. Successive bounces do not change the output. Thus, the output is debounced.

- *Integrating debouncers.* The RC constant of the integrator determines the rate at which the capacitor charges up toward the supply voltage once the ground connection via the switch has been removed. As long as the capacitor voltage does not exceed the logic one threshold value, the V_{out} signal will continue to be recognized as a logic zero. This solution is shown in Figure 6.10c.

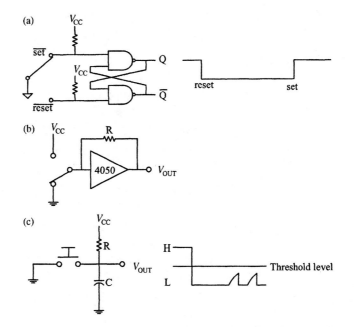

Figure 6.10 Hardware debouncing techniques. (a) Set–reset circuit. (b) CMOS gate debouncer. (c) Integrating RC circuit debounce.

Software Debouncing Techniques

The easiest software solution to the key bounce problem is the *wait-and-see* technique. When the input drops, indicating that the switch might be closed, the program will wait for 10 ms and look at the same key again. If it is still low, the program decides that the key has indeed been pressed. If it is high, the program decides that the input signal was noise or that the input was bouncing—if it was bouncing, it will certainly be clear later if the key was actually pressed. In either case, the program returns to wait for the input to drop. The instruction sequence that performs keyboard debouncing is as follows:

```
debnce:
db_0:       lcall   wt_10ms         ; wait for 10 ms
            jb      P1.0,temp_1     ; is the key 0 indeed pressed?
            mov     A,#0            ; yes.
            ljmp    get_code        ; look up the ASCII code of 0
temp_1:     ljmp    scan_1
db_1:       lcall   wt_10ms         ; wait for 10 ms
            jb      P1.1,temp_2     ; is the key 1 indeed pressed?
            mov     A,#1            ; yes
            ljmp    get_code        ; look up the ASCII code of 1
temp_2:     ljmp    scan_2
db_2:       lcall   wt_10ms         ; wait for 10 ms
            jb      P1.2,temp_3     ; is the key 2 indeed pressed?
            mov     A,#2            ; yes
            ljmp    get_code        ; look up the ASCII code of 2
temp_3:     ljmp    scan_3
db_3:       lcall   wt_10ms         ; wait for 10 ms
            jb      P1.3,temp_4     ; is the key 3 indeed pressed?
            mov     A,#3            ; yes
            ljmp    get_code        ; look up the ASCII code of 3
temp_4:     ljmp    scan_4
db_4:       lcall   wt_10ms         ; wait for 10 ms
            jb      P1.0,temp_5     ; is the key 4 indeed pressed?
            mov     A,#4            ; yes
            ljmp    get_code        ; look up the ASCII code of 4
temp_5:     ljmp    scan_5
db_5:       lcall   wt_10ms         ; wait for 10 ms
            jb      P1.1,temp_6     ; is the key 5 indeed pressed?
            mov     A,#5            ; yes
            ljmp    get_code        ; look up the ASCII code of 5
temp_6:     ljmp    scan_6
```

```
db_6:       lcall   wt_10ms         ; wait for 10 ms
            jb      P1.2,temp_7     ; is the key 6 indeed pressed?
            mov     A,#6            ; yes
            ljmp    get_code        ; look up the ASCII code of 6
temp_7:     ljmp    scan_7
db_7:       lcall   wt_10ms         ; wait for 10 ms
            jb      P1.3,temp_8     ; is the key 7 indeed pressed?
            mov     A,#7            ; yes
            ljmp    get_code        ; look up the ASCII code of 7
temp_8:     ljmp    scan_8
db_8:       lcall   wt_10ms         ; wait for 10 ms
            jb      P1.0,temp_9     ; is the key 8 indeed pressed?
            mov     A,#8            ; yes
            ljmp    get_code        ; look up the ASCII code of 8
temp_9:     ljmp    scan_9
db_9:       lcall   wt_10ms         ; wait for 10 ms
            jb      P1.1,temp_A     ; is the key 9 indeed pressed?
            mov     A,#9            ; yes
            ljmp    get_code        ; look up the ASCII code of 9
temp_A:     ljmp    scan_A
db_A:       lcall   wt_10ms         ; wait for 10 ms
            jb      P1.2,temp_B     ; is the key A indeed pressed?
            mov     A,#10           ; yes
            ljmp    get_code        ; look up the ASCII code of A
temp_B:     ljmp    scan_B
db_B:       lcall   wt_10ms         ; wait for 10 ms
            jb      P1.3,temp_C     ; is the key B indeed pressed?
            mov     A,#11           ; yes
            ljmp    get_code        ; look up the ASCII code of B
temp_C:     ljmp    scan_C
db_C:       lcall   wt_10ms         ; wait for 10 ms
            jb      P1.0,temp_D     ; is the key C indeed pressed?
            mov     A,#12           ; yes
            ljmp    get_code        ; look up the ASCII code of C
temp_D:     ljmp    scan_D
db_D:       lcall   wt_10ms         ; wait for 10 ms
            jb      P1.1,temp_E     ; is the key D indeed pressed?
            mov     A,#13           ; yes
            ljmp    get_code        ; look up the ASCII code of D
```

```
temp_E:      ljmp    scan_E
db_E:        lcall   wt_10ms         ; wait for 10 ms
             jb      P1.2,temp_F     ; is the key E indeed pressed?
             mov     A,#14           ; yes
             ljmp    get_code        ; look up the ASCII code of E
temp_F:      ljmp    scan_F
db_F:        lcall   wt_10ms         ; wait for 10 ms
             jnb     P1.3,getc       ; is the key F indeed pressed?
             ljmp    scan
getc:        mov     A,#15           ; yes
             ljmp    get_code        ; lookup the ASCII code of F
```

The subroutine *wt_10ms* simply waits for 10 ms and return. This routine can be implemented by program loops or timer function. The timer version of the delay routine will be discussed in Chapter 7.

6.7.3 ASCII Code Table Lookup

After the key has been debounced, the program should look up the ASCII table and send the corresponding ASCII code to the CPU. The instruction sequence for looking up the ASCII code in a table is

```
get_code:    mov     DPTR,#key_tab
             movc    A,@A+DPTR       ; look up the ASCII code table
             lcall   display         ; send the character for display
             ljmp    scan            ; continue to scan the keypad
key_tab:     db      '0123456789ABCDEF'
             END
```

After looking up the ASCII code, the program calls the *display* routine to display the digit and then jumps back to the beginning of the scanning subroutine. The display routine is not shown here.

6.8 SIMPLE OUTPUT DEVICES

A microcontroller is often connected to several different kinds of output devices. These output devices include light-emitting diodes (LED), seven-segment displays constructed from LEDs, liquid-crystal displays (LCDs), motors, digital-to-analog converters, vacuum tube devices such as fluorescent displays, printers, and so on.

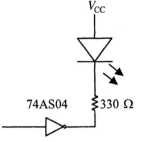

Figure 6.11 An LED connected to a CMOS inverter through a current limiting resistor.

V_{CC}

74AS04   330 Ω

6.8.1 A Single LED

An LED can illuminate if it is forward biased and has enough current flowing through it. The current required to light an LED may range from a few to more than 10 mA. The voltage drop across the LED when it is forward biased can range from about 1.6 to more than 2 V.

LED indicators are easy to be interfaced with the microcontroller if the interface circuit has at least 10 mA of current available to drive the LED. LEDs require series resistors to limit the current passing through them, as depicted in Figure 6.11. The voltage drop across the lighted LED is about 2.0 V in this circuit. (The LED nominally drops 1.65 V, but in practice the drop more often is closer to 2.0 V.) The remaining 3 V is dropped across the series current-limiting resistor. To limit the current to 10 mA, a 300-Ω resistor should be used. In this example, a 330-Ω resistor is used because it is the resistor closest in value available. This interface, or one that is similar, must be used if the current available to drive the LED is less than 10 mA.

All four I/O ports of the MCS-51/52 can drive LED devices using the circuit as shown in Figure 6.11.

Example 6.2 Use the MCS-51/52 port 1 pins P1.2, P1.1, and P1.0 to drive green, yellow, and red LEDs. Light the green LED for 1 s, then the yellow LED for 1 s, and then the red LED for 1 s and then repeat.

Solution: The circuit connection is shown in Figure 6.12. The 74AS04 can sink 20 mA of current when its output is low.

Port 1 of the MCS-51/52 must output appropriate values to turn LEDs on and off. A two-level loop is used to create the 1 s delay. The inner loop creates a 5-ms delay whereas the outer loop simply repeats the inner loop for 200 times to create a time delay of 1 s. Due to the subroutine call and loop overhead, the actual delay is 806 ms longer for a 12-MHz crystal oscillator. The program is as follows:

```
LED_light:    mov    P1,#04H        ; turn on green, turn off yellow and red
              lcall  wt_1sec        ; wait for 1 s
              mov    P1,#02H        ; turn on yellow, turn off green and red
              lcall  wt_1sec        ; wait for 1 s
              mov    P1,#01H        ; turn on red, turn off green and yellow
```

```
                    lcall    wt_1sec        ; wait for 1 s
                    ajmp     LED_light      ; repeat for ever
; The following routine creates a one-second delay
wt_1sec:            mov      R1,#200        ; initialize outer loop count to 200
L1:                 mov      R0,#250        ; initialize inner loop count to 250
L2:                 push     ACC            ; 2 machine cycles
                    pop      ACC            ; "
                    push     ACC            ; "
                    pop      ACC            ; "
                    push     ACC            ; "
                    pop      ACC            ; "
                    push     ACC            ; "
                    pop      ACC            ; "
                    nop                     ; 1 machine cycle
                    nop      ; "
                    djnz     R0,L2          ; 2 machine cycles
                    djnz     R1,L1          ; 2 machine cycles
                    ret                     ; 2 machine cycles
```

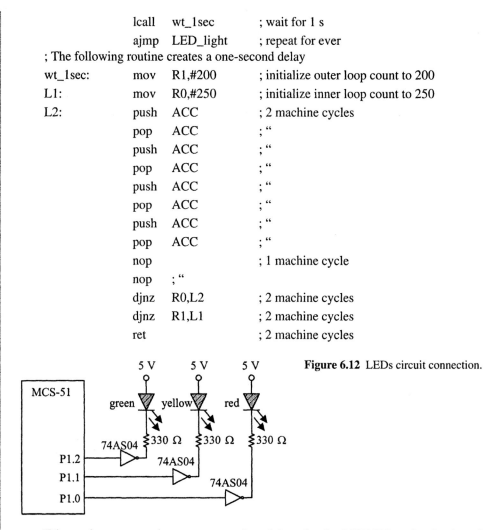

Figure 6.12 LEDs circuit connection.

When using program loops to create time delays for the MCB520 evaluation board, we need to make some changes because

- One machine cycle consists of 4 instead of 12 oscillator cycles.
- The DS87C520 crystal oscillator frequency is 33 MHz.

One machine cycle in a DS87C520 running at 33 MHz is 121.21 ns ($4 \times 1000/33$ ns). It should be fairly straightforward to modify the above instruction sequence to create a delay of 1 s.

6.8.2 The Seven-Segment Display

A seven-segment display consists of seven LED segments (a, b, c, d, e, f, g). Seven-segment displays come in either common-anode or common-cathode form. In a *common-anode display*, the anodes of all seven LEDs are tied together and a segment will be lighted whenever a low voltage is applied at the corresponding segment input and the common anode is connected to high. In a common-cathode display, the cathodes of all seven LEDs are tied together and a segment will be lighted if a high voltage is applied to the corresponding segment input and the common cathode is connected to the ground. Diagrams of a common-cathode and a common-anode seven-segment display are shown in Figure 6.13. The current required to light a segment is similar to that required to light an LED.

Seven-segment displays are mainly used to display binary-coded decimal (BCD) digits. Any parallel port of the MCS-51/52 can be used to drive seven-segment displays. One port is adequate if there is only one seven segment to be driven. The total supply current of the 8XC51FX (shown in Table 6.3) is not enough to drive the seven-segment display directly, but this problem can be solved by adding a buffer chip such as 74ALS244. The circuit shown in Figure 6.14 uses port 1 to drive a common-cathode seven-segment display.

The output high voltage (V_{OH}) of the 74ALS244 is about 3 V. Since the voltage drop of one LED segment is about 1.7 V, a 100-Ω current-limiting resistor will limit the current to about 13 mA, which should be adequate to light an LED segment. The light patterns shown in Table 6.4 require that segments a, . . . , g be connected from the second most significant bit to the least significant bit of the output port.

There is often a need to display multiple BCD digits, and this can be achieved by using the time-multiplexing technique, which will be discussed shortly. An example of a circuit that can display four BCD digits is shown in Figure 6.15. In Figure 6.15, the common cathode of each display is connected to the collector of a 2N2222 transistor.

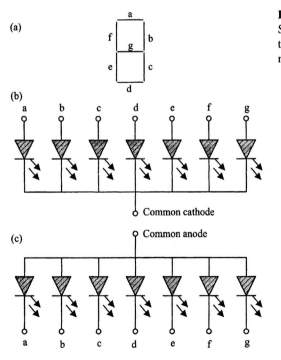

(a)

(b)

Common cathode

(c)   Common anode

Figure 6.13 Seven-segment displays. (a) Seven-segment display. (b) Common-cathode seven-segment display. (c) Common-anode seven-segment display.

TABLE 6.3
Total Supply Current of the 8XC51FX

Operation Mode	Operating Frequency (MHz)	Total Supply Current (mA)	
		Typical	Max
Active mode	12	15	30
	16	20	38
	24	28	56
	33	35	56
Idle mode	12	5	7.5
	16	6	9.5
	24	7	13.5
	33	7	15
Power-down mode		5 μA	75 μA

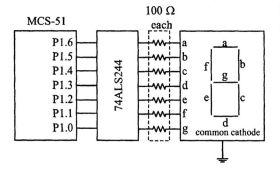

Figure 6.14 The MCS-51 drives a single seven-segment display.

TABLE 6.4
BCD to Seven-Segment Decoder

BCD Digit	Segments							Corresponding Hex Number
	a	b	c	d	e	f	g	
0	1	1	1	1	1	1	0	7EH
1	0	1	1	0	0	0	0	30H
2	1	1	0	1	1	0	1	6DH
3	1	1	1	1	0	0	1	79H
4	0	1	1	0	0	1	1	33H
5	1	0	1	1	0	1	1	5BH
6	1	0	1	1	1	1	1	5FH
7	1	1	1	0	0	0	0	70H
8	1	1	1	1	1	1	1	7FH
9	1	1	1	1	0	1	1	7BH

When a port 3 pin is high, the connected 2N2222 transistor will be turned on and be driven into the saturation region. The common cathode of the display will then be pulled down to low (0.1~0.2 V), allowing the display to be lighted. The value of the base resistor

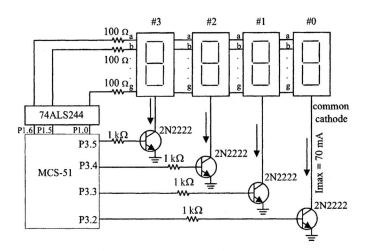

Figure 6.15 MCS-51 drives four seven-segment displays.

must be chosen so that the 2N2222 transistor is driven into saturation region when a P3 pin outputs a high value. By turning the four transistors on and off many times in a second, four digits can be displayed simultaneously. A 2N2222 can sink from 100 to 300 mA of current. The maximum current that flows into the common cathode is about 70 mA (7 × 10 mA = 70 mA) and hence can be handled by a 2N2222 transistor.

It is not difficult to verify that the 2N2222 transistors in Figure 6.15 are driven into saturation region when their base voltages are high and this problem will be left as an exercise problem.

Example 6.3 Write a sequence of instructions to display 1 on the #0 seven-segment display.

Solution: To display a 1 on the display #0, the numbers 30H and 04H must be written into ports P1 and P3, respectively. The number 30H is the segment pattern of digit 1. The following instruction sequence allows only the display #0 to illuminate:

```
mov    P1,#30H        ; output the segment pattern of digit 1
anl    P3,#C3H        ; turn off all displays
orl    P3,#04H        ; allow the display #0 to light
```

The second and the third instructions in the above set the pin P3.2 to 1 and pins P3.5~P3.3 to 0. The circuit in Figure 6.15 can display four BCD digits simultaneously by using the time-multiplexing technique, in which each seven-segment display is lighted in turn for a short period of time and then turned off. When one display is lighted, all other displays are turned off. Within 1 s, each seven-segment display is turned on and then turned off many times. Because of the *persistence of vision*, all four displays will appear to be lighted simultaneously and continuously. The idea is illustrated in the flowchart in Figure 6.16; in this example, each digit is lighted for 2.5 ms at a time.

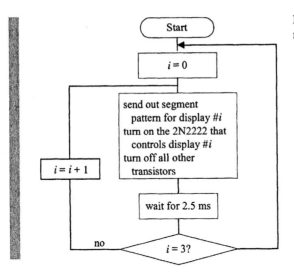

Figure 6.16 Program logic flow for time-multiplexing displays.

Example 6.4 Display 4321 on the four seven-segment displays shown in Figure 6.15.

Solution: Display digits 4, 3, 2, and 1 on the seven-segment displays #3, #2, #1, and #0, respectively. Write the numbers in Table 6.5 into the P1 and P3 registers, respectively. Use the following assembler directives to create Table 6.5:

```
display:    DB   33H,20H
            DB   79H,10H
            DB   6DH,08H
            DB   30H,04H
```

TABLE 6.5
Display Pattern of Example 6.4

Seven-Segment Display	Displayd BCD Digit	Port 1 Pattern	Port 3 Value
#3	4	33H	20H
#2	3	79H	10H
#1	2	6DH	08H
#0	1	30H	04H

The following program will turn on each seven-segment display for 2.5 ms at a time. Thus each seven-segment display will be turned on and off 100 times per second.

```
              org    4000H          ; starting address of the program
              mov    DPTR,#display  ; place the base address of the table in DPTR
  forever:    mov    B,#0           ; initialize the loop count
  next:       mov    A,B
              movc   A,@A+DPTR      ; get the light pattern
              mov    P1,A
```

```
            inc     B
            mov     A,B
            movc    A,@A+DPTR        ; get the transistor control value
            mov     P3,A
            inc     B
; The following instructions create a delay of 2.5 ms
            mov     R1,#125
L1:         push    ACC              ; 2 machine cycles
            pop     ACC              ; "
            push    ACC              ; "
            pop     ACC              ; "
            push    ACC              ; "
            pop     ACC              ; "
            push    ACC              ; "
            pop     ACC              ; "
            nop                      ; 1 machine cycle
            nop                      ; "
            djnz    R1,L1            ; 2 machine cycles
            cjne    B,#8,next
            ljmp    forever          ; start from the beginning of the table

display:    DB      33H,20H
            DB      79H,10H
            DB      6DH,08H
            DB      30H,04H
            END
```

6.8.3 Driving Liquid-Crystal Displays Using the MCS-51/52 Parallel Ports

The liquid-crystal display (LCD), which is found on many digital wrist watches, calculators, telephones, facsimile machines, point-of-sale (POS) terminals, electronic typewriters, measuring instruments, etc., is among the most familiar output devices. Unlike the LED display, the main advantage of the LCD display is that it has very high contrast so it can be seen extremely well in very bright light. The main problem with the LCD is that it requires a light source in dimly lit environments. However, the light consumes more power than the entire display.

Figure 6.17 illustrates the basic construction of an LCD display. The LCD type of display that is most common allows light to pass through it whenever it is activated. Earlier LCD displays absorbed light. Activation of a segment requires a low-frequency bipolar

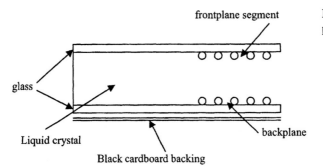

Figure 6.17 A liquid-crystal display (LCD).

excitation voltage of 30–1000 Hz. The polarity of this voltage must change, or else the LCD will not be able to change very quickly.

The LCD functions in the following manner. When a voltage is applied across the LCD segment, it sets up an electrostatic field that aligns the crystals in the liquid. This alignment allows light to pass through the segment. If no voltage is applied across a segment, the crystals appear to be opaque because they are randomly aligned. The ac excitation voltage applied to each segment ensures random alignment. In a digital watch, the segments appear to be darkened when they are activated because light passes through the segment to a black cardboard backing that absorbs all light. The area surrounding the activated segment appears brighter in color because the randomly aligned crystals reflect much of the light. In a *backlit* computer display, the segment appears to grow brighter because of a light placed behind the display; the light is allowed to pass through the segment when it is activated.

Many manufacturers have developed color LCD displays for use in computers and small color televisions. LCD is the only display used in notebook computers. It uses three segments (dots) for each picture element (pixel), and the three dots are filtered so that they pass red, blue, and green light. By varying the number of dots and the amount of time each dot is active, just about any color and intensity can be displayed. White color consists of 59% green, 30% red, and 11% blue light. Secondary colors are magenta (red and blue), cyan (blue and green), and yellow (red and green). Any other colors, not just secondary colors, can be obtained by mixing red, green, and blue light.

LCD needs a driving circuit to work. To simplify the design and interfacing, the driving circuit and LCD are often integrated into a single module. Shown in Figure 6.18 is the block diagram of an integrated LCD module manufactured by Hitachi.

The Hitachi LM015 can display one line of 16 characters. The microcontroller needs to provide only several initialization bytes to set up the display for an operating mode to

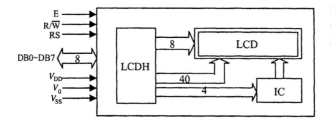

Figure 6.18 Block diagram of the character display module LM015 by Hitachi.

fit the project, then supply ASCII data of those characters to be displayed. The display has one register into which commands are sent, and one register into which data to be displayed are sent. These two registers are differentiated by the RS input. The data lines (DB7~DB0) are used to transfer both commands (clearing, homing, cursor positioning, etc.) and data (characters to be displayed). Incoming bytes will be treated as commands when RS is low and as data to be displayed when RS is high. We need to allocate a memory space to this device and use the address decoder to select it for data transfer. The E input is normally connected to the address decoder output. In Figure 6.19, the address space 6000H~7FFFH is assigned to the LM015. The circuit connection allows the microcontroller to send commands and data to the LCD and also to read the status from the LCD.

The commands to the LC015 can be classified into four types:

- Designate functions such as display format, data length, etc.
- Give internal RAM addresses.
- Perform data transfer with internal RAM.
- Others.

A subset of LM015 commands is shown in Table 6.6. These commands take much longer than a machine cycle to execute. Therefore, we need to insert time delay between any two commands or data sent to the LM015. For example, the procedure to send the string "87C51FB" is shown in Table 6.7. In Table 6.7, an appropriate delay must be added between two consecutive commands sent to the LM015. These steps can easily be translated into appropriate MCS-51 instructions.

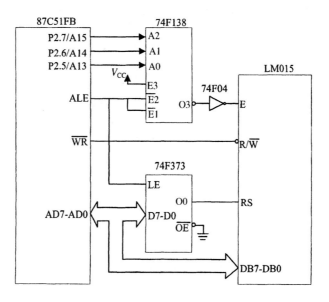

Figure 6.19 The circuit connection between LM015 and the MCS-51.

TABLE 6.6
A Subset of LM015 Commands[a]

Instruction	Command Code	Description	Execution Time
Clear display	0000 0 0 0 1	Clears all display and returns the cursor to the home poisition (address 0)	82 μs~1.64 ms
Return home	0000 0 0 1 x	Returns the cursor to home position; returns the display being shifted to the original position; display data RAM (DD/RAM) contents remain unchanged	40μs~1.6 ms
Entry mode set	0000 0 1 I/D S	Sets the cursor move direction and specifies to shift or not to shift	40 μs
Display on/off control	0000 1 D C B	Sets on/off of all display (D), cursor on/off (C), and blink of cursor position character (B)	40 μs
Function set	0011 N F xx	Sets interface 8-bit data, number of display lines (N), and character font (F)	120 μs
Write data to DD RAM or CG	Write data	Writes data into DD RAM or CG RAM	120 μs
Read data from CG or DD RAM	Read data	Read data from DD RAM or CG RAM	40 μs

[a] I/D = 1, increment; 0, decrement. C = 1, cursor on; 0, cursor off. S = 1, be accompanied with display shift. B = 1, blink cursor position. N = 1, 2 lines; 0, 1 line. F = 1, 5 $\times$ 10 dots; 0, 5 $\times$ 7 dots. CG RAM, character generator RAM. DD RAM, display data RAM.

TABLE 6.7
Steps for Sending "87C51FB" to the LM015

No.	Instruction	Operation	
1	power on		Initialize; no display appears
2	0011 00xx		Select 8-bit operation, 1-line display, and 5 $\times$ 7 font
3	0000 1110	_	Turn on display and cursor; Entire display is in space
4	0000 0110	_	Set mode to increment the address by one and to shift the cursor to the right of write to the DD/CG RAM; display is not shifted
5	0011 1000	8_	Write "8"
6	0011 0111	87_	Write "7"
7	0100 0011	87C_	Write "C"
8	0011 0101	87C5_	Write "5"
9	0011 0001	87C51_	Write "1"
10	0100 0110	87C51F_	Write "F"
11	0100 0010	87C51FB_	Write "B"

6.8.4 Interfacing with the D/A Converter (DAC) Using the MCS-51/52 Parallel Ports

Digital-to-analog conversion is required when a digital code must be converted to an analog signal. For example, an 8-bit DAC with a step voltage of 0.01 V will generate output voltages between 0.0 and 2.55 V with 0.01 V step. A 00000000B input to this type of DAC generates

0.0 V output. A 11111111B input to the DAC generates 2.55 V output. Any voltage in this range is generated with the appropriate digital number applied to the input. The maximum output voltage is called *full-scale*.

The step voltage is not always 0.01 V. Step voltages vary with the full-scale voltage of the converter. For example, if an 8-bit DAC has a full-scale voltage of +5.0 V, the step voltage is +5.0 V/255 or 0.0196 V per step. The step voltage is always the full-scale voltage divided by $2^n - 1$. A 10-bit converter using +5.0 V as full-scale has a step voltage of +5.0 V/($2^{10} - 1$) or +5.0 V/1023, which is 0.00489 V per step.

The analog signal can be used to control the output level of another system, for example, the flow level of a fluid system or the volume level of a stereo system. A general DAC consists of a network of precision resistors, input switches, and level shifters that activates the switches that convert a digital code to an analog voltage or current. A DAC may also contain input or output buffers, amplifiers, and internal references.

The AD7248A manufactured by Analog Device is a 12-bit DAC that produces an output voltage proportional to the digital input code. Figure 6.20 illustrates the pin-out of the AD7248A. This device functions with a single power supply with a range of +12 to +15 V. The AD7248A can interface directly with most microprocessor and microcontroller buses and ports. For single supply operation, two output ranges of 0 to +5 V and 0 to +10 V are available. These two ranges plus an additional ±5 V range are available with dual power supplies.

Pin Functions

V_{SS} (*Negative supply voltage*). 0 V for single supply operation.

R_{OFS} (*Bipolar OFS offset resistor*). This provides access to the on-chip application resistors and allows different output voltage ranges.

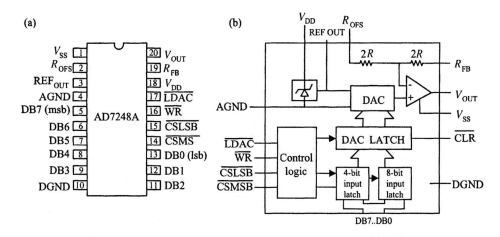

Figure 6.20 AD7248A pin assignment (a) and block diagram (b). (Redrawn with permission of Analog Devices.)

REF OUT   (*Reference output*). This on-chip reference is provided at this pin and is used when configuring the D/A converter for bipolar (both negative and positive) outputs.

AGAND   (*Analog ground*). Normally connected to the ground of the analog system.

DGAND   (*Digital ground*). Normally connected to the ground of the digital system.

DB7–DB0   (*Data bit 7 to data bit 0*). Digital input pins.

$\overline{\text{CSMSB}}$ (*Chip select for MS nibble*). This signal selects the upper 4 bits of the input latch.

$\overline{\text{CSLSB}}$ (*Chip select for LS byte*). *This signal selects the lower 8 bits of the input latch.*

$\overline{\text{WR}}$ (*Write input*). This is used in conjunction with CSMSB and CSLSB to load data into the input latch of the AD7248A.

$\overline{\text{LDAC}}$ (*Load DAC input*). This is an asynchronous input, which when active, transfers data from input latch to the DAC latch.

V_{DD}   (*Positive power supply*). Where a +12 to +15 V DC voltage is applied.

R_{FB}   (*Feedback resistor*). This resistor allows access to the amplifier's feedback loop.

V_{OUT}   (*Output voltage*). Three different output voltage ranges can be chosen: 0 to +5 V, 0 to +10 V or −5 V to +5 V.

Operation of the AD7248A

The internal scaling resistors provided on the AD7248A allow three output voltage ranges. The AD7248A can provide unipolar output ranges of 0 to +5 V or 0 to +10 V and a bipolar output range of −5 V to +5 V. The reference voltage REF OUT (referred to as V_{REF} later) is 5 V and is generated by an internal Zener diode.

Unipolar 0 V to +10 V Configuration.   This configuration is achieved by connecting the bipolar offset resistor, R_{OFS}, to AGND and connecting R_{FB} to V_{OUT}. This configuration is shown in Figure 6.21. V_{SS} should be connected to −12 ~ −15 V if dual supply performance is required. Otherwise, it should be grounded. Assume the digital code is X then the corresponding analog voltage output is given by the following equation:

$$V_X = 2 \times V_{REF} \times X \div 2^{12} \tag{6.1}$$

Unipolar 0 V to +5 V Configuration.   This configuration is achieved by tying R_{OFS}, R_{FB}, and V_{OUT} (in Figure 6.21) together. For this output range the AD7248A can operate on single supply ($V_{SS} = 0$ V) or dual supply. Assume the digital code is X, then the corresponding analog voltage output can be calculated by the following equation:

$$V_X = V_{REF} \times X \div 2^{12} \tag{6.2}$$

Bipolar −5 V to +5 V Configuration.   This configuration is achieved by connecting the R_{OFS} input to REF OUT and connecting R_{FB} to V_{OUT}. The AD7248A must operate on dual supply to achieve this output range. Assume the digital code is X, then the corresponding analog output voltage can be calculated by the following equation:

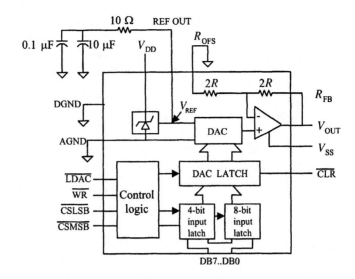

Figure 6.21 Unipolar (0 to ÷ 10 V) configuartion. (Redrawn with permission of Analgo Devices.)

$$V_X = V_{REF} (X - 2^{11})/2048 \qquad (6.3)$$

Loading Data into the AD7248A. The input loading structure in the AD7248A is configured for interfacing with a microprocessor with an 8-bit wide data bus. This device contains two 12-bit latches—an input latch and a DAC latch. The data held in the DAC latch determines the analog output from the converter. The truth table for the AD7248A operation control is shown in Table 6.8.

$\overline{CSMSB}$, $\overline{CSLSB}$, and $\overline{WR}$ control the loading of data from the external data bus to the input latch. The eight data inputs on the AD7248A accept right justified data. These data are loaded into the input latch in two separate write operations. The signals $\overline{CSLSB}$

TABLE 6.8
AD7248A Control Truth Table

$\overline{CSLSB}$	$\overline{CSMSB}$	$\overline{WR}$	$\overline{LDAC}$	Function
L	H	L	H	Loads LS byte into input latch
L	H	↑	H	Latches LS byte into input latch
↑	H	L	H	Latches LS byte into input latch
H	L	L	H	Loads MS nibble into input latch
H	L	↑	H	Latches MS nibble into input latch
H	↑	L	H	Latches MS nibble into input latch
H	H	H	L	Loads input latch into DAC latch
H	H	H	↑	Loads input latch into DAC latch
H	L	L	L	Loads MS nibble into input latch and loads input latch into DAC latch
H	H	H	H	No data transfer operation

and $\overline{WR}$ control the loading of the lower 8 bits into the 12-bit-wide latch. $\overline{CSMSB}$ and $\overline{WR}$ control the loading of the upper 4 bits. All control inputs are level triggered, and input data for either the lower byte or upper 4 bits are latched into the input latches on the rising edge of $\overline{WR}$ (or $\overline{CSMSB}$ or $\overline{CSLSB}$). The order in which the data are loaded into the input latch is not important.

The data in the input latch is loaded into the DAC latch on the rising edge of the $\overline{LDAC}$ signal. An alternate scheme for writing data to the AD7248A is to tie the $\overline{CSMSB}$ and $\overline{LDAC}$ inputs together. In this case exercising $\overline{CSLSB}$ and $\overline{WR}$ latches the lower eight bits into the input latch. The second write, which exercises $\overline{CSMSB}$, $\overline{WR}$, and $\overline{LDAC}$, loads the upper four bits to the input latch and at the same time transfers the 12-bit data to the DAC latch. This automatic transfer mode updates the output of the AD7248A in two write operations. This scheme works equally well for $\overline{CSLSB}$ and $\overline{LDAC}$ tied together provided the upper four bits are loaded to the input latch followed by a write to the lower eight bits of the input latch.

Hardware Connection between the AD7248A and the MCS-51.   Figure 6.22 shows a connection diagram between the AD7248A and the MCS-51 microcontroller. The AD7248A is configured in the automatic transfer mode. The signal P3.0 is pulsed to load data into the lower byte of the input latch. Pulsing the P3.1 signal, after the upper four bits of data have been set up on port 1, updates the output of the AD7248A. The $\overline{WR}$ input is tied low in this application because spurious address strobes on $\overline{CSLSB}$ and $\overline{CSMSB}$ do not occur.

Example 6.5   Assume the AD7248A is connected to the MCS-51 using the circuit in Figure 6.22 and is configured to operate in unipolar mode using the circuit shown in Figure 6.21. Write an instruction sequence to convert the value 120H to analog signal from the V_{OUT} pin.

Solution: Before outputting any value to port P1, set P3.0 and P3.1 to high. There are four steps in outputting data to the AD7248A:

STEP 1   Place the lower byte into the P1 register.

STEP 2   Set $\overline{CSLSB}$ and $\overline{CSMSB}$ ($\overline{LDAC}$ also) to low and high, respectively.

STEP 3   Place the upper 4 bits into the P1 register.

STEP 4   Set $\overline{CSLSB}$ and $\overline{CSMSB}$ ($\overline{LDAC}$ also) to high and low, respectively.

The following instruction sequence will load the value 120H into the AD7248A and then this digital value will be converted to analog signal output:

```
mov   P1,#20H        ; send the lower byte to port P1
mov   P3,#02H        ; latch the lower byte into the AD7248A
mov   P1,#01H        ; send the upper nibble to port P1
mov   P3,#01H        ; latch the upper nibble into DAC and start
. . .                ; the D/A conversion
```

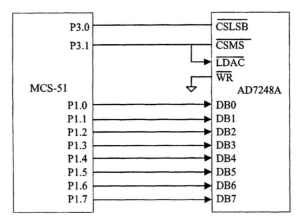

Figure 6.22 Hardware connection between the MCS-51 and AD7248A.

Example 6.6 For the same circuit connection, write a program to generate a sawtooth waveform with a magnitude equal to 5 V from the V_{OUT} pin.

Solution: We need to output the value from 000H to 800H to the AD7248A to generate a sawtooth waveform ranging from 0 to 5 V. The program is as follows:

```
forever:    mov    R0,#0            ; use R1..R0 as loop count &
            mov    R1,#0            ; initialize R1..R0 to 0
next:       mov    P1,R0            ; send out the digital value to be converted
            mov    P3,#02H          ; latch the lower byte into the AD7248A
            mov    P1,R1            ; send out the upper nibble to be converted
            mov    P3,#01H          ; latch the upper nibble and start conversion
            inc    R0               ; increment the loop count
            mov    A,R0             ; check loop count
            jnz    next             ; if the lower byte is not zero, then continue
            inc    R1               ; if the lower byte equals zero, then
                                    ; increment upper nibble
            cjne   R1,#08H,next     ; if not reach the upper limit, continue
            ajmp   forever          ; start all over again when reach the peak
                                    ; value
            END
```

Example 6.7 Calculate the voltage outputs corresponding to the digital codes 10H, 20H, 40H, 60H, 80H, 100H, and 200H for the three output configurations.

Solution: Apply Equations 6.1, 6.2, and 6.3, the voltages corresponding to these digital codes are computed and listed in Table 6.9.

TABLE 6.9
Voltage Outputs from DAC AD7248A[a]

	Configuration		
Digital Code	0 ~ 10 V	0 ~ 5 V	−5 ~ +5 V
0000 0001 0000	0.039	0.0195	−4.961
0000 0010 0000	0.078	0.0391	−4.922
0000 0100 0000	0.156	0.0781	−4.883
0000 0110 0000	0.234	0.1172	−4.844
0000 1000 0000	0.312	0.1562	−4.688
0001 0000 0000	0.625	0.3125	−4.375
0010 0000 0000	1.250	0.6250	−3.750

[a] All values in volts.

6.9 THE I8255 PROGRAMMABLE PERIPHERAL INTERFACE

The MCS-51 has very limited number of I/O ports. If external memory is needed, then both port 0 and 2 cannot be used for I/O. If more I/O ports are needed, there are three solutions:

- Add parallel interface chip(s) to expand the number of parallel ports. The Intel programmable peripheral interface (PPI) chip i8255 is a parallel interface chip that can be added to the MCS-51 to expand its number of parallel ports.
- Choose the member (8XC51GB) that has serial peripheral interface and its supporting chips. This alternative will be discussed in Chapter 10.
- Choose a member that has more I/O ports.

Besides the limited number of I/O ports, the MCS-51 does not have any I/O port that has the handshake capability. Some I/O device requires handshake signals to synchronize the data transfer. The solution to this problem is to use some peripheral chip that has this capability. An example is the Intel i8255.

The Intel i8255 PPI has three 8-bit ports: ports A, B, and C. Ports A and B can be programmed as either input or output, port A can also be programmed as bidirectional, and port C can be programmed as either input, output, or a pair of 4-bit bidirectional control ports (one for port A and one for port B). Furthermore, port C lines can be individually set or reset to generate strobe signals for controlling external devices.

The signals and internal organization of the i8255 are shown in Figure 6.23. In Figure 6.23, signals A1–A0 select the registers within the PPI as follows:

A1	A0	Port selected
0	0	Port A
0	1	Port B
1	0	Port C
1	1	Control (write only)

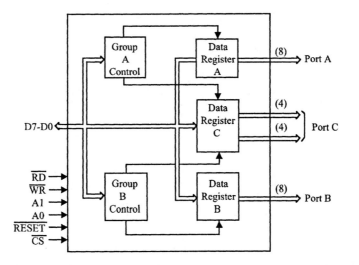

Figure 6.23 Intel i8255 programmable peripheral interface. (Redrawn with permission of Intel.)

6.9.1 Operation of the i8255

Address inputs A1 and A0 select one of the four i8255 registers: port A data, port B data, port C data, and control registers. The control register controls the overall operation of the i8255. Depending on the setting of its most significant bit, the control register serves two functions: when set to 1, *mode definition*; when cleared to 0, *bit set–reset*. The mode definition format and bit set–reset format of the control register are illustrated in Figures 6.24 and 6.25. Any of the eight bits of port C can be set or reset by writing a value into the port C control register as shown in Figure 6.25.

6.9.2 i8255 Operation Modes

The i8255 has three operation modes: mode 0, mode 1, and mode 2.

Mode 0 (Basic Input and Output). This functional configuration provides simple input and output operations for each of the three ports. No "handshaking" is required; data are simply written onto or read from a specified port.

In mode 0,

- There are two 8-bit ports and two 4-bit ports.
- Any port can be input or output.
- Outputs are latched.
- Inputs are not latched.
- Sixteen different input/output configurations are possible in this mode.

Mode 1 (Strobed Input/Output). This functional configuration provides a means for transferring I/O data to or from a specified port in conjunction with strobes or "handshaking"

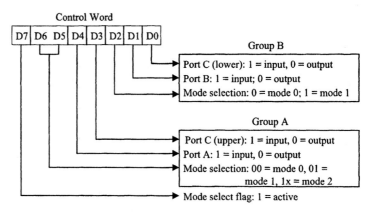

Figure 6.24 i8255 control register mode definition format.

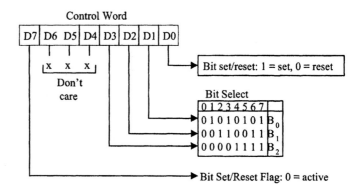

Figure 6.25 i8255 control register bit set–reset format.

signals. In mode 1, port A and port B use the lines on port C to generate or accept these "handshaking" signals.

In mode 1, three ports are divided into two groups. Each group contains one 8-bit port and one 4-bit control/data port. The 8-bit data port can be either input or output. Both input and output are latched. The 4-bit port is used for control and status of the 8-bit data port. The functions of port C pins are illustrated in Table 6.10.

The function of a port C pin depends on whether its associated port is input or output. For example, when port A is configured for input, the pins PC7 and PC6 are used as general-purpose I/O whose directions are set by bit 3 of the control register. The signal transactions for mode 1 input and output are shown in Figures 6.26 and 6.27, respectively.

In Figure 6.26, when the input buffer is not full, the input device places data on input port pins and pulses the $\overline{\text{STB}}$ signal. The falling edge of the $\overline{\text{STB}}$ signal latches data into the input port data register and sets the input buffer full flip-flop. The i8255 asserts the interrupt request signal INTR and the CPU reads the data in the interrupt service routine. After the

TABLE 6.10
Port C Pin Functions in Mode 1[a]

	Pin Function			
Pin	Port A as Input	Port A as Output	Port B as Input	Port B as Output
PC7	I/O	OBF$_A$	NA	NA
PC6	I/O	ACK$_A$	NA	NA
PC5	IBF$_A$	I/O	NA	NA
PC4	STB$_A$	I/O	NA	NA
PC3	INTR$_A$	INTR$_A$	NA	NA
PC2	NA	NA	STB$_B$	ACK$_B$
PC1	NA	NA	IBF$_B$	OBF$_B$
PC0	NA	NA	INTR$_B$	INTR$_B$

[a] OBF$_X$ (X = A or B), output buffer full flip-flop. The OBF will go low to indicate that the CPU has written data out to the specified port. $\overline{ACK}_X$, acknowledge input. A low on this pin informs the i8255 that the data from port A or B have been accepted. INTR$_X$, interrupt request. A high on this pin can be used to interrupt the CPU when an output device has accepted data transmitted by the CPU. $\overline{STB}_X$, strobe input. A low on this input loads data into the input latch. IBF$_X$, input buffer full. A high on this pin indicates that data have been loaded into the input latch.

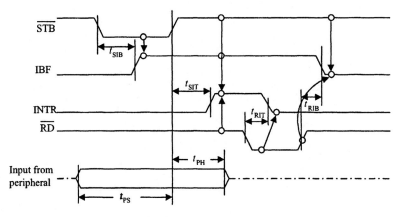

Figure 6.26 Mode 1 input timing diagram.

input data have been read, the input buffer full flag is cleared. This process will be repeated if there are more data to be input.

In Figure 6.27, when the output buffer is not full and the CPU is interrupted, the CPU writes data to the i8255. For a delay of t_{WB} after the rising edge of the WR signal, data appear on i8255 port pins. The $\overline{OBF}$ signal, which stands for output buffer full, is asserted by the write operation. The falling edge of the $\overline{OBF}$ signal latches data into the output device and the output device asserts the $\overline{ACK}$ signal to acknowledge the receipt of data.

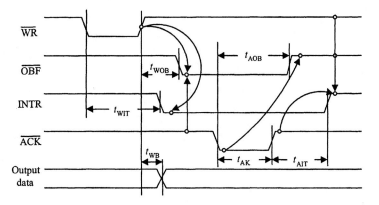

Figure 6.27 Mode 1 output timing diagram.

Mode 2 (Strobed Bidirectional Bus I/O). This configuration provides a means for communicating with a peripheral device or structure on a single 8-bit bus for both transmitting and receiving data. "Handshaking" signals are provided to maintain proper bus flow discipline in a manner similar to mode 1.

In mode 2, only port A is used. Port A becomes an 8-bit bidirectional bus port whereas 5 bits (PC3~PC7) of port C are used as control port. Both input and output are latched. Functions of port C pins are shown in Table 6.11.

The signal transactions for mode 2 operation are shown in Figure 6.28. Like mode 1 operation, data I/O can be either hardware (interrupt) driven or software (polling) driven.

Data output. In software-driven approach, the software tests the $\overline{\text{OBF}}$ signal to determine whether the output buffer is empty. If it is, then data are written out via the *mov* instruction.

TABLE 6.11
Port C Pin FUnctins in Mode 2[a]

Pin	Pin Function
PC7	$\overline{\text{OBF}}_A$
PC6	$\overline{\text{ACK}}_A$
PC5	IBF_A
PC4	$\overline{\text{STB}}_A$
PC3	INTR_A
PC2	I/O
PC1	I/O
PC0	I/O

[a] OBF_A output buffer full. The OBF will go low to indicate that the CPU has written data out to port A. $\overline{\text{ACK}}_A$, acknowledge input. A low on this pin enables the tristate output buffer of port A to send out data. INTR_A, interrupt request. A high on this pin can be used to interrupt the CPU for both input and output. $\overline{\text{STB}}_A$, strobe input. A low on this input loads data into the input latch. IBF_A, input buffer full. A high on this pin indicates that data have been loaded into the input latch.

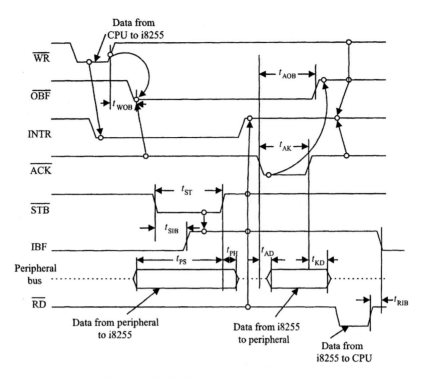

Figure 6.28 i8255 mode 2 signal transactions.

The external circuitry also monitors the $\overline{\text{OBF}}$ signal to decide if the microprocessor has sent new data to the i8255. As soon as the output circuitry sees logic 0 on $\overline{\text{OBF}}$, it sends back the $\overline{\text{ACK}}$ signal to remove data from the output buffer. The low level of the $\overline{\text{ACK}}$ signal causes the $\overline{\text{OBF}}$ signal to go high and also enables the three-state output buffer so that data may be read.

In interrupt-driven approach, the software first enables the i8255 to interrupt the microprocessor. When the output buffer is empty (indicated by the high level of $\overline{\text{OBF}}$ pin), it generates an interrupt request to the CPU. The CPU outputs a byte to the i8255 in the interrupt service routine. The byte written into the i8255 causes the $\overline{\text{OBF}}$ signal to go low, which informs the output device to latch the data. The output device asserts the $\overline{\text{ACK}}$ signal to acknowledge the receipt of the data, which causes the $\overline{\text{OBF}}$ signal to become inactive.

Data input. In software-driven approach, the program tests the IBF signal to determine if data have been strobed into the buffer. If IBF is low, the input device places data on port A pins and asserts the $\overline{\text{STB}}$ signal to strobe data into the input buffer. After this, the IBF signal goes high. When the user program detects that the IBF signal is high, it reads the data from the input buffer. The IBF signal goes low after the data are read. This process will be repeated as long as there are data to be input.

In interrupt-driven approach, the software enables the i8255 to interrupt the micropro-cessor. Whenever the IBF signal is low, the input device places data on the port pins and asserts the $\overline{\text{STB}}$ signal to strobe data into the input buffer. After data are strobed into the input buffer, the IBF signal is asserted and an interrupt is generated. The CPU reads the data from the input buffer when executing the interrupt service routine. Reading data brings the IBF signal to low, which further causes the $\overline{\text{STB}}$ signal to go high.

Example 6.8 Assume that the base address of the i8255 is 8000H and the address signals A1 and A0 from the MCS-51 are connected to the corresponding pins of the i8255. Write down instructions to configure the i8255 to operate in mode 0:

- Port A for input
- Port B for output
- Upper port C for input
- Lower port C for output

Solution: The setting of the control register is as follows:

- bit 7: set to 1 to choose mode select
- bits 6 and 5: set to 00 to configure port A for mode 0 operation
- bit 4: set to 1 to configure port A for input
- bit 3: set to 1 to configure upper port C pins for input
- bit 2: set to 0 to configure port B for mode 0 operation
- bit 1: set to 0 to configure port B for output
- bit 0: set to 0 to configure lower port C pins for output

We need to write the binary value 10011000_2 into the control register. The following instructions will configure the i8255 as desired:

```
mov    DPTR,#8003H      ; point DPTR to the control register
mov    A,#98H           ; place the control word into accumulator A
movx   @DPTR,A          ; write out the contents of accumulator A
```

Example 6.9 Assume the base address of the i8255 is at 8000H and the address signals A1 and A0 from the MCS-51 are connected to the corresponding pins of the i8255. Write down the instructions to configure port A for output in mode 1 and port B for input also in mode 1. Configure the unused port C pins (PC4 and PC5) as general input.

Solution: To configure pins PC4 and PC5 for input, the bit 3 of the control register must be set to 1. The value to be written into the control register is 10101110_2. The following instructions will configure the i8255 as desired:

```
mov    DPTR,#8003H      ; place address of the control register in DPTR
mov    A,#AEH           ; place the control word in accumulator A
movx   @DPTR,A          ; write out the control word
```

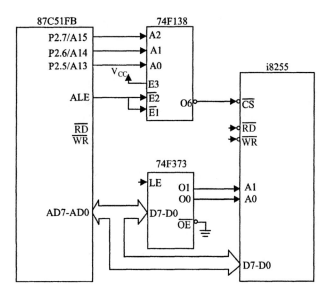

Figure 6.29 The circuit connection between the i8255 and the MCS-51.

6.9.3 Interfacing the i8255 with the 87C51FX

Interfacing the i8255 with the 87C51FX is very straightforward. The data pins D7–D0 can be connected directly to the data pins (port P0) of the microcontroller. Two address inputs A1 and A0 of the i8255 can be connected directly to the lowest two address pins (A1 and A0) from the 87C51FX.

An address space must be allocated to the i8255 registers so that the 87C51FX can access them. Assume we need to add some other components to the 87C51FX in addition to the i8255. Also assume that the 87C51FX memory space is assigned in 8-KB blocks and the address space C000H~DFFFH is assigned to the i8255. The part of the circuit that includes the i8255 and an address decoder is shown in Figure 6.29.

Example 6.10 Perform a timing analysis to verify that the timing requirements for both the 82C55A and the 87C51FX are satisfied in the circuit connections shown in Figure 6.29. A 12-MHz 87C51FX is used in this example.

    Solution: The signal transactions of the CPU side read and write cycles are illustrated in Figures 6.30 and 6.31 and the timing parameters are listed in Table 6.12.

    The address-input-to-output-valid propagation delay of the 74F138 is 8 ns at room temperature. The signal E3 is tied to high permanently. E1 and E2 are connected to ALE. The address decoder output will become valid 8 ns after the falling edge of ALE.

    With regard to the 74F373 latch, the propagation delay of concern to us is the delay from the falling edge of LE to output valid. This delay is 11.5 ns at room temperature.

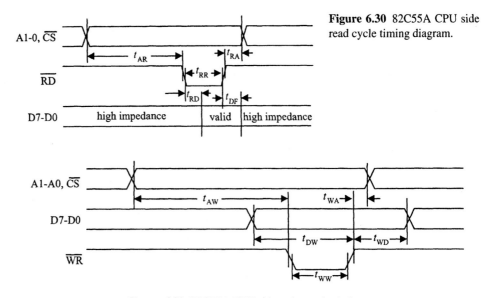

Figure 6.30 82C55A CPU side read cycle timing diagram.

Figure 6.31 82C55A CPU side write cycle timing.

TABLE 6.12
82C55A CPU Side Read and Write Cycle Timing Parameters

Symbol	Parameter	Min (ns)	Max (ns)
t_{AR}	Address stable before $\overline{RD}\downarrow$	0	
t_{RA}	Address hold time after $\overline{RD}\uparrow$	0	
t_{RR}	$\overline{RD}$ pulse width	150	
t_{RD}	Data delay from $\overline{RD}\downarrow$		120
t_{DF}	$\overline{RD}\uparrow$ to data floating	10	75
t_{RV}	Recovery time between $\overline{RD}/\overline{WR}$	200	
t_{AW}	Address stable before $\overline{WR}\downarrow$	0	
t_{WA}	Address hold time after $\overline{WR}\uparrow$	20	
t_{WW}	$\overline{WR}$ pulse width	100	
t_{DW}	Data setup time before $\overline{WR}\uparrow$	30	
t_{WD}	Data hold time after $\overline{WR}\uparrow$	30	

The MCS-51 treats the 82C55A as an external memory component. Therefore, we must use the MCS-51 external memory read and write cycle timing diagrams (Figures 4.15 and 4.16) to do the analysis.

During a read bus cycle, the following parameters of the 87C51FX and the 82C55A must be satisfied:

Address Stable before the Falling Edge of the RD Signal (t_{AR}). The 82C55A requires the address input to be stable for 0 ns before the falling edge of the RD signal. Since the address signals A1A0 are latched into the 74F373 by the falling edge of the ALE, the actual value of t_{AR} can be calculated by the following expression:

$$t_{AR} = T_{LLWL} - 74F373 \text{ propagation delay}$$
$$= 200 \sim 300 \text{ ns} - 11.5 \text{ ns} = 188.5 \sim 288.5 \text{ ns}$$

Therefore, the requirement is satisfied.

Address Hold Time after the Rising Edge of the RD Signal (t_{RA}). The requirement is 0 ns. The address inputs A1 and A0 are from the 74F373 latch. The earliest time for the address to change is when the ALE signal latches new value into the 74F373 in the next bus cycle. Its hold time is calculated as follows and is shown in Figure 6.32.

$$t_{RA} = T_{WHLH} + T_{LHLL} + 74F373 \text{ propagation delay}$$
$$= (43 \text{ ns} \sim 123 \text{ ns}) + 127 \text{ ns} + 11.5 \text{ ns}$$
$$= 181.5 \text{ ns} \sim 261.5 \text{ ns}$$

Read Pulse Width (t_{RR}). The 12-MHz 87C51FX provides a 400-ns pulse width for the $\overline{RD}$ signal and is longer than the requirement (150 ns).

RD Low to Valid Data In (T_{RLDV}). The 12-MHz 87C51FX requires external data to be valid no later than 252 ns after the $\overline{RD}$ signal goes low. The 82C55A provides data no later than 120 ns after the $\overline{RD}$ signal goes low. This requirement is satisfied.

Data Hold Time after $\overline{RD}$ (T_{RHDX}). The 12-MHz 87C51FX requires 0 ns data hold time after the rising edge of the RD signal. The 82C55A holds data valid at least 10 ns after the rising edge of $\overline{RD}$ (t_{DF}). Therefore, this requirement is also satisfied.

During a write bus cycle, the following parameters of the 87C51FX and the 82C55A must be satisfied:

Recovery Time between $\overline{RD}/\overline{WR}$ (t_{RV}). The 82C55A requires a recovery time of 200 ns between the $\overline{RD}$ and $\overline{WR}$ signals. The actual value is calculated as follows and is shown in Figure 6.33:

$$t_{RV} = T_{WHLH} + T_{LHLL} + T_{LLWL}$$
$$= (43 \text{ ns} \sim 123 \text{ ns}) + 127 \text{ ns} + (200 \text{ ns} \sim 300 \text{ ns})$$
$$= 370 \text{ ns} \sim 550 \text{ ns}$$

The calculation result shows that this requirement is satisfied.

Address Stable before the Falling Edge of the $\overline{WR}$ Signal (t_{AW}). The 82C55A requires the address signal to be stable for 0 ns before the falling edge of the $\overline{WR}$ signal. The calculation of this value is identical to that for t_{AR} and hence this requirement is satisfied.

Address Hold Time after the Rising Edge of the $\overline{WR}$ Signal (t_{WA}). The 82C55A requires address signals to be stable for at least 20 ns after the rising edge of the $\overline{WR}$ signal. The calculation of this value is identical to that of t_{RA}. Therefore, this requirement is satisfied.

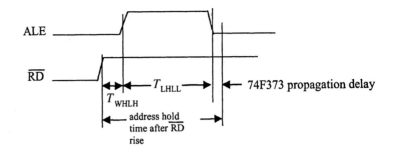

Figure 6.32 Calculation of address hold time after RD rise.

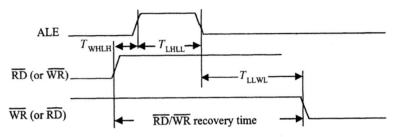

Figure 6.33 $\overline{\text{RD}}/\overline{\text{WR}}$ recovery time calculation.

$\overline{\text{WR}}$ **Pulse Width (t_{WW}).** The 82C55A requires the $\overline{\text{WR}}$ signal to be low for at least 100 ns during a write cycle. The 87C51FX asserts the $\overline{\text{WR}}$ signal (low) for at least 400 ns (T_{WLWH}). Therefore, this requirement is satisfied.

Data Setup Time before the Rising Edge of $\overline{\text{WR}}$ (t_{DW}). The calculation of the actual value of this parameter is as follows and is illustrated in Figure 6.34:

$$t_{\text{DW}} = T_{\text{QVWX}} + T_{\text{WLWH}}$$
$$= 33 \text{ ns} + 400 \text{ ns}$$
$$= 433 \text{ ns}$$

Therefore, this requirement is satisfied.

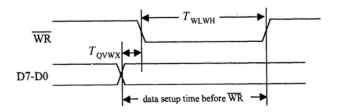

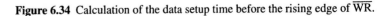

Figure 6.34 Calculation of the data setup time before the rising edge of $\overline{\text{WR}}$.

Data Hold Time after the Rising Edge of $\overline{\text{WR}}$ (t_{WD}). The 87C51FX holds data valid for 33 ns after the rising edge of $\overline{\text{WR}}$ (T_{WHQX}) and is slightly longer than the requirement.

From the above analysis, we conclude that all the timing requirements for read and write cycles are satisfied. Therefore, the 87C51FX can read from and write into the 82C55A without any problem.

6.9.4 Centronics Printer Interface

The standard Centronics printer interface allows the transfer of byte-wide, parallel data under the control of two handshake signals, Data Strobe and ACK (acknowledge). Short data setup (50 ns) and hold (100 ns) times are required. The Centronics interface provides the following signals:

- *D7–D0*: Data pins (input to the printer)
- *Busy*: Output from the printer. This signal indicates that the printer is busy printing.
- *PE*: Output from the printer. When PE is high, the printer is in error due to an internal condition such as being out of paper or a malfunction.
- *Select*: Output from the printer. This signal indicates that the printer is connected to the computer.
- $\overline{Data\ Strobe}$. Input to the printer. This signal is an input to the printer and latches data into the printer.
- $\overline{Ack}$: Acknowledge. Ack is active low and is an output from the printer.

PE, Select, and Busy are status signals and are not all needed in any particular printer design. The Centronics interface timing is shown in Figure 6.35.

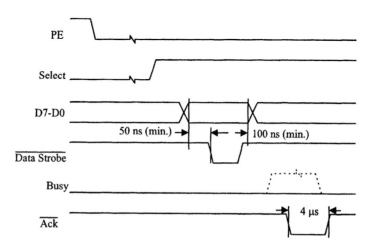

Figure 6.35 Centronics printer interface timing.

Example 6.11 Interface a Centronics printer with the 87C51FB via the port A of the 82C55A. Use the 82C55A I/O port timing parameters shown in Table 6.13 to verify that all the timing requirements are satisfied.

TABLE 6.13
82C55A-2 I/O Port Timing Parameters

Symbol	Parameter	Min (ns)	Max (ns)
t_{WB}	WR = 1 to output		35
t_{IR}	Peripheral data before RD	0	
t_{HR}	Peripheral data after RD	0	
t_{AK}	ACK pulse width	200	
t_{ST}	STB pulse width	100	
t_{PS}	Peripheral data before STB high	20	
t_{PH}	Peripheral data after STB high	50	
t_{AD}	ACK = 0 to output		175
t_{KD}	ACK = 1 to output float	20	250
t_{WOB}	WR = 1 to OBF = 0		150
t_{AOB}	ACK = 0 to OBF = 1	150	
t_{STB}	STB = 0 to IBF = 1		150
t_{RIB}	RD = 1 to IBF = 0		150
t_{RIT}	RD = 0 to INTR = 0		200
t_{SIT}	STB = 1 to INTR = 1	150	
t_{AIT}	ACK = 1 to INTR = 1	200	
t_{WIT}	WR = 0 to INTR = 0	200	
t_{RES}	Reset pulse width	500	

Solution: Connect the Centronics printer and the 82C55A as shown in Figure 6.36. Use the mode 1 output configuration to interface with the Centronics printer. Refering to Figure 6.27, we need to verify that both the data setup and hold times relative to the falling edge of $\overline{\text{Data Strobe}}$ signal are satisfied. Since the data setup time is the delay

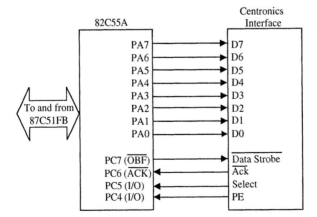

Figure 6.36 Interfacing a Centronics printer with the 82C55A.

from the moment that the data are valid until the falling edge of the $\overline{\text{Data Strobe}}$ signal (connected to $\overline{\text{OBF}}$), it can be calculated as follows:

$$t_{su} = t_{WOB} - t_{WB}$$
$$= 150 \text{ ns} - 35 \text{ ns}$$
$$= 115 \text{ ns} > 50 \text{ ns (requirement)}$$

The data hold time is the delay from the falling edge of $\overline{\text{Data Strobe}}$ until port data becomes invalid. This delay cannot be calculated from Figure 6.27. However, it is easy to tell that it is longer than t_{AOB} and t_{AOB} ($= 150$ ns) is longer than the requirement 100 ns. Therefore, both timing parameters are satisfied.

Example 6.12 Write a subroutine to initialize the 82C55A so that it operates in mode 1 output and set both pins PC5 and PC4 for input.

Solution: The setting of 82C55A control registers is as follow:

- bit 7: set to 1 to select mode definition format
- bits 6 and 5: set to 01 to select mode 1
- bit 4: set to 0 to set port A for output
- bit 3: set to 1 to set the upper port C pins (PC5 and PC4) for input
- bit 2: don't care. Set to 0
- bit 1: don't care. Set to 0
- bit 0: don't care. Set to 0

The subroutine must check to see if the printer is already on-line and also check if there is any error before initializing the printer. The subroutine is as follows:

```
portc       equ     C002H           ; 82C55A port C data register
prt         equ     C003H           ; 82C55A control register address
prt_init:   mov     DPTR,#portc
wait_ol:    movx    A,@DPTR         ; wait for the printer to be turned on
            anl     A,#20H          ; "
            jz      wait_ol         ; "
wait_noer:  movx    A,@DPTR         ; wait for the printer error to be corrected
            anl     A,#10H          ; "
            jnz     wait_noer       ; "
            inc     DPTR            ; point DPTR to the printer control
                                    ; register
            mov     A,#A8H          ; initialize the printer
            movx    @DPTR,A         ; "
            ret
```

Example 6.13 Write a subroutine to output a character and a subroutine to output a string to the printer described in Example 6.11. The starting address of the string is passed in the DPTR register. The string is terminated by a null character. The character to be output is passed in accumulator A. Use polling method to print the character and the string.

Solution: Before the microcontroller can send a character to the printer, it must make sure that the output buffer is empty, i.e., the OBF signal (PC7) must be high. The print character subroutine is as follows:

```
prt_stat    equ     C002H               ; 82C55A port C data register
                                         ; address
printer     equ     C000H               ; 82C55A port A is the printer port
prt_char:   push    DPL
            push    DPH
            push    ACC                 ; save the character to be output
here:       mov     DPTR,#prt_stat      ; place the address of printer status
                                        ; in DPTR
            movx    A,@DPTR
            anl     A,#80H              ; check the OBF signal
            jnz     here               ; wait until the output buffer is empty
            mov     DPTR,#printer       ; place the printer address in DPTR
            pop     ACC                 ; get back the character to be output
            movx    @DPTR,A             ; output the character
            pop     DPH
            pop     DPL
            ret
```

The print string subroutine simply reads a character from the string and calls the print character subroutine to print it until the null character is encountered.

```
prt_strg:   push    ACC                 ; save accumulator A
next:       movx    A,@DPTR             ; get the next character
            jz      exit                ; reach the end of the string?
            lcall   prt_char            ; call the print character subroutine
            inc     DPTR                ; move to the next character
            sjmp    next                ; go to get the next character
exit:       pop     ACC                 ; restore accumulator A
            ret
```

Example 6.14 Suppose the INTR pin of the 82C55A is connected to the INT1 pin of the 87C51FB. Write a subroutine to print a character and a subroutine to print a string using the interrupt-driven approach. The starting address of the string to be output is passed in DPTR.

Solution: To use the interrupt-driven approach, the caller of the subroutine that prints a character must enable the interrupt. If the caller just wants to output a single character, it should include the following instructions to make the call:

```
movx   A,@DPTR        ; get the character to be printed
mov    IE,#84H         ; enable INT1 interrupt
 . . .                 ; do something else (but not change A)
```

The subroutine that prints a string will enable the INT1 interrupt. The caller of this routine should include the following instructions to make the call:

```
mov     DPTR,#string   ; place starting address of the string in DPTR
lcall   prt_strg       ; make the subroutine call
 . . .
```

The printer will request an interrupt only when it is ready to print the next character. The subroutine that prints a character should be written as the service routine of the INT1 interrupt. The service routine of the INT1 interrupt should be written as follows:

```
            org     0013H          ; starting address of the INT1 service
                                   ; routine
            ljmp    prt_char       ; make the subroutine call
            org     xxxxH          ; starting address of the prt_char
                                   ; subroutine
prt_char:   push    DPL
            push    DPH
            mov     DPTR,#C000H    ; place the printer port address in DPTR
            movx    @DPTR,A        ; print the character
            pop     DPH
            pop     DPL
            inc     DPTR           ; move the DPTR to point to the next
                                   ; character
            reti
```

The subroutine that prints a string will enable the INT1 interrupt and then stay in a loop to check if the character pointed to by the DPTR is a null character:

```
prt_strg:   orl     IE,#84H        ; enable printer interrupt
loop:       movx    A,@DPTR        ; get the character to be printed
            jnz     loop           ; is it a null character?
            anl     IE,#FBH        ; disable printer interrupt
            ret
```

6.10 SUMMARY

This chapter discussed in detail many issues and techniques related to I/O. When performing I/O operation, the microcontroller actually deals with registers. The microcontroller needs to configure the control register so that the I/O port may operate in the appropriate mode and configuration. When inputting data, the microcontroller reads from the data register. When outputting data, the microcontroller writes into the data register. The key concept in input is "the microcontroller must wait until the input device has placed valid data in the data register then reads it." The key concept for output is that "the microcontroller must wait until the data in the data register of the interface chip have been fetched by the output device then sends the next character to the data register of the interface chip."

There are two aspects in I/O synchronization: the synchronization between the CPU and the interface chip and the synchronization between the interface chip and the I/O device. Timing requirements and electrical load must be considered and taken care of before any I/O operation may be successful. DIP switches and keyboards are used as examples of input devices. Mechanical key switches have bouncing problem and must be debounced. Both hardware and software techniques are available for doing keyboard debouncing. There are three steps in keyboard input: keyboard scanning, debouncing, and ASCII code lookup.

LEDs, seven-segment displays, LCDs, and D/A converters are common output devices. Examples are provided to demonstrate the interfacing to these devices. Electrical load considerations are also illustrated in those examples.

When an application requires more parallel ports or handshake capability, the Intel i8255 can be used. An example is used to demonstrate the interfacing between the 87C51FB and the i8255. Timing verification is demonstrated in that example.

Centronics printer interface has been very popular in the last 20 years and is still being used in many printers. Examples are provided to illustrate the interfacing and programming of this interface.

6.11 EXERCISES

6.1 What is isolated I/O? What is memory-mapped I/O?

6.2 Describe interlocked input handshaking and pulsed input handshaking.

6.3 *Traffic light controller*. Use port 1 pins to drive two sets of green, yellow, and red LEDs to simulate traffic light controller. The traffic light patterns and durations for the east–west and north–south traffic are given in Table 6E.1 Write a program to control the light patterns, and connect the circuit to demonstrate the changes in lights.

6.4 Perform an analysis to show that the 2N2222 transistors in Figure 6.15 are operating in saturation region when they are turned on. Assume that the current gain β is 150.

6.5 Write a program to generate a waveform as shown in Figure 6E.1 for the DAC circuit in Figure 6.22.

TABLE 6E.1
Traffic Light Pattern

East–West			North–South			Durations
Green	Red	Yellow	Green	Red	Yellow	(s)
1	0	0	0	1	0	20
0	0	1	0	1	0	4
0	1	0	1	0	0	15
0	1	0	0	0	1	3

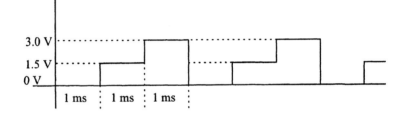

Figure 6E.1 A periodic waveform to be generated.

6.6 For the circuit shown in Figure 6E.2, write a program to perform keyboard scanning, debouncing, and ASCII table lookup, and then send the input data for display. Display only the most recently entered four keys. The keys entered earlier will be shifted out. Use registers R3...R6 to hold the last four keys. Assume the subroutine *display* already exists. Your program needs only to call it. The MC14051 is an analog multiplexor that has three select inputs (A, B, and C), eight data inputs (X0–X7), one inhibit input, and one common output (X). The common output is active high. When data input is selected by the select signals, its voltage will be passed to the common output.

6.7 Suppose the 87C51FB microcontroller does not have enough I/O ports for some applications and the 82C55A is chosen to provide the needed I/O ports. The 82C55A will be used to drive six seven-segment displays. Show a circuit connection that will work and also write a program to display the time of day. Configure the 82C55A to operate in mode 0.

6.8 Suppose common-anode seven-segment displays are used instead of common-cathode seven-segment displays. Show the changes that must be made in the circuit shown in Figure 6.15. What needs to be modified in Table 6.3 for the seven-segment pattern?

6.9 Use Equations 6.1, 6.2, and 6.3 to calculate the voltage outputs corresponding to the digital codes 24H, 32H, 80H, 96H, 120H, 160H, 240H, and 320H for the three possible configurations of the AD7248A.

6.10 The National Semiconductor 74C922 is a 16-key encoder that performs keypad scanning and debouncing. The pin assignment is shown in Figure 6E.3. The data out value for each

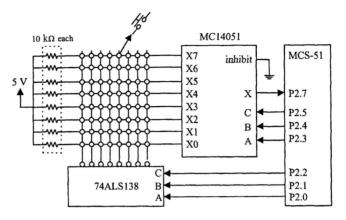

Figure 6E.2 64-key keyboard interfaced with the MCS-51.

Figure 6E.3 Pin assignment of 74C922.

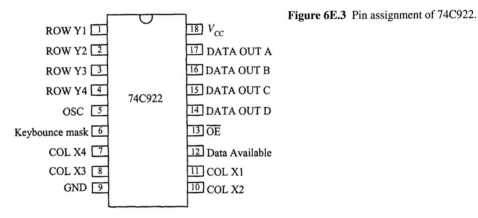

BCD digit is its own value. That is, the data out value for 0 is 0, for 1 is 1, and so on. It has a *data available* output that can remind the microcontroller to read the keypad inputs. Suppose the address space 4000H~5FFFH is assigned to the 74C922. Connect the 74C922 to the 87C51FB as shown in Figure 6E.4. Write a main program to enable keypad interrupt and initialize the DPTR to the starting address of a buffer *key_buf*. The main program then stays in a loop until the key (in accumulator A) pressed is an F. Then the main program disables the keypad interrupt and exits the loop. Whenever the keypad has been pressed, it asserts the data available pin, which in turn interrupts the microcontroller. Write an interrupt service routine to read the keypad and look up the ASCII code and leave it in accumulator A and return.

6.12 LAB EXERCISES AND ASSIGNMENTS

Do the following experiments with the MCB520 evaluation board. Since we need to use serial port 1 to download our programs into the board, we cannot use the pins associated with serial

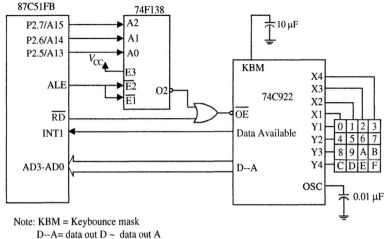

Figure 6E.4 The circuit connection between 74C922 and the 87C51FB. KBM, keybounce mask; D–A, data out D ~ data out out A.

port 1 (P1.2 and P1.3). Use P3.0 and P3.1 to replace P1.2 and P1.3, respectively. The INT button on the MCB520 evaluation board is connected to the INT0 pin (P3.2).

6.1 Interrupt-driven input experiment. The purpose of this lab is to practice interrupt-driven input. You will apply four interrupt pulses to the INT0 pin. Each interrupt pulse will cause 1 byte to be read from an 8-DIP switch. Connect the 8-DIP switch to port 1 as shown in Figure 6.5 (remember to replace P1.2 and P1.3 with P3.0 and P3.1). The procedure is as follows:

STEP 1   Write a main program that performs the following operations:

   a. Initializes the INT0 interrupt count *int_cnt* to 4.
   b. Uses R1 as a pointer to an internal memory buffer *in_buf*.
   c. Stays in a wait loop and keeps checking the interrupt count *int_cnt*; when *int_cnt* is decremented to 0, the main program disables the INT0 and returns to the monitor.

STEP 2   Write an INT0 service routine that performs the following operations:

   a. Reads the 8-DIP switch and saves the value at the memory location pointed to by *R1*. In this step you need to combine the values from port 1 and port 3.
   b. Increments the buffer pointer *R1* by 1.
   c. Decrements the INT0 interrupt count *int_cnt* by 1.

STEP 3   Set up the 8-DIP switch properly so that it represents the value that the user wants to input to the microcontroller.

STEP 4   Press the INT button to inform the microcontroller to read the 8-DIP switch.

STEP 5   Repeats Steps 3 and 4 four times and then stop.

6.2 *Seven-segment display experiment.* Use ports P1 and P3 of the DS87C520 to drive two seven-segment displays. Use port 1 and port P3 pins to drive the segment patterns and two port 3 pins to drive the bases of 2N2222 transistors. The collectors are connected to the common cathodes of the seven-segment displays. Write a program to perform the following operations:

Display the values from 00 to 59 three times and stop. Display each value for 1 s each time before changing to the next value.

7

TIMER FUNCTION

7.1 OBJECTIVES

After completing this chapter, you should be able to

- use timer function to measure the pulse width, period, frequency, duty cycle of a signal, and the phase shift between two different signals.
- use timer function to capture the arrival time of an event and/or use it as a time reference.
- use timer function to generate digital waveforms
- use watchdog function to detect software problems
- explain the operations of step motors and DC motors.
- use timer function to control step and DC motors

7.2 INTRODUCTION

In a microcontroller, *physical time* is represented by the count value of a timer. By interpreting the count value of a timer properly, many timer applications can be realized. There are many applications that require a dedicated timer system, including

- time delay creation
- elapsed time measurement
- pulse width, period, and frequency measurement
- event counting
- time-of-day tracking
- periodic interrupt generation to remind the processor to perform routine tasks
- waveform generation
- time reference
- motor control

Without a dedicated timer system, some of these applications would be very difficult to implement. The MCS-51 microcontrollers include powerful timer systems to support these applications. The original MCS-51 microcontrollers provide two 16-bit timers (Timer 0 and 1). Timer 2 is added to the MCS-52 series microcontrollers. The programmable counter array (PCA) is added to the 8XC51FX and the 8XC51GB. The capabilities of Timers 0, 1, 2 and the programmable counter array are listed in Table 7.1.

Both Timer 0 and Timer 1 can be used as timers or counters. A timer can be used to create a time delay whereas a counter can be used to count external events that occurred within a time interval. An event is represented by a signal edge (falling or rising). Both timers can generate interrupts to the CPU.

In addition to being used as a timer/counter, Timer 2 can also be used to capture the arrival time of an event when being configured in capture mode. Timer 2 is more flexible than Timer 0 and Timer 1 because it can be programmed to count up or count down when programmed in its auto-reload mode.

Programmable counter arrays (PCA) are added to the 8XC51FX and 8XC51GB series microcontrollers. The 8XC51FX has one PCA whereas the 8XC51GB has two PCAs (PCA and PCA1). The PCA consists of one free-running timer and five capture/compare modules. Each of these five capture/compare modules can

- capture the arrival time of the falling and/or rising edge of an unknown signal.
- compare the timer value with that of a preloaded compare register. This function can be used to create a time delay.
- toggle a signal when the timer is equal to the preloaded compare register.

TABLE 7.1
Capabilities of the Intel MCS-51 Timer Subsystem

Timer Subsystem	Capabilities	Available in
Timer 0	Mode 0: 13-bit counter/timer Mode 1: 16-bit counter/timer Mode 2: 8-bit auto-reload counter/timer Mode 3: Two separate 8-bit counters	MCS-51 MCS-52 8XC51FX 8XC51GB
Timer 1	Mode 0–2: identical to those in Timer 0 Mode 3: holds its contents	Sames as above
Timer 2	16-bit auto reload up or down counter 16-bit capture Baud-rate generation Programmable clock out	MCS-52 8XC51FX 8XC51GB
PCA	One 16-bit free-running timer and five 16-bit compare/capture modules 16-bit capture, positive-edge triggered 16-bit capture, negative-edge triggered 16-bit capture, both edges triggered 16-bit software timer 16-bit high speed output 8-bit pulse width modulator Watchdog timer (on module 4 only)	8XC51FX 8XC51GB
PCA1	Same as PCA except that watchdog timer is not supported	8XC51GB

- invoke a reset when the PCA timer matches the value stored in the compare register (available only in module 4). The PCA1 of the 8XC51GB does not have this function.
- serve as a pulse width modulator output.

Signal pins related to timer functions include the following:

T0 (P3.4).   Timer 0 external input

T1 (P3.5).   Timer 1 external input

T2 (P1.0).   External count input to timer/counter 2, clock out

T2EX (P1.1).   Timer/counter 2 capture/reload trigger and direction control

ECI (P1.2).   External count input to the PCA

CEX0 (P1.3).   External I/O for compare/capture module 0

CEX1 (P1.4).   External I/O for compare/capture module 1

CEX2 (P1.5).   External I/O for compare/capture module 2

CEX3 (P1.6).   External I/O for compare/capture module 3

CEX4 (P1.7),   External I/O for compare/capture module 4

These pins serve *alternate functions* when being used as timer functions. An alternate function can be activated only if its corresponding bit latch in the port special function register contains a 1. Otherwise the port pin is stuck at 0. We need to write 1s to these pins before using them for alternate functions.

7.3 TIMER 0 AND TIMER 1

Both Timer 0 and Timer 1 are 16-bit timers. Each consists of two 8-bit registers, THx and TLx ($x = 0$ and 1). Both can be configured to operate either as a timer or an event counter.

In the timer function, the TLx register is incremented every machine cycle. Thus it can be thought of as counting machine cycles. Since a machine cycle consists of 12 oscillator periods, the count rate is 1/12 of the oscillator frequency.

In the counter function, the register is incremented in response to a 1-to-0 transition at its corresponding external input pin—T0 or T1. In this function, the external input is sampled during the S5P2 of every machine cycle (see Section 1.10.4). When the sample shows a high in one cycle and a low in the next cycle, the count is incremented. The new count value appears in the register during S3P1 of the cycle following the one in which the transition was detected. Since it takes two machine cycles to recognize a 1-to-0 transition, the maximum count rate is 1/24 of the oscillator frequency. There are no restrictions on the duty cycle of the external input signal, but to ensure that a given level is sampled at least once before it changes, it should be held for at least one full machine cycle.

In addition to the timer or counter selection, Timer 0 and Timer 1 have four operating modes. The TMOD register selects the operation modes and the TCON register controls the operations of Timer 0 and 1.

7.3.1 Timer 0 and Timer 1 Operation Modes

Programming the TMOD register as illustrated in Figure 7.1 sets the operation modes of Timer 0 and Timer 1.

Mode 0. Either Timer 0 or Timer 1 in mode 0 is an 8-bit counter with a divide-by-32 prescaler. Figure 7.2 shows the mode 0 operation for either timer. In this mode, the timer register is configured as a 13-bit register. As the counter rolls over from all 1s to all 0s, it sets the timer interrupt flag TFx. The counter input is enabled to the timer when TR$x = 1$ and either GATE $= 0$ or INT$x = 1$. (Setting GATE $= 1$ allows the timer to be controlled by external input INTx, to facilitate pulse width measurements.) TRx and TFx are control bits in the TCON register.

address = 89H	Timer 1				Timer 0			not bit addressable
	GATE	C/$\overline{T}$	M1	M0	GATE	C/$\overline{T}$	M1	M0
	7	6	5	4	3	2	1	0

GATE: When GATE = 1, Timer/Counter 0 or 1 is enabled only while INT0 or INT1 pin is high and TR0 or TR1 control bit is set. When GATE = 0, Timer 0 or 1 is enabled whenever TR0 or TR1 contorl bit is set.

C/$\overline{T}$: Timer or Counter Selector. Clear for timer operation. Set for counter operation (input from T0 or T1).

M1 M0: Operation mode

0	0	8-bit timer/counter. THx with TLx as a 5-bit prescaler.
0	1	16-bit timer/counter. THx and TLx are cascaded; there is no prescaler.
1	0	8-bit auto-reload timer/counter. THx holds a value which is to be reloaded into TLx each time it overflows.
1	1	(Timer 0) TL0 is an 8-bit timer/counter controlled by the standard timer 0 control bits. TH0 is an 8-bit timer controlled by Timer 1 control bits. (Timer 1) timer/counter stopped.

Figure 7.1 TMOD timer/counter mode control register.

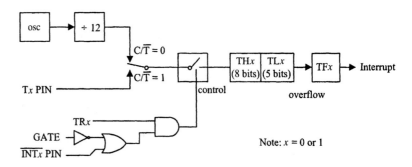

Figure 7.2 Timer/Counter 0 or 1 in mode 0: 13-bit counter.

The contents of the TCON register are shown in Figure 7.3. The 13-bit timer register consists of all 8 bits of TH*x* and the lower 5 bits of TL*x*. The upper 3 bits of TL*x* are indeterminate and should be ignored. Setting the run flag (TR*x*) does not clear these registers.

Mode 1. Mode 1 is the same as mode 0 except that the timer register uses all 16 bits. In this mode, TH*x* and TL*x* are cascaded. There is no prescaler.

Mode 2. As shown in Figure 7.4, mode 2 configures the timer register as an 8-bit counter (TL*x*) with automatic reload. An overflow from TL*x* not only sets TF*x*, but also reloads TL*x* with the contents of TH*x*. The reload leaves TH*x* unchanged.

address
= 88H   bit addressable

TF1	TR1	TF0	TR0	IE1	IT1	IE0	IT0
7	6	5	4	3	2	1	0

TF1: *Timer 1 overflow flag*. Set by hardware on timer/counter overflow. Cleared by hardware when processor vectors to interrupt routine.

TR1: *Timer 1 run control*. Timer 1 is turned on when this bit is set to 1.

TF0: *Timer 0 overflow flag*. Set by hardware on timer/counter overflow. Cleared by hardware when processor vectors to interrupt routine.

TR0: *Timer 0 run control*. Timer 0 is turned on when this bit is set to 1.

IE1: *Interrupt 1 flag*. Set by hardware when external interrupt 1 edge/level is detected. If INT1 is edge-triggered, then IE1 will be cleared by hardware after interrupt is processed.

IT1: *Interrupt 1 type control bit*. Set/cleared by software to specify falling edge/low level triggered external interrupt 1.

IE0: *Interrupt 0 flag*. Set by hardware when external interrupt 0 edge/level is detected. If INT0 is edge-triggered, then IE1 will be cleared by hardware after interrupt is processed.

IT0: *Interrupt 0 type control bit*. Set/cleared by software to specify falling edge/low level triggered external interrupt 0.

Figure 7.3 TCON: timer/counter control register.

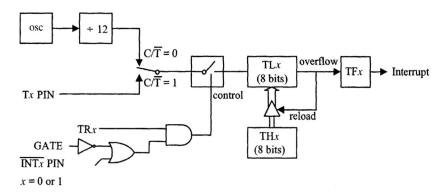

Figure 7.4 Timer/Counter 0 and 1 in mode 2: 8-bit auto-reload.

Mode 3. Timer 1 in mode 3 simply holds its contents. The effect is the same as setting TR1 = 0. Timer 0 in mode 3 establishes TL0 and TH0 as two separate counters. The logic for mode 3 on Timer 0 is shown in Figure 7.5. TL0 uses the Timer 0 control bits: C/$\overline{T}$, GATE, TR0, INT0, and TF0. TH0 is locked into a timer function (counting machine cycles) and takes over the use of TR1 and TF1 from Timer 1. Thus TH0 now controls the Timer 1 interrupt.

Mode 3 is useful for applications that require an extra 8-bit timer or counter. When Timer 0 is in mode 3, Timer 1 can still count oscillator cycles in modes 0, 1, and 2 but can neither interrupt the CPU nor set the flag; Timer 1 can still be used by the serial port as a baud rate generator, or in any application not requiring an interrupt.

7.3.2 Applications of Timer 0 and Timer 1

Timer 0 and Timer 1 can be used to create time delays, measure the pulse width of an unknown signal, measure the frequency or period of a periodic waveform, count external events, and so on.

Time Delay Creation.   Assume the oscillator output frequency is f_{osc}, then its period is $1/f_{osc}$ s. When choosing the *oscillator output ÷ 12* as the clock source to the timer, the period of the clock input to the timer becomes $12/f_{osc}$ s. Suppose the time delay to be created is X seconds, then the number of timer counts equivalent to the time delay can be computed by the following expression:

$$\text{timer count} = X \div (12/f_{osc}) \tag{7.1}$$

Depending on the duration of the time delay to be created, this number may or may not be larger than $2^{16} - 1$. If this number is smaller than 2^{16}, this time delay can be created by placing the timer count into the Timer 1 or 0 register and choosing mode 1. Otherwise, the number of timer overflows must be used in order to create this delay.

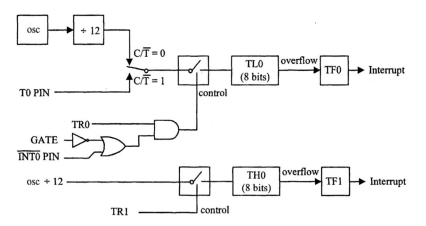

Figure 7.5 Timer/Counter 0 and 1 in mode 3: two 8-bit counters.

Example 7.1 Assume the 87C51FB microcontroller is controlled by an oscillator running at 12 MHz. Write a program to create a time delay of 20 ms.

Solution: The period of a machine cycle is $12/12$ MHz $= 1\ \mu s$. Suppose the oscillator $\div\ 12$ output is used as the clock source of Timer 1, then 20 ms corresponds to 20,000 counts. By placing the value of 45,535 ($65{,}535 - 20{,}000$) into Timer 1 registers (TH1 and TL1), Timer 1 will overflow in 20 ms. The procedure to create a delay of 20 ms is as follows:

STEP 1 Configure Timer 1 to operate in mode 1 and choose oscillator $\div\ 12$ as the clock input.

STEP 2 Pull the INT1 pin to high.

STEP 3. Place the value of 61DFH (45535) into the Timer 1 register and wait until the overflow flag is set to 1.

The program to create a delay of 20 ms will be written as a subroutine and the caller of this subroutine uses the following instruction to make the subroutine call:

```
lcall   dly20ms      ; call the delay subroutine
 . . .
```

The delay subroutine is as follows:

```
dly20ms:    mov   TMOD,#00010000B   ; set up Timer 1 in mode 1
            clr   TF1               ; clear Timer 1 overflow flag
            mov   TH1,#61H          ; place the upper byte of the count
                                    ; in TH1
            mov   TL1,#DFH          ; place the lower byte of the count
                                    ; in TL1
            setb  TR1               ; enable Timer 1 to operate
wait:       jnb   TF1,wait          ; wait until TF1 is set to 1
            ret
```

There is an overhead of 10 machine cycles in the delay subroutine. If we want to be more exact, this overhead should be added into the value to be placed in the timer register.

To create a time delay longer than 65.5 ms, we need to keep track of the number of times the timer overflows. For example, to create a delay of 1 s, we can

1. write a loop that creates a time delay of 50 ms and
2. repeat the loop for 20 times.

Example 7.2 Assume the 87C51FB microcontroller is controlled by an oscillator running at 12 MHz. Write a program to create a time delay of 1 s.

Solution:

```
loop_cnt     set    R2                  ; use R2 as the loop count
```

```
dly1s:      mov   loop_cnt,#20      ; need to repeat the delay sequence 20
                                    ; times
            clr   ET1              ; disable Timer 1 interrupt
            mov   TMOD,#10H        ; set up Timer 1 in mode 1
again:      clr   TF1              ; clear Timer 1 overflow flag
            mov   TH1,#3CH         ; place 15535 into Timer 1 register so that
            mov   TL1,#AFH         ; it overflows in 50 ms
            setb  TR1              ; enable Timer 1 to operate
wait:       jnb   TF1,wait         ; wait until TF1 is set to 1
            djnz  loop_cnt,again   ; wait until 50 ms delay is repeated 20
                                    ; times

            ret
```

Measurement of Pulse Width. Connect the unknown signal to either the INT1 or the INT0 pin depending on which timer is used and load the chosen timer with 0. When the signal is high, the timer is allowed to count. Select the mode 1 operation. If the pulse duration is not longer than $2^{16} - 1$ machine cycles, the pulse width (in machine cycles) is equal to the timer final count. Otherwise, it is necessary to keep track of the number of timer overflows. The procedure for measuring the pulse width is as follows:

STEP 1   Connect the unknown signal to the INT1 pin. Invert the signal if it is a negative-going pulse.

STEP 2   Configure Timer 1 to operate in mode 1 and select oscillator $\div$ 12 as the clock input to the timer.

STEP 3   Clear the TF1 flag to 0 and also initialize the Timer 1 overflow count to 0.

STEP 4   Write a Timer 1 overflow interrupt service routine that increments the overflow count by 1 and returns.

STEP 5   Write an INT1 interrupt service routine that decrements its interrupt count by 1.

STEP 6.   Select falling edge interrupt from INT1 pin. Enable Timer 1 overflow interrupt. Initialize the INT1 interrupt count to 1. Enable Timer 1 to run.

STEP 7.   Wait until the INT1 interrupt count is decremented to 0. Then the pulse width of the unknown signal is given by the following expression:

$$\text{Pulse width} = (\text{timer overflow count} \times 2^{16} + \text{timer count}) \text{ machine cycles} \quad (7.2)$$

Example 7.3 Assume the 87C51FB microcontroller is controlled by an oscillator running at 12 MHz. Connect the unknown signal to be measured to the INT1 pin. Write a program to measure its pulse width.

Solution: Two bytes are used to hold the overflow count of Timer 1 in this example.

```
pw_l          set    R0                 ; low byte of pulse width
pw_h          set    R1                 ; high byte of pulse width
t1ov_cntl     set    R2                 ; use R2 & R3 as the Timer 1 overflow
                                        ; count
t1ov_cnth     set    R3                 ; "
int_cnt       set    R4                 ; INT1 interrupt count
              org    0013H              ; INT1 interrupt vector
int1_hnd:     dec    int_cnt            ; decrement the INT1 interrupt count
              reti
              org    01BH               ; Timer 1 overflow interrupt vector
t1_hndler:    ljmp   inc_ovcnt          ; jump to increment Timer 1 overflow
                                        ; count
              org    yyyyH
inc_ovcnt:    mov    A,t1ov_cntl        ; increment timer overflow count by 1
              add    A,#1               ; "
              mov    t1ov_cntl,A        ; "
              mov    A,t1ov_cnth        ; "
              addc   A,#0               ; "
              mov    t1ov_cnth,A        ; "
              reti
              org    xxxxH              ; starting address of the main program
              setb   P3.3               ; enable alternate function of INT1
              mov    TL1,#0             ; initialize Timer 1 register to 0
              mov    TH1,#0             ; "
              mov    t1ov_cntl,#0       ; initialize Timer 1 overflow count to 0
              mov    t1ov_cnth,#0       ;
              mov    int_cnt,#1         ; initialize INT1 interrupt count to 1
              mov    tmod,#90H          ; configure Timer 1 to gated, timer,
                                        ; mode 1
              setb   IT1                ; choose falling edge interrupt for INT1
              orl    IE,#8CH            ; enable INT1 and Timer 1 overflow
                                        ; interrupts
              clr    TF1                ; clear Timer 1 overflow flag
              setb   TR1                ; enable Timer 1 to run
measure:      mov    A,int_cnt          ; check if the INT1 falling edge arrived
              jnz    measure
              mov    pw_l,TL1           ; save lower byte of pulse width
              mov    pw_h,TH1           ; save upper byte of pulse width
              end
```

Frequency Measurement. To measure the frequency of an unknown signal, Timer 1 or 0 must be configured to operate in counter mode. Initialize the counter to 0. By using the unknown signal as the clock input to the counter and using another timer to create a delay of 1 s the frequency can be measured.

Example 7.4 There is a signal with unknown frequency. Use Timer 1 and Timer 0 to measure its frequency. Describe the procedure of measurement and convert the procedure to a program. Assume the frequency is not higher than 65,535 so that there is no need to keep track of timer overflows.

Solution: Connect the unknown signal to the P3.4/T0 pin and choose this signal as the clock input to Timer 0. Configure Timer 0 to operate as a counter in mode 1 without external gating signal. Configure Timer 1 to operate as a timer in mode 1 without external gating signal. Initialize the Timer 0 register to 0. Use Timer 1 to create a time delay of 1 s. Place the value 3CAFH in Timer 1 register to create a 50 ms delay for each Timer 1 overflow. At the end of 1 s, the final count in Timer 0 is the frequency of the unknown signal. The program is as follows:

```
t1_ovcnt    set    R0              ; use R0 as the Timer 1 overflow count
freq_l      set    R1              ; use R1 to hold the lower byte of
                                   ; frequency
freq_h      set    R2              ; use R2 to hold the upper byte of
                                   ; frequency
            org    2000H           ; starting address of the main program
            setb   P3.4            ; enable alternate function input of T0
            mov    TMOD,#15H       ; configure Timer 1 and Timer 0 as
                                   ; described
            mov    t1_ovcnt,#20    ; initialize Timer 1 overflow count to 20
            mov    TH0,#0          ; initialize Timer 0 register to 0
            mov    TL0,#0          ; "
            clr    ET1             ; disable Timer 1 interrupt
            setb   TR1             ; enable Timer 1 to run
            setb   TR0             ; enable Timer 0 to operate
again:      clr    TF1             ; clear Timer 1 overflow flag
            mov    TH1,#3CH        ; place the upper byte of the count in TH1
            mov    TL1,#AFH        ; place the lower byte of the count in TL1
wait:       jnb    TF1,wait        ; wait until TF1 is set to 1
            djnz   t1_ovcnt,again  ; wait until 50 ms delay is repeated 20
                                   ; times
            mov    freq_l,TL0      ; save the frequency
            mov    freq_h,TH0      ; "
            . . .
```

When the unknown signal's frequency is higher than $2^{16} - 1$, it is necessary to keep track of the number of Timer 0 overflows to obtain the correct frequency value. The execution time of the Timer 1 overflow interrupt is four machine cycles. In Figure 5.4, the time it takes to sample the interrupt signal until the interrupt service routine is started is about four machine cycles for the timer interrupt. The service time for a timer overflow interrupt is eight machines cycles (spent on incrementing the overflow count and the instruction RETI). As long as the timer overflow flag is cleared before the next overflow occurs, the timer overflow count will be correct. Since Timer 0 and Timer 1 are not stopped when the interrupt is being serviced, the highest frequency that can be measured will be equal to the highest number of falling edges that can be detected at the T0 pin. The signal must stay high for one machine cycle and low for at least one machine cycle for the edge to be detected. Therefore the highest frequency that can be measured can be calculated by the following equation:

$$f_{\max} = f_{osc} \div 12 \div 2 = f_{osc}/24 \tag{7.3}$$

7.4 TIMER 2

Timer 2 is a 16-bit timer/counter that can operate either as a timer or as an event counter. This is selected by the C/T2 bit in the T2CON register. The contents of the T2CON register are shown in Figure 7.6. Timer 2 has three operation modes: capture, auto-reload, and baud rate generation.

7.4.1 Timer 2 Capture Mode

In the capture mode there are two options selected by bit EXEN2 in T2CON. If EXEN2 = 0, Timer 2 is a 16-bit counter that on overflow sets bit TF2 in T2CON. This bit can then be used to generate an interrupt. If EXEN2 = 1, Timer 2 still does the above, but with the added feature that a 1-to-0 transition at external input T2EX causes the current value in the Timer 2 registers, TH2 and TL2, to be captured into registers RCAP2H and RCAP2L, respectively. In addition, the transition at T2EX causes bit EXF2 in T2CON to be set. The EXF2 bit, like TF2, can generate an interrupt. The capture mode is illustrated in Figure 7.7.

7.4.2 Timer 2 Auto-Reload Mode (Up or Down Counter)

Timer 2 can be programmed to count up or down when configured in its 16-bit auto-reload mode. This feature is invoked by a bit named DCEN (down counter enable) located in the T2MOD register. On reset the DCEN bit is set to 0 so that Timer 2 will default to count up. When DCEN is set, Timer 2 can count up or down depending on the value of the T2EX pin. The contents of the T2MOD register are shown in Figure 7.8.

T2CON   Address = 0C8H   Bit Addressable

TF2	EXF2	RCLK	TCLK	EXEN2	TR2	C/$\overline{T2}$	CP/$\overline{RL2}$
7	6	5	4	3	2	1	0

TF2:   Timer 2 overflow flag set by a Timer 2 overflow and must be cleared by software. TF2 will not be set when either RCLK = 1 or TCLK = 1

EXF2:   Timer 2 external flag set when either a capture or a reload is caused by a negative transition on the pin T2EX and EXEN2 = 1. When Timer 2 interrupt is enabled EXF2 = 1 will cause the CPU to vector to the Timer 2 interrupt routine. EXF2 must be cleared by software. EXF2 does not cause an interrupt in up/down counter mode (DCEN = 1).

RCLK: Receive clock flag. When set, causes the serial port to use Timer 2 overflow pulses for its receive clock in serial port modes 1 and 3. RCLK = 0 causes Timer 1 overflows to be used for the receive clock.

TCLK: Transmit clock flag. When set, causes the serial port to use Timer 2 overflow pulses for its transmit clock in serial port modes 1 and 3. TCLK = 0 causes Timer 1 overflows to be used for the transmit clock.

EXEN2:   Timer 2 external enable flag. When set, allows a capture or reload to occur as a result of a negative transition on the pin T2EX if Timer 2 is not being used to clock the serial port. EXEN2 = 0 causes Timer 2 to ignore events at the pin T2EX.

TR2:   Start/stop control for timer 2. A logic 1 starts the timer.

C/$\overline{T2}$:   Timer or counter select. (Timer 2)
         0 = internal timer (OSC/12 or OSC/2 in baud rate generation mode).
         1 = external event counter (falling edge triggered).

CP/$\overline{RL2}$:   Capture/Reload flag. When set, captures will occur on negative transitions at the T2EX pin if EXEN2 = 1. When cleared, auto-reloads will occur either with Timer 2 overflows or negative transitions at T2EX when EXEN2 = 1. When either RCLK = 1 or TCLK = 1, this bit is ignored and the timer is forced to auto-reload on Timer 2 overflow.

Figure 7.6 T2CON: Timer/Counter 2 control register.

Figure 7.9 shows that Timer 2 automatically counts up when DCEN = 0. In this mode there are two options selected by bit EXEN2 in T2CON. If EXEN2 = 0, Timer 2 counts up to 0FFFFH and then sets the TF2 flag on overflow. The overflow also causes the timer registers to be reloaded with the 16-bit value in RCAP2H and RCAP2L. If EXEN2 = 1, a 16-bit reload can be triggered either by an overflow or by a 1-to-0 transition at external input T2EX. This transition also sets the EXF2 bit. Either the TF2 or EXF2 bit can generate the Timer 2 interrupt if it is enabled.

Setting the DCEN bit enables Timer 2 to count up or down as shown in Figure 7.10. In this mode the T2EX pin controls the direction of count. Logic 1 at the T2EX pin makes Timer 2 count up. The timer will overflow at 0FFFFH and set the TF2 bit, which can then generate an interrupt if it is enabled. This overflow also causes the 16-bit value in RCAP2H and RCAP2L to be reloaded into the timer registers, TH2 and TL2, respectively.

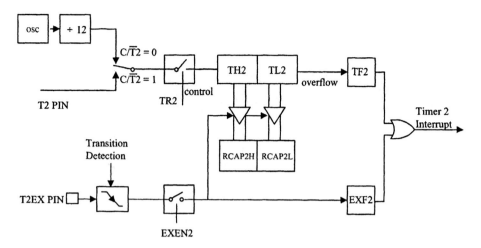

Figure 7.7 Timer 2 in capture mode.

T2MOD Address = 0C9H   Not bit addressable

--	--	--	--	--	--	T2OE	DCEN
7	6	5	4	3	2	1	0

T2OE: Timer 2 Output Enable Bit

DCEN: Down Count Enable bit. When set, this allows Timer 2 to be
       configured as an up/down counter.

Figure 7.8 T2MOD: Timer 2 control register.

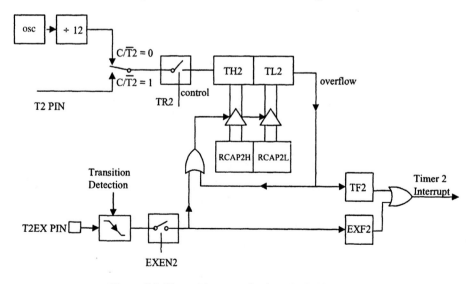

Figure 7.9 Timer 2 in auto-reload mode (DCEN = 0).

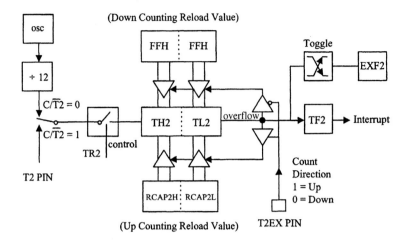

Figure 7.10 Timer 2 in auto-reload mode (DCEN = 1).

A logic 0 at T2EX makes Timer 2 count down. Now the timer underflows when TH2 and TL2 equal the values stored in RCAP2H and RCAP2L. The underflow sets the TF2 bit and causes 0FFFFH to be reloaded into the timer registers.

The EXF2 bit toggles whenever Timer 2 overflows or underflows. This bit can be used as a seventeenth bit of resolution if desired. In this operation mode, EXF2 does not generate an interrupt.

7.4.3 Timer 2 Baud Rate Generation Mode

The baud rate generation mode is selected by setting the RCLK and/or TCLK bits in the T2CON register. When RCLK = 1, serial port uses Timer 2 overflow pulses as receive clock in serial port modes 1 and 3. RCLK = 0 causes Timer 1 overflow pulses to be used for receive clock. When TCLK = 1, the serial port uses Timer 2 overflow pulses for its transmit clock in serial port modes 1 and 3. TCLK = 0 causes Timer 1 overflow pulses to be used for the transmit clock. This subject will be discussed in more detail in Section 9.4.3.

7.4.4 Programmable Clock Out

A 50% duty cycle clock can be programmed to come out on P1.0. This pin, besides being a regular I/O pin, has two alternate functions. It can be programmed (1) to input the external clock for Timer/Counter 2 or (2) to output a 50% duty cycle clock ranging from 61 Hz to 4 MHz at a 16-MHz operating frequency.

To configure Timer/Counter 2 as a clock generator, bit $C/\overline{T}2$ (in T2CON) must be cleared and bit T2OE in T2MOD must be set. Bit TR2 (T2CON.2) also must be set to start the timer.

The clock-out frequency depends on the oscillator frequency and the reload value of Timer 2 capture registers (RCAP2H, RCAP2L) as shown in this equation:

$$\text{Clock-out frequency} = \frac{\text{Oscillator frequency}}{4 \times (65536 - \text{RCAP2H, RCAP2L})} \tag{7.4}$$

In the clock-out mode Timer 2 rollover will not generate an interrupt. This is similar to when Timer 2 is used as a baud-rate generator. It is possible to use Timer 2 as a baud-rate generator and a clock generator simultaneously. Note, however, that the baud-rate and clock-out frequencies cannot be determined independently of one another since they both use the values in RCAP2H and RCAP2L.

7.4.5 Applications of Timer 2

Like Timer 1 and Timer 0, Timer 2 can be used to create time delays and measure frequencies. In addition, Timer 2 can also be used to measure the period of an unknown signal. The period of a signal can be measured by capturing two consecutive falling edges of a signal as shown in Figure 7.11.

Taking the difference of the two captured values gives the period in number of machine cycles. For some very slow signals, the timer may have overflowed many times before two consecutive falling edges are captured. Timer overflows must be kept track of for such slow signals. Let

tovcnt	= the Timer 2 overflow count
diff	= edge2 − edge1 (because 2's complement addition is used to perform a subtract operation, this will give the correct magnitude if edge1 is larger than edge 2)
edge1	= the captured time of the first edge
edge2	= the captured time of the second edge

The period of the signal can be calculated using the following equations:

Case 1:   edge2 ≥ edge1

$$\text{Period} = tovcnt \times 2^{16} + diff \tag{7.5}$$

Case 2:   edge2 < edge1

$$\text{Period} = (tovcnt - 1) \times 2^{16} + diff \tag{7.6}$$

In Case 2, the Timer 2 overflows at least once even if the period is shorter than $2^{16} - 1$ machine cycles. Therefore, we need to subtract one from the timer overflow count to obtain the correct result.

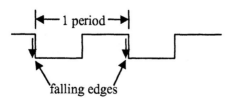

Figure 7.11 Period measurement.

Example 7.5 Use Timer 2 to measure the period of an unknown signal. Assume the unknown signal has been connected to the T2EX pin.

Solution: We will use the polling method to capture the first falling edge and include a Timer 2 interrupt-handling routine to keep track of the number of Timer 2 overflows. When the first falling edge arrives, the program initializes the Timer 2 register to 0 and clears both the TF2 and EXF2 flags and enables Timer 2 interrupt. Since Timer 2 has only one interrupt vector, its service routine must check the cause of the interrupt. If the interrupt is caused by timer register overflow, it simply increments the overflow count and return. If the interrupt is caused by the arrival of the second edge, it stops Timer 2. Two bytes are reserved for this purpose so that we can measure a period as long as $2^{32} - 1$ machine cycles. The period is obtained by appending the difference of the two captured edges to the overflow count. The logic flow of the program is illustrated in Figure 7.12. The T2CON register must be programmed as follows for period measurement:

- Clear TF2 (bit 7) and EXF2 (bit 6)
- Clear RCLK (bit 5) and TCLK (bit 4) to 0
- Set EXEN2 (bit 3) to 1 to enable capture
- Set TR2 (bit 2) to 1 to enable Timer 2
- Clear C/$\overline{T2}$ (bit 1) to 0 to choose timer mode
- Set CP/$\overline{RL2}$ (bit 0) to 1 to enable capture on the falling edge of the T2EX pin

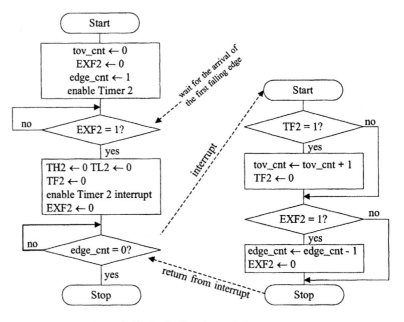

Figure 7.12 Logic flow for period measurement.

Write the value 0DH into the T2CON register for this configuration.

The program for measuring the period is as follows:

```
tov_cntH     set    R0              ; upper byte of Timer 2 overflow
                                    ; count

tov_cntL     set    R1              ; lower byte of Timer 2 overflow
                                    ; count

period_H     set    R2              ; period in machine cycles
period_L     set    R3              ; "
edge_cnt     set    R4
             org    00H             ; starting address of reset service
                                    ; routine

             ljmp   main
             org    02BH            ; Timer 2 interrupt vector
             ljmp   t2_ISR          ; jump to the service routine of
                                    ; interrupt

             org    xxxxH           ; starting address of the main
                                    ; program
main:        mov    edge_cnt,#1     ; initialize the edge count to 1
             setb   P1.1            ; enable T2EX alternate function
             mov    tov_cntH,#0     ; initialize Timer 2 overflow count
             mov    tov_cntL,#0     ; to 0
             mov    T2CON,#0DH      ; clear two flags, initialize & enable
                                    ; Timer 2

             mov    IE,#00H         ; disable all interrupt at the
                                    ; beginning
edge_1st:    jnb    TF2,edge_1st    ; wait for the arrival of the first falling
                                    ; edge
             mov    period_H,RCAP2H ; save the first edge
             mov    period_L,RCAP2L ; "
             clr    EXF2            ; clear that flag immediately
             clr    TF2             ; also clear the Timer 2 overflow flag
             orl    IE,#A0H         ; enable Timer 2 interrupt
wait_lp:     mov    A,edge_cnt      ; has the second edge arrived?
             jnz    wait_lp
             mov    A,RCAP2H        ;
             clr    C               ; clear the carry flag
             subb   A,period_H      ; compare the upper byte first
             jc     e1_larger       ; is the first edge larger?
             jz     upper_eq        ; are upper bytes equal?
; the upper byte of the first edge is smaller and subtraction starts from the lower byte
```

```
e2_larger:    mov    A,RCAP2L         ; place the lower byte of the second
                                      ; edge in A
              clr    C                ; clear the carry before subtraction
              subb   A,period_L       ; compute the difference of the
                                      ; lower bytes
              mov    period_L,A       ; "
              mov    A,RCAP2H         ; compute the difference of the
                                      ; upper byte
              subb   A,period_H       ;
              mov    period_H,A       ; place the upper byte of the
                                      ; difference in period
              ajmp   exit
e1_larger:    mov    A,tov_cntL       ; decrement the overflow count by 1
              clr    C                ; "
              subb   A,#1             ; "
              mov    tov_cntL,A       ; "
              mov    A,tov_cntH       ; "
              subb   A,#0             ; "
              mov    tov_cntH,A       ; "
              ajmp   e2_larger
upper_eq:     mov    A,RCAP2L         ; compare the lower half
              clr    C
              subb   A,period_L
              jnc    e2_larger        ; the second edge is larger or both
                                      ; edges are equal
              ajmp   e1_larger        ; the first edge is larger
exit:         . . . .                 ; do something else
t2_ISR:       jnb    TF2,check_ed     ; is the interrupt caused by timer
                                      ; overflow?
              mov    A,tov_cntL       ; yes, increment the overflow count by 1
              add    A,#1             ; "
              mov    tov_cntL,A       ; "
              mov    A,tov_cntH       ; "
              addc   A,#0             ; "
              mov    tov_cntH,A       ; "
              clr    TF2              ; also clear the TF2 bit
check_ed:     jnb    EXF2,quit        ; is interrupt caused by the second
                                      ; edge?
              dec    edge_cnt         ; decrement the edge count
              clr    EXF2             ; clear the EXF2 flag
```

| | | anl | IE,#5F | | ; disable Timer 2 interrupt |
| quit: | | reti | | | |

The auto-reload mode of Timer 2 makes the creation of time delay longer than $2^{16} - 1$ machine cycles slightly easier. This mode can also facilitate the generation of periodic interrupts, which is useful in many applications. One application would be the tracking of time of day.

Example 7.6 Use Timer 2 to create a time delay of 1 s. Assume that the 87C51FB is controlled by a 12-MHz crystal oscillator.

Solution: Configure Timer 2 to operate in auto-reload mode using the TF2 flag to reload the timer register. Enable Timer 2 overflow interrupt and generate 50 ms time delay for each overflow. Load the value 15535 (3CAF in hex) into the Timer 2 register so that it overflows in 50,000 machine cycles. Configure the T2CON register as follows:

- clear TF2 and EXF2 flags
- clear RCLK and TCLK to 0
- clear EXEN2 to disable external reload
- enable Timer 2 (set the TR2 bit)
- select timer mode (set the C/T2 bit to 0)
- select reload by timer overflow (clear bit 0)

For this configuration, load the value 00000100_2 into the T2CON register. Load 0 into the T2MOD register to select count up and disable Timer 2 output.

The program is written as a subroutine as follows:

ov_cnt		set	R0	; use this register to keep track of
				; remaining overflows
		org	2BH	; Timer 2 interrupt vector
		dec	ov_cnt	;
		clr	TF2	;
		reti		
delay_1s:		clr	TF2	
		mov	TH2,#3CH	; initialize Timer 2 registers to 3CAFH
		mov	TL2,#AFH	; "
		mov	RCAP2H,#3CH	; initialize RCAP2H register
		mov	RCAP2L,#AFH	; initialize RCAP2L register
		mov	ov_cnt,#20	; initialize the timer overflow count
				; to 20
		mov	T2MOD,#00	; select timer mode and disable output
		mov	T2CON,#04H	; initialize T2CON register and enable
				; Timer 2

```
                orl   IE,#A0H              ; enable Timer 2 interrupt
    here:       mov   A,ov_cnt             ; is ov_cnt decremented to 0?
                jnz   here
                ret                        ; one second delay is ended
```

Example 7.7 *Time-of-day tracking*. Assume that the 87C51FB is controlled by a 12-MHz crystal oscillator. Use Timer 2 to keep track of the current time of day.

Solution: Here, we are not concerned about how the current time of day is entered. Only the part of updating the current time will be presented. The procedure to keep track of the current time of day is very straightforward:

STEP 1 Use three registers to hold the hour, minute, and second of the current time.

STEP 2 Configure Timer 2 to operate as described in the previous example.

STEP 3 Update the current time every second.

Use registers R0, R1, and R2 to hold the hour, minute, and second of the current time. Use a 24-h system. The program is as follows:

```
    hour        set   R0
    minute      set   R1
    second      set   R2
    ov_cnt      set   R3
                org   2BH                  ; Timer 2 interrupt vector
                dec   ov_cnt
                clr   TF2
                reti
                org   100H                 ; starting address of the program
                clr   TF2                  ; clear the TF2 flag
                mov   T2MOD,#00            ; select timer mode and disable output
                mov   T2CON,#04H           ; initialize T2CON register
                mov   TH2,#3CH             ; initialize Timer 2 registers to 3CAFH
                mov   TL2,#AFH             ; "
                mov   RCAP2H,#3CH          ; initialize RCAP2H register
                mov   RCAP2L,#AFH          ; initialize RCAP2L register
                orl   IE,#A0H              ; enable Timer 2 interrupt
    forever:    mov   ov_cnt,#20           ; initialize the timer overflow count
                                           ; to 20
    here:       mov   A,ov_cnt             ; wait until 1 s is over
                jnz   here                 ; "
                inc   second               ; increment the second
```

cjne	second,#60, forever	; need to update minute?
mov	second,#0	; reset second to 0
inc	minute	; increment the minute
cjne	minute,#60, forever	; need to update hour?
mov	minute,#0	; reset minute to 0
inc	hour	; increment hour
cjne	hour,#24,forever	; need to reset hour to 0?
mov	hour,#0	; reset hour to 0
ljmp	forever	; repeat
end		

Timer 2 cannot capture the rising edge of a signal. This may be inconvenient for some applications, for example, the measurement of pulse width. If Timer 2 can also capture the rising edge of a signal, the measurement of pulse width becomes very simple. The user program simply captures two consecutive edges and takes their difference. This may be one of the reasons that led to the addition of PCA.

The capture mode of Timer 2 has other applications:

Event arrival time recording. There are applications that need to compare the arrival times of several different events. Timer 2 may serve this purpose along with other channels of PCA.

Interrupt generation. The T2EX signal can serve as an edge-sensitive interrupt source.

Event counting. An event can be represented by a signal edge. The capture mode of Timer 2 can be used in combination with one other timer to count the number of events that occur during an interval. An event counter can be set up and incremented by the Timer 2 (in capture mode) interrupt service routine. This application is illustrated in Figure 7.13.

Example 7.8 Use the Timer 2 programmable clock-out mode to create a 4-kHz digital waveform with 50% duty cycle. Assume $f_{OSC} = 12$ MHz.

Solution: Use Equation 7.4, the 16-bit value to be written into (RCAP2H; RCAP2L) is FD12H. The following instruction sequence will accomplish the job:

mov	T2CON,#04H	; enable Timer 2 and select timer mode
mov	T2MOD,#02H	; enable Timer 2 output
mov	RCAP2H,#FDH	; place the upper byte of FD12H in RCAP2H
mov	RCAP2L,#12H	; place the lower byte of FD12H in RCAP2L
setb	P1.0	; enable clock-out alternate function

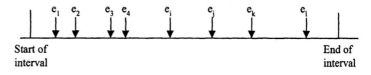

Start of
interval

End of
interval

Figure 7.13 Using Timer 2 capture mode for counting events.

7.5 PROGRAMMABLE COUNTER ARRAY

The programmable counter array (PCA) consists of a 16-bit timer/counter and five 16-bit compare/capture modules as shown in Figure 7.14. The PCA timer/counter serves as a common time base for the five modules and is the only timer that can service the PCA. Its clock input can be programmed to count any one of the following signals:

- oscillator output ÷ 12
- oscillator output ÷ 4
- Timer 0 overflow
- external input on ECI (P1.2)

Each compare/capture module can be programmed in any one of the following modes:

- rising and/or falling edge capture
- software timer
- high-speed output
- pulse width modulator

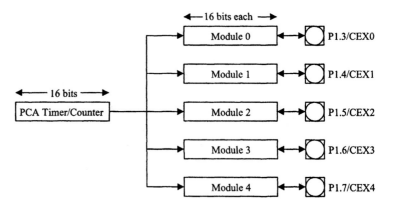

Figure 7.14 Programmable counter array.

Module 4 can also be programmed as a watchdog timer.

When the compare/capture module is programmed in the capture, software timer, or high speed output mode, an interrupt can be generated when the module performs its function. All five modules plus PCA timer overflows share the same interrupt vector.

As mentioned at the beginning of this chapter, the 8XC51GB has two PCAs called PCA and PCA1. The following discussion (includes text and figures) addresses only PCA but is also applicable to PCA1 with the following exceptions:

1. The module 4 of PCA1 does not support watchdog timer.
2. All the special function registers and bits have 1s added to their names (see Table 7.2).
3. Port 4 is the interface for PCA1:
   P4.2 ECI1
   P4.3 C1EX0
   P4.4 C1EX1
   P4.5 C1EX2
   P4.6 C1EX3
   P4.7 C1EX4
4. There is one additional bit added to C1CON to allow both PCAs to be enabled simultaneously. This bit is called CRE and occupies bit position 5 of C1CON. Its bit address is 0EDH. When CRE is set both CR and CR1 must be set to enable PCA1.

TABLE 7.2
PCA and PCA1 SFRs

SFRs		Bits	
PCA	**PCA1**	**PCA**	**PCA1**
CCON	C1CON	EC1	ECI1
CMOD	C1MOD	CEX0	C1EX0
CCAPM0	C1CAPM0	CEX1	C1EX1
CCAPM1	C1CAPM1	CEX2	C1EX2
CCAPM2	C1CAPM2	CEX3	C1EX3
CCAPM3	C1CAPM3	CEX4	C1EX4
CCAPM4	C1CAPM4	CCF0	C1CF0
CL	CL1	CCF1	C1CF1
CCAP0L	C1CAP0L	CCF2	C1CF2
CCAP1L	C1CAP1L	CCF3	C1CF3
CCAP2L	C1CAP2L	CCF4	C1CF4
CCAP3L	C1CAP3L	CR	CR1
CCAP4L	C1CAP4L	CF	CF1
CH	CH1		
CCAP0H	C1CAP0H		
CCAP1H	C1CAP1H		
CCAP2H	C1CAP2H		
CCAP3H	C1CAP3H		
CCAP4H	C1CAP4H		

7.5.1 PCA 16-Bit Timer/Counter

The PCA has a free-running 16-bit timer/counter consisting of registers CH and CL (hold the higher and lower bytes of the count value). These two registers can be read from or written into any time. Figure 7.15 shows a block diagram of this timer. The clock input can be selected from the following four sources:

- Oscillator output ÷ 12
  The CL register is incremented at S5P2 of every machine cycle.
- Oscillator output ÷ 4
  The CL register is incremented at S1P2, S3P2, and S5P2 of every machine cycle.
- Timer 0 overflow
  The CL register is incremented at S5P2 of the machine cycle when Timer 0 overflows. This mode allows a programmable input frequency to the PCA.
- External input
  The CL register is incremented at the first one of S1P2, S3P2, and S5P2 of every machine cycle after a 1-to-0 transition is detected on the ECI pin (P1.2). P1.2 is sampled at S1P2, S3P2, and S5P2 of every machine cycle. The maximum input frequency in this mode is equal to crystal oscillator frequency ÷ 8.

The CH register is incremented two oscillator periods after CL overflows. The mode register CMOD contains the count pulse select bits (CPS1 and CPS0) to specify the clock input. The contents of the CMOD register are shown in Figure 7.16. This register also contains the ECF bit that enables the PCA counter overflow to generate the PCA interrupt. In addition, the user has the option of turning off the PCA timer during idle mode by setting the counter idle bit (CIDL). The watchdog timer enable bit (WDTE) will be discussed in a later section.

The CCON register, shown in Figure 7.17, contains two more bits that are associated with the PCA timer/counter. The CF bit gets set by hardware when the counter overflows, and the CR bit is set or cleared to turn the counter on or off. The other five bits in this register are the event flags for the compare/capture modules and will be discussed in a later section.

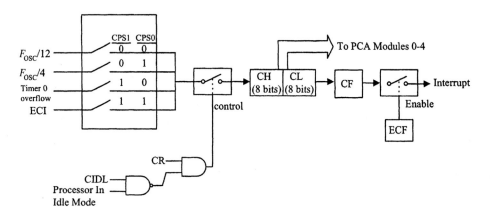

Figure 7.15 PCA timer/counter. (Redrawn with permission of Intel.)

CMOD   Address = 0D9H   Not Bit Addressable

CIDL	WDTE	--	--	--	CPS1	CPS0	ECF
7	6	5	4	3	2	1	0

CIDL: Counter Idle Control. CIDL = 0 programs the PCA counter to continue functioning during idle mode. CIDL = 1 programs it to be gated off during idle.

WDTE: Watchdog Timer Enable. WDTE = 0 disables Watchdog Timer function on PCA module 4. WDTE = 1 enables it.

CPS1:   PCA Count Enable Select bit 1.

CPS0:   PCA Count Enable Select bit 0.

CPS1	CPS0	Selected PCA Input
0	0	Internal clock, $f_{OSC} \div 12$
0	1	Interanl clock, $f_{OSC} \div 4$
1	0	Timer 0 overflow
1	1	External clock at ECI/P1.2 pin

ECF: PCA Enable Counter Overflow interrupt. ECF = 1 enables CF bit in CCON to generate an interrupt. ECF = 0 disables that function of CF.

Figure 7.16 CMOD: PCA counter mode register.

CCON   Address = 0D8H   Bit Addressable

CF	CR	--	CCF4	CCF3	CCF2	CCF1	CCF0
7	6	5	4	3	2	1	0

CF: PCA Counter Overflow flag. Set by hardware when the counter rolls over. CF flags an interrupt if bit ECF in CMOD is set. CF may be set by either hardware or software but can be cleared only by software.

CR: PCA Counter Run control bit. Set by software to turn the PCA counter on. Must be cleared by software to turn the PCA counter off.

CCF4:   PCA module 4 interrupt flag. Set by the hardware when a match or capture occurs. Must be cleared by software.

CCF3:   PCA module 3 interrupt flag. Set by the hardware when a match or capture occurs. Must be cleared by software.

CCF2:   PCA module 2 interrupt flag. Set by the hardware when a match or capture occurs. Must be cleared by software.

CCF1:   PCA module 1 interrupt flag. Set by the hardware when a match or capture occurs. Must be cleared by software.

CCF0:   PCA module 0 interrupt flag. Set by the hardware when a match or capture occurs. Must be cleared by software.

Figure 7.17 CCON PCA counter control register.

7.5.2 Capture/Compare Modules

Each of the five compare/capture modules can perform the following six functions:

- 16-bit capture, positive-edge (rising-edge) triggered
- 16-bit capture, negative-edge (falling-edge) triggered

CCAPMn (n = 0,..,4)   Address = 0DAH..0DEH   Not Bit Addressable

--	ECOMn	CAPPn	CAPNn	MATn	TOGn	PWMn	ECCFn
7	6	5	4	3	2	1	0

ECOMn: Enable comparator. ECOMn = 1 enables the comparator function

CAPPn: Capture positive, CAPPn = 1 enables positive edge capture.

CAPNn: Capture negative, CAPNn = 1 enables negative edge capture.

MATn: Match. When MATn = 1, a match of the PCA counter with this module's compare/capture register causes the CCFs bit in CCON to be set, flagging an interrupt.

TOGn: Toggle. When TOGn = 1, a match of the PCA counter with this module's compare/capture register causes the CEXn pin to toggle.

PWMn: Pulse Width Modulation Mode. PWMn = 1 enables the CEXn pin to be used as a pulse width modulated output.

ECCFn: Enable CCF interrupt. Enables compare/capture flag CCFn in the CCON register to generate an interrupt.

Figure 7.18 CCAPMn: PCA module compare/capture register.

- 16-bit capture, both positive-edge and negative-edge triggered
- 16-bit software timer
- 16-bit high-speed output
- 8-bit pulse width modulation

In addition, module 4 can be used as a watchdog timer. The modules can be programmed in any combination of the different modes.

Each module has a mode register called CCAPMn (n = 0, 1, 2, 3, or 4) to select which function it will perform. The CCAPMn register is shown in Figure 7.18. The ECCFn bit enables the PCA interrupt when a module's event flag is set. The event flag (CCFn) is contained in the CCON register and is set when a capture event, software timer, or high-speed output event occurs for a given module.

Each module also has a pair of 8-bit compare/capture registers (CCAPnH and CCAPnL) associated with it. These registers store the time when a capture event occurred or when a compare event should occur. For the PWM mode, the high byte register CCAPnH controls the duty cycle of the waveform.

Example 7.9 Configure PCA module 0 to capture the rising edge of the signal applied to the CEX0 pin. Use oscillator output *osc ÷ 12* as the clock source of the timer.

Solution: Three registers need to be programmed:

CMOD register: This application does not care about watchdog function or counter idle control. Disable both. Bits 2 and 1 of the CMOD register should be set to 00 to choose the appropriate PCA clock source. PCA overflow interrupt is not needed. Set the bit 0 to 0. Therefore write the value 00H into the CMOD register.

CCON register: The PCA counter must be enabled and all flags should be cleared at the beginning. Write the value 40H into the CCON register.

CCAPM0 register: For module 0,

- Bit ECOM0 (bit 6): set to 0 to disable the comparator
- Bit CAPP0 (bit 5): set to 1 to capture positive (rising) edge
- Bit CAPN0 (bit 4): set to 0 to disable falling edge capture
- Bit MAT0 (bit 3): set to 0 to disable module 0 comparator
- Bit TOG0 (bit 2): set to 0 so that CEX0 pin will not toggle when PCA counter matches the compare/capture registers of module 0
- Bit PWM0 (bit 1): cleared to disable pulse modulation output
- Bit ECCF0 (bit 0): cleared to disable CCF interrupt

Therefore, the value 20H should be written into the CCAPM0 register. The following instructions will accomplish the intended configuration:

```
mov    CMOD,#00H        ; configure the PCA CMOD register
mov    CCON,#40H        ; configure the PCA CCON register
mov    CCAPM0,#20H      ; configure the PCA CCAPM0 register
```

7.5.3 Sixteen-Bit Capture Mode

The PCA can capture both the positive and negative transitions of a signal. This gives the flexibility to measure periods, pulse widths, duty cycles, and phase differences on up to five separate inputs. Setting the CAPPn and/or CAPNn *in* the CCAPMn mode register selects the input trigger—positive and/or negative transition—for module n. The functioning of the capture mode is illustrated in Figure 7.19.

The external input pins CEX0 through CEX4 are sampled for a transition. When a valid transition is detected (positive and/or negative edge), hardware loads the 16-bit value of the PCA timer (CH, CL) into the module's capture registers (CCAP*n*H, CCAP*n*L). On a capture, the module's event flag (CCF*n*) in the CCON register is set, and an interrupt is flagged if the ECCF*n* bit in the mode register CCAPM*n* is set. The PCA interrupt will then be generated if it is enabled. Since the hardware does not clear an event flag when the interrupt is vectored to, the flag must be cleared in software.

In the interrupt service routine, the 16-bit capture value must be saved in RAM before the next capture event occurs. A subsequent capture on the same CEX*n* pin will write over the previous capture values in CCAP*n*H and CCAP*n*L.

Like the capture mode of Timer 2, the PCA 16-bit capture mode can be used to measure the period of an unknown signal. Since the PCA 16-bit capture mode can capture both positive and negative signal edges, it can also be used to measure the pulse width of an unknown signal. As shown in Figure 7.20, the pulse width can be measured by capturing two consecutive edges of an unknown signal—one positive and one negative.

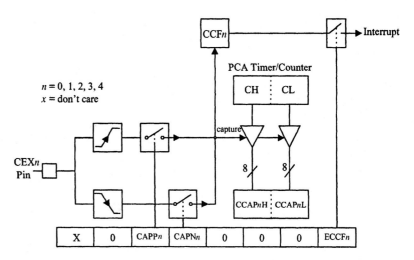

Figure 7.19 PCA 16-bit capture mode. (Redrawn with permission of Intel.)

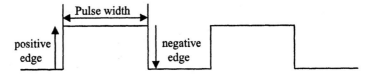

Figure 7.20 Pulse width measurement.

Since the pulse width may be much longer than what a 16-bit register can accommodate, the user software needs to keep track of the number of the PCA timer overflows. Let

ovcnt   = the PCA timer overflow count
edge1   = the captured time of the first edge
edge2   = the captured time of the second edge
diff   = edge2 − edge1

Then the pulse width can be calculated using the following equations:

Case 1:   edge2 ≥ edge1

$$\text{Pulse width} = ovcnt \times 2^{16} + diff \tag{7.7}$$

Case 2:   edge2 < edge1

$$\text{Pulse width} = (ovcnt - 1) \times 2^{16} + diff \tag{7.8}$$

Example 7.10 Suppose an unknown signal is connected to the CEX0 pin. Write a subroutine to measure the pulse width of this signal.

Solution: The procedure for measuring the pulse width is as follows:

STEP 1   Configure the PCA counter and module 0 accordingly.

STEP 2   Wait for the arrival of the first edge of the CEX0 signal.

STEP 3   Enable PCA counter overflow interrupt and initialize the overflow count to 0.

STEP 4   For each PCA counter overflow, increment the overflow count by 1.

STEP 5   Wait for the arrival of the next signal edge. Take the difference of the two captured edges to compute the pulse width.

The registers CCON, CMOD, and CCAPM0 must be configured properly:

The CCON register: Clear all the flags and enable the PCA timer to run. Write the value 40H into CCON.

The CMOD register: Choose *osc ÷ 12* as the clock source of the PCA timer and enable PCA timer overflow interrupt. Disable watchdog timer and choose to gate off the PCA timer during idle mode. Write the value 81H into CMOD.

The CCAPM0 register: Disable the comparator function, capture both edges, disable match, disable toggling, disable pulse width modulation, and disable capture interrupt. Write the value 30H into the CCAPM0 register.

The program is as follows:

```
tov_cntH      set    R0              ; PCA counter overflow count high
                                     ; byte
tov_cntL      set    R1              ; PCA counter overflow count low
                                     ; byte
pw_H          set    R2              ; pulse width high byte
pw_L          set    R3              ; pulse width low byte
              org    033H            ; PCA interrupt vector
              jmp    pca_handler     ; jump to the service routine of PCA
                                     ; interrupt
              org    xxxxH           ; starting address of the real PCA
                                     ; handler
pca_hndler:   anl    CCON,#7FH       ; clear CF flag
              mov    A,tov_cntL      ; increment the PCA timer overflow
                                     ; count by 1
              add    A,#1            ; "
              mov    tov_cntL,A      ; "
              mov    A,tov_cntH      ; "
              addc   A,#0            ; "
```

```
                          mov     tov_cntH,A          ; "
                          reti
                          org     yyyyH               ; starting address of the program
         pulse:           setb    P1.3                ; enable CEX0 alternate function
                          mov     tov_cntH,#0         ; initialize PCA timer overflow count
                                                      ; to 0
                          mov     tov_cntL,#0         ; "
                          mov     CCON,#40H           ; initialize the PCA CCON register
                          mov     CMOD,#81H           ; initialize the PCA CMOD register
                          mov     CCAPM0,#30H         ; enable PCA module 0 to capture
                                                      ; both edges
                          mov     IE,#00H             ; disable all interrupts at the
                                                      ; beginning
                          setb    CR                  ; enable the PCA timer to run
                          clr     CF                  ; make sure PCA timer flag is cleared
         first_ed:        jnb     CCF0,first_ed       ; wait for the arrival of the first edge
                          mov     pw_H,CCAP0H         ; save the rising edge
                          mov     pw_L,CCAP0L         ; "
                          clr     CF                  ; clear the PCA timer overflow flag
                          clr     CCF0                ; also clear the module 0 capture flag
                          orl     IE,#C0H             ; enable PCA interrupt
         second_ed:       jnb     CCF0,second_ed      ; wait for the arrival of the second
                                                      ; edge
                          clr     EC                  ; disable PCA interrupt
                          mov     A,CCAP0H            ;
                          clr     C                   ; clear the carry flag
                          subb    A,pw_H              ; compare the upper bytes first
                          jc      e1_larger           ; is the first edge larger?
                          jz      upper_eq            ; are upper bytes equal?
; the upper byte of the first edge is smaller and subtraction starts from the
; lower bytes
         e2_larger:       mov     A,CCAP0L            ; place the lower byte of the second
                                                      ; edge in A
                          clr     C                   ; clear the carry before subtraction
                          subb    A,pw_L              ;
                          mov     pw_L,A              ; put the lower byte of difference
                                                      ; back to pw_L
                          mov     A,CCAP0H
                          subb    A,pw_H              ; take the difference of the upper bytes
                          mov     pw_H,A              ; place the upper byte of the difference
                                                      ; in pw_H
```

```
              ret
e1_larger:    clr     C                        ; subtract the overflow count by 1
              mov     A,tov_cntL               ; "
              subb    A,#1                     ; "
              mov     tov_cntL,A               ; "
              mov     A,tov_cntH               ; "
              subb    A,#0                     ; "
              mov     tov_cntH,A               ; "
              ajmp    e2_larger
upper_eq:     mov     A,CCAP0L                 ; compare the lower half
              clr     C
              subb    A,pw_L
              jc      e1_larger                ; second edge is smaller
              ajmp    e2_larger                ; second edge is not smaller
              end
```

The *duty cycle* of a digital waveform can be measured by dividing the pulse width by the period of the signal. The *phase difference* is defined for two signals having the same frequency but do not coincide at their rising and falling edges. The phase difference is illustrated in Figure 7.21.

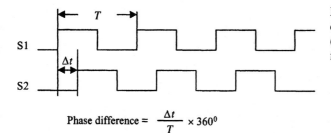

Figure 7.21 Definition of phase difference between two signals (these two signals have the same frequency).

$$\text{Phase difference} = \frac{\Delta t}{T} \times 360^0$$

The procedure for measuring the phase difference of two signals is as follows:

STEP 1 Capture the rising (or falling) edge of the first signal using one PCA module.

STEP 2 Capture the rising (or falling) edge of the second signal using another PCA module.

STEP 3 Capture the second rising (or falling) edge of the first signal to compute the period of the signal.

STEP 4 Compute the phase difference using the equation shown in Figure 7.21.

7.5.4 Sixteen-Bit Software Timer and High-Speed Output

The high-speed output (HSO) mode toggles a CEXn pin when a match occurs between the PCA timer and a preloaded value in a module's compare register. For this mode, the TOGn

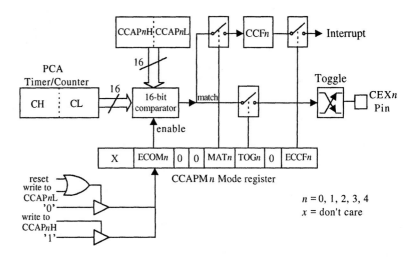

Figure 7.22 High-speed output circuit operation. (Redrawn with permission of Intel.)

bit in the CCAPM*n* register needs to be set in addition to the ECOM*n* and MAT*n* bits as seen in Figure 7.22. The user also has the option of flagging an interrupt when a match event occurs by setting the ECCF*n* bit.

The HSO mode is more accurate than toggling port pins in software because the toggle occurs before branching to an interrupt. That is, interrupt latency will not affect the accuracy of the output. If the user does not change the compare registers in an interrupt routine, the next toggle will occur when the PCA timer rolls over and matches the last compare value.

To use the software timer mode,

1. Make a copy of the PCA timer (CH, CL) value
2. Add to this copy a value equal to the desired time delay
3. Store the sum into the module compare registers (CCAP*n*H, CCAP*n*L)

We have the option of specifying the signal on the selected pin to be toggled.

Example 7.11 Assume that the 87C51FB is running with a 12-MHz crystal oscillator. Use the PCA module 0 to create a time delay of 1 s.

Solution: Choose *osc* ÷ *12* as the clock input to the PCA timer. Since the PCA timer is 16 bit, it will overflow every 65.5 ms (2^{16} machine cycles). To create a 1-s delay, we will need to perform multiple software comparisons. For example, we can perform 20 software compare operations, with each software comparison creating a time delay of 50 ms. Use register R0 to keep track of the number of software compare operations remaining to be performed.

```
cnt         set    R0              ; software comparison counter
one_sec     equ    20              ; the number of software compare to be
                                    ; performed
```

```
50ms_L      equ     50H             ; the lower and upper bytes of the
                                    ; number to be
50ms_H      equ     C3H             ; added to create a 50 ms delay
            org     33H             ; the PCA interrupt vector
            ljmp    pca_ISR         ; jump to the actual PCA service routine
            org     4000H           ; starting address of the main program
            mov     CMOD,#80H       ; choose osc ÷ 12 as clock input, disable
                                    ; PCA timer overflow interrupt, gate off
                                    ; counter when in idle mode, and disable
                                    ; watchdog timer
            mov     CCON,#40H       ; enable PCA timer and clear all flags
            mov     CCAPM0,#49H     ; enable module 0 comparator, CCF
                                    ; interrupt, and
                                    ; match but disable the reset functions
            orl     IE,#C0H         ; enable PCA interrupt
            mov     cnt,#one_sec    ; initialize the software compare
                                    ; counter to 20
            mov     A,CL            ; add 50 ms delay and store it
            add     A,#50ms_L       ; "
            mov     CCAP0L,A        ; "
            mov     A,CH            ; "
            addc    A,#50ms_H       ; "
            mov     CCAP0H,A        ; "
loop:       mov     A,cnt           ; is one second over?
            jnz     loop            ; "
            anl     IE,#BFH         ; disable PCA interrupt
            . . .
pca_ISR:    anl     CCON,#5EH       ; clear CF and CCF0 flags
            dec     cnt             ; decrement the software compare
                                    ; counter by 1
            mov     A,CCAP0L        ; start the next software compare
                                    ; operation on module 0 with 50 ms
                                    ; delay
            add     A,#50ms_L       ; "
            mov     CCAP0L,A        ; "
            mov     A,CCAP0H        ; "
            addc    A,#50ms_H       ; "
            mov     CCAP0H,A        ; "
            reti
```

Example 7.12 Assume that the 87C51FB is running with a 12-MHz crystal oscillator. Generate a 1-kHz digital waveform with 40% duty cycle.

Solution: A digital waveform with 40% duty cycle is shown in Figure 7.23.

Figure 7.23 A digital waveform with 40% duty cycle.

If we use $osc \div 12$ as the clock input to the PCA timer; the period of the waveform to be generated is then 1 ms and is equal to 1000 machine cycles. The procedure for generating the specified waveform is as follows:

STEP 1 Set the CEX0 pin to high.

STEP 2 Perform a software compare operation with 400 as the delay to be added to the copy of the PCA timer (or compare register after the first one).

STEP 3 Wait until the PCA timer equals the module 0 compare registers.

STEP 4 Start the next software compare operation by adding 600 to the module 0 compare registers.

STEP 5 Repeat Steps 2 to 4 forever.

The program is in the following:

```
dly_flg      set    R0              ; if dly_flg = 0, use 600 as delay;
                                    ; otherwise use 400

             org    33H             ; PCA interrupt vector
             ljmp   pca_ISR         ; jump to the real interrupt service
                                    ; routine

             org    xxxxH
pca_ISR:     anl    CCON,#5EH       ; clear CF and CCF0 flags
             mov    A,dly_flag      ; check the delay flag
             jnz    add_400         ; add 400 as delay
             mov    A,CCAP0L        ; start the next software compare
                                    ; operation on module 0 with 600 μs
                                    ; delay (600 = 258H)
             add    A,#58H          ; "
             mov    CCAP0L,A        ; "
             mov    A,CCAP0H        ; "
             addc   A,#02H          ; "
             mov    CCAP0H,A        ; "
             mov    dly_flag,#1     ; toggle the flag
```

```
                reti
add_400:

                mov     A,CCAP0L       ; start the next software compare
                                       ; operation on module 0 with 400 μs
                                       ; delay (400 = 190H)
                add     A,#90H         ; "
                mov     CCAP0L,A       ; "
                mov     A,CCAP0H       ; "
                addc    A,#01H         ; "
                mov     CCAP0H,A       ; "
                mov     dly_flag,#0    ; toggle the flag
                reti
                org     4000H          ; starting address of the main program
                mov     CMOD,#80H      ; choose osc ÷ 12 as clock input, disable
                                       ; PCA timer overflow interrupt, gate
                                       ; off counter when in idle mode;
                                       ; disable watchdog timer
                mov     CCON,#40H      ; enable PCA timer and clear all flags
                mov     CCAPM0,#4DH    ; enable module 0 comparator, CCF,
                                       ; interrupt match, toggle; disable PWM0
                orl     IE,#C0H        ; enable PCA interrupt
                mov     A,CL           ; start the first software compare
                add     A,#90H         ; with delay equal to 400 (190H)
                mov     CCAP0L,A       ; "
                mov     A,CH           ; "
                addc    A,#01H         ; "
                mov     CCAP0H,A       ; "
                setb    CEX0           ; set CEX0 pin to high & enable
                                       ; alternate function
                clr     dly_flag       ; initialize the delay flag to 0
                Ajmp    forever        ; do something else
                end
```

7.5.5 Pulse Width Modulation Mode

Any or all of the five PCA modules can be programmed to be a pulse width modulator (PWM). The PWM output can be used to convert digital data to an analog signal by simple external circuitry. The frequency of the PWM depends on the clock sources for the PCA timer. With a 16-MHz crystal the maximum frequency of the PWM waveform is 15.6 kHz.

The PCA generates 8-bit PWMs by comparing the low byte of the PCA timer (CL) with the low byte of the compare registers (CCAPnL). As shown in Figure 7.24, when

CL < CCAPnL the output is low. When CL $\geq$ CCAPnL the output is high. The value in CCAPnL controls the duty cycle of the waveform. To change the value in CCAPnL without glitches, the user must write the new value to the high byte register (CCAPnH). This value is then shifted by hardware into CCAPnL when CL rolls over from 0FFH to 00H, which corresponds to the next period of the output.

CCAPnH can contain any integer from 0 to 255 to vary the duty cycle from 100 to 0.4%. To calculate the CCAPnH value for a given duty cycle, use the following equation:

$$CCAP_nH = 256\,(1 - \text{duty cycle}) \tag{7.9}$$

where duty cycle is expressed as a fraction.

The frequency of the PWM output will depend on which of the four clock inputs is chosen for the PCA timer. The maximum frequency is 15.6 kHz at 16 MHz. Refer to Table 7.3 for a summary of the different PWM frequencies possible with the PCA.

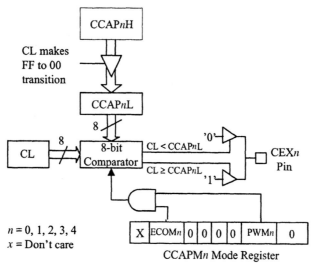

Figure 7.24 PCA 8-bit PWM mode. (Redrawn with permission of Intel.)

TABLE 7.3
PWM Frequencies

| | PWM Frequency | |
PCA Timer Mode	12 MHz	16 MHz
1/12 oscillator frequency	3.9 kHz	5.2 kHz
1/4 oscillator frequency	11.8 kHz	15.6 kHz
Timer 0 overflow		
8-bit	15.5 kHz	20.3 kHz
16-bit	0.06 kHz	0.08 kHz
8-bit auto-reload	3.9 kHz to 15.3 Hz	5.2 kHz to 20.3 Hz
External input (max)	5.9 kHz	7.8 kHz

Example 7.13 Write an instruction sequence to initialize module 0 so that a PWM signal with 50% duty cycle is generated.

Solution: Choose *osc* ÷ *12* as the clock input to the PCA timer. Load the value 80H into the CMOD register. Write the value 42H into the CCAPM0 to enable the comparator and PWM0. The following instruction sequence will configure module 0 as desired:

```
mov   CMOD,#80H        ; choose osc ÷ 12 as clock input to PCA timer
mov   CL,#00H          ; reset PCA timer to 0
mov   CH,#00H          ; "
mov   CCAPM0,#42H      ; configure module 0 for PWM
mov   CCAP0L,#80H      ; choose 50% duty cycle
mov   CCAP0H,#80H      ;
setb  CR               ; enable the PCA timer
setb  P1.3             ; enable CEX0 alternate function
```

The PWM function has been used extensively in motor control. This application will be discussed in a later section.

7.5.6 Watchdog Timer Mode

A watchdog timer is a circuit that automatically invokes a reset unless the system being watched sends regular hold-off signals to the watchdog timer. These circuits are used in applications that are subject to electrical noise, power glitches, electrostatic discharges, etc., or where high reliability is required.

The watchdog timer function is available only in PCA module 4. In this mode, every time the count in the PCA timer matches the value stored in module 4's compare registers, an internal reset is generated. The operation of the watchdog timer is illustrated in Figure 7.25. The bit that selects this mode is WDTE in the CMOD register. Module 4 must be set up in either compare mode as a software timer or high-speed output mode.

When the PCA watchdog timer times out, it resets the chip just like a hardware reset, except that it does not drive reset pin high.

To hold off the reset, the user has three options:

1. Periodically change the compare value so it will never match the PCA timer.
2. Periodically change the PCA timer value so it will never match the compare value.
3. Disable the watchdog by clearing the WDTE bit before a match occurs and then later reenable it.

The first two options are more reliable because the watchdog timer is never disabled as in option #3. The second option is not recommended if other PCA modules are being used since this timer is the time base for all five modules. Thus, in most applications the first solution is the best option. If a watchdog timer is not needed, module 4 can still be used in other modes.

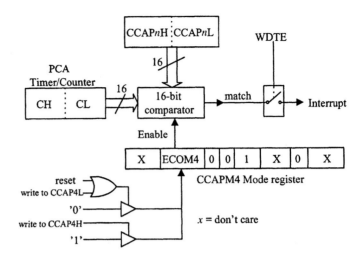

Figure 7.25 Watchdog timer mode. (Redrawn with permission of Intel.)

7.6 MOTOR CONTROL

Two types of motors are commonly connected to microcontroller-based systems: the DC motor and the step motor. The DC motor is an analog motor and the step motor is a digital motor. Step motors are available in small sizes that produce low torque. The DC motor is available in almost any size and is therefore more common to many applications, especially those that require a large torque.

7.6.1 The Step Motor

Step motors, also known as stepping or stepper motors, are essentially incremental motion devices. A step motor receives a rectangular pulse train and responds by rotating its shaft a certain number of degrees as dictated by the number of pulses in the pulse train. Usually the pulse train is controlled by means of a microcontroller or an electronic circuit.

Since the motion in a step motor is generally governed by counting the number of pulses, no feedback loops and sensors are needed for controlling a step motor. Therefore, step motors are excellent devices for position control in an open loop system. They are relatively inexpensive and simple in construction and can be made to step in equal increments in either direction. Step motors are excellent candidates for applications such as printers, XY plotters, electric typewriters, control of floppy disk drives, robots, and numerical control of machine tools. Step motors are generally used in a range from 1 W to about 3 hp.

To illustrate the operation principles of a step motor, a simplified construction diagram of a two-phase four-pole permanent magnet step motor is shown in Figure 7.26. In this diagram, the motor has two wires leading into it. In fact various versions have four, five, six and sometimes more.

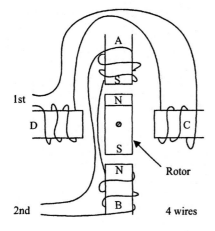

Figure 7.26 Step motor internal construction.

In Figure 7.26, the rotor is a permanent magnet that pivots on its center. There are two loops of wire, each loop forming its own electromagnet and each having a different polarity.

If a voltage is applied such that the polarity of the pole segment A is south and that of B is north the rotor magnet will line up as shown. As long as there is a voltage applied to the coil, the magnet will stay in this position. This holding position will stay as long as there is no significant force applied against it and the voltage is sufficient to provide a large enough current through the coil and consequently magnetic attraction.

If the voltage is removed from the second loop and then applied to the first loop, pole segments A and B will have no magnetic attraction and pole segments C and D will have. Assume that pole segment C goes south and D goes north. The magnet will take up a new position and be rotated 90° clockwise as shown in Figure 7.27.

To obtain further clockwise movement we remove the voltage from the first coil and reapply it to the second coil but this time in the reverse direction such that the polarity of the pole segment A is north and that of B is south as shown in Figure 7.28.

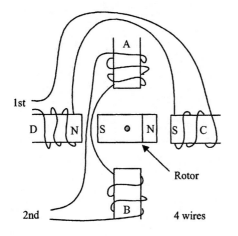

Figure 7.27 New position of the step motor.

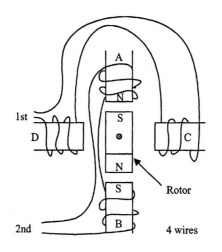

Figure 7.28 The third position of the step motor.

The magnet rotates further 90°. To get it to rotate again we remove the voltage from the second coil and reapply it to the first, again in a reverse direction. This time the polarity of the pole segment C will be north and that of D will be south. Again this is another 90° movement. To arrive at where the rotor started, remove the voltage from the first coil and reapply it to the second coil in a direction such that pole segment A is south and B is north (as shown in Figure 7.26).

To obtain another rotation, simply repeat the same sequence. This sequence gives a clockwise rotation.

To rotate in the counterclockwise direction, simply reverse the polarities of pole segments C and D in Figures 7.27 and 7.29. Figure 7.30 shows the counterclockwise sequence.

In Figures 7.26 to 7.29, the rotor rotates 90° in each step (from one pole segment to another). This is called a *full step* and is the commonest way to move the rotor of a step

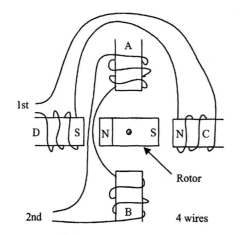

Figure 7.29 The fourth position of the step motor.

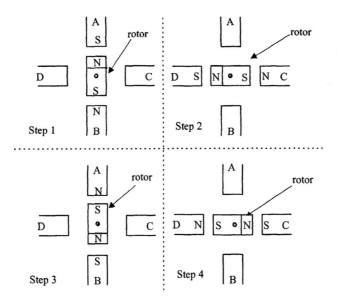

Figure 7.30 Full-step counterclockwise operation of step motor.

motor. The step motor may also be operated with half steps. A *half step* occurs when the rotor (in a four-pole step) is moved to eight discrete positions (45°).

To operate the step motor in half steps, sometimes both loops of wires may have to be on at the same time. When two coils in close proximity are energized there is a resultant magnetic field whose center will depend on the relative strengths of the two magnetic fields. Figure 7.31 illustrates the half-stepping sequence.

The step sizes of step motors vary from approximately 0.72° to 90°. However, the most common step sizes are 1.8°, 7.5°, and 15°. The steps of 90° or even 45° resolution are too crude for many applications.

The actual stator (the stationary electromagnets) of a real motor has more segments on it than previously indicated. One example is shown in Figure 7.32. The rotor is also a little bit different and is also shown in Figure 7.32.

In Figure 7.32, the stator has eight individual sections on it and hence there is 45° between two adjacent sections. The rotor has six sections on it as shown and hence there is 60° between two adjacent sections. Using the principle of a vernier mechanism the actual movement of the rotor for each step would be 60 − 45 or 15°. In Figure 7.32, pole segments A, C, E, and G are wired together and so are pole segments B, D, F, and H. Assume that pole segments A, C, E, and G are polarized so that

- A has a north polarity on it
- C has a north polarity on it
- E has a south polarity on it
- G has a south polarity on it

The rotor will be lined up accordingly. To rotate the rotor 15° clockwise, we need to remove the current applied to the first set of pole pieces and apply it to the second set so that

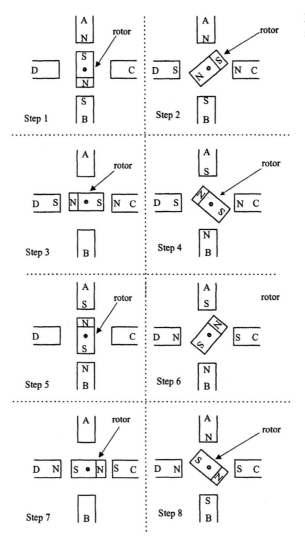

Figure 7.31 Half-step operation of step motor.

- B has a south polarity on it
- D has a south polarity on it
- F has a north polarity on it
- H has a north polarity on it

If we want to rotate the rotor 15° counterclockwise pole pieces B, D, F, and H would have opposite polarities on them.

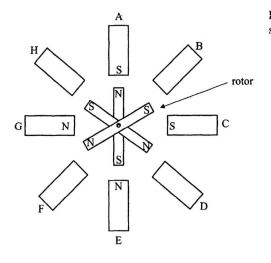

Figure 7.32 Actual internal construction of step motor.

Step Motor Drivers

Driving a step motor involves applying a series of voltages to the coils of the motor. A subset of coils is energized at a time to cause the motor to rotate one step. The pattern of coils energized must be followed exactly for the motor to work correctly. The pattern will vary depending on the mode used on the motor.

The four-pole step motor illustrated in Figures 7.26–7.29 can be driven directly by transistors as shown in Figure 7.33. The interface shown in Figure 7.33 requires that the microcontroller output the drive pattern to make the motor rotate.

The diodes in Figure 7.33 are called *fly back diodes* and are used to protect the transistors from reverse biases. The transistor loads are the windings in the step motor. The windings are inductors, storing energy as a magnetic field. When the current is cut off, the inductor dispenses its stored energy in the form of an electric current. This current attempts to flow through the transistor, reversely biasing its collector-emitter pair. The diodes are placed to prevent this current from going through the transistors.

For higher-torque applications the normal full-step sequence is used. This sequence is shown in Table 7.4. For lower-torque applications the half-step mode is used and its sequence is shown in Table 7.5. To control the motor, the microcontroller must output the values in the table in the sequence shown. Tables 7.4 and 7.5 are circular in that after the last step, the next output must be the first step. The values may be output in the order shown to rotate the motor one direction or in reverse order to rotate it in the reverse direction.

It is essential that the order be preserved even if the motor is stopped for a while. The next step to restart the motor must be the next sequential step following the last step used.

The mechanical inertia of the motor will require a short delay (a few milliseconds) between two steps to prevent the motor from missing steps. The amount of delay is determined by the maximum allowable step rate (supplied by the manufacturer) for the motor.

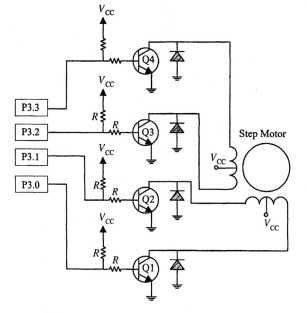

Figure 7.33 Driving a step motor.

TABLE 7.4

Full-Step Sequence for Clockwise Rotation

Step	Q1 P3.0	Q2 P3.1	Q3 P3.2	Q4 P3.3	Value
1	On	Off	On	Off	1010
2	On	Off	Off	On	1001
3	Off	On	Off	On	0101
4	Off	On	On	Off	0110
1	On	Off	On	Off	1010

TABLE 7.5

Half-Step Sequence for Clockwise Rotation

Step	Q1 P3.0	Q2 P3.1	Q3 P3.2	Q4 P3.3	Value
1	On	Off	On	Off	1010
2	On	Off	Off	Off	1000
3	On	Off	Off	On	1001
4	Off	Off	Off	On	0001
5	Off	On	Off	On	0101
6	Off	On	Off	Off	0100
7	Off	On	On	Off	0110
8	Off	Off	On	Off	0010
1	On	Off	On	Off	1010

Example 7.14 Write a subroutine to turn the four-pole step motor with the direction and number of revolutions supplied by the caller. There must be a 1 ms delay between two steps. Use the full-step sequence.

Solution: Assume the direction of the rotation and the number of revolutions are passed in registers R0 and R1. The value of 1 specifies clockwise rotation and the value of 0 specifies counterclockwise rotation. The subroutine is as follows:

```
;clockwise step sequence
clstep1          equ    0FAH
clstep2          equ    0F9H
clstep3          equ    0F5H
clstep4          equ    0F6H
; counterclockwise step sequence
ccstep1          equ    0FAH
ccstep2          equ    0F6H
ccstep3          equ    0F5H
ccstep4          equ    0F9H
1ms_H            equ    FCH              ; the upper byte of 64535
1ms_L            equ    17H              ; the lower byte of 64535
step_rotate:     cjne   R0,#0,cl_loop    ; rotate in clockwise direction?
cc_loop:         mov    P3,#ccstep1      ; counterclockwise first step
                 lcall  delay            ; delay for 1 ms
cc_loop2:        mov    P3,#ccstep2      ; counterclockwise second step
                 lcall  delay            ; delay for 1 ms
                 mov    P3,#ccstep3      ; counterclockwise third step
                 lcall  delay            ; delay for 1 ms
                 mov    P3,#ccstep4      ; counterclockwise fourth step
                 lcall  delay            ; delay for 1 ms
                 mov    P3,#ccstep1      ; counterclockwise step one
                 lcall  delay            ; delay for 1 ms
                 djnz   R1,cc_loop2
                 ret
cl_loop:         mov    P3,#clstep1      ; clockwise first step
                 lcall  delay            ; delay for 1 ms
cl_loop2:        mov    P3,#clstep2      ; clockwise second step
                 lcall  delay            ; delay for 1 ms
                 mov    P3,#clstep3      ; clockwise third step
                 lcall  delay            ; delay for 1 ms
                 mov    P3,#clstep4      ; clockwise fourth step
                 lcall  delay            ; delay for 1 ms
```

```
                    mov    P3,#clstep1       ; clockwise step one
                    lcall  delay             ; delay for 1 ms
                    djnz   R1,cl_loop2
                    ret
; the following routine uses Timer 1 to create 1 ms delay
delay:              mov    TMOD,#10H         ; set up Timer 1 in mode 1
                    clr    TF1               ; clear Timer 1 overflow flag
                    mov    TH1,#1ms_H        ; place the upper byte of the count in
                                             ; TH1
                    mov    TL1,#1ms_L        ; place the lower byte of the count in
                                             ; TL1
                    setb   TR1               ; enable Timer 1 to run
wait:               jnb    TF1,wait          ; wait until 1 ms is over
                    ret
```

7.6.2 DC Motors

DC motors are used extensively in control systems as positioning devices because their speeds as well as their torques can be precisely controlled over a wide range. The DC motor differs from the step motor in that it has a permanent magnetic field. The armature is a coil in the DC motor. When a voltage and a subsequent current flow are applied to the armature, the motor begins to spin. The DC voltage applied across the armature determines the speed of rotation.

The microcontroller can digitally control the angular velocity of a DC motor by monitoring the feedback lines and driving the output lines. Almost every application that uses a DC motor requires it to reverse its direction of rotation or vary its speed. Reversing the direction is simply done by changing the polarity of the voltage applied to the motor. Varying the speed requires changing the voltage level of the input to the motor, and that means changing the input level to the motor driver. In a digitally controlled system, the analog signal to the driver must come from some form of D/A converter. But adding a D/A converter to the circuit adds to the chip count, which means higher cost, higher power consumption, and reduced reliability of the system. The other alternative is to vary the pulse width of a digital signal input to the motor. By varying the pulse width the average voltage delivered to the motor changes and so does the speed of the motor. The MCS-51 microcontroller PCA PWM mode can be used to control the DC motor.

The 8XC51FX series can interface with the DC motor through a driver as shown in Figure 7.34. This configuration, a closed loop circuit, takes up only three I/O pins. The line controlling direction can be a regular port pin but the speed control line must be one of the port 1 pins, which corresponds to a PCA module selected for PWM.

Although some DC motors operate at 5 V or less, the 8X51FX cannot supply the necessary current to drive a motor directly. The minimum current requirement of any

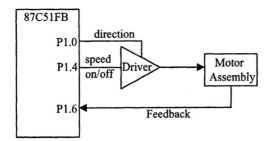

Figure 7.34 Simplified circuit diagram for DC motor control.

practical motor is higher than any microcontroller can supply. Depending on the size and rating of the motor, a suitable driver must be selected to take control signals from the 8XC51FX and deliver the necessary voltage and current to the motor.

A motor draws its maximum current when it is fully loaded and starts from a stand still condition. This factor must be taken into account when choosing a driver. However, if the application requires reversing the motor, the current demand will even be higher. As the motor's speed increases, it's power consumption decreases. Once the speed of a motor reaches a steady state, the current depends on the load and the voltage across the motor.

Drivers

Standard motor drivers are available in many current and voltage ratings. Examples are L292 and L293. The L293 has four channels and can output up to 1 A of current per channel with a supply voltage of 36 V. It has separate logic supply and takes logical input (0 or 1) to enable or disable each channel. The L293D also includes clamping diodes needed to protect the driver from the back electromagnetic frequency (EMF) generated during motor reversal. The pin assignment and block diagram of the L293 are shown in Figure 7.35. There are two supply voltages: V_{SS} and V_S. V_{SS} is the logic supply voltage, which can be from 4.5 to 36 V (normally 5.0 V). V_S is the supply voltage and can be as high as 36 V.

Feedback

The DC motor controller needs information to adjust the voltage output to the motor driver circuit. The most important information is the speed of the motor and must be fed back from the motor by a sensing device. The sensing device may be an optical encoder, infrared detector, Hall effect sensor, etc. Whatever the means of sensing, the result is a signal, which is fed to the controller. The microcontroller can use the feedback to determine the speed and position of the motor. Then it can make adjustments to increase or decrease the speed, reverse the direction, or stop the motor.

Assume that a Hall effect transistor is mounted on the shaft of a DC motor. Two magnets, which are 180° apart, are mounted on the DC motor. As shown in Figure 7.36, every time the Hall effect transistor passes through the magnetic field, it generates a pulse. The PCA can capture the passing time of the pulse. The time between two captures is half

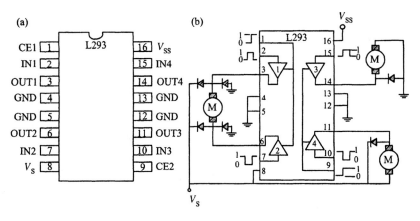

Figure 7.35 Motor driver L293 pin assignment and motor connection. (a) Pin assignment. (b) Motor connection.

of a revolution. Thus the motor speed can be calculated. By storing the value of the capture registers each time, and comparing it with its previous value, the controller can constantly measure and adjust the speed of the motor. Using this method a motor can be run at a precise speed or synchronized with another event.

The schematic of a motor-control system is illustrated in Figure 7.37. The PWM output from the CEX1 pin is connected to one end of the motor whereas the pin P1.0 is connected to the other end of the motor. The circuit is connected so that the motor will rotate clockwise when the voltage of the P1.0 pin is 0 while the PWM output from CEX1 is nonzero (positive). The direction of motor rotation is illustrated in Figure 7.38. By applying appropriate voltages on P1.0 and CEX1 (P1.4), the motor can rotate clockwise, counterclockwise, or even stop. Module 3 captures the feedback from the Hall effect transistor.

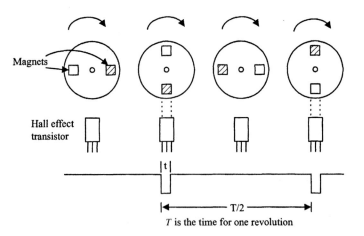

Figure 7.36 The output waveform of the Hall effect transistor.

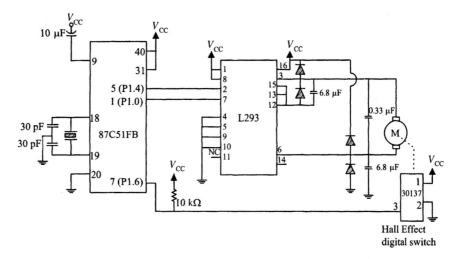

Figure 7.37 Schematic of a motor-control system. All diodes are the same and could be any one of the 1N4000 series.

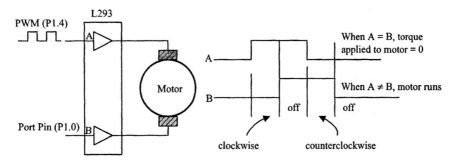

Figure 7.38 The L293 motor driver..

Example 7.15 For the circuit connection in Figure 7.37, write a program that uses PCA modules and other port pins to fulfill the following requirements:

- Maintain a constant motor speed.
- Monitor the motor speed and increase/decrease the PWM output duty cycle by 5% whenever the DC motor speed is slower/faster than the previous measurement. Remember that the duty cycle of the PWM output cannot be higher than 100% and cannot be lower than 0.4%.
- Set the duty cycle of the PWM output to 50% at the beginning.

Solution: The procedure to accomplish the requirements is as follows:

STEP 1   Set the pin P1.0 to 0 V and output a 50% duty cycle from the pin P1.4 to turn the motor clockwise at the beginning. Allow some amount of time (say 10 s) for the motor to reach a steady speed. Use PCA module 3 to capture the speed information fed back from the motor.

STEP 2   Use two flags (*incs* and *decs*) to indicate if the motor speed should be increased or decreased. Initialize these flags to 0 to indicate that the motor speed should not be changed.

STEP 3   Enable capture interrupt and stay in a loop checking the flags. If the *incs* flag is 1, then clear the flag and increase the duty cycle by 5%. If the *decs* flag is 1, then clear the flag and decrease the duty cycle by 5%.

STEP 4   Write a capture interrupt service routine to compute the current motor speed and compare it with the previous speed. Set the *incs* flag to 1 if the current motor speed is slower than the previous speed. Set the *decs* flag to 1 if the current motor speed is faster than the previous speed.

Program the CCON, CMOD, CCAPM1, CL, CH, CCAP1H, CCAP1L, and CCAPM3 registers as follows:

1. The *CCON register*: Clear all PCA flags to 0 and disable the PCA timer. Write the value 00H into the CCON.
2. The *CMOD register*: Gate off the PCA timer during idle mode, disable watchdog timer, choose *osc ÷ 12* as the clock input to the PCA, and disable PCA counter overflow interrupt. Write the value 80H into the CMOD register.
3. The *CCAPM1 register*: Enable comparator, no edge capture, no match, no toggle, enable PWM, disable CCF1 interrupt. Write the value 42H into the CCAPM1 register.
4. The *CL register*: Place 0 in this register as its initial value.
5. The *CH register*: Place 0 in this register as its initial value.
6. The *CCAP1H register:* Place 128 in this register to set the duty cycle to 50%.
7. The *CCAP1L register:* Place 128 in this register to set the duty cycle to 50%.
8. The *CCAPM3 register:* Disable comparator, enable positive-edge capture, disable match, disable toggle, disable PWM, enable CCF flag interrupt. Write the value 21H into this register.

To change the duty cycle by 5%, add or subtract 12 from the CCAP1H register. Since the initial value of the CCAP1H register is 128, it is not divisible by 12. The last value of the CCAP1H is 248 before it is increased to 255. The last value of the CCAP1H is 8 before it is decreased to 0.

There is no need to compare the speeds until the third edge is captured. Two flags are used for this purpose: the flag *ist_edge* is used to indicate that we are waiting for the first edge; the flag *pre_spd* is used to indicate that there is no previous speed to be compared.

The program that implements this procedure is as follows:

```
incs        bit    00H            ; motor speed increase flag
decs        bit    01H            ; motor speed decrease flag
ist_edge    bit    02H            ; flag to indicate the capture edge is
                                  ; the first one
```

```
pre_spd       bit    03H           ; flag to indicate the previous speed
                                    ; is available
cmp_cnt       set    R0            ; compare operation counter
old_sphi      set    R1            ; previous speed high byte
old_splo      set    R2            ; previous speed low byte
new_sphi      set    R3            ; new speed high byte
new_splo      set    R4            ; new speed low byte
tmp_hi        set    R5            ; the high byte of a 16-bit value
tmp_lo        set    R6            ; the low byte of a 16-bit value
50ms_L        equ    50H           ; the lower and upper bytes of the
                                    ; number to be
50ms_H        equ    C3H           ; added to create a 50 ms delay

              org    33H           ; the PCA interrupt vector
              ljmp   pca_isr       ; jump to the real PCA service
                                    ; routine
              org    4000H         ; starting address of main program
              setb   P1.4          ; enable CEX1 alternate function
              setb   P1.6          ; enable CEX3 alternate function
              setb   ist_edge      ; indicate the current capture is the
                                    ; first edge
              clr    pre_spd       ; initial speed not available yet
              mov    CCON,#00H     ; initialize PCA control
              mov    CMOD,#80H     ; initialize PCA mode
              mov    CCAPM1,#42H   ; enable PWM on module 1
              mov    CL,#00H       ; start PCA timer from 0
              mov    CH,#00H       ; "
              mov    CCAP1H,#128   ; initialize PWM duty cycle to 50%
              mov    CCAP1L,#128   ; initialize PWM duty cycle to 50%
              mov    CCAPM3,#21H   ; capture positive edge and enable
                                    ; interrupt on capture
              setb   CR            ; enable PCA timer
              clr    incs          ; clear increase motor speed flag
              clr    decs          ; clear decrease motor speed flag
              acall  delay10s      ; wait for 10 s to allow motor to
                                    ; stabilize
forever:      jnb    incs,chk_dec  ; should motor speed be increased?
              clr    incs
              mov    A,CCAP1H      ; check the current duty cycle
              jz     forever       ; duty cycle is already 100%
              cjne   A,#8,dec_12   ; can regular formula be used?
```

```
                        mov    CCAP1H,#0            ; set duty cycle to 100%
                        ajmp   forever              ; continue
        dec_12:         clr    C
                        subb   A,#12                ; increase the duty cycle by 5%
                        mov    CCAP1H,A             ; "
                        ajmp   forever              ; continue
        chk_dec:        jnb    decs,forever         ; need to lower the motor speed?
                        clr    decs
                        mov    A,CCAP1H             ; check the current duty cycle
                        cjne   A,#255,chk_248       ; can duty cycle be decremented
                                                    ; any further?
                        ajmp   forever              ; no action be taken and continue
        chk_248:        cjne   A,#248,inc_12        ; can regular formula be used?
                        mov    CCAP1H,#255          ; decrease the duty cycle to 0.4%
                        ajmp   forever              ; continue
        inc_12:         add    A,#12                ; decrease the duty cycle by 5%
                        mov    CCAP1H,A             ; "
                        ajmp   forever
; The following subroutine uses module 2 to create a 10-s delay
        delay10s:       mov    CCAPM2,#48H          ; enable compare, enable match,
                                                    ; disable interrupt on setting of the
                                                    ; CCF flag, disable others on
                                                    ; module 2
                        mov    cmp_cnt,#200         ; prepare to perform 200 compare
                                                    ; operation
                        mov    A,CL                 ; perform the first compare operation
                        add    A,#50ms_L            ; on module 2 with 50 ms delay
                        mov    CCAP2L,A             ; "
                        mov    A,CH                 ; "
                        addc   A,#50ms_H            ; "
                        mov    CCAP2H,A             ; "
                        clr    CCF2                 ; clear the flag to avoid false success
        wait:           jnb    CCF2,wait            ; wait until the compare is successful
                        clr    CCF2
                        djnz   cmp_cnt,next
                        ajmp   exit
        next:           mov    A,CCAP2L             ; start the next compare operation
                        add    A,#50ms_L            ; "
                        mov    CCAP2L,A             ; "
                        mov    A,CCAP2H             ; "
```

```
              addc   A,#50ms_H              ; "
              mov    CCAP2H,A               ; "
              ajmp   wait
exit:         ret
pca_isr:      jnb    ist_edge,cap_2         ; is this the first captured edge?
              clr    ist_edge               ; indicate that first edge has
                                            ; been captured
              mov    tmp_hi,CCAP3H          ; save for next computation
              mov    tmp_lo,CCAP3L          ; "
              clr    CCF3                   ; reset PCA interrupt flag
              reti
cap_2:        clr    C
              mov    A,CCAP3L               ; subtract old capture from new
              subb   A,tmp_lo               ; capture
              mov    new_splo,A             ; "
              mov    A,CCAP3H               ; "
              subb   A,tmp_hi               ; "
              mov    new_sphi,A             ; "
              mov    tmp_lo,CCAP3L          ; save the current capture value
              mov    tmp_hi,CCAP3H          ; for next
              jb     pre_spd,cmpare         ; compare if previous speed is
                                            ; available
              setb   pre_spd                ; indicate that previous speed is
                                            ; now available
              mov    old_splo,new_splo      ; current new speed becomes old
              mov    old_sphi,new_sphi      ; speed for next time
              reti
; CEX3 captures the time that the motor takes to rotate half a cycle (in number of
; machine cycles). The longer the time, the slower the speed is.
cmpare:       mov    A,new_splo             ; compare current and old speed
              clr    C                      ; "
              subb   A,old_splo             ; "
              mov    A,new_sphi             ; "
              subb   A,old_sphi             ; "
              jz     quit                   ; no change in speed?
              jc     slowdown               ; is the new speed faster than the
                                            ; previous one?
              setb   incs                   ; new speed is slower (set the
                                            ; slow down flag)
              ajmp   quit                   ; "
```

```
slowdown:    setb    decs                    ; set the speed up motor flag
quit:        mov     old_splo,new_splo       ; current speed becomes old speed
             mov     old_sphi,new_sphi       ; in next capture
             reti
```

Electrical Braking

Once a DC motor is running, it picks up momentum. Turning off the voltage to the motor does not make it stop immediately because the momentum will keep it turning. After the voltage is shut off, the momentum will gradually wear off due to friction. If the application does not require an abrupt stop, then by removing the driving voltage, the motor can be brought to a gradual stop.

An abrupt stop may be essential to an application in which the motor must run a few turns and stop very quickly at a predetermined point. This could be achieved by electrical braking.

Electrical braking is done by reversing the voltage applied to the motor. The length of time that the reversing voltage is applied must be precisely calculated to ensure a quick stop while not starting it in the reverse direction. There is no simple formula to calculate when to start and how long to maintain braking. It varies from motor to motor and application to application. But it can be perfected through trial and error.

In a closed loop system, the feedback can be used to determine where or when to start braking and when to discontinue. Again, this is application dependent.

In Figure 7.38, the motor can be braked by (1) reducing the duty cycle of PWM output (at P1.4) to 0.4% and (2) setting the port pin P1.0 output to high for an appropriate amount of time.

The following subroutine will do the electrical braking:

```
brake_mot:   setb    P1.0            ; reverse the voltage applied to the
                                     ; motor
             mov     CCAP1H,#FFH     ; reduce the PWM duty cycle to 0.4%
             lcall   brake_time      ; wait for an amount of time deter-
                                     ; mined by the routine brake_time
             clr     P1.0            ; reduce voltage to 0 to stop the motor
             ret
```

The subroutine *brake_time* is a simple routine that creates a delay required to stop the motor. This routine is similar to several delay routines that are discussed in this chapter.

7.7 DS87C520 TIMERS

Like any other MCS-52 microcontroller, the DS87C520 has three timers: Timer 0, 1, and 2. They are identical to their counterparts in any MCS-52 microcontroller except for the clock input. When configured in timer mode, either *osc ÷ 4* or *osc ÷ 12* can be selected as the clock input for each timer, respectively. The DS87C520 does this selection via the CKCON register (located at 8EH). The bit 5 (T2M), bit 4 (T1M), and bit 3 (T0M) select the clock source for Timer 2, Timer 1, and Timer 0, respectively. When set to 0, *osc ÷ 12* is selected as the clock input. Otherwise, *osc ÷ 4* is selected. After reset, *osc ÷ 12* is selected as the clock input of all timers.

7.8 SUMMARY

Many applications require a timer. Without a timer the following applications will become impossible or very difficult to implement:

- the measurement of pulse width, frequency, period, duty cycle, and phase difference
- the detection of certain events
- the creation of time delays
- the generation of waveforms

The basic MCS-51 microcontroller provides Timer 0 and Timer 1. There are two pins associated with the operations of Timers 0 and 1: INTx and Tx ($x = 0$ or 1). The Tx pin is chosen as the clock input in counter mode. When in gated mode, the high level of the INTx pin allows the timer to count. This feature allows us to measure the pulse width of an unknown signal. Registers TCON and TMOD control the operations of Timers 0 and 1. There are four operation modes for Timers 0 and 1: modes 0, 1, 2, and 3.

- In mode 0, THx ($x = 0$ or 1) is an 8-bit timer/counter with 5 bits of TLx ($x = 0$ or 1) as the prescaler.
- In mode 1, Timers 0 and 1 act as a 16-bit timer/counter.
- In mode 2, TL1 and TL0 act as 8-bit timers/counters that will be reloaded from TH1 and TH0, respectively, when they overflow.
- In mode 3, Timer 1 simply holds its value. TH0 and TL0 are two separate 8-bit counters. TL0 uses the Timer 0 control bits: C/T, GATE, TR0, INT0, and TF0. TH0 is locked into timer function and takes over the use of TR1 and TF1 from Timer 1. TH0 now controls the interrupt of Timer 1.

Timers 0 and 1 can be used to create delays, count external events, measure pulse width, and generate interrupts.

Timer 2 is added to the MCS-52 series microcontrollers. Registers T2CON and T2MOD control the operation of Timer 2. Two signal pins are related to the operation of Timer 2: T2 (P1.0) and T2EX (P1.1). T2 is count input when in counter mode. T2EX pin serves as the trigger and direction control on capture, reload, and counting. Timer 2 can count up or count down. Timer 2 has three operation modes: capture, auto-reload, and baud rate generation.

- In capture mode, the falling edge of the T2EX pin will transfer the values of TH2 and TL2 into RCAP2H and RCAP2L, respectively.

- In auto-reload mode, the values stored in RCAP2H and RCAP2L will be loaded into TH2 and TL2 when Timer 2 (TH2 and TL2) overflows.
- In baud rate generation mode, the overflow of Timer 2 will be used as a clock signal to generate baud rate. More details will be discussed in Chapter 9.

When not being used as the clock source for Timer 2, the T2 (P1.0) pin can be configured for generating a 50% duty cycle clock with frequency ranging from 61 Hz to 4 MHz (the T2OE bit of the T2MOD register must be set to 1). The frequency is determined by Equation 7.4.

In addition to creating delays and counting events, Timer 2 can capture the arrival time of a falling edge and count up and count down. Timer 2 is more flexible than Timers 0 and Timer 1 because its timer register can be reloaded automatically on an overflow.

The 8XC51FX series microcontrollers add a programmable counter array (PCA) that is even more versatile for the following capabilities:

- 16-bit capture, rising-edge triggered
- 16-bit capture, falling-edge triggered
- 16-bit capture, both rising-edge and falling-edge triggered
- 16-bit software timer (called compare function in some other microcontrollers)
- 16-bit high-speed output
- 8-bit pulse width modulation (PWM)

The PCA consists of a 16-bit timer/counter and five 16-bit compare/capture modules. Six signal pins are related to the operation of PCA: ECI (P1.2), CEX0 (P1.3), CEX1 (P1.4), CEX2 (P1.5), CEX3 (P1.6), and CEX4 (P1.7). Registers CMOD and CCON control the operation of the PCA main timer (CH and CL). Each PCA module uses the CCAPMn (n = 0,..., 4) register to control its operation and uses CCAPnH and CCAPnL to capture the arrival times of signal edges or hold the value for comparison during the compare operation. A PCA module may toggle its associated signal pin voltage on a match in a compare operation. This feature allows the PCA module to generate digital waveforms of any duty cycle.

The module 4 of the PCA can also be used as a watchdog timer. The watchdog timer will reset the CPU if it is not taken care of within a preset time limit. The watchdog function is often used to detect software errors. All PCA modules can be configured as pulse width modulators. A pulse width modulator can be used to approximate a D/A converter, which can be used to control a DC motor.

The 8XC51GB microcontroller adds programmable counter array PCA1 in addition to the PCA. The PCA1 is identical to the PCA with the exception that module 4 does not implement the watchdog function.

A step motor is digital in the sense that it can move in discrete steps. The rotor of the step motor is a bar magnet that pivots on its center. Surrounding the rotor are pole segments wound with wires. By turning the current flowing around the pole segments on and off in a predefined order, the rotor can be rotated clockwise or counterclockwise. To achieve very fine rotation steps, there must be many pole segments surrounding the rotor.

The current flowing around the pole segments can be controlled by a microcontroller. The microcontroller sends out control signals to drive the step motor. By applying the control signals according to some predefined sequence, the step motor can be rotated clockwise or counterclockwise. There must be some delay between applying two different sets of control signals to the step motor. This delay can be created easily with a timer function.

A DC motor will spin faster when the applied voltage is higher. The microcontroller can control the angular velocity of a DC motor by monitoring the feedback lines and driving the input lines. Almost every application that uses a DC motor requires it to reverse its direction of rotation or vary its speed. Reversing the direction is done by changing the polarity of the voltage applied to the motor. Varying the speed requires changing the voltage level of the input to the motor, and that means changing the input level to the motor driver. In a digitally controlled system, the analog signal to the driver must come from some form of D/A converter. Adding a D/A converter adds to the chip count. An alternative is to change the pulse width of the digital signal applied to the motor driver. By varying the pulse width the average voltage delivered to the motor changes and so does the speed of the motor. The MCS-51 microcontroller PCA PWM function can be used to control the DC motor. Sometimes we need to brake a DC motor. When a DC motor is turning, it picks up momentum. Turning off the voltage to the motor will not stop the motor immediately. To stop the DC motor abruptly, we need to reverse the voltage applied to the DC motor.

A DC motor control system is illustrated in Figure 7.37. In Figure 7.37, the control system consists of a 87C51FB, a L293 motor driver, and a Hall effect switch. The L293 DC motor driver shifts the PWM voltage to a level appropriate for the DC motor. The Hall effect transistor outputs are used to measure the speed of the DC motor.

7.9 EXERCISES

Assume a 12-MHz crystal oscillator is used to control the 87C51FB microcontroller for the following problems if the frequency of the oscillator is not specified.

7.1 Write a program to control Timer 2 to create a time delay of 1 s.

7.2 How many machine cycles can Timers 0 and 1s count (in mode 0) before the timers overflow?

7.3 Write a program to measure the period of a signal connected to the CEX0 pin.

7.4 Write a program to measure the duty cycle of the digital signal connected to the CEX0 pin. Assume the signal period is not longer than 10 s so that the PCA counter will not overflow more than 167 times during the measurement process.

7.5 Write a program to generate a 2-kHz digital waveform with 50% duty cycle from the CEX0 pin.

7.6 Write a program to compute the phase difference between two signals applied to pins CEX0 and CEX1. Assume these two signals have the same frequency and their period is not longer than 65 ms so that we do not need to keep track of timer overflow in order to measure it.

7.7 What value should be placed in CCAP*n*H to get 30 and 80% duty cycle PWM pulse outputs from the CEX*n* pin?

7.8 Write a program to generate 10 pulses from the CEX4 pin. Each pulse has 40% high and 60% low. The pulse width is 400 μs.

7.9 Write a subroutine to turn the four-pole step motor with the direction and number of revolutions supplied by the caller. There must be a 5-ms delay between two steps. Use half-step sequence.

7.10 Describe how to generate a 1-MHz digital waveform with 50% duty cycle from the P1.0 pin?

7.11 Describe how to generate a 200-kHz digital waveform with 50% duty cycle from the P1.0 pin?

7.12 What is the highest frequency of the signal that can be measured by Timer 1 of a 24-MHz 87C51FA microcontroller?

7.13 Compare the four waveform generation methods mentioned in this chapter: (1) use software to set and reset a port pin, (2) use Timer 2 clock-out mode, (3) use the PCA high-speed output mode, and (4) use pulse width modulator.

7.10 LAB EXERCISES AND ASSIGNMENTS

Do the following experiments on the MCB520 or other evaluation board. By default, the DS87C520 microcontroller uses *osc* $\div$ *12* as the clock signal to Timers 0, 1, and 2. Although there are other options, we will ignore them in these experiments. Avoid using Timer 1 because Timer 1 has been used by MCB520 to generate baud rate for serial port.

7.1 *Time delay creation.* Use port 1 pins P1.4, P1.5, P1.6, and P1.7 to drive green, yellow, red, and blue LEDs, respectively. Use Timer 2 to create time delays to control the on and off of each LED. Turn on one LED at a time for 1 s. Turn on LEDs in this sequence: green, yellow, red, blue, and repeat.

7.2 *Frequency measurement.* Use Timer 0 and Timer 2 to measure the frequency of an unknown signal. The procedure is as follows:

1. Connect the signal to the T3.4 (T0) pin.
2. Connect the signal to an oscilloscope and a frequency counter.
3. Use Timer 2 to create a 1-s time base for measuring the frequency.
4. Use registers R2 to hold overflow count of Timer 0. Use R3 and R4 to hold the final values in TH0 and TL0, respectively.
5. Enable Timer 0 overflow interrupt.
6. Write a Timer 0 interrupt service routine to accumulate the Timer 0 overflows, The Timer 0 interrupt service routine simply increases the overflow count by 1.

7. Repeat the measurement for the following frequency ranges:
   a. 10 to 99 Hz
   b. 100 to 999 Hz
   c. 1 kHz to 9999 Hz
   d. 10 kHz to 99 kHz
   e. 100 kHz to 400 kHz

7.3 *Waveform generation.* Use Timer 2 to generate digital waveforms from the P1.0 pin. The procedure is as follows:

1. Connect the P1.0 pin to the oscilloscope input.
2. Write a main program that generates waveforms with the following frequencies and 50% duty cycle:
   a. 100 Hz   **b.** 400 Hz   **c.** 800 Hz   **d.** 1 kHz
   e. 2 kHz   **f.** 3 kHz   **g.** 4 kHz   **h.** 5 kHz
3. Display each waveform for 10 s. Use Timer 0 or Timer 1 to generate this time delay.
4. Repeat this operation forever.

8

ANALOG-TO-DIGITAL CONVERTER

8.1 OBJECTIVES

After completing this chapter, you should be able to

- explain the A/D conversion process
- describe the successive-approximation A/D conversion method
- interpret the A/D conversion result
- perform voltage scaling and level shifting
- use the Intel 8XC51GB's 8-bit A/D converter to perform A/D conversion
- measure and display the barometric pressure using a pressure sensor, an A/D converter, and seven-segment displays
- measure and display the temperature using a temperature sensor, an A/D converter, and seven-segment displays
- measure and display the humidity using a humidity sensor, an A/D converter, and seven-segment displays
- use an external A/D converter with any MCS-51 microcontroller

8.2 INTRODUCTION

An analog signal has a continuous set of values over a given range, in contrast to the discrete values of digital signals. Almost any measurable quantity, for example, voltage, current, weight, temperature, speed, humidity, pressure, height, brightness, and time, is analog in nature. To be processed by a digital computer, analog signals must be represented in the digital form; thus an analog-to-digital (A/D) converter is required.

An A/D converter can deal only with electrical voltage. A nonelectric quantity must be converted into a voltage before A/D conversion can be performed. Conversion from a nonelectric quantity to a voltage requires the use of a *transducer.* For example, a temperature sensor is used to convert a temperature into a voltage. However, the transducer output may not be appropriate for processing by the A/D converter. A voltage level shifter and a scaler

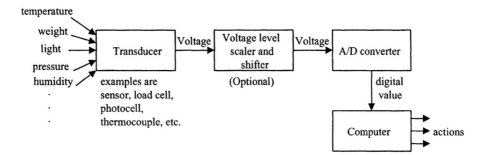

Figure 8.1 The A/D conversion system.

are often needed to transform the voltage output into the range that can be handled by the A/D converter. The overall process is illustrated in Figure 8.1.

The accuracy of an A/D converter is dictated by the number of bits used to represent the analog quantity. The greater the number of bits, the better the accuracy. Because of the progress in very large-scale integration (VLSI) technology, more and more microcontrollers have incorporated an on-chip A/D converter. Most of them have 8-bit precision and some of them even have 10-bit precision. For higher precision, the user still needs to look for an off-chip A/D converter.

The Intel 8XC51GB microcontroller has an 8-channel, 8-bit, multiplexed input, successive-approximation analog-to-digital converter with sample-and-hold circuitry to minimize rapidly changing input signals. MCS-51 variants from other vendors even incorporate 10-bit A/D converters. Examples are Philips 83C552 and 87C552 and Siemens 80C515A, 80C517A, 80535, 80C535A, 80C537A, and SABC503.

Almost all microcontrollers use the successive-approximation method to implement the A/D conversion. This method will be illustrated in the next section.

8.3 SUCCESSIVE-APPROXIMATION METHOD

The block diagram of a successive-approximation A/D converter is shown in Figure 8.2. A successive-approximation A/D converter approximates the analog signal to n-bit code in n steps. It first initializes the successive-approximation register (SAR) to zero and then performs a series of assumptions, starting with the most significant bit and proceeding toward the least significant bit. The algorithm of the successive-approximation method is illustrated in Figure 8.3. It assumes that the SAR has n bits. For every bit of the SAR, the algorithm

- assumes the bit to be a 1
- converts the value of the SAR to an analog voltage
- compares the D/A output with the analog input
- clears the bit to 0 if the D/A output is larger (which indicates that the guess is wrong)

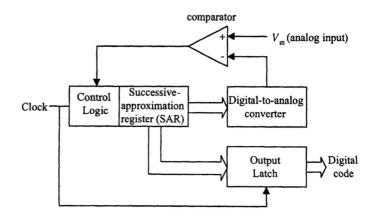

Figure 8.2 Block diagram of a successive-approximation A/D converter.

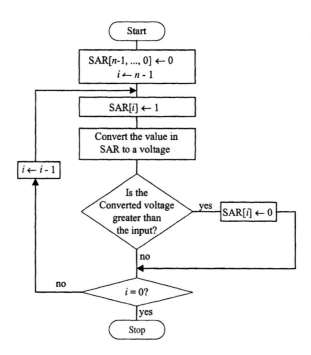

Figure 8.3 Successive-approximation A/D conversion method.

8.4 VOLTAGE LEVEL SCALING AND SHIFTING

Not all the transducer outputs are appropriate for an A/D converter. An A/D converter often needs a circuit to scale and/or shift the transducer output to fit ins input range. This chapter discusses a few circuits that perform the voltage scaling and level shifting.

8.4.1 Optimal Voltage Range for the A/D Converter

An A/D converter needs a *low-reference voltage* (V_{LREF}) and a *high-reference voltage* (V_{HREF}) to perform the conversion. The low-reference voltage is often set to 0 V and the high-reference voltage is often set to the power supply voltage V_{CC}. Most A/D converters are ratiometric, i.e.,

- a 0-V analog input is converted to the digital value 0
- a V_{CC} analog input is converted to the digital value $2^n - 1$
- an X volt input will be converted to the digital value $X \times (2^n - 1) \div V_{CC}$

where n is the number of bits the A/D converter uses to represent a conversion result. The value n is also called the *resolution* of the A/D converter.

Since the A/D converter is ratiometric, the optimal voltage range for the A/D converter is 0~V_{CC} as long as the V_{LREF} and the V_{HREF} are set to 0 V and V_{CC}, respectively. The A/D conversion result x corresponds to an analog voltage given by the following equation:

$$V_x = V_{LREF} + (range \times x) \div (2^n - 1) \tag{8.1}$$

where, V_x is the analog voltage corresponding to the converted result x and $range = V_{HREF} - V_{LREF}$.

Example 8.1 Assume there is a 10-bit A/D converter with $V_{LREF} = 1$ V and $V_{HREF} = 4$ V. Find the corresponding voltage values for A/D conversion results of 20, 100, 400, 500, and 900.

Solution:

$$range = V_{HREF} - V_{LREF} = 4 \text{ V} - 1 \text{ V} = 3 \text{ V}$$

The voltages corresponding to the results of 20, 100, 400, 500, and 900 are

$$1 \text{ V} + (20 \times 3) \div (2^{10} - 1) = 1.058 \text{ V}$$
$$1 \text{ V} + (100 \times 3) \div (2^{10} - 1) = 1.29 \text{ V}$$
$$1 \text{ V} + (400 \times 3) \div (2^{10} - 1) = 2.17 \text{ V}$$
$$1 \text{ V} + (500 \times 3) \div (2^{10} - 1) = 2.47 \text{ V}$$
$$1 \text{ V} + (900 \times 3) \div (2^{10} - 1) = 3.64 \text{ V}$$

8.4.2 Voltage Scaling Circuit

There are situations in which the transducer output voltages are in the range of 0~V_Z, where V_Z < power supply. The voltage scaling circuit can be used to improve the accuracy of the A/D conversion because it allows the A/D converter to utilize its full range. The diagram of this circuit is shown in Figure 8.4. The voltage gain of this circuit is given by the following equation:

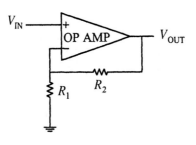

Figure 8.4 A voltage scaler.

$$A_V = \frac{V_{OUT}}{V_{IN}} = \frac{R_1 + R_2}{R_1} = 1 + \frac{R_2}{R_1} \qquad (8.2)$$

The transducer output is applied to the V_{IN} terminal whereas V_{OUT} should be connected to the A/D converter input.

Example 8.2 Assume the transducer output voltage ranges from 0 V to 120 mV. Choose the appropriate values of R_1 and R_2 to scale this range to 0 ~ 5 V.

Solution:

$$5 \text{ V} \div 120 \text{ mV} = 41.67$$

$$\therefore R_2/R_1 = 40.67$$

By trial and error, by choosing 1.5 kΩ for R_1, then R_2 should be 61 kΩ; the closest standard resistor is 62 kΩ for R_2.

8.4.3 Voltage Shifting Circuit

There are transducers whose outputs are in the range of V_1~V_2 (V_1 can be negative and V_2 < V_{CC}) instead of in the range of 0 V ~ V_{CC}. To improve the accuracy of A/D conversion, we can use a voltage shifting circuit to convert the transducer output so that it falls in the full range of 0 V ~ V_{CC}.

There are a few OP AMP circuits that can perform voltage level shifting. An example is shown in Figure 8.5c. This circuit consists of a summing circuit (Figure 8.5a) and a voltage inverter (Figure 8.5b). The voltage V_{IN} comes from the transducer output whereas V_1 is an adjusting voltage. By choosing appropriate values for V_1 and resistors, the desired voltage shifting can be achieved.

Example 8.3 Choose the appropriate values of resistors and the adjusting voltage so that the circuit in Figure 8.5c can shift the voltage range from −2 V~6 V to 0 V~8 V.

Solution: Applying Equation 8.5,

$$0 = -2 \times (R_f/R_1) - (R_f/R_2)V_1$$

$$8 = 6 \times (R_f/R_1) - (R_f/R_2)V_1$$

By choosing $R_0 = R_1 = R_f = 20$ kΩ and $V_1 = -12$ V, then $R_2 = 120$ kΩ.

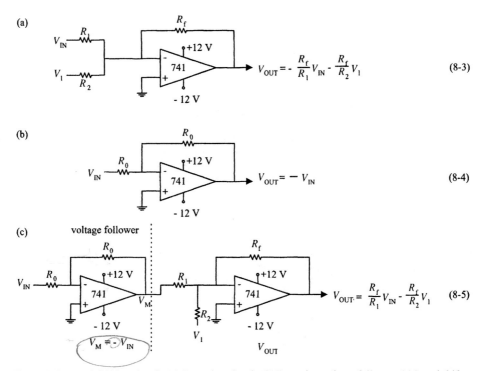

Figure 8.5 Level shifting circuit. (a) Summing circuit. (b) Inverting voltage follower. (c) Level shifter.

Example 8.4 Choose the appropriate values of resistors and adjusting voltage to shift and scale the transducer output voltage from $-50\sim150$ mV to $0\sim5$ V so that it becomes more suitable for the A/D converter.

Solution: Applying Equation 8.5,

$$0 \text{ V} = (-50\text{mV}) \times (R_f/R_1) - (R_f/R_2)V_1$$
$$5 \text{ V} = (150\text{mV}) \times (R_f/R_1) - (R_f/R_2)V_1$$

$R_f/R_1 = 25$; by choosing $R_1 = 1.2$ kΩ, then $R_f = 30$ kΩ. By choosing $V_1 = -5$ V, then $R_2 = 120$ kΩ. Choose R_0 to be 10 kΩ arbitrarily.

From the above two examples, we see that the selection of resistor values and the voltage V_1 is a trial-and-error process at best.

8.5 THE INTEL 8XC51GB A/D CONVERTER

The Intel 8XC51GB (X = 0, or 3, or 7) is an enhanced version of 8XC51FA and has the same instruction set and architecture as the existing MCS-51 microcontroller products. In addition to having six 8-bit I/O ports, the 8XC51GB also has eight dedicated analog inputs (ACH7-ACH0) for the A/D converter. The A/D converter contained in the 8XC51GB has 8-bit resolution and uses the successive-approximation method to perform the conversion. The conversion of one sample takes 26 machine cycles.

8.5.1 Registers Related to the A/D Converter

The 8XC51GB has 10 registers related to the A/D converter: the ACON control register, the ACMP comparison result register, and eight result registers with one for each channel (AD0–AD7). The contents of the ACON and ACMP are shown in Figures 8.6 and 8.7, respectively.

8.5.2 The Modes of the A/D Converter

The lowest two bits of the ACON register select the *trigger* and *input modes* of the A/D converter. The *comparison mode* is always enabled once the A/D converter is enabled.

A/D Trigger Mode

Setting the ATM bit (bit 0) of the ACON register enables the A/D external trigger mode. In this mode, the A/D conversions begin when a falling edge is detected at the TRIGIN pin. There is no edge detector on the TRIGIN pin; it is sampled once every machine cycle. A negative edge is recognized when TRIGIN is high in one machine cycle and low in the next. For this reason, TRIGIN should be held high for at least one machine cycle and low for one

Address = 097H		ACON				Not Bit Addressable	
—	—	AIF	ACE	ACS1	ACS0	AIM	ATM
7	6	5	4	3	2	1	0

AIF: *A/D interrupt flag*. Set by hardware upon completion of a conversion cycle. Triggers an interrupt if interrupt is enabled. Must be cleared by software.

ACE: *A/D conversion enable*. When set, the converter is operational. When cleared, no conversions occur.

ACS1-ACS0: *A/D converter select*. Used in select mode to choose which analog channel will be converted four times.
   0   0: channel ACH0 is selected
   0   1: channel ACH1 is selected
   1   0: channel ACH2 is selected
   1   1: channel ACH3 is selected

AIM: *Analog input mode*. When set, select mode is activated. When cleared, scan mode is activated.

ATM: *Analog trigger mode*. When cleared, A/D conversions are triggered internally and occur whenever ACE = 1. When set, A/D conversions begin on the falling edge of the TRIGIN pin.

Figure 8.6 The ACON register.

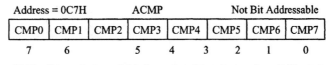

Address = 0C7H		ACMP				Not Bit Addressable	
CMP0	CMP1	CMP2	CMP3	CMP4	CMP5	CMP6	CMP7
7	6	5	4	3	2	1	0

CMP*x*: Comparison result bit for analog channel *x*. *x* = 0, ..., 7. If set, the
voltage at analog input channel *x* is greater than that on the
COMPREF pin. If cleared, the voltage at the input channel is less
than COMPREF.

Figure 8.7 A/D comparison register ACMP.

machine cycle. Once the falling edge is detected, the A/D conversions begin on the next
machine cycle and complete when channel 7 is converted. After channel 7 is converted,
AIF is set and the conversions halt until another trigger is detected while ACE = 1. External
triggers are ignored while a conversion cycle is in progress.

If internal trigger mode is selected, conversions begin as soon as the ACE bit is set.
Conversion cycles continue until ACE is cleared.

A/D Input Mode

The 8XC51GB has two input modes: *scan mode* and *select mode*. Setting the AIM bit of
the ACON register activates select mode. In scan mode the analog conversions occur in
the sequence ACH0, ACH1, ACH2, ACH3, ACH4, ACH5, ACH6, and ACH7. The result
of each conversion is placed in the corresponding A/D result register: AD0, AD1, AD2,
AD3, AD4, AD5, AD6, and AD7. In select mode, one of the lower four analog inputs
(ACH0–ACH3) is converted four times and these four results are placed in the lower four
result registers (AD0 through AD3). After the first four conversions are complete the cycle
continues with ACH4 through ACH7. The rest of the conversion results are placed in their
associated result registers.

A/D Comparison Mode

The A/D comparison mode is always active while the A/D converter is enabled. The comparison mode is used to compare each analog input with an external reference voltage applied
to COMPREF. Whenever the A/D converter is triggered, each bit in ACMP is updated as
each analog conversion is completed, starting with channel 0 up to channel 7 regardless
of whether select or scan mode is invoked. The comparison mode can provide a quicker
"greater-than or less-than" decision than that performed with software and it is more code
efficient. It can also be used to convert the analog inputs into digital inputs with a variable
threshold. If the comparison mode is not used, COMPREF should be tied to V_{CC} or V_{SS}.

8.5.3 A/D Converter Operating Condition

The 8XC51GB can operate with a V_{CC} of 4.0–6.0 V. The analog reference low-input AV_{SS}
should be connected to 0 V. The analog reference high-input AV_{REF} can be anywhere between
4.5 and 5.5 V but cannot be higher than V_{CC}. Tying AV_{REF} to V_{CC} is probably the best way.

The eight analog inputs should be between AV_{SS} and AV_{REF}. The 8XC51GB is guaranteed to operate correctly between 0 and 70°C.

8.6 THE PROCEDURE FOR USING THE A/D CONVERTER

The procedure for using the A/D converter is as follows:

STEP 1   Connect the hardware properly. Connect the A/D-related signal pins as follows:

V_{CC}:   5 V
V_{SS}:   0 V
AV_{REF}:   5 V
AV_{SS}:   0 V

COMPREF: 0 V (or 5 V)

TRIGIN: 0 V (or 5 V) when the external trigger mode is not used. Otherwise, connect it to the appropriate trigger input.

ACHx pin: analog voltage to be converted (must be scaled and shifted properly).

STEP 2   Select the appropriate channel (s) and operation modes by programming the ACON register. The A/D conversion will be started as soon as the ACE bit is set to 1.

STEP 3   Wait until the AIF flag is set, then collect the A/D conversion results and store them in memory.

Example 8.5 Write an instruction to configure the 8XC51GB A/D converter to operate with the following environment:

- scan mode
- convert all eight channels
- internal trigger mode

Solution: The setting of the ACON register is as follows:

bits 7 and 6: not implemented; set to 00
bit 5: is a status flag; should be set to 0
bit 4: set to 1 to enable the A/D converter
bits 3 and 2: don't cares for scan mode; set to 00
bit 1: set to 0 to select the scan mode
bit 0: set to 0 to choose internal trigger mode

Therefore, we should write the value 10H into the ACON register. Use the following instruction to configure the A/D converter:

    mov   ACON,#10H

Example 8.6 Write a small program to test if the A/D converter of an 87C51GB-based single board computer works properly.

Solution: The procedure for testing the A/D converter is as follows:

STEP 1 Apply a known dc voltage value to each analog input pin (ACH0–ACH7).

STEP 2 Run a small program that performs an A/D conversion on each channel and then stops.

STEP 3 Check the A/D conversion results with the expected value.

STEP 4 Apply different dc voltages to each analog input pin and rerun the program.

Rerun the program once for each new value and check the result.

For this testing purpose, the ACON register should be configured as follows:

bits 7 and 6: don't cares; set to 00

bit 5: a status flag; set to 0

bit 4: enable the A/D converter; set to 1

bits 3 and 2: don't care; set to 00

bit 1: choose scan mode; set to 0

bit 0: choose internal triggered; set to 0

Write the value 10H into the ACON register to configure the A/D converter. The program is as follows:

```
        mov   ACON,#10H      ; configure and enable the A/D converter
loop:   mov   A,ACON         ; prepare to test the AIF bit
        anl   A,#20H          ; test the AIF bit
        jz    loop            ; is A/D conversion completed?
; The A/D conversion results are available for checking after the loop. This program may
; exit to the evaluation board monitor program so that the user can examine the AD
; registers
        .
        .
        .
```

8.7 MEASURING THE BAROMETRIC PRESSURE

Sensortechnics Inc. manufactures a barometric pressure transducer (BPT) kit that has three external connectors: $+V_S$, GND, and V_{OUT}. The operating parameters are listed in Table 8.1. This product can be found in an Electronic Components Catalog prepared by Farnell Inc.

TABLE 8.1
BPT Parameters[a]

Parameter	Value
Reference conditions	$V_S = 9.0$ V, T (ambient) $= 25°C$, RL $= 100$ kΩ
Supply voltage	7–24 V dc
Operating pressure	800–1100 mbar
Breakdown pressure	2 bar
Voltage output (span)	5.0 ± 500 mV
Operating temperature	-40 to $85°C$
Compensated range	-10 to $60°C$
Nonlinearity and hysteresis	0.1% FSO (max)
Repeatability	0.2% FSO (typical)
Temperature shift (-10 to $60°C$)	0.3% FSO/$10°C$ (max)
Response time	1 msec (typical)
Long term stability	0.1% FSO (typical)

[a] Manufacturer's Type No. 144SC0811-BARO.

The BPT is a calibrated and signal conditioned transducer that provides a true 4.5–5.5 V output in the barometric pressure ranging from 800 to 1100 mbar. Internal voltage regulation allows the device to operate on a power supply between 7 and 24 V. Applications include barometry, weather stations, and absolute pressure compensation in sensitive equipment. A potentiometer is provided to adjust for changes in altitude. The transducer is designed for use in noncorrosive, nonionic media, e.g., dry air and gasses.

Since the voltage output of BPT is from 4.5 to 5.5 V, a voltage shifting circuit is needed to get the best conversion result from the 87C51GB A/D converter.

Example 8.7 Design a circuit to shift and scale the BPT's output voltage from 4.5~5.5 V to 0~5 V.

Solution: The circuit that consists of the BPT and voltage shifter is shown in Figure 8.8. Appling Equation 8.5, we obtain

$$0V = 4.5 \times (R_f/R_1) - V_1 \times (R_f/R_2)$$

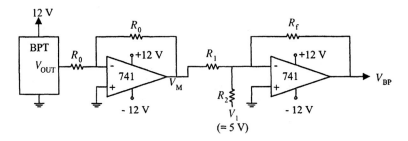

Figure 8.8 Barometric pressure sensor output voltage scaling and shifting circuit.

$$5 \text{ V} = 5.5 \times (R_f/R_1) - V_1 \times (R_f/R_2)$$

By setting V_1 to 5 V and R_f to 150 kΩ, R_1 and R_2 are 30 and 33 kΩ, respectively. Choose 10 kΩ for R_0.

Example 8.8 Write a program to monitor and display the barometric pressure constantly and update the display every second for the circuit shown in Figure 8.9. Assume the crystal oscillator frequency is 12 MHz.

Solution: The pressure data will be displayed in four BCD digits. Since the A/D conversion result 0 represents a pressure of 800 mbar whereas the conversion result 255 represents a pressure of 1100 mbar, the translation from A/D conversion result to pressure cannot be exact. To simplify the calculation and speed up the program, a table is used to translate an A/D conversion result to its corresponding barometric pressure. Two bytes are needed to hold each entry. Two tables are used because of the limitation of the MCS-51/52's index addressing mode. One table holds the upper two digits and the other table holds the lower two digits. The barometric pressure for the A/D conversion result X is given by the following equation:

$$P_X = 800 + (X \times 300 \div 255) \tag{8.6}$$

The barometric pressure will be measured and the display will be updated once every second. The procedure is as follows:

STEP 1   Initialize the A/D converter by writing the value 10H into the ACON register.

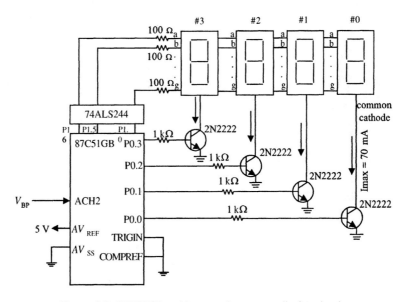

Figure 8.9 87C51GB and barometric pressure display circuit.

STEP 2 Blank out the display.

STEP 3 Perform one A/D conversion. When it is done, send it for display.

STEP 4 Display the current barometric pressure for 1 s.

STEP 5 Go to Step 3.

The program is as follows:

```
              org    4000H              ; starting address of the program
              mov    ACON,#10H          ; initialize and enable the A/D
                                        ; converter
              mov    P1,#00H            ; blank out the display
wait_ad:      mov    A,ACON             ; wait for the A/D conversion to be
                                        ; completed
              anl    A,#20H             ; check the AIF bit
              jz     wait_ad            ; is A/D completed?
              anl    ACON,#DFH          ; clear the AIF flag
              mov    A,AD2              ; get the A/D result of ACH2
; look up the barometric table to find the corresponding barometric pressure
              mov    DPTR,#prestab_H
              movc   A,@A+DPTR
              mov    B,A                ; save a copy in B
              mov    A,AD2
              mov    DPTR,#prestab_L    ; get the lower two digits
              movc   A,@A+DPTR          ; "
              mov    R4,A               ; save a copy
              anl    A,#0FH             ; mask the upper four bits
              mov    DPTR,#dis_pat
              movc   A,@A+DPTR          ; look up the display pattern
              mov    R0,A
              mov    A,R4               ; get back the lower two digits
              anl    A,#F0H             ; mask the lower four bits
              rr     A                  ; shift to the lower four bits
              rr     A                  ; "
              rr     A                  ; "
              rr     A                  ; "
              movc   A,@A+DPTR          ; look up the display pattern
              mov    R1,A               ; put it in display buffer
              mov    A,B                ; get back the upper two digits
              anl    A,#0FH             ; mask the upper four bits
              movc   A,@A+DPTR          ; look up the display pattern
```

```
            mov    R2,A                ; save the display pattern of
                                       ; hundreds digit
            mov    A,B                 ; get back the upper two digits
            anl    A,#F0H              ; mask the second most significant
                                       ; digit
            rr     A                   ; shift to the lowest four bits
            rr     A                   ; "
            rr     A                   ; "
            rr     A                   ; "
            movc   A,@A+DPTR           ; look up the display pattern
            mov    R5,#250             ; set up the display loop count
disp_lp:    mov    P1,A                ; output the most significant
                                       ; digit (msd)
            mov    P0,#08H             ; turn on the msd
            lcall  wait_1ms            ; wait for 1 ms
            mov    P1,R2               ; display the second msd
            mov    P0,#04H             ; "
            lcall  wait_1ms            ; wait for 1 ms
            mov    P1,R1               ; display the second least significant
                                       ; digit (lsd)
            mov    P0,#02H             ; "
            lcall  wait_1ms            ; wait for 1 ms
            mov    P1,R0               ; display the lsd
            mov    P0,#01H             ; "
            lcall  wait_1ms            ; wait for 1 ms
            djnz   R5,disp_lp          ; does 1 s expire?
            ljmp   wait_ad             ; repeat forever
; the following subroutine creates 1 ms delay
wait_1ms:   mov    R6,#200             ; set up loop count
here:       nop                        ; 1 μs
            nop                        ; 1 μs
            nop                        ; 1 μs
            djnz   R6,here             ; 2 μs
            ret
; seven-segment display pattern table
dis_pat:    DB     7EH,30H,6DH,79H,33H,5BH,5FH,70H,7FH,7BH
; The A/D conversion result-to-pressure lookup table is organized as a 13 by 20
; matrix with the last row containing only nine entries
prestab_H   DB     08H,08H,08H,08H,08H,08H,08H,08H,08H,08H,08H,08H,08H
            DB     08H,08H,08H,08H,08H,08H,08H,08H,08H,08H,08H,08H,08H
```

```
            DB      08H,08H,08H,08H,08H,08H,08H,08H,08H,08H,08H,08H,08H
            DB      08H,08H,08H,08H,08H,08H,08H,08H,08H,08H,08H,08H,08H
            DB      08H,08H,08H,08H,08H,08H,08H,08H,08H,08H,08H,08H,08H
            DB      08H,08H,08H,08H,08H,08H,08H,08H,08H,08H,08H,08H,08H
            DB      08H,08H,08H,08H,08H,08H,08H,09H,09H,09H,09H,09H,09H
            DB      09H,09H,09H,09H,09H,09H,09H,09H,09H,09H,09H,09H,09H
            DB      09H,09H,09H,09H,09H,09H,09H,09H,09H,09H,09H,09H,09H
            DB      09H,09H,09H,09H,09H,09H,09H,09H,09H,09H,09H,09H,09H
            DB      09H,09H,09H,09H,09H,09H,09H,09H,09H,09H,09H,09H,09H
            DB      09H,09H,09H,09H,09H,09H,09H,09H,09H,09H,09H,09H,09H
            DB      09H,09H,09H,09H,09H,09H,09H,09H,09H,09H,09H,09H,09H
            DB      09H,10H,10H,10H,10H,10H,10H,10H,10H,10H,10H,10H,10H
            DB      10H,10H,10H,10H,10H,10H,10H,10H,10H,10H,10H,10H,10H
            DB      10H,10H,10H,10H,10H,10H,10H,10H,10H,10H,10H,10H,10H
            DB      10H,10H,10H,10H,10H,10H,10H,10H,10H,10H,10H,10H,10H
            DB      10H,10H,10H,10H,10H,10H,10H,10H,10H,10H,10H,10H,10H
            DB      10H,10H,10H,10H,10H,10H,10H,10H,10H,10H,10H,10H,10H
            DB      10H,10H,10H,10H,10H,10H,10H,10H,11H
prestab_L   DB      00H,01H,02H,04H,05H,06H,07H,08H,09H,11H,12H,13H,14H
            DB      15H,16H,18H,19H,20H,21H,22H,24H,25H,26H,27H,28H,29H
            DB      31H,32H,33H,34H,35H,36H,38H,39H,40H,41H,42H,44H,45H
            DB      46H,47H,48H,49H,51H,52H,53H,54H,55H,56H,58H,59H,60H
            DB      61H,62H,64H,65H,66H,67H,68H,69H,71H,72H,73H,74H,75H
            DB      76H,78H,79H,80H,81H,82H,84H,85H,86H,87H,88H,89H,91H
            DB      92H,93H,94H,95H,96H,98H,99H,00H,01H,02H,04H,05H,06H
            DB      07H,08H,09H,11H,12H,13H,14H,15H,16H,18H,19H,20H,21H
            DB      22H,24H,25H,26H,27H,28H,29H,31H,32H,33H,34H,35H,36H
            DB      38H,39H,40H,41H,42H,44H,45H,46H,47H,48H,49H,51H,52H
            DB      53H,54H,55H,56H,58H,59H,60H,61H,62H,64H,65H,66H,67H
            DB      68H,69H,71H,72H,73H,74H,75H,76H,78H,79H,80H,81H,82H
            DB      84H,85H,86H,87H,88H,89H,91H,92H,93H,94H,95H,96H,98H
            DB      99H,00H,01H,02H,04H,05H,06H,07H,08H,09H,11H,12H,13H
            DB      14H,15H,16H,18H,19H,20H,21H,22H,24H,25H,26H,27H,28H
            DB      29H,31H,32H,33H,34H,35H,36H,38H,39H,40H,41H,42H,44H
            DB      45H,46H,47H,48H,49H,51H,52H,53H,54H,55H,56H,58H,59H
            DB      60H,61H,62H,64H,65H,66H,67H,68H,69H,71H,72H,73H,74H
            DB      75H,76H,78H,79H,80H,81H,82H,84H,85H,86H,87H,88H,89H
            DB      91H,92H,93H,94H,95H,96H,98H,99H,00H
            END
```

8.8 MEASURING THE TEMPERATURE

The National Semiconductor LM34 is a precise Fahrenheit temperature sensor. This device is rated to operate in the temperature range of $-50 \sim +300°F$. LM34 does not require any external calibration or trimming to provide typical accuracies of $\pm 1/2°F$ at room temperature and $\pm 1.5°F$ in the full $-50 \sim +300°F$ range.

The LM34 has the following features:

- calibrated directly in degrees of Fahrenheit
- linear $+10.0$ mV/°F scale factor (i.e., sensor output voltage increases 10.0 mV for an increase of 1°F in temperature)
- rated for the full $-50 \sim +300°F$ range
- suitable for remote applications
- operates from 5 to 30 V
- less than 90-mA current drain
- low self-heating, 0.18°F in still air
- typical nonlinearity $\pm 0.5°F$
- low-impedance output, 0.4 Ω for 1-mA load

The LM34 has only three pins as shown in Figure 8.10. There are two possible circuit connections for the LM34 as shown in Figure 8.11.

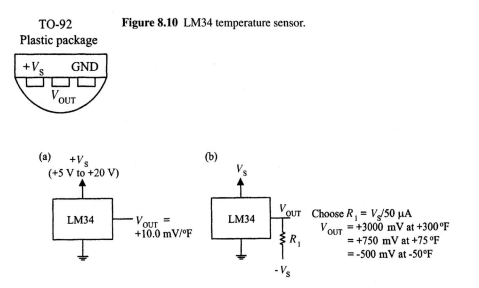

TO-92
Plastic package

Figure 8.10 LM34 temperature sensor.

Figure 8.11 Circuit connection for the LM34. (a) Circuit connection for $+5$ to $+300°F$. (b) Circuit connection for -50 to $+300°F$.

Example 8.9 Use the National Semiconductor temperature sensor LM34 to display the room temperature in Fahrenheit in three integral digits and one fractional digit. This circuit should be able to display the temperature from −50 up to 120°F.

Solution: The seven-segment display has a segment **h** that allows the decimal point to be displayed. Since the position of the decimal point is fixed for our purpose, this pin can be tied to V_{CC} or ground so that our program does not need to control it.

For the given temperature range, the voltage output of the temperature will be from −500 mV to 1.2 V. We need to use a level shifter circuit to shift and scale it to between 0 and 5 V. The connection between the temperature sensor and the scaling circuit is shown in Figure 8.12.

Since only one analog source is to be converted, any channel can be used. We will use ACH2 to perform the A/D conversion. The output voltage V_X from the temperature sensor LM34 is from −0.5 to +1.2 V. To get a better A/D conversion result, we need to scale and shift it to between 0 and +5 V. Using Equation 8.5, the values of the resistors and the adjusting voltage are computed to be

- $R_0 = 10K$
- $R_1 = 68K$
- $R_2 = 680K$
- $R_f = 200K$
- $V_1 = -5$ V

The display circuit will be identical to that of Figure 8.9. The most significant to least significant digits will be displayed on seven-segment displays #3 to #0. The h segment of display #1 will be tied to 5 V so that the decimal point is always lighted.

The A/D conversion result 0 corresponds to temperature −50°F whereas the result 255 corresponds to +120°F. The resolution of the converter is 170/255°F per step. It will be easier to use a lookup table instead of performing division to compute the corresponding temperature. The corresponding temperature of the A/D conversion result X can be computed using the following equation:

$$T_X = (X \times 170 \div 255) - 50 \tag{8.7}$$

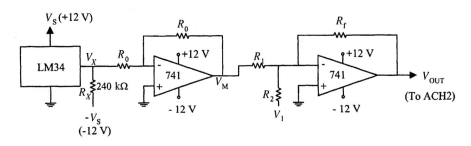

Figure 8.12 Temperature sensor and level scaling circuit connection.

Displaying the segment **g** and blanking out the other segments of the most significant digit can show the negative temperature. The display pattern value for the negative sign is 01H and will be placed at the end of the display pattern table (eleventh entry). The negative sign will be represented as letter A in the A/D result translation table so that it refers to the last entry of the display pattern table. Since each temperature reading has four BCD digits, two translation tables will be established. One table holds the upper two digits and the other table holds the lower two digits.

The program is as follows:

```
             mov    ACON,#10H          ; initialize and enable the A/D
                                       ; converter
             mov    P1,#00H            ; blank out the display
wait_ad      mov    A,ACON             ; wait for the A/D conversion to be
             anl    A,#20H             ; completed
             jz     wait_ad            ; "
             anl    ACON,#DFH          ; clear the AIF flag
             mov    A,AD2              ; get the A/D result of ACH2
; look up the temperature table to find the corresponding temperature
             mov    DPTR,#temtab_H
             movc   A,@A+DPTR
             mov    B,A                ; save a copy in B
             mov    A,AD2
             mov    DPTR,#temtab_L     ; get the lower two digits
             movc   A,@A+DPTR          ; "
             mov    R4,A               ; save a copy
             anl    A,#0FH             ; mask out the upper four bits
             mov    DPTR,#dis_pat
             movc   A,@A+DPTR          ; look up the display pattern
             mov    R0,A               ; save the pattern of the least
                                       ; significant digit (lsd)
             mov    A,R4               ; get back the lower two digits
             anl    A,#F0H             ; mask out the lower four bits
             rr     A                  ; shift to the lower four bits
             rr     A                  ; "
             rr     A                  ; "
             rr     A                  ; "
             movc   A,@A+DPTR          ; look up the display pattern
             mov    R1,A               ; save pattern of the second lsd
             mov    A,B                ; get back the upper two digits
             anl    A,#0FH             ; mask the upper four bits
```

```
                movc   A,@A+DPTR          ; look up the display pattern
                mov    R2,A               ; save pattern of the second most
                                          ; significant digit (msd)
                mov    A,B                ; get back the upper two digits
                anl    A,#F0H             ; mask the second msd
                rr     A                  ; shift to the lowest four bits
                rr     A                  ; "
                rr     A                  ; "
                rr     A                  ; "
                movc   A,@A+DPTR          ; get the pattern of the msd
                mov    R5,#250            ; set up the display loop count
disp_lp:        mov    P1,A               ; output the msd
                mov    P0,#08H            ; turn on the msd
                lcall  wait_1ms           ; wait for 1 ms
                mov    P1,R2              ; display the second msd
                mov    P0,#04H            ; "
                lcall  wait_1ms           ; wait for 1 ms
                mov    P1,R1              ; display the second lsd
                mov    P0,#02H            ; "
                lcall  wait_1ms           ; wait for 1 ms
                mov    P1,R0              ; display the lsd
                mov    P0,#01             ; "
                lcall  wait_1ms           ; wait for 1 ms
                djnz   R5,disp_lp         ; does one second expire?
                ljmp   wait_ad            ; repeat forever
; the following subroutine creates 1 ms delay
wait_1ms:       mov    R6,#200            ; set up loop count
here:           nop                       ; 1 μs
                nop                       ; 1 μs
                nop                       ; 1 μs
                djnz   R6,here            ; 2 μs
                ret
; the following is the seven-segment display pattern table
dis_pat:        DB     7EH,30H,6DH,79H,33H,5BH,5FH,70H,7FH,7BH,01H
; the following is the temperature lookup table
temtab_H:       DB     A5H,A4H,A4H,A4H,A4H,A4H,A4H,A4H,A4H,A4H,A4H,A4H,A4H
                DB     A4H,A4H,A4H,A3H,A3H,A3H,A3H,A3H,A3H,A3H,A3H,A3H,A3H
                DB     A3H,A3H,A3H,A3H,A3H,A2H,A2H,A2H,A2H,A2H,A2H,A2H
                DB     A2H,A2H,A2H,A2H,A2H,A2H,A2H,A1H,A1H,A1H,A1H,A1H,A1H
```

```
            DB    A1H,A1H,A1H,A1H,A1H,A1H,A1H,A1H,A1H,A0H,A0H,A0H,A0H
            DB    A0H,A0H,A0H,A0H,A0H,A0H,A0H,A0H,A0H,A0H,00H,00H,00H
            DB    00H,00H,00H,00H,00H,00H,00H,00H,00H,00H,00H,00H,01H
            DB    01H,01H,01H,01H,01H,01H,01H,01H,01H,01H,01H,01H,01H
            DB    01H,02H,02H,02H,02H,02H,02H,02H,02H,02H,02H,02H,02H
            DB    02H,02H,02H,03H,03H,03H,03H,03H,03H,03H,03H,03H,03H
            DB    03H,03H,03H,03H,03H,04H,04H,04H,04H,04H,04H,04H,04H
            DB    04H,04H,04H,04H,04H,04H,04H,05H,05H,05H,05H,05H,05H
            DB    05H,05H,05H,05H,05H,05H,05H,05H,05H,06H,06H,06H,06H
            DB    06H,06H,06H,06H,06H,06H,06H,06H,06H,06H,06H,07H,07H
            DB    07H,07H,07H,07H,07H,07H,07H,07H,07H,07H,07H,07H,07H
            DB    08H,08H,08H,08H,08H,08H,08H,08H,08H,08H,08H,08H,08H
            DB    08H,08H,08H,08H,09H,09H,09H,09H,09H,09H,09H,09H,09H
            DB    09H,09H,09H,09H,09H,10H,10H,10H,10H,10H,10H,10H,10H
            DB    10H,10H,10H,10H,10H,10H,10H,10H,11H,11H,11H,11H,11H
            DB    11H,11H,11H,11H,11H,11H,11H,11H,12H
temtab_L:   DB    00H,93H,87H,80H,73H,67H,60H,53H,46H,40H,33H,26H,20H
            DB    13H,07H,00H,93H,87H,80H,73H,67H,60H,53H,47H,40H,33H
            DB    27H,20H,13H,07H,00H,93H,87H,80H,73H,67H,60H,53H,47H
            DB    40H,33H,27H,20H,13H,07H,00H,93H,87H,80H,73H,67H,60H
            DB    53H,47H.40H,33H,27H,20H,13H,07H,00H,93H,87H,80H,73H
            DB    67H,60H,53H,47H,40H,33H,27H,20H,13H,07H,00H,07H,13H
            DB    20H,27H,33H,40H,47H,53H,60H,67H,73H,80H,87H,93H,00H
            DB    07H,13H,20H,27H,33H,40H,47H,53H,60H,67H,73H,80H,87H
            DB    93H,00H,07H,13H,20H,27H,33H,40H,47H,53H,60H,67H,73H
            DB    80H,87H,93H,00H,07H,13H,20H,27H,33H,40H,47H,53H,60H
            DB    67H,73H,80H,87H,93H,00H,07H,13H,20H,27H,33H,40H,47H
            DB    53H,60H,67H,73H,80H,87H,93H,00H,07H,13H,20H,27H,33H
            DB    40H,47H,53H,60H,67H,73H,80H,87H,93H,00H,07H,13H,20H
            DB    27H,33H,40H,47H,53H,60H,67H,73H,80H,87H,93H,00H,07H
            DB    13H,20H,27H,33H,40H,47H,53H,60H,67H,73H,80H,87H,93H
            DB    00H,07H,13H,20H,27H,33H,40H,47H,53H,60H,67H,73H,80H
            DB    87H,93H,00H,07H,13H,20H,27H,33H,40H,47H,53H,60H,67H
            DB    73H,80H,87H,93H,00H,07H,13H,20H,27H,33H,40H,47H,53H
            DB    60H,67H,73H,80H,87H,93H,00H,07H,13H,20H,27H,33H,40H
            DB    47H,53H,60H,67H,73H,80H,87H,93H,00H
            END
```

8.9 MEASURING THE HUMIDITY

The IH-3605 is a humidity sensor made by HyCal Engineering, which is a division of Honeywell. The IH-3605 humidity sensors provides a linear output from 0.8 to 3.9 V in the full range of 0–100% *relative humidity* (RH) when excited by a 5-V power supply. It can operate in a range of 0–100% RH, −40 to 185°F.

The pins of the IH-3605 are shown in Figure 8.13. The specifications of the IH-3605 are listed in Table 8.2. The IH-3605 is light sensitive and should be shielded from bright light for best results. The IH-3605 can resist contaminant vapors such as organic solvents, chlorine, and ammonia. It is unaffected by water condensate as well. Because of this capability, the IH-3605 has been used in refrigeration, drying, instrumentation, meteorology, etc.

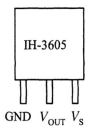

Figure 8.13 HyCal IH-3605 humidty sensor.

GND V_{OUT} V_S

TABLE 8.2
Specifications of IH-3605

Specification	Description
Total accuracy	±2% RH, 0–100% RH at 25°C
Interchangeability	±5% RH up to 60% RH, ±8% RH at 90% RH
Operating temperature	−40 to 85°C (−40 to 185°F)
Storage temperature	−51 to 110°C (−60 to 230°F)
Linearity	±0.5% RH typical
Repeatibility	±0.5% RH
Humidity stability	±1% RH typical at 50% RH in 5 years
Temperature effect on 0% RH voltage	±0.007% RH/°C (negligible)
Temperature effect on 100% span voltage	−0.22% RH/°C
Output voltage	$V_{OUT} = (V_S)(0.16$ to $0.78)$ nominal relative to supply voltage for 0–100% RH, i.e., 1–4.9 V for 6.3 V supply; 0.8–3.9 V for 5 V supply; sink capability 50 μA; drive capability 5 μA typical; low pass 1-kH filter required; turn on time < 0.1 s to full output
V_S supply requirement	4 to 9 V, regulated or use output/supply ratio; calibrated at 5 V
Current requirement	200 μA typical at 5 V, increased to 2 mA at 9 V

Example 8.10 Construct a humidity measurement system that consists of the 87C51GB, an IH-3605 humidity sensor and four seven-segment displays.

Solution: The schematic of this system is shown in Figure 8.14. Since the humidity does not change very quickly, it is adequate to measure it once every second. The voltage output from the humidity sensor will be between 0.8 and 3.9 V for the 5-V power supply. For the 8-bit A/D converter of the 87C51GB, 0.8 and 3.9 V inputs correspond to the A/D conversion result of 40 (or 41) and 198 (or 199), respectively. These two values correspond to 0 and 100% relative humidity, respectively. A lookup table will be used to translate the A/D conversion result to relative humidity. The relative humidity is calculated using the following expression:

$$RH = (X - 0.8 \times 255 \div 5) \div (3.9 \times 255 \div 5 - 0.8 \times 255 \div 5) \times 100\% \quad (8.8)$$

The relative humidity will be measured to one fractional digit. Three integral digits and one fractional digit are used in this example. Assign 0% RH to the A/D conversion results 40 and 41. Assign 100% RH to the A/D conversion result 199. For table lookup purposes, we subtract 40 from the A/D result before using it to look up the humidity table.

The procedure for measuring and displaying the humidity is as follows:

STEP 1   Configure the A/D converter parameters.

STEP 2   Take one humidity sample and convert it to digital value.

STEP 3   Look up the humidity table and display it for 1 s.

STEP 4   Repeat Steps 2 and 3 forever.

In Figure 8.14 a 1-kΩ resistor and a 0.16-μF capacitor are used as the required 1-kHz low pass filter.

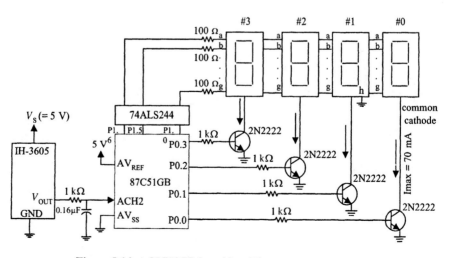

Figure 8.14 A 87C51GB-based humidity measurement system.

The program is as follows:

```
                mov     ACON,#10H            ; enable A/D, select scan mode,
                                             ; internal trigger
                mov     P1,#00H              ; blank out the display
wait_ad         mov     A,ACON               ;
                anl     A,#20H               ; check the AIF bit
                jz      wait_ad              ; is A/D completed?
                anl     ACON,#DFH            ; clear the AIF flag
                mov     A,AD2                ; get the A/D result of ACH2
                clr     C                    ; subtract 40 from A/D result before
                subb    A,#40                ; using it to look up the humidity
                mov     R5,A                 ; make a backup copy
; look up the humidity table to find the corresponding relative humidity
                mov     DPTR,#humtab_H       ; get the higher two digits of the
                                             ; humidity
                movc    A,@A+DPTR
                mov     B,A                  ; save a copy in B
                mov     A,R5
                mov     DPTR,#humtab_L       ; get the lower two digits of the
                movc    A,@A+DPTR            ; humidity
                mov     R4,A                 ; save a copy
                anl     A,#0FH               ; mask the upper four bits
                mov     DPTR,#dis_pat
                movc    A,@A+DPTR            ; look up the display pattern
                mov     R0,A                 ; save the pattern of the fractional
                                             ; digit of RH
                mov     A,R4                 ; get back the lower two digits
                anl     A,#F0H               ; mask the lower four bits
                rr      A                    ; shift to the lower four bits
                rr      A                    ; "
                rr      A                    ; "
                rr      A                    ; "
                movc    A,@A+DPTR            ; look up the display pattern
                mov     R1,A                 ; save the pattern of the ones
                                             ; digit of RH
                mov     A,B                  ; get back the upper two digits
                anl     A,#0FH               ; mask out the upper four bits
                movc    A,@A+DPTR            ; look up the display pattern
                mov     R2,A                 ; save the pattern of the tens
                                             ; digit of RH
```

```
                    mov     A,B              ; get back the upper two digits
                    anl     A,#0FH           ; mask out the upper four bits
                    movc    A,@A+DPTR        ; look up the display pattern
                    mov     R2,A             ; save the pattern of the tens
                                             ; digit of RH

                    mov     A,B              ; get back the upper two digits
                    anl     A,#F0H           ; mask out the second most
                                             ; significant digit
                    rr      A                ; shift to the lowest four bits
                    rr      A                ; "
                    rr      A                ; "
                    rr      A                ; "
                    movc    A,@A+DPTR        ; get the pattern of the hundreds
                                             ; digit of RH

                    mov     R5,#250          ; set up the display loop count
disp_lp:            mov     P1,A             ; display the most
                    mov     P0,#08H          ; significant digit (msd)
                    lcall   wait_1ms         ; wait for 1 ms
                    mov     P1,R2            ; display the second msd
                    mov     P0,#04H          ; "
                    lcall   wait_1ms         ; wait for 1 ms
                    mov     P1,R1            ; display the second lease
                    mov     P0,#02H          ; significant digit (lsd)
                    lcall   wait_1ms         ; wait for 1 ms
                    mov     P1,R0            ; display the lsd
                    mov     P0,#01           ; "
                    lcall   wait_1ms         ; wait for 1 ms
                    djnz    R5,disp_lp       ; does 1 s expire?
                    ljmp    wait_ad          ; repeat forever
; the following subroutine creates 1 ms delay
wait_1ms:           mov     R6,#200          ; set up loop count
here:               nop                      ; 1 $\mu$s
                    nop                      ; 1 $\mu$s
                    nop                      ; 1 $\mu$s
                    djnz    R6,here          ; 2 $\mu$s
                    ret
dis_pat             DB      7EH,30H,6DH,79H,33H,5BH,5FH,70H,7FH,7BH
humtab_H            DB      00H,00H,00H,00H,00H,00H,00H,00H,00H,00H,00H,00H,00H
                    DB      00H,00H,00H,00H,01H,01H,01H,01H,01H,01H,01H,01H,01H
```

	DB	01H,01H,01H,01H,01H,01H,01H,01H,02H,02H,02H,02H,02H
	DB	02H,02H,02H,02H,02H,02H,02H,02H,02H,02H,03H,03H,03H
	DB	03H,03H,03H,03H,03H,03H,03H,03H,03H,03H,03H,03H,04H
	DB	04H,04H,04H,04H,04H,04H,04H,04H,04H,04H,04H,04H,04H
	DB	04H,04H,05H,05H,05H,05H,05H,05H,05H,05H,05H,05H,05H
	DB	05H,05H,05H,05H,05H,06H,06H,06H,06H,06H,06H,06H,06H
	DB	06H,06H,06H,06H,06H,06H,06H,06H,07H,07H,07H,07H,07H
	DB	07H,07H,07H,07H,07H,07H,07H,07H,07H,07H,07H,08H,08H
	DB	08H,08H,08H,08H,08H,08H,08H,08H,08H,08H,08H,08H,08H
	DB	09H,09H,09H,10H
humtab_L	DB	00H,00H,08H,14H,20H,27H,33H,39H,46H,52H,58H,64H,71H
	DB	77H,83H,90H,96H,02H,09H,15H,21H,28H,34H,40H,47H,53H
	DB	59H,66H,72H,78H,85H,91H,97H,04H,10H,16H,23H,29H,35H
	DB	41H,48H,54H,60H,67H,73H,80H,86H,92H,99H,05H,11H,18H
	DB	24H,30H,36H,43H,50H,55H,62H,68H,74H,81H,87H,93H,00H
	DB	06H,12H,19H,25H,31H,38H,44H,50H,57H,63H,69H,76H,82H
	DB	88H,95H,01H,07H,14H,20H,26H,32H,39H,45H,52H,58H,64H
	DB	70H,77H,83H,90H,96H,02H,08H,15H,21H,27H,34H,40H,46H
	DB	53H,59H,65H,72H,78H,84H,90H,97H,03H,10H,16H,22H,29H
	DB	35H,41H,48H,54H,60H,67H,73H,80H,86H,92H,98H,04H,11H
	DB	17H,24H,30H,36H,42H,49H,55H,61H,68H,74H,80H,87H,93H
	DB	00H,06H,12H,18H,25H,31H,37H,43H,50H,56H,63H,69H,75H
	DB	82H,88H,94H,00H
	END	

8.10 USING THE EXTERNAL A/D CONVERTER ADC0820

The National Semiconductor ADC0820 is an 8-bit microprocessor compatible A/D converter with track/hold function. The 8-bit ADC0820 offers a 1.5 μs conversion time and dissipates only 75 mW of power.

For ease of interface with microprocessors, the ADC0820 has been designed to appear as a memory location or an I/O port without the need for external interfacing logic. The ADC0820 needs only a single 5 V power to operate. It has tristate output to interface with the microprocessor bus. The analog input can be anywhere between 0 and 5 V. The pin assignment of the ADC 0820 is shown in Figure 8.15.

8.10.1 Pin Functions of the AD0820

V_{IN}:   *Analog input*; range $= GND \leq V_{IN} \leq V_{CC}$

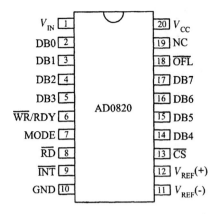

Figure 8.15 The AD0820 A/D converter.

DB7~DB0:   *Tristate data output* (MSB ~ LSB)

Mode: *Mode selection input.* When low, the AD0820 is configured to RD mode. When high, the AD0820 is configured to WR-RD mode.

$\overline{\text{WR}}$/RDY: In the **WR-RD** mode (when the mode input is high), with $\overline{\text{CS}}$ low, the conversion is started on the falling edge of $\overline{\text{WR}}$. Approximately 800 ns after the signal $\overline{\text{WR}}$'s rising edge, the result of the conversion will be transferred to the output latch, provided that the $\overline{\text{RD}}$ signal does not go low before this time period. In the **RD** mode (when mode input is low), this signal is used as RDY and becomes an open-drain output. RDY will go low after the falling edge of $\overline{\text{CS}}$; RDY will go tristate when the result of the conversion is strobed into the output latch. It is used to simplify the interface with a microprocessor system.

$\overline{\text{RD}}$:   *Read signal.* In WR-RD mode, with $\overline{\text{CS}}$ low, the tristate data outputs will be activated when $\overline{\text{RD}}$ goes low. $\overline{\text{RD}}$ can also be used to increase the speed of the converter by reading data prior to the preset internal time out (t_I ~ 800 ns). If this is done, the data result transferred to output latch is latched after the falling edge of the $\overline{\text{RD}}$. In RD mode, with $\overline{\text{CS}}$ low, the conversion will start when $\overline{\text{RD}}$ goes low. The $\overline{\text{RD}}$ signal will enable the tristate data outputs at the completion of conversion. The condition that the RDY signal goes tristate and the INT signal goes low indicates the completion of the conversion.

$\overline{\text{INT}}$:   *Interrupt.* In **WR-RD** mode, the condition that the $\overline{\text{INT}}$ signal goes low indicates that the conversion is completed and the data result is in the output latch. $\overline{\text{INT}}$ will go low about 800 ns after the rising edge of $\overline{\text{WR}}$ or after the falling edge of $\overline{\text{RD}}$, if $\overline{\text{RD}}$ goes low prior to the 800 ns time-out interval. $\overline{\text{INT}}$ is reset by the rising edge of $\overline{\text{RD}}$ or $\overline{\text{CS}}$. In **RD** mode, the condition that the $\overline{\text{INT}}$ signal goes low indicates that the conversion is completed and the result is in the output latch. $\overline{\text{INT}}$ is reset by the rising edge of $\overline{\text{RD}}$ or $\overline{\text{CS}}$.

$V_{REF}(-)$:   Low reference voltage.

$V_{REF}(+)$:   High reference voltage.

$\overline{CS}$:   *Chip select.* $\overline{CS}$ must be low for the $\overline{RD}$ or $\overline{WR}$ to be recognized by the converter.

$\overline{OFL}$:   Overflow output—if the analog input is higher than the $V_{REF}(+)$, OFL will be low at the end of conversion. It can be used to cascade two or more devices to have more resolution (9, 10 bits). This output is always active and does not go into tristate as DB7-DB0.

8.10.2 Digital Interface

The ADC0820 has two basic interface modes that are selected by strapping the MODE pin high or low.

RD Mode

With the MODE pin grounded, the converter is set to read mode. In this configuration, a complete conversion is done by pulling $\overline{RD}$ low until output data appear. The $\overline{INT}$ goes low at the end of the conversion. The RDY output can be used to signal a processor that the converter is busy or can also serve as a system transfer acknowledge signal. It takes 1.6 ms to complete the A/D conversion in this mode. The signal transactions of this mode are shown in Figure 8.16.

WR Then RD Mode

With the MODE pin tied high, the A/D will be set up for the WR-RD mode. Here, a conversion is started with the $\overline{WR}$ input brought low; however, there are two options for reading the output data that relate to interface timing. If an interrupt driven scheme is desired, the user can wait for $\overline{INT}$ to go low before reading the conversion result. $\overline{INT}$ typically goes

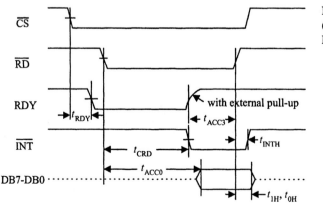

Figure 8.16 RD Mode timing. (Redrawn with permission of National Semiconductor.)

low 800 ns after the signal $\overline{WR}$'s rising edge. However, if a shorter conversion time is desired, the processor need not wait for $\overline{INT}$ and can exercise a read only 600 ns after the rising edge of $\overline{WR}$. If this is done, $\overline{INT}$ will immediately go low and data will appear at the outputs. The signal transactions of this mode are shown in Figure 8.17.

Stand-Alone Operation in WR-RD Mode

For stand-alone operation in WR-RD mode, $\overline{CS}$ and $\overline{RD}$ can be tied low and a conversion can be started with the falling edge of $\overline{WR}$. Data will be valid approximately 800 ns following $\overline{WR}$'s rising edge. The signal transactions of stand-alone mode are shown in Figure 8.18. Timing parameters related to the ADC0820 operation are listed in Table 8.3.

From Figures 8.16, 8.17, and 8.18, we conclude that it would be the easiest to use WR-RD stand-alone mode. The WR-RD mode has a slightly shorter conversion time.

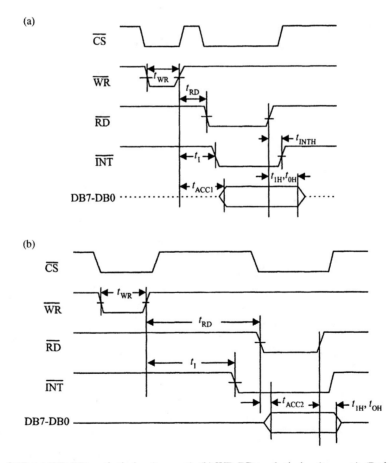

Figure 8.17 (a) WR-RD mode timing ($t_{RD} < t_I$). (b) WR-RD mode timing ($t_{RD} > t_I$). (Redrawn with permission of National Semiconductor.

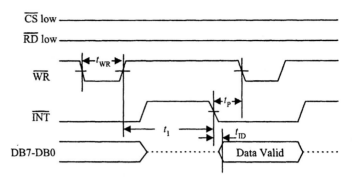

Figure 8.18 WR-RD stand-along operation timing. (Redrawn with permission of National Semiconductors.)

TABLE 8.3
ADC0820 Timing Parameters[a]

Symbol	Parameter	Typical[b]	Tested Limit[c]	Design Limit[d]	Unit
t_{CRD}	Conversion time for RD mode	16		2.5	ns
t_{ACC0}	Access time from falling edge of RD to output valid	$t_{CRD}+20$		$t_{CRD}+50$	μs
$t_{CWR\text{-}RD}^e$	Conversion time for WR-RD mode			1.52	μs
t_{WR}	Write time	50 μs (max)	600 ns		ns
t_{RD}	Read time		600 ns	280	ns
t_{ACC1}	Access time from falling edge of RD to output valid	190 ($C_L = 15$ pF) 210 ($C_L = 100$ pF)		320 120	ns ns
t_{ACC2}	Access time from falling edge of RD to output valid	70 ($C_L = 15$ pF) 90 ($C_L = 100$ pF)		150	ns ns
t_{ACC3}	Access time from falling edge of RDY to output valid	30 ($C_L = 15$ pF)			ns
t_I	Internal comparison time	800 ($C_L = 50$ pF)		1300 200	ns
$t_{1H} \, t_{0H}$	Tristate control	100 ($R_L = 1$ K,$C_L = 10$ pF)		225	ns
t_{INTH}	Delay from rising edge of WR to rising edge of INT	125 ($C_L = 50$ pF)		100	ns
t_{RDY}	Delay from CS to RDY	50 ($C_L = 50$ pF, pin 7 = 0)		50	ns
t_{ID}	Delay from INT to output valid	20			ns
t_P	Delay from end of conversion to next conversion			500	ns

Source: From National Semiconductor.
[a] Accuracy may degrade if t_{WR} or t_{RD} is shorter than the minimum value specified.
[b] Typicals are at 25°C and represent most likely parametric norm.
[c] Tested limits are guaranteed to National Semiconductor's average outgoing quality level.
[d] Design limits are guaranteed but not 100% tested.
[e] $t_{CWR\text{-}RD}$ is measured when $t_{WR} = 600$ ns and $t_{RD} = 600$ ns.

8.10.3 Interfacing the ADC0820 with the 87C51FB

As described earlier, the ADC0820 can be interfaced with the microcontroller as a memory device (a memory space needs to be assigned to the ADC) or an I/O device. When should we use the ADC0820 as a memory device and when should we use it as an I/O device? The answer depends on whether the product at which we are working has external memory devices. If there are other external memory devices, then it is not inconvenient to add another memory device to the design as long as there is still memory space unassigned. Otherwise, it would be easier to use it as an I/O device.

Example 8.11 Describe how to use the 87C51FB to drive an ADC0820 to perform A/D conversion and write a program to start an A/D conversion, read the result, and leave it in accumulator A. Assume that the 87C51FB has no external memory device and ports 1 and 3 are available for interfacing.

Solution: We will use port 1 to connect to the data outputs DB7-DB0 and use port 3 pin P3.0 to drive the $\overline{WR}$ pin. The circuit connection is shown in Figure 8.19.

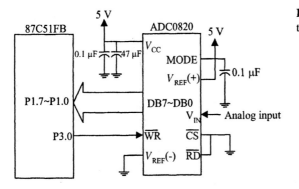

Figure 8.19 Circuit connection between the 87C51FB and the ADC0820.

To start an A/D conversion, we must pull the signal P3.0 to low and then set it to high. The conversion result will be available 800 ns (shorter than one machine cycle) later.
The instruction sequence is as follows:

```
clr     P3.0        ; pull WR to low
setb    P3.0        ; pull WR to high
mov     P1,#FFH      ; configure port P1 for input
mov     A,P1        ; read conversion result into accumulator A
```

After reading the A/D conversion result, we can do any processing on these data. There are A/D converters with serial interface, that is, the microcontroller reads the converter's result bit serially. They will be discussed in Chapter 10.

8.11 SUMMARY

The A/D converter is useful in data acquisition applications. An A/D conversion converts an analog voltage into a digital value. The number of bits used in representing the analog voltage determines the accuracy of the A/D conversion. The most popular A/D conversion method used today is called the successive-approximation method. Most A/D converters are ratiometric, i.e., the A/D result is proportional to the input voltage.

An A/D converter needs a high-reference voltage and a low-reference voltage to perform the conversion. The best conversion result can be obtained when the analog input covers the whole range from the low-reference voltage to the high-reference voltage. A voltage scaling and shifting circuit can achieve this goal. This circuit is also called a *signal-conditioning* circuit. For convenience, the high-reference voltage is often set to the power supply voltage whereas the low-reference voltage is often set to ground. A data acquisition system usually includes a sensor that converts the nonelectrical physical quantity into a voltage. The sensor output may need a signal conditioning circuit to achieve better conversion accuracy.

The Intel 8XC51GB provides an 8-channel, 8-bit A/D converter. The 8XC51GB has 10 registers related to the A/D converter: the ACON control register, the ACMP comparison register, and eight result registers for eight channels. The ACON register configures the operation of the A/D. We can configure the input trigger mode, A/D input mode, and A/D comparison mode by programming the ACON register. The A/D converter is started when the ACE bit of the ACON register is set to 1. The conversion of one sample takes 26 machine cycles.

All of the sensors discussed in this chapter have three external connections: $+V_S$, GND, and V_{OUT}. The barometric pressure transducer (BPT) kit produces a 4.5–5.5 V output over the barometric pressure range from 800 to 1100 mbar. It can operate over a power supply between 7 and 24 V. Applications include barometry, weather stations, and absolute pressure compensation in sensitive equipment. We need to add a shifting and scaling circuit to translate its voltage output to between 0 and V_{CC} so that the whole dynamic range of an A/D converter can be utilized. Since the barometric pressure range is not a power of 2, we use a table to look up the corresponding barometric pressure for each conversion result. A display circuit can be added to display the pressure.

The temperature sensor LM34 made by National Semiconductor can be used to measure the temperature in the range from -50 to $+300°F$. The output voltage of LM34 increases by $+10.0$ mV per degree of temperature increment in the Fahrenheit scale. LM34 can operate over a power supply of 5 ~ 30 V. A signal conditioning circuit is required if we use LM34 in measuring room temperature since its output voltage is in a small range. A lookup table should be used to find the corresponding temperature for each A/D conversion result.

The IH-3605 is a humidity sensor made by HyCal Engineering. The IH-3605 provides a linear output of 0.8 ~ 3.9 V over the full range from 0 to 100% relative humidity (RH) when excited by a 5 V power supply. It can operate over a temperature range from -40 to $+185°F$. A 1-kHz low-pass filter is required for the operation of this sensor (connected to the V_{OUT} pin). A signal conditioning circuit is not required. Table lookup is still a good method to find the corresponding relative humidity for each A/D conversion result. The humidity table is based on Equation 8.8.

Many MCS-51 members do not have an on-chip A/D converter. For some applications, the resolution of the A/D converter of the 8XC51GB (or other MCS-51 variants with on-chip A/D converter) may not be adequate. In these situations, using an off-chip A/D converter is the only choice. The ADC0820 from National Semiconductor is an 8-bit A/D converter with parallel interface. The A/D conversion from the ADC0820 can be read back via an input port or data bus (when ADC0820 is treated as a memory device). The conversion of each sample takes about 800 ns from the rising edge of the $\overline{\text{WR}}$ signal.

8.12 EXERCISES

8.1 Explain the difference between digital and analog signals.

8.2 How long does it take to convert the voltages of four channels on the 87C51GB that operates with a 16-MHz oscillator?

8.3 Given an A/D converter with 8-bit resolution, what will be the analog input voltages for the conversion results of 20, 40, 75, 120, 180, 210, 240? Assume $V_{\text{LREF}} = 1$ V, $V_{\text{HREF}} = 4$ V, $V_{\text{CC}} = 5$ V.

8.4 Given an A/D converter with 10-bit resolution, what will be the analog input voltages for the conversion results of 80, 120, 200, 256, 384, 512, 640, 896, and 960? Assume $V_{\text{LREF}} = 0$ V, $V_{\text{HREF}} = 5$ V, $V_{\text{CC}} = 5$ V.

8.5 Assume that you are given a voltage output from a transducer that can be as low as 0 V and as high as 200 mV. Use the circuit shown in Figure 8.4 to scale the output voltage to 0~5 V. Compute the appropriate value for each resistor.

8.6 Assume that you are given a voltage output from a transducer that can be as low as 0 V and as high as 500 mV. Use the circuit shown in Figure 8.4 to scale the output voltage to 0~5 V. Compute the appropriate value for each resistor.

8.7 Assume that you are given a transducer voltage output with a range of −80 ~ 200 mV. Use the circuit in Figure 8.5 to shift and scale it to the range of 0~5 V.

8.8 Assume that the output voltage of a transducer is in the range of −100~150 mV. Use the circuit in Figure 8.5 to shift and scale it to the range of 0~5 V.

8.9 The LM35 is a Centigrade temperature sensor made by National Semiconductor Inc. This device has three external connection pins like the LM34. The pin assignment and circuit connection for converting temperature are shown in Figure 8E.1. Use this device to construct a circuit to display the room temperature in Celsius. Assume the temperature range is from 0 to 42.5°C.

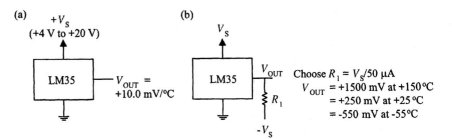

Figure 8E.1 Circuit connection for the LM35. (a) Circuit connection for +2 to +150°C. (b) Circuit connection for −50 to +300°F.

8.13 LAB EXERCISES AND ASSIGNMENTS

The MCB520 does not have an on board A/D converter. We need to add an external A/D converter to perform experiments on A/D conversion. There are two types of A/D converters. The first type has parallel interface and allows the microcontroller to read back the conversion result in one or two read operations. The second type has serial interface with which the A/D conversion result must be shifted to the microcontroller bit serially. The second type is much smaller because fewer pins are needed.

8.1 *Signal conditioning experiment.* Build a signal conditioning circuit that can shift and scale the voltage from the range of −1~+3 V to the range of 0~5 V. The lab procedure is as follows:

STEP 1   Compute the values for R_0, R_1, R_2, and R_f and also choose an appropriate value for V_1 for the circuit in Figure 8.5.

STEP 2   Set V_{in} to −1, −0.5, 0, 0.5, 1, 1.5, 2.0, 2.5, and 3.0 V and measure the voltage V_{OUT} for each of these V_{in} values. What value of V_{OUT} do you get for each of these V_{in} values? What is the theoretical value of V_{OUT} corresponding to each V_{in}?

Do the following two lab experiments after you have read Section 10.13 or after you have studied Chapter 10.

8.2 *Verifying the functioning of an A/D converter.* Use the 10-bit serial A/D converter ADC1031 from National Semiconductor to do this experiment. Refer to Figure 10.35. The purpose of this experiment is to verify that the A/D converter at hand works properly. Use a 5-V power supply for the A/D converter. After the A/D conversion is completed, we need to use the serial method (one bit at a time) to read the result from the converter. The lab procedure is as follows:

STEP 1   Connect the circuit properly.

- Use P1.6 and P1.7 as DO and S_{CLK}, respectively.
- Use Timer 2 to generate programmable clock out (from P1.0 pin) and use it as the conversion clock C_{CLK}. What values should be placed in RCAP2H and RCAP2L to generate a 4.125-MHz clock signal from P1.0?

- Connect 5 and 0 V to the V_{CC} and GND pins, respectively.
- Tie the CS pin to ground permanently.
- Connect V_{REF} to V_{CC}.

STEP 2   Adjust the function generator output to the range of 0~5 V and connect it to the V_{IN} input of the A/D converter. Set the frequency to about 2 kHz. Please note that the frequency of V_{IN} is not critical.

STEP 3   Write a program that reads 64 conversion results and stores them in external memory from locations 2000H to 207FH. Use 2 bytes for each conversion result. Check to see if the conversion results demonstrate a periodic pattern.

The ADC1031 shifts out data starting from the most significant bit on the falling edge of the C_{CLK} signal. To read the A/D conversion from the ADC1031, do the following: Clear accumulator A to 0 before shifting data in from the A/D converter. To read a bit, set the C_{CLK} signal to high and then pull it to low. The bit value will then be available on the DO pin. Transfer this bit (from P1.6) to the C flag. Use an RLC instruction to shift the bit into accumulator A. Repeat this process twice and save accumulator A in an external memory location. Repeat the shift process eight more times and read in the lower 8 bits and store it in the next memory location and you have read the conversion result for one sample. Store it in 2 bytes of external data memory.

8.3 *Digital thermometer.* Use the LM34 Fahrenheit temperature sensor, the mA741 op amp, the MCB520 evaluation board, and an external serial 10-bit A/D converter ADC1031 (described in Chapter 10) to construct a digital thermometer. The temperature should be displayed in three integral digits and one fractional digit. The requirements are as follows:

1. The temperature range is from 0 to 110°F.
2. Use four seven-segment displays to display the temperature reading, which must include one fractional digit. Use the Motorola MC14489 seven-segment display driver to control the seven-segment displays. The function of the MC14489 is described in Section 10.9.
3. Use a water bath to change the ambient temperature to the LM34. Remember to insulate the LM34 so that it does not get wet.
4. Measure the temperature 10 times every second and display the average of the measurements.
5. Update the temperature once every second.

9

SERIAL COMMUNICATION
PORT

9.1 OBJECTIVES

After completing this chapter, you should be able to

- define different types of data links
- explain the fours aspects of the EIA-232-E interface standard
- explain the data transmission process for the EIA-232-E interface standard
- explain the types of data transmission errors that occur in serial data communication
- establish a null modem connection
- explain the operation of the serial port
- wire the serial port pins to a EIA-232 connector
- use the mode 0 of the serial port to interface with serial memory chips such as an X24C44
- program the serial port to do data transfer

9.2 INTRODUCTION

Serial data communication has been widely used in long-distance data communication and in situations that do not need high-speed transfer rate. There are two types of serial data communication: synchronous and asynchronous. Synchronous serial data communication uses a separate clock signal to synchronize the receiver and the transmitter. Asynchronous serial data communication does not need a separate clock signal to synchronize the data transfer. Asynchronous serial data transfer proceeds character by character. Each character is framed by a start bit and a stop bit. The receiver needs to identify the start bit and stop bit to receive data correctly. We will discuss synchronous serial data transfer in Chapter 10.

Either a dedicated or public phone line can be used as a medium for asynchronous serial data communication. A basic data communication link is shown in Figure 9.1. A computer or a terminal can be at each end of the link. The communication link consists of data terminal equipment (DTE) and an associated modem [a type of data communication equipment

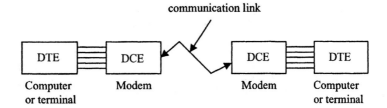

Figure 9.1 A data communication system.

(DCE)] at each end. The term *modem* is derived from the process of accepting digital bits, changing them into a form suitable for analog transmission (modulation), sending the signal to the other station, and transforming it back to its original digital representation (demodulation).

There are two types of communication links, point to point and multipoint (also called multidrop), as illustrated in Figure 9.2. In the former, the two end stations communicate as peers; in the latter, one device is designated as the master (primary) and the others as slaves (secondaries). Each multipoint station has its own unique address, with the primary station controlling all data transfers over the communication link.

A communication link may consist of either two or four wires. A two-wire link provides a signal and a ground, and a four-wire link provides two such pairs. A communication link can be used in three different ways:

1. *Simplex link.* The line is dedicated to either transmission or reception, but not both.
2. *Half-duplex link.* The communication link can be used for either transmission or reception, but in only one direction at a time.
3. *Full-duplex link.* The transmission and reception can proceed simultaneously. This link requires four wires.

Many standards have been proposed to facilitate data communication. An early but still popular one is the RS-232. This standard has experienced several revisions since its first debut in 1960. The latest revision, RS-232-E, was done in July 1991.

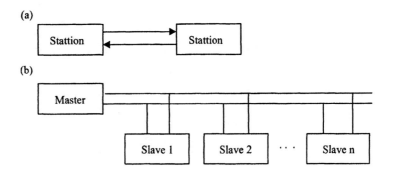

Figure 9.2 Point-to-point (a) and multipoint (b) communication links.

Data communication engineers and technicians use the term *mark* to indicate a binary 1 and *space* to indicate a binary 0. The terms *high* and *low* are confusing when applied to serial communication because the logic levels used on a serial communication circuit may not be those used in standard TTL and CMOS digital circuits. The RS-232 standard, for example, represents a binary 0, or space, with a positive voltage and a binary 1, or mark, with a negative voltage.

9.3 THE EIA-232-E (OR RS-232) STANDARD

The RS-232 standard published by the Electronic Industry Association (EIA) is one of the most widely used physical interfaces in the world and is most prevalent in North America. The EIA has replaced the prefix RS (recommended standard) with the prefix EIA. The change represents no change to the standard, but was made to allow easier identification of the source of the standard. We will mix the uses of RS-232 and EIA-232 throughout this chapter.

EIA-232-E can apply to the following data communication schemes:

- Serial communications
- Synchronous and asynchronous
- Dedicated leased or private lines
- Switched service
- Two wire or four wire
- Point to point or multipoint

There are four aspects in the EIA-232-E interface: mechanical, functional, procedural, and electrical.

9.3.1 EIA-232-E Mechanical Characteristics

EIA-232-E uses a 25-pin plug connector for all interface circuits. This plug connector is shown in Figure 9.3. A summary of EIA-232-E signals is listed in Table 9.1.

9.3.2 Functions of EIA-232-E Interchange Circuits

The EIA-232-E interface provides one primary channel and one secondary channel. Since the secondary channel is rarely used, only the functions of signals in the primary channel will be discussed.

Circuit AB—Signal common (pin 7). This circuit establishes the common ground reference potential for all interchange circuits.

Circuit BA—Transmitted data (pin 2). The DTE transmits data from this pin to its associated DCE.

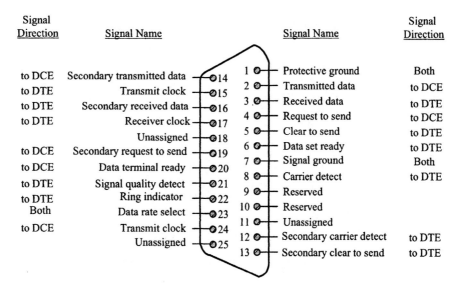

Signal Direction	Signal Name		Signal Name	Signal Direction
to DCE	Secondary transmitted data	14		
to DTE	Transmit clock	15		
to DTE	Secondary received data	16		
to DTE	Receiver clock	17		
	Unassigned	18		
to DCE	Secondary request to send	19		
to DCE	Data terminal ready	20		
to DTE	Signal quality detect	21		
to DTE	Ring indicator	22		
Both	Data rate select	23		
to DCE	Transmit clock	24		
	Unassigned	25		
		1	Protective ground	Both
		2	Transmitted data	to DCE
		3	Received data	to DTE
		4	Request to send	to DCE
		5	Clear to send	to DTE
		6	Data set ready	to DTE
		7	Signal ground	Both
		8	Carrier detect	to DTE
		9	Reserved	
		10	Reserved	
		11	Unassigned	
		12	Secondary carrier detect	to DTE
		13	Secondary clear to send	to DTE

Figure 9.3 EIA-232-E connector and pin assignment.

Circuit BB—*Received data (pin 3).* A DTE receives data from this pin.

Circuit CA—*Request to send (pin 4).* This signal is also abbreviated as RTS. The DTE asserts this signal to its associated DCE when it has data to transmit. On a half-duplex channel, the ON condition maintains the DCE in the transmit mode and inhibits the receive mode. The OFF condition maintains the DCE equipment in the receive mode.

The rules for the use of this pin are as follows:
1. A transition from OFF to ON instructs the DCE to enter a transmit mode.
2. The DCE takes necessary actions and turns on circuit CB (clear to send, pin 5).
3. A transition from ON to OFF instructs the DCE to complete transmission of all data that were sent across circuit BA (pin 2).
4. The DCE turns off circuit CB (clear to send, pin 5) in response.
5. Circuit CA (pin 4) cannot be turned on again until circuit CB (pin 5) is turned off by the DCE.

Circuit CB—*Clear to send (pin 5).* A DCE asserts this signal (abbreviated as CTS) to indicate that it is ready to transmit data, or, for a dialing DCE, whether or not it can accept dialing or control signals. The OFF condition is an indication to the DTE that it should not transfer data across the interface on interchange circuit BA (pin 2).

Circuit CC—*DCE ready (pin 6).* Signals on this circuit are used to indicate the status of the local DCE. The ON condition on this circuit indicates the following conditions:

1. The local DCE is connected to a communications channel (off hook in switched service).

TABLE 9.1
EIA-232-E Signals

Pin Number	Circuit	Description
1	—	Shield
2	BA	Transmitted data
3	BB	Received data
4	CA/CJ	Request to send/ready for receiving[a]
5	CB	Clear to send
6	CC	DCE
7	AB	Signal common
8	CF	Received line signal detector
9	—	(Reserved for testing)
10	—	(Reserved for testing)
11	—	Unassigned[b]
12	SCF/CI	Secondary received line signal detection/data range selector (DCE source)[c]
13	SCB	Secondary clear to send
14	SBA	Secondary transmitted data
15	DB	Transmitter signal element timing (DCE source)
16	SBB	Secondary received data
17	DD	Received signal element timing
18	LL	Local loopback
19	SCA	Secondary request to send
20	CD	DTE ready
21	RL/CG	Remote loopback/signal quality detector
22	CE	Ring indicator
23	CH/CI	Data signal rate selector (DTE/DCE source)[c]
24	DA	Transmitter signal element timing (DTE source)
25	TM	Test mode

[a] When hardware flow control is required, circuit CA may take on the functionality of circuit CJ. This is one change from the former EIA-232.

[b] Pin 11 is unassigned. It will not be assigned in future versions of EIA-232. However, in international standard ISO 2110, this pin is assigned to select transmit frequency.

[c] For designs using interchange circuit SCF, interchange circuits CH and CI are assigned to pin 23. If SCF is not used, CI is assigned to pin 12.

2. The local DCE has completed any timing functions required by the switching system and the transmission of any discrete answer tone.

3. The local DCE is not in test (local or remote), talk, or dial mode.

The OFF condition on this circuit indicates one of the following conditions:

1. It is not ready to operate.

2. It has detected a problem.

3. For switched operation, it has detected a disconnect indication.

The OFF condition shall appear at all other times and shall be an indication that the DTE is to disregard signals appearing on any other interchange circuit with the exception of circuit CE (ring indicator, pin 22)

Circuit CD—DTE ready (pin 20). Signals on this circuit are used to control switching of the DCE to the communication channel. The ON condition prepares the DCE for connection with the communication channel and maintains the connection established by external means (manual calling, manual answering, or automatic calling). When the station is equipped for automatic answering of received calls and is in the automatic answering mode, the connection to the line occurs only in response to a combination of a ringing signal and the ON condition of circuit CD. However, the DTE is normally permitted to present the ON condition on circuit CD whenever it is ready to transmit or receive data. With switched lines, circuit CD shall not be turned on again until circuit CC (DCE ready) is turned off by the DCE.

Circuit CE—Ring Indicator (pin 22). The ON condition of this circuit indicates that a ringing signal is being received on the communication channel. The ring indicator is used to direct the receiving I/O driver to activate data terminal ready (if it is OFF). One of its other important functions is to alert the I/O driver to check the calling modem's carrier.

Circuit CF—Received line signal detector (pin 8). The ON condition on this circuit is presented when the DCE is receiving a signal. The OFF condition indicates that no signal is being received or that signal is unsuitable for demodulation. The OFF condition of circuit CF shall cause circuit BB (received data) to be clamped to the binary one (MARK) condition. This circuit is more commonly called "*carrier detect*" (DCD). Its use varies for the half-duplex and full-duplex operations:

1. Half-duplex: A carrier is on the line and the local interface's request to send is OFF.
2. Full-duplex: A carrier is on the line and the remote interface's request to send is ON.

Circuit CG—Remote loopback/signal quality detector (pin 21). Signals on this circuit are used to indicate whether or not there is a high probability of an error in the received data. An ON condition is maintained whenever there is no reason to believe that an error has occurred.

Circuit CH—Data signal rate selector (pin 23). Signals on this circuit are used to select between the two data signaling rates in the case of dual rate synchronous DCEs or the two ranges of data signaling rates in the case of dual range nonsynchronous DCEs. An ON condition shall select the higher data signaling rate or range of rates.

Circuit CI—Data signal rate selector (pin 23 or pin 12). Signals on this circuit are used to select between the two data signaling rates in the case of dual rate synchronous DCEs or the two ranges of data signaling rates in the case of dual nonsynchronous DCEs. An ON condition shall select the higher data signaling rate or range of rates.

Circuit DA—Transmitter signal element timing (DTE source, pin 24). Signals on this circuit are used to provide the transmitting signal converter with signal element timing information. The ON to OFF transition shall nominally indicate the center of each signal element on circuit BA (transmitted data). When circuit DA is implemented in the DTE, the DTE shall nominally provide timing information on this circuit whenever the DTE is in a power ON condition.

Circuit DB—Transmitter signal element timing (DCE source, pin 15). Signals on this circuit are used to provide the DTE with signal element timing information. The DTE shall provide a data signal on circuit BA (transmitted data) in which the transitions between signal elements normally occur at the time of the transitions from OFF to ON condition of the signal on circuit DB. When circuit DB is implemented in the DCE, the DCE shall normally provide timing information on this circuit whenever DCE is in a power ON condition.

Circuit DD—Receiver signal element timing (DCE source, pin 17). Signals on this circuit are used to provide the DTE with received signal element timing information. The transition from ON to OFF condition indicates the center of each signal element on circuit BB (received data). Timing information on circuit DD shall be provided at all times when circuit CF is in the ON condition.

The timing pins are not required for asynchronous systems but are necessary for synchronous devices because synchronous data streams do not have the start/stop timing bits. In summary, the timing pins are used as follows:

PIN	Name	Source
15	Transmit timing	Transmitting DCE
17	Receive timing	Receiving DCE
24	Transmit timing	Transmitting DTE

9.3.3 The EIA-232-E Procedural Characteristics

This aspect of the standard describes how data communication is proceeded across the interface. The sequence of events that occurs during data transmission using the EIA-232-E is easiest to understand by studying examples. In the first example, two DTEs are connected with a point-to-point link (shown in Figure 9.4) using an asynchronous dedicated-line modem:

1. Signal reference connections are made.
2. DTEs turn ON pin 20 (DTR) to indicate readiness and DCEs turn on pin 6 (DCE ready).
3. DTE X requests a transmission with pin 4 (RTS) turned on. DCE X sends out a carrier signal to DCE Y and turns on pin 5 (CTS) to DTE X. DCE Y detects the carrier signal and turns on pin 8 (carrier detect) to DTE Y.
4. DTE X begins transmitting application data over pin 2 to DCE X. Pin 24 synchronizes DTE X and DCE X. Data are modulated and transmitted to DCE Y, which demodulates data and transmits to DTE Y using pin 3. DCE Y sends the proper timing signals to DTE Y on pin 17.
5. The end of transmission (EOT) procedures cause DTE X to turn OFF pin 4, which instructs DCE X to turn OFF its carrier signal. DCE Y detects the carrier being turned OFF and turns OFF pin 8 to Y.

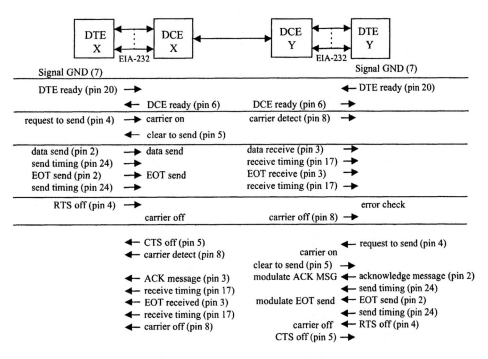

Figure 9.4 EIA-232-E communication.

6. In responds to the DTE X's data, DTE Y transmits its own data using the same process as in events 1 through 5.

In the second example, two DTEs exchange data through a telephone line. Now one of the DTEs (initiator) must dial the phone (automatically or manually) to establish the connection. An additional lead is required for this application: ring indicator (CE).

Data transmission in this configuration can be divided into three steps:

STEP 1 *Establishing the connection.* The following events occur during this step:

1. The transmit DTE asserts the data-terminal-ready (DTR) signal to indicate to the local modem that it is ready to make a call.
2. The local modem opens the phone circuit and dials the destination number. The number can be stored in the modem or transmitted to the modem by the computer via the transmit-data pin.
3. The remote modem detects a ring on the phone line and asserts ring-indicator (RI) to indicate to the remote DTE that a call has arrived.
4. The remote DTE asserts the DTR signal to accept the call.
5. The remote modem answers the call by sending a carrier signal to the local modem via the phone line. It also asserts the DSR signal to inform the remote DTE that it is ready for data transmission.

6. The local modem asserts both the DSR and DCD (data carrier detect) signals to indicate that the connection is established and it is ready for data communication.

7. For full-duplex data communication, the local modem also sends a carrier signal to the remote modem. The remote modem then asserts DCD signal.

STEP 2 *Data transmission.* The following events occur during this step:

1. The local DTE asserts the RTS signal when it is ready to send data.

2. The local modem responds by asserting the CTS signal.

3. The local DTE sends data bit serially to the local modem over the transmit-data pin. The local modem then modulates its carrier signal to transmit the data to the remote modem.

4. The remote modem receives the modulated signal from the local modem, demodulates it to recover the data, and sends it to the remote DTE over the receive-data pin.

STEP 3 *Disconnection.* Disconnection requires only two steps:

1. When the local DTE has finished the data transmission, it drops the RTS signal.

2. The local modem then deasserts the CTS signal and drops the carrier (equivalent to hanging up the phone).

9.3.4 The EIA-232-E Electrical Characteristics

The equivalent circuit of the EIA-232-E interface circuit is shown in Figure 9.5. The signal on an interchange circuit is in marking condition when the voltage (V_1) is less than -3 V with respect to circuit AB (signal common). The signal is considered to be in a spacing condition when the voltage (V_1) is greater than 3 V with respect to AB. The region between $+3$ and -3 V is a transition region. The marking condition is to represent a binary 1 and the spacing condition is used to represent a binary 0. The circuit functions are considered ON when the circuit is in a spacing condition and OFF when the circuit is in a marking condition.

The open-circuit generator voltage (V_0) with respect to signal ground (AB) in any circuit is not allowed to exceed 25 V in magnitude. When the receiver open-circuit voltage (E_L) is zero, the potential (V_1) ranges between 5 and 15 V.

The signal transmitted across the interface point must adhere to the following conventions:

1. Signals entering the transition region shall proceed through it to the opposite signal state.

2. No reversal of voltage is permitted while the signal is in the transition region.

3. The time to pass through the transition region shall not exceed 1 ms.

4. The data and timing interchange circuits must have the transition time requirements shown in Table 9.2.

In asynchronous transfer mode, the following rules are followed to guarantee correct data transmission:

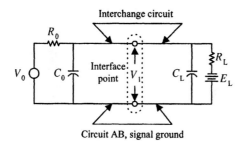

Figure 9.5 EIA-232-E interchange equivalent circuit.

Circuit AB, signal ground

V_0: The open-circuit generator voltage.
R_0: The generator internal DC resistance.
C_0: The total effective capacitance associated with the generator, measured at the interface point and including any cable to the interface point.
V_1: The voltage at the interface point.
C_L: The total effective capacitance associated with the receiver measured at the interface point and including any cable to the interface point.
R_L: The receiver load DC resistance.
E_L: The open circuit receiver voltage (bias).

TABLE 9.2
Transition Times for Data and Timing Interchange Circuits

Unit Interval (UI) Duration	Maximum Transition Time Allowed
$UI \geq 25$ ms	1 ms
25 ms $\geq UI \geq \mu s$	4% of UI
$125 \, \mu s \geq UI$	$5 \, \mu s$

1. Data are transferred character by character.
2. A character consists of one start bit, 7 or 8 data bits, an optional parity bit, and 1 or 1½, or 2 stop bits.
3. The start bit is 0.
4. The least significant bit (lsb) is transferred first and the most significant bit (msb) is transferred last.
5. The stop bit is 1.

Example 9.1 Draw the waveforms of letter A in the CMOS (or TTL) and EIA-232-E interface using the EIA-232-E format. Assume the format of 1 start bit, 8 data bits, 1 stop bit, and no parity bit.

Solution: The ASCII code of letter A is 41H (01000001). Since the least significant bit is transmitted first, the data pattern for letter A in the EIA-232-E format will be binary value 0100000101. The waveforms in CMOS and EIA-232-E format are shown in Figure 9.6.

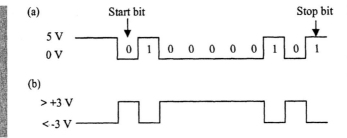

Figure 9.6 A comparison of signal pattern of letter "A." (a) Signal pattern for letter "A" in CMOS (or TTL). (b) Signal pattern for letter "A" in EIA-232-E format.

Example 9.2 What is the overhead of EIA-232-E data transmission using the format of 1 start bit, 8 data bit, 1 stop bit, and 1 parity bit.

Solution: For each character transferred, 11 bits must be transmitted. Therefore, the overhead is $3 \div 11 \times 100\% = 27.3\%$.

Example 9.3 How much time does it take to transmit 100 characters using the EIA-232-E interface at the data rate of 9600 bits per second. Assume the format of 1 start bit, 8 data bits, 1 stop bit, and no parity bit.

Solution: For each character transferred, 10 bits are transmitted. Each bit takes 104 μs (= 1 s $\div$ 9600). Thus each character takes 10×104 μs = 1.04 ms to transmit. The transmission of 100 characters will take 104 ms.

9.3.5 Data Transmission Errors

The following types of errors may occur during the data transfer using asynchronous serial transmission:

- Framing error: A framing error occurs when a received character is improperly framed by the start and stop bits; it is detected by the absence of stop bit. This error indicates a synchronization error, faulty transmission, or a break condition.
- Receiver overrun: One or more characters in the data stream were lost. That is, a character or a number of characters were received but were not read from the buffer before the subsequent characters were received.
- Parity error: A parity error occurs when an odd number of bits change value. It can be detected by a parity error detector circuit.

9.3.6 Null Modem Connection

When two DTEs are located very close, it makes no sense to use modems to connect them. However, for two computers to communicate with each other directly using the EIA-232-E interface, the interface circuit must be connected in such a way that these two computers are fooled into thinking that they are connected through modems. This connection method is called *null modem*. The null modem connection is shown in Figure 9.7. Since the data transmission is not through a phone line, the ring indicator is not needed. The transmitter-timing and receiver-timing signals are not needed either.

9.3.7 Interfacing a Microprocessor with the EIA-232-E Interface

The microprocessor outputs data in parallel format and is different from that in the EIA-232-E standard. On the other hand, the EIA-232-E standard uses different voltage levels and polarity to transmit data. For a microprocessor to talk to the EIA-232-E interface, the following operations must be performed:
On transmission:

1. Convert data from parallel to serial format.
2. Add start, stop, and optionally parity bits to the serial data.
3. Translate the voltage levels of the converted data stream to those of the EIA-232-E standard.

On reception:

1. Translate the voltage levels of the incoming data stream to those used in the micro-processor.
2. Detect the start and stop bits.
3. Optionally perform parity checking.
4. Convert serial data into parallel format.

In the past, a separate interface chip does most of these operations (excluding voltage level translation). The voltage level translation is done by a separate transceiver chip. The Intel 8251, Zilog 8530, and Motorola 6850 are examples of serial interface chips. The MAX232 series from MAXIM and MC145403 from Motorola are examples of RS-232 transceiver chips. Therefore a microprocessor-based serial communication system

Pin	Circuit name	DTE	DTE
22	Ring indicator	CE	CE
20	Data terminal ready	CD	CD
8	Data carrier detect	CF	CF
6	Data set ready	CC	CC
5	Clear to send	CB	CB
4	Request to send	CA	CA
3	Received data	BB	BB
2	Transmitted data	BA	BA
24	Transmitter timing	DA	DA
17	Receiver timing	DD	DD
7	Signal ground	AB	AB

Figure 9.7 Null modem connection.

should include the trio of a microprocessor, a serial interface chip, and an RS-232 voltage transceiver chip. The serial interface function has been incorporated in most microcontroller chips.

9.4 THE MCS-51/52 SERIAL INTERFACE

The serial port in the MCS-51/52 is full duplex. It has separate registers for the data to be transmitted and the data to be received. However, we access these two registers by referring to the same register SBUF. Writing to SBUF loads the transmit register, and reading from SBUF accesses a physically separate receive register.

9.4.1 The Serial Port Control Register SCON

The contents of the SCON register are shown in Figure 9.8. This register contains not only the mode selection bits, but also the ninth data bits for transmission and receiving (TB8 and RB8), and the serial port interrupt bits (TI and RI).

9.4.2 Serial Operation Modes

The serial port can operate in four modes:

Mode 0: Serial data enter and exit through the RXD pin. The TXD pin outputs the shift

Address = 98H   Bit addressable

SM0	SM1	SM2	REN	TB8	RB8	TI	RI
7	6	5	4	3	2	1	0

SM0	SM1	Mode	Description	Baud rate
0	0	0	shift register	$f_{OSC}/12$
0	1	1	8-bit UART	variable
1	0	2	9-bit UART	$f_{OSC}/64$ or $f_{OSC}/32$
1	1	3	9-bit UART	variable

SM2: Enables the multiprocessor communication feature in modes 2 and 3. In mode 2 or 3, if SM2 is set to 1 then RI will not be activated if the received 9th data bit is 0. In mode 1, if SM2 = 1 then RI will not be activated if a valid stop bit was not received. In mode 0, SM2 should be 0.

REN: Enable serial reception. Set to 1 to enable. Set to 0 to disable.

TB8: The 9th data bit that will be transmitted in modes 2 and 3.

RB8: The 9th bit that was received in mode 2 and 3. If SM2 = 0, RB8 is the stop bit that was received. In mode 0, RB8 is not used.

TI: Transmit interrupt bit. Set by the hardware at the end of the 8th bit in mode 0, or at the beginning of the stop bit in other modes, in any serial transmission.

RI: Received interrupt bit. Set by hardware at the end of the 8th bit time in mode 0, or halfway through the stop bit time in other modes, in any serial reception.

Figure 9.8 SCON: serial port control register.

clock. Eight bits are transmitted/received with least significant bit first. The baud rate is fixed at 1/12 of the oscillator frequency.

Mode 1: Ten bits are transmitted or received: a start bit, 8 data bits, and 1 stop bit. On reception, the stop bit goes into bit RB8 of the SCON register. The baud rate is variable.

Mode 2: Eleven bits are transmitted or received: 1 start bit, 8 data bits, a programmable ninth data bit, and a stop bit. On reception, the ninth data bit goes into bit RB8 of the SCON register, while the stop bit is ignored. The baud rate is programmable to either 1/32 or 1/64 of the oscillator frequency.

Mode 3: Eleven bits are transmitted or received: a start bit, 8 data bits, a programmable ninth data bit, and a stop bit. In fact, mode 3 is identical to mode 2 in all aspects except the baud rate. The baud rate in mode 3 is variable.

In all four modes, transmission is initiated by any instruction that uses SBUF as the destination register. Reception is initiated in mode 0 by the condition RI = 0 and REN = 1. Reception is initiated in other modes by the incoming start bit if REN = 1.

9.4.3 Baud Rates

The baud rate in mode 0 is fixed at $f_{OSC}/12$. The baud rate in mode 2 depends on the value of bit SMOD in special function register PCON. If SMOD = 0 (which is the value on reset), the baud rate is 1/64 of the oscillator frequency. If SMOD = 1, the baud rate is 1/32 of the oscillator frequency.

In the MCS-51, the baud rates in modes 1 and 3 are determined by the Timer 1 overflow rate. In the MCS-52, these baud rates can be determined by Timer 1, or by Timer 2, or by both (one for transmission and the other for receiving).

Using Timer 1 to Generate Baud Rate

When Timer 1 is used as the baud rate generator, the baud rate in modes 1 and 3 are determined by the Timer 1 overflow rate and the value of SMOD is as follows:

$$\text{Modes 1, 3 baud rate} = 2^{\text{SMOD}} \div 32 \times (\text{Timer 1 overflow rate}) \tag{9.1}$$

The Timer 1 interrupt should be disabled in this application. The Timer 1 itself can be configured for either "timer" or "counter" operation, and in any of its three running modes. In most applications, it is configured for timer operation in the 8-bit auto-reload mode (high nibble of TMOD = 0010B). In this case, the baud rate is given by the formula

$$\text{Modes 1, 3 Baud Rate} = 2^{\text{SMOD}} \div 32 \times f_{OSC} \div [12 \times (256 - \text{TH1})] \tag{9.2}$$

Table 9.3 lists various commonly used baud rates and how they can be obtained from Timer 1.

TABLE 9.3
Timer 1 Generated Commonly Used Baud Rates

Baud Rate	f_{OSC} (MHz)	SMOD	Timer 1 C/$\overline{T}$	Mode	Reload Value
Mode 0 max: 1 MHz	12	x	x	x	x
Mode 2 max: 375K	12	1	x	x	x
Mode 1, 3: 62.5K	12	1	0	2	FFH
19.2K	11.059	1	0	2	FDH
9.6K	11.059	0	0	2	FDH
4.8K	11.059	0	0	2	FAH
2.4K	11.059	0	0	2	F4H
1.2 K	11.059	0	0	2	E8H
137.5	11.059	0	0	2	1DH
110	6	0	0	2	72H
110	12	0	0	1	FEEBH

Using Timer 2 to Generate Baud Rates

In the MCS-52, Timer 2 is selected as the baud rate generator by setting TCLK and/or RCLK in the T2CON register. The baud rates for transmission and receiving can be simultaneously different. Setting RCLK and TCLK puts Timer 2 into its baud rate generator mode.

The baud rate generator mode is similar to the auto-reload mode, in that a rollover in TH2 causes the Timer 2 registers to be reloaded with the 16-bit value in registers RCAP2H and RCAP2L, which are set by software.

The baud rates in modes 1 and 3 are determined by Timer 2's overflow rate as follows:

$$\text{Modes 1, 3 baud rate} = \text{Timer 2 overflow rate} \div 16 \qquad (9.3)$$

The Timer can be configured for either "timer" or "counter" operation. In most applications, it is configured for "timer" operation. The timer operation is a little different for Timer 2 when it is used as a baud rate generator. As a timer it would increment every machine cycle (thus at 1/12 the oscillator frequency). As a baud rate generator, however, it increments every state time (thus at one-half the oscillator frequency). In this case the baud rate is given by the formula

$$\text{Modes 1, 3 baud rate} = f_{OSC} \div \{32 \times [65536 - (\text{RCAP2H, RCAP2L})]\} \qquad (9.4)$$

where (RCAP2H, RCAP2L) is the contents of RCAP2H and RCAP2L taken as a 16-bit unsigned integer.

When used as a baud rate generator, a rollover in TH2 does not set TF2, and will not generate an interrupt. Therefore, the Timer 2 interrupt does not have to be disabled when Timer 2 is in the baud rate generator mode. In baud rate generator mode, the pin T2EX is not related to the reload of Timer 2 and can be used as an extra external interrupt if it is desired.

It should be noted that when Timer 2 is running in timer function in the baud rate generator mode, do not try to read or write TH2 or TL2. Under these conditions the timer is being incremented every state time, and the result of a read or write may not be accurate. The RCAP registers may be read, but should not be written to, because a write might overlap a reload and cause write and/or reload error. Turn the timer off (clear TR2) before accessing the Timer 2 or RCAP registers, in this case.

Timer 2 as a baud rate generator is shown in Figure 9.9.

Table 9.4 lists commonly used baud rates and also how they can be generated from Timer 2. Although we have the choice of using either Timer 2 or Timer 1 overflow to generate baud rate for a serial port, we need to consider which one is more accurate. For example, to generate the baud rate of 9600, using Timer 1 overflow is more accurate than using Timer 2 overflow. We can use Equations 9.2 and 9.4 to check the accuracies of both methods.

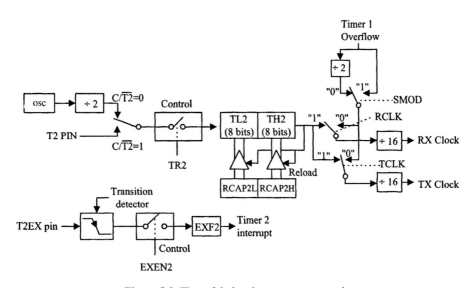

Figure 9.9 Timer 2 in baud rate generator mode.

TABLE 9.4
Timer 2 Generated Commonly Used Baud Rates

Baud Rate	Oscillator Frequency (MHz)	Timer 2	
		RCAP2H	RCAP2L
375K	12	FF	FF
9.6K	12	FF	D9
4.8K	12	FF	B2
2.4K	12	FF	64
1.2K	12	FE	C8
300	12	FB	1E
110	12	F2	AF
300	6	FD	8F
110	6	F9	57

9.4.4 The Detection of Start Bit and Determination of Bit Values

Reception is initiated by a detected 1-to-0 transition at the RXD pin. For this purpose, RXD is sampled at a rate of 16 times whatever baud rate has been established. When a transition is detected, the divide-by-16 counter is immediately reset, and 1FFH is written into the input shift register. Resetting the divide-by-16 counter aligns its rollovers with the boundaries of the incoming bit times.

The 16 states of the counter divide each bit time into 16ths. At the seventh, eighth, and ninth counter states of each bit time, the bit detector samples the value of RXD. The value accepted is the value that was seen in at least two of the three samples. This is done for noise rejection. If after the detection of 1-to-0 transition, the bit value is determined to be a 0, a valid start bit is detected. If the bit value is determined not to be a 0, the circuit will reset itself and go back to looking for another 1-to-0 transition.

The seventh, eighth, and ninth counter states of a bit time is also used to determine the value of each data bit.

Please note that other serial communication chips may use a clock whose frequency is 32 or 64 times that of the receive data rate to sample the incoming data. They may use slightly different methods to detect the start bit and determine the bit value.

9.4.5 Multiprocessor Communications

Modes 2 and 3 have a special provision for multiprocessor communications (in a multipoint link). In these modes, nine data bits are received. The ninth one goes into RB8 of the SCON register. Then comes a stop bit. The port can be programmed so that when the stop bit is received, the serial port interrupt will be activated only if RB8 = 1. Setting bit SM2 in the SCON register enables this feature. A way to use this feature in multiprocessor systems is as follows:

> When the master processor wants to transmit a block of data to one of the slaves, it first sends out an address byte that identifies the target slave. An address byte differs from a data byte in that the ninth bit is 1 in an address byte and 0 in a data byte. With SM2 = 1, no slave will be interrupted by a data byte. An address byte, however, will interrupt all slaves, so that each slave can examine the received byte and see if it is being addressed. The addressed slave will clear its SM2 bit and prepare to receive the data bytes that will be coming. The slaves that were not being addressed leave their SM2s set and go on about their business, ignoring the coming data bytes.

SM2 has no effect in mode 0, and in mode 1 can be used to check the validity of the stop bit. In a mode 1 reception, if SM2 = 1, the receive interrupt will not be activated unless a valid stop bit is received.

9.5 APPLICATIONS OF MODE 0

There are many peripheral chips having serial interfaces, i.e., data are transferred into and out of them bit serially. Although the serial port mode 0 is not completely compatible with those peripheral chips, it can still be used. In this section we will learn how to use mode 0 to interface the Xicor serial nonvolatile SRAM X24C44 with the MCS-51/52.

9.5.1 X24C44 Serial Nonvolatile Static RAM

The X24C44 is a 256-bit serial NOVRAM (nonvolatile RAM) internally configured as 16 16-bit words of RAM overlaid bit by bit with a nonvolatile E²PROM. The X24C44 has the standard hardware RECALL and STORE inputs plus the ability to perform these same operations under software control, thereby freeing two microcontroller port pins for other tasks. The pin assignment of the X24C44 is shown in Figure 9.10.

The Xicor NOVRAM design allows data to be transferred between these two memory arrays by means of software commands or external hardware inputs. A store operation (RAM to E²PROM) is completed in 5 ms or less and a recall operation (E²PROM to RAM) is completed in 2 μs or less. Xicor NOVRAMs are designed for unlimited write operations to RAM, from either the host or recalls from E²PROM and a minimum 1,000,000 store operations.

9.5.2 X24C44 Pin Descriptions

Chip Enable (CE).   The CE (chip enable) pin must be high to enable all read/write operations. CE must remain high following a read or write command until the data transfer is complete.

Serial Clock (SK).   The serial clock input is used to clock all data into and out of the device.

Data In and Data Out.   Data in (DI) is the serial data input and data out (DO) is the serial data output. The DO pin is in high impedance state except during data output cycles in response to a read instruction.

$\overline{Store}$.   The low voltage at the store pin will initiate an internal transfer of data from RAM to the E²PROM array.

$\overline{Recall}$.   The low voltage at the recall pin will initiate an internal transfer of data from E²PROM to the RAM array.

9.5.3 X24C44 Operation

The X24C44 contains an 8-bit instruction register. It is accessed via the DI input, with data being clocked in on the rising edge of SK; CE must be high during the entire data transfer cycle.

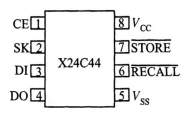

Figure 9.10 X24C44 NOVRAM.

Table 9.5 contains a list of the instructions and their operation codes. The most significant bit of all instructions is a logic one (high); bits 6 through 3 are either RAM address bits (A) or don't cares (X) and bits 2 through 0 are the operation codes. The X24C44 requires the instruction to be shifted in with the MSB first.

After CE goes high, the X24C44 will not begin to interpret the data stream until a 1 has been shifted in on DI. Therefore, CE may be brought high to indicate the start condition of an instruction before the X24C44 begins any action.

Either a software RCL instruction or a low on the $\overline{\text{RECALL}}$ pin will initiate a transfer of E²PROM data into RAM. The software or hardware recall operation sets an internal "previous recall" latch. This latch is reset on power-up and must be intentionally set by the user to enable any write or store operations.

Internally the X24C44 contains a "write-enable" latch. This latch must be set for either writes to the RAM or store operations to the E²PROM. The WREN instruction sets the latch and the WRDS instruction resets the latch, disabling both RAM writes and E²PROM stores, effectively protecting the nonvolatile data from corruption. The write-enable latch is automatically reset on power-up.

Either the software STO instruction or a low on the $\overline{\text{STORE}}$ input will initiate a transfer of data from RAM to E²PROM. To safeguard against unwanted store operations, the following conditions must be true:

- STO instruction is issued or $\overline{\text{STORE}}$ input is low.

- The internal "write-enable" latch must be set (WREN instruction issued).

- The "previous recall" latch must be set.

Once the store cycle is initiated, all other device functions are inhibited. On completion of the store cycle, the write-enable latch is reset.

The write instruction contains the 4-bit address of the word to be written. The write instruction is immediately followed by the 16-bit word to be written. CE must go low before the next rising edge of SK. If CE is brought low prematurely (after the instruction but before 16 bits of data are transferred), the instruction register will be reset and the data that were shifted in will be written to RAM.

TABLE 9.5
Xicor X24C44 Instruction Set

Instruction	Format l_2 l_1 l_0	Operation
WRDS	1XXXX000	Reset write enable latch (disable writes and stores)
STO	1XXXX001	Stores RAM data in E²PROM
Reserved	1XXXX010	N/A
WRITE	1AAAA011	Write data into RAM address AAAA
WREN	1XXXX100	Set write enable latch
RCL	1XXXX101	Recall E²PROM data into RAM
READ	1AAAA11X	Read data from RAM address AAAA

Reprinted with permission of Xicor.

If CE is kept high for more than 24 SK clock cycles (8-bit instruction plus 16-bit data), the data already shifted-in will be overwritten.

The READ instruction contains the 4-bit address of the word to be accessed. Unlike the other six instructions, I_0 of the instruction word is a "don't care." This provides two advantages. In a design that ties both DI and DO together, the absence of an eighth bit in the instruction allows the host time to convert an I/O line from an output to an input. Second, it allows for valid data output during the ninth SK clock cycle.

D0, the first bit output during a read operation, is truncated. That is, it is internally clocked by the falling edge of the eighth SK clock; all succeeding bits are clocked by the rising edge of SK.

9.5.4 The X24C44 Read and Write Timing

A read operation to the X24C44 takes 24 clock cycles to complete and each shift clock takes at least 1 μs. The timing diagram of a read operation (16-bit access) is shown in Figure 9.11. A write operation also takes 24 clock cycles to complete. The timing diagram of a 16-bit write is shown in Figure 9.12. A nondata instruction takes eight clock cycles to write into the X24C44. The timing of a nondata operation is shown in Figure 9.13.

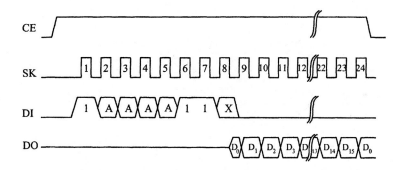

Figure 9.11 Xicor X24C44 read operation. Bit 8 read instruction is don't care. (Reprinted with permission of Xicor.)

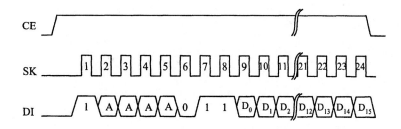

Figure 9.12 Xicor X24C44 write cycle timing. (Redrawn with permission of Xicor.)

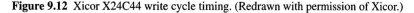

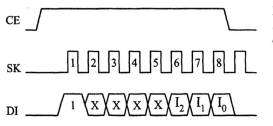

Figure 9.13 Xicor X24C44 nondata operations. (Redrawn with permission of Xicor.)

9.5.5 Interfacing the X24C44 with the MCS-51/52

The X24C44 can directly interface with the MCS-51/52 without external circuitry. DI and DO of the X24C44 can be tied together. Shown in Figure 9.14 is the basic configuration to interface the X24C44 with the MCS-51/52.

Port 3 pin 1 (P3.1) is the clock output for both transmit and receive modes and port 3 pin 0 (P3.0) is used for bidirectional data transfers. The clock frequency is 1/12 of the crystal oscillator input frequency. Assume a 12-MHz oscillator is used in this circuit because the highest data transfer frequency for the X24C44 is 1 MHz. The CE pin is tied to any free I/O pin (P1.2 in this example).

The serial port of the MCS-51/52 transmits lsb first, but the instruction format for the X24C44 shows the instruction to be transmitted msb first. This requires a simple transposition of the instruction, msb for lsb. However, the memory is effectively a FIFO, so the data to be stored need not be transposed.

Figures 9.11 to 9.13 show that the X24C44 expects CE to go from low to high when SK is low so that the first bit of data can be clocked into the X24C44 on the first rising edge of the SK. The data are sampled to see if it is "0" (a don't care state) or a "1," which is recognized as an instruction start. The MCS-51/52 places both P3.1 and P3.0 in the high state when not actively transmitting. The X24C44 internally gates CE and SK; therefore, toggling the port pin controlling CE to a high effectively generates the first rising edge of SK, and also clocks in the high present at P3.0 (DI). This indicates the start of an instruction prior to any shifting operation by the MCS-51/52 serial port. This will require dropping the leading "1" from the instruction. All the instructions must be reversed. The reversed instructions are shown in Table 9.6.

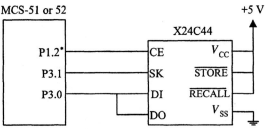

Figure 9.14 Basic circuit connection between the MCS-51/52 and the X24C44. *Can be any available I/O pin.

Note: * can be any available I/O pin

TABLE 9.6
Instruction Pattern for Serial Port Mode 0

Instruction	Original Bit Pattern								Reversed Pattern							
	7	6	5	4	3	2	1	0	7	6	5	4	3	2	1	0
WRDS	1	X	X	X	X	0	0	0	X	0	0	0	X	X	X	X
STO	1	X	X	X	X	0	0	1	X	1	0	0	X	X	X	X
Reserved	1	X	X	X	X	0	1	0	X	0	1	0	X	X	X	X
WRITE	1	A	A	A	A	0	1	1	X	1	1	0	A	A	A	A
WREN	1	X	X	X	X	1	0	0	X	0	0	1	X	X	X	X
RCL	1	X	X	X	X	1	0	1	X	1	0	1	X	X	X	X
READ	1	A	A	A	A	1	1	X	1	X	1	1	A	A	A	A

The MCS-51/52 will still generate eight rising clock edges on P3.1 for each byte to be loaded into the shift register, effectively providing the X24C44 with nine clocks for the first byte. For the single byte instruction, the ninth clock and data bit are ignored by the X24C44.

Writing

The write instruction is issued by the MCS-51/52 in the same manner as the single byte instructions. The msb (eighth bit) of the instruction byte is clocked in on the equivalent ninth clock rising edge. This bit is recognized as the first data bit of the transfer and is initially written into the addressed word's bit position zero. The MCS-51/52 will continue to transmit two more bytes of actual data. The lsb (bit 0) of the first byte will be physically located in bit position one and all subsequent bits will also be offset by one. The msb (sixteenth data bit) of the word will be written into bit position zero, overwriting the last bit of the instruction byte.

Reading

Reading data back from the RAM array is similar. The X24C44 begins to shift data out during the instruction cycle. After the instruction is shifted out, the MCS-51/52 must turn around P3.0 and configure it as input. CE and SK are static during this period and the DO output will remain unchanged until after the rising edge of the first MCS-51/52 receives data clock. Therefore, the first data shifted into the MCS-51/52 will be from bit position one, equivalent to the lsb originally written.

The DO output of the X24C44 is always in the high-impedance state unless it is outputting data in response to a READ command. Therefore, the serial port of the MCS-51/52 need not be dedicated to a serial interface.

9.5.6 Programming the X24C44 for Data Transfer

Special program code is needed to write data into and read data from the X24C44. To send out a byte via the serial port using mode 0, the SCON register should be configured as follows:

SM1 and SM0:   set to 00 to select mode 0.

SM2:   set to 0 in mode 0

REN: set to 0 to disable receiving

TB8 and RB8:   not used, set to 00

TI and RI: set to 0

Write the value 00H into the SCON register.

    To configure the serial port for receives in mode 0, set the REN bit to 1 and all other bits to 0. Write the value 10H into the SCON register.

    Assuming the CE signal is set and reset properly by the caller, the following routine outputs a byte to the X24C44:

```
send_byte:      mov   SCON,#00H     ; configure serial port to mode 0 output
                mov   SBUF,A         ; send out the byte in accumulator A
send_lp:        mov   C,SCON.1       ; loop until data are shifted out (check TI bit)
                jnc   send_lp
                ret
```

    Assuming the caller sets and resets the CE signal before and after making the subroutine call, the following routine inputs a byte (in A) from the serial port using mode 0:

```
read_byte:      mov   SCON,#10H      ; initialize the serial port for mode 0 input
read_lp:        mov   C,SCON.0       ; receive loop while data are being received
                jnc   read_lp        ; (RI bit)
                mov   A,SBUF          ; place the character in A
                ret
```

    There is an addressing problem when writing data into the X24C44. If the address is not reversed, the data may not be written into the intended location. However, this causes no problem. We can read back the same data using the same address when performing a read operation.

Example 9.4 Write a subroutine to output the 16-bit word in registers R2 and R1 to the X24C44 (address specified in R3) via serial port mode 0.

Solution: The first step is to send out the write instruction (with address specified in the instruction) and then the 16-bit data word.

```
CE              EQU   P1.2
write           EQU   60H            ; write instruction to address 0
wr_word:        setb  CE             ; enable write to the X24C44
                mov   A,R3           ; place address in A
                orl   A,#write       ; combine the write instruction with address
                lcall send_byte      ; send write instruction to the X24C44
```

```
        mov    A,R2          ; output the upper byte
        lcall  send_byte     ; "
        mov    A,R1          ; output the lower byte
        lcall  send_byte     ; "
        clr    CE            ; disable the serial memory
        ret
```

Example 9.5 Write a subroutine to input the 16-bit word at location specified in R3 from X24C44 and return the 16-bit word in registers R2 and R1 via serial port in mode 0.

Solution: The first step is output the read instruction.

```
CE            EQU    P1.2
read          EQU    B0H          ; reversed read instruction (address 0)
rd_word:      setb   CE           ; enable access to the X24C44
              mov    A,R3         ; place address in A
              orl    A,#read      ; combine the read instruction with address
              lcall  send_byte    ; send out the read instruction
              lcall  read_byte    ; read the upper byte
              mov    R2,A         ; put it in R2
              lcall  read_byte    ; read the lower byte
              mov    R1,A
              clr    CE           ; disable access to the X24C44
              ret
```

All other instructions can be sent to the X24C44 by performing the following steps:

STEP 1 Set the CE pin to high.

STEP 2 Place the instruction in accumulator A.

STEP 3 Call the subroutine *send_byte*.

STEP 4 Set the CE pin to low.

9.6 APPLICATIONS OF MODE 1

The mode 1 of the serial port can be used to communicate with the RS-232 interface. The polarities and ranges of voltages of serial port and the RS-232 interface are different. A voltage translation circuit is needed to translate the voltage levels of the serial port signals to and from those of the corresponding RS-232 signals.

The RS-232 transceivers from MAXIM, the MC145403 from Motorola, and similar products from other companies can translate the voltage levels back and forth between the RS-232 interface and the serial port. In this section, we will discuss the MAX202E/232E chip from MAXIM to do the voltage translation.

A MAX202E/232E requires only a 5-V power supply to convert a 0- and 5-V input to a +10- and −10-V output. A MAX202E/232E has two RS-232 drivers and two RS-232 receivers. The pin assignment and circuit connection of the RS-202E/232E are shown in Figure 9.15. Adding an RS-232 transceiver chip will then allow the MCS-51/52 serial port to communicate with the EIA-232-E interface circuit. An example of such a circuit is shown in Figure 9.16.

The connection enclosed by dotted lines is a null-modem connection, which allows the serial port to talk to a PC via a standard RS-232 cable without using a modem.

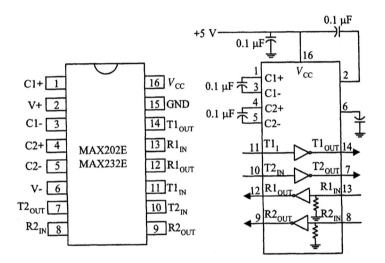

Figure 9.15 MAX202E/232E.

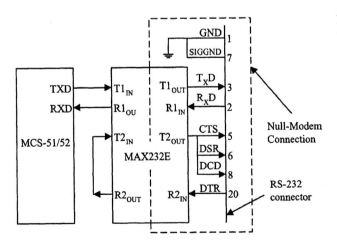

Figure 9.16 Circuit connection between MCS-51/52 and MAX232E.

Example 9.6 Write an instruction sequence to initialize the MCS-51/52 serial port to operate with the following parameters:

- baud rate 9600
- one start bit, eight data bits, and one stop bit (mode 1 operation)
- disable interrupt for receiving and transmission
- enable receiving and transmission

Solution: The value to be written into the SCON register is 01010000_2. To disable receive and transmit interrupt, clear the bit 4 of the IE register. The baud rate is controlled by the Timer 1 overflow rate. To set the baud rate to 9600, we should choose the following parameters:

- use a 11.059-MHz crystal oscillator
- set the upper four bits of the TMOD register to 0100—this value sets the timer mode and chooses the mode 2 operation of Timer 1.
- set the Timer 1 reload value to be FDH—this value is to be reloaded into the TL1 register from TH1 every time the TL1 timer overflows.
- set the SMOD bit (bit 7) of the PCON register to 0.

The following subroutine will satisfy the requirements:

```
SC_init:    clr    IE.4            ; disable serial port interrupt
            anl    TMOD,#0FH       ; set the upper 4 bits of TMOD to 0100
            orl    TMOD,#40H       ; "
            mov    TL1,#FDH        ; set the initial and reload values of Timer 1
            mov    TH1,#FDH        ; "
            anl    PCON,#7F        ; clear the SMOD bit of PCON to 0
            mov    T2CON,#00       ; clear bits 5 and 4 to 00 to use Time 1
                                   ; overflow for baud rate generation
            mov    SCON,#50H       ; initialize the serial port and enable receive
            ret                    ; and transmit
```

Example 9.7 Write a subroutine that reads a character from the serial port using the polling method. The character will be returned in accumulator A. Assume the serial port has been initialized using the routine in Example 9.6.

Solution: The subroutine will continuously test the RI bit (bit 0) of the SCON register until it is set and read the SBUF register.

```
get_char:   jnb    SCON.0,get_char    ; poll the RI bit of SCON
            mov    A,SBUF             ; read the character in SBUF register
            ret
```

Example 9.8 Write a subroutine to output the character in accumulator A from the serial port using the polling method. Assume the serial port has been initialized using the routine in Example 9.6.

Solution: The subroutine will continuously check the TI bit (bit 1) of the SCON register until it is set and then send the character in accumulator A to the SBUF register.

```
put_char:      jnb    SCON.1,put_char    ; poll the TI bit of SCON
               mov    SBUF,A             ; output the character
               ret
```

Example 9.9 Write a subroutine to output a string terminated by a null character. The starting address of the string is in the DPTR register.

Solution: This routine will call the put_char routine to output the string.

```
put_string:    movx   A,@DPTR            ; get a character from the string
               jz     exit               ; is this the end of the string
               lcall  put_char           ; call the put_char routine to output the
                                         ; character
               inc    DPTR               ; move to the next character
               ajmp   put_string         ; go to output the next character
exit:          ret
```

Example 9.10 Write a subroutine to input a string from the serial port. The address of the buffer memory to hold the string is passed in DPTR.

Solution: This routine will call the get_char routine to input the string. A string is terminated by the carriage return (CR) character.

```
CR             equ    0DH                ; ASCII code of carriage return
get_string:    lcall  get_char           ; read a character
               cjne   A,#CR,keep_go      ; is this the end of the input string
               mov    A,#0               ; terminate the string by a null
               movx   @DPTR,A            ; character
               ret
keep_go:       movx   @DPTR,A            ; save the character in the buffer
                                         ; memory
               inc    DPTR               ; move the pointer
               ajmp   get_string         ; continue
```

The polling method should be used only if the microcontroller has nothing else to do when waiting for input and output to complete. The interrupt-driven method is recommended if we want the microcontroller to perform other functions while waiting for the I/O operation to be completed.

The procedure for interrupt-driven serial port I/O (mode 1) is as follows:

Reading/Outputting a Single Character

STEP 1   Enable serial port interrupt.

STEP 2   Write a serial port interrupt service routine.

STEP 3   Wait for serial port interrupt to occur.

STEP 4   Check the cause of the serial port interrupt. If the serial port interrupt is caused by transmit then write the character in accumulator A into the SBUF register and return. If the interrupt is caused by receive-buffer-full, then read the character in SBUF and return.

The interrupt vector of the serial port is 23H. The first instruction of the serial port service routine is a jump instruction. A possible service routine for the serial port interrupt is as follows:

```
                org    23H
                ljmp   serial_IO
                . . .
                org    xxxxH
serial_IO:      jnb    SCON.1,check_Rx    ; is interrupt caused by transmit-
                                          ; buffer-empty?
                mov    SBUF,A             ; send out the character in A
check_Rx:       jnb    SCON.0,exit        ; is interrupt caused by receive-
                                          ; buffer-full?
                mov    A,SBUF             ; get the character in SBUF
exit:           reti
```

The receive operation needs a memory buffer to hold the input string. The output string routine also needs a buffer to hold the string to be output. A pointer is needed for each operation. Assume external memory is used as buffer memory. Assume that the DPTR register and the register pair (R6, R7) are used as the pointer to the input buffer and the pointer to the string to be output, respectively. The serial_IO service routine must be modified. The modification is to update the buffer pointer. The modified serial I/O interrupt service routine is as follows:

```
                org    23H
                ljmp   ser_ISR
                ...
                org    xxxxH
ser_ISR:        jnb    SCON.1,check_Rx    ; is interrupt caused by transmit-
                                          ; buffer-empty?
                mov    SBUF,A             ; send out the character in A
```

```
; R6 is the most significant byte of the pointer
              mov    A,R7              ; add 1 to the transmit buffer
              add    A,#1              ; pointer
              mov    R7,A              ; "
              mov    A,R6              ; "
              addc   A,#0              ; "
              mov    R6,A              ; "
check_Rx:     jnb    SCON.0,exit       ; is interrupt caused by receive
                                       ; buffer full?
              mov    A,SBUF            ; get the character in SBUF
              movx   @DPTR,A           ; save it in external buffer
                                       ; memory
              inc    DPTR              ; update the DPTR register
exit:         reti
```

The above interrupt routine supports full-duplex communication. The routine that inputs the string enables the serial port interrupt and then waits for the serial port interrupt. When the CR character is received, it disables the serial port interrupt. Serial port interrupt should be disabled in a full-duplex communication only when both reception and transmission are not needed.

Example 9.11 Write a subroutine to read a string from the serial port (maybe connected to a terminal keyboard) using the interrupt-driven approach.

Solution: The subroutine is as follows:

```
CR            equ    0DH               ; ASCII code for CR
getstr_int:   mov    DPTR,#in_buf      ; put starting address of input buffer in
                                       ; DPTR
              orl    IE,#90H           ; enable serial port interrupt
              clr    A                 ; clear accumulator A
; the following instruction will wait for receive interrupt until the CR character is
; received
rd_loop:      cjne   A,#CR,rd_loop     ; loop until CR character is read
              ret
```

Example 9.12 Write a subroutine to output the string pointed to by the register pair (R6,R7) using the *interrupt-driven* approach.

Solution: A string is terminated by the null character.

```
putstr_int:   push   DPH               ; save DPTR
```

```
                        push    DPL             ; "
                        orl     IE,#90H         ; enable serial port interrupt
; a transmit interrupt may occur in any one of the following five instructions
wr_loop:                mov     DPH,R6          ; use DPTR as the pointer to the string
                        mov     DPL,R7          ; "
                        movx    A,@DPTR         ; get the character pointed to by DPTR
                        jnz     wr_loop         ; not done yet?
                        pop     DPL             ; restore DPTR
                        pop     DPH             ; "
                        ret
```

9.7 APPLICATIONS OF MODE 2 AND MODE 3

Mode 2 and mode 3 are mainly used in multipoint data link communications. A complete discussion of multipoint data link is beyond the scope of this text. We will only briefly explore how mode 2 and mode 3 may be used in this environment.

In a multipoint data link, there is usually a controlling unit called *master*. The remaining units are called *slaves*. The master directs the activities of the slaves. Each slave has its own unique address. The address is usually 8 bits. An address byte is sent on the same link. Slaves must be able to determine if a byte is an address byte or a data byte. Mode 2 and mode 3 provide easy ways to solve this problem. Depending on the value of the tenth bit, a character is considered as an address (1) or a data (0) byte.

A communication protocol is needed to govern the communication activities between the master and slaves. The message sent to a slave should follow a predefined format so that no misunderstanding will occur. A message consists of several characters. The first character is always the address byte. Following the address byte is a command that tells the slave what to do. A command may consist of one or a few characters depending on the size of the command set. Following the command are the optional data bytes. A slave can send or receive data to or from the master in response to the request from the master.

After the power-on reset, all the slaves may have their SM2 bits of the SCON registers set to one so that they are expecting to receive address bytes. If the tenth bit (11-bit character) of the coming byte is a 1, all slaves will compare it with their addresses. The slave that was addressed will clear the SM2 bit of its SCON register and then wait for command or data bytes to come. Those slaves that were not selected will not change their SM2 bits and continue on their own business. A special character such as "$" is used to mark the end of a message.

The EIA-485 is a standard that specifies the electrical characteristics for multipoint data links. The standard is similar to EIA-422-A, which allows the generators and receivers to operate by using either standard. However, EIA-485 does not specify other character-istics normally in the EIA standards, such as pin assignments, timing, or signal quality characteristics for complete equipment interfacing. Although EIA-485 does not specify the particular type of cable, it does define cable characteristics for the following parameters:

- signaling rate (and therefore the unit interval)
- minimum voltage signal transmitted to the receiver
- maximum acceptable distortion
- cable length requirement

9.8 THE DS87C520 SERIAL PORTS

The Dallas Semiconductor microcontroller DS87C520 has two identical serial ports: port 0 and 1. Like serial port 0, port 1 has one control register (SCON1, located at C0H) and one buffer register (SBUF1, located at C1H). The contents of SCON1 are identical to that of SCON0.

The bit 7 (SMOD_0) of the PCON register controls the baud rate doubling for serial port 0 whereas the bit 7 (SMOD_1) of the WDCON register controls the baud rate doubling for serial port 1. When set to 1, the baud rate will be double that defined by the baud rate equation discussed earlier.

The MCB520 evaluation board uses serial port 1 to communicate with the PC. The configuration of serial port 1 is as follows:

- Baud rate is set to 9600 (9549 to be exact).
- Use Timer 1 overflow to generate baud rate.
- Timer 1 reload value (placed in TH1) is CAH.
- Choose *osc ÷ 4* as the clock input of Timer 1 (bit 4 of the CKCON register is set to 1).
- Choose serial port 1 baud rate doubling (bit 7 of the WDCON register is set to 1).

Since Timer 1 is being used for baud rate generation for serial port 1, we should not use it for other purposes to maintain communication with the MCB520 evaluation board. It is not advisable to change the setting of serial port 1 because that will interfere with MON51's communication with the evaluation board. There is no need to reinitialize serial port 1 to do any I/O operation.

The I/O routines for port 1 can be modified from those of port 0 described in Examples 9.7 through 9.10.

9.9 SUMMARY

The various versions of the EIA-232 standard were defined to facilitate data communication over the public phone line. This standard was defined for asynchronous serial data communication. The EIA-232-E standard has four aspects: electrical, mechanical, procedural, and functional. For a short distance, modems are not needed for two DTEs to be connected by using a connection called *null modem*. This is achieved by connecting signals in such a way as to fool two computers into thinking that they are connected through modems.

The EIA-232-E standard uses a higher voltage (than the CMOS voltage level) to achieve reliable communication. A serial interface chip is needed to connect the microprocessor to the EIA-232-E interface. This interface chip converts parallel data from the microprocessor into serial format and adds a start bit, 1 to 2 stop bits, and the optional parity bit so that the data conform to the characteristics of the EIA-232-E requirement. It also converts the serial data coming from the EIA-232-E interface into parallel format before they are forwarded to the microprocessor. Since the outputs of the serial interface chip are in CMOS levels, which are different from those of the EIA-232-E levels, a transceiver chip is needed to perform the voltage conversion.

Only a small subset of the 25 signals defined in the EIA-232 standard is needed in the serial communication. These signals include

- Pin 2: transmit data (TxD)
- Pin 3: receive data (RxD)
- Pin 4: request to send (RTS)
- Pin 5: clear to send (CTS)
- Pin 6: DCE ready (DSR)
- Pin 7: signal ground
- Pin 8: carrier detect (DCD)
- Pin 20: DTE ready (DTR)

For data communications over the public phone system, one additional signal is required: ring indicator. The data communications in this environment involve three steps:

STEP 1   Establishing the connection

STEP 2   Data transmission

STEP 3   Disconnection

Errors may occur during a data communication process. The most common errors include framing, receiver overrun, and parity error. A framing error occurs when the start and stop bits improperly frame a received character. A framing error is detected by a missing stop bit. A receiver-overrun error occurs when one or multiple characters are received but not read by the processor. A parity error occurs when an odd number of bits changes value.

The MCS-51 serial interface is full duplex. It has separate registers for the data to be transmitted and the data received. However, the user accesses these two registers by referring to the same register SBUF. The SCON register allows us to select the operation mode and enable receive. For 9-bit data format, the most significant bit is taken or placed from or in the SCON register. The lowest two bits of the SCON register are used for recording the transmission and reception status (TI and RI bits).

The MCS-51 serial communication port has four operation modes: modes 0, 1, 2, and 3.

- Mode 0: Data are shifted in and out through the RXD pin. The TXD pin outputs the shift clock. Eight bits are transmitted or received for each character with the least significant bit first. The baud rate is fixed at 1/12 of the oscillator frequency.
- Mode 1: Ten bits are transmitted and received for each character: 1 start bit, 8 data bits, and 1 stop bit. The baud rate is variable.
- Mode 2: Eleven bits are transmitted or received: 1 start bit, 9 data bits, and 1 stop bit. The baud rate is variable.
- Mode 3: Eleven bits are transmitted and received for each character: 1 start bit, 9 data bits, and 1 stop bit. The baud rate is variable.

Depending on the operation mode, the baud rate used in the serial interface can be fixed at 1/12 of the oscillator frequency, or generated by Timer 1 overflows, or generated by Timer 2 overflows. The baud rates at different modes are determined by Equations 9.1 to 9.3.

A reception is initiated by a detected 1-to-0 transition at pin RXD. The RXD signal is sampled at a rate that is 16 times of whatever baud rate has been established. The majority function of the seventh, eighth, and ninth samples determines whether a valid start bit is received and the data bit value after the valid start bit has been received.

Mode 0 can be used to interface with the 256-bit SRAM X24C44. The X24C44 is a 256-bit serial nonvolatile SRAM internally configured as a 16 16-bit word of RAM overlaid bit for bit with a nonvolatile E^2PROM. The X24C44 contains an 8-bit instruction register. To transfer data to the X24C44, we need to send an appropriate command followed by the 16-bit data word. To read data from the X24C44, we send in an 8-bit read command and then read back the 16-bit data word bit serially. After power-up, we can send in a command to recall data from EEPROM to SRAM or store RAM data into EEPROM.

The major application of mode 1 is to communicate with the EIA-232 interface. An RS-232 transceiver is needed to translate the voltage levels back and forth between the MCS-51/52 serial port and the EIA-232-E standard. A null-modem connection is normally constructed on the MCS-51 board. Using the serial interface allows us to communicate with the MCS-51 microcontroller using a PC.

Mode 2 and mode 3 are mainly for multipoint environment. A brief description of the functioning of a multipoint data link is given at the end of the chapter.

9.10 EXERCISES

9.1 How many types of communication links are there? Explain each of them.

9.2 How long does it take to transmit 1000 characters using the 19200 baud rate. Each character consists of 8 data bits, 1 start bit, and 1 stop bit.

9.3 Delineate the waveform of the letter d in the DTE (CMOS) and EIA-232-E interfaces. Assume that the format of 1 start bit, 8 data bits, and 1 stop bit is used.

9.4 Delineate the waveform of the letter *M* in the DTE (CMOS) and EIA-232-E interfaces. Assume that the format of 1 start bit, 8 data bits, and 1 stop bit is used.

9.5 Write down an instruction sequence to configure the serial port to operate with the following parameters:

- mode 1 operation
- baud rate 19200
- interrupt-driven transmission and receiving
- use Timer 1 overflow to generate baud rate

9.6 Assume that the Xicor X24C44 is interfaced with the MCS-51 serial port. Write down an instruction sequence to set the write-enable latch (using the WREN instruction) and recall E^2PROM data into RAM (use the RCL instruction).

9.7 Assume that the Xicor X24C44 is interfaced with the MCS-51 serial port. Write down an instruction sequence to store RAM data in E^2PROM (use the STO instruction) and reset the enable latch (use the WRDS instruction).

9.8 Write down an instruction sequence to initialize every memory location in the X24C44 to 00H.

9.9 Use the polling method. Write a subroutine to output the binary number contained in accumulator A in two hex digits. You can call the *put_char* routine to output the hex digits.

9.10 Modify the subroutine in Example 9.9 to expand the CR or LF character into the CR/LF or LF/CR pair. This has the effect of moving the cursor to the beginning of the next line on the screen.

9.11 Suppose the serial port of the MCS-51 is connected to a keyboard and accepts input from the keyboard. The user of the terminal wants the characters that have been entered to be echoed on the screen to determine if they have been entered correctly. At some other time, the user does not want to echo what has been entered. Use a flag to indicate whether the entered characters should be echoed. Modify the routine in Example 9.8 to accommodate this requirement.

9.11 LAB EXERCISES AND ASSIGNMENTS

9.1 Run the MON51 terminal program in a DOS command window to talk to the MCB520 evaluation board. Write a program to simulate the log-in session on any mini- or mainframe computer. Your program should perform the following steps:

1. The program begins by outputting the following message:

Welcome to the MCB520 Evaluation Board!
User Name:

2. After putting out this message, the program waits for you to type in your user name, which should be terminated by the CR character.

3. After entering your user name, the program outputs the following prompt:

   Password:

4. The program then waits for you to enter the password. After the user name and password are entered, the program starts to search the user name/password table to see if the user name and password match. The table contains 15 pairs of user names and passwords. If the user name and password are correct, the program outputs the following message:

   log in successful!

5. If *log-in* is not successful, the program should output the following message and repeat the log-in process:

   Invalid password or user name.

9.2 Write a program to be run on the MCB520 evaluation board to read in an array of 15 numbers. Each number consists of two decimal digits and will be entered from a PC keyboard. To read one number, the program outputs the following prompt:

Please enter a two-digit decimal number:

The user then enters a two-digit decimal number. If the number contains an invalid digit or is longer than two digits, the program will ask the user to reenter a valid number.

Each prompt should appear on a separate line. After 15 two-digit decimal numbers have been entered, the program sorts the array and computes its average value and outputs them on the screen. The following message should appear on the screen at the end of program execution:

The given array is: xx xx xx xx xx xx xx xx xx xx xx xx xx xx xx

The average of the array is: yy

The sorted array is: zz zz zz zz zz zz zz zz zz zz zz zz zz zz zz

10

SERIAL EXPANSION PORT

10.1 OBJECTIVES

After completing this chapter, you should be able to

- describe the serial expansion port (SEP) of the 8XC51GB
- connect the SEP with one or multiple peripherals with serial interface
- simulate the operation of SEP
- use SEP and multiple HC589s to add parallel input ports to the 8XC51GB
- use SEP and multiple HC595s to add parallel output ports to the 8XC51GB
- use the SEP and M14489(s) to drive multiple seven-segment displays
- use the SEP with interface to Xicor serial EEPROMs
- use the SEP with interface to an A/D converter with serial interface

10.2 INTRODUCTION

The number of pins on an 8-bit microcontroller is very limited. However, it is desirable to implement as many I/O functions as possible on that limited number of pins. In the real world, many applications do not require a high data rate. Although using parallel interface can satisfy the data transmission needs of these applications, it prevents more functions from being implemented on the same number of pins.

The solution to this dilemma is to use serial data transfer. Several vendors have introduced protocols to facilitate serial data transfer. For example, Motorola's Serial Peripheral Interface (SPI), Philips' Inter-Integrated Circuits (I²C), National Semiconductor's Microwire, and Intel's Serial Expansion Ports (SEP). All of these serial interfaces have a clock to synchronize data transfer and one or two pins to carry data. The device that generates the clock signal and controls the data transfer is called *master*. Other devices are called *slaves*.

Many vendors are producing peripheral chips with serial interface to work with microcontrollers from these companies. The Intel SEP interface is implemented in the 8XC51GB and the 8XC152JX series microcontrollers. The SEP can work with many peripheral chips with serial interface. Examples of peripheral devices with serial interface include LED display drivers, LCD drivers, SRAMs, flash memories, EEPROMs, phase-locked loops (PLL), clock/timer chips, A/D converters, D/A converters, shift registers, and so on.

The SEP uses two signal pins: P4.0 as clock (SEPCLK) and P4.1 as data pin (SEPDAT). We can select whether the idle state of the clock is high or low and whether the data are sampled/output on the rising or falling edge of the clock. Four different data rates are possible: $f_{OSC}/12, f_{OSC}/24, f_{OSC}/48$, and $f_{OSC}/96$.

Three new special function registers have been added to support the SEP. The SEPCON register is used to select the clock's phase and polarity, to choose the baud rate, to enable reception, and to enable the SEP. Data are transferred through the SEPDAT register. The SEPSTAT register contains error bits and the interrupt flag.

10.3 THE SEP-RELATED REGISTERS

The SEPCON register defines all the operating parameters for the SEP. Its contents are illustrated in Figure 10.1.

The SEPSTAT register reflects the status of SEP operation. Its contents are shown in Figure 10.2.

The SEP transmission does not allow access to either the SEPCON or the SEPDAT register when the previous SEP transmission is not yet completed. Whenever that happens,

SEPCON   address = 0D7H

Not bit addressable   reset value = xx00 0000B

—	—	SEPE	SEPREN	CLKPOL	CLKPH	SEPS1	SEPS0
7	6	5	4	3	2	1	0

SEPE: *SEP enable*. Must be set to enable any SEP operation.

SEPREN: *SEP receive enable*. After SEPREN is set, 8 clock pulses are genearted to clock in received data. SEPREN is cleared by hardware after 8 bits have been received.

CLKPOL: *Clock polarity*. If cleared, the idle state of the clock pin is low. If set, the idle state of the clock pin is high.

CLKPH: *Clock phase*. When cleared, the 8XC51GB samples data on the first phase edge of the clock and transfers data on the second phase edge of the clock (i.e., if CLKPOL = 0, data are sampled on the rising edges of the clock and transferred on the falling edges). When CLKPH is set, data are sampled on the second phase edges and transferred on the first edges.

SEPS1: *SEP speed select*. Used to select the data rate according to the SEPS0 following table.

SEPS1	SEPS0	Data Rate
0	0	$f_{OSC}/12$
0	1	$f_{OSC}/24$
1	0	$f_{OSC}/48$
1	1	$f_{OSC}/96$

Figure 10.1 SEP control register.

SEPSTAT Address -- 0F7H
not bit addressable   reset value = xxxx x000B

—	—	—	—	—	SEPFWR	SEPFRD	SEPIF
7	6	5	4	3	2	1	0

SEPFWR: *SEP fault write bit*. Set if an attempt is made to read or write the
SEPDATA register or write the SEPCON register while a
transmission is in progress. Must be cleared by software.

SEPFRD: *SEP fault read bit*. Set if an attempt is made to read or write the
SEPDATA register or write the SEPCON register while a
reception is in progress. Must be cleared by software.

SEPIF: *SEP interrupt flag*. Set by hardware when a transmission or
reception is complete. Flags an interrupt if one is enabled. Must be
cleared by software.

Figure 10.2 The SEP SEPSTAT register.

it is recorded as a fault in the SEPSTAT register. The completion of a SEP transmission will
be flagged in the SEPSTAT register.

The SEP has a data register called SEPDAT. Any data to be transmitted must be written
into this register. The received data are also stored in this register.

10.4 THE SEP OPERATION

The SEP has four operation modes that determine the inactive level of the clock pin and
which edge of the clock is used for transmission or reception. These four modes are shown
in Figure 10.3. Figure 10.3 shows that the meaning of a data bit is always determined at the
center of a bit time. We must be careful not to use modes 1 and 3 in receive mode. Table
10.1 shows how SEP modes are determined.

Prior to any SEP data transfers, we should initialize the clock phase, polarity, and rate.
If SEPE = 1, transmission occurs when a byte is written into the SEPDAT register. The
data are shifted out msb first.

Receptions are initiated by setting the SEPREN and SEPE bits. Once the SEPREN bit
is set, the 87C51GB sends out eight pulses on the clock pin. Data are received msb first.

If we attempt to read or write the SEPDAT register or write to the SEPCON register
while the SEP is transmitting or receiving, an error bit is set. The SEPFWR bit is set if the
action occurs while the SEP is transmitting. The SEPFRD bit is set if the action is attempted
while the SEP is receiving. There is no interrupt associated with these bits. The bits remain
set until cleared by software. The attempted read or write is ignored and the reception and
transmission in progress are not affected.

10.5 SEP-COMPATIBLE PERIPHERAL CHIPS

Many companies provide peripheral chips with serial interface to support the serial bus
protocols provided by Intel, Motorola, National Semiconductor, Philips, and so on. Periph-

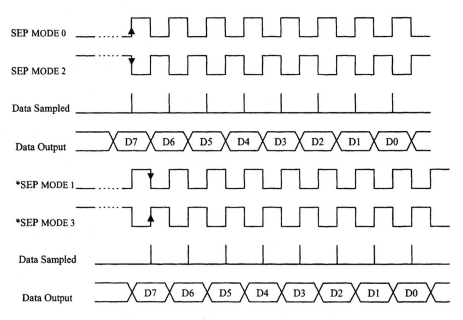

Figure 10.3 SEP modes. *Cannot be used for the receive mode.

TABLE 10.1
Determination of SEP Modes

CLKPOL	CLKPH	SEP Mode
0	0	Mode 0
0	1	Mode 1
1	0	Mode 2
1	1	Mode 3

eral interface chips have a smaller footprint because fewer pins are needed. A partial list of peripheral chips with serial interface is given in Table 10.2.

10.6 SIMULATING THE SEP

The SEP function is convenient to use when the number of data bits to be transferred is a multiple of eight. When the data to be transferred are not a multiple of 8 bits, the SEP might be clumsy to use. In this situation, a software technique can be used to simulate the SEP operation. On the other hand, in the MCS-51/52 family, only the 8XC51GB and the 8XC152JX series implement the SEP function. Other members must use simulation to interface with those peripheral chips with serial interface. A peripheral device would use either the falling or the rising clock edges to shift data in or out.

The procedure for shifting data out on the rising edges of the clock signal is as follows:

TABLE 10.2
Peripheral Chips with Serial Interface

Vendor	Part Number	Description
Analog Device	AD7823	Single-channel 8-bit A/D converter (135 kSPS)
	AD7810	Single-channel 10-bit A/D converter (350 kSPS)
	AD7818	Single-channel 10-bit A/D converter (100 kSPS)
	AD7892	Single-channel 12-bit A/D converter (600 kSPS)
	AD7721	Single-channel 12-bit A/D converter (468 kSPS)
	AD7895	Single-channel 12-bit A/D converter (250 kSPS, 8-pin)
	AD7853/L	Single-channel 12-bit A/D converter (200/100 kSPS)
	AD7893	Single-channel 12-bit A/D converter (117 kSPS, 8-pin)
	AD7896	Single-channel 12-bit A/D converter (100 kSPS, 8-pin)
	AD7851	Single-channel 14-bit A/D converter (333 kSPS)
	AD7894	Single-channel 14-bit A/D converter (163 kSPS)
	AD7723	Single-channel 16-bit A/D converter (470 kSPS)
	AD977A	Single-channel 16-bit A/D converter (200 kSPS)
	AD7722	Single-channel 16-bit A/D converter (200 kSPS)
	AD977	Single-channel 16-bit A/D converter (100 kSPS)
	AD7811	4-channel 10-bit A/D converter (350 kSPS)
	AD7812	8-channel 10-bit A/D converter (350 kSPS)
	AD7817	4-channel 10-bit A/D converter (100 kSPS)
	AD7858	8-channel 12-bit A/D converter (200 kSPS)
	AD7888	8-channel 12-bit A/D converter (200 kSPS)
	AD7858L	8-channel 12-bit A/D converter (100 kSPS)
	AD7890	8-channel 12-bit A/D converter (83 kSPS)
	AD7891	8-channel 12-bit A/D converter (45 kSPS)
	AD7856	8-channel 14-bit A/D converter (330 kSPS)
	AD7564	Quad 12-bit D/A converter
	DAC8800	Octal 8-bit D/A converter
	AD7568	Octal 12-bit D/A converter
	AD7849A/B	Single-channel 16-bit D/A converter
	DAC8420	Quad 12-bit D/A converter
	AD8300	12-bit D/A converter
	DAC8512	12-bit D/A converter
	AD420	16-bit D/A converter
	AD7303	8-bit D/A converter
	AD8522	12-bit D/A converter
	AD7304	Quad 8-bit D/A converter
	AD7804	Quad 10-bit D/A converter
	DAC8420	Quad 12-bit D/A converter
	AD7834	Quad 14-bit D/A converter
	DAC8841	Octal 8-bit D/A converter
	AD7808	Octal 10-bit converter
Motorola	MC28HC14	256-byte EEPROM in 8-pin DIP
	MC14021	8-bit input port
	MC74HC165	8-bit input port
	MC74LS165	8-bit input port
	MC74HC589	8-bit parallel-in/serial-out shift register
	MC74HC595	8-bit serial-in/parallel-out shift register
	MC74LS673	16-bit output port
	MC144115	16-segment nonmuxed LCD driver
	MC144117	4-digit LCD driver nonmuxed
	MC14549	A/D converter successive approximation register
	MC14559	A/D converter successive approximation register
	MC14489	5-digit 7-segment LED display decoder/driver
	MC14499	4-digit 7-segment LED display decoder/driver
	MC145000	Serial input multiplexed LCD driver (master)

Continued

TABLE 10.2
Continued

Vendor	Part Number	Description
	MC145001	Serial input multiplexed LCD driver (slave)
	MC145453	LCD driver with serial interface
	MC144110	6 six-bit D/A converter
	MC144111	4 six-bit D/A converter
	MC144040	8-bit A/D converter
	MC144051	8-bit A/D converter
	MC145050	10-bit A/D converter
	MC145051	10-bit A/D converter
	MC145053	10-bit A/D converter
	MC68HC68T1	Real-time clock
	MCCS1850	Serial real-time clock
	MC145155	Serial input PLL FS
	MC145156	Serial input PLL FS
	MC145157	Serial input PLL FS
	MC145158	Serial input PLL FS
	MC145159	Serial input PLL FS
	MC145170	Serial input PLL FS
National	ADC0811	8-bit 11-channel A/D converter
Semiconductor	ADC0819	8-bit 19-channel A/D converter
	ADC0831	8-bit serial I/O A/D converter with mux option
	ADC0832	8-bit serial I/O A/D converter with mux option
	ADC0834	8-bit serial I/O A/D converter with mux option
	ADC0838	8-bit serial I/O A/D converter with mux option
	ADC0833	8-bit 4-channel serial I/O A/D converter
	ADC08031	8-bit high-speed serial I/O A/D converter
	ADC08032	8-bit high-speed serial I/O A/D converter
	ADC08034	8-bit high-speed serial I/O A/D converter
	ADC08038	8-bit high-speed serial I/O A/D converter
	ADC08131	8-bit high-speed serial I/O A/D converter
	ADC08132	8-bit high-speed serial I/O A/D converter
	ADC08134	8-bit high-speed serial I/O A/D converter
	ADC08138	8-bit high-speed serial I/O A/D converter
	ADC08231	8-bit high-speed serial I/O A/D converter
	ADC08234	8-bit high-speed serial I/O A/D converter
	ADC08238	8-bit high-speed serial I/O A/D converter
	ADC1031	10-bit A/D converter with analog mix
	ADC1034	10-bit A/D converter with analog mix
	ADC1038	10-bit A/D converter with analog mix
	ADC10731	10-bit plus sign A/D converter with analog mux
	ADC10732	10-bit plus sign A/D converter with analog mux
	ADC10734	10-bit plus sign A/D converter with analog mux
	ADC10738	10-bit plus sign A/D converter with analog mux
	ADC10831	10-bit plus sign A/D converter with analog mux
	ADC10832	10-bit plus sign A/D converter with analog mux
	ADC10834	10-bit plus sign A/D converter with analog mux
	ADC10838	10-bit plus sign A/D converter with analog mux
	ADC12030	12-bit self-calibrating plus sign A/D converter
	ADC12032	12-bit self-calibrating plus sign A/D converter
	ADC12034	12-bit self-calibrating plus sign A/D converter
	ADC12038	12-bit self-calibrating plus sign A/D converter
	ADC12L030	3.3 V 12-bit self-calibrating plus sign A/D converter
	ADC12L032	3.3 V 12-bit self-calibrating plus sign A/D converter
	ADC12L034	3.3 V 12-bit self-calibrating plus sign A/D converter
	ADC12L038	3.3 V 12-bit self-calibrating plus sign A/D converter

Continued

TABLE 10.2

Continued

Vendor	Part Number	Description
	ADC12130	12-bit self-calibrating plus sign A/D converter
	ADC12132	12-bit self-calibrating plus sign A/D converter
	ADC12138	12-bit self-calibrating plus sign A/D converter
	DAC0854	Quad 8-bit D/A converter with voltage output
	DAC1054	Quad 10-bit D/A converter with voltage output
RCA	CDP68H68A1	10-bit A/D converter
	CDP68HC68R1	128×8-bit SRAM
	CDP68HC68R2	256×8-bit SRAM
	CDP68HC68T1	Real-time clock
Signetics	PCx2100	40-segment LCD duplex driver
	PCx2110	60-segment LCD duplex driver
	PCx2111	64-segment LCD duplex driver
	PCx2112	32-segment LCD duplex driver
	PCx3311	DTMF generator with parallel inputs
	PCx3312	DTMF generator with I^{2}C bus inputs
	PCx8570A	256×8 SRAM
	PCx8571	128×8 SRAM
	PCx8573	Clock/timer
	PCx8474	8-bit remote I/O expander
	PCx8476	1:4 mux LCD driver
	PCx8477	32/64 segment LCD driver
	PCx8491	8-bit, 4-channel A/D converter and D/A converter
	SAA1057	PLL tuning circuit: 512 kHz to 120 MHz
	SAA1060	32-segment LED driver
	SAA1061	16-segment LED driver
	SAA1062A	20-segment LED driver
	SAA1063	Flourescent display driver
	SAA1300	Switching circuit
	SAA3019	Clock/timer
	SAA3028	I/R transcoder
	SAB3013	Hex 6-bit D/A converter
	SAB3035	PLL digital tuning circuit with 8 D/A converters
	SAB3036	PLL digital tuning curcuit
	SAB3037	PLL digital tuning circuit with 4 D/A converters
	SAA5240	Teletext controller chip—625 line system
	TDA3820	Digital stereo sound control IC
	TEA6000	MUSTI: FM/RF system
	TDA1534A	14-bit A/D converter—serial output
	TDA1540P,D	14-bit A/D converter—serial output
	NE5036	6-bit A/D converter—serial output
Sprague	UCN4810/5810	Power driving output port
	UAA2022/2023	16-bit power output port
Xicor	X2444	16×16 nonvolatile SRAM with serial I/O
	X2444I	16×16 nonvolatile SRAM with serial I/O
	X2444M	16×16 nonvolatile SRAM with serial I/O (military)
	X2402	256×8 serial E^{2}PROM
	X2402I	256×8 serial E^{2}PROM
	X2404	512×8 E^{2}PROM with serial I/O
	X2404I	512×8 E^{2}PROM with serial I/O
	X2404M	512×8 E^{2}PROM with serial I/O
	X24C04	512×8 E^{2}PROM with serial I/O
	X24C04I	512×8 E^{2}PROM with serial I/O
	X24C16	2048×8 E^{2}PROM with serial I/O

Continued

TABLE 10.2
Continued

Vendor	Part Number	Description
	X24C16I	2048 × 8 E²PROM with serial I/O
	X24C16M	2048 × 8 E²PROM with serial I/O
MAXIM	MAX5351	13-bit D/A converter voltage output using 3.3 V supply
	MAX5353	12-bit D/A converter voltage output using 3.3 V supply
	MAX551	12-bit D/A converter current output using 2.7 V supply
	MAX7543	12-bit D/A converter current output using 3.3 V supply
	MAX5043	12-bit D/A converter current output using 3.3 V supply
	MAX5151	13-bit D/A converter voltage output using 2.7~3.6 V supply
	MAX5153	13-bit D/A converter voltage output using 2.7~3.6 V supply
	MAX5155	12-bit D/A converter voltage output using 2.7~3.6 V supply
	MAX5157	12-bit D/A converter voltage output using 2.7~3.6 V supply
	MAX1110	8-channel 8-bit A/D converter using 2.7~5.5 V supply
	MAX1111	4-channel 8-bit A/D converter using 2.7~5.5 V supply
	MAX1241	1-channel 12-bit A/D converter using 3~5.5 V supply
	MAX1247	4-channel 12-bit A/D converter using 2.7~5.25 V supply
	MAX147	8-channel 12-bit A/D converter using 2.7~5.25 V supply
	MAX1240	1-channel 12-bit A/D converter using 3~5.5 V supply
	MAX1246	4-channel 12-bit A/D converter using 2.7~5.25 V supply
	MAX146	8-channel 12-bit A/D converter using 2.7~5.25 V supply
	MAX1243	1-channel 10-bit A/D converter using 2.7~5.25 V supply
	MAX1249	4-channel 10-bit A/D converter using 2.7~5.25 V supply
	MAX148	8-channel 10-bit A/D converter using 2.7~5.25 V supply
	MAX1242	1-channel 10-bit A/D converter using 2.7~5.25 V supply
	MAX1248	4-channel 10-bit A/D converter using 2.7~5.25 V supply
	MAX149	8-channel 10-bit A/D converter using 2.7~5.25 V supply

STEP 1   Set the clock to low.

STEP 2   Apply the data bit on the port pin that is connected to the serial data input pin of the peripheral device.

STEP 3   Pull the clock to high.

STEP 4   Repeat Steps 1 to 3 as many times as needed.

To shift data out on the falling edges, swap Steps 1 and 3.

Example 10.1 Assume the 87C51FB is interfaced with a peripheral chip with serial interface. The data input and clock pins of the peripheral chip are connected to 87C51FB's P1.6 and P1.7, respectively. Write an instruction sequence to shift the contents of accumulator A to the peripheral chip on the rising edges of the clock signal. Shift out the most significant bit first.

Solution: The instruction sequence is as follows:

```
        mov   R2,#8        ; use R2 as the loop count
loop:   rlc   A            ; shift the msb to CY flag
```

```
            clr     P1.7        ; set the clock signal to low
            clr     P1.6        ; set data bit value to 0
            bcc     shift_0     ; is msb = 0?
            setb    P1.6        ; output a 1
shift_0:    setb    P1.7        ; generate a rising edge on the clock pin
            djnz    R2,loop
```

The procedure for shifting data from the peripheral chip into accumulator A on the rising edges of the clock signal is as follows:

STEP 1 Pull the clock pin to low.

STEP 2 Pull the clock pin to high.

STEP 3 Move the data bit value into the carry flag CY.

STEP 4 Rotate accumulator A left through carry.

STEP 5 Repeat Steps 1 to 4 as many times as needed (no more than eight times). Swap Steps 1 and 2 to shift data on the falling edges of the clock signal.

Example 10.2 Assume there is a peripheral chip with serial interface connected to the 87C51FB. Pins P1.6 and P1.7 are connected to the peripheral chip's data pin and clock pin, respectively. Write an instruction sequence to shift data in on the falling edges of the clock signal. The most significant bit is shifted in first. Assume the peripheral chip data are 8 bits in length.

Solution: The instruction sequence is as follows:

```
            mov     R2,#8       ; use R2 as the loop count
in_loop:    setb    P1.7        ; set the clock signal to high
            clr     P1.7        ; generate a falling edge on clock pin
            mov     CY,P1.6
            rlc     A           ; shift data bit into accumulator A
            djnz    R2,in_loop
```

10.7 INTERFACING THE 74HC589 WITH THE SEP

The 74HC589 is an 8-bit serial- or parallel-input to serial-output shift register. Its block diagram is shown in Figure 10.4. The 74HC589 can accept serial or parallel data input and shift it out serially. The highest shift clock rate for the 74HC589 is 6 MHz at room temperature. One application of the 74HC589 is to expand the number of input ports to the microcontroller.

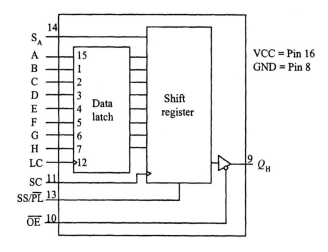

Figure 10.4 74HC589 block diagram.

VCC = Pin 16
GND = Pin 8

10.7.1 74HC589 Pins

The functions of the 74HC589 signal pins are as follows:

A, B, C, D, E, F, G, and *H*:   *Parallel data inputs.* Data on these inputs are stored in the data latch on the rising edge of the latch clock input.

SA: *Serial data input.* Data on this pin are shifted into the shift register on the rising edges of the shift clock input if the SS/PL signal is high. Data on this pin are ignored when the serial-shift/parallel-load signal is low.

SS/$\overline{PL}$:   *Shift register mode control.* When a high level is applied to this pin, the shift register is allowed to shift data serially. When a low level is applied, the shift register accepts parallel data from the data latch.

SC: *Serial-shift clock.* A low-to-high transition on this input shifts datum on the serial data input into the shift register; datum on stage H is shifted out from Q_H, where it is replaced by the datum previously stored in stage G.

LC: *Data latch clock.* A low-to-high transition on this input loads the parallel data on inputs A–H into the data latch.

$\overline{OE}$:   *Active low-output enable.* A high level applied to this pin forces the Q_H output into a high-impedance state. A low level enables the output. This control does not affect the state of the input latch or the shift register.

Q_H output: *Serial data output.* This is a three-state output from the last stage of the shift register.

10.7.2 Circuit Connections of the 74HC589 and the SEP

Depending on the number of input ports that we want to add to the 8XC51GB, we can interface as many 74HC589s to the 8XC51GB as desired. The circuit connection between

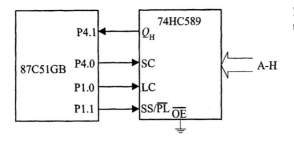

Figure 10.5 Circuit connection between the 87C51GB and 74HC589.

the 74HC589 and the 8X51GB is shown in Figure 10.5. In Figure 10.5, the H bit is shifted into the 87C51GB and becomes the most significant input to the microcontroller. Bit A is the least significant bit.

Example 10.3 Assume the A–H pins in Figure 10.5 are connected to an 8-DIP switch. Write a program to read in a byte into accumulator A from the 8-DIP switch.

Solution: We need to enable the alternate function of pins P4.0 and P4.1. This can be achieved by setting the bit latch of these two bits to 1:

```
orl    P4,#03H    ; activate the alternate function
```

The SEPCON register should be configured as follows:

- SEPE: set to 1 to enable the SEP function
- SEPREN: set to 0 to disable SEP receive mode
- CLKPOL and CLKPH: set to 00 (select mode 0) to shift in data on the rising edges
- SEPS1 and SEPS0: set to 00 to set the shift clock rate to $f_{OSC}/12$

Thus the following instruction will configure the SEP properly:

```
mov    SEPCON,#20H
```

Before reading the 74HC589, we need to load the value of the 8-DIP switch into the data latch in parallel. This can be achieved by the following two instructions:

```
clr    P1.0    ; load external data into
setb   P1.0    ; data latch
```

The next step is to transfer this byte into the shift register, which can be done by

```
clr    P1.1    ; select the parallel load mode
```

The next step is to select the shift mode:

```
setb   P1.1
```

Now we can start the serial transfer that reads a byte into the SEPDAT register:

```
              orl    SEPCON,#10H    ; enable SEP receive
wait_sep:     mov    A,SEPSTAT      ; test SEPIF flag
```

```
           anl     A,#01H                 ; "
           jz      wait_sep               ; is the byte shifted in yet?
           anl     SEPSTAT,#FEH           ; clear the SEPIF flag
```

The complete instruction sequence is as follows:

```
           mov     SEPCON,#20H
           clr     P1.0                   ; load external data into
           setb    P1.0                   ; data latch
           clr     P1.1                   ; transfer the byte to the shift register
           setb    P1.1                   ; select serial shift mode
           orl     SEPCON,#10H            ; enable SEP receive
wait_sep:  mov     A,SEPSTAT              ; wait until the byte has been shifted in
           anl     A,#01H                 ; "
           jz      wait_sep               ; "
           anl     SEPSTAT,#FEH           ; clear the SEPIF flag
```

There are several ways to connect multiple 74HC589s to the 8XC51GB. One method is illustrated in Figure 10.6. Using this method, multiple bytes can be loaded into 74HC589s simultaneously and then shifted into the 8XC51GB bit serially. The procedure for shifting in multiple bytes is as follows:

STEP 1   Program the SEP with appropriate operating parameters.

STEP 2   Set the LC pin to low and then pull it to high; this will load the external data into data latches in parallel.

STEP 3   Set P1.1 to low to select parallel mode, which will load the contents of the data latches into their associated shift registers.

STEP 4   Set P1.1 to high to select serial-shift mode.

STEP 5   Enable the SEP receive by setting the SEPREN bit of the SEPCON register. This will shift in 1 byte.

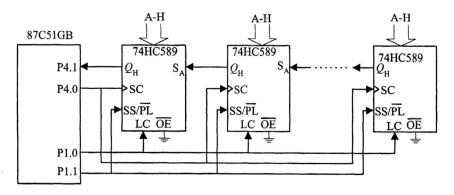

Figure 10.6 Serial connection of multiple 74HC589s to the 87C51GB.

STEP 6   Wait until the SEPIF flag in the SEPSTAT register is set to 1 and save the byte in a buffer.

STEP 7   Clear the SEPIF flag and go to Step 5 as many times as needed, and save the data in the buffer.

Example 10.4 Assume there are six 74HC589s connected to the 87C51GB as shown in Figure 10.6. Write a program to read in 6 bytes and store them at memory locations 40H~45H.

Solution: The program is as follows:

```
                mov    SEPCON,#20H      ; configure SEP, enable SEP, disable
                                        ; receive
                clr    P1.0             ; load external data into data latches
                setb   P1.0             ; "
                clr    P1.1             ; transfer data into shift registers in
                                        ; parallel
                setb   P1.1             ; select shift mode
                mov    B,#6             ; set up the loop count
                mov    R1,#40H          ; use R1 as the internal SRAM
                                        ; pointer
next_char:      orl    SEPCON,#10H      ; enable SEP receive
wait_sep:       mov    A,SEPSTAT        ; test SEPIF flag
                anl    A,#01H           ; "
                jz     wait_sep         ; "
                anl    SEPSTAT,#FEH     ; clear the SEPIF flag
                mov    @R1,SEPDAT       ; save the byte
                inc    R1               ; move the pointer
                djnz   B,next_char      ; continue to shift in data if not
                                        ; done yet
                end
```

Another way to connect multiple 74HC589s is to tie all the QH pins together and then use other port pins to selectively enable one of the 74HC589s to shift out data to the 87C51GB. The circuit connection for this method is shown in Figure 10.7. This circuit configuration allows the user to selectively input data from a specific 74HC589. The procedure for loading a byte from a specific 74HC589 into the SEPDAT register is as follows:

STEP 1   Configure the SEPCON register and set up appropriate parameters.

STEP 2   Set P1.0 to low and then pull it to high to load external data into all data latches in parallel.

STEP 3   Set P1.1 to low to load the contents of data latches into the shift registers.

STEP 4　Set P1.1 to high to select serial-shift mode.

STEP 5　Set the port 3 pin that selects the specified 74HC589 to low to enable its shift register to output data. Other port 3 pins are set to high.

STEP 6　Set the SEPREN bit of the SEPCON register to 1 to start the SEP receive. Wait until the byte has been shifted in.

STEP 7　Clear the SEPIF flag and repeat Steps 5 and 6 as many times as needed.

This procedure can be readily translated into an assembly program.

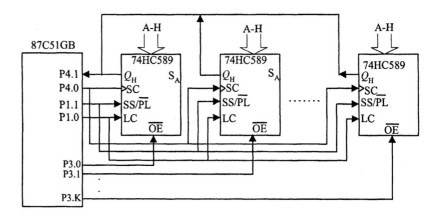

Figure 10.7　Parallel connection of multiple 74HC589s to the 87C51GB.

10.8 INTERFACING THE 74HC595 WITH THE SEP

The 74HC595 is a serial-in/parallel-out shift register. Its block diagram and pin assignment are shown in Figure 10.8. The 74HC595 consists of an 8-bit shift register and an 8-bit D-type latch with three-state parallel outputs. The shift register accepts serial data and provides a serial output. The shift register and the latch have independent clock inputs. This device also has an asynchronous reset input. The maximum shift clock rate is 6 MHz at room temperature.

10.8.1 74HC595 Pins

The functions of the 74HC595 pins are as follows:

- **A**: *Serial data input*. The data on this pin are shifted into the 8-bit serial-shift register.
- **SC**: *Shift clock*. A low-to-high transition on this input causes the data at the serial input pin to be shifted into the 8-bit shift register.

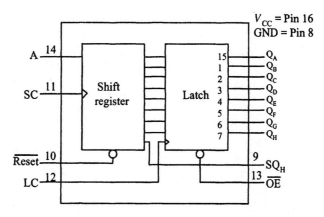

Figure 10.8 74HC595 block diagram and pin assignment.

- $\overline{Reset}$: *Active low reset.* A low on this pin resets the shift register portion of this device only. The 8-bit latch is not affected.
- *LC*: *Latch clock.* A low-to-high transition on this pin loads the shift register data into the latch.
- $\overline{OE}$: *Output enable.* A low on this pin allows the data from the latch to be presented at the outputs. A high on this input forces the outputs (Q_A–Q_H) into high-impedance state. This pin does not affect the serial output.
- Q_A-Q_H: *Noninverted, three-state, latch outputs.*
- SQ_H: *Serial data output.* This is the output of the eighth stage of the 8-bit shift register. This output does not have tristate capability.

10.8.2 Circuit Connections of the 74HC595 and the SEP

Depending on the number of output ports that we want to add to the 8XC51GB, we can interface as many 74HC595s with the 8XC51GB as desired. The circuit connection between the 74HC595 and the 8X51GB is shown in Figure 10.9.

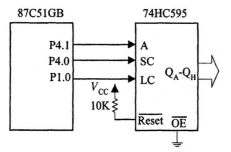

Figure 10.9 Connecting a 74HC595 to the 87C51GB.

Example 10.5 Assume that the Q_A–Q_G pins of the circuit in Figure 10.9 are connected to the segment inputs of a common-cathode seven-segment display. The common cathode is grounded permanently. Write down an instruction sequence to display the digit 5 on it.

Solution: Since the most significant bit is shifted out from the SEP first, it will be shifted to the Q_H pin of the 74HC595. The least significant bit will be shifted to the Q_A pin. Connect $Q_G \ldots Q_A$ to segments g...a, respectively. We need to send out the binary value 01101101_2 via the SEP to display the digit 5. The SEPCON register should be configured as follows:

- SEPE bit: set to 1 to enable SEP
- SEPREN bit: set to 0 to disable SEP receive
- CLKPOL & CLKPH: set to 00 (mode 0) to shift data out on rising edges
- SEPS1 & SEPS0: set to 00 to choose $f_{OSC}/12$ as its data rate

Write the value 20H into the SEPCON register to set up this configuration. The following instruction sequence will display 5 on the seven-segment display:

```
            mov   SEPCON,#20H      ; configure the SEP
            mov   SEPDAT,#6DH      ; send out 5's display pattern
sep_wait:   mov   A,SEPSTAT        ; test the SEPIF flag
            anl   A,#01H           ; "
            jz    sep_wait         ; has the byte been shifted out?
            mov   SEPSTAT,#00      ; clear the SEPIF flag
```

Many parallel ports can be added to the 87C51GB by using the SEP system and multiple 74HC595s. Figure 10.10 shows a method of connecting multiple 74HC595s to the SEP subsystem. The procedure for outputting multiple bytes using this connection is as follows:

STEP 1 Configure the SEP by writing an appropriate value into the SEPCON register. Enable the SEP transmission at this step.

STEP 2 Write a byte into the SEPDAT register to trigger clock pulses from the P4.0 pin. Clear the SEPIF flag in the SEPSTAT register.

STEP 3 Repeat Step 2 as many times as needed.

STEP 4. Set the P1.1 pin to low and then pull it to high to load the data into output latches from shift registers. After this step, the Q_H–Q_A pins of each 74HC595 contain a new value.

Example 10.6 Assume that there are four 74HC595s connected to the 87C51GB in series as shown in Figure 10.10. Write an instruction sequence to send the ASCII codes of A to D to these four 74HC595s.

Solution: Use the same configuration as in Example 10.3. The following instruction sequence will output the ASCII codes of A to D to the four 74HC595s:

```
            mov   SEPCON,#20H      ; configure the SEP
            mov   B,#04            ; set up the loop count
            mov   R0,#41H          ; place the ASCII code of A in R0
```

next_char:	mov	SEPDAT,R0	; send out one byte
sep_wait:	mov	A,SEPSTAT	; test the SEPIF flag
	anl	A,#01	; "
	jz	sep_wait	; has the byte been sent out already?
	mov	SEPSTAT,#0	; clear the SEPIF flag
	inc	R0	; increase the ASCII code by 1
	djnz	B,next_char	; have we output four characters yet?
	clr	P1.1	; load the ASCII codes to output
	setb	P1.1	; latches

Another method of expanding the number of parallel output ports is to connect multiple 74HC595s in parallel to the SEP subsystem, as shown in Figure 10.11.

With this connection, we can selectively output data to any 74HC595 by setting the

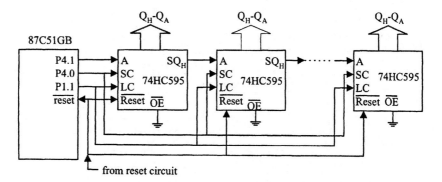

Figure 10.10 Serial connection of multiple 74HC595s to the 87C51GB.

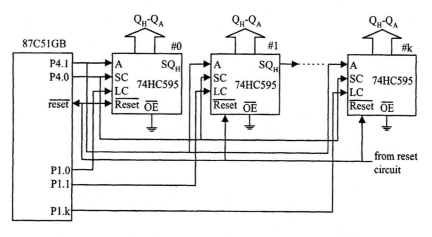
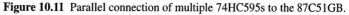

Figure 10.11 Parallel connection of multiple 74HC595s to the 87C51GB.

corresponding port 1 pin after the data has been shifted to that 74HC595. The procedure for outputting data to I/O devices connected to the 74HC595s is as follows:

STEP 1   Configure the SEP by writing an appropriate value to the SEPCON register. Enable SEP transfer at this step.

STEP 2   Write a data byte into the SEPDAT register to trigger SEP data transfer.

STEP 3   Set the P1.i pin to low and then pull it to high to load the byte from the shift register of the 74HC595 #i into its output latch.

10.9 INTERFACING WITH THE SEVEN-SEGMENT DISPLAY DRIVER MC14489

The Motorola MC14489 is a light-emitting-diode driver that can directly interface with individual lamps, seven-segment displays, or various combinations of both. LEDs wired with common cathodes are driven in a multiplexed-by-5 fashion. Communication with a microcontroller is via a synchronous serial port. The MC14489 requires only a current-setting resistor to operate.

A single MC14489 can drive any one of the following: a 5-digit display plus decimals, a 4½-digit display plus decimals and sign, or 25 lamps. A special technique allows driving 5½ digits. A configuration register allows the drive capability to be partitioned to suit many additional applications. The on-chip decoder outputs seven-segment numbers 0 to 9, hexadecimal characters A to F, plus 15 letters and symbols.

10.9.1 The Signal Pins of MC14489

The diagram and the pin assignment are illustrated in Figure 10.12.
    The functions of the MC14489 pins are as follows:

Data In: *Serial data input.* The bit stream begins with the most significant bit and is shifted in on the rising edges of clock. When the device is not cascaded, the bit pattern is either 1 byte long to change the configuration register or 3 bytes long to update the display register. For two chips cascaded, the pattern is either 4 or 6 bytes, respectively. The display does not change or flicker during shifting, which allows slow serial data rate.

Clock: *Serial data clock input.* Low-to-high transitions on clock shift bits available at data in, while high-to-low transitions shift bits from data out. To guarantee proper operation of the power-on reset (POR) circuit, the clock pin must not be floated or toggled during power-up. That is, the clock pin must be stable until the V_{DD} pin reaches at least 3 V. The highest clock frequency is 4 MHz.

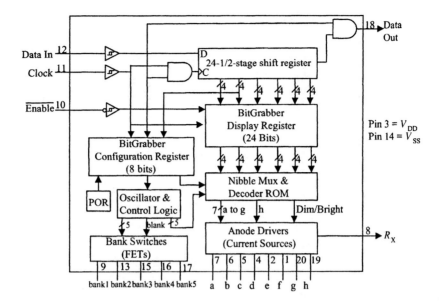

Figure 10.12 MC14489 multicharacter LED driver. (Copyright of Motorola, reprinted with permission.)

Enable: *Active low enable input.* This pin allows the MC14489 to be used on a serial bus, sharing data in and clock with other peripherals. When enable is in the inactive state, data out is forced to the low state, and shifting is inhibited. To transfer data to the device, this pin must be taken low. When the transfer is done, we must pull it to high. The low-to-high transition of enable transfers data to either the configuration or display register, depending on the data stream length.

Data Out: *Serial data output.* Data are transferred out of the shift register through the data out pin on the falling edges of the clock signal. When cascaded, this pin is connected to the data in pin of the next device. Data out can be fed back to a microcontroller to perform a wraparound test of serial data.

R_X: *External current-setting resistor.* A resistor tied between this pin and ground (V_{SS}) determines the peak segment drive current at pins **a** through **h**. This resistor ties to a current mirror with an approximate current gain of 10 when bit 23 of the shift register is a 1. With bit 23 set to 0, the peak current is reduced to half. Values of R_X range from 700 Ω to infinity. When $R_X = \infty$ (open circuit), the display is extinguished. The relationship between R_X and the segment current is shown in Figure 10.13.

a through h: *Anode-driver current sources.* These outputs are closely matched current sources that directly tie to the anodes of external discrete LEDs (lamps) or display segment LEDs. When used with lamps, outputs **a**, **b**, **c**, and **d** are used to independently control up to 20 lamps. Output **h** is used to control up to 5 lamps dependently. For lamps, the *No Decode* mode is selected via the configuration register, and **e**, **f**, and **g** are forced inactive. When used with segmented displays, outputs a through g drive segments **a** to **g**, respectively. Output **h** is used to drive the decimal point. If unused, **h** should be left open.

Bank 1 through Bank 5:   *Diode-Bank FET switches.* These outputs can handle up to 320 mA and are tied to the common cathodes of segment displays or the cathodes of lamps directly. The display is refreshed at a minimal 1 kHz rate.

V_{DD}:   *Most positive power supply.*

V_{SS}:   *Most negative power supply.*

10.9.2 The Operation of the MC14489

The configuration register controls the operation of the MC14489. The contents of the configuration register are shown in Figure 10.14.

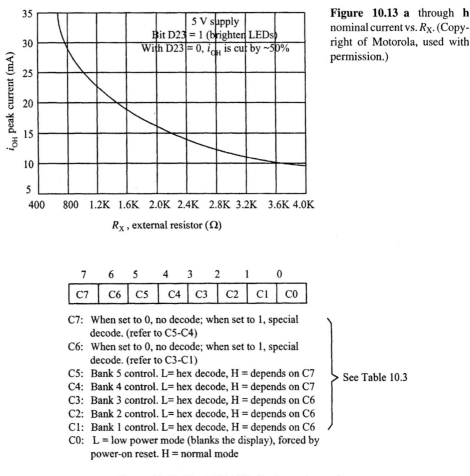

Figure 10.13 a through **h** nominal current vs. R_X. (Copyright of Motorola, used with permission.)

C7: When set to 0, no decode; when set to 1, special decode. (refer to C5–C4)
C6: When set to 0, no decode; when set to 1, special decode. (refer to C3–C1)
C5: Bank 5 control. L= hex decode, H = depends on C7
C4: Bank 4 control. L= hex decode, H = depends on C7
C3: Bank 3 control. L= hex decode, H = depends on C6
C2: Bank 2 control. L= hex decode, H = depends on C6
C1: Bank 1 control. L= hex decode, H = depends on C6
C0: L = low power mode (blanks the display), forced by power-on reset. H = normal mode

⎫
⎬ See Table 10.3
⎭

Figure 10.14 The MC14489 Configuration register.

Before sending data for display, we need to configure the operation of this device. The MC14489 has two modes: *hex decode* mode and *special decode* mode. In the hex decode mode, regular hex digits (from 0, 1,...9, A, B, C, D, E, and F) are displayed. In the special decode mode, the annunciators and some letters can be displayed. In either mode, displays can be made dimmer or brighter by clearing or setting the first bit of the display data sent to the MC14489. The MC14489 segment decoder function is illustrated in Table 10.3.

When there are no more than five digits to be displayed, one MC14489 is adequate. The circuit connection is shown in Figure 10.15. When there are only five digits to be displayed, the digit controlled by bank 5 is shifted out first, followed by the digit controlled by bank 4, and so on. Three bytes will be shifted out when there are five digits to be displayed. The first four bits of the display data are used to select the decimal point to be displayed and select whether to dim the displays or not. The use of the most significant four bits of the display data sent to the MC14489 is illustrated in Figure 10.16.

TABLE 10.3
Triple-Mode Segment Decoder Function Table

Bank Nibble Value					Seven-Segment Display Characters		Lamp Conditions			
	Binary				Hex Decode (Invoked via	Special Decode (Invoked via	No Decode[a] (Invoked via Bits C1 to C7)			
Hex	msb			lsb	Bits C1 to C5)	Bits C1 to C7	d	c	b	a
$0	0	0	0	0	0					
$1	0	0	0	1	1	c				On
$2	0	0	1	0	2	H			On	
$3	0	0	1	1	3	h			On	On
$4	0	1	0	0	4	J		On		
$5	0	1	0	1	5[b]	L		On		On
$6	0	1	1	0	6	n		On	On	
$7	0	1	1	1	7	o		On	On	On
$8	1	0	0	0	8[c]	P	On			
$9	1	0	0	1	9[d]	r	On			On
$A	1	0	1	0	A	U	On		On	
$B	1	0	1	1	B	u	On		On	On
$C	1	1	0	0	C	y	On	On		
$D	1	1	0	1	D	-	On	On		On
$E	1	1	1	0	E	=	On	On	On	
$F	1	1	1	1	F	o	On	On	On	On

Source: Copyright of Motorola, reprinted with permission.

[a] In the *No Decode Mode*, outputs e, f, and g are unused and are all forced inactive. Output h's decoding is unaffected, i.e., unchanged from the other modes. The No Decode mode is used for three purposes: (1) individually controlling lamps; (2) controlling a half digit with sign; and (3) controlling annunciators—examples: AM, PM, UHF, kV, mm, Hg.

[b] Can be used as "cap S."

[c] Can be used as "cap B."

[d] Can be used as "small g."

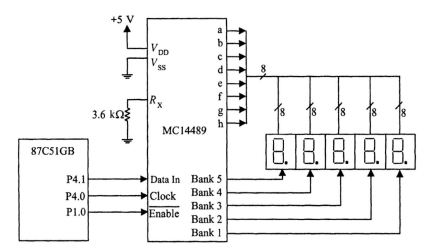

Figure 10.15 87C51GB driving 5 seven-segment displays using an MC14489.

D23 D22 D21 D20

Figure 10.16 Use of the most significant 4 bits of the display data.

0	0	0	= all h outputs inactive
0	0	1	= activate h in bank 1
0	1	0	= activate h in bank 2
0	1	1	= activate h in bank 3
1	0	0	= activate h in bank 4
1	0	1	= activate h in bank 5
1	1	0	= activate h in both banks 1 and 2
1	1	1	= activate h in all banks

L = dim LEDs, H = brighten LEDs

Example 10.7 Write a program to display 527.45 from bank 5 to bank 1 in Figure 10.15. Use the normal brightness to display these five digits.

Solution: The control byte to be written into the configuration register is as follows:

bit 7:   no decode, set to 0
bit 6:   no decode, set to 0
bit 5:   bank 5 hex decode, set to 0
bit 4:   bank 4 hex decode, set to 0
bit 3:   bank 3 hex decode, set to 0
bit 2:   bank 2 hex decode, set to 0
bit 1:   bank 1 hex decode, set to 0
bit 0:   normal mode, set to 1

The display data are shown in Figure 10.17.

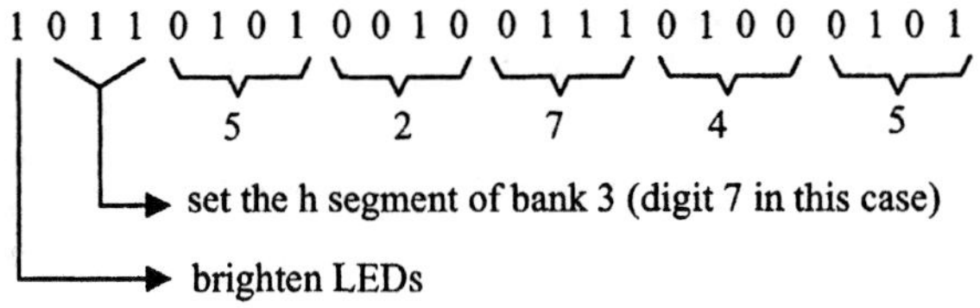

1 0 1 1 0 1 0 1 0 0 1 0 0 1 1 1 0 1 0 0 0 1 0 1

 5   2   7   4   5

→ set the h segment of bank 3 (digit 7 in this case)

→ brighten LEDs

Figure 10.17 Display data for Example 10.7.

The SEPCON register should be configured as follows:

bit 5 (SEPE):   set to 1 to enable SEP

bit 4 (SEPREN):   set to 0 to disable SEP receive

bits 3 and 2 (CLKPOL and CLKPH):   set to 00 to use rising edges to shift data out

bits 1 and 0 (CLKS1 and CLKS0):   set to 00 to choose $f_{OSC} \div 12$ as the data rate

Write the value of 20H to configure SEP.
The program is as follows:

```
                mov   SEPCON,#20H      ; configure SEP subsystem
                clr   P1.0             ; enable SEP data transfer to the
                                       ; MC14489
                mov   SEPDAT,#01H      ; send data to configure the MC14489
sep_wait0:      mov   A,SEPSTAT        ; check the SEPIF bit
                anl   A,#01H           ; "
                jz    sep_wait0        ; is SEP transfer complete?
                setb  P1.0             ; load configuration data into
                                       ; configuration register
                anl   SEPSTAT,#FEH     ; clear the SEPIF flag
                clr   P1.0             ; allow data to be shifted into the
                                       ; MC14489
                mov   SEPDAT,#B5H      ; send out the first byte
sep_wait1:      mov   A,SEPSTAT        ; check the SEPIF bit
                anl   A,#01H           ; "
                jz    sep_wait1        ; is SEP transfer complete?
                anl   SEPSTAT,#FEH     ; clear the SEPIF flag
                mov   SEPDAT,#27H      ; send out the second byte
sep_wait2:      mov   A,SEPSTAT        ; check the SEPIF bit
                anl   A,#01H           ; "
                jz    sep_wait2        ; is SEP transfer complete?
                anl   SEPSTAT,#FEH     ; clear the SEPIF flag
                mov   SEPDAT,#45H      ; send out the third byte
sep_wait3:      mov   A,SEPSTAT        ; check the SEPIF bit
                anl   A,#01H           ; "
```

```
        jz    sep_wait3        ; is SEP transfer complete?
        anl   SEPSTAT,#FEH     ; clear the SEPIF flag
        setb  P1.0             ; load display data into display
                               ; register

        end
```

10.9.3 Cascading the MC14489s

Nothing special is needed to cascade multiple MC14489s together. It is done by connecting the data out pin of the current MC14489 to the data in pin of the next MC14489. Shown in Figure 10.18 is the example of cascading three MC14489s.

Before sending display data, these MC14489s must be configured. Seven bytes of data must be sent in. The first byte shifted in is used as the configuration byte for the MC14489 #3; the fourth byte shifted in is used as the configuration byte of the MC14489 #2; the last byte shifted in is used as the configuration byte of the MC14489 #1. The remaining four bytes are not used for configuration purpose. The configuration information is shown in Figure 10.19.

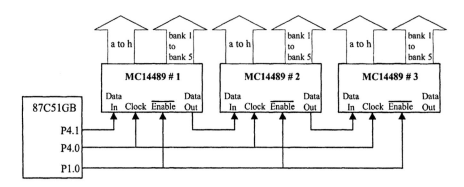

Figure 10.18 Cascading three MC14489s.

1st byte	2nd byte	3rd byte	4th byte	5th byte	6th byte	7th byte (last)
Configuration register of device #3	don't care	don't care	Configuration register of device #2	don't care	don't care	Configuration register of device #1

→ Time

Figure 10.19 Configuration information for three cascaded MC14489s.

Example 10.8 Write a program to display the following information (temperature at 14:20 of August 2, 1997) on the 15 seven-segment displays driven by the three MC14489s shown in Figure 10.18:

30.5°C 14 20 08 02 97

Solution: The character for degree can be represented by the special decode character of hex digit F (see Table 10.3). The letter *C* can be represented by hex digit C in hex decode mode. All the other characters can be represented by digits in regular hex decode mode. The left-most five characters of the above information are to be displayed on displays driven by the MC14489 #1. The middle five characters are to be displayed on the displays driven by the MC14489 #2. The right-most five characters are to be displayed on the displays driven by the MC14489 #3.

The configuration data for these three MC14489s are as follows:

MC14489 #1:

C7:   set to 0 to select no decode

C6:   set to 1 to select special decode (need to display degree character on bank 2)

C5:   set to 0 to select hex decode

C4:   set to 0 to select hex decode

C3:   set to 0 to select hex decode

C2:   set to 1 to select special decode

C1:   set to 0 to select hex decode

C0:   set to 1 to select normal mode

MC14489 #2 and #3:

C7 and C6:   set to 0 to select no decode

C5 to C1:   set to 0 to select hex decode

C0:   set to 1 to select normal mode

The configuration data of MC14489 #3 must be sent out first and hence the complete configuration data are 01xxxx01xxxx45H. Here, x stands for don't care and we will use 0 for it.

The right-most five characters of the display data 80297 must be sent out first, followed by the middle five characters 14200, then followed by the left-most five characters 30.5°C. The overall display data are for MC14489 #1 (Figure 10.20), MC14489 #2 (Figure 10.21), and MC14489 #3 (Figure 10.22).

The program that displays the specified information is as follows:

```
        org    4000H            ; starting address of the program
        mov    SEPCON,#20H       ; configure SEP operation
        clr    P1.0              ; enable SEP data transmission
        mov    DPTR,#conf_dat    ; place the address of configuration
                                 ; data in R0
```

1 1 0 0 0 0 1 1 0 0 0 0 0 1 0 1 1 1 1 1 1 1 0 0   **Figure 10.21** Display data for
     3   0   5   ▫   C   MC14489 #1.
     → set the h segment of bank #4 digit 0
     → brighten LEDs

1 0 0 0 0 0 0 1 0 1 0 0 0 0 1 0 0 0 0 0 0 0 0 0   **Figure 10.21** Display data for
     1   4   2   0   0   MC14489 #2.
     → all h segments inactive
     → brighten LEDs

1 0 0 0 1 0 0 0 0 0 0 0 0 0 1 0 1 0 0 1 0 1 1 1   **Figure 10.22** Display data for
     8   0   2   9   7   MC14489 #3.
     → all h segments inactive
     → brighten LEDs

```
              mov    B,#7              ; use B as byte count
loop_con:     mov    A,#0              ; send 1 byte to SEP
              movc   A,@A+DPTR         ; "
              mov    SEPDAT,A          ; "
sep_wait1:    mov    A,SEPSTAT         ; test the SEPIF bit
              anl    A,#01H            ; "
              jz     sep_wait1         ; is transmission complete?
              anl    SEPSTAT,#FEH      ; clear the SEPIF flag
              inc    DPTR              ; move the table pointer
              djnz   B,loop_con        ; are all configuration data transferred?
              setb   P1.0              ; load the configuration data into
                                       ; config. reg.
              clr    P1.0              ; enable SEP transfer again
              mov    B,#9              ; set up transfer byte count
              mov    DPTR,#disp_dat    ; place the address of display
                                       ; data in R0
loop_dt:      mov    A,#0              ; send one byte to SEP
              movc   A,@A+DPTR         ; "
              mov    SEPDAT,A          ; "
sep_wait2:    mov    A,SEPSTAT         ; test the SEPIF bit
              anl    A,#01H            ; "
              jz     sep_wait2         ; is transmission complete?
              anl    SEPSTAT,#FEH      ; clear the SEPIF flag
              inc    DPTR              ; move the table pointer
```

```
                    djnz   B,loop_dt           ; are all display data transferred?
                    setb   P1.0                ; load display data into display latch
                    nop
conf_dat            DB     01H,00H,00H,01H,00H,00H,45H
disp_dat            DB     88H,02H,97H,81H,42H,00H,C3H,05H,FCH
                    end
```

10.10 THE XICOR SERIAL E²PROM

The Xicor X24165 is a 16384 bit serial E²PROM, internally organized as 2048×8. The Xicor E²PROMs are designed and tested for applications requiring extended endurance. Data retention is specified to be longer than 100 years.

The pin configuration of the X24165 is shown in Figure 10.23.

The SCL and SDA are serial clock and data input, respectively. Three address inputs (S2, $\overline{S1}$, S0) allow up to eight devices to share a common two-wire bus. Address inputs are used to set the least significant three bits of the seven-bit slave address. The inputs are static and should be tied high or low, forming one unique address per device.

The write-protect (WP) input controls the hardware write protect feature. When held low, hardware write protection is disabled and the X24165 can be written normally. When this input is held high, and the WPEN bit in the write protect register is set high, write protection is enabled, and writes are disabled to the selected blocks as well as the write protect register itself.

10.10.1 Device Operation

The X24165 supports the synchronous serial data transfer protocol and can serve as a slave only. The rules that the X24165 needs to follow are described in the following:

Clock and Data Conventions

Data states on the SDA line can change only when SCL is low. The SDA state changes when SCL is high are reserved for indicating start and stop conditions.

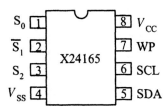

Figure 10.23 Xicor X24165 E²PROM.

Start and Stop Conditions

All commands must be preceded by the start condition. The start condition is a high-to-low transition of SDA when SCL is high. All communications must be terminated by a stop condition, which is a low-to-high transition of SDA when SCL is high. The definitions of start and stop are illustrated in Figure 10.24. The stop condition is also used to place the device into standby mode after a read sequence. A stop condition can be issued only after the transmitting device has released the bus.

Acknowledge

Acknowledge is a software convention used to indicate successful data transfer. The transmitting device, either master or slave, will release the bus after transmitting 8 bits. During the ninth clock cycle the receiver will pull the SDA line to low to acknowledge that it received the 8 bits of data. Refer to Figure 10.25.

The X24165 will always respond with an acknowledgment after recognition of a start condition and its slave address. If both the device and a write operation have been selected, the X24165 will respond with an acknowledgment after the receipt of each subsequent 8-bit word.

In the read mode the X24165 will transmit 8 bits of data, release the SDA line, and monitor the line for an acknowledgment. If an acknowledgment is detected and no stop condition is generated by the master, the X24165 will continue to transmit data. If an acknowledgment is not detected, the X24165 will terminate further data transmissions. The

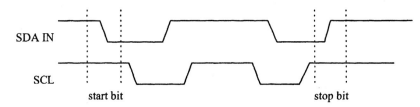

Figure 10.24 Xicor X24165 definitions of start and stop. (Redrawn with permission of Xicor.)

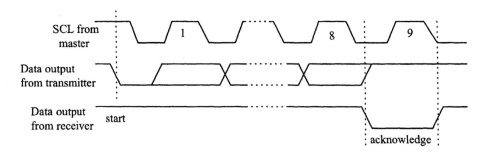

Figure 10.25 Xicor X24165 acknowledge response from receiver. (Redrawn with permission of Xicor.)

master must then issue a stop condition to return the X24165 to the standby power mode and place the device into a known state.

Device Addressing

Following a start condition the master must send the address of the slave it is accessing. The format of the slave address is shown in Figure 10.26. The most significant bit is a 1. Bit 6 to bit 4 are device select bits. A system can have up to eight X24165s on the bus. The eight addresses are defined by the state of the S0, S1, and S2 inputs. S1 of the slave address must be inverse of the S1 input pin.

Bits 3 to 1 are an extension of the memory array's address and are concatenated with the 8 bits of address in the word address field, providing direct access to the whole 2048 × 8 array.

The least significant bit of the slave address defines the operation to be performed. When set high a read operation is performed; when set low a write operation is performed.

Following the start condition, the X24165 monitors the SDA bus by comparing the slave address device type identifier. On a match the X24165 outputs an acknowledgment on the SDA line. Depending on the state of the R/W bit, the X24165 will execute a read or a write operation.

10.10.2 Write Operations

We can perform a byte write or a page write to the X24165.

Byte Write

For a write operation, the X24165 requires a second address field. This address field is the word address, comprised of 8 bits, providing access to any one of the 2048 words in the array. On receipt of the word address, the X24165 responds with an acknowledgment and awaits the next 8 bits of data, again responding with an acknowledgment. The master then terminates the transfer by generating a stop condition, at which time the X24165 begins the internal write cycle to the nonvolatile memory. While the internal write cycle is in progress the X24165 inputs are disabled, and the device will not respond to any requests from the master. The byte write sequence is illustrated in Figure 10.27.

Page Write

The X24165 is capable of a 32-byte page write operation. It is initiated in the same manner as the byte write operation, but instead of terminating the write cycle after the first data

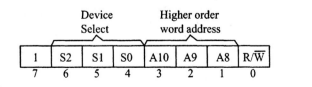

Figure 10.26 Slave address.

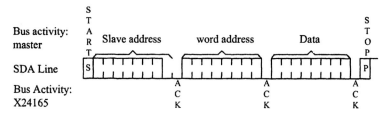

Figure 10.27 Xicor X24165 byte write format. (Redrawn with permission of Xicor.)

word is transferred, the master can transmit up to 31 more words. After the receipt of each word, the X24165 will respond with an acknowledgment.

After the receipt of each word, the five low-order address bits are internally incremented by one. The high-order bits of the word address remain constant. Should the master transmit more than 32 words prior to generating the stop condition, the address counter will "roll over" and the previously written data will be overwritten. As with the byte write operation, all inputs are disabled until completion of the internal write cycle. The page write sequence is illustrated in Figure 10.28.

Acknowledge Polling

A byte-write operation takes no more than 10 ms (5 ms typical) to complete. This maximal write cycle time can be reduced using the acknowledge polling. To initiate acknowledge polling, the master issues a start condition followed by the slave address byte for a write or read operation. If the device is still busy with the write cycle, then no ACK will be returned. If the device has completed the write operation, an ACK will be returned and the host can then proceed with the read or write operation.

10.10.3 Read Operations

Read operations are initiated in the same manner as write operations with the exception that the $R/\overline{W}$ bit of the slave address is set high. There are three basic read operations: current address read, random read, and sequential read.

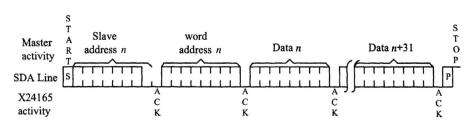

Figure 10.28 Xicor X24165 page write sequence. (Redrawn with permission of Xicor.)

To terminate a read operation, the master must either issue a stop condition during the ninth clock cycle or hold SDA high during the ninth clock cycle and then issue a stop condition.

Current Address Read

Internally the X24165 contains an address counter that maintains the address of the last word read, incremented by one after a read operation. Therefore, if the last access read was to address n, the next read operation would access data from address $n + 1$. On receipt of the slave address with the R/$\overline{\text{W}}$ set high, the X24165 issues an acknowledgment and transmits the 8-bit word. The read operation is terminated by the master, by not responding with an acknowledgment and by issuing a stop condition. The sequence of transactions is illustrated in Figure 10.29.

Random Read

Random read operations allow the master to access any memory location in a random manner. Prior to issuing the slave address with the R/$\overline{\text{W}}$ bit set high, the master must first perform a "dummy" write operation. The master issues the start condition, and the slave address with the R/$\overline{\text{W}}$ bit set low, followed by the word address it is to read. After the word address acknowledgment, the master immediately reissues the start condition and the slave address with the R/$\overline{\text{W}}$ bit set high. This will be followed by an acknowledgment from the X24165 and then by the 8-bit word. The master terminates the read operation by not responding to the acknowledgment and by issuing a stop condition. The complete sequence is illustrated in Figure 10.30.

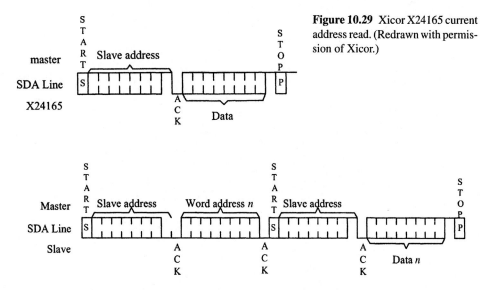

Figure 10.29 Xicor X24165 current address read. (Redrawn with permission of Xicor.)

Figure 10.30 Xicor X24165 random read sequence. (Redrawn with permission of Xicor.)

Sequential Read

Sequential reads can be initiated as either a current address read or a random access read. The first word is transmitted as in other modes, however, the master now responds with an acknowledgment, indicating it requires additional data. The X24165 continues to output data for each acknowledgment received. The read operation is terminated by the master by not responding with an acknowledgment and then issuing a stop condition.

The data output is sequential, with the data from address n followed by the data from $n + 1$. The address counter for read operations increments all address bits allowing the entire memory contents to be serially read during one operation. At the end of the address space (address 2047), the counter rolls over to 0 and the X24165 continues to output data for each acknowledgment received. The complete sequence is shown in Figure 10.31.

10.10.4 Write Protect Register

The write protect register is located at the highest address, 7FFH. The write protect register is written by performing a random write of 1 byte directly to address 7FFH. The state of the write protect register can be read by performing a random read at address 7FFH at any time. The contents of the write protect register are shown in Figure 10.32.

The bits WEL and RWEL are volatile latches that power-up in the low state. A write to any address other than 7FFH will be ignored until the WEL bit is set high. The WEL

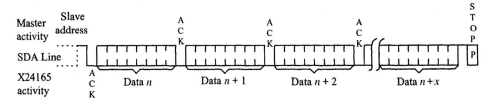

Figure 10.31 Xicor X24165 sequential read sequence. (Redrawn with permission of Xicor.)

7	6	5	4	3	2	1	0
WPEN	0	0	BP1	BP0	RWEL	WEL	0

Figure 10.32 Write protect register.

WPEN: Write protect enable bit. Is used along with the WP pin to provide memory protection

BP1 & BP0: Block protect bits.

BP1	BP0	Protected address	comment
0	0	None	
0	1	600H ~ 7FFH	upper 1/4
1	0	400H ~ 7FFH	upper 1/2
1	1	000H ~ 7FFH	full array

RWEL: Register write enable latch. When 0, writes disabled. When 1, writes enabled.

WEL: Write enable latch. When 0, writes disabled. When 1, writes enabled.

bit is set by writing the binary value 0000001x to address 7FFH. The RWEL bit controls write to the block protect bits. RWEL is set by first setting WEL to 1 and then writing the binary value 0000011x to address 7FFH. RWEL must be set in order to change the block protect bits, BP1 and BP0, or the WPEN bit. RWEL is reset when the block protect bits or the WPEN bit are changed, or when the chip powers up again.

A three-step sequence is required to change the nonvolatile block protect bits or write protect enable bit:

STEP 1   Set WEL to 1 (write 00000010 to address 7FFH).

STEP 2   Set RWEL to 1 (write 00000110 to address 7FFH).

STEP 3   Set BP1, BP0, and/or WPEN bits (write w00yz010 to address 7FFH).

Step 3 is a nonvolatile write cycle, requiring 10 ms to complete. RWEL must be 0 in step 3; if w00yz110 is written to address 7FFH, RWEL is set but WPEN, BP1, and BP0 are not changed.

The write protect (WP) pin and the write protect enable (WPEN) bit in the write protect register control the programmable hardware write protection feature. The hardware write protection feature is illustrated in Table 10.4.

10.10.5 Interfacing X24165 with the MCS-51/52

The X24165 can interface with any member of the MCS-51/52 family. As long as there are two I/O pins available we can use them to connect to the X24165. A circuit that interfaces the 87C51FB with the X24165 is illustrated in Figure 10.33.

We need to know the timing of the X24165 before data transfer can proceed. The timing diagram and the timing parameters are shown in Figure 10.34 and Table 10.5, respectively.

All data transfer requires a start command to the X24165. There are two timing parameters to be satisfied for the start command: $t_{SU:STA}$ (4.7 μs) and $t_{HD:DAT}$ (4 μs). The start command can be implemented by a software subroutine as follows:

```
SDAbit      equ    0
SCLbit      equ    1
start:      setb   P1.SDAbit
            setb   P1.SCLbit
            nop                    ; provide minimum t_SU:STA time
```

TABLE 10.4
Write Protect Status Table

WP	WPEN	Memory Array (Not Block Protected)	Memory Array (Block Protected)	BP Bits	WPEN Bit
0	x	Writable	Protected	Writable	Writable
x	0	Writable	Protected	Writable	Writable
1	1	Writable	Protected	Protected	Protected

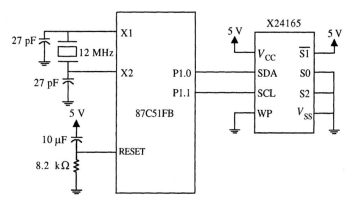

Figure 10.33 Hardware connection for interfacing an X24165 with the 87C51FB.

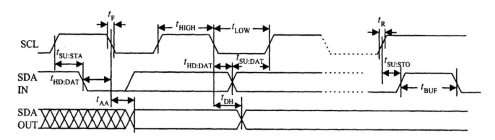

Figure 10.34 Xicor X24165 bus timing. (Redrawn with permission of Xicor.)

TABLE 10.5
X24165 Bus Timing Parameters

Symbol	Parameter	Minimum	Maximum	Units
f_{SCL}	SCL clock frequency	0	100	kHz
T_I	Noise suppression time (Constant at SCL, SDAs)		100	ns
t_{AA}	SCL low to SDA data out valid	0.3	3.5	μs
t_{BUF}	Time the bus must be free before a new transmission can start	4.7		μs
t_{HD-STA}	Start condition hold time	4		μs
t_{LOW}	Clock low period	4.7		μs
t_{HIGH}	Clock high period	4		μs
$t_{SU:STA}$	Start condition setup time	4.7		μs
$t_{HD:DAT}$	Data in hold time	0		μs
$t_{SU:DAT}$	Data in setup time	250		ns
t_R	SDA and SCL rise time		1	μs
t_F	SDA and SCL fall time		300	ns
$t_{SU:STO}$	Stop condition setup time	4.7		μs
t_{DH}	Data out hold time	300		ns

```
        nop                 ; "
        nop                 ; "
        nop                 ; "
        nop                 ; "
        clr    P1.SDAbit    ; create the falling edge for SDA
        nop                 ; provide minimum t_HD:DAT for SDA
        nop                 ; "
        nop                 ; "
        nop                 ; "
        clr    P1.SCLbit    ; force SCL to low
        ret
```

A stop command is needed to end the data transmission. The stop condition setup time ($t_{SU:STO}$) must be satisfied for the stop command. A stop command can be implemented by a software routine:

```
stop:   clr    P1.SDAbit    ; force SDA line to low
        setb   P1.SCLbit    ; bring up the SCL pin to high
        nop
        nop
        nop
        nop
        nop
        setb   P1.SDAbit    ; generate a rising edge on SDA pin
        ret
```

Except for the 8XC51GB and the 8XC152JX series, other MCS-51/52 microcontrollers do not have SEP subsystems; therefore we need to generate a clock pulse to synchronize the data transfer using software. The following subroutine generates a clock pulse and also returns the value of the SDA pin using the C flag:

```
clkpulse:   setb  p1.SCLbit              ; SCL clock starts from high
            nop
            nop
            clr   C
            jnb   P1.SDAbit,clock_lo
            setb  C                       ; set C to 1 if SDA bit is 1
clock_lo:   clr   P1.SCLbit
            ret
```

Acknowledgment is needed in many data transfers. Either the microcontroller or the X24165 may generate acknowledgment. The microcontroller needs to know when the

X24165 sends out acknowledgment in response to the data transfer. We need two subroutines for this purpose: the subroutine *outack* sends out acknowledgment to the X24165 whereas the subroutine *getack* reads the acknowledgment. If the X24165 acknowledges the subroutine *getack* will return 0 in carry flag C.

```
outack:     clr     P1.SDAbit       ; SDA line should be low for acknowledge
            ajmp    clkpulse        ; sends out a high to low clock pulse & return
getack:     setb    P1.SDAbit       ; force SDA line to high
            acall   clkpulse        ; generate a clock pulse
            ret
```

The routine *outack* returns to its caller via the *clkpulse* subroutine.

An address is required to perform a read or write operation to the X24165 serial memory. The following routine prepares the slave address in the format described earlier and sends it to the X24165. The page number (passed in DPTR) and the operation to be performed (passed in C; 0 = write; 1 = read) are the inputs to this subroutine:

```
send_addr:  mov     A,DPH           ; page number high address
            rlc     A               ; merge command bit with the upper 3
                                    ; address bits
            orl     A,#DeviceID     ; combine with the device select bits
            ajmp    outbyte         ; send the slave address
```

The parameter DeviceID is in the following format:

1xxx0000

where xxx is the device ID.

The subroutine *outbyte* shifts out a byte, most significant bit first, through the assigned SDA/SCL lines on port 1. The data to be shifted out are in accumulator A.

```
outbyte:    setb    C
out_loop:   rlc     A
            jnc     out_0
            setb    P1.SDAbit
            ajmp    out_1
out_0:      clr     P1.SDAbit
out_1:      acall   clkpulse        ; clock the data bit into the serial
                                    ; memory
            cjne    A,#80H,out_next ; is it done?
            ajmp    getack          ; check for an acknowledgment from
                                    ; device and return
out_next:   clr     C               ; loop until all bits are sent
            ajmp    out_loop        ; "
```

The procedure of random read is illustrated in Figure 10.30. A random read returns the contents of the specified serial memory location. The routine *rand_rd* reads the byte pointed to by DPTR.

```
rand_rd:    acall   start           ; send a start command
            clr     C               ; [C=0] set write operation bit
            acall   send_addr       ; send the slave address byte
            mov     A,DPL           ; load the lower byte of the page
            acall   outbyte         ; send out the address
            mov     A,DPH
            acall   start           ; start
            setb    C               ; specify a read operation
            acall   send_addr       ; sent the slave address byte
            acall   inbyte          ; shift in a byte
            setb    P1.SDAbit       ; stop read operation
            acall   clkpulse        ; "
            jmp     stop            ; "
```

The routine *rand_rd* calls the subroutine *inbyte* to shift in a byte. The *inbyte* routine is as follows:

```
inbyte:     mov    R2,#8            ; use this value as a loop count
            setb   P1.SDAbit        ; make pin P1.SDA an input pin
inloop:     acall  clkpulse         ; clock the serial memory and shift it into
            rlc    A                ; accumulator A (the data bit is returned in C)
            djnz   R2,inloop
            ret
```

The X24165 allows us to perform sequential read up to 32 bytes. The routine *seqread* performs sequential read from the X24165. This routine assumes that the starting address has been initialized by the *rand_rd* routine. The SRAM buffer to hold the bytes is pointed to by R1. The number of bytes to be read is in R0.

```
seqread:    acall   start
            setb    C               ; specify the read operation to be
                                    ; performed
            acall   send_addr       ; send the slave address byte
read_lp:    acall   inbyte          ; start reading from the current address
            mov @   R1,A            ; save the byte in buffer
            inc     R1              ; move the buffer pointer
            djnz    R0,read_next    ; if not done, we need to acknowledge
; The following three instructions stop the read operation
            setb        p1.SDAbit
```

```
                       acall    clkpulse
                       ajmp     stop                ; jump to stop and return to caller
        read_next:     acall    outack              ; send out acknowledge
                       ajmp     read_lp             ; continue
```

To perform a write operation to the X24165, we need to make sure it is not write protected. Since the WPR register controls the write protection feature, it must be configured properly. To configure the WPEN and block protection bits in the WPR register, both the WEL and RWEL bits must be set to 1. These two bits are reset to 0 when the device is first powered up. The WPR register must be configured properly using the three-step sequence described in Section 10.10.4.

The first step is to set the WEL bit to 1 by calling the subroutine *setwel*. This routine calls the subroutine *addr_wpr* to transfer the address of the WPR register into the X24165. The routines *addr_wpr* and *setwel* are as follows:

```
  addr_wpr:    mov    DPTR,#7FFH       ; place the address of WPR in DPTR
               acall  start            ; issue a start command to X24165
               clr    C                ; specify a write operation
               acall  send_addr        ; send out the device ID and upper 3
                                       ; address bits
               mov    A,DPL            ; send out the lower 8 address bits and
                                       ; return to
               ajmp   outbyte          ; the caller
  setwel:      acall  addr_wpr         ; send out the address of the WPR
                                       ; register
               mov    A,#02H           ; value to set the WEL bit
               acall  outbyte          ; send out the WEL bit
               ajmp   stop             ; issue the stop command and return to
                                       ; the caller
```

The second step is to set the RWEL bit of the WPR register to 1 by calling the subroutine *setrwel*.

```
  setrwel:     acall  addr_wpr         ; send out the address of the WPR register
               mov    A,#06H           ; value to set the RWEL bit to 1
               acall  outbyte          ; shift out the value
               ajmp   stop             ; issue the stop command and return to the caller
```

In normal operation, we may need to change the block protection feature of the device. To do that, we need to make sure that both the WEL and RWEL bits are set to 1. The routine *enpro_wpr* enables us to change the contents of the WPR register. This routine returns the initial value of the WPR register in A.

```
enpro_wpr:      mov     DPTR,#7FFH      ; place the address of the WPR register
                                        ; in DPTR
                acall   rand_rd         ; read the WPR register
                mov     20H,A           ; make a backup copy of A
                jb      1,chk_rwel      ; check the RWEL bit if the WEL bit is 1
                acall   setwel          ; send the set WEL bit command
chk_rwel:       jb      2,no_op         ; is the RWEL bit set already?
                acall   setrwel         ; issue the set RWEL bit command
no_op:          mov     A,20H           ; restore the initial value of WPR in A
                ret
```

The third step is to update block protect bits (BP1 and BP0) and/or the WPEN bit. Here we will use two separate subroutines to change block protect bits and the WPEN bit.

```
; The block protect bits are passed by using the lowest two bits of accumulator A
setBP:          anl     A,#03H          ; mask out the upper 6 bits
                swap    A               ; move block protect bits to the right
                rr      A               ; position
                mov     R0,A            ; make a backup copy of A
                acall   enpro_wpr       ; enable the WPR register to be changed
                anl     A,#10000110B    ; prepare the new block protect value to
                orl     A,R0            ; be written into the WPR register
                mov     R0,A            ; make a backup copy
                acall   addr_wpr        ; send out the address of the WPR register
                mov     A,R0            ; restore A
                acall   outbyte         ; output the new value to WPR
                ajmp    stop            ; issue a stop command
; The following routine sets the WPEN bit to the value of carry flag C
ch_wpen:        clr     A               ; place the new WPEN bit value in the
                                        ; MSB of A
                rrc     A               ; and clear out the other 7 bits
                mov     R2,A            ; make a backup copy of A
                acall   enpro_wpr       ; enable the WPR register to be
                                        ; changed
                anl     A,#9AH          ; mask out bits 6, 5, 2, and 0
                orl     A,#02H          ; make sure the WEL bit is set
                orl     A,R2            ; set the WPEN bit as required
                mov     R2,A            ; make a backup copy
                acall   addr_wpr        ; send out the address of the WPR
                                        ; register
                mov     A,R2            ; shift out the new WPR pattern
```

```
                    acall   outbyte          ; "
                    ajmp    stop             ; issue a stop command and return to the
                                             ; caller
```

A byte-write operation is performed according to the sequence described in Figure 10.27. The subroutine that does the byte-write operation is as follows:

```
; The following routine writes the byte contained in R2 into the serial memory
; location at DPTR
wr_byte:    acall   start            ; issue the start command
            clr     c                ; indicate the write operation to be performed
            acall   send_addr        ; send the device ID and upper 3 address bits
            mov     A,DPL            ; send out the word address (lower 8 address
            acall   outbyte          ; bits)
            mov     A,R2            ; load the data to be output into accumulator A
            acall   outbyte          ; output the data byte
            ajmp    stop             ; issue the stop command and return
```

To perform a page-write operation, simply follow the sequence described in Figure 10.28. The following two parameters are needed:

- Starting address of RAM buffer: passed in R0
- Starting address of the serial memory to be written (programmed): passed in DPTR

The following subroutine will write the page (32 bytes) stored in RAM buffer to the serial memory X24165:

```
pagesize    equ     32
wr_page:    acall   start            ; issue start command
            clr     C                ; indicate a write operation
            acall   send_addr        ; send out the device ID and upper 3
                                     ; address bits
            mov     A,DPL            ; output the lower 8 address bits
            anl     A,#E0H           ; mask the lowest five address bits
            acall   outbyte          ; and write it out
            mov     R2,#pagesize     ; use the page size as the loop count
next_byte:  mov     A,@R0            ; get one byte to be output
            acall   outbyte          ; send it out
            inc     R0               ; move the buffer pointer
            djnz    R2,next_byte     ; repeat until all of the bytes have been
                                     ; sent out
            ajmp    stop             ; issue the stop command
```

The E²PROM with serial interface is useful in applications that need to record data in the field for further processing, for example, recording the ins and outs of birds' or animals' resident places.

10.11 INTERFACING WITH A/D CONVERTERS WITH SERIAL INTERFACE

Many companies manufacture A/D converters with serial interface. The ADC1031 from National Semiconductor is a 10-bit A/D converter with serial interface. The ADC1031 can operate on a single 5-V power supply. Each analog sample takes no more than 13.7 μs to convert for a 3-MHz clock input. The pin assignment of the ADC1031 is shown in Figure 10.35.

The ADC1031 consumes no more than 20 mW power and can shift the conversion result out at the rate of 1 MHz. Major applications of the ADC1031 include engine control, process control, instrumentation, and test equipment.

10.11.1 The ADC1031 Signal Pins

The functions of the ADC1031 signal pins are as follows:

S_{CLK}:   *Serial data clock input.* The clock applied to this input controls the rate at which the serial data exchange occurs. The falling edge shifts the data resulting from the previous A/D conversion out on DO. CS enables the above function.

C_{CLK}:   *Conversion clock input.* The clock frequency applied to this input can be from 700 kHz to 4 MHz.

DO: *The data output pin.* The A/D conversion result (D0-D9) is output on this pin. The most significant bit is shifted out first.

$\overline{CS}$:   *Chip select.* When this pin is low, the falling edge of the S_{CLK} shifts out the previous A/D conversion result on the DO pin.

V_{REF}:   *Analog voltage reference.* This input cannot be higher than V_{CC} + 50 mV.

V_{IN}:   *Analog input voltage.*

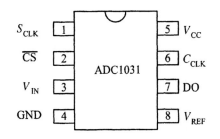

Figure 10.35 The ADC1031 A/D converter.

10.11.2 Device Operation

The CS pin of the ADC1031 cannot be left low continuously. When the CS pin is high, the DO pin will be in a high-impedance state. S_{CLK} and C_{CLK} can be tied together. However, the total conversion time will increase because the maximum clock frequency is now 1 MHz. The V_{REF} can be tied to V_{CC} to simplify the connection. Like most A/D converters, the ADC1031 is ratiometric and the conversion is done automatically.

10.11.3 Using the ADC1031 to Measure Mass Airflow

The Microbridge AWM3300V is a mass airflow sensor manufactured by Honeywell. A block diagram of the AWM3300V is shown in Figure 10.36.

The Microbridge mass airflow sensor AWM3300V is designed to measure the airflow. Its applications include air-conditioning, medical ventilation/anesthesia control, gas analyzers, gas metering, fume cabinet, and process control.

The AWM3300V operates on a single 10 V $\pm$ 10 mV power supply. The sensor output voltage corresponding to the airflow rate of 0 ~ 1.0 liter/min is 1.0 ~ 5 V. The AWM3300V can operate in the temperature range of -25 to $85°C$. It takes 3 ms for the output voltage to settle after power-up.

To simplify the conversion of A/D result to airflow, we need to use a circuit shifter to shift the output of the AWM3300 from 1~5 V to 0~5 V. The circuit in Figure 8.5c will be used. The values for resistors and V_1 are

$$V_1 = 5V, R_1 = 24K, R_f = 30K, R_2 = 120K, R_0 = 20K.$$

The circuit connection of the AWM3300V to Op-Amps is shown in Figure 10.37.

The circuit connection between the ADC1031 and the MCS-51 is illustrated in Figure 10.38. The 3-MHz clock is created by Timer 2 programmable clock output. After the setup of the circuit, the A/D conversion is started automatically. The microcontroller may need to wait for 3 ms for the sensor to settle. Since the A/D conversion takes no more than 13.7 μs to complete at 3 MHz, the MCS-51 should be able to read a valid result after a time delay that is longer than 3 ms.

In the following we will create a time delay of 5 ms so that the MCS-51 can read the valid conversion result.

1. Place the value of 60535 (EC77H) into the Timer 1 register so that it overflows in 5 ms.

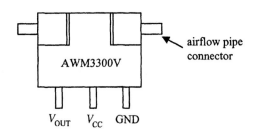

Figure 10.36 Microbridge AWM3300V.

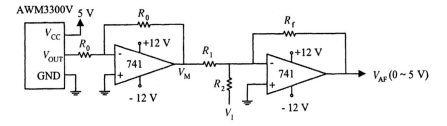

Figure 10.37 Level shifter circuit for the AWM3300V output.

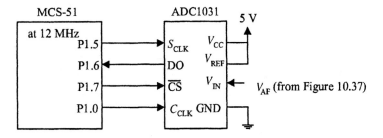

Figure 10.38 Connection between the MCS-51 and the ADC1031.

2. Configure Timer 1 to operate in mode 1 by loading the value 10H into the TMOD register.

The following instruction sequence creates a delay of 5 ms:

```
              mov   TMOD,#10H      ; set up Timer 1 in mode 1
              clr   TF1            ; clear Timer 1 overflow flag
              mov   TH1,#ECH       ; place the upper byte of the count in TH1
              mov   TL1,#77H       ; place the lower byte of the count in TL1
              setb  TR1            ; enable Timer 1 to operate
wait_5ms:     jnb   TF1,wait 5ms   ; wait until TF1 is set to 1
              clr   TR1
```

To use Timer 2 to generate a clock signal to be connected to the C_{CLK} pin, do the following:

- Set Timer 2 to timer mode and enable it by placing the value 04H into T2CON.
- Enable Timer 2 output by setting the T2OE bit in the T2MOD register.
- Place the value FFH into RCAP2H and RCAP2L registers.

The following instructions will generate a 3-MHz clock signal with 50% duty cycle from the P1.0 pin:

```
        mov   RCAP2H,#FFH
        mov   RCAP2L,#FFH
        mov   T2CON,#04H
        setb  T2OE
```

After making sure that the A/D conversion has started, we may read back the A/D conversion result. Two bytes are needed to hold the 10-bit conversion result. To shift the A/D result into the MCS-51/52, a falling edge on the S_{CLK} pin must be created. The following instruction sequence will read in the 10-bit A/D conversion result and store it in registers R2 and R3:

```
              clr   A
              clr   P1.7        ; enable DO pin of the ADC1031 to shift
                                ; out data
              setb  P1.6        ; set up P1.6 as an input
              mov   R1,#2       ; prepare to shift in the most significant
                                ; 2 bits
shift_lp1:    setb  P1.5        ; create a falling edge
              clr   P1.5        ; "
              mov   C,P1.6      ; copy a bit of A/D conversion result to C
              rlc   A           ; shift the new bit to the lsb of A
              djnz  R1,shift_lp1 ; are the upper 2 bits A/D conversion
                                ; shifted in yet?
              mov   R2,A
              clr   A           ; prepare to shift in the lower 8 bits
              mov   R1,#8       ; set up loop count
shift_lp2:    setb  P1.5        ; create a falling edge
              clr   P1.5        ; "
              mov   C,P1.6      ; copy a bit of A/D conversion result to C
              rlc   A           ; shift the new bit to the lsb of A
              djnz  R1,shift_lp2 ; have we done with shifting?
              mov   R3,A        ; save the lower 8 bits in register R3.
              setb  P1.7        ; disable DO output
```

The A/D conversion result 0 ~ 1023 corresponds to a mass airflow rate of 0 to 1000 ml/min. If accuracy is not very critical, we can simply translate the A/D conversion result 0 ~ 1000 to mass airflow 0 ~ 1000 ml/min, respectively, and assign anything higher than 1000 as the airflow rate 1000 ml/min. This will reduce the complexity and the length of our program. If accuracy is very critical, other methods need to be used. This problem will be left as an exercise.

The A/D conversion result can be displayed using the MC14489 and seven-segment displays. This is also very straightforward and hence will be left as an exercise.

10.12 D/A CONVERTERS WITH SERIAL INTERFACE

The AD7303 is a dual-channel, 8-bit voltage output DAC that operates from a single +2.7 to +5.5 V supply. This device uses a three-wire serial interface that operates at a clock rate up to 30 MHz. The device has a 16-bit input register; 8 bits act as data bits for the DACs, and the remaining 8 bits make up a control register.

The on-chip control register is used to address the relevant DAC, to power-down the complete device or an individual DAC, to select internal or external reference, and to provide a synchronous loading facility for simultaneous update of the DAC outputs with a software LDAC function. The block diagram and signal pins are shown in Figure 10.39.

10.12.1 The AD7303 Signal Pins

The functions of signal pins are as follows:

$V_{OUT}A$ **and** $V_{OUT}B$:   *Analog output voltage from DAC A and DAC B.*

REF: *External reference input.* This can be used as the reference for both DACs, and is selected by setting the INT/EXT bit in the control register to logic one. The range on this reference input is 1 V to $V_{DD}/2$.

SCLK: *Serial clock.* Data are clocked into the input shift register on the rising edges of the serial clock input. Data can be transferred at rates up to 30 MHz.

DIN: *Serial data input.* This device has a 16-bit shift register, 8 bits for data and 8 bits for control.

$\overline{SYNC}$:   *Level triggered control input (active low).* The low level of the SYNC signal enables the input shift register and data will be shifted in on the rising edges of the

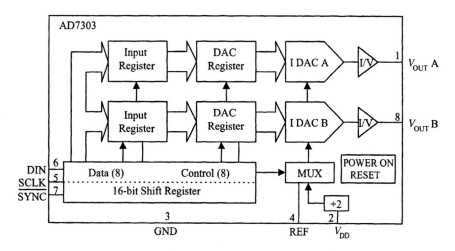

Figure 10.39 Functional block diagram of AD7303.

SCLK clock. The rising edge of the SYNC signal causes the relevant registers to be updated.

10.12.2 Functional Description

The reference voltage to the AD7303 can be internal or external. Internal reference voltage is set to $V_{DD}/2$. External reference voltage can be anywhere between 1.0 V and $V_{DD}/2$. The selection of the reference voltage is via a bit in the control register. The output voltage from either DAC is

$$V_{OUT}A/B = 2 \times V_{REF} \times (N/255)$$

where N is the decimal equivalent of the code loaded into the DAC register and ranges from 0 to 255.

When using the internal reference voltage, external reference should not be connected to the REF pin. In a noisy environment it is recommended that a $0.1\text{-}\mu F$ capacitor be connected to the REF pin to provide added decoupling even if the internal reference is selected.

An active low SYNC enables the shift register to receive data from the serial data input DIN. Data are clocked into the shift register on the rising edge of the serial clock. The shift register is 16 bits wide. The first 8 bits are control bits and the second 8 bits are data bits for the DACs. Each transfer must consist of a 16-bit transfer. Data are sent msb first and can be transmitted in one 16-bit write or two 8-bit writes. The SYNC input to the DAC should remain low until all 16 bits have been transferred to the shift register.

The contents and meaning of each bit of the shift register are shown in Table 10.6.

LDAC, A/B, CR1, and CR0 bits as illustrated in Table 10.7 control the data loading to the DACs.

TABLE 10.6
Contents of the AD7303 Shift Register

Bit Location	Mnemonic	Description
DB15	$\overline{INT}$/EXT	Selects between internal and external references
DB14	X	Undefined
DB13	LDAC	Load DAC bit for synchronous update of DAC outputs
DB12	PDB	Power-down DAC B
DB11	PDA	Power-down DAC A
DB10	$\overline{A}$/B	Address bit to select either DAC A or DAC B
DB9	CR1	Control bit 1 used in conjunction with CR0 to implement the various data loading functions
DB8	CR0	Control bit 0 used in conjunction with CR1 to implement the various data loading functions
DB7–DB0	Data	These bits contain the data used to update the outputs of the DACs

TABLE 10.7
Loading Control Bits

LDAC	$\overline{A}/B$	CR1	CR0	Function Implemented
0	x	0	0	Both DAC registers loaded from shift register
0	0	0	1	Update DAC A input register from shift register
0	1	0	1	Update DAC B input register from shift register
0	0	1	0	Update DAC A DAC register from input register
0	1	1	0	Update DAC B DAC register from input register
0	0	1	1	Update DAC A DAC register from shift register
0	1	1	1	Update DAC B DAC register from shift register
1	0	x	x	Load DAC A input register from shift register and update both DAC A and DAC B DAC registers
1	1	x	x	Load DAC B input register from shift register and update both DAC A and DAC B DAC registers

10.12.3 Interfacing the AD7303 with MCS-51 and 8XC51GB

Interfacing the AD7303 with MCS-51 or 8XC51GB is straightforward. Three pins are needed: one pin is used as data pin, the second pin is used as shift clock, and the third pin is connected to SYNC pin.

A D/A converter has many applications, for example, it can be used as a digitally programmable window detector. A digitally programmable upper/lower limit detector using the two DACs in the AD7303 is shown in Figure 10.40. The upper and lower limits for the test are loaded to DACs A and B, which in turn set the limits on the CMP04. The CMP04 is a quad analog comparator manufactured by Analog Devices. If a signal at the V_{IN} input is not within the programmed window, an LED will indicate the fail condition.

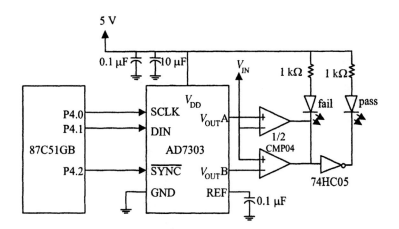

Figure 10.40 Window detector using the AD7303.

Example 10.9 Write a program to set the upper and lower limits for checking V_{IN} to 4.5 and 2 V, respectively.

Solution: Since the AD7303 shifts in data on the rising edge of SCLK, choose mode 0 operation of the SEP. Select the SEP speed to be $f_{OSC}/12$. Write the value 20H into the SEPCON register to set up the desired parameters and enable the SEP operation.

The circuit in Figure 10.40 uses internal reference. The voltage outputs for $V_{OUT}A$ and $V_{OUT}B$ should be set to 4.5 and 2.0 V, respectively. We need to write digital values 230 (E6) and 102 (66H) into DAC registers A and B, respectively.

Send the value 21E6H to the AD7303 to set up the upper window limit. The value 21H updates the input register A from the shift register. Send the value 2566H to the AD7303 to set up the lower window limit. The value 25H updates the input register B from the shift register.

The following program will implement the window detector:

```
                mov   SEPCON,#20H    ; enable the SEP subsystem
                clr   P4.2           ; pull the SYNC pin to low to enable
                                     ; data shifting
; The following instructions set up the upper limit of the window
                mov   SEPDAT,#21H    ; send the control byte to the AD7303
sep_waituu:     mov   A,SEPSTAT      ; "
                anl   A,#01H         ; "
                jz    sep_waituu     ; "
                anl   SEPSTAT,FEH    ; clear the SEPIF flag
                mov   SEPDAT,#E6H    ; send the upper limit value to the
                                     ; AD7303
sep_waitul:     mov   A,SEPSTAT      ; "
                anl   A,#01H         ; "
                jz    sep_waitul     ; "
                anl   SEPSTAT,FEH    ; clear the SEPIF flag
                setb  P4.2           ; pull SYNC to high to complete the
                                     ; transfer
; The following instructions set up the lower limit of the window
                clr   P4.2           ; pull SYNC to low to enable SEP
                                     ; shifting
                mov   SEPDAT,#25H    ; send the control byte to the AD7303
sep_waitlu:     mov   A,SEPSTAT      ; "
                anl   A,#01H         ; "
                jz    sep_waitlu     ; '
                anl   SEPSTAT,FEH    ; clear the SEPIF flag
                mov   SEPDAT,#66H    ; send the lower limit value to the
                                     ; AD7303
sep_waitll:     mov   A,SEPSTAT      ; "
```

```
        anl    A,#01H              ; "
        jz     sep_waitll          ; '
        anl    SEPSTAT,FEH         ; clear the SEPIF flag
        setb   P4.2                ; pull the SYNC to high to complete
                                   ; the transfer
        end
```

10.13 SUMMARY

The number of signal pins of an 8-bit microcontroller is quite limited. However, it is desirable to implement as many I/O functions as possible on that limited number of pins. In the real world, many applications do not need high data rate. Although using parallel data transfer can satisfy the data transmission need of these applications, it prevents more functions from being implemented on the same number of pins. The solution to this dilemma is to use serial data transfer. Philips' I²C, National Semiconductor's Microwire, Motorola's SPI, and Intel's Serial Expansion Port are examples of synchronous serial interface.

The SEP allows the 8XC51GB series microcontrollers to use two pins for data transfer in serial format. Other microcontrollers from Intel can also use a simulated method to transfer data in serial format. Many applications that do not need the on-chip A/D function of the 8XC51GB will use this option to interface with peripherals with serial interface. Two parties are involved in serial data transfer: a master and one or more slaves. The master supplies the clock to synchronize the data transfer. A slave can respond only to the data transfer. The Intel 8XC51GB series microcontrollers provide two signals for serial data transfer. However, most peripheral chips require an additional enable signal to perform serial data transfer.

Three registers are related to the SEP function. The SEPCON register allows us to enable the SEP function, select the data rate, clock polarity, and clock phase for data shifting. The SEPDAT register holds the data to be transferred using the SEP port. The SEPSTAT is the status register that records the SEP interrupt flag and error conditions for the previous SEP data transfer. An SEP output is started by writing a byte into the SEPDAT register with the SEPE bit of SEPCON set to 1. Setting the SEPE and SEPREN bits of SEPCON starts SEP input.

The 74HC589 is a shift register with parallel and serial data inputs and serial data output. Adding the 74HC589s can increment the number of parallel input ports.

The 74HC595 is a shift register with parallel and serial data outputs and serial data input. Adding the 74HC595s can expand the number of parallel output ports.

The MC14489 is a seven-segment display driver with serial interface. One MC14489 can drive up to five seven-segment displays. Multiple MC14489s can be cascaded to drive more than five seven-segment displays at the same time. An 8-bit configuration data byte must be sent before sending display data to the MC14489. Configuration and display data are shifted from the data in pin on the rising edge of the clock pin when the $\overline{\text{Enable}}$ signal is low. An external resistor is needed to set the brightness of LEDs driven by the MC14489.

The Xicor 24165 is a 2K × 8 E²PROM with serial interface. The X24165 has three address inputs, which allow up to eight X24165s to be added to the microcontroller at the same time. To start a data transfer, the microcontroller must send out a start command, followed by the address information and the direction of the data transfer (read or write). We can perform random byte write, page write, current address read, random read, and sequential read to or from the X24165. A significant amount of programming is needed to access the X24165.

The ADC1031 is a 10-bit A/D converter with serial interface. The ADC1031 operates on a 5-V power supply. Each analog sample takes no more than 13.7 μs to convert. The AWM3300V is a mass airflow sensor manufactured by Honeywell. The sensor output 1.0~5 V corresponds to the airflow rate of 0 ~ 1.0 liter/min. To improve the A/D accuracy, we can add a signal conditioning circuit to shift and scale the voltage output of the sensor to 0 ~ 5 V. By combining the use of an ADC1031 and an AWM3300, we can measure the mass airflow in a process plant.

The AD7303 is a dual-channel, 8-bit voltage output DAC that operates from a single +2.7 to +5.5-V power supply. This device uses a three-wire serial interface that operates at a clock rate up to 30 MHz. The device has a 16-bit input register; 8 bits act as data bits for the DACs and the remaining 8 bits act as a control register. One of the applications of the AD7303 is to detect if a signal falls within a window.

10.14 EXERCISES

10.1 Give a value to be written into the SEPCON register so that it will enable the SEP; select the falling clock edge to shift in data at the data rate of $f_{OSC}/24$. This value will also enable receive.

10.2 Give a value to be written into the SEPCON register so that it will enable the SEP; select the rising edge to shift out data bits at the frequency of $f_{OSC}/12$.

10.3 Write a program to read a byte from the 74HC589 controlled by pin P3.2 in Figure 10.7.

10.4 Write a program to output the values of 41H and 50H to the 74HC595s controlled by P1.2 and P1.0 in Figure 10.11, respectively.

10.5 Show a circuit that can drive four seven-segment displays using the 74HC595s and the 87C51FB.

10.6 Give a set of values to be written into the MC14489s to display the value of 92.6°F 16 35 09 20 97. How many MC14489s are needed?

10.7 Show a circuit that uses four MC14489s and seven-segment displays to display the current relative humidity, temperature, minute, hour, month, date, and year. Write a program to display the value 98.5H 65.4°F 12 00 09 16 97. The numbers are right justified. The most significant digit is not lighted.

10.8 Write a subroutine to clear the WEL bit of the WPR register of the X24165.

10.9 Write a subroutine to read a byte using the current address of the X24165.

10.10 Write a subroutine to poll the ACK signal until it is set after a write operation to the X24165.

10.11 Add four seven-segment displays to the circuit shown in Figure 10.38 and display the mass airflow. Update the display once every second. Write a program to perform the A/D conversion and update the display.

10.12 Use an 87C51FB to replace the 87C51GB in Figure 10.40 and write a program to set the upper and lower limits of the window. Use EQU directives to define upper and lower window limits.

10.13 What values should be written into the AD7303 in Figure 10.39 to set the upper and lower window limits to be 3.6 and 2.4 V, respectively.

10.15 LAB EXERCISES AND ASSIGNMENTS

10.1 **Keyboard scanning and debouncing.** Connect the 16-key (or a 24-key) keypad as shown in Figure 6.8 and use the MC14489 to display the entered hex digits. The entered digits should be shifted from the right to the left when more digits are entered. Use one MC14489 so that five hex digits can be displayed at a time. Write a main program to scan the keypad. The keypad should be blanked out at the beginning. Whenever a key is pressed, the program should perform the debounce operation. If the debounce program shows that the key is indeed pressed, the main program should update the display. If the user enters more than five digits, only the last five digits will be displayed.

10.2 **Temperature and time-of-day display.** Use the LM35 temperature sensor shown in Figure 8E.1 to measure the current temperature and two MC14489s to drive seven-segment displays. The current time of day is entered via serial port 1. The lab procedure is as follows:

STEP 1 Connect the circuit properly.

STEP 2 Write a program to read the current time in the order of hour, minute, and second. Each parameter is entered in two BCD digits. The hour digits are entered first.

STEP 3 Update the time using Timer 2.

STEP 4 Measure the room temperature once every second and update the displays also once every second.

APPENDIX A: MCS-51 INSTRUCTION EXECUTION TIMES

Mnemonic[a]		Description	Byte	Number of Machine Cycles	Oscillator Period
Arithmetic operations					
ADD	A,Rn	Add register to accumulator	1	1	12
ADD	A,direct	Add direct byte to accumulator	2	1	12
ADD	A,@Ri	Add indirect RAM to accumulator	1	1	12
ADD	A,#data	Add immediate data to accumulator	2	1	12
ADDC	A,Rn	Add register to accumulator with carry	1	1	12
ADDC	A,direct	Add direct byte to accumulator with carry	2	1	12
ADDC	A,@Ri	Add indirect RAM to accumulator with carry	1	1	12
ADDC	A,#data	Add immediate data to accumulator with carry	2	1	12
SUBB	A,Rn	Subtract register from accumulator with borrow	1	1	12
SUBB	A,direct	Subtract direct byte from accumulator with borrow	2	1	12
SUBB	A,@Ri	Subtract indirect RAM from accumulator with borrow	1	1	12
SUBB	A,#data	Subtract immediate data from accumulator with borrow	2	1	12
INC	A	Increment accumulator	1	1	12
INC	Rn	Increment register	1	1	12
INC	direct	Increment direct byte	2	1	12
INC	@Ri	Increment indirect RAM	1	1	12
INC	DPTR	Increment data pointer	1	1	12
DEC	A	Decrement accumulator	1	1	12
DEC	Rn	Decrement register	2	1	12
DEC	direct	Decrement direct byte	1	1	12
DEC	@Ri	Decrement indirect RAM	1	2	24
MUL	AB	Multiply A and B	1	4	48
DIV	AB	Divide A by B	1	4	48
DA	A	Decimal adjust accumulator	1	1	12

Continued

Mnemonic[a]		Description	Byte	Number of Machine Cycles	Oscillator Period
Logical operations					
ANL	A,Rn	AND register to accumulator	1	1	12
ANL	A,direct	AND direct byte to accumulator	2	1	12
ANL	A,@Ri	AND indirect RAM to accumulator	1	1	12
ANL	A,#data	AND immediate data to accumulator	2	1	12
ANL	direct,A	AND accumulator to direct byte	2	1	12
ANL	direct,#data	AND immediate data to direct byte	3	2	24
ORL	A,Rn	OR register to accumulator	1	1	12
ORL	A,direct	OR direct byte to accumulator	2	1	12
ORL	A,@Ri	OR indirect RAM to accumulator	1	1	12
ORL	A,#data	OR immediate data to accumulator	2	1	12
ORL	direct,A	OR accumulator to direct byte	2	1	12
ORL	direct,#data	OR immediate data to direct byte	3	2	24
XRL	A,Rn	Exclusive-OR register to accumulator	1	1	12
XRL	A,direct	Exclusive-OR direct byte to accumulator	2	1	12
XRL	A,@Ri	Exclusive-OR indirect RAM to accumulator	1	1	12
XRL	A,#data	Exclusive-OR immediate data to accumulator	2	1	12
XRL	direct,A	Exclusive-OR accumulator to direct byte	2	1	12
XRL	direct,#data	Exclusive-OR immediate data to direct byte	3	2	24
CLR	A	Clear accumulator	1	1	12
CPL	A	Complement accumulator	1	1	12
RL	A	Rotate accumulator left	1	1	12
RLC	A	Rotate accumulator left through carry	1	1	12
RR	A	Rotate accumulator right	1	1	12
RRC	A	Rotate accumulator right through carry	1	1	12
SWAP	A	Swip nibbles within accumulator	1	1	12
Data transfer					
MOV	A,Rn	Move register to accumulator	1	1	12
MOV	A,direct	Move direct byte to accumulator	2	1	12
MOV	A,@Ri	Move indirect RAM to accumulator	1	1	12
MOV	A,#data	Move immediate data to accumulator	2	1	12
MOV	Rn,A	Move accumulator to register	1	1	12
MOV	Rn,direct	Move direct byte to register	2	2	24
MOV	Rn,#data	Move immediate data to register	2	1	12
MOV	direct,A	Move accumulator to direct byte	2	1	12
MOV	direct,Rn	Move register to direct byte	2	2	24
MOV	direct,direct	Move direct byte to direct byte	3	2	24
MOV	direct,@Ri	Move indirect RAM to direct byte	2	2	24
MOV	direct,#data	Move immediate data to direct byte	3	2	24

Continued

Mnemonic[a]		Description	Byte	Number of Machine Cycles	Oscillator Period
MOV	@Ri,A	Move accumulator to indirect RAM	1	1	12
MOV	@Ri,direct	Move direct byte to indirect RAM	2	2	24
MOV	@Ri,#data	Move immediate data to indirect RAM	2	1	12
MOV	DPTR,#data16	Load data pointer with a 16-bit constant	3	2	24
MOVC	A,@A+DPTR	Move code byte relative to DPTR to accumulator	1	2	24
MOVC	A,@A+PC	Move code byte relative to PC to accumulator	1	2	24
MOVX	A,@Ri	Move external (8-bit address) RAM to accumulator	1	2	24
MOVX	A,@DPTR	Move external (16-bit address) RAM to accumulator	1	2	24
MOVX	@Ri,A	Move accumulator to external RAM (8-bit address)	1	2	24
MOVX	@DPTR,A	Move accumulator to external RAM (16-bit address)	1	2	24
PUSH	direct	Push direct byte onto stack	2	2	24
POP	direct	Pop direct byte from stack	2	2	24
XCH	A,Rn	Exchange register with accumulator	1	1	12
XCH	A,direct	Exchange direct byte with accumulator	2	1	12
XCH	A,@Ri	Exchange indirect RAM with accumulator	1	1	12
XCHD	A,@Ri	Exchange low order digit of indirect RAM with accumulator	1	1	12
Boolean variable manipulation					
CLR	C	Clear carry	1	1	12
CLR	bit	Clear direct bit	2	1	12
SETB	C	Set carry	1	1	12
SETB	bit	Set direct bit	2	1	12
CPL	C	Complement carry	1	1	12
CPL	bit	Complement direct bit	2	1	12
ANL	C,bit	AND direct bit with carry	2	2	24
ANL	C,/bit	AND complement of direct bit with carry	2	2	24
ORL	C,bit	OR direct bit with carry	2	2	24
ORL	C,/bit	OR complement of direct bit with carry	2	2	24
MOV	C,bit	Move direct bit to carry	2	1	12
MOV	bit,C	Move carry to direct bit	2	2	24
JC	rel	Jump if carry is set	2	2	24
JNC	rel	Jump if carry is not set	2	2	24
JB	bit,rel	Jump if direct bit is set	3	2	24
JNB	bit,rel	Jump if direct bit is not set	3	2	24
JBC	bit,rel	Jump if direct bit is set and clear it	3	2	24

Continued

Mnemonic[a]		Description	Byte	Number of Machine Cycles	Oscillator Period
Program branching					
ACALL	addr11	Absolute subroutine call	2	2	24
LCALL	addr16	Long subroutine call	3	2	24
RET		Return from subroutine	1	2	24
RETI		Return from interrupt	1	2	24
AJMP	addr11	Absolute jump	2	2	24
LJMP	addr16	Long jump	3	2	24
SJMP	rel	Short jump (relative address)	2	2	24
JMP	@A+DPTR	Jump indirect relative to the DPTR	1	2	24
JZ	rel	Jump if accumulator is zero	2	2	24
JNZ	rel	Jump if accumulator is not zero	2	2	24
CJNE	A,direct,rel	Compare direct byte to accumulator and jump if not equal	3	2	24
CJNE	A,#data,rel	Compare immediate data to accumulator and jump if not equal	3	2	24
CJNE	Rn,#data,rel	Compare immediate data to register and jump if not equal	3	2	24
CJNE	@Ri,#data,rel	Compare immediate data to indirect RAM and jump if not equal	3	2	24
DJNZ	Rn,rel	Decrement register and jump if not equal to zero	2	2	24
DJNZ	direct,rel	Decrement direct byte and jump if not equal to zero	3	2	24
NOP		No operation	1	1	12

[a]Ri, R1 or R0; Rn, R7 . . . R0.

APPENDIX B: SPECIAL FUNCTION REGISTERS

Address	Symbol	Bit 7	Bit 6	Bit 5	Bit 4	Bit 3	Bit 2	Bit 1	Bit 0
80H	P0	P0.7	P0.6	P0.5	P0.4	P0.3	P0.2	P0.1	P0.0
81H	SP								
82H	DPL								
83H	DPH								
84H	DPL1[a]								
85H	DPH1[a]								
86H	DPS[a]	0	0	0	0	0	0	0	SEL
87H	PCON	SMOD_0	SMOD0	—	—	GF1	GF0	STOP	IDLE
88H	TCON	TF1	TR1	TF0	TR0	IE1	IT1	IE0	M0
89H	TMOD	GATE	C/$\overline{\text{T}}$	M1	M0	GATE	C/$\overline{\text{T}}$	M1	M0
8AH	TL0								
8BH	TL1								
8CH	TH0								
8DH	TH1								
8EH	CKCON[a]	WD1	WD0	T2M	T1M	T0M	MD2	MD1	MD0
90H	P1	P1.7	P1.6	P1.5	P1.4	P1.3	P1.2	P1.1	P1.0
98H	SCON0	SM0/FE_0	SM1_0	SM2_0	REN_0	TB8_0	RB8_0	TI_0	RI_0
99H	SBUF0								
A0H	P2	P2.7	P2.6	P2.5	P2.4	P2.3	P2.2	P2.1	P2.0
A8H	IE	EA	EC	ET2	ES0	ET1	EX1	ET0	EX0
B0H	P3	P3.7	P3.6	P3.5	P3.4	P3.3	P3.2	P3.1	P3.0
B8H	IP	—	PS1	PT2	PS0	PT1	PX1	PT0	PX0
C0H	SCON1[a]	SM0/FE_1	SM1_1	SM2_1	REN_1	TB8_1	RB8_1	TI_1	RI_1
C1H	SBUF1[a]								
C8H	T2CON	TF2	EXF2	RCLK	TCLK	EXEN2	TR2	C/$\overline{\text{T2}}$	CP/$\overline{\text{RL2}}$
C9H	T2MOD	—	—	—	—	—	—	T2OE	DCEN
CAH	RCAP2L								
CBH	RCAP2H								
CCH	TL2								
CDH	TH2								
D0H	PSW	CY	AC	F0	RS1	RS0	OV	FL	P
D8H	WDCON[a]	SMOD_1	POR	EPF1	PF1	WDIF	WTRF	EWT	RWT
D8H	CCON	CF	CR	—	CCF4	CCF3	CCF2	CCF1	CCF0

Continued

Address	Symbol	Bit 7	Bit 6	Bit 5	Bit 4	Bit 3	Bit 2	Bit 1	Bit 0
D9H	CMOD	CIDL	WDTE	—	—	—	CPS1	CPS0	ECF
DAH	CCAPM0	—	ECOM0	CAPP0	CAPN0	MAT0	TOG0	PWM0	ECCF0
DBH	CCAPM1	—	ECOM1	CAPP1	CAPN1	MAT1	TOG1	PWM1	ECCF1
DCH	CCAPM2	—	ECOM2	CAPP2	CAPN2	MAT2	TOG2	PWM2	ECCF2
DDH	CCAPM3	—	ECOM3	CAPP3	CAPN3	MAT3	TOG3	PWM3	ECCF3
DEH	CCAPM4	—	ECOM4	CAPP4	CAPN4	MAT4	TOH4	PWM4	ECCF4
E0H	ACC								
E9H	CL								
EAH	CCAP0L								
EBH	CCAP1L								
ECH	CCAP2L								
EDH	CCAP3L								
EEH	CCAP4L								
F0H	B								
F9H	CH								
FAH	CCAP0H								
FBH	CCAP1H								
FCH	CCAP2H								
FDH	CCAP3H								
FEH	CCAP4H								

[a]Exists only in DS87C520.

APPENDIX C: MCS-51/52 INTERRUPT VECTORS

Interrupt Source	Vector Address
INT0 external interrupt	0003H
Timer 0 interrupt	000BH
INT1 external interrupt	0013H
Timer 1 interrupt	001BH
Serial port interrupt	0023H
Timer 2 interrupt	002BH

APPENDIX D: STANDARD VALUES OF COMMERCIALLY AVAILABLE RESISTORS

Ohms (Ω)					Kiloohms ($\kappa\Omega$)		Megaohms ($M\Omega$)	
0.10	1.0	10	100	1000	10	100	1.0	10.0
0.11	1.1	11	110	1100	11	110	1.1	11.0
0.12	1.2	12	120	1200	12	120	1.2	12.0
0.13	1.3	13	130	1300	13	130	1.3	13.0
0.15	1.5	15	150	1500	15	150	1.5	15.0
0.16	1.6	16	160	1600	16	160	1.6	16.0
0.18	1.8	18	180	1800	18	180	1.8	18.0
0.20	2.0	20	200	2000	20	200	2.0	20.0
0.22	2.2	22	220	2200	22	220	2.2	22.0
0.24	2.4	24	240	2400	24	240	2.4	
0.27	2.7	27	270	2700	27	270	2.7	
0.30	3.0	30	300	3000	30	300	3.0	
0.33	3.3	33	330	3300	33	330	3.3	
0.36	3.6	36	360	3600	36	360	3.6	
0.39	3.9	39	390	3900	39	390	3.9	
0.43	4.3	43	430	4300	43	430	4.3	
0.47	4.7	47	470	4700	47	470	4.7	
0.51	5.1	51	510	5100	51	510	5.1	
0.56	5.6	56	560	5600	56	560	5.6	
0.62	6.2	62	620	6200	62	620	6.2	
0.68	6.8	68	680	6800	68	680	6.8	
0.75	7.5	75	750	7500	75	750	7.5	
0.82	8.2	82	820	8200	82	820	8.2	
0.91	9.1	91	910	9100	91	910	9.1	

APPENDIX E: VENDORS OF SOFTWARE AND HARDWARE DEVELOPMENT TOOLS

Software Tools Vendors

Company	Address	Tools
2500AD Software	109 Brookdale Ave., P.O. Box 480 Buena Vista, CO 81211 (800) 843-8144	Assembler, C compiler, simulator
Avocet Systems Inc.	120 Union St., Rockport, ME 04856 (800) 448-8500 (207) 236-9055 www.avocetsystems.com	Assembler, C compiler, simulator, debugger
BSO Tasking	International 333 Elm Street, Dedham, MA 02026-4530 (800) 458-8276 (617) 320-9400 www.bsotasking.com	Assembler, C compiler, simulator, debugger, integrated development environment
Chiptools Inc.	1232 Stavebank Rd., Mississauga, Ontario, Canada L5G 2V2 (801) 274-6244 www.chiptools.com	Borland-like debugger
Crossware Products	Old Post House, Silver Street, Litling-ton, Royston, Herts, SG8 0QE, UK +44 (0) 1763 853500 www.crossware.com	Assembler, C compiler, simulator
Dunfield Development Systems	P.O. Box, 31044, Nepean, Ontario, Canada K2B 8S8 (613) 256-5820 www.dunfield.com	Assembler, C compiler, debugger, integrated development environment
Franklin Software	888 Saratoga Ave., #2 San Jose, CA 95129 (408) 296-8051 www.fsinc.com	Assembler, C compiler, debugger, integrated development environment
IAR Systems Software, Inc.	One Maritime Plaza, San Francisco, CA 94111 (415) 765-5500 www.iar.com	Assembler, C compiler, integrated development environment
Keil Software	16990 Dallas Parkway, Suite 120, Dallas, TX 75248 (800) 348-8051 (214) 735-8052 www.keil.com	Assembler, C compiler, debugger, integrated development environment
Systronics	555S. 300 east #21 Salt Lake City, UT 84111 (905) 274-6244 www.systron.com	Basic compiler

Continued

Company	Address	Tools
Production Language Corp.	P.O. Box, 109, Weatherford, TX 76086 (800) 525-6289 (817) 599-8363 www.plcorp.com	Assembler, C compiler, debugger, integrated development environment
Hi-Tech Software	P.O. Box 103, Alderly QLD 4051, Australia (+61-7) 300-5011 www.hitech.com.au	Assembler, C compiler, debugger, integrated development environment
Intermetrics Microsystems Software	733 Concord Ave. Cambridge, MA 02138 (613) 829-3196	Assembler, C compiler, debugger
Mandeno Granville Electronics, Ltd.	128 Grange Rd., Auckland 3, New Zealand (+64) 9 6301 720	C compiler
Micro Computer Control	P.O. Box 275, 17 Model Ave. Hopewell, NJ 08525 (609) 466-1751 www.mcc-us.com	Assembler, C compiler

Board Products Vendors

Company	Address	Products
Binary Technology	463 Autumn Lane, Carlisle, MA 01741 (978) 369-9556	8051 evaluation board
Blue Earth Research	410 Belle Ave. Mankato, MN 56001 (507) 387-4001	8031-based development kits
Ceibo USA	7 Edgestone Ct. Florissant, MO 63033 (800) 833-4084 www.ceibo.com	DB-51 evaluation board
Hitech Equipment Corp.	9400 Activity Rd. San Diego, CA 92126 (619) 566-1892 www.hte.com	Single board computers based on 8031, 8032, and 80552
Intel Corp.	2200 Mission College Blvd. Santa Clara, CA 95052-8118 (800) 468-8188 www.intel.com	FX51 Target Board
Keil Software	16990 Dallas Parkway, Suite 120, Dallas, TX 75248 (800) 348-8051 (214) 735-8052 www.keil.com	MCB520 evaluation board based on 33 MHz Dallas 87C520
Micromint	4 Park Street Vernon, CT 06066 (800) 635-3355 (860) 871-6170 www.micromint.com	80C52-based evaluation board
New Micros Inc.	1601 Chalk Hill Rd. Dallas, TX 75212 (214) 339-2204 www.newmicros.com	Siemens 80535-based evaluation board
Rostek inc.	P.O. Box 6719 South Bend, IN 46660 (219) 272-3239	Philips 80552-based evaluation board PU552

APPENDIX F: SUMMARY OF MCS-51 VARIANTS

Device	Features
Atmel: 2125 O'Nel Drive, San Jose, CA 95131, (800) 365-3375 (408) 441-0311, www.atmel.com	
AT1051	64 bytes SRAM, 1 KB flash memory, 20 pins, 1 16-bit timer, 1 UART, 24 MHz
AT2051	128 bytes SRAM, 2 KB flash memory, 20 pins, 2 16-bit timers, 1 UART, 24 MHZ
AT89C51	128 bytes SRAM, 4 KB flash memory, 32 I/O pins, 2 16-bit timers, 1 UART, 24 MHz
AT89C52	256 bytes SRAM, 8 KB flash memory, 32 I/O pins, 3 16-bit timers, 1 UART, 24 MHz
AT89C55	256 bytes SRAM, 20 KB flash memory, 32 I/O pins, 3 16-bit timers, 1 UART, 33 MHz
AT89LS8252	256 bytes SRAM, 8K flash memory, 2K EEPROM, 32 I/O pins, 3 16-bit timers, 1 UART, 1 SPI, two DPTRs, 12 MHz
AT89S8252	256 bytes SRAM, 8K flash memory, 2K EEPROM, 32 I/O pins, 3 16-bit timers, 1 UART, 1 SPI, two DPTRs, watchdog timer, 24 MHz
AT89LV51	128 bytes SRAM, 4 KB flash memory, 32 I/O pins, 2 16-bit timers, 1 UART, 12 MHz
AT89LV52	256 bytes SRAM, 8 KB flash memory, 32 I/O pins, 3 16-bit timers, 1 UART, 12 MHz
AT89LV55	256 bytes SRAM, 20 KB flash memory, 32 I/O pins, 3 16-bit timers, 1 UART, 12 MHz
AT89S53	256 bytes SRAM, 12 KB flash memory, 32 I/O pins, 3 16-bit timers, 1 UART, SPI, 2 DPTRs, watchdog timer, 24 MHz
AT89S4D12	256 bytes SRAM, 128K flash memory, 5 I/O pins, 12-MHz on-chip oscillator, SPI, 2 DPTRs, 3.3 power supply
AT89C4051	128 bytes SRAM, 4K flash memory, 20 pins, analog comparator, 2 16-bit timers, 1 UART, 16 MHz
Dallas Semiconductor: 4401 South Beltwood Parkway, Dallas, TX 75244-3292, (214) 450-0448, www.dalsemi.com	
DS80C310	256 bytes SRAM, 4 clocks/machine cycle, 3 16-bit timers, 32 I/O pins, 2 DPTRs, 1 UART, 0~33 MHz
DS80C320	256 bytes SRAM, 4 clocks/machine cycle, 3 16-bit timers, 32 I/O pis, 2 DPTRs, 2 UART, watchdog timer, 0~33 MHz
DS87C520	256 bytes SRAM, 16 KB EPROM, 1 KB XRAM,[a] 4 clocks/machine cycle, 3 16-bit timers, 32 I/O pins, 2 DPTRs, 2 UARTs, watchdog timer, power management mode, 0~33 MHz
DS87C530	256 bytes SRAM, 16 KB EPROM, 1 KB XRAM, 4 clocks/machine cycle, 3 16-bit timers, 32 I/O pins, 2 DPTRs, 2 UARTs, watchdog timer, power management mode, real-time clock, 0~33 MHz
Intel: 2200 Mission College Blvd. P.O. Box 58119, Santa Clara, CA 95052-8119, (408) 765-8080	
8031AH	128 bytes SRAM, 32 I/O pins, 2 16-bit timers, 1 UART, 12 MHz
8051AH	128 bytes SRAM, 4 KB ROM, 32 I/O pins, 2 16-bit timers, 1 UART, 12 MHz
8051AHP	128 bytes SRAM, 4 KB ROM, 32 I/O pins, 2 16-bit timers, 1 UART, 12 MHz, 1 lock
8751H	128 bytes SRAM, 4 KB EPROM, 32 I/O pins, 2 16-bit timers, 1 UART, 12 MHz
8751BH	128 bytes SRAM, 4 KB EPROM, 32 I/O pins, 2 16-bit timers, 1 UART, 12 MHz, 2 locks
8032AH	256 bytes SRAM, 32 I/O pins, 3 16-bit timers, 1 UART, 12 MHz
8052AH	256 bytes SRAM, 8 KB ROM, 32 I/O pins, 3 16-bit timers, 1 UART, 12 MHz

Continued

451

Device	Features
8752BH	256 bytes SRAM, 8 KB EPROM, 32 I/O pins, 3 16-bit timers, 1 UART, 12 MHz, 2 locks
80C31BH	128 bytes SRAM, 32 I/O pins, 2 16-bit timers, 1 UART, 12, 16 MHz
80C51BH	128 bytes SRAM, 4 KB ROM, 32 I/O pins, 2 16-bit timers, 1 UART, 12, 16 MHz
80C51BHP	128 bytes SRAM, 4 KB ROM, 32 I/O pins, 2 16-bit timers, 1 UART, 12, 16 MHz, 1 lock
87C51	128 bytes SRAM, 4 KB EPROM, 32 I/O pins, 2 16-bit timers, 1 UART, 12, 16, 20, 24 MHz, 3 locks
80C32	256 bytes SRAM, 32 I/O pins, 3 16-bit timers, 1 UART, 12, 16, 20, 24 MHz, 3 locks
80C52	256 bytes SRAM, 8 KB ROM, 32 I/O pins, 3 16-bit timers, 1 UART, 12, 16, 20, 24 MHz, 1 lock
87C52	256 bytes SRAM, 8 KB EPROM, 32 I/O pins, 3 16-bit timers, 1 UART, 12, 16, 20, 24 MHz, 3 locks
80C54	256 bytes SRAM, 16 KB ROM, 32 I/O pins, 3 16-bit timers, 1 UART, 12, 16, 20, 24 MHz, 1 lock
87C54	256 bytes SRAM, 16 KB EPROM, 32 I/O pins, 3 16-bit timers, 1 UART, 12, 16, 20, 24 MHz, 3 locks
80C58	256 bytes SRAM, 32 KB ROM, 32 I/O pins, 3 16-bit timers, 1 UART, 12, 16, 20, 24 MHz, 1 lock
87C58	256 bytes SRAM, 32 KB EPROM, 32 I/O pins, 3 16-bit timers, 1 UART, 12, 16, 20, 24 MHz, 3 locks
80L52	256 bytes SRAM, 8 KB ROM, 32 I/O pins, 3 16-bit timers, 1 UART, 12, 16, 20 MHz, 1 lock
87L52	256 bytes SRAM, 8 KB OTP ROM, 32 I/O pins, 3 16-bit timers, 1 UART, 12, 16, 20, MHz, 3 locks
80L54	256 bytes SRAM, 16 KB ROM, 32 I/O pins, 3 16-bit timers, 1 UART, 12, 16, 20, MHz, 1 lock
87L54	256 bytes SRAM, 16 KB OTP ROM, 32 I/O pins, 3 16-bit timers, 1 UART, 12, 16, 20, 24 MHz, 3 locks
80L58	256 bytes SRAM, 32 KB ROM, 32 I/O pins, 3 16-bit timers, 1 UART, 12, 16, 20, MHz, 1 lock
87L58	256 bytes SRAM, 32 KB OTP ROM, 32 I/O pins, 3 16-bit timers, 1 UART, 12, 16, 20, 24 MHz, 3 locks
80C51FA	256 bytes SRAM, 32 I/O pins, 3 16-bit timers, 1 PCA, 1 UART, 12, 16 MHz
83C51FA	256 bytes SRAM, 8 KB ROM, 32 I/O pins, 3 16-bit timers, 1 PCA, 1 UART, 12, 16 MHz
87C51FA	256 bytes SRAM, 8 KB EPROM, 32 I/O pins, 3 16-bit timers, 1 PCA, 1 UART, 3 locks, 12, 16, 20, 24 MHz
83C51FB	256 bytes SRAM, 16 KB ROM, 32 I/O pins, 3 16-bit timers, 1 PCA, 1 UART, 1 lock, 12, 16, 20, 24 MHz
87C51FB	256 bytes SRAM, 16 KB EPROM, 32 I/O pins, 3 16-bit timers, 1 PCA, 1 UART, 3 locks, 12, 16, 20, 24 MHz
83C51FC	256 bytes SRAM, 32 KB ROM, 32 I/O pins, 3 16-bit timers, 1 PCA, 1 UART, 1 lock, 12, 16, 20, 24, MHz
87C51FC	256 bytes SRAM, 32 KB EPROM, 32 I/O pins, 3 16-bit timers, 1 PCA, 1 UART, 3 locks, 12, 16, 20, 24 MHz
80L51FA	256 bytes SRAM, 32 I/O pins, 3 16-bit timers, 1 PCA, 1 UART, 12, 16, 20 MHz
83L51FA	256 bytes SRAM, 8 KB ROM, 32 I/O pins, 3 16-bit timers, 1 PCA, 1 UART, 1 lock, 12, 16, 20, MHz
87L51FA	256 bytes SRAM, 8 KB OTP ROM, 32 I/O pins, 3 16-bit timers, 1 PCA, 1 UART, 3 locks, 12, 16, 20 MHz
83L51FB	256 bytes SRAM, 16K ROM, 32 I/O pins, 3 16-bit timers, 1 PCA, 1 UART, 1 lock, 12, 16, 20 MHz

Continued

Device	Features
87L51FB	256 bytes SRAM, 16 KB OTP ROM, 32 I/O pins, 3 16-bit timers, 1 PCA, 1 UART, 3 locks, 12, 16, 20 MHz
83L51FC	256 bytes SRAM, 32K ROM, 32 I/O pins, 3 16-bit timers, 1 PCA, 1 UART, 1 lock, 12, 16, 20, MHz
87L51FC	256 bytes SRAM, 32 KB OTP ROM, 32 I/O pins, 3 16-bit timers, 1 PCA, 1 UART, 3 locks, 12, 16, 20 MHz
80C51GB	256 bytes SRAM, 48 I/O pins, 3 16-bit timers, 2 PCAs, 1 UART, 8-bit A/D, 12, 16 MHz
83C51GB	256 bytes SRAM, 8K ROM, 48 I/O pins, 3 16-bit imers, 2 PCAs, 1 UART, 8-bit A/D, 1 lock, 12, 16 MHz
87C51GB	256 bytes SRAM, 8K EPROM, 48 I/O pins, 3 16-bit timers, 2 PCAs, 1 UART, 8-bit A/D, 3 locks, 12, 16 MHz
80C152JA	256 bytes SRAM, 40 I/O pins, 2 16-bit timers, 1 UART, 1 SEP, DMA, 16.5 MHz
80C152JB	256 bytes SRAM, 56 I/O pins, 2 16-bit timers, 1 UART, 1 SEP, DMA, 16.5 MHz
83C152JA	256 bytes SRAM, 8K ROM, 40 I/O pins, 2 16-bit timers, 1 UART, 1 SEP, DMA, 16.5 MHz
80C51SL-BG	256 bytes SRAM, 24 I/O pins, 2 16-bit timers, 1 UART, 8-bit A/D, 16 MHz
81C51SL-BG	256 bytes SRAM, 8K ROM (with BIOS), 24 I/O pins, 2 16-bit timers, 1 UART, 8-bit A/D, 16 MHz
83C51SL-BG	256 bytes SRAM, 8K ROM, 24 I/O pins, 2 16-bit timers, 1 UART, 8-bit A/D, 16 MHz
80C51SLAH	256 bytes SRAM, 24 I/O pins, 2 16-bit timers, 1 UART, 8-bit A/D, 16 MHz
81C51SLAH	256 bytes SRAM, 16K ROM (with BIOS), 24 I/O pins, 2 16-bit timers, 1 UART, 8-bit A/D, 16 MHz
83C51SLAH	256 bytes SRAM, 16K ROM, 24 I/O pins, 2 16-bit timers, 1 UART, 8-bit A/D, 16 MHZ
87C51SLAH	256 bytes SRAM, 16K EPROM, 24 I/O pins, 2 16-bit timers, 1 UART, 8-bit A/D, 16 MHZ

ISSI: 2231 Lawson Lane, Santa Clara, CA 95054, (800) 379-4774, www.issi.com

Device	Features
IS80C51	128 bytes SRAM, 4 KB ROM, 32 I/O pins, 2 16-bit timers, 1 UART, 40 MHz
IS80C52	256 bytes SRAM, 8 KB ROM, 32 I/O pins, 3 16-bit timers, 1 UART, 40 MHz
IS89C51	128 bytes SRAM, 4 KB flash, 32 I/O pins, 2 16-bit timers, 1 UART, 40 MHz
IS89C52	256 bytes SRAM, 8 KB flash, 32 I/O pins, 3 16-bit timers, 1 UART, 40 MHz

OKI: U.S. Administration, Three University Plaza, Hackensack, NJ 07601 Tel: (201) 646-0011

Device	Features
83C154	256 bytes SRAM, 16K ROM, 32 I/O pins, 3 16-bit timers, 1 UART, 12 MHz

Phillips: 811 East Arques Ave. P.O. Box 3409, Sunnyvale, CA 94088-3409, (800) 447-1500

Device	Features
80C451	128 bytes SRAM, 52 I/O pins, 2 16-bit timers, 1 UART, 12 MHz
83C451	128 bytes SRAM, 4 KB ROM, 52 I/O pins, 2 16-bit timers, 1 UART, 12 MHz
87C451	128 bytes SRAM, 4 KB OTP EPROM, 52 I/O pins, 2 16-bit timers, 1 UART, 12 MHz
80C51	128 bytes SRAM, 4 KB ROM, 32 I/O pins, 3 16-bit timers, 1 UART, 33 MHz
87C51	128 bytes SRAM, 4 KB OTP EPROM, 32 I/O pins, 2 16-bit timers, 1 UART, 33MHz
80C31	128 bytes SRAM, 32 I/O pins, 1 16-bit timer, 1 UART, 33 MHz
80C550	128 bytes SRAM, 32 I/O pins, 8-bit A/D, watchdog timer, 2 16-bit timers, 1 UART, 16 MHz
83C550	128 bytes SRAM, 4K ROM, 32 I/O pins, 8-bit A/D, watchdog timer, 2 16-bit timers, 1 UART, 16 MHz
87C550	128 bytes SRAM, 4K OTP EPROM, 32 I/O pins, 8-bit A/D, watchdog timer, 2 16-bit timers, 1 UART, 16 MHz
80C552	256 bytes SRAM, 48 I/O pins, 10-bit A/D, watchdog timer, 3 16-bit timers, 2 PWMs, 1 UART, 12C bus, 16, 24, 33 MHz
83C552	256 bytes SRAM, 8K ROM, 48 I/O pins, 10-bit A/D, watchdog timer, 3 16-bit timers, 2 PWMs, 1 UART, 12C bus, 16, 24, 33 MHz

Continued

Device	Features
87C522	256 bytes SRAM, 8K EPROM, 48 I/O pins, 10-bit A/D, watchdog timer, 3 16-bit timers, 2 PWMs, 1 UART, 12C, 16, 24, 33 MHz
80C575	256 bytes SRAM, 32 I/O pins, watchdog timer, 3 16-bit timers, 1 PCA, 1 UART, on-chip oscillator, 4 analog comparators, 16 MHz
83C575	256 bytes SRAM, 8K ROM, 32 I/O pins, watchdog timer, 3 16-bit timers, 1 PCA, 1 UART, on-chip oscillator, 4 analog comparators, 16 MHz
87C575	256 bytes SRAM, 8K EPROM, 32 I/O pins, watchdog timer, 3 16-bit timers, 1 PCA, 1 UART, on-chip oscillator, 4 analog comparators, 16 MHz
80C652	256 bytes SRAM, 32 I/O pins, watchdog timer, 2 16-bit timers, 12C bus, 1 UART, 16, 20 MHz
83C652	256 bytes SRAM, 8K ROM, 32 I/O pins, watchdog timer, 2 16-bit timers, I2C bus, 1 UART, 16, 20 MHz
87C652	256 bytes SRAM, 8K EPROM, 32 I/O pins, watchdog timer, 2 16-bit timers, I2C bus, 1 UART, 16, 20 MHz
80C851	128 bytes SRAM, 256 EEPROM, 52 I/O pins, 2 16-bit timers, 1 UART, 16 MHz
83C851	128 bytes SRAM, 4K ROM, 256 EEPROM, 52 I/O pins, 2 16-bit timers, 1 UART, 16 MHz
80C453	256 bytes SRAM, 2 16-bit timers, 56 I/O pins, 1 UART, 16 MHz
83C453	256 bytes SRAM, 8K ROM, 2 16-bit timers, 56 I/O pins, 1 UART, 16 MHz
87C453	256 bytes SRAM, 8K EPROM, 2 16-bit timers, 56 I/O pins, 1 UART, 16 MHz
83C145 (for TV and video)	256 bytes SRAM, 8K ROM, on screen display controller, three video outputs, 128 × 10 bits display SRAM, character generator ROM, 8 text shadowing modes, 8 6-bit PWMs, 1 14-bit PWM, D/A converter, 37 I/O pins, 2 16-bit timers, 12 + 12 V outputs, 1 UART
83C845	Same as 83C145 except that 83C845 has 12K ROM
83C055	Same as 83C145 except that 83C845 has 16K ROM
87C845	Same as 83C145 except that 83C845 has 16K OTP ROM
80C34	256 bytes SRAM, 3 16-bit timers, 32 I/O pins, 1 UART, 24 MHz
80C54	256 bytes SRAM, 16K ROM, 3 16-bit timers, 32 I/O pins, 1 UART, 24 MHz
87C54	256 bytes SRAM, 16K EPROM, 3 16-bit timers, 32 I/O pins, 1 UART, 24 MHz
83CE654	256 bytes SRAM, 16K ROM, 2 16-bit timers, 32 I/O pins, 1 UART, I2C bus, EMC, 16 MHz
83C654	256 bytes SRAM, 16K ROM, 2 16-bit timers, 32 I/O pins, 1 UART, 12C bus, 24 MHZ
P80CE559	1.5K SRAM, 2 16-bit timers, 48 I/O pins, 10-bit A/D, watchdog timer, PLL oscillator, PCA, 2 PWMs, 1 UART, I2C bus, 24 MHz
P83CE559	Same as P80CE559 but has 48K ROM
P80CE558	1K SRAM, 2 16-bit timers, 48 I/O pins, 10-bit A/D, watchdog timer, PLL oscillator, PCA, 2 PWMs, 1 UART, I2C bus, 16MHz
P83CE558	Same as P80CE558 but has 32K ROM
P89CE558	Same as P80CE558 but has 32K flash memory
OM5202	512 bytes SRAM, 3 16-bit timers, 32 I/O pins, 1 UART, I2C bus, watchdog timer, 16 MHz
OM5232	Same as OM5202 but has 8K ROM
OM5234	Same as OM5202 but has 16K ROM
OM5238	Same as OM5202 but has 32K ROM
80C528	512 bytes SRAM, 3 16-bit timers, 32 I/O pins, 1 UART, I2C bus, watchdog timer, 16 MHz
83C528	Same as 80C528 but has 32K ROM
83C055	256 bytes SRAM, 16K ROM, on screen display controller, three video outputs, 128 × 10 bits display SRAM, character generator ROM, 8 text shadowing modes, 8 6-bit PWMs, 1 14-bit PWM, D/A converter, 37 I/O pins, 2 16-bit timers, 12 + 12 V outputs, 1 UART
87C055	Same as 83C055 but as 16K OTP EPROM
83C504	256 bytes SRAM, 16K ROM, 2 16-bit timers, 32 I/O pins, 1 UART, 24-by-8 divide, watchdog timer, 24 MHz
87C504	Same as 83C504 but has 16K EPROM

Continued

Device	Features
80C58	256 bytes SRAM, 3 16-bit timers, 32 I/O pins, 1 UART, 16 MHz
87C58	Same as 80C58 but has 32 K EPROM
80C562	256 bytes SRAM, 2 16-bit timers, 1 PCA, 48 I/O pins, 8-bit ADC, 2 PWMs, 1 UART, watchdog timer, 12 MHz
83C562	Same as 80C562 but has 8K ROM
80C851	128 bytes SRAM, 256 bytes EEPROM, 2 16-bit timers, 32 I/O pins, 1 UART, 16 MHz
83C851	Same as 80C851 but has 4K ROM
80C32	256 bytes SRAM, 3 16-bit timers, 32 I/O pins, 1 UART, 16, 24, 33 MHz
87C52	Same as 80C32 but has 8K EPROM
80C31	128 bytes SRAM, 2 16-bit timers, 32 I/O pins, 1 UART, 12, 16, 24, 33 MHz
80C51	Same as 80C31 but has 4K ROM
87C51	Same as 80C31 but has 4K EPROM
80C34	256 bytes SRAM, 3 16-bit timers, 32 I/O pins, 1 UART, 24 MHz
80C54	Same as 80C34 but has 16K ROM
87C54	Same as 80C34 but has 16K EPROM
83C749	64 bytes SRAM, 2K ROM, 1 16-bit timer, 8-bit PWM, 28-pin DIP, 8-bit A/D, 1 UART, 16 MHz
87C749	Same as 83C749 but has 2K EPROM
P83C524	512 bytes SRAM, 16K ROM, 3 16-bit timers, 32 I/O pins, I2C bus, watchdog, 1 UART, 16 MHz
83C542	256 bytes SRAM, 4K ROM, 2 16-bit timers, 44 pins, ACCESS.bus interface, ISA interface, 16 MHz
87C542	Same as 83C542 but has 4K EPROM
83C748	64 bytes SRAM, 1 16-bit timer, 10-bit fixed rate timer, 24 pins, 16 MHz
87C748	Same as 83C748 but has 2K EPROM
P80CE598	512 bytes SRAM, 2 16-bit timers, 1 PCA, 2 PWMs, 48 I/O pins, 1 UART, CAN-controller, watchdog timer, 10-bit A/D, improved EMC, 16 MHz
P83CE598	Same as P80CE598 but has 32K ROM
P80C592	512 bytes SRAM, 2 16-bit timers, 1 PCA, 2 PWMs, 48 I/O pins, 1 UART, CAN-controller, watchdog timer, 10-bit A/D, 16 MHz
P83C592	Same as 80C592 but has 16K ROM
83L51FB	256 bytes SRAM, 16K ROM, 3 16-bit timers, PCA, 32 I/O pins, 1 UART, 16 MHz
87L51FB	Same as 83C51FB but has 16K EPROM
80C51FA	256 bytes SRAM, 3 16-bit timers, PCA, 32 I/O pins, 1 UART, 16, 24, 33 MHz
83C51FA	Same as 80C51FA but has 8K ROM
87C51FA	Same as 80C51FA but has 8K EPROM
83C51FB	256 bytes SRAM, 16K ROM, 3 16-bit timers, PCA, 32 I/O pins, 1 UART, 16, 24, 33 MHz
87C51FB	Same as 83C51FB but has 16K EPROM
83C508	256 bytes SRAM, 32K ROM, 2 16-bit timers, 32 I/O pins, 1 UART, 24-by-16 bit divide, 24-by-16-bit multiply, 24 MHz
87C508	Same as 83C508 but has 32K EPROM
87L51FA	256 bytes SRAM, 8K EPROM, 3 16-bit timers, PCA, 32 I/O pins, 1 UART
87L51FA	Same as 87L51FA but has 16K EPROM
87C51FC	Same as 87C51FA but has 32K EPROM
87C654	256 bytes SRAM, 16K EPROM, 2 16-bit timers, 32 I/O pins, I2C bus, 1 UART, 16, 20 MHz
87C528	Same as 80C828 but has 32K EPROM
87C524	Same as 80C524 but has 16K EPROM
83C752	64 bytes SRAM, 2K ROM, 1 16-bit timer, 8-bit A/D, 1 8-bit PWM, 28-pin, I2C bus, 12 MHz
87C752	Same as 83C752 but has 2K EPROM
83C751	64 bytes SRAM, 2K ROM, 1 16-bit timer, 24-pin, I2C bus, 12 MHz
87C751	Same as 83C751 but has 2K EPROM
83C750	64 bytes SRAM, 1K ROM, 1 16-bit timer, 24-pin, I2C bus, 40 MHz

Continued

Device	Features
87C750	Same as 83C750 but has 1K EPROM
83C576	256 bytes SRAM, 8K ROM, 32 I/O pins, 3 16-bit timers, 1 PCA, watchdog timer, 2 8-bit PWMs, 28-pin DIP, 10-bit A/D, 1 UART, 4 analog comparator, UPI interface, 6–16 MHz
87C576	Same as 83C576 but has 8K EPROM

Siemens Components, Inc.: Integrated Circuit Division, 10950 N. Tantau Ave., Cupertino, CA 95014, (800) 777-4363

Device	Features
SAB 8031A	Same as Intel 8031H and runs at 12 MHz
SAB 8031A-16	Same as SAB 8031A but runs at 16 MHz
SAB 8031A-20	Same as SAB 8031A but runs at 20 MHz
SAB 8051A	Same as SAM 8031A with on-chip 4K ROM
SAB 8051A-16	Same as SAB 8051A but runs at 16 MHz
SAB 8032B	Same as Intel 8032H and runs at 12 MHz
SAB 8032B-16	Same as SAB 8032B but runs at 16 MHz
SAB 8032B-20	Same as SAB 8032B but runs at 20 MHz
SAB 8052B	Same as SAB 8032B but has 8K ROM
SAB 8052B-16	Same as SAB 8052B but runs at 16 MHz
SAB 8052B-20	Same as SAB 8052B but runs at 20 MHz
SAB 80515	256 bytes SRAM, 8K ROM, 6 I/O ports, 8-bit A/D, 3 16-bit timers, PCA, 1 UART, watchdog timer, 12 MHz
SAB 80535	An SAB 80515 without 8K ROM
SAB C501-L	Same as 80C32, ROMLESS, 12, 16 MHz
SAB C501-R	Same as 80C52, 12, 20, 40 MHz
SAB C502-L	Same as 80C32 ROMLESS plus 256 bytes XRAM, 8 data pointers, 2 watchdogs, 12, 20 MHz
SAB C502-R	Same as C502-L plus 16K ROM, 12, 20, MHz
SAB C502-2H	Hybrid version of SAB C502-R with 16K EEPROM, 12 MHz
SAB C503-L	Same as 80C32 plus 10-bit A/D, 2 watchdogs, 12, 20 MHz
SAB C503-R	Same as 80C52 plus 10-bit A/D, 2 watchdogs, 12, 20 MHz
SAB C503-1H	Hybrid version of SAB C503-R with 8K EEPROM
SAB 80C32	CMOS version of SAB 8032, runs at 12 MHz
SAB 80C32-16	CMOS version of SAB 8032, runs at 16 MHz
SAB 80C32-20	CMOS version of SAB 8032, runs at 20 MHz
SAB 80C52	CMOS version of SAB 8052 with 8K ROM, 12 MHz
SAB 80C52-16	16-MHz version of SAB 80C52
SAB 80C52-20	20-MHz version of SAB 80C52
SAB 80C535	CMOS version of the SAB 80535 with power saving modes, 12 MHz
SAB 80C535-16	16-MHz version of 80C535
SAB 80C515	80C535 with 8K ROM, 12 MHz
SAB 80C515-16	16-MHz version of 80C515
SAB 80C515H-3J	Hybrid combination of 80C515 with 8K EEPROM, 12 MHz
SAB 80C515A	256 bytes SRAM, 1K XRAM, 48 I/O pins, 3 16-bit timers, 1 PCA, 2 watchdog timers, 2 8-bit PWMs, 10-bit A/D, 1 UART, 4 analog comparators, UPI interface, 18 MHz
SAB 80C515A-5	Same as 80C515A with 32K ROM, 18 MHz
SAB 83C515H-5J	Hybrid combination of 80C515A with 32K PROM, 18 MHz
SAB 80C537	256 bytes SRAM, 9 I/O ports, 4 16-bit timers, 1 PCAs with 21 PWMs, 2 8-bit PWMs, fast 32-bit division, 16-bit multiplication, 8 data pointers, 8-bit A/D, 2 UART, 12 MHz
SAB 80C537-16	16-MHz version of SAB 80C537
SAB 80C517	An 80C537 with 8K ROM, 12 MHz
SAB 80C517-16	16-MHz version of SAB 80C517
SAB 80C517H-3J	Hybrid combination of SAB 80C517 with 8K EEPROM, 12 MHz
SAB 80C517A	256 bytes SRAM, 2K XRAM, 84 PLCC, 4 16-bit timers, PCAs with 21 PWMs, 2 watchdog timers, 10-bit A/D, 2 UARTs, 8 data pointers, fast 32-bit division, 16-bit multiplication, 18 MHz

Continued

Device	Features
SAB 80C517A-5	SAB 80C517A with 32K ROM, 18 MHz
SAB 80C517AH-5J	Hybrid combination of 80C517A with 32K EEPROM, 18 MHz
SAB 80C32	CMOS version of SAB 8032, 12 MHz
SAB 80C32-16	16-MHz version of SAB 80C32
SAB 80C32-20	20-MHz version of SAB 80C32
SAB 80C52	CMOS version of SAB 8052, 8K ROM, 12 MHz
SAB 80C52-16	16-MHz version of SAB 80C52
SAB 80C52-20	20-MHz version of SAB 80C52
SAB 80C535	CMOS version of SAB 80535, 12 MHz
SAB 80C535-16	16-MHz version of SAB 80C535
SAB 80C515	SAB 80C535 with 8K ROM, 12 MHz
SAB 80C515-16	16-MHz version of SAB 80C515
SAB 80C515H-3J	Hybrid combination of 80C515 with 8K EEPROM, 12 MHz
SAB 80C515A	256 bytes SRAM, 1 KB XRAM, 10-bit A/D, 3 16-bit timers, 2 watchdog timers, 1 PCA, 18 MHz
SAB 80C515A-5	Same as 80C515A with 32K ROM, 18 MHz
SAB 80C515AH-5J	Hybrid combination of 80C515A with 32K ROM, 18 MHz
SAB 80C537	256 bytes SRAM, 9 I/O ports, 8-bit A/D, 4 timers, PCAs with 21 PWMs, fast 32-bit division, 16-bit multiplication, 8 data pointers, 2 watchdogs, 12 MHz

[a] XRAM, extra internal SRAM, which can be accessed using the MOVX instruction.

APPENDIX G: MCS-51 INSTRUCTION SET

INSTRUCTION DEFINITIONS

ACALL   addr11

Function: Absolute Call

Description: ACALL unconditionally calls a subroutine located at the indicated address. The instruction increments the PC twice to obtain the address of the following instruction, then pushes the 16-bit result onto the stack (low-order byte first) and increments the Stack Pointer twice. The destination address is obtained by successively concatenating the five high-order bits of the incremented PC, opcode bits 7-5, and the second byte of the instruction. The subroutine called must therefore start within the same 2K block of the program memory as the first byte of the instruction following ACALL. No flags are affected.

Example: Initially SP equals 07H. The label "SUBRTN" is at program memory location 0345 H. After executing the instruction,

ACALL   SUBRTN

at location 0123H, SP will contain 09H, internal RAM locations 08H and 09H will contain 25H and 01H, respectively and the PC will contain 0345H.

Bytes: 2

Cycles: 2

Encoding: | a10 a9 a8 1 | 0 0 0 1 | | a7 a6 a5 a4 | a3 a2 a1 a0 |

Operation: ACALL

$(PC) \leftarrow (PC) + 2$

$(SP) \leftarrow (SP) + 1$

$((SP)) \leftarrow (PC_{7-0})$

$(SP) \leftarrow (SP) + 1$

$((SP)) \leftarrow (PC_{15-8})$

$(PC_{10-0}) \leftarrow$ page address

ADD   A, \<src-byte\>

Function: Add

Description: ADD adds the byte variable indicated to the Accumulator, leaving the result in the Accumulator. The carry and auxiliary-carry flags are set, respectively, if there is a carry-out from bit 7 or bit 3, and cleared otherwise. When adding unsigned integers, the carry flag indicates an overflow occurred.

Reprinted with permission of Intel.

OV is set if there is a carry-out of bit 6 but not out of bit 7, or a carry-out of bit 7 but not bit 6; otherwise OV is cleared. When adding signed integers, OV indicates a negative number produced as the sum of two positive operands, or a positive sum from two negative operands.

Four source operand addressing modes are allowed: register, direct, register-indirect, or immediate.

Example: The Accumulator holds 0C3H (11000011B) and register 0 holds 0AAH (10101010B). The instruction,

ADD   A,R0

will leave 6DH (01101101B) in the Accumulator with the AC flag cleared and both the carry flag and OV set to 1.

ADD   A,Rn

Bytes:	1
Cycles:	1

Encoding: | 0 0 1 0 | 1 r r r |

Operation: ADD
$(A) \leftarrow (A) + (Rn)$

ADD   A,direct

Bytes:	2
Cycles:	1

Encoding: | 0 0 1 0 | 0 1 0 1 | | direct address |

Operation: ADD
$(A) \leftarrow (A) + (direct)$

ADD   A,@Ri

Bytes:	1
Cycles:	1

Encoding: | 0 0 1 0 | 0 1 1 i |

Operation: ADD
$(A) \leftarrow (A) + ((R_i))$

ADD   A,#data

Bytes:	2
Cycles:	1

Encoding: | 0 0 1 0 | 0 1 0 0 | | immediate data |

Operation: ADD
$(A) \leftarrow (A) + \# data$

ADDC   A, <src-byte>

Function: Add with Carry

Description: ADDC simultaneously adds the byte variable indicated, the carry flag and the Accumulator contents, leaving the result in the Accumulator. The carry and auxiliary-carry flags are set, respectively, if there is a carry-out from bit 7 or bit 3, and cleared otherwise. When adding unsigned integers, the carry flag indicates an overflow occurred.

OV is set if there is a carry-out of bit 6 but not out of bit 7, or a carry-out of bit 7 but not out of bit 6; otherwise OV is cleared. When adding signed integers, OV indicates a negative number produced as the sum of two positive operands or a positive sum from two negative operands.

Four source operand addressing modes are allowed: register, direct, register-indirect, or immediate.

Example: The accumulator holds 0C3H (11000011B) and register 0 holds 0AAH (10101010B) with the carry flag set. The instruction,

ADDC   A, R0

will leave 6EH (01101110B) in the Accumulator with AC cleared and both the Carry flag and OV set to 1.

ADDC   A,Rn

Bytes: 1

Cycles: 1

Encoding: | 0 0 1 1 | 1 r r r |

Operation: ADDC

$(A) \leftarrow (A) + (C) + (R_n)$

ADDC   A,direct

Bytes: 2

Cycles: 1

Encoding: | 0 0 1 1 | 0 1 0 1 | | direct address |

Operation: ADDC

$(A) \leftarrow (A) + (C) + (direct)$

ADDC   A,@Ri

Bytes: 1

Cycles: 1

Encoding: | 0 0 1 1 | 0 1 1 i |

Operation: $(A) \leftarrow (A) + (C) + ((R_i))$

ADDC   A,#data

Bytes: 2

Cycles: 1

Encoding: | 0 0 1 1 | 0 1 0 0 | | immediate data |

Operation: ADDC

$(A) \leftarrow (A) + (C) + \# data$

AJMP   addr11

Function: Absolute Jump

Description: AJMP transfers program execution to the indicated address, which is formed at run-time by concatenating the high-order five bits of the PC (*after* incrementing the PC twice), opcode bits 7-5, and the second byte of the instruction. The destination must therefore be within the same 2K block of program memory as the first byte of the instruction following AJMP.

Example: The label "JMPADR" is at program memory location 0123H. The instruction,

AJMP   JMPADR

is at location 0345H and will load the PC with 0123H.

Bytes: 2

Cycles: 2

Encoding: | a10 a9 a8 0 | 0 0 0 1 | | a7 a6 a5 a4 | a3 a2 a1 a0 |

Operation: AJMP
$(PC) \leftarrow (PC) + 2$
$(PC_{10-0}) \leftarrow$ page address

ANL   \<dest-byte\>, \<src-byte\>

Function: Logical-AND for byte variables

Description: ANL performs the bitwise logical-AND operation between the variables indicated and stores the results in the destination variable. No flags are affected.

The two operands allow six addressing mode combinations. When the destination is the Accumulator, the source can use register, direct, register-indirect, or immediate addressing; when the destination is a direct address, the source can be the Accumulator or immediate data.

Note: When this instruction is used to modify an output port, the value used as the original port data will be read from the output data latch, *not* the input pins.

Example: If the Accumulator holds 0C3H (11000011B) and register 0 holds 55H (01010101B) then the instruction,

ANL,   A,R0

will leave 41H (01000001B) in the Accumulator.

When the destination is a directly addressed byte, this instruction will clear combinations of bits in any RAM location or hardware register. The mask byte determining the pattern of bits to be cleared would either be a constant contained in the instruction or a value computed in the Accumulator at run-time. The instruction,

ANL   P1, #01110011B

will clear bits 7, 3, and 2 of output port 1.

ANL   A,Rn

Bytes: 1
Cycles: 1

Encoding: | 0 1 0 1 | 1 r r r |

Operation: ANL
$(A) \leftarrow (A) \wedge (Rn)$

ANL   A,direct

Bytes: 2
Cycles: 1

Encoding: | 0 1 0 1 | 0 1 0 1 | | direct address |

Operation: ANL
$(A) \leftarrow (A) \wedge (direct)$

ANL   A,@Ri

Bytes: 1
Cycles: 1

Encoding: | 0 1 0 1 | 0 1 1 i |

Operation: ANL
$(A) \leftarrow (A) \wedge ((Ri))$

ANL   A,#data

Bytes: 2

Cycles: 1

Encoding: | 0 1 0 1 | 0 1 0 0 | | immediate data |

Operation: ANL

$$(A) \leftarrow (A) \wedge \# \text{ data}$$

ANL   direct,A

Bytes: 2

Cycles: 1

Encoding: | 0 1 0 1 | 0 0 1 0 | | direct address |

Operation: ANL

$$(\text{direct}) \leftarrow (\text{direct}) \wedge (A)$$

ANL   direct,#data

Bytes: 3

Cycles: 2

Encoding: | 0 1 0 1 | 0 0 1 1 | | direct address | immediate data |

Operation: ANL

$$(\text{direct}) \leftarrow (\text{direct}) \wedge \# \text{ data}$$

ANL   C, <src-bit>

Function: Logical-AND for bit variables

Description: If the Boolean value of the source bit is a logical 0 then clear the carry flag; otherwise leave the carry flag in its current state. A slash ("/") preceding the operand in the assembly language indicates that the logical complement of the addressed bit is used as the source value, *but the source bit itself is not affected.* No other flags are affected.

Only direct addressing is allowed for the source operand.

Example: Set the carry flag if, and only if, P1.0 = 1, ACC.7 = 1, and OV = 0;

MOV   C,P1.0   ;LOAD CARRY WITH INPUT PIN STATE

ANL   C,ACC.7   ;AND CARRY WITH ACCUM. BIT 7

ANL   C,/OV   ;AND WITH INVERSE OF OVERFLOW FLAG

ANL   C,bit

Bytes: 2

Cycles: 2

Encoding: | 1 0 0 0 | 0 0 1 0 | | bit address |

Operation: ANL

$$(C) \leftarrow (C) \wedge (\text{bit})$$

ANL   C,/bit

Bytes: 2

Cycles: 2

Encoding: | 1 0 1 1 | 0 0 0 0 | | bit address |

Operation: ANL

$$(C) \leftarrow (C) \wedge \neg (\text{bit})$$

CJNE   <dest-byte>, <src-byte>, rel

Function: Compare and Jump if Not Equal.

Description: CJNE compares the magnitudes of the first two operands, and branches if their values are not equal. The branch destination is computed by adding the signed relative-displacement in the last instruction byte to the PC, after incrementing the PC to the start of the next instructioin. The carry flag is set if the unsigned integer value of <dest-byte> is less than the unsigned integer value of <src-byte>; otherwise, the carry is cleared. Neither operand is affected.

The first two operands allow four addressing mode combinations: the Accumulator may be compared with any directly addressed byte or immediate data, and any indirect RAM location or working register can be compared with an immediate constant.

Example: The Accumulator contains 34H. Register 7 contains 56H. The first instruction in the sequence,

```
        CJNE   R7, # 60H, NOT_EQ
;              . . .   . . . .          ; R7 = 60H.
NOT_EQ:     JC     REQ_LOW              ; IF R7 < 60H.
;              . . .   . . . .          ; R7 > 60H.
```

sets the carry flag and branches to the instruction at label NOT_EQ. By testing the carry flag, this instruction determines whether R7 is greater or less than 60H.

If the data being presented to Port 1 is also 34H, then the instruction,

```
WAIT:       CJNE   A,P1, WAIT
```

clears the carry flag and continues with the next instruction in sequence, since the Accumulator does equal the data read from P1. (If some other value was being input on P1, the program will loop at this point until the P1 data changes to 34H).

CJNE A,direct,rel

Bytes: 3

Cycles: 2

Encoding: | 1 0 1 1 | 0 1 0 1 | | direct address | | rel, address |

Operation: $(PC) \leftarrow (PC) + 3$
IF $(A) <> (direct)$
THEN
       $(PC) \leftarrow (PC) + relative\ offset$
IF $(A) < (direct)$
THEN
       $(C) \leftarrow 1$
ELSE
       $(C) \leftarrow 0$

CJNE   A,#data,rel

Bytes: 3

Cycles: 2

Encoding: | 1 0 1 1 | 0 1 0 0 | | immediate data | | rel. address |

Operation: $(PC) \leftarrow (PC) + 3$
IF $(A) <> data$
THEN
       $(PC) \leftarrow (PC) + relative\ offset$
IF $(A) < data$
THEN
       $(C) \leftarrow 1$
ELSE
       $(C) \leftarrow 0$

CJNE   Rn, #data,rel

Bytes: 3

Cycles: 2

Encoding: | 1 0 1 1 | 1 r r r | | immediate data | | rel. address |

Operation: (PC) ← (PC) + 3
IF (Rn) <> *data*
THEN
   (PC) ← (PC) + *relative offset*
IF (Rn) < *data*
THEN
   (C) ← 1
ELSE
   (C) ← 0

CJNE   @Ri,#data,rel

Bytes: 3

Cycles: 2

Encoding: | 1 0 1 1 | 0 1 1 i | | immediate data | | rel. address |

Operation: (PC) ← (PC) + 3
IF ((Ri)) <> *data*
THEN
   (PC) ← (PC) + *relative offset*
IF ((Ri)) < *data*
THEN
   (C) ← 1
ELSE
   (C) ← 0

CLR   A

Function: Clear Accumulator

Description: The Accumulator is cleared (all bits set on zero). No flags are affected.

Example: The Accumulator contains 5CH (01011100B). The instruction,
CLR   A
will leave the Accumulator set to 00H (00000000B).

Bytes: 1

Cycles: 1

Encoding: | 1 1 1 0 | 0 1 0 0 |

Operation: CLR
(A) ← 0

CLR   bit

Function: Clear bit

Description: The indicated bit is cleared (reset to zero). No other flags are affected. CLR can operate on the carry flag or any directly addressable bit.

Example: Port 1 has previously been written with 5DH (01011101B). The instruction,
CLR   P1.2
will leave the port set to 59H (01011001B).

CLR   C

Bytes: 1

Cycles: 1

Encoding: | 1 1 0 0 | 0 0 1 1 |

Operation: CLR

$(C) \leftarrow 0$

CLR   bit

Bytes: 2

Cycles: 1

Encoding: | 1 1 0 0 | 0 0 1 0 | | bit address |

Operation: CLR

$(bit) \leftarrow 0$

CPL   A

Function: Complement Accumulator

Description: Each bit of the Accumulator is logically complemented (one's complement). Bits which previously contained a one are changed to a zero and vice-versa. No flags are affected.

Example: The Accumulator contains 5CH (01011100B). The instruction,

CPL   A

will leave the Accumulator set to 0A3H (10100011B).

Bytes: 1

Cycles: 1

Encoding: | 1 1 1 1 | 0 1 0 0 |

Operation: CPL

$(A) \leftarrow \neg (A)$

CPL   bit

Function: Complement bit

Description: The bit variable specified is complemented. A bit which had been a one is changed to zero and vice-versa. No other flags are affected. CLR can operate on the carry or any directly addressable bit.

Note: When this instruction is used to modify an output pin, the value used as the original data will be read from the output data latch, *not* the input pin.

Example: Port 1 has previously been written with 5BH (01011101B). The instruction sequence,

CPL   P1.1

CPL   P1.2

will leave the port set to 5BH (01011011B).

CPL   C

Bytes: 1

Cycles: 1

Encoding: | 1 0 1 1 | 0 0 1 1 |

Operation: CPL

$(C) \leftarrow \neg (c)$

CPL   bit

Bytes: 2

Cycles: 1

Encoding: | 1 0 1 1 | 0 0 1 0 | | bit address |

Operation: CPL

(bit) ← ¬ (bit)

DA   A

Function: Decimal-adjust Accumulator for Addition

Description: DA A adjust the eight-bit value in the Accumulator resulting from the earlier addition of two variables (each in packed-BCD format), producing two four-bit digits. Any ADD or ADDC instruction may have been used to perform the addition.

If Accumulator bits 3-0 are greater than nine (xxx1010-xxxx1111), or if the AC flag is one, six is added to the Accumulator producing the proper BCD digit in the low-order nibble. This internal addition would set the carry flag if a carry-out of the low-order four-bit field propagated through all high-order bits, but it would not clear the carry flag otherwise.

If the carry flag is now set, or if the four high-order bits now exceed nine (1010xxx-1111xxxx), these high-order bits are incremented by six, producing the proper BCD digit in the high-order nibble. Again, this would set the carry flag if there was a carry-out of the high-order bits, but wouldn't clear the carry. The carry flag thus indicates if the sum of the original two BCD variables is greater than 100, allowing multiple precision decimal addition. OV is not affected.

All of this occurs during the one instruction cycle. Essentially, this instruction performs the decimal conversion by adding 00H, 06H, 60H, or 66H to the Accumulator, depending on initial Accumulator and PSW conditions.

Note: DA A *cannot* simply convert a hexadecimal number in the Accumulator to BCD notation, nor does DA A apply to decimal subtration.

Example: The Accumulator holds the value 56H (01010110B) representing the packed BCD digits of the decimal number 56. Register 3 contains the value 67H (01100111B) representing the packed BCD digits of the decimal number 67. The carry flag is set. The instruction sequence.

ADDC   A,R3

DA   A

will first perform a standard twos-complement binary addition, resulting in the value 0BEH (10111110) in the Accumulator. The carry and auxiliary carry flags will be cleared.

The Decimal Adjust instruction will then alter the Accumulator to the value 24H (00100100B), indicating the packed BCD digits of the decimal number 24, the low-order two digits of the decimal sum of 56, 67, and the carry-in. The carry flag will be set by the Decimal Adjust instruction, indicating that a decimal overflow occurred. The true sum 56, 67, and 1 is 124.

BCD variables can be incremented or decremented by adding 01H or 99H. If the Accumulator initially holds 30H (representing the digits of 30 decimal), then the instruction sequence,

ADD   A,#99H

DA A

will leave the carry set and 29H in the Accumulator, since $30 + 99 = 129$. The low-order byte of the sum can be interpreted to mean $30 - 1 = 29$.

Bytes: 1

Cycles: 1

Encoding: | 1 1 0 1 | 0 1 0 0 |

Operation: DA

-contents of Accumulator are BCD

IF $[[(A_{3-0}) > 9] \vee [(AC) = 1]]$

$$\text{THEN}(A_{3\text{-}0}) \leftarrow (A_{3\text{-}0}) + 6$$
$$\text{AND}$$
$$\text{IF} \quad [[(A_{7\text{-}4}) > 9] \vee [(C) = 1]]$$
$$\text{THEN } (A_{7\text{-}4}) \leftarrow (A_{7\text{-}4}) + 6$$

DEC   byte

Function: Decrement

Description: The variable indicated is decremented by 1. An original value of 00H will underflow to 0FFH. No flags are affected. Four operand addressing modes are allowed: accumulator, register, direct, or register-indirect.

Note: When this instruction is used to modify an output port, the value used as the original port data will be read from the output data latch, *not* the input pins.

Example: Register 0 contains 7FH (01111111B). Internal RAM locations 7EH and 7FH contain 00H and 40H, respectively. The instruction sequence,

DEC   @R0

DEC   R0

DEC   @R0

will leave register 0 set to 7EH and internal RAM locations 7EH and 7FH set to 0FFH and 3FH.

DEC   A

Bytes: 1

Cycles: 1

Encoding: | 0 0 0 1 | 0 1 0 0 |

Operation: DEC
$$(A) \leftarrow (A) - 1$$

DEC   Rn

Bytes: 1

Cycles: 1

Encoding: | 0 0 0 1 | 1 r r r |

Operation: DEC
$$(Rn) \leftarrow (Rn) - 1$$

DEC   direct

Bytes: 2

Cycles: 1

Encoding: | 0 0 0 1 | 0 1 0 1 | | direct address |

Operation: DEC
$$(direct) \leftarrow (direct) - 1$$

DEC   @Ri

Bytes: 1

Cycles: 1

Encoding: | 0 0 0 1 | 0 1 1 i |

Operation: DEC
$$((Ri)) \leftarrow ((Ri)) - 1$$

DIV   AB

Function: Divide

Description: DIV AB divides the unsigned eight-bit integer in the Accumulator by the unsigned eight-bit integer in register B. The Accumulator receives the integer part of the quotient; register B receives the integer remainder. The carry and OV flags will be cleared.

Exception: if B had originally contained 00H, the values returned in the Accumulator and B-register will be undefined and the overflow flag will be set. The carry flag is cleared in any case.

Example: The Accumulator contains 251 (0FBH or 11111011B) and B contains 18 (12H or 00010010B). The instruction,

DIV   AB

will leave 13 in the Accumulator (0DH or 00001101B) and the value 17 (11H or 00010001B) in B, since $251 = (13 \times 18) + 17$. Carry and OV will both be cleared.

Bytes: 1

Cycles: 4

Encoding: | 1 0 0 0 | 0 1 0 0 |

Operation: DIV
$(A)_{15\text{-}8}$
$(B)_{7\text{-}0}$ $\leftarrow (A)/(B)$

DJNZ   \<byte\>,\<rel-addr\>

Function: Decrement and Jump if Not Zero

Description: DJNZ decrements the location indicated by 1, and branches to the address indicated by the second operand if the resulting value is not zero. An original value of 00H will underflow to 0FFH. No flags are affected. The branch destination would be computed by adding the signed relative-displacement value in the last instruction byte to the PC, after incrementing the PC to the first byte of the following instruction.

The location decremented may be a register or directly addressed byte.

Note: When this instruction is used to modify an output port, the value used as the original port data will be read from the output data latch, *not* the input pins.

Example: Internal RAM locations 40H, 50H, and 60H contain the value 01H, 70H, and 15H, respectively. The instruction sequence,

DJNZ   40H,LABEL_1
DJNZ   50H,LABEL_2
DJNZ   60H,LABEL_3

will cause a jump to the instruction at label LABEL_2 with the values 00H, 6FH, and 15H in the three RAM locations. The first jump was *not* taken because the result was zero.

This instruction provides a simple way of executing a program loop a given number of times, or for adding a moderate time delay (from 2 to 512 machine cycles) with a single instruction. The instruction sequence.

```
            MOV   R2,#8
TOGGLE:     CPL   P1.7
            DJNZ  R2,TOGGLE
```

will toggle P1.7 eight times, causing four output pulses to appear at bit 7 of output Port 1. Each pulse will last three machine cycles; two for DJNZ and one to alter the pin.

DJNZ   Rn,rel

Bytes: 2

Cycles: 2

Encoding: | 1 1 0 1 | 1 r r r | | rel.address |

Operation: DJNZ

$(PC) \leftarrow (PC) + 2$

$(Rn) \leftarrow (Rn) - 1$

IF (Rn) > 0 or (Rn) < 0

THEN

$(PC) \leftarrow (PC) + rel$

DJNZ   direct,rel

Bytes: 3

Cycles: 2

Encoding: | 1 1 0 1 | 0 1 0 1 | | direct address | | rel.address |

Operation: DJNZ

$(PC) \leftarrow (PC) + 2$

$(direct) \leftarrow (direct) - 2$

IF (direct) > 0 or (direct) < 0

THEN

$(PC) \leftarrow (PC) + rel$

INC   <byte>

Function: Increment

Description: INC increments the indicated variable by 1. An original value of 0FFH will overflow to 00H. No flags are affected. Three addressing modes are allowed: register, direct, or register-indirect.

Note: When this instruction is used to modify an output port, the value used as the original port data will be read from the output data latch, *not* the input pins.

Example: Register 0 contains 7EH (01111110B). Internal RAM locations 7EH and 7FH contain 0FFH and 40H, respectively. The instruction sequence,

INC   @R0

INC   R0

INC   @ R0

will leave register 0 set to 7FH and internal RAM locations 7EH and 7FH holding (respectively) 00H and 41H.

INC   A

Bytes: 1

Cycles: 1

Encoding: | 0 0 0 0 | 0 1 0 0 |

Operation: INC

$(A) \leftarrow (A) + 1$

INC   Rn

Bytes: 1

Cycles: 1

Encoding: | 0 0 0 0 | 1 r r r |

Operation: INC

$(Rn) \leftarrow (Rn) + 1$

INC direct

Bytes: 2
Cycles: 1
Encoding: | 0 0 0 0 | 0 1 0 1 | | direct address |
Operation: INC
                   (direct) ← (direct) + 1

INC @Ri

Bytes: 1
Cycles: 1
Encoding: | 0 0 0 0 | 0 1 1 i |
Operation: INC
                   ((Ri)) ← ((Ri)) + 1

INC DPTR

Function: Increment Data Pointer
Description: Increment the 16-bit data pointer by 1. A 16-bit increment (modulo 2^{16}) is performed; an overflow of the low-order byte of the data pointer (DPL) from 0FFH to 00H will increment the high-order byte (DPH). No flags are affected.

This is the only 16-bit register which can be incremented.
Example: Registers DPH and DPL contain 12H and 0FEH, respectively. The instruction sequence,

INC   DPTR
INC   DPTR
INC   DPTR

will change DPH and DPL to 13H and 01H.
Bytes: 1
Cycles: 2
Encoding: | 1 0 1 0 | 0 0 1 1 |
Operation: INC
                   (DPTR) ← (DPTR) + 1

JB bit,rel

Function: Jump if Bit set
Description: If the indicated bit is a one, jump to the address indicated; otherwise proceed with the next instruction. The branch destination is computed by adding the signed relative-displacement in the third instruction byte to the PC, after incrementing the PC to the first byte of the next instruction. *The bit tested is not modified.* No flags are affected.
Example: The data present at input port 1 is 11001010B. The Accumulator holds 56 (01010110B). The instruction sequence,

JB   P1.2,LABEL1
JB   ACC.2,LABEL2

will cause program execution to branch to the instruction at label LABEL2.
Bytes: 3
Cycles: 2
Encoding: | 0 0 1 0 | 0 0 0 0 | | bit address | | rel.address |

Operation: JB

(PC) ← (PC) + 3

IF (bit) = 1

THEN

(PC) ← (PC) + rel

JBC   bit,rel

Function: Jump if Bit is set and Clear bit

Description: If the indicated bit is one, branch to the address indicated; otherwise proceed with the next instruction. *The bit will not be cleared if it is already a zero.* The branch destination is computed by adding the signed relative-displacement in the third instruction byte to the PC, after incrementing the PC to the first byte of the next instruction. No flags are affected.

Note: When this instruction is used to test an output pin, the value used as the original data will be read from the output data latch, *not* the input pin.

Example: The Accumulator holds 56H (01010110B). The instruction sequence,

JBC   ACC.3,LABEL1

JBC   ACC.2,LABEL2

will cause program execution to continue at the instruction identified by the label LABEL2, with the Accumulator modified to 52H (01010010B).

Bytes: 3

Cycles: 2

Encoding: | 0001 | 0000 | | bit address | | rel.address |

Operation: JBC

(PC) ← (PC) + 3

IF (bit) = 1

THEN

(bit) ← 0

(PC) ← (PC) + rel

JC   rel

Function: Jump if Carry is set

Description: If the carry flag is set, branch to the address indicated; otherwise proceed with the next instruction. The branch destination is computed by adding the signed relative-displacement in the second instruction byte to the PC, after incrementing the PC twice. No flags are afflected.

Example: The carry flag is cleared. The instruction sequence,

JC   LABEL1

CPL   C

JC   LABEL 2

will set the carry and cause program execution to continue at the instruction identified by the label LABEL2.

Bytes: 2

Cycles: 2

Encoding: | 0100 | 0000 | | rel.address |

Operation: JC

(PC) ← (PC) + 2

IF (C) = 1

THEN

(PC) ← (PC) + rel

JMP   @A + DPTR

Function: Jump indirect

Description: Add the eight-bit unsigned contents of the Accumulator with the sixteen-bit data pointer, and load the resulting sum to the program counter. This will be the address for subsequent instruction fetches. Sixteen-bit addition is performed (modulo 2^{16}): a carry-out from the low-order eight bits propagates through the higher-order bits. Neither the Accumulator nor the Data Pointer is altered. No flags are affected.

Example: An even number from 0 to 6 is in the Accumulator. The following sequence of instructions will branch to one of four AJMP instructions in a jump table starting at JMP_TBL:

```
               MOV   DPTR,#JMP_TBL
               JMP   @A + DPTR
JMP_TBL:       AJMP  LABEL0
               AJMP  LABEL1
               AJMP  LABEL2
               AJMP  LABEL3
```

If the Accumulator equals 04H when starting this sequence, execution will jump to label LABEL2. Remember that AJMP is a two-byte instruction, so the jump instructions start at every other address.

Bytes: 1

Cycles: 2

Encoding: | 0 1 1 1 | 0 0 1 1 |

Operation: JMP
(PC) ← (A) + (DPTR)

JNB   bit,rel

Function: Jump if Bit Not set

Description: If the indicated bit is a zero, branch to the indicated address; otherwise proceed with the next instruction. The branch destination is computed by adding the signed relative-displacement in the third instruction byte to the PC, after incrementing the PC to the first byte of the next instruction. *The bit tested is not modified.* No flags are affected.

Example: The data present at input port 1 is 11001010B. The Accumulator holds 56H (01010110B). The instruction sequence,

```
JNB   P1.3,LABEL1
JNB   ACC.3,LABEL2
```

will cause program execution to continue at the instruction at label LABEL2.

Bytes: 3

Cycles: 2

Encoding: | 0 0 1 1 | 0 0 0 0 | | bit address | | rel.address |

Operation: JNB
(PC) ← (PC) + 3
IF (bit) = 0
        THEN (PC) ← (PC) + rel.

JNC   rel

Function: Jump if Carry not set

Description: If the carry flag is a zero, branch to the address indicated; otherwise proceed with the next instruction. The branch destination is computed by adding the signed relative-displacement in the second instruction byte to the PC, after incrementing the PC twice to point to the next instruction. The carry flag is not modified.

Example: The carry flag is set. The instruction sequence,

JNC   LABEL1

CPL   C

JNC   LABEL2

will clear the carry and cause program execution to continue at the instruction identified by the label LABEL2.

Bytes: 2

Cycles: 2

Encoding: | 0 1 0 1 | 0 0 0 0 | | rel.address |

Operation: JNC

(PC) ← (PC) + 2

IF (C) = 0

          THEN (PC) ← (PC) + rel

JNZ   rel

Function: Jump if Accumulator Not Zero

Description: If any bit of the Accumulator is a one, branch to the indicated address; otherwise proceed with the next instruction. The branch destination is computed by adding the signed relative-displacement in the second instruction byte to the PC, after incrementing the PC twice. The Accumulator is not modified. No flags are affected.

Example: The Accumulator originally holds 00H. The instruction sequence,

JNZ   LABEL1

INC   A

JNZ   LABEL2

will set the Accumulator to 01H and continue at label LABEL2.

Bytes: 2

Cycles: 2

Encoding: | 0 1 1 1 | 0 0 0 0 | | rel.address |

Operation: JNZ

(PC) ← (PC) + 2

IF (A) ≠ 0

          THEN (PC) ← (PC) + rel

JZ   rel

Function: Jump if Accumulator Zero

Description: If all bits of the Accumulator are zero, branch to the address indicated; otherwise proceed with the next instruction. The branch destination is computed by adding the signed relative-displacement in the second instruction byte to the PC, after incrementing the PC twice. The Accumulator is not modified. No flags are affected.

Example: The Accumulator originally contains 01H. The instruction sequence,

JZ   LABEL1

DEC   A

JZ   LABEL2

will change the Accumulator to 00H and cause program execution to continue at the instruction identified by the label LABEL2.

Bytes: 2

Cycles: 2

Encoding: | 0 1 1 0 | 0 0 0 0 | | rel.address |

Operation: JZ

$(PC) \leftarrow (PC) + 2$

IF $(A) = 0$

THEN $(PC) \leftarrow (PC) + rel$

LCALL   addr16

Function: Long call

Description: LCALL calls a subroutine located at the indicated address. The instruction adds three to the program counter to generate the address of the next instruction and then pushes the 16-bit result onto the stack (low byte first), incrementing the Stack Pointer by two. The high-order and low-order bytes of the PC are then loaded, respectively, with the second and third bytes of the LCALL instruction. Program execution continues with the instruction at this address. The subroutine may therefore begin anywhere in the full 64K-byte program memory address space. No flags are affected.

Example: Initially the Stack Pointer equals 07H. The label "SUBRTN" is assigned to program memory location 1234H. After executing the instruction,

LCALL   SUBRTN

at location 0123H, the Stack Pointer will contain 09H, internal RAM locations 08H and 09H will contain 26H and 01H, and the PC will contain 1234H.

Bytes: 3

Cycles: 2

Encoding: | 0 0 0 1 | 0 0 1 0 | | addr15-addr8 | | addr7-addr0 |

Operation: LCALL

$(PC) \leftarrow (PC) + 3$

$(SP) \leftarrow (SP) + 1$

$((SP)) \leftarrow (PC_{7-0})$

$(SP) \leftarrow (SP) + 1$

$((SP)) \leftarrow (PC_{15-8})$

$(PC) \leftarrow addr_{15-0}$

LJMP   addr16

Function: Long Jump

Description: LJMP causes an unconditional branch to the indicated address, by loading the high-order and low-order bytes of the PC (respectively) with the second and third instruction bytes. The destination may therefore be anywhere in the full 64K program memory address space. No flags are affected.

Example: The label "JMPADR" is assigned to the instruction at program memory location 1234H. The instruction,

LJMP   JMPADR

at location 0123H will load the program counter with 1234H.

Bytes: 3

Cycles: 2

Encoding: | 0 0 0 0 | 0 0 1 0 | | addr15-addr8 | | addr7-addr0 |

Operation: LJMP

$(PC) \leftarrow addr_{15-0}$

MOV   \<dest-byte\>,\<scr-byte\>

Function: Move byte variable

Description: The byte variable indicated by the second operand is copied into the location specified by the first operand. The source byte is not affected. No other register or flag is affected.

This is by far the most flexible operation. Fifteen combinations of source and destination addressing modes are allowed.

Example: Internal RAM location 30H holds 40H. The value of RAM location 40H is 10H. The data present at input port 1 is 11001010B (0CAH).

MOV	R0,#30H	;R0 < = 30H
MOV	A,@R0	;A < = 40H
MOV	R1,A	;R1 < = 40H
MOV	B,@R1	;B < = 10H
MOV	@R1,P1	;RAM (40H) < = 0CAH
MOV	P2,P1	;P2 #0CAH

leaves the value 30H in register 0, 40H in both the Accumulator and register 1, 10H in register B, and 0CAH (11001010B) both in RAM location 40H and output on port 2.

MOV   A,Rn

Bytes: 1

Cycles: 1

Encoding: | 1 1 1 0 | 1 r r r |

Operation: MOV
                (A) ← (Rn)

**MOV   A,direct*

Bytes: 2

Cycles: 1

Encoding: | 1 1 1 0 | 0 1 0 1 | | direct address |

Operation: MOV
                (A) ← (direct)

MOV   A,@Ri

Bytes: 1

Cycles: 1

Encoding: | 1 1 1 0 | 0 1 1 i |

Operation: MOV
                (A) ← ((Ri))

MOV   A,#data

Bytes: 2

Cycles: 1

Encoding: | 0 1 1 1 | 0 1 0 0 | | immediate data |

Operation: MOV
                (A) ← #data

---

*MOV A,ACC is not a valid instruction.

MOV   Rn,A

Bytes: 1
Cycles: 1
Encoding: | 1 1 1 1 | 1 r r r |
Operation: MOV
                (Rn) ← (A)

MOV   Rn,direct

Bytes: 2
Cycles: 2
Encoding: | 1 0 1 0 | 1 r r r | | direct addr. |
Operation: MOV
                (Rn) ← (direct)

MOV   Rn,#data

Bytes: 2
Cycles: 1
Encoding: | 0 1 1 1 | 1 r r r | | immediate data |
Operation: MOV
                (Rn) ← #data

MOV   direct,A

Bytes: 2
Cycles: 1
Encoding: | 1 1 1 1 | 0 1 0 1 | | direct address |
Operation: MOV
                (direct) ← (A)

MOV   direct,Rn

Bytes: 2
Cycles: 2
Encoding: | 1 0 0 0 | 1 r r r | | direct address |
Operation: MOV
                (direct) ← (Rn)

MOV   direct,direct

Bytes: 3
Cycles: 2
Encoding: | 1 0 0 0 | 0 1 0 1 | | dir.addr.(src) | | dir.addr.(dest) |
Operation: MOV
                (direct) ← (direct)

MOV   direct,@Ri

Bytes: 2
Cycles: 2

Encoding: | 1 0 0 0 | 0 1 1 i | | direct addr. |
Operation: MOV
           (direct) ← ((Ri))

MOV   direct,#data

Bytes: 3
Cycles: 2
Encoding: | 0 1 1 1 | 0 1 0 1 | | direct address | | immediate data |
Operation: MOV
           (direct) ← #data

MOV   @Ri,A

Bytes: 1
Cycles: 1
Encoding: | 1 1 1 1 | 0 1 1 i |
Operation: MOV
           ((Ri)) ← (A)

MOV   @Ri,direct

Bytes: 2
Cycles: 2
Encoding: | 1 0 1 0 | 0 1 1 i | | direct addr. |
Operation: MOV
           ((Ri)) ← (direct)

MOV   @Ri,#data

Bytes: 2
Cycles: 1
Encoding: | 0 1 1 1 | 0 1 1 i | | immediate data |
Operation: MOV
           ((RI)) ← #data

MOV   <dest-bit>,<src-bit>

Function: Move bit data
Description: The Boolean variable indicated by the second operand is copied into the location specified by the first operand. One of the operands must be the carry flag; the other may be any directly addressable bit. No other register or flag is affected.
Example: The carry flag is originally set. The data present at input Port 3 is 11000101B. The data previously written to output Port 1 is 35H (00110101B).

                  MOV   P1.3,C
                  MOV   C,P3.3
                  MOV   P1.2,C

              will leave the carry cleared and change Port 1 to 39H (00111001B).

MOV   C,bit

Bytes: 2

Cycles: 1

Encoding: | 1 0 1 0 | 0 0 1 0 | | bit address |

Operation: MOV

(C) ← (bit)

MOV   bit,C

Bytes: 2

Cycles: 2

Encoding: | 1 0 0 1 | 0 0 1 0 | | bit address |

Operation: MOV

(bit) ← (C)

MOV   DPTR,#data16

Function: Load Data Pointer with a 16-bit constant

Description: The Data Pointer is loaded with the 16-bit constant indicated. The 16-bit constant is located at the second and third bytes of the instruction. The second byte (DPH) is the high-order byte, while the third byte (DPL) holds the low-order byte. No flags are affected.

This is the only instruction which moves 16 bits of data at once.

Example: The instruction

MOV   DPTR,#1234H

will load the value 1234H into the Data Pointer: DPH will hold 12H and DPL will hold 34H.

Bytes: 3

Cycles: 2

Encoding: | 1 0 0 1 | 0 0 0 0 | | immed.data15-8 | immed.data7-0 |

Operation: MOV

(DPTR) ← #data$_{15-0}$

DPH □ DPL ← #data$_{15-8}$ □ #data$_{7-0}$

MOVC   A,@A+<base-reg>

Function: Move Code byte

Description: The MOVC instructions load the Accumulator with a code byte, or constant from program memory. The address of the byte fetched is the sum of the original unsigned eight-bit Accumulator contents and the contents of a sixteen-bit base register, which may be either the Data Pointer or the PC. In the latter case, the PC is incremented to the address of the following instruction before being added with the Accumulator; otherwise the base register is not altered. Sixteen-bit addition is performed so a carry-out from the low-order eight bits may propagate through higher-order bits. No flags are affected.

Example: A value between 0 and 3 is in the Accumulator. The following instructions will translate the value in the Accumulator to one of four values defined by the DB (define byte) directive.

```
REL_PC:    INC A
           MOVC  A,@A+PC
           RET
           DB        66H
           DB        77H
           DB        88H
           DB        99H
```

If the subroutine is called with the Accumulator equal to 01H, it will return with 77H in the Accumulator. The INC A before the MOVC instruction is needed to "get around" the RET instruction above the table. If several bytes of code separated the MOVC from the table, the corresponding number would be added to the Accumulator instead.

MOVC   A,@A + DPTR

Bytes: 1
Cycles: 2
Encoding: | 1 0 0 1 | 0 0 1 1 |
Operation: MOVC
                  (A) ← ((A) + (DPTR))

MOVC   A,@A + PC

Bytes: 1
Cycles: 2
Encoding: | 1 0 0 0 | 0 0 1 1 |
Operation: MOVC
                  (PC) ← (PC) + 1
                  (A) ← ((A) + (PC))

MOVX   <dest-byte>,<src-byte>

Function: Move External

Description: The MOVX instructions transfer data between the Accumulator and a byte of external data memory, hence the "X" appended to MOV. There are two types of instructions, differing in whether they provide an eight-bit or sixteen-bit indirect address to the external data RAM.

In the first type, the contents of R0 or R1 in the current register bank provide an eight-bit address multiplexed with data on P0. Eight bits are sufficient for external I/O expansion decoding or for a relatively small RAM array. For somewhat larger arrays, any output port pins can be used to output higher-order address bits. These pins would be controlled by an output instruction preceding the MOVX.

In the second type of MOVX instruction, the Data Pointer generates a sixteen-bit address. P2 outputs the high-order eight address bits (the contents of DPH) while P0 multiplexes the low-order eight bits (DPL) with data. The P2 Special Function Register retains its previous contents while the P2 output buffers are emitting the contents of DPH. This form is faster and more efficient when accessing very large data arrays (up to 64K bytes), since no additional instructions are needed to set up the output ports.

It is possible in some situations to mix the two MOVX types. A large RAM array with its high-order address lines driven by P2 can be addressed via the Data Pointer, or with code to output high-order address bits to P2 followed by a MOVX instruction using R0 or R1.

Example: An external 256 byte RAM using multiplexed address/data lines (e.g., an Intel 8155 RAM/I/O/Timer) is connected to the 8051 Port 0. Port 3 provides control lines for the external RAM. Ports 1 and 2 are used for normal I/O. Registers 0 and 1 contain 12H and 34H. Location 34H of the external RAM holds the value 56H. The instruction sequence,

MOVX   A,@R1
MOVX   @R0,A

copies the value 56H into both the Accumulator and external RAM location 12H.

MOVX   A,@Ri

Bytes: 1

Cycles: 2

Encoding: | 1 1 1 0 | 0 0 1 i |

Operation: MOVX
                 (A) ← ((Ri))

MOVX   A,@DPTR

Bytes: 1

Cycles: 2

Encoding: | 1 1 1 0 | 0 0 0 0 |

Operation: MOVX
                 (A) ← ((DPTR))

MOVX   @Ri,A

Bytes: 1

Cycles: 2

Encoding: | 1 1 1 1 | 0 0 1 i |

Operation: MOVX
                 ((Ri)) ← (A)

MOVX   @DPTR,A

Bytes: 1

Cycles: 2

Encoding: | 1 1 1 1 | 0 0 0 0 |

Operation: MOVX
                 (DPTR) ← (A)

MUL   AB

Function: Multiply

Description: MUL AB multiplies the unsigned eight-bit integers in the Accumulator and register B. The low-order byte of the sixteen-bit product is left in the Accumulator, and the high-order byte in B. If the product is greater than 255 (0FFH) the overflow flag is set; otherwise it is cleared. The carry flag is always cleared.

Example: Originally the Accumulator holds the value 80 (50H). Register B holds the value 160 (0A0H). The instruction,

                  MUL   AB

                  will give the product 12,800 (3200H), so B is changed to 32H (00110010B) and the Accumulator is cleared. The overflow flag is set, carry is cleared.

Bytes: 1

Cycles: 4

Encoding: | 1 0 1 0 | 0 1 0 0 |

Operation: MUL
                 $(A)_{7-0}$ ← (A) × (B)
                 $(B)_{15-8}$

NOP

Function: No Operation

Description: Execution continues at the following instruction. Other than the PC, no registers or flags are affected.

Example: It is desired to produce a low-going output pulse on bit 7 of Port 2 lasting exactly 5 cycles. A simple SETB/CLR sequence would generate a one-cycle pulse, so four additional cycles must be inserted. This may be done (assuming no interrupts are enabled) with the instruction sequence,

```
CLR    P2.7
NOP
NOP
NOP
NOP
SETB   P2.7
```

Bytes: 1

Cycles: 1

Encoding: | 0 0 0 0 | 0 0 0 0 |

Operation: NOP
$(PC) \leftarrow (PC) + 1$

ORL   <dest-byte> <src-byte>

Function: Logical-OR for byte variables

Description: ORL performs the bitwise logical-OR operation between the indicated variables, storing the results in the destination byte. No flags are affected.

The two operands allow six addressing mode combinations. When the destination is the Accumulator, the source can use register, direct, register-indirect, or immediate addrressing; when the destination is a direct address, the source can be the Accumulator or immediate data.

Note: When this instruction is used to modify an output port, the value used as the original port data will be read from the output data latch, *not* the input pins.

Example: If the Accumulator holds 0C3H (11000011B) and R0 holds 55H (01010101B) then the instruction,

ORL   A,R0

will leave the Accumulator holding the value 0D7H (11010111B).

When the destination is a directly addressed byte, the instruction can set combinations of bits in any RAM location or hardware register. The pattern of bits to be set is determined by a mask byte, which may be either a constant data value in the instruction or a variable computed in the Accumulator at run-time. The instruction,

ORL   P1,#00110010B

will set bits 5, 4, and 1 of output Port 1.

ORL   A,Rn

Bytes: 1

Cycles: 1

Encoding: | 0 1 0 0 | 1 r r r |

Operation: ORL
$(A) \leftarrow (A) \vee (Rn)$

ORL   A,direct

Bytes: 2

Cycles: 1

Encoding: | 0 1 0 0 | 0 1 0 1 | | direct address |

Operation: ORL
$(A) \leftarrow (A) \lor (direct)$

ORL   A,@Ri

Bytes: 1
Cycles: 1
Encoding: | 0 1 0 0 | 0 1 1 i |
Operation: ORL
$(A) \leftarrow (A) \lor ((Ri))$

ORL   A,#data

Bytes: 2
Cycles: 1
Encoding: | 0 1 0 0 | 0 1 0 0 | | immediate data |
Operation: ORL
$(A) \leftarrow (A) \lor \#data$

ORL   direct,A

Bytes: 2
Cycles: 1
Encoding: | 0 1 0 0 | 0 0 1 0 | | direct address |
Operation: ORL
$(direct) \leftarrow (direct) \lor (A)$

ORL   direct,#data

Bytes: 3
Cycles: 2
Encoding: | 0 1 0 0 | 0 0 1 1 | | direct addr. | | immediate data |
Operation: ORL
$(direct) \leftarrow (direct) \lor \#data$

ORL   C,<src-bit>

Function: Logical-OR for bit variables

Description: Set the carry flag if the Boolean value is a logical 1; leave the carry in its current state otherwise. A slash ("/") preceding the operand in the assembly language indicates that the logical complement of the addressed bit is used as the source value, but the source bit itself is not affected. No other flags are affected.

Example: Set the carry flag if and only if P1.0 = 1, ACC.7 = 1, or OV = 0:

                  MOV   C,P1.0   ;LOAD CARRY WITH INPUT PIN P1.0
                  ORL   C,ACC.7   ;OR CARRY WITH THE ACC. BIT 7
                  ORL   C,/OV   ;OR CARRY WITH THE INVERSE OF OV.

ORL   C,bit

Bytes: 2
Cycles: 2

Encoding: | 0 1 1 1 | 0 0 1 0 | | bit address |

Operation: ORL

$(C) \leftarrow (C) \vee (bit)$

ORL   C,/bit

Bytes: 2

Cycles: 2

Encoding: | 1 0 1 0 | 0 0 0 0 | | bit address |

Operation: ORL

$(C) \leftarrow (C) \vee (bit)$

POP   direct

Function: Pop from stack.

Description: The contents of the internal RAM location addressed by the Stack Pointer is read, and the Stack Pointer is decremented by one. The value read is then transferred to the directly addressed byte indicated. No flags are affected.

Example: The Stack Pointer originally contains the value 32H, and internal RAM locations 30H through 32H contain the values 20H, 23H, and 01H, respectively. The instruction sequence,

POP   DPH

POP   DPL

will leave the Stack Pointer equal to the value 30H and the Data Pointer set to 0123H. At this point the instruction,

POP   SP

will leave the Stack Pointer set to 20H. Note that in this special case the Stack Pointer was decremented to 2FH before being loaded with the value popped (20H).

Bytes: 2

Cycles: 2

Encoding: | 1 1 0 1 | 0 0 0 0 | | direct address |

Operation: POP

$(direct) \leftarrow ((SP))$

$(SP) \leftarrow (SP) - 1$

PUSH   direct

Function: Push onto stack

Description: The Stack Pointer is incremented by one. The contents of the indicated variable is then copied into the internal RAM location addressed by the Stack Pointer. Otherwise no flags are affected.

Example: On entering an interrupt routine the Stack Pointer contains 09H. The Data Pointer holds the value 0123H. The instruction sequence,

PUSH   DPL

PUSH   DPH

will leave the Stack Pointer set to 0BH and store 23H and 01H in internal RAM locations 0AH and 0BH, respectively.

Bytes: 2

Cycles: 2

Encoding: | 1 1 0 0 | 0 0 0 0 | | direct address |

Operation:	PUSH
	$(SP) \leftarrow (SP) + 1$
	$((SP)) \leftarrow (direct)$

RET

Function:	Return from subroutine
Description:	RET pops the high- and low-order bytes of the PC successively from the stack, decrementing the Stack Pointer by two. Program execution continues at the resulting address, generally the instruction immediately following an ACALL or LCALL. No flags are affected.
Example:	The Stack Pointer originally contains the value 0BH. Internal RAM locations 0AH and 0BH contain the values 23H and 01H, respectively. The instruction,
	RET
	will leave the Stack Pointer equal to the value 09H. Program execution will continue at location 0123H.
Bytes:	1
Cycles:	2
Encoding:	0 0 1 0 | 0 0 1 0
Operation:	RET
	$(PC_{15-8}) \leftarrow ((SP))$
	$(SP) \leftarrow (SP) - 1$
	$(PC_{7-0}) \leftarrow ((SP))$
	$(SP) \leftarrow (SP) - 1$

RETI

Function:	Return from interrupt
Description:	RETI pops the high- and low-order bytes of the PC successively from the stack, and restores the interrupt logic to accept additional interrupts at the same priority level as the one just processed. The Stack Pointer is left decremented by two. No other registers are affected; the PSW is *not* automatically restored to its pre-interrupt status. Program execution continues at the resulting address, which is generally the instruction immediately after the point at which the interrupt request was detected. If a lower- or same-level interrupt had been pending when the RETI instruction is executed, the one instruction will be executed before the pending interrupt is processed.
Example:	The Stack Pointer originally contains the value 0BH. An interrupt was detected during the instruction ending at location 0122H. Internal RAM locations 0AH and 0BH contain the values 23H and 01H, respectively. The instruction,
	RETI
	will leave the Stack Pointer equal to 09H and return program execution to location 0123H.
Bytes:	1
Cycles:	2
Encoding:	0 0 1 1 | 0 0 1 0
Operation:	RETI
	$(PC_{15-8}) \leftarrow ((SP))$
	$(SP) \leftarrow (SP) - 1$
	$(PC_{7-0}) \leftarrow ((SP))$
	$(SP) \leftarrow (SP) - 1$

RL   A

Function:	Rotate Accumulator Left

Description:	The eight bits in the Accumulator are rotated one bit to the left. Bit 7 is rotated into the bit 0 position. No flags are affected.
Example:	The Accumulator holds the value 0C5H (11000101B). The instruction,

RL   A

leaves the Accumulator holding the value 8BH (10001011B) with the carry unaffected.

Bytes:	1
Cycles:	1
Encoding:	0010 | 0011
Operation:	RL

$(A_n + 1) \leftarrow (An)$ $n = 0 - 6$
$(A0) \leftarrow (A7)$

RLC   A

Function:	Rotate Accumulator Left through the Carry flag
Description:	The eight bits in the Accumulator and the carry flag are together rotated one bit to the left. Bit 7 moves into the carry flag; the original state of the carry flag moves into the bit 0 position. No other flags are affected.
Example:	The Accumulator holds the value 0C5H (11000101B), and the carry is zero. The instruction,

RLC   A

leaves the Accumulator holding the value 8BH (10001010B) with the carry set.

Bytes:	1
Cycles:	1
Encoding:	0011 | 0011
Operation:	RLC

$(An + 1) \leftarrow (An)$ $n = 0 - 6$
$(A0) \leftarrow (C)$
$(C) \leftarrow (A7)$

RR   A

Function:	Rotate Accumulator Right
Description:	The eight bits in the Accumulator are rotated one bit to the right. Bit 0 is rotated into the bit 7 position. No flags are affected.
Example:	The Accumulator holds the value 0C5H (11000101B). The instruction,

RR   A

leaves the Accumulator holding the value 0E2H (11100010B) with the carry unaffected.

Bytes:	1
Cycles:	1
Encoding:	0000 | 0011
Operation:	RR

$(An) \leftarrow (A_n + 1)$ $n = 0 - 6$
$(A7) \leftarrow (A0)$

RRC   A

Function:	Rotate Accumulator Right through Carry flag

Description: The eight bits in the Accumulator and the carry flag are together rotated one bit to the right. Bit 0 moves into the carry flag; the original value of the carry flag moves into the bit 7 position. No other flags are affected.

Example: The Accumulator holds the value 0C5H (11000101B), the carry is zero. The instruction,

RRC   A

leaves the Accumulator holding the value 62 (01100010B) with the carry set.

Bytes: 1

Cycles: 1

Encoding: | 0 0 0 1 | 0 0 1 1 |

Operation: RRC

$(A_n) \leftarrow (A_n + 1)$ $n = 0 - 6$

$(A7) \leftarrow (C)$

$(C) \leftarrow (A0)$

SETB   <bit>

Function: Set Bit

Description: SETB sets the indicated bit to one. SETB can operate on the carry flag or any directly addressable bit. No other flags are affected.

Example: The carry flag is cleared. Output Port 1 has been written with the value 34H (00110100B). The instructions,

SETB   C

SETB   P1.0

will leave the carry flag set to 1 and change the data output on Port 1 to 35H (00110101B).

SETB   C

Bytes: 1

Cycles: 1

Encoding: | 1 1 0 1 | 0 0 1 1 |

Operation: SETB

$(C) \leftarrow 1$

SETB   bit

Bytes: 2

Cycles: 1

Encoding: | 1 1 0 1 | 0 0 1 0 | | bit address |

Operation: SETB

$(bit) \leftarrow 1$

SJMP   rel

Function: Short Jump

Description: Program control branches unconditionally to the address indicated. The branch destination is computed by adding the signed displacement in the second instruction byte to the PC, after incrementing the PC twice. Therefore, the range of destinations allowed is from 128 bytes preceding this instruction to 127 bytes following it.

Example: The label "RELADR" is assigned to an instruction at program memory location 0123H. The instruction,

SJMP   RELADR

will assemble into location 0100H. After the instruction is executed, the PC will contain the value 0123H.

(*Note:* Under the above conditions the instruction following SJMP will be at 102H. Therefore, the displacement byte of the instruction will be the relative offset (0123H-0102H) = 21H. Put another way, an SJMP with a displacement of 0FEH would be a one-instruction infinite loop.)

Bytes: 2

Cycles: 2

Encoding: | 1 0 0 0 | 0 0 0 0 | | rel. address |

Operation: SJMP
$(PC) \leftarrow (PC) + 2$
$(PC) \leftarrow (PC) + rel$

SUBB   A,<src-byte>

Function: Subtract with borrow

Description: SUBB subtracts the indicated variable and the carry flag together from the Accumulator, leaving the result in the Accumulator. SUBB sets the carry (borrow) flag if a borrow is needed for bit 7, and clears C otherwise. (If C was set *before* executing a SUBB instruction, this indicates that a borrow was needed for the previous step in a multiple precision subtraction, so the carry is subtracted from the Accumulator along with the source operand.) AC is set if a borrow is needed for bit 3, and cleared otherwise. OV is set if a borrow is needed into bit 6, but not into bit 7, or into bit 7, but not bit 6.

When subtracting signed integers OV indicates a negative number produced when a negative value is subtracted from a positive value, or a positive result when a positive number is subtracted from a negative number.

The source operand allows four addressing modes: register, direct, register-indirect, or immediate.

Example: The Accumulator holds 0C9H (11001001B), register 2 holds 54H (01010100B), and the carry flag is set. The instruction,

SUBB   A,R2

will leave the value 74H (01110100B) in the accumulator, with the carry flag and AC cleared but OV set.

Notice that 0C9H minus 54H is 75H. The difference between this and the above result is due to the carry (borrow) flag being set before the operation. If the state of the carry is not known before starting a single or multiple-precision subtraction, it should be explicitly cleared by a CLR C instruction.

SUBB   A,Rn

Bytes: 1

Cycles: 1

Encoding: | 1 0 0 1 | 1 r r r |

Operation: SUBB
$(A) \leftarrow (A) - (C) - (Rn)$

SUBB   A,direct

Bytes: 2

Cycles: 1

Encoding: | 1 0 0 1 | 0 1 0 1 | | direct address |

Operation: SUBB
$(A) \leftarrow (A) - (C) - (direct)$

SUBB   A,@Ri

Bytes:	1
Cycles:	1
Encoding:		1 0 0 1	0 1 1 i	
Operation:	SUBB
	$(A) \leftarrow (A) - (C) - ((Ri))$

SUBB   A,#data

Bytes:	2
Cycles:	1
Encoding:		1 0 0 1	0 1 0 0		immediate data	
Operation:	SUBB
	$(A) \leftarrow (A) - (C) - \#data$

SWAP   A

Function:	Swap nibbles within the Accumulator
Description:	SWAP A interchanges the low- and high-order nibbles (four-bit fields) of the Accumulator (bits 3-0 nd bits 7-4). The operation can also be thought of as a four-bit rotate instruction. No flas are affected.
Example:	The Accumulator holds the value 0C5H (11000101B). The instruction,
	SWAP A
	leaves the Accumulator holding the value 5CH (01011100B).
Bytes:	1
Cycles:	1
Encoding:		1 1 0 0	0 1 0 0	
Operation:	SWAP
	$(A_{3-0}) \overset{\leftarrow}{\underset{\rightarrow}{}} (A_{7-4})$

XCH   A,<byte>

Function:	Exchange Accumulator with byte variable
Description:	XCH loads the Accumulator with the contents of the indicated variable, at the same time writing the original Accumulator contents to the indicated variable. The source/destination operand can use register, direct, or register-indirect addressing.
Example:	R0 contains the address 20H. The Accumulator holds the value 3FH (00111111B). Internal RAM location 20H holds the value 75H (01110101B). The instruction,
	XCH A,@R0
	will leave RAM location 20H holding the values 3FH (00111111B) and 75H (01110101B) in the accumulator.

XCH   A,Rn

Bytes:	1
Cycles:	1
Encoding:		1 1 0 0	1 r r r	
Operation:	XCH
	$(A) \overset{\leftarrow}{\underset{\rightarrow}{}} (Rn)$

XCH   A,direct

Bytes: 2

Cycles: 1

Encoding: | 1 1 0 0 | 0 1 0 1 | | direct address |

Operation: XCH

(A) $\overset{\leftarrow}{\rightarrow}$ (direct)

XCH   A,@Ri

Bytes: 1

Cycles: 1

Encoding: | 1 1 0 0 | 0 1 1 i |

Operation: XCH

(A) $\overset{\leftarrow}{\rightarrow}$ ((Ri))

SCHD   A,@Ri

Function: Exchange Digit

Description: XCHD exchanges the low-order nibble of the Accumulator (bits 3-0), generally representing a hexadecimal or BCD digit, with that of the internal RAM location indirectly addressed by the specified register. The high-order nibbles (bits 7-4) of each register are not affected. No flags are affected.

Example: R0 contains the address 20H. The Accumulator holds the value 36H (00110110B). Internal RAM location 20H holds the value 75H (01110101B). The instruction,

XCHD   A,@R0

will leave RAM location 20 H holding the value 76H (01110110B) and 35H (00110101B) in the Accumulator.

Bytes: 1

Cycles: 1

Encoding: | 1 1 0 1 | 0 1 1 i |

Operation: XCHD

$(A_{3-0}) \overset{\leftarrow}{\rightarrow} ((Ri_{3-0}))$

XRL   <dest-byte>,<src-byte>

Function: Logical Exclusive-OR for byte variables.

Description: XRL performs the bitwise logical Exclusive-OR operation between the indicated variables, storing the results in the destination. No flags are affected.

The two operands allow six addressing mode combinations. When the destination is the Accumulator, the source can use register, direct, register-indirect, or immediate addressing; when the destination is a direct address, the source can be the Accumulator or immediate data.

(*Note:* When this instruction is used to modify an output port, the value used as the original port data will be read from the output data latch, *not* the input pins.)

Example: If the Accumulator holds 0C3H (11000011B) and register 0 holds 0AAH (10101010B) then the instruction,

XRL   A,R0

will leave the Accumulator holding the value 69H (01101001B).

When the destination is a directly addressed byte, this instruction can complement combinations of bits in any RAM location or hardware register. The pattern of bits to be complemented is then determined by a mask byte, either a constant contained in the instruction or a variable computed in the Accumulator at run-time. The instruction,

XRL P1, #00110001B
will complement bits 5, 4, and 0 of output Port 1.

XRL   A,Rn

Bytes: 1
Cycles: 1
Encoding: | 0 1 1 0 | 1 r r r |
Operation: XRL
$(A) \leftarrow (A) \veebar (Rn)$

XRL   A,direct

Bytes: 2
Cycles: 1
Encoding: | 0 1 1 0 | 0 1 0 1 | | direct address |
Operation: XRL
$(A) \leftarrow (A) \veebar (direct)$

XRL   A,@Ri

Bytes: 1
Cycles: 1
Encoding: | 0 1 1 0 | 0 1 1 i |
Operation: XRL
$(A) \leftarrow (A) \veebar ((Ri))$

XRL   A,#data

Bytes: 2
Cycles: 1
Encoding: | 0 1 1 0 | 0 1 0 0 | | immediate data |
Operation: XRL
$(A) \leftarrow (A) \veebar \#data$

XRL   direct,A

Bytes: 2
Cycles: 1
Encoding: | 0 1 1 0 | 0 0 1 0 | | direct address |
Operation: XRL
$(direct) \leftarrow (direct) \veebar (A)$

XRL   direct,#data

Bytes: 3
Cycles: 2
Encoding: | 0 1 1 0 | 0 0 1 1 | | direct address | | immediate data |
Operation: XRL
$(direct) \leftarrow (direct) \veebar \#data$

APPENDIX H: DALLAS DS87C520/DS8C520 DATASHEET

FEATURES

- 80C52 compatible
  - 8051 pin and instruction set compatible
  - Four 8-bit I/O ports
  - Three 16-bit timer/counters
  - 256 bytes scratchpad RAM

- Large On-chip Memory
  - 16KB Program Memory
  - 1 KB extra on-chip SRAM for MOVX

- ROMSIZE Feature
  - Selects internal ROM size from 0 to 16KB
  - Allows access to entire external memory map
  - Dynamically adjustable by software
  - Useful as boot block for external FLASH

- High-Speed Architecture
  - 4 clocks/machine cycle (8051 = 12)
  - Runs DC to 33 MHz clock rates
  - Single-cycle instruction in 121 ns
  - Dual data pointer
  - Optional variable length MOVX to access fast/slow RAM/peripherals

- Power Management Mode
  - Programmable clock source to save power
  - CPU runs from (crystal/64) or (crystal/1024)
  - Provides automatic hardware and software exit

- EMI Reduction Mode disables ALE

- Two full-duplex hardware serial ports

- High integration controller includes:
  - Power-fail reset
  - Early-warning power-fail interrupt
  - Programmable Watchdog timer

- 13 total interrupt sources with 6 external

- Available in 40-pin PDIP, 44-pin PLCC, 44-pin TQFP, and 40-pin windowed CERDIP

- Factory Mask DS83C520 or EPROM (OTP) DS87C520

491

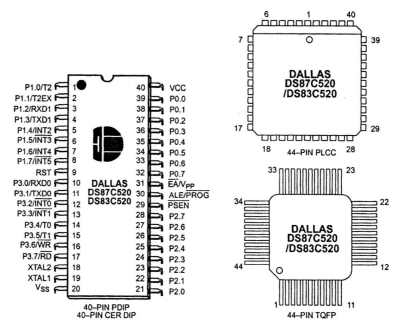

Figure H.1 Package outline

DESCRIPTION

The DS87C520/DS83C520 is a fast 8051 compatible microcontroller. It features a redesigned processor core without wasted clock and memory cycles. As a result, it executes every 8051 instruction between 1.5 and 3 times faster than the original for the same crystal speed. Typical applications will see a speed improvement of 2.5 imes using the same code and the same crystal. The DS87C520/DS83C520 offers a maximum crystal speed of 33 MHz, resulting in apparent execution speeds of 82.5 MHz (approximately 2.5 ×).

The DS87C520/DS83C520 is pin compatible with all three packages of the standard 8051 and includes standard resources such as three timer/counters, serial port, and four 8-bit I/O ports. It features 16KB of EPROM or Mask ROM with an extra 1KB of data RAM. Both OTP and windowed packages are available.

Besides greater speed, the microcontroller includes a second full hardware serial port, seven additional interrupts, programmable watchdog timer, brown-out monitor, and power-fail reset. The device also provides dual data pointers (DPTRs) to speed block data memory moves. It also can adjust the speed of MOVX data memory access from two to nine machine cycles for flexibility in selecting external memory and peripherals.

A new Power Management Mode (PMM) is useful for portable applications. This feature allows software to select a lower speed clock as the main time base. While normal operation has a machine cycle rate of 4 clocks per cycle, the PMM runs the process at 64 or 1024 clocks per cycle. For example, at 12 MHz, standard operation has a machine cycle of 3 MHz. In Power Management Mode, software can select either 187.5 KHz or 11.7 KHz machine cycle rate. There is a corresponding reduction in power consumption when the processor runs slower.

The EMI reduction feature allows software to select a reduced emission mode. This disables the ALE signal when it is unneeded.

The DS83C520 is a factory Mask ROM version of the DS87C520 designed for high-volume, cost-sensitive applications. It is identical in all respects to the DS87C520, except that the 16KB of EPROM is replaced by a user-supplied application program. All references to features of the DS87C520 will apply to the DS83C520, with the exception of EPROM-specific features where noted. Please contact your local Dallas Semiconductor sales representative for ordering information.

TABLE H.1
Ordering Information

Part Number	Package	Max. Clock Speed	Temperature Range
DS87C520-MCL	40-pin plastic DIP	33 MHz	0°C to 70°C
DS87C520-QCL	44-pin PLCC	33 MHz	0°C to 70°C
DS87C520-ECL	44-pin TQFP	33 MHz	0°C to 70°C
DS87C520-MNL	40-pin plastic DIP	33 MHz	-40°C to +85°C
DS87C520-QNL	44-pin PLCC	33 MHz	-40°C to +85°C
DS87C520-ENL	44-pin TQFP	33 MHz	-40°C to +85°C
DS87C520-WCL	40-pin windowed CERDIP	33 MHz	0°C to 70°C
DS83C520-MCL	40-pin plastic DIP	33 MHz	0°C to 70°C
DS83C520-QCL	44-pin PLCC	33 MHz	0°C to 70°C
DS83C520-ECL	44-pin TQFP	33 MHz	0°C to 70°C

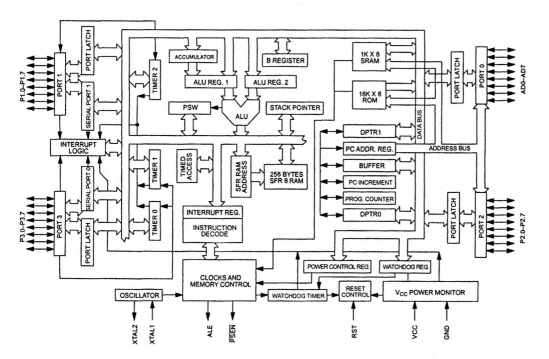

Figure H-2 DS87C520/DS83C520 Block diagram

H.1 COMPATIBILITY

The DS87C520/DS83C520 is a fully static CMOS 8051 compatible microcontroller designed for high performance. In most cases the DS87C520/DS83C520 can drop into an existing socket for the 8xc51 family to improve the operation

TABLE H.2

Pin Description

Dip	PLCC	TQFP	Signal Name	Description
40	44	38	V_{CC}	V_{CC} - +5V.
20	22, 23, 1	16, 17, 39	GND	GND–Digital circuit ground.
9	10	4	RST	**RST - Input.** The RST input pin contains a Schmitt voltage input to recognize external active high Reset inputs. The pin also employs an internal pull-down resistor to allow for a combination of wired OR external Reset sources. An RC is not required for power-up, as the device provides this function internally.
18 19	20 21	14 15	XTAL2 XTAL 1	**XTAL 1, XTAL 2.** The crystal oscillator pins XTAL 1 and XTAL 2 provide support for parallel resonant, AT cut crystals. XTAL 1 acts also as an input if there is an external clock source in place of a crystal. XTAL 2 serves as the output of the crystal amplifier.
29	32	26	$\overline{PSEN}$	**PSEN–Output.** The Program Store Enable output. This signal is commonly connected to optional external ROM memory as a chip enable. $\overline{PSEN}$ will provide an active low pulse and is driven high when external ROM is not being accessed.
30	33	27	ALE	**ALE–Output.** The Address Latch Enable output functions as a clock to latch the external address LSB from the multiplexed address/data bus on Port 0. This signal is commonly connected to the latch enable of an external 373 family transparent latch. ALE has a pulse width of 1.5 XTAL 1 cycles and a period of four XTAL 1 cycles. ALE is forced high when the DS87C520/DS83C520 is in a Reset condition. ALE can also be disabled by writing ALEOFF=1 (PMR.2). When ALEOFF=1 ALE is forced high. AFE operates independently of ALEOF during external memory accesses.
39 38 37 36 35 34 33 32	43 42 41 40 39 38 37 36	37 36 35 34 33 32 31 30	P0.0 (AD0) P0.1 (AD1) P0.2 (AD2) P0.3 (AD3) P0.4 (AD4) P0.5 (AD5) P0.6 (AD6) P0.7 (AD7)	**Port 0 (AD0-7)–I/O.** Port 0 is an open-drain 8-bit bi-directional I/O port. As an alternate function Port 0 can function as the multiplexed address/data bus to access off-chip memory. During the time when ALE is high, the LSB of a memory address is presented. When ALE falls to a logic 0, the port transitions to a bi-directional data bus. This bus is used to read external ROM and read/write external RAM memory or peripherals. When used as a memory bus, the port provides active high drivers. The reset condition of Port 0 is tri-state. Pull-up resistors are required when using Port 0 as an I/O port.
1-8	2-9	40-44	P1.0-P1.7	**Port 1–I/O.** Port 1 functions as both an 8-bit bi-directional I/O port and an alternate functional interface for Timer 2 I/O, new Extenal Interrupts, and new Serial Port 1. The reset condition of Port 1 is with all bits at a logic 1. In this state, a weak pull-up holds the port high. This condition also serves as an input state, a weak pull-up holds the port high. This condition also serves as an input mode, since any external circuit that writes to the port will overcome the weak pull-up. When software writes a 0 to any port pin, the DS87C520/DS83C520 will activate a strong pull-down that remains on until either a 1 is written or a reset occurs. Writing a 1 after the port has been at 0 will cause a strong transition driver to turn on, followed by a weaker sustaining pull-up. Once the momentary strong driver turns off, the port again becomes the output high (and input) state. The alternate modes of Port 1 are outlines as follows.

			Port	Alternate	Function
1	2	40	P1.0	T2	External I/O for Timer/Counter 2
2	3	41	P1.1	T2EX	Timer/Counter 2 Capture/Reload Trigger
3	4	42	P1.2	RXD1	Serial Port 1 Input
4	5	43	P1.3	TXD1	Serial Port 1 Output
5	6	44	P1.4	INT2	External Interrupt 2 (Positive Edge Detect)
6	7	1	P1.5	$\overline{INT3}$	External Interrupt 3 (Negative Edge Detect)
7	8	2	P1.6	INT4	External Interrupt 4 (Positive Edge Detect)
8	9	3	P1.7	$\overline{INT5}$	External Interrupt 5 (Negative Edge Detect)

Continued

TABLE H.2
Continued

Dip	PLCC	TQFP	Signal Name	Description
21 22 23 24 25 26 27 28	24 25 26 27 28 29 30 31	18 19 20 21 22 23 24 25	P2.0 (A8) P2.1 (A9) P2.2 (A10) P2.3 (A11) P2.4 (A12) P2.5 (A13) P2.6 (A14) P2.7 (A15)	**Port 2 (A8-15)–I/O.** Port 2 is a bi-directional I/O port. The reset condition of Port 2 is logic high. in this state, a weak pull-up holds the port high. This condition also serves as an input mode, since any external circuit that writes to the port will overcome the weak pull-up. When software writes a 0 to any port pin, the DS87C520/DS83C520 will activate a strong pull-down that remains on until either a 1 is written or a reset occurs. Writing a 1 after the port has been at 0 will cause a strong transition driver to turn on, followed by a weaker sustaining pull-up. Once the momentary strong driver turns off, the port again becomes both the output high and input state. As an alternate function Port 2 can function as MSB of the external address bus. This bus can be used to read external ROM and read/write external RAM memory or peripherals.
10-17	11, 13-19	5, 7-13	P3.0-P3.7	**Port 3–I/O.** Port 3 functions as both an 8-bit bi-directional I/O port and an alternate functional interface for External Interrupts, Serial Port 0, Timer 0 and 1 inputs, and $\overline{RD}$ and $\overline{WR}$ strobes. The reset condition of Port 3 is with all bits at a logic 1. In this state, a weak pull-up holds the port high. This condition also serves as an input mode, since any external circuit that writes to the port will overcome the weak pull-up. When software writes a 0 to any port pin, the DS87C520/DS83C520 will activate a strong pull-down that remains on until either a 1 is written or a reset occurs. Writing a 1 after the port has been at 0 will cause a strong transition driver to turn on, followed by a weaker sustaining pull-up. Once the momentary strong driver turns off, the port again becomes both the output high and input stage. The alternate modes of Port 3 are outlined below.

				Port	Alternate	Mode
10	11	5		P3.0	RXD0	Serial Port 0 Input
11	13	7		P3.1	TXD0	Serial Port 0 Output
12	14	8		P3.2	$\overline{INT0}$	External Interrupt 0
13	15	9		P3.3	$\overline{INT1}$	External Interrupt 1
14	16	10		P3.4	T0	Timer 0 External Input
15	17	11		P3.5	T1	Timer 1 External Input
16	18	12		P3.6	$\overline{WR}$	External Data Memory Write Strobe
17	19	13		P3.7	$\overline{RD}$	External Data Memory Read Strobe

Dip	PLCC	TQFP	Signal Name	Description
31	35	29	$\overline{EA}$	**$\overline{EA}$–Input.** Connect to ground to force the DS87C520/DS83C520 to use an external ROM. The internal RAM is still accessible as determined by register settings. Connect $\overline{EA}$ to V_{CC} to use internal ROM.
— 	12 34	6 28	NC	**NC–Reserved.** These pins should not be connected. They are reserved for use with future devices in this family.

significantly. While remaining familiar to 8051 family users, it has many new features. In general, software written for existing 8051 based systems works without modification on the DS87C520/DS83C520. The exception is critical timing since the High-Speed Micro performs its instructions much faster than the original for any given crystal selection. The DS87C520/DS83C520 runs the standard 8051 family instruction set and is pin compatible with DIP, PLCC or TQFP packages.

The DS87C520/DS83C520 provides three 16-bit timer/counters, full-duplex serial port (2), 256 bytes of direct RAM plus 1KB of extra MOVX RAM. I/O ports have the same operation as a standard 8051 product. Timers will default to a 12 clock per cycle operation to keep their timing comptabile with original 8051 family systems. However, timers are individually programmable to run at the new 4 clocks per cycle if desired. The PCA is not supported.

The DS87C520/DS83C520 provides several new hardware features implemented by new Special Function Registers. A summary of these SFRs is provided below.

H.2 PERFORMANCE OVERVIEW

The DS87C520/DS83C520 features a high speed 8051 compatible core. Higher speed comes not just from increasing the clock frequency, but from a newer, more efficient design.

This updated core does not have the dummy memory cycles that are present in a standard 8051. A conventional 8051 generates machine cycles using the clock frequency divided by 12. In the DS87C520/DS83C520, the same machine cycle takes four clocks. Thus the fastest instruction, 1 machine cycle, executes three times faster for the same crystal frequency. Note that these are identical instructions. The majority of instructions on the DS87C520/DS83C520 will see the full 3 to 1 speed improvement. Some instructions will get between 1.5 and 2.4 to 1 improvement. All instructions are faster than the original 8051.

The numercial average of all opcodes gives approximately a 2.5 to 1 speed improvement. Improvement of individual programs will depend on the actual instructions used. Speed sensitive applications would make the most use of instructions that are three times faster. However, the sheer number of 3 to 1 improved opcodes makes dramatic speed improvements likely for any code. These architecture improvements produce a peak instruction cycle in 121 ns (8.25 MIPs). The Dual Data Pointer feature also allows the user to eliminate wasted instructions when moving blocks of memory.

H.3 INSTRUCTION SET SUMMARY

All instructions in the DS87C520/DS83C520 perform the same functions as their 8051 counterparts. Their effect on bits, flags, and other status functions is identical. However, the timing of each instruction is different. This applies both in absolute and relative number of clocks.

For absolute timing of real-time events, the timing of software loops can be calculated using a table in the High-Speed Microcontroller User's Guide. However, counter/timers default to run at the older 12 clocks per increment. In this way, timer-based events occur at the standard intervals with software executing at higher speed. Timers optionally can run at 4 clocks per increment to take advantage of faster processor operation.

The relative time of two instructions might be different in the new architecture than it was previously. For example, in the original architecture, the "MOVX A,@DPTR" instruction and the "MOV direct, direct" instruction used two machine cycles or 24 oscillator cycles. Therefore, they required the same amount of time. In the DS87C520/DS83C520, the MOVX instruction takes as little as two machine cycles or eight oscillator cycles but the "MOV direct,direct" uses three machine cycles or 12 oscillator cycles. While both are faster than their original counterparts, they now have different execution times. This is because the DS87C520/DS83C520 usually uses one instruction cycle for each instruction byte. The user concerned with precise program timing should examine the timing of each instruction for familiarity with the changes. Note that a machine cycle now requires just four clocks, and provides one ALE pulse per cycle. Many instructions require only one cycle, but some require five. In the original architecture, all were one or two cycles except for MUL and DIV. Refer to the High-Speed Microcontroller User's Guide for details and individual instruction timing.

H.4 SPECIAL FUNCTION REGISTERS

Special Function Registers (SFRs) control most special features of the DS87C520/DS83C520. This allows the DS87C520/DS83C520 to have many new features but use the same instruction set as the 8051. When writing software to use a new feature, an equate statement defines the SFR to an assembler or compiler. This is the only change needed to access the new function. The DS87C520/DS83C520 duplicates the SFRs contained in the standard 80C52. Table H.3 shows the register addresses and bit locations. Many are standard 80C52 registers. The High-Speed Microcontroller User's Guide describes all SFRs.

TABLE H.3
Special Function Register Locations (*New functions are in bold*)

Register	Bit 7	Bit 6	Bit 5	Bit 4	Bit 3	Bit 2	Bit 1	Bit 0	Address
P0	P0.7	P0.6	P0.5	P0.4	P0.3	P0.2	P0.1	P0.0	80h
SP									81h
DPL									82h
DPH									83h
DPL1									84h
DPH1									85h
DPS	0	0	0	0	0	0	0	**SEL**	86h
PCON	SMOD_0	**SMOD0**	—	—	GF1	GF0	STOP	IDLE	87h
TCON	TF1	TR1	TF0	TR0	IE1	IT1	IE0	IT0	88h
TMOD	GATE	C/$\overline{T}$	M1	M0	GATE	C/$\overline{T}$	M1	M0	89h
TL0									8Ah
TL1									8Bh
TH0									8Ch
TH1									8Dh
CKCON	WD1	WD0	T2M	T1M	T0M	MD2	MD1	MD0	8Eh
PORT1	P1.7	P1.6	P1.5	P1.4	P1.3	P1.2	P1.1	P1.0	90h
EXIF	**IE5**	**IE4**	**IE3**	**IE2**	**XT/$\overline{RG}$**	**RGMD**	**RGSL**	**BGS**	91h
SCON0	SM0/FE_0	SM1_0	SM2_0	REN_0	TB8_0	RB8_0	TI_0	RI_0	98h
SBUF0									99h
P2	P2.7	P2.6	P2.5	P2.4	P2.3	P2.2	P2.1	P2.0	A0h
IE	EA	ES1	ET2	ES0	ET1	EX1	ET0	EX0	A8h
SADDR0									A9h
SADDR1									AAh
P3	P3.7	P3.6	P3.5	P3.4	P3.3	P3.2	P3.1	P3.0	B0h
IP	—	PS1	PT2	PS0	PT1	PX1	PT0	PX0	B8H
SADEN0									B9h
SADEN1									BAh
SCON1	SM0/FE_1	SM1_1	SM2_1	REN_1	TB8_1	RB8_1	TI_1	RI_1	C0H

Continued

TABLE H.3
Continued

Register	Bit 7	Bit 6	Bit 5	Bit 4	Bit 3	Bit 2	Bit 1	Bit 0	Address
SBUF1	SB7	SB6	SB5	SB4	SB3	SB2	SB1	SB0	C1h
ROMSIZE	—	—	—	—	—	RMS2	RMS1	RMS0	C2h
PMR	CD1	CD0	SWB	—	XTOFF	ALEOFF	DME1	DME0	C4h
STATUS	PIP	HIP	LIP	XTUP	SPTA1	SPRA1	SPTA0	SPRA0	C5h
TA									C7h
T2CON	TF2	EXF2	RCLK	TCLK	EXEN2	TR2	C/$\overline{T2}$	CP/$\overline{RL2}$	C8h
T2MOD	—	—	—	—	—	—	T2OE	DCEN	C9h
RCAP2L									CAh
RCAP2H									CBh
TL2									CCh
TH2									CDh
PSW	CY	AC	F0	RS1	RS0	OV	FL	P	D0h
WDCON	SMOD_1	POR	EPFI	PFI	WDIF	WTRF	EWT	RWT	D8h
ACC									E0h
EIE	—	—	—	EWDI	EX5	EX4	EX3	EX2	E8h
B									F0h
EIP	—	—	—	PWDI	PX5	PX4	PX3	PX2	F8h

H.5 MEMORY RESOURCES

Like the 8051, the DS87C520/DS83C520 uses three memory areas. These are program (ROM), data (RAM), and scratchpad RAM (registers). The DS87C520 contains on-chip quantities of all three areas.

The total memory configuration of the DS87C520/DS83C520 is 16KB of ROM, 1KB of data SRAM and 256 bytes of scratchpad or direct RAM. The 1KB of data space SRAM is read/write accessible and is memory mapped. This on-chip SRAM is reached by the MOVX instruction. It is not used for executable memory. The scratchpad area is 256 bytes of register mapped RAM and is identical to the RAM found on the 80C52. There is no conflict or overlap among the 256 bytes and the 1KB as they use different addressing modes and separate instructions.

H.6 PROGRAM MEMORY ACCESS

On-chip ROM begins at address 0000h and is contiguous through 3FFFh (16KB). Exceeding the maximum address of on-chip ROM will cause the device to access off-chip memory. However, the maximum on-chip decoded address is selectable by software using the ROMSIZE™ feature. Software can cause the DS87C520/DS83C520 to behave like a device with less on-chip memory. This is beneficial when overlapping external memory, such as Flash, is used.

The maximum memory size is dynamically variable. Thus a portion of memory can be removed from the memory map to access off-chip memory, then restored to access on-chip memory. In fact, all of the on-chip memory can be removed from the memory map allowing the full 64KB memory space to be addressed from off-chip memory. ROM addresses that are larger than the selected maximum are automatically fetched from outside the part via Ports 0 and 2. A depiction of the ROM memory map is shown in Figure 2.

The ROMSIZE register is used to select the maximum on-chip decoded address for ROM. Bits RMS2, RMS1, RMS0 have the following affect.

RMS2	RMS1	RMS0	Maximum on-chip ROM Address
0	0	0	0KB
0	0	1	1KB/03FFh
0	1	0	2KB/07FFh
0	1	1	4KB/0FFFh
1	0	0	8KB/1FFFh
1	0	0	16KB (default)/3FFFh
1	1	0	Invalid–reserved
1	1	1	Invalid–reserved

The reset default condition is a maximum on-chip ROM address of 16KB. Thus no action is required if this feature is not used. When accessing external program memory, the first 16KB would be inaccessible. To select a smaller effective ROM size, software must alter bits RMS2-RMS0. Altering these bits requires a Timed Access procedure as explained later.

Care should be taken so that changing the ROMSIZE register does not corrupt program execution. For example, assume that a DS87C520/DS83C520 is executing instructions from internal program memory near the 12KB boundary (~3000h) and that the ROMSIZE register is currently configured for a 16KB internal program space. If software reconfigures the ROMSIZE register to 4KB (0000h–0FFFh) in the current state, the device will immediately jump to external program execution because program code from 4KB to 16KB (1000h–3FFFh) is no longer located on-chip. This could result in code misalignment and execution of an invalid instruction. The recommended method is to modify the ROMSIZE register from a location in memory that will be internal (or external) both before and after the operation. In the above example, the instruction which modifies the ROMSIZE register should be located below the 4KB (1000h) boundary, so that it will be unaffected by the memory modification. The same precaution should be applied if the internal program memory size is modified while executing from external program memory.

Off-chip memory is accessed using the multiplexed address/data bus on P0 and the MSB address on P2. While serving as a memory bus, these pins are not I/O ports. This convention follows the standard 8051 method of expanding on-chip memory. Off-chip ROM access also occurs if the $\overline{EA}$ pin is a logic 0. $\overline{EA}$ overrides all bit settings. The $\overline{PSEN}$ signal will go active (low) to serve as a chip enable or output enable when Ports 0 and 2 fetch from external ROM.

H.7 DATA MEMORY ACCESS

Unlike many 8051 derivatives, the DS87C520/DS83C520 contains on-chip data memory. It also contains the standard 256 bytes of RAM accessed by direct instructions. These areas are separate. The MOVX instruction accesses the on-chip data memory. Although physically on-chip, software treats this area as though it was located off-chip. The 1KB of SRAM is between address 0000h and 03FFh.

Access to the on-chip data RAM is optional under software control. When enabled by software, the data SRAM is between 0000h and 03FFh. Any MOVX instruction that uses this area will go the on-chip RAM while enabled. MOVX addresses greater than 03FFh automatically go to external memory through Ports 0 and 2.

When disabled, the 1KB memory area is transparent to the system memory map. Any MOVX directed to the space 0000h and FFFFh goes to the expanded bus on Ports 0 and 2. This also is the default condition. This default allows the DS87C520/DS83C520 to drop into an existing system that uses these addresses for other hardware and still have full compatibility.

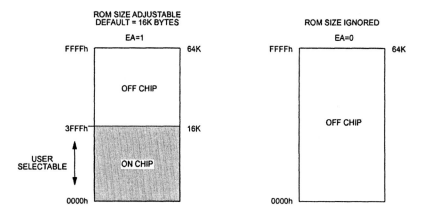

Figure H.3 ROM Memory Map. The erasure window should be covered without regard to the programmed/unprogrammed state of the EPROM. Otherwise, the device may not meet the AC and DC parameters listed on the datasheet.

TABLE H.4
Data Memory Access Control

DME1	DME0	Data Memory Address	Memory Function
0	0	0000h–FFFFh	External Date Memory *Default condition*
0	1	0000h–03FFh	Internal SRAM Data Memory
		0400h–FFFFh	External Data Memory
1	0	Reserved	Reserved
1	1	0000h–03FFh	Internal SRAM Data Memory
		0400h–FFFBh	Reserved—no external access
		FFFCh	Read access to the status of lock bits
		FFFDh–FFFFh	Reserved—no external access

Notes on the status byte read at FFFCh with DME 1, 0 = 1, 1; Bits 2–0 reflect the programmed status of the security lock bits LB2–LB0. They are individually set to a logic 1 to correspond to a security lock bit that has been programmed. These status bits allow software to verify that the part has been locked before running if desired. The bits are read only.
Note: After internal MOVX SRAM has been initialized, changing DME0/1 bits will have no effect on the contents of the SRAM.

The on-chip data area is software selectable using two bits in the Power Management Register at laocation C4h. This section is dynamically programmable. Thus access to the on-chip area becomes transparent to reach off-chip devices at the same addresses. The control bits are DME1 (PMR.1) and DME0 (PMR.0). They have the following operation:

H.8 STRETCH MEMORY CYCLE

The DS87C520/DS83C520 allows software to adjust the speed of off-chip data memory access. The microcontroller is capable of performing the MOVX in as few as two instruction cycles. The on-chip SRAM uses this speed and any MOVX instruction directed internally uses two cycles. However, the time can be stretched for interface to external devices. This allows access to both fast memory and slow memory or peripherals with no glue logic. Even in high-speed systems, it may not be necessary or desirable to perform off-chip data memory access at full speed. In addition, there are a variety of memory mapped peripherals such as LCDs or UARTs that are slow.

The Stretch MOVX is controlled by the Clock Control Register at SFR locatioin 8Eh as described below. It allows the user to select a Stretch value between zero and seven. A Stretch of zero will result in a two machine cycle MOVX. A Stretch of seven will result in a MOVX of nine machine cycles. Software can dynamically change this value depending on the particular memory or peripheral.

On reset, the Stretch value will default to a one resulting in a three cycle MOVX for any external access. Therefore, off-chip RAM access is not at full speed. This is a convenience to existing designs that may not have fast RAM in place. Internal SRAM access is always at full speed regardless of the Stretch setting. When desiring maximum speed, software should select a Stretch value of zero. When using very slow RAM or peripherals, select a larger Stretch value. Note that this affects data memory only and the only way to slow program memory (ROM) access is to use a slower crystal.

Using a Stretch value between one and seven causes the microcontroller to stretch the read/write strobe and all related timing. Also, setup and hold times are increased by one clock when using any Stretch greater than 0. This results in a wider read/write strobe and relaxed interface timing, allowing more time for memory/peripherals to respond. The timing of the variable speed MOVX is in the Electrical Specifications. Table H.5 shows the resulting strobe widths for each Stretch value. The memory Stretch uses the Clock Control Special Function Register at SFR location 8Eh. The Stretch value is selected using bits CKCON.2-0. In the table, these bits are referred to as M2 through M0. The first Stretch (default) allows the use of common 120 ns RAMs without dramatically lengthening the memory access.

H.9 DUAL DATA POINTER

The timing of block moves of data memory is faster using the Dual Data Pointer (DPTR). The standard 8051 DPTR is a 16-bit value that is used to address off-chip data RAM or peripherals. In the DS87C520/DS83C520, this data pointer is called DPTR0, located at SFR address 82h and 83h. These are the original locations. Using DPTR requires no modification of standard code. The new DPTR at SFR 84 h and 85h is called DPTR1. The DPTR Select bit (DPS) chooses the active pointer. Its location is the lsb of the SFR location 86h. No other bits in register 86h have any effect and are 0. The user switches between data pointers by toggling the lsb of register 86h. The increment (INC) instruction is the fastest way to accomplish this. All DPTR-related instructions use the currently selected DPTR for any activity. Therefore it takes only one instruction to switch from a source to a destination address. Using the Dual Data Pointer saves code from needing to save source and destination addresses when doing a block move. The software simply switches between DPTR0 and 1 once software loads them. The relevant register locations are as follows:

DPL	82h	Low byte original DPTR
DPH	83h	High byte original DPTR
DPL1	84h	Low byte new DPTR
DPH1	85h	High byte new DPTR
DPS	86h	DPTR Select (lsb)

TABLE H.5
Data Memory Cycle Stretch Values

| CKCON.2-0 | | | | $\overline{\text{RD}}$ or $\overline{\text{WR}}$ Strobe | Strobe Width Time |
M2	M1	M0	Memory Cycles	Width in Clocks	@ 33 MHz
0	0	0	2 (forced internal)	2	60 ns
0	0	1	3 (default external)	4	121 ns
0	1	0	4	8	242 ns
0	1	1	5	12	364 ns
1	0	0	6	16	485 ns
1	0	1	7	20	606 ns
1	1	0	8	24	727 ns
1	1	1	9	28	848 ns

H.10 POWER MANAGEMENT

Along with the standard Idle and power down (Stop) modes of the standard 80C52, the DS87C520/DS83C520 provides a new Power Management Mode. This mode allows the processor to continue functioning, yet to save power compared with full operation. The DS87C520/DS83C520 also features several enhancements to Stop mode that make it more useful.

H.11 POWER MANAGEMENT MODE (PMM)

Power Management Mode offers a complete scheme of reduced internal clock speeds that allow the CPU to run software but to use substantially less power. During default operation, the DS87C520/DS83C520 uses four clocks per machine cycle. Thus the instruction cycle rate is Clock/4. At 33 MHz crystal speed, the instruction cycle speed is 8.25 MHz (33/4). In PMM, the microcontroller continues to operate but uses an internally divided version of the clock source. This creates a lower power state without external components. It offers a choice of two reduced instruction cycle speeds (and two clock sources—discussed below). The speeds are (Clock/64) and (Clock/1024).

Software is the only mechanism to invoke the PMM. Table H.6 illustrates the instruction cycle rate in PMM for several common crystal frequencies. Since power consumption is a direct function of operating speed, PMM 1 eliminates most of the power consumption while still allowing a reasonable speed of processing. PMM 2 runs very slow and provides the lowest power consumption without stopping the CPU. This is illustrated in Table H.7.

Note that PMM provides a lower power condition than Idle mode. This is because in Idle mode, all clocked functions such as timers run at a rate of crystal divided by 4. Since wake-up from PMM is as fast as or faster than from Idle and PMM allows the CPU to operate (even if doing NOPs), there is little reason to use Idle mode in new designs.

TABLE H.6
Instruction Cycle Rate

Crystal Speed	Full Operation (4 Clocks)	PMM 1 (64 Clocks)	PMM 2 (1024 Clocks)
1.8432 MHz	460.8 KHz	28.8 KHz	1.8 KHz
11.0592 MHz	2.765 MHz	172.8 KHz	10.8 KHz
22 MHz	5.53 MHz	345.6 KHz	21.6 KHz
25 MHz	6.25 MHz	390.6 KHz	24.4 KHz
33 MHz	8.25 MHz	515.6 KHz	32.2 KHz

TABLE H.7
Operating Current Estimates in PMM

Crystal Speed	Full Operation (4 Clocks)	PMM 1 (64 Clocks)	PMM 2 (1024 Clocks)
1.8432 MHz	3.1 mA	1.2 mA	1.0 mA
3.57 MHz	5.3 mA	1.6 mA	1.1 mA
11.0592 MHz	15.5 mA	4.8 mA	4.0 mA
16 MHz	21 mA	7.1 mA	6.0 mA
22 MHz	25.5 mA	8.3 mA	6.5 mA
25 MHz	31 mA	9.7 mA	8.0 mA
33 MHz	36 mA	12.0 mA	10.0 mA

H.12 CRYSTALESS PMM

A major component of power consumption in PMM is the crystal amplifier circuit. The DS87C520/DS83C520 allows the user to switch CPU operation to an internal ring oscillator and turn off the crystal amplifier. The CPU would then have a clock source of approximately 2–4 MHz, divided by either 4, 64, or 1024. The ring is not accurate, so software can not perform precision timing. However, this mode allows an additional saving of between 0.5 and 6.0 mA depending on the actual crystal frequency. While this saving is of little use when running at 4 clocks per instruction cycle, it makes a major contribution when running in PMM1 or PMM2.

H.13 PMM OPERATION

Software invokes the PMM by setting the appropriate bits in the SFR area. The basic choices are divider speed and clock source. There are three speeds (4, 64, and 1024) and two clock sources (crystal and ring). Both the decisions and the controls are separate. Software will typically select the clock speed first. Then, it will perform the switch to ring operation if desired. Lastly, software can disable the crystal amplifier if desired.

There are two ways of exiting PMM. Software can remove the condition by reversing the procedure that invoked PMM or hardware can (optionally) remove it. To resume operation at a divide by 4 rate under software control, simply select 4 clocks per cycle, then crystal based operatioin if relevant. When disabling the crystal as the time base in favor of the ring oscillator, there are timing restrictions associated with restarting the crystal operation. Details are described below.

There are three registers containing bits that are concerned with PMM functions. They are Power Management Register (PMR; C4h), Status (STATUS; C5h), and External Interrupt Flag (EXIF; 91H).

H.13.1 Clock Divider

Software can select the instruction cycle rate by selecting bits CD1 (PMR.7) and CD0 (PRM.6) as follows:

CD1	CD0	Cycle rate
0	0	Reserved
0	1	4 clocks (default)
1	0	64 clocks
1	1	1024 clocks

The selection of instruction cycle rate will take effect after a delay of one instruction cycle. Note that the clock divider choice applies to all functions including timers. Since baud rates are altered, it will be difficult to conduct serial communication while in PMM. There are minor restrictions on accessing the clock selection bits. The processor must be running in a 4 clock state to select either 64 (PMM1) or 1024 (PMM2) clocks. This means software cannot go directly from PMM1 to PMM2 or vice versa. It must return to a 4 clock rate first.

H.13.2 Switchback

To return to a 4 clock rate from PMM, software can simply select the CD1 and CD0 clock control bits to the 4 clocks per cycle state. However, the DS87C520/DS83C520 provides several hardware alternatives for automatic Switchback. If Switchback is enabled, then the DS87C520/DS83C520 will automatically return to a 4 clock per cycle speed when an interrupt occurs from an enabled, valid external interrupt source. A Switchback will also occur when a UART detects the beginning of a serial start bit if the serial receiver is enabled (REN=1). Note the beginning of a start bit does not generate an interrupt; this occurs on reception of a complete serial word. The automatic Switchback on detection of a start bit allows hardware to correct baud rates in time for a proper serial reception. A switchback will also occur when a byte is written to SBUF0 or SBUF1 for transmission.

Switchback is enabled by setting the SWB bit (PMR.5) to a 1 in software. For an external interrupt, Switchback will occur only if the interrupt source could really generate the interrupt. For example, if $\overline{INT0}$ is enabled but has a low priority setting, then Switchback will not occur on $\overline{INT0}$ if the CPU is servicing a high priority interrupt.

H.13.3 Status

Information in the Status register assists decisions about switching into PMM. This register contains information about the level of active interrupts and the activity on the serial ports.

The DSC87C520/DS83C520 supports three levels of interrupt priority. These levels are Power-fail, High, and Low. Bits STATUS.7-5 indicate the service status of each level. If PIP (Power-fail Interrupr Priority; STATUS.7) is a 1, then the processor is servicing this level. If either HIP (High Interrupt Priority; STATUS.6) or LIP (Low Interrupt Priority; STATUS.5) is high, then the corresponding level is in service.

Software should not rely on a lower priority level interrupt source to remove PMM (Switchback) when a higher level is in service. Check the current priority service level before entering PMM. If the current service level locks out a desired Switchback source, then it would be advisable to wait until this condition clears before entering PMM.

Alternately, software can prevent an undesired exit from PMM by entering a low priority interrupt service level before entering PMM. This will prevent other low priority interrupts from causing a Switchback.

Status also contains information about the state of the serial ports. Serial Port Zero Receive Activity (SPRA0; STATUS.0) indicates a serial word is being received on Serial Port 0 when this bit is set to a 1. Serial Port Zero Transmit Activity (SPTA0; STATUS.1) indicates that the serial port is still shifting out a serial transmission. STATUS.2 and STATUS.3 provide the same information for Serial Port 1, respectively. These bits should be interrogated before entering PMM1 or PMM2 to ensure that no serial port operations are in progress. Changing the clock divisor rate during a serial transmission or reception will corrupt the operation.

H.13.4 Crystal/Ring Operation

The DS87C520/DS83C520 allows software to choose the clock source as an independent selection from the instruction cycle rate. The user can select crystal-based or ring oscillator-based operation under software control. Power-on reset default is the crystal (or external clock) source. The ring may save power depending on the actual crystal speed. To save still more power, software can then disable the crystal amplifier. This process requires two steps. Reversing the process also requires two steps.

The XT/$\overline{RG}$ bit (EXIF.3) selects the crystal or ring as the clock source. Setting XT/$\overline{RG}$ = 1 selects the crystal. Setting XT/$\overline{RG}$ = 0 selects the ring. The RGMD (EXIF.2) bit serves as a status bit by indicating the active clock source. RGMD = 0 indicates the CPU is running frm the crystal. RGMD = 1 indicates it is running from the ring. When operating from the ring, disable the crystal amplifier by setting the XTOFF bit (PMR.3) to a 1. This can only be done when XT/$\overline{RG}$ = 0.

When changing the clock source, the selection will take effect after a one instruction cycle delay. This applies to changes from crystal to ring and vice versa. However, this assumes that the crystal amplifier is running. In most cases, when the ring is active, software previously disabled the crystal to save power. If ring operation is being used and the system must switch to crystal operation, the crystal must first be enabled. Set the XTOFF bit to a 0. At this time, the crystal oscillation will begin. The DS87C520/DS83C520 then provides a warm-up delay to make certain that the frequency is stable. Hardware will set the XTUP bit (STATUS.4) to a 1 when the crystal is ready for use. Then software should write XT/$\overline{RG}$ to a 1 to begin operating from the crystal. Hardware prevents writing XT/$\overline{RG}$ to a 1 before XTUP = 1. The delay between XTOFF = 0 and XTUP = 1 will be 65,536 crystal clocks in addition to the crystal cycle startup time.

Switchback has no effect on the clock source. If software selects a reduced clock divider and enables the ring, a Switchback will only restore the divider speed. The ring will remain as the time base until altered by software. If there is serial activity, Switchback usually occurs with enough time to create proper baud rates. This is not true if the crystal is off and the CPU is running from the ring. If sending a serial character that wakes the system from crystaless PMM, then it should be a dummy character of no importance with a subsequent delay for crystal startup.

ENTER POWER MANAGEMENT MODE

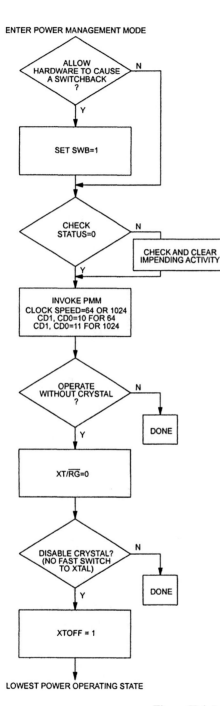

LOWEST POWER OPERATING STATE

EXITING POWER MANAGEMENT MODE

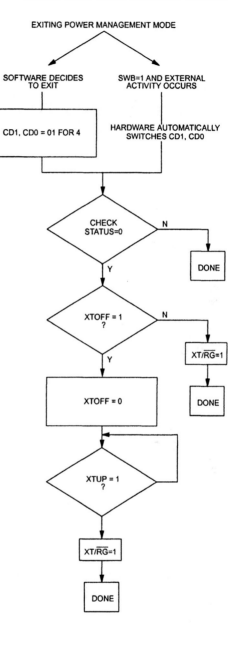

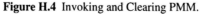

Figure H.4 Invoking and Clearing PMM.

TABLE H.8
PMM Control and Status Bit Summary

Bit Name	Location	Function	Reset	Write Access
XT/$\overline{\text{RG}}$	EXIF.3	Control. XT$\overline{\text{RG}}$ = 1, runs from crystal or external clock; XT/$\overline{\text{RG}}$ = 0, runs from internal ring oscillator.	X	0 to 1 only when XTUP = 1 and XTOFF = 0
RGMD	EXIF.2	Status. RGMD = 1, CPU clock = ring; RGMD = 0, CPU clock = crystal.	0	None
CD1, CD0	PMR.7, PMR.6	Control. CD1,0 = 01, 4 clocks; CS1,0 = 10, PMM1; CD1,0 = 11, PMM2.	0, 1	Write CD1,0 = 10 or 11 only from CD1, 0 = 01
SWB	PMR.5	Control. SWB = 1, hardware invokes switchback to 4 clocks, SWB = 0, no hardware switchback.	0	Unrestricted
XTOFF	PMR.3	Control. Disables crystal operation after ring is selected.	0	1 only when XT/$\overline{\text{RG}}$ = 0
PIP	STATUS.7	Status. 1 indicates a power-fail interrupt in service.	0	None
HIP	STATUS.6	Status. 1 indicates high priority interrupt in service.	0	None
LIP	STATUS.5	Status. 1 indicates low priority interrupt in service.	0	None
XTUP	STATUS.4	Status. 1 indicates that the crystal has stabilized.	1	None
SPTA1	STATUS.3	Status. Serial transmission on serial port 1.	0	None
SPRA1	STATUS.2	Status. Serial word reception on serial port 1.	0	None
SPTA0	STATUS.1	Status. Serial transmission on serial port 0.	0	None
SPRA0	STATUS.0	Status. Serial word reception on serial port 0.	0	None

Figure H.4 illustrates a typical decision set associated with PMM. Table H.8 is a summary of the bits relating to PMM and its operation.

H.14 IDLE MODE

Setting the lsb of the Power Control register (PCON; 87h) invokes the Idle mode. Idle will leave internal clocks, serial ports and timers running. Power consumption drops because the CPU is not active. Since clocks are running, the Idle power consumption is a function of crystal frequency. It should be approximately 1/2 of the operational power at a given frequency. The CPU can exit the Idle state with any interrupt or a reset. Idle is available for backward software comptability. The system can now reduce power consumption to below Idle levels by using PMM1 or PMM2 and running NOPs.

H.15 STOP MODE ENHANCEMENTS

Setting bit 1 of the Power Control register (PCON; 87h) invokes the Stop mode. Stop mode is the lowest power state since it turns off all internal clocking. The I_{CC} of a standard Stop mode is approximately 1 μA (but is specified in the Electrical Specifications). The CPU will exit Stop mode from an external interrupt or a reset condition. Internally generated interrupts (timer, serial port, watchdog) are not useful since they require clocking activity.

The DS87C520/DS83C520 provides two enhancements to the Stop mode. As documented below, the DS87C520/DS83C520 provides a band-gap reference to determine Power-fail Interrupt and Reset thresholds. The default state is that the band-gap reference is off while in Stop mode. This allows the extremely low power state mentioned above. A user can optionally choose to have the band-gap enabled during Stop mode. With the band-gap reference enabled, PFI and Power-fail Reset are functional and are a valid means for leaving Stop mode. This allows software to detect and compensate for a brown-out or power supply sag, even when in Stop mode. In Stop mode with the band-gap enabled, I_{CC} will be approximately 50 μA compared with 1 μA with the band-gap off. If a user does not require a Power-fail Reset or Interrupt while in Stop mode, the band-gap can remain disabled. Only the most power sensitive applications should turn off the band-gap, as this results in an uncontrolled power-down condition.

The control of the band-gap reference is located in the Extended Interrupt Flag register (EXIF; 91h). Setting BGS (EXIF.0) to a 1 will keep the band-gap reference enabled during Stop mode. The default or reset condition is with the bit at a logic 0. This results in the band-gap being off during Stop mode. Note that this bit has no control of the reference during full power, PMM, or Idle modes.

The second feature allows an additional power saving option while also making Stop easier to use. This is the ability to start instantly when exiting Stop mode. It is the internal ring oscillator that provides this feature. This ring can be a clock source when exiting Stop mode in response to an interrupt. The benefit of the ring oscillator is as follows.

Using Stop mode turns off the crystal oscillator and all internal clocks to save power. This requires that the oscillator be restarted when exiting Stop mode. Actual start-up time is crystal dependent, but is normally at least 4 ms. A common recommendation is 10 ms. In an application that will wake-up, perform a short operation, then return to sleep, the crystal start-up can be longer than the real transaction. However, the ring oscillator will start instantly. Running from the ring, the user can perform a simple operation and return to sleep before the crystal has even started. If a user selects the ring to provide the start-up clock and the processor remains running, hardware will automatically switch to the crystal once a power-on reset interval (65,536 clocks) has expired. Hardware uses this value to assure proper crystal start even though power is not being cycled.

The ring oscillator runs at approximately 2–4 MHz but will not be a precise value. Do not conduct real-time precision operations (including serial communication) during this ring period. Figure 3 shows how the operation would compare when using the ring, and when starting up normally. The default state is to exit Stop mode without using the ring oscillator.

The RGSL—Ring Select bit at EXIF.1 (EXIF; 91h) controls this function. When RGSL = 1, the CPU will use the ring oscillator to exit Stop mode quickly. As mentioned above, the processor will automatically switch from the ring to the crystal after a delay of 65,536 crystal clocks. For a 3.57 MHz crystal, this is approximately 18 ms. The processor sets a flag called RGMD-Ring Mode, located at EXIF.2, that tells software that the ring is being used. The bit will be a logic 1 when the ring is in use. Attempt no serial communication or precision timing while this bit is set, since the operating frequency is not precise.

H.16 EMI REDUCTION

The DS87C520/DS83C520 allows software to reduce EMI. One of the major contributors to radiated noise in an 8051 based system is the toggling of ALE. The DS87C520 allows software to disable ALE when not used by setting the ALE OFF (PMR.2) bit to a 1. When ALEOFF = 1, ALE will still toggle during an off-chip MOVX. However, ALE will remain in a static mode when performing on-chip memory access. The default state of ALEOFF = 0 so ALE toggles at a frequency of XTAL/4.

H.17 PERIPHERAL OVERVIEW

The DS87C520/DS83C520 provides several of the most commonly needed peripheral functions in microcomputer-based systems. These new functions include a second serial port, Power-fail Reset, Power-fail Interrupt, and a programmable Watchdog Timer. These are described below, and more details are available in the High-Speed Microcontroller User's Guide.

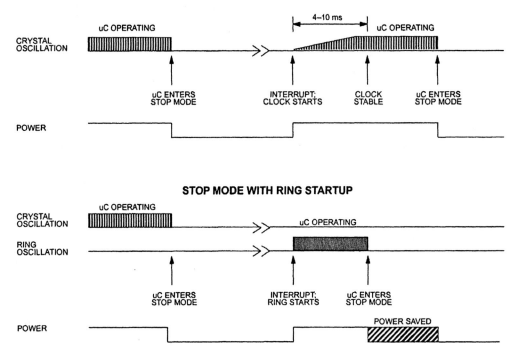

Figure H.5 Ring oscillator exit from Stop mode. *Note:* Diagram assumes that the operation following Stop requires less than 18 ms to complete.

H.18 SERIAL PORTS

The DS87C520/DS83C520 provides a serial port (UART) that is identical to the 80C52. In addition it includes a second hardware serial port that is a full duplicate of the standard one. This port optionally uses pins P1.2 (RXD1) and P1.3 (TXD1). It has duplicate control functions included in new SFR lications.

Both ports can operate simultaneously but can be at different baud rates or even in different modes. The second serial port has similar control registers (SCON1 at C0h, SBUF1 at C1h) to the original. The new serial port can only use Timer 1 for timer generated baud rates.

H.19 TIMER RATE CONTROL

There is one important difference between the DS87C520/DS83C520 and 8051 regarding timers. The original 8051 used 12 clocks per cycle for timers as well as for machine cycles. The DS87C520/DS83C520 architecture normally uses four clocks per machine cycle. However, in the area of timers and serial ports, the DS87C520/DS83C520 will default to 12 clocks per cycle on reset. This allows existing code with real-time dependencies such as baud rates to operate properly.

If an application needs higher speed timers or serial baud rates, the user can select individual timers to run at the 4 clock rate. The Clock Control register (CKCON; 8Eh) determines these timer speeds. When the relevant CKCON bit is a logic 1, the DS87C520/DS83C520 uses four clocks per cycle to generate timer speeds. When the bit is a 0, the DS87C520/DS83C520 uses 12 clocks for timer speeds. The reset condition is a 0. CKCON.5 selects the speed of Timer 2. CKCON.4 selects Timer 1 and CKCON.3 selects Timer 0. Unless a user desires very fast timing, it is unnecessary to alter these bits. Note that the timer controls are independent.

H.20 POWER-FAIL RESET

The DS87C520/DS83C520 uses a precision band-gap voltage reference to decide if V_{CC} is out of tolerance. While powering up, the internal monitor circuit maintains a reset state until V_{CC} rises above the V_{RST} level. Once above this level, the monitor enables the crystal oscillator and counts 65,536 clocks. It then exits the reset state. This power-on reset (POR) interval allows time for the oscillator to stabilize.

A system needs no external components to generate a power-related reset. Anytime V_{CC} drops below V_{RST}, as in power failure or a power drop, the monitor will generate and hold a reset. It occurs automatically, needing no action from the software. Refer to the Electrical Specifications for the exact value of V_{RST}.

H.21 POWER-FAIL INTERRUPT

The voltage reference that sets a precise reset threshold also generates an optional early warning Power-Fail Interrupt (PFI). When enabled by software, the processor will vector to program memory address 0033h if V_{CC} drops below V_{PFW}. PFI has the highest priority. The PFI enable is in the Watchdog Control SFR (WDCON-D8h). Setting WDCON.5 to a logic 1 will enable the PFI. Application software can also read the PFI flag at WDCON.4. A PFI condition sets this bit to a 1. The flag is independent of the interrupt enable and software must manually clear it.

H.22 WATCHDOG TIMER

To prevent software from losing control, the DS87C520/DS83C520 includes a programmable Watchdog Timer. The Watchdog is a free running timer that sets a flag if allowed to reach a preselected time-out. It can be (re)started by software.

A typical application is to select the flag as a reset source. When the Watchdog times out, it sets its flag which generates reset. Software must restart the timer before it reaches its time-out or the processor is reset.

Software can select one of four time-out values. Then, it restarts the timer and enables the reset function. After enabling the rest function, software must then restart the timer before its expiration or hardware will reset the CPU. Both the Watchdog Reset Enable and the Watchdog Restart control bits are protected by a "Timed Access" circuit. This prevents errant software from accidentally clearing the Watchdog. Time-out values are precise since they are a function of the crystal frequency as shown in Table H.8. For reference, the time periods at 33 MHz also are shown.

The Watchdog also provides a useful option for systems that do not require a reset circuit. It will set an interrupt flag 512 clocks before setting the reset flag. Software can optionally enable this interrupt source. The interrupt is independent of the reset. A common use of the interrupt is during debug, to show developers where the Watchdog times out. This indicates where the Watchdog must be restarted by software. The interrupt also can serve as a convenient time-base generator or can wake-up the processor from power saving modes.

The Watchdog function is controlled by the Clock Control (CKCON–8Eh), Watchdog Control (WDCON–D8h), and Extended Interrupt Enable (EIE–E8h) SFRs. CKCON.7 and CKCON.6 are WD1 and WD0 respectively and they select the Watchdog time-out period as shown in Table H.9.

As shown, the Watchdog Timer uses the crystal frequency as a time base. A user selects one of four counter values to determine the time-out. These clock counter lengths are $2^{17} = 131,072$ clocks; $2^{20} = 1,048,576$; $2^{23} = 8,388,608$ clocks; and $2^{26} = 67,108,864$ clocks. The times shown in Table H.8 above are with a 33 MHz crystal frequency. Once

TABLE H.9
Watchdog Time-Out Values

WD1	WD0	Interrupt Time-Out	Time (33MHz)	Reset Time-Out	Time (33 MHz)
0	0	2^{17} clocks	3.9718 ms	2^{17} + 512 clocks	3.9874 ms
0	1	2^{20} clocks	31.77 ms	2^{20} + 512 clocks	31.79 ms
1	0	2^{23} clocks	254.20 ms	2^{23} + 512 clocks	254.21 ms
1	1	2^{56} clocks	2033.60 ms	2^{26} + 512 clocks	2033.62 ms

the counter chain has completed a full interrupt count, hardware will set an interrupt flag. Regardless of whether the user enables this interrupt, there are then 512 clocks left until the reset flag is set. Software can enable the interrupt and reset individually. Note that the Watchdog is a free running timer and does not require an enable. There are five control bits in special function registers that affect the Watchdog Timer and two status flags that report to the user. WDIF (WDCON.3) is the interrupt flag that is set at timer termination when there are 512 clocks remaining until the reset flag is set. WTRF (WDCON.2) is the flag that is set when the timer has completely timed out. This flag is normally associated with a CPU reset and allows software to determine the reset source. EWT (WDCON.1) is the enable for the Watchdog timer reset function. RWT (WDCON.0) is the bit that software uses to restart the Watchdog Timer. Setting this bit restarts the timer for another full interval. Application software must set this bit before the time-out. Both of these bits are protected by Timed Access discussed below. As mentioned previously, WD1 and 0 (CKCON.7 and 6) select the time-out. Finally, the user can enable the Watchdog Interrupt using EWDI (EIE.4). The Special Function Register map is shown above.

H.23 INTERRUPTS

The DS87C520/DS83C520 provides 13 interrupt sources with three priority levels. The Power-fail Interrupt (PFI) has the highest priority. Software can assign high or low priority to other sources. All interrupts that are new to the 8051 family, except for the PFI, have a lower natural priority than the originals.

TABLE H.10
Interrupt Sources and Priorities

Name	Description	Vector	Natural Priority	8051/Dallas
PFI	Power-Fail Interrupt	33h	1	DALLAS
$\overline{INT0}$	External Interrupt 0	03h	2	8051
TF0	Timer 0	0Bh	3	8051
$\overline{INT1}$	External Interrupt 1	13h	4	8051
TF1	Timer 1	1Bh	5	8051
SCON0	TI0 or RI0 from serial port 0	23h	6	8051
TF2	Timer 2	2Bh	7	8051
SCON1	TI1 or RI1 from serial port 1	3Bh	8	DALLAS
INT2	External Interrupt 2	43h	9	DALLAS
$\overline{INT3}$	External Interrupt 3	4Bh	10	DALLAS
INT4	External Interrupt 4	53h	11	DALLAS
$\overline{INT5}$	External Interrupt 5	5Bh	12	DALLAS
WDT1	Watchdog Time-Out Interrupt	63h	13	DALLAS

H.24 TIMED ACCESS PROTECTION

It is useful to protect certain SFR bits from an accidental write operation. The Timed Access procedure stops an errant CPU from accidentally changing these bits. It requires that the following instructions precede a write of a protected bit.

```
MOV   0C7,#0AAH
MOV   0C7h,#55h
```

Writing an AAh then a 55h to the Timed Access register (location C7h) opens a 3 cycle window for write access. The window allows software to modify a protected bit(s). If these instructions do not immediately precede the write operation, then the write will not take effect. The protected bits are:

EXIF.0	BGS	Band-gap Select
WDCON.6	POR	Power-on Reset flag
WDCON.1	EWT	Enable Watchdog Reset
WDCON.0	RWT	Restart Watchdog
WDCON.3	WDIF	Watchdog Interrupt Flag
ROMSIZE.2	RMS2	ROM size select 2
ROMSIZE.1	RMS1	ROM size select 1
ROMSIZE.0	RMS0	ROM size select 0

H.25 EPROM PROGRAMMING

The DS87C520 follows standards for a 16KB EPROM version in the 8051 family. It is available in a UV erasable, ceramin windowed package and in plastic packages for one-time user-programmable versions. The part has unique signature information so programmers can support its specific EPROM options. ROM-specific features are described later in this data sheet.

Most commercially available device programmers will directly support Dallas Semiconductor microcontrollers. If your programmer does not, please contact the manufacturer for updated software.

H.26 PROGRAMMING PROCEDURE

The DS87C520 should run from a clock speed between 4 and 6 MHz when being programmed. The programming fixture should apply address information for each byte to the address lines and the data value to the data lines. The control signals must be manipulated as shown in Table H.11. The diagram in Figure H.5 shows the expected electrical connection for programming. Note that the programmer must apply addresses in demultiplexed fashion to Ports 1 and 2 with data on Port 0. Waveforms and timing are provided in the Electrical Specifications.

Program the DS87C520 as follows:

1. Apply the address value,
2. Apply the data value,
3. Select the programming option from Table H.10 using the control signals,
4. Increase the voltage on V_{PP} from 5V to 12.75V if writing to the EPROM,
5. Pulse the $\overline{PROG}$ signal five times for EPROM array and 25 times for encryption table, lock bits, and other EPROM bits,
6. Repeat as many times as necessary.

TABLE H.11
EPROM Programming Modes

Mode		RST	$\overline{PSEN}$	ALE/$\overline{PROG}$	EA/VPP	P2.6	P2.7	P3.3	P3.6	P3.7
Program Code Data		H	L	PL	12.75V	L	H	H	H	H
Verify Code Data		H	L	H	H	L	L	L	H	H
Program Encryption Array Address 0-3Fh		H	L	PL	12.75V	L	H	H	L	H
Program Lock Bits	LB1	H	L	PL	12.75V	H	H	H	H	H
	LB2	H	L	PL	12.75V	H	H	H	L	L
	LB3	H	L	PL	12.75V	H	L	H	H	L
Program Option Register Address FCh		H	L	PL	12.75V	L	H	H	L	L
Read Signature or Option Registers 30, 31, 60, FCh		H	L	H	H	L	L	L	L	L

*PL indicates pulse to a logic low.

H.27 SECURITY OPTIONS

The DS87C520 employs a standard three-level lock that restricts viewing of the EPROM contents. A 64-byte Encryption Array allows the authorized user to verify memory by presenting the data in encrypted form.

H.27.1 Lock Bits

The security lock consists of three lock bits. These bits select a total of four levels of security. Higher levels provide increasing security but also limit application flexibility. Table H.12 shows the security settings. Note that the programmer cannot directly read the state of the security lock. User software has access to this information as described in the Memory section.

TABLE H.12
DS87C520 EPROM Lock Bits

Level	Lock Bits			Protection
	LB1	LB2	LB3	
1	U	U	U	No program lock. Encrypted verify if encryption table was programmed.
2	P	U	U	Prevent MOVC instructions in external memory from reading program bytes in internal memory. $\overline{EA}$ is sampled and latched on reset. Allow no further programming of EPROM.
3	P	P	U	Level 2 plus no verify operation. Also, prevent MOVX instructions in external memory from reading SRAM (MOVX) in internal memory.
4	P	P	P	Level 3 plus no external execution.

H.27.2 Encryption Array

The Encryption Array allows an authorized user to verify EPROM without allowing the true memory to be dumped. During a verify, each byte is Exclusive NORed (XNOR) with a byte in the Encryption Array. This results in a true representation of the EPROM while the Encryption is unprogrammed (FFh). Once the Encryption Array is programmed in a non-FFh state, the verify value will be encrypted.

For encryption to be effective, the Encryption Array must be unknown to the party that is trying to verify memory. The entire EPROM also should be a non-FFh state or the Encryption Array can be discovered.

The Encryption Array is programmed as shown in Table H.10. Note that the programmer cannot read the array. Also note that the verify operation always uses the Encryption Array. The array has no impact while FFh. Simply programming the array to a non-FFh state will cause the encryption to function.

H.28 OTHER EPROM OPTIONS

The DS87C520 has user selectable options that must be set before beginning software execution. These options use EPROM bits rather than SFRs.

Program the EPROM selectable options as shown in Table H.10. The Option Register sets or reads these selections. The bits in the Option Control Register have the following function:

Bit 7–4   Reserved, program to a 1.

Bit 3   Watchdog POR default. Set=1; Watchdog reset function is disabled on power-up. Set = 0; Watchdog reset function is enabled automatically.

Bit 2–0   Reserved. Program to a 1.

H.29 SIGNATURE

The Signature bytes identify the product and programming revision to EPROM programmers. This information is at programming addresses 30h, 31h, and 60h.

Address	Value	Meaning
30h	DAh	Manufacturer
31h	20h	Model
60h	01h	Extension

H.30 ROM-SPECIFIC FEATURES

The DS83C520 supports a subset of the EPROM features found on the DS87C520.

H.31 SECURITY OPTIONS

H.31.1 Lock Bits

The DS83C520 employs a lock that restricts viewing of the ROM contents. When set, the lock will prevent MOVC instructions in external memory from reading program bytes in internal memory. When locked, the $\overline{EA}$ pin is sampled

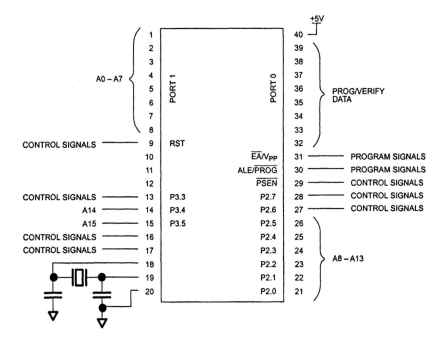

Figure-H.6 EPROM Programming Configuration

and latched on reset. The lock setting is enabled or disabled when the devices are manufactured according to customer specifications. The lock bit cannot be read in software, and its status can only be determined by observing the operation of the device.

H.31.2 Encryption Array

The DS83C520 Encryption Array allows an authorized user to verify ROM without allowing the true memory contents to be dumped. During a verify, each byte is Exclusive NORed (XNOR) with a byte in the Encryption Array. This results in a true representation of the ROM while the Encryption is unprogrammed (FFh). Once the Encryption Array is programmed in a non-FFh state, the Encryption Array is programmed (or optionally left unprogrammed) when the devices are manufactured according to customer specifications.

H.32 DS83C520 ROM VERIFICATION

The DS83C520 memory contents can be verified using a standard EPROM programmer. The memory address to be verified is placed on the pins shown in Figure H.6, and the programming control pins are set to the levels shown in Table H.11. The data at that location is then asserted on port 0.

H.33 DS83C520 SIGNATURE

The Signature bytes identify the DS83C520 to EPROM programmers. This information is at programming addresses 30h, 31h, and 60h. Most designers will find little use for the feature, and it is included only for compatibility.

Address	Value	Meaning
30h	DAh	Manufacturer
31h	21h	Model
60h	01h	Extension

H.34 ABSOLUTE MAXIMUM RATINGS*

- Voltage on Any Pin Relative to Ground   −0.3V to +7.0V
- Operating Temperature   0°C to 70°C
- Storage Temperature   −55°C to +125°C
- Soldering Temperature   260°C for 10 seconds

H.35 NOTES FOR DC ELECTRICAL CHARACTERISTICS

All parameters apply to both commercial and industrial temperature operation unless otherwise noted.

1. All voltages are referenced to ground.
2. Active current is measured with a 33 MHz clock source driving XTAL 1, v_{CC} = RST = 5.5V, all other pins disconnected.
3. Idle mode current is measured with a 33 MHz clock source driving XTAL 1, V_{CC} = 5.5V, RST at ground, all other pins disconnected.
4. Stop mode current measured with XTAL 1 and RST grounded, V_{CC} = 5.5V, all other pins disconnected. This value is not guaranteed. Users that are sensitive to this specification should contact Dallas Semiconductor for more information.
5. When addressing external memory.
6. RST = V_{CC}. This condition mimics operation of pins in I/O mode. Port 0 is tristated in reset and when at a logic high state during I/O mode.
7. During a 0 to 1 transition, a one-shot drives the ports hard for two clock cycles. This measurement reflects port in transition mode.
8. Ports 1, 2, and 3 source transition current when being pulled down externally. It reaches its maximum at approximately 2V.
9. $0.45 < V_{IN} < V_{CC}$. Not a high impedance input. This port is a weak address holding latch in Bus Mode. Peak current occurs near the input transition point of the latch, approximately 2V.
10. $0.45 < V_{IN} < V_{CC}$. RST = V_{CC}. This condition mimics operation of pins in I/O mode.

---

*This is a stress rating only and functional operation of the device at these or any other conditions above those indicated in the operation sections of this specification is not implied. Exposure to absolute maximum rating conditions for extended periods of time may affect reliability.

DC Electrical Characteristics. (0°C to 70°C; V_{CC} = 4.0V to 5.5V)

Parameter	Symbol	Min	Typ	Max	Units	Notes
Supply Voltage	V_{CC}	4.5	5.0	5.5	V	1
Power-fail Warning	V_{PFW}	4.25	4.38	4.5	V	1
Minimum Operating Voltage	V_{RST}	4.0	4.13	4.25	V	1
Supply Current Active Mode @ 33 MHz	I_{CC}		30		mA	2
Supply Current Idle Mode @ 33 MHz	I_{IDLE}		15		mA	3
Supply Current Stop Mode Band-gap Disabled	I_{STOP}		1		μA	4
Supply Current Stop Mode, Band-gap Enabled	I_{SPBG}		50		μA	4
Input Low Level	V_{IL}	−0.3		+0.8	V	1
Input High Level	V_{IH}	2.0		V_{CC}+0.3	V	1
Input High Level XTAL 1 and RST	V_{IH2}	3.5		V_{CC}+0.3	V	1
Output Low Voltage, Ports 1 and 3 @ I_{OL} = 1.6 mA	V_{OL1}		0.15	0.45	V	1
Output Low Voltage Ports 0 and 2, $\overline{ALE}$, $\overline{PSEN}$ I_{OL} = 3.2 mA	V_{OL2}		0.15	0.45	V	1
Output High Voltage Ports 1, 2, 3, ALE, $\overline{PSEN}$ @ I_{OH} = −50 μA	V_{OH1}	2.4			V	1,6
Output High Voltage Ports 1, 2, 3 @ I_{OH} = −1.5 mA	V_{OH2}	2.4			V	1,7
Output High Voltage Port 0, 2, ALE, $\overline{PSEN}$ in Bus Mode I_{OH} = −8 mA	V_{OH3}	2.4			V	1,5
Input Low Current Ports 1, 2, 3 @ 0.45V	I_{IL}			−55	μA	
Transition Current from 1 to 0 Ports 1, 2, 3 @ 2V	I_{TL}			−650	μA	8
Input Leakage Port 0, and $\overline{EA}$ pins, I/O Mode	I_L	−10		+10	μA	10
Input Leakage Port 0, Bus Mode	I_L	−300		+300	μA	9
RST Pull-down Resistance	R_{RST}	50		170	$\kappa\Omega$	

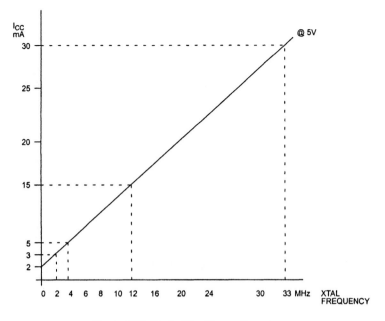

Figure H.7 Typical I_{CC} Versus Frequency.

AC Electrical Characteristics. (0°C to 70°C; V_{CC} = 4.0V to 5.5V)

Parameter	Symbol	33 MHz Min	33 MHz Max	Variable Clock Min	Variable Clock Max	Units
Oscillator Frequency	$1/t_{CLCL}$	0	33	0	33	MHz
ALE Pulse Width	t_{LHLL}	40		$1.53t_{CLCL}-5$		ns
Port 0 Address Valid to ALE Low	t_{AVLL}	10		$0.5t_{CLCL}-5$		ns
Address Hold after ALE low	t_{LLAX1}	10		$0.5t_{CLCL}-5$		ns
ALE Low to Valid Instruction In	t_{LLIV}		56		$2.5t_{CLCL}-20$	ns
ALE Low to $\overline{PSEN}$ Low	t_{LLPL}	10		$0.5t_{CLCL}-5$		ns
$\overline{PSEN}$ Pulse Width	t_{PLPH}	55		$26_{CLCL}-5$		ns
$\overline{PSEN}$ Low to Valid Instr. In	t_{PLIV}		41		$2t_{CLCL}-20$	ns
Input Instruction Hold after $\overline{PSEN}$	t_{PXIX}	0		0		ns
Input Instruction Float after $\overline{PSEN}$	t_{PXIZ}		26		$t_{CLCL}-5$	ns
Port 0 Address to Valid Instr. In	t_{AVIV}		71		$3t_{CLCL}-20$	ns
Port 2 Address to Valid Instr. In	t_{AVIV2}		81		$3.5t_{CLCL}-25$	ns
$\overline{PSEN}$ Low to Address Float	t_{PLAZ}		0		0	ns

H.36 NOTES FOR AC ELECTRICAL CHARACTERISTICS

All parameters apply to both commercial and industrial temperature range operation unless otherwise noted. All signals characterized with load capacitance of 80 pF except Port 0, ALE, $\overline{PSEN}$, $\overline{RD}$ and $\overline{WR}$ with 100 pF. Interfacing to memory devices with float times (turn off times) over 25 ns may cause contention. This will not damage the parts, but will cause an increase in operating current.

MOVX Characteristics. (0°C to 70°C; V_{CC} = 4.0V to 5.5V)

Parameter	Symbol	Variable Clock Min	Variable Clock Max	Units	Stretch
Data Access ALE Pulse Width	t_{LHLL2}	$1.5t_{CLCL} -5$		ns	$t_{MCS} = 0$
		$2t_{CLCL} -5$			$t_{MCS} > 0$
Address Hold after ALE Low for MOVX Write	t_{LLAX2}	$0.5t_{CLCL} -5$		ns	$t_{MCS} = 0$
		$t_{CLCL} -5$			$t_{MCS} > 0$
$\overline{RD}$ Pulse Width	t_{RLRH}	$2t_{CLCL} -5$		ns	$t_{MCS} = 0$
		$t_{MCS} -10$			$t_{MCS} > 0$
$\overline{WR}$ Pulse Width	t_{WLWH}	$2t_{CLCL} -5$		ns	$t_{MCS} = 0$
		$t_{MCS} -10$			$t_{MCS} > 0$
$\overline{RD}$ Low to Valid Data In	t_{RLDV}		$2t_{CLCL} -20$	ns	$t_{MCS} = 0$
			$t_{MCS} -20$		$t_{MCS} > 0$
Data Hold after Read	t_{RHDX}	0		ns	
Data Float after Read	t_{RHDZ}		$t_{CLCL} -5$	ns	$t_{MCS} = 0$
			$2t_{CLCL} -5$		$t_{MCS} > 0$
ALE Low to Valid Data In	t_{LLDV}		$2.5t_{CLCL} -20$	ns	$t_{MCS} = 0$
			$t_{MCS} + t_{CLCL} -40$		$t_{MCS} > 0$
Port 0 Address to Valid Data In	t_{AVDV1}		$3t_{CLCL} -20$	ns	$t_{MCS} = 0$
			$t_{MCS} + 1.5t_{CLCL} -20$		$t_{MCS} > 0$
Port 2 Address to Valid Data In	t_{AVDV2}		$3.5t_{CLCL} -20$	ns	$t_{MCS} = 0$
			$t_{MCS} + 2t_{CLCL} -20$		$t_{MCS} > 0$
ALE Low to $\overline{RD}$ or $\overline{WR}$ Low	t_{LLWL}	$0.5t_{CLCL} -5$	$0.5t_{CLCL} +5$	ns	$t_{MCS} = 0$
		$t_{CLCL} -5$	$t_{CLCL} +5$		$t_{MCS} > 0$
Port 0 Address to $\overline{RD}$ or $\overline{WR}$ Low	t_{AVWL1}	$t_{CLCL} -5$		ns	$t_{MCS} = 0$
		$2t_{CLCL} -5$			$t_{MCS} > 0$
Port 2 Address to $\overline{RD}$ or $\overline{WR}$ Low	t_{AVWL2}	$1.5t_{CLCL} -10$		ns	$t_{MCS} = 0$
		$2.5t_{CLCL} -10$		ns	$t_{MCS} > 0$
Data Valid to $\overline{WR}$ Transition	t_{QVWX}	-5		ns	
Data Hold after Write	t_{WHQX}	$t_{CLCL} -5$		ns	$t_{MCS} = 0$
		$2t_{CLCL} -5$			$t_{MCS} > 0$
$\overline{RD}$ Low to Address Float	t_{RLAZ}		$0.5t_{CLCL} -5$	ns	
$\overline{RD}$ or $\overline{WR}$ High to ALE High	t_{WHLH}	0	10	ns	$t_{MCS} = 0$
		$t_{CLCL} -5$	$t_{CLCL} +5$		$t_{MCS} > 0$

NOTE: t_{MCS} is a time period related to the Stretch memory cycle selection. The following table shows the value of t_{MCS} for each Stretch selection

M2	M1	M0	MOVX Cycles	t_{MCS}
0	0	0	2 machine cycles	0
0	0	1	3 machine cycles (default)	$4\,t_{CLCL}$
0	1	0	4 machine cycles	$8\,t_{CLCL}$
0	1	1	5 machine cycles	$12\,t_{CLCL}$
1	0	0	6 machine cycles	$16\,t_{CLCL}$
1	0	1	7 machine cycles	$20\,t_{CLCL}$
1	1	0	8 machine cycles	$24\,t_{CLCL}$
1	1	1	9 machine cycles	$28\,t_{CLCL}$

External Clock Characteristics. (0°C to 70°C; V$_{CC}$ = 4.0V to 5.5V)

Parameter	Symbol	Min	Typ	Max	Units	Notes
Clock High Time	t$_{CHCX}$	10			ns	
Clock Low Time	t$_{CLCX}$	10			ns	
Clock Rise Time	t$_{CLCH}$			5	ns	
Clock Fall Time	t$_{CHCL}$			5	ns	

Serial Port Mode 0 Timing Characteristics. (0°C to 70°C; V$_{CC}$ = 4.0V to 5.5V)

Parameter	Symbol	Min	Typ	Max	Units	Notes
Serial Port Clock Cycle time	t$_{XLXL}$					
SM2 = 0, 12 clocks per cycle			12t$_{CLCL}$		ns	
SM2 = 1, 4 clocks per cycle			4t$_{CLCL}$		ns	
Output Data Setup to Clock Rising	t$_{QVXH}$					
SM2 = 0, 12 clocks per cycle			10t$_{CLCL}$		ns	
SM2 = 1, 4 clocks per cycle			3t$_{CLCL}$		ns	
Output Data Hold from Clock Rising	t$_{XHQX}$					
SM2 = 0, 12 clocks per cycle			2t$_{CLCL}$		ns	
SM2 = 1, 4 clocks per cycle			t$_{CLCL}$		ns	
Input Data Hold after Clock Rising	t$_{XHDX}$					
SM2 = 0, 12 clocks per cycle			t$_{CLCL}$		ns	
SM2 = 1, 4 clocks per cycle			t$_{CLCL}$		ns	
Clock Rising Edge to Input Data Valid	t$_{XHDV}$					
SM2 = 0, 12 clocks per cycle			11t$_{CLCL}$		ns	
SM2 = 1, 4 clocks per cycle			3t$_{CLCL}$		ns	

H.37 EXPLANATION OF AC SYMBOLS

In an effort to remain compatible with the original 8051 family, this device specifies the same parameters as such devices, using the same symbols. For completeness, the following is an explanation of the symbols.

t Time
A Address
C Clock
D Input data
H Logic level high
L Logic level low
I Instruction
P $\overline{PSEN}$
Q Output data
R $\overline{RD}$ signal
V Valid
W $\overline{WR}$ signal
X No longer a valid logic level
Z Tristate

Power Cycle Timing Characteristics. (0°C to 70°C; V_{CC} = 4.0V to 5.5V)

Parameter	Symbol	Min	Typ	Max	Units	Notes
Cycle Start-up Time	t_{CSU}		1.8		ms	1
Power-on Reset Delay	t_{POR}			65,536	t_{CLCL}	2

H.38 NOTES FOR POWER CYCLE TIMING CHARACTERISTICS

1. Start-up time for crystals varies with load capacitance and manufacturer. Time shown is for an 11.0592 MHz crystal manufactured by Fox.
2. Reset delay is a synchronous counter of crystal oscillations after crystal start-up. At 33 MHz, this time is 1.99 ms.

EPROM Programming and Verification. (21°C to 27°C; V_{CC} = 4.5V to 5.5V)

Parameter	Symbol	Min	Typ	Max	Units	Notes
Programming Voltage	V_{PP}	12.5		13.0	V	1
Programming Supply Current	I_{PP}			50	mA	
Oscillator Frequency	$1/t_{CLCL}$	4		6	MHz	
Address Setup to $\overline{PROG}$ Low	t_{AVGL}	$48t_{CLCL}$				
Address Hold after $\overline{PROG}$	t_{GHAX}	$48t_{CLCL}$				
Data Setup to $\overline{PROG}$ Low	t_{DVGL}	$48t_{CLCL}$				
Data Hold after $\overline{PROG}$	t_{GHDX}	$48t_{CLCL}$				
Enable High to V_{PP}	t_{EHSH}	$48t_{CLCL}$				
V_{PP} Setup to $\overline{PROG}$ Low	t_{SHGL}	10			μs	
V_{PP} Hold after $\overline{PROG}$	t_{GHSL}	10			μs	
$\overline{PROG}$ Width	t_{GLGH}	90		110	μs	
Address to Data Valid	t_{AVQV}			$48t_{CLCL}$		
Enable Low to Data Valid	t_{ELQV}			$48t_{CLCL}$		
Data Float after Enable	t_{EHQZ}	0		$48t_{CLCL}$		
$\overline{PROG}$ High to $\overline{PROG}$ Low	t_{GHGL}	10			μs	

NOTE: 1. All voltages are referenced to ground.

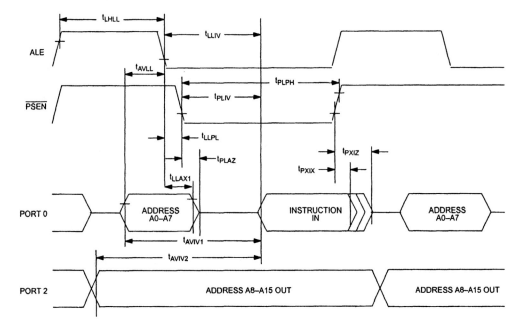

Figure H.8 External Program Memory Read Cycle

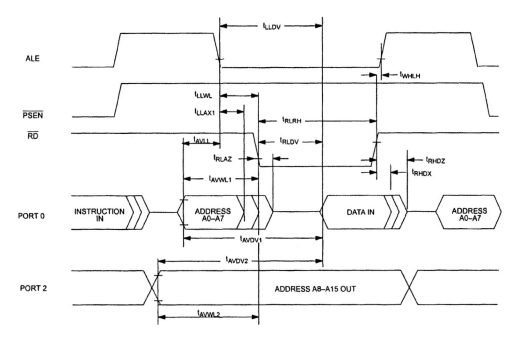

Figure H.9 External Data Memory Read Cycle

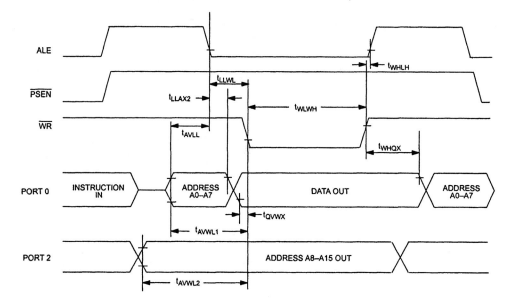

Figure H.10 External Data Memory Write Cycle

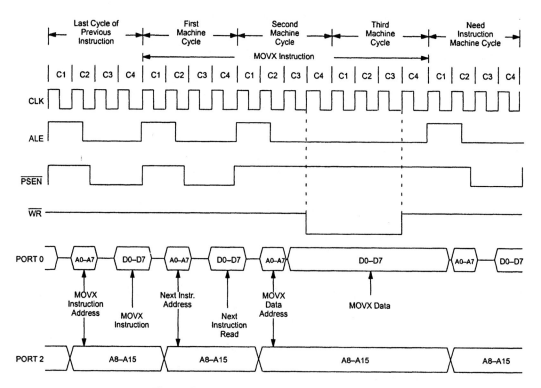

Figure H.11 Data Memory Write with Stretch = 1

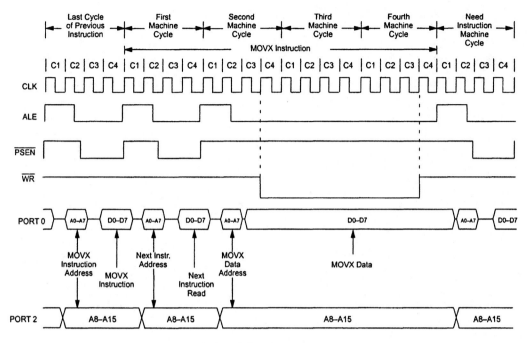

FOUR CYCLE DATA MEMORY WRITE
STRETCH VALUE=2

Figure H.12 Data Memory Write with Stretch = 2

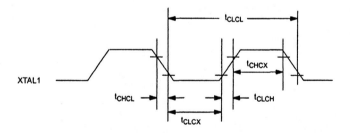

Figure H.13 External Clock Drive

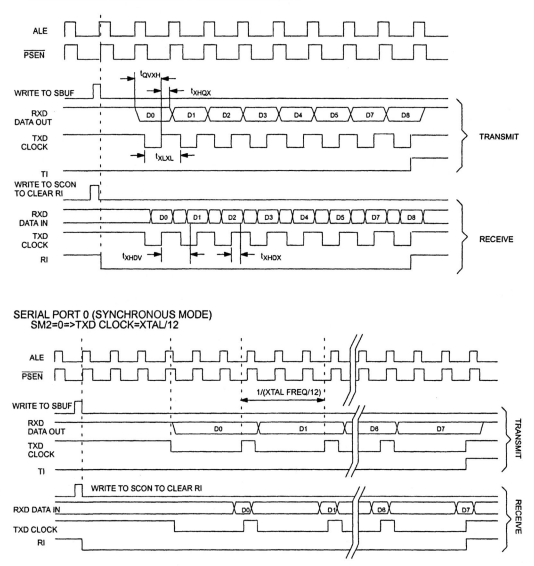

Figure H.14 Serial Port Mode 0 Timing

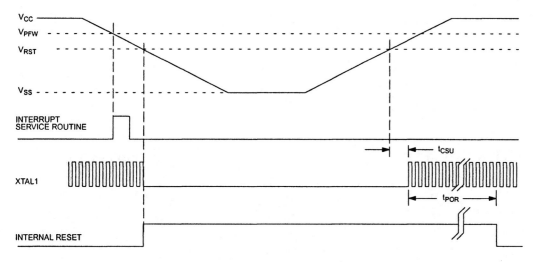

Figure H.15 Power Cycle Timing

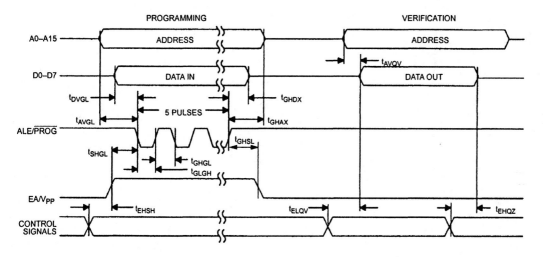

Figure H.16 EPROM Programming and Verification Waveforms

40–PIN PDIP (600 MIL)

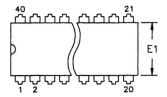

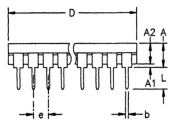

DIMENSIONS ARE IN INCHES.

PKG	40-PIN	
DIM	MIN	MAX
A	–	0.200
A1	0.015	–
A2	0.140	0.160
b	0.014	0.022
c	0.008	0.012
D	1.980	2.085
E	0.600	0.625
E1	0.530	0.555
e	0.090	0.110
L	0.115	0.145
eB	0.600	0.700

56–G5000–000

Figure H.17 40-Pin PDIP (600 MIL)

40–PIN CER DIP

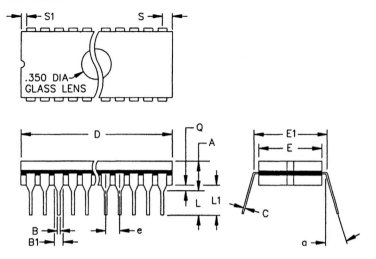

DIMENSIONS ARE IN INCHES.

PKG	40-PIN	
DIM	MIN	MAX
A	–	0.225
B	0.014	0.023
B1	0.038	0.065
C	0.006	0.015
D	-	2.096
E	0.510	0.620
E1	0.590	0.630
e	100 BSC	
L	0.125	0.200
L1	0.150	–
Q	0.020	0.060
S	–	0.098
S1	0.005	–
a	0°	15°

56–G4008–001

Figure H.18 40-Pin CER DIP

44–PIN PLCC

NOTE:
⚠ PIN−1 IDENTIFIER TO BE LOCATED IN ZONE INDICATED.
2. CONTROLLING DIMENSIONS ARE IN INCHS

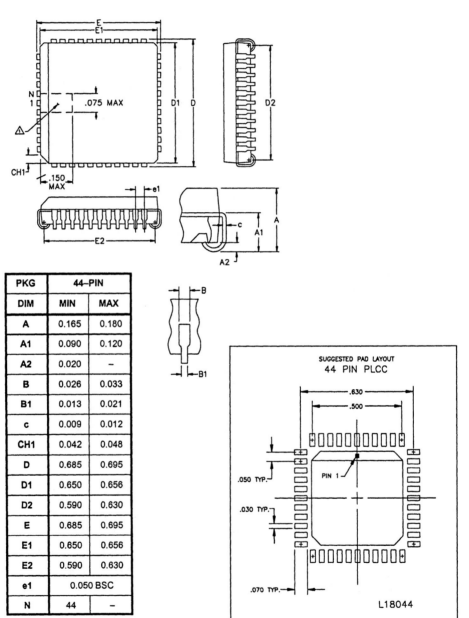

PKG	44–PIN	
DIM	MIN	MAX
A	0.165	0.180
A1	0.090	0.120
A2	0.020	–
B	0.026	0.033
B1	0.013	0.021
c	0.009	0.012
CH1	0.042	0.048
D	0.685	0.695
D1	0.650	0.656
D2	0.590	0.630
E	0.685	0.695
E1	0.650	0.656
E2	0.590	0.630
e1	0.050 BSC	
N	44	–

56–G4003–001

Figure H.19 44-Pin PLCC

44–PIN TQFP

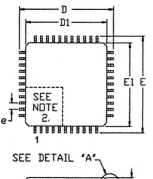

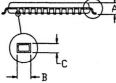

SEE DETAIL 'A'

NOTES:

1. DIMENSIONS D1 AND E1 INCLUDE MOLD MISMATCH, BUT DO NOT INCLUDE MOLD PROTRUSION; ALLOWABLE PROTRUSION IS 0.25 MM PER SIDE.
2. DETAILS OF PIN 1 IDENTIFIER ARE OPTIONAL BUT MUST BE LOCATED WITHIN THE ZONE INDICATED.
3. ALLOWABLE DAMBAR PROTRUSION IS 0.08 MM TOTAL IN EXCESS OF THE B DIMENSION; AT MAXIMUM MATERIAL CONDITION. PROTRUSION NOT TO BE LOCATED ON LOWER RADIUS OR FOOT OF LEAD.
4. CONTROLLING DIMENSIONS: MILLIMETERS.

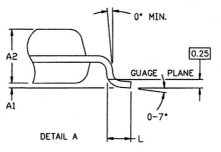

PKG	44–PIN	
DIM	MIN	MAX
A	–	1.20
A1	0.05	0.15
A2	0.95	1.05
D	11.80	12.20
D1	10.00 BSC	
E	11.80	12.20
E1	10.00 BSC	
L	0.45	0.75
e	0.80 BSC	
B	0.30	0.45
C	0.09	0.20

56–G4012–001

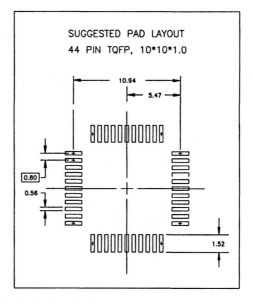

Figure H.20 44-Pin TQFP

H.39 DATA SHEET REVISION SUMMARY

The following represent the key differences between 11/01/95 and 02/20/97 version of the CD87C520 data sheet. Please review this summary carefully.

1. Update ALE pin description.
2. Add note pertaining to erasure window.
3. Add note pertaining to internal MOVX SRAM.
4. Change not 10 from RST = 5.5V to RST = V_{CC}.
5. Change serial port mode 0 timing diagram label from t_{QVXL} to t_{QVXH}.

GLOSSARY

Absolute addressing   An addressing mode, used with ACALL and AJMP, that specifies the lowest 11-bit address of the destination instruction.

Accumulator   A register in a computer that contains an operand to be used in an arithmetic operation.

Active bus   A bus that has a pull-up device.

A/D converter   A circuit that can convert an analog voltage into a digital value.

A/D input mode   The method that the 8XC51GB selects to convert analog input voltage into digital value. Two methods are available: scan mode and select mode.

A/D trigger mode   The method that the 8XC51GB uses to start the A/D conversion. Two methods are available: external trigger and internal trigger mode.

Address access time   The amount of time it takes for a memory component to send out valid data to the external data pins after address signals have been applied (assuming that all other control signals have been asserted).

Addressing   The application of a unique combination of high and low logic levels to select a corresponding unique memory location.

Array   An ordered set of elements of the same type. The elements of the array are arranged so that there are a zeroth, first, second, third, and so forth. Array may be one, two, or multidimensional.

Arithmetic logic unit (ALU)   The part of the processor in which all arithmetic and logic operations are performed.

Assembler A   Program that converts a program in assembly language into machine instructions so that it can be executed in a computer.

Assembler directive   A command to the assembler for defining data and symbols, setting assembler and linking conditions, and specifying output format. Assembler directives do not produce machine code.

Assembly instruction   A mnemonic representation of a machine instruction.

Binary-coded decimal (BCD)   A coding method that uses four binary digits to represent a decimal digit. The binary codes 0000_2–1001_2 correspond to decimal digits 0–9.

Bit inherent   An addressing method, specifying only the carry flag, that does not need an extra byte to specify the bit operand.

Bus   A set of conducting wires or signal lines through which the processor of a computer communicates with memory and I/O devices.

Bus cycle timing diagram   A diagram that describes the transitions of all the involved signals during a read or write operation.

Bus transaction   The activities that transfer data over a bus.

Capture mode   An operation mode available in Timer 2 and PCA modules that will load the timer value into a register when the signal edge arrives. Timer 2 can capture only the falling edge. The PCA modules can capture both rising and falling edges.

Central processing unit (CPU)   The combination of registers, ALU, and the control unit.

Centronics printer interface   A widely adopted printer interface protocol that uses pulse mode handshake protocol to achieve synchronization of data transfer.

Chip enable signal   A signal that can be driven to allow and disallow data to be read from or written into the I/O interface chip or memory components.

Column major order   A method that stores matrix elements in memory column by column.

Comment field   An optional field in an assembly program line, added for documentation purpose. The comment field starts with the seimcolon ";" and is ignored by the assembler.

Computer   A computer consists of hardware and software. The hardware consists of four major parts: the central processing unit, the memory unit, the input unit, and the output unit. Software is a sequence of instructions that controls the operations of the hardware.

Contact bounce   A problem that occurs in mechanical-type key switches when the switch contacts do not come to rest immediately after the key is pressed.

Control unit   The part of the processor that decodes and monitors the execution of instructions. It arbitrates the use of the computer resources and makes sure that all computer operations are performed in proper order.

Cross assembler   An assembler that runs on one computer but generates machine instructions that will be executed by another computer that has a different instruction set.

Data communication equipment (DCE)   Usually refers to equipment such as a modem, concentrator, or router.

Data hold time   The length of time over which the data must remain stable after the edge of the control signal that latches the data is asserted.

Data setup time   The amount of time over which the data must remain stable before the edge of the control signal that latches the data is asserted.

Data terminal equipment (DTE)   Usually refers to a computer or a terminal.

Debounce   The process of minimizing the effect of key bounce so that the processor can read the correct data.

Direct addressing   A byte appended to the opcode byte that is used to select either an internal register or an internal RAM byte as an operand.

Dynamic memories   Memory devices that require periodic refreshing of the stored information, even when power is on.

Electrical braking   An operation performed to stop a DC motor aburptly. Electrical braking is done by reversing the voltage applied to the motor.

Electrically erasable programmable read-only memory (EEPROM)   A type of read-only memory that can be erased and reprogrammed by electrical signals. EEPROM allows each individual location inside the chip to be erased and reprogrammed.

Electronic Industry Association   (EIA)

Erasable programmable read-only memory (EPROM)   A type of read-only memory that can be erased by subjecting it to strong ultraviolet light. It can be reprogrammed by using an EPROM programmer. A quartz window on top of the EPROM allows light to be shone directly on the silicon chip inside.

Event   An event can be anything: pieces on an assembly line, cycles of an incoming signal, or units of time. An event is often represented by the rising or falling edge of a signal.

Exception   A software interrupt, such as an illegal opcode, an overflow, division by zero, or an underflow.

Fall time   The amount of time a digital signal takes to go from logic high to logic low.

Flash memory   A type of read-only memory that can be programmed and erased electrically. However, it does not allow individual locations to be erased—the user can erase only the whole chip.

Floating signal   An undriven signal.

Flowchart   A diagram that shows the structure and logic flow of a program.

Framing error   A data communication error in which a received character is not properly framed by the start and stop bits.

Full-duplex link   A four-wire communication link that allows both transmission and receptioin to proceed simultaneously.

Global memory   The memory that is available for all programs in a computer system.

Half-duplex link   A communication link that can be used for either transmission or reception, but only in one direction at a time.

Hall Effect   The phenomenon in which the motion of the magnetic lines of a permanent magnet perpendicular to a crystal induces a voltage between the two faces of the crystal.

This effect has been utilized to construct key switches, detecting the motion of objects, and so on.

Handshake   A method of synchronizing data transfer between the interface chip and the I/O device. Two handshake signals are required—one handshake signal is asserted by the interface chip and the other is asserted by the I/O device. The interface chip initiates the handshake cycle by asserting one of the handshake signals to indicate that it wants more data during an input operation or that it has data on the data pins during an output operation. The input device places data on the data pins and asserts the other handshake signal to indicate the availability of data. The output device asserts the second handshake signal to indicate that it has accepted the data. Both handshake signals are then deasserted one after the other according to the predefined order.

High-speed output   A function provided in the PCA, which compares the PCA timer to the preloaded value in a module's compare register in every machine cycle. When they are equal, it will toggle the level of the associated pin. This function is often used to generate digital waveforms.

Idle   A continuous logic high on the RxD line for one complete character time.

Idle mode   A power-saving mode in which the MCS-51/52 CPU stops executing instruction while retaining the values of special function registers and on-chip RAM.

Illegal opcode   A binary bit pattern of the opcode byte for which an operation is not defined.

Immediate   An addressing method in which the byte or two bytes following the opcode of an MCS-51 instruction is used as the operand of the instruction.

Indexed addressing   An addressing method that uses a base register (either PC or DPTR) and an offset (in A) in forming the memory address for a JMP or MOVC instruction.

Indirect addressing   An addressing method that uses a register to hold the actual address that will be used in data movement.

Inter-Integrated Circuits (I^2C)   A serial data transfer protocol proposed by Philips.

Interrupt   An unusual event that requires the CPU to stop normal program execution and perform some service to the unusual event.

Interrupt-driven I/O method   A method of synchronizing data transfer between the microprocessor and the interface chip. The interface chip interrupts the microprocessor when it is ready. The microprocessor reads data from or writes data into the interface chip in the interrupt service routine.

Interrupt priority   The order in which the CPU will service interrupts when all of them occur at the same time.

Interrupt service   The service provided to a pending interrupt by CPU execution of a program called a service routine.

Interrupt vector   The starting address of an interrupt service routine.

Interrupt vector table   A table that stores all interrupt vectors.

Isolated I/O   An I/O method in which the microprocessor has separate instructions for performing I/O operations and has separate memory space for I/O devices.

Keyboard scanning   A process for detecting which key is pressed in a keyboard device. The key switches of a keyboard are organized into rows and columns. Keyboard scanning proceeds row by row and column by column.

Label field   The first field in an assembly program line; it is used by the programmer to identify memory locations in the program or data areas of the assembly module.

Light-emitting diode (LED)   A diode that emits light when it is forward biased and there is enough current flowing through it.

Liquid crystal display (LCD)   A display in which liquid crystals are organized into segments or pixels (for color). Light can pass through a segment or a pixel when it is activated and aligned.

Load cell   A transducer that can convert a weight into a voltage.

Long addressing   An addressing method, used only with LCALL and LJMP, that specifies a 16-bit address for the destination instruction.

Machine cycle   A term that is used to refer to the execution time of MCS-51 instructions and is equal to 12 oscillator periods.

Machine instruction   A set of binary digits, which tells the computer what operation to perform.

Mark   A term used to indicate a binary 1.

Maskable interrupts   Interrupts that can be ignored by the CPU. This type of interrupts can be disabled by setting a mask bit or by clearing an enable bit.

Masked ROM (MROM)   A type of ROM that is programmed when it is fabricated.

Matrix   A two-dimensional data structure that is organized into rows and columns. The elements of a matrix are of the same length and are access by using their row and column numbers (i, j) where i is the row number and j is the column number.

Memory   Storage for software and information.

Memory capacity   The total amount of information that a memory device can store; also called memory density.

Memory-mapped I/O   An I/O method in which the same instruction set is used to perform I/O operations and memory references. I/O registers and memory components occupy the same memory space.

Memory organization   A description of the number of bits that can be read from or written into a memory chip during a read or write operation.

Memory space   The range of addresses and size of a type of memory that the CPU can access.

Microcontroller   A computer system implemented on a single, very large-scale integrated circuit. A microcontroller contains everything in a microprocessor and may contain memories, an I/O device interface, a timer circuit, an A/D converter, etc.

Microprocessor   A CPU packaged in a single integrated circuit.

Modem   A device that can accept digital bits and change them into a form suitable for analog transmission (modulation) and can also receive a modulated signal and transform it back to its original representation (demodulation).

Multidrop   A data communication scheme in which more than two stations share the same data link. One station is designated as the master and the other stations are designated as slaves. Each station has its own unique address, with the primary station controlling all data transfers over the link.

Multiprecision arithmetic   Arithmetic performed on numbers that are larger than the word length of a computer.

Multitasking   A computer technique in which CPU time is divided into slots that are usually 10 to 20 ms in length. When multiple programs are resident in the main memory waiting for execution, the operating system assigns a program to be executed to one time slot. At the end of a time slot or when a program is waiting for completion of I/O, the operating system takes over and assigns another program to be executed.

Native assembler   An assembler that runs on one machine and generates machine instructions to be executed on either the same machine or a different machine having the same instruction set.

Negative edge   Falling edge of a signal.

Nibble   A group fo 4-bit information.

Nonmaskable interrupts   Interrupts that the CPU cannot ignore.

Nonvolatile memory   Memory that retains stored information even when power to the memory is removed.

Null modem   A circuit connection between two DTEs in which the leads are interconnected in such a way as to fool both DTEs into thinking that they are connected to modems. A null modem is used only for short-distance interconnections.

Object code   The sequence of machine instructions resulting from the process of assembling and/or compiling a source program.

Operand field   The third field in an assembly program line; if an operand field is present, it follows the operation field and is separated from the operation field by at least one space.

Operation field   The second field in an assembly program line; it contains the mnemonic names for machine instructions and assembler directives.

Parameter passing   The process and mechanism of sending parameters from a caller to a subroutine, where they are used in computations; parameters can be sent to a subroutine using CPU registers, the stack, or global memory.

Parity error   An error in which an odd number of bits change value; it can be detected by a parity checking circuit.

Passive bus   A bus that does not have a pull-up device.

Peripheral devices   Pieces of equipment that exchange data with a computer.

Photocell   A device that can convert a light intensity into a voltage.

Physical time   A time represented by the counter of a timer.

Point-to-point   A data communication scheme in which two stations communicate as peers.

Polling   A method of synchronizing data transfer between a microprocessor and an interface chip. The microprocessor keeps reading the interface chip status register until it is sure that the interface chip has valid data or is ready to receive more data and then it proceeds with the I/O operation.

Pop   The operation that removes the top element from a stack.

Positive edge   The rising edge of a signal.

Power-down mode   A power-saving mode in which the MCS-51/52 stops the oscillator while retaining the values of special function registers and on-chip RAM.

Power-saving mode   An operation mode in which less power is consumed. In CHMOS technology, the low-power mode is implemented by either slowing down the clock frequency or turning off some circuit modules within a chip.

Program   A set of instructions that the computer hardware executes to perform some sequence of operations.

Program counter (PC)   A register that keeps track of the address of the next instruction to be executed.

Program loop   A sequence of instructions that will be executed repeatedly for a finite or infinite number of times.

Program status word (PSW)   The register in the MCS-51 CPU that keeps track of program execution status and controls the program execution.

Programmable read-only memory (PROM)   A type of ROM that allows the end user to program it once and only once using a device called a PROM programmer.

Pulse width modulation   A function provided in the PCA, which may vary the duty cycle of a digital signal based on the comparison result of the low byte (CAPnL) of the compare registers and the low byte of the PCA timer (CL).

Push   The operation that adds a new element to the top of the stack.

Random access memory (RAM)   A type of memory that allows read and write access to every location inside the memory chip. Furthermore, read and write accesses take the same amount of time for any location inside the chip.

Read-only memory (ROM)   A type of memory that is nonvolatile in the sense that when power is removed from ROM and then reapplied, the original data are still there. ROM data can be read—not written only during normal computer operation.

Receiver overrun   A data communication error in which a character or a number of characters were received but not read from buffer before the following characters were received.

Refresh   An operation performed on dynamic memories to retain the stored information during normal operation.

Refresh period   The time interval within which each location of a DRAM chip must be refreshed at least once to retain its stored information.

Register   A storage location in the CPU that is used to hold data and/or a memory address during the execution of an instruction.

Register inherent   An addressing mode in which the register operand is specified directly by the opcode byte.

Relative addressing mode   An addressing mode, used only with certain jump instruction, that specifies the distance of jump.

Reset   A signal or operation that sets the flip-flops and registers of a chip or microprocessor to some predefined values or states so that the circuit or microprocessor can start from a known state.

Return address   The address of the instruction that immediately follows the subroutine call instruction (either ACALL or LCALL).

Row major order   A method that stores the matrix elements in memory row by row.

Rise time   The amount of time a digital signal takes to go from logic low to logic high.

Serial expansion port (SEP)   A serial port available in Intel 8XC51GB series microcontrollers. The SEP uses two wires for data transfer.

Serial memory   A kind of memory that uses serial format to exchange data with processors.

Serial peripheral interface (SPI)   A serial data transfer protocol proposed by Motorola. SPI is available in most 8-bit microcontrollers manufactured by Motorola. SPI uses four pins for data transfer.

Simplex link   A line dedicated to either transmission or reception, but not both.

Single-step operation   An instruction execution mode in which the CPU is interrupted after the execution of one instruction of the user program. This operation mode is often used to perform program debugging.

Software timer   A function provided in the PCA, which compares the PCA timer to the preloaded value in a module's compare register in every machine cycle. When they are equal, a flag will be set and an interrupt can optionally be generated.

Source code   A program written in either assembly language or high-level language; also called a source program.

Space   A data communication term used to indicate a binary 0.

Stack   A last-in–first-out data structure whose elements can be accessed only from one end. A stack structure has a top and a bottom. A new item can be added only to the top, and the stack elements can be removed only from the top.

Stack pointer   An MCS-51 register that points to the top byte of the stack memory.

Static memories   Memory devices that do not require periodic refreshing to retain the stored information as long as power is applied.

String   A sequence of characters.

Strobe method   A method of synchronizing data transfer between the interface chip and the I/O device. During input, the input device asserts a strobe signal to latch data into the interface chip data register. During output, the interface chip asserts a strobe signal to latch data into the output device.

Subroutine call   The process of invoking a subroutine to perform the desired operations. The MCS-51/52 has ACALL and LCALL instructions for making subroutine calls.

Successive approximation method   An A/D conversion method that starts from the most significant bit to the least significant bit and does the following for each bit:

- guesses the bit to be a 1
- converts the value of the successive approximation register to an analog voltage
- compares the converted analog voltage with the input voltage
- clears the bit to 0 if the converted analog voltage is larger (which indicates that the guess is wrong)

Thermocouple   A transducer that can convert a high temperature into a voltage.

Transducer   A device that can convert a nonelectric quantity into a voltage.

Transpose   An operation that converts the rows of a matrix into columns and vice versa.

Trap   A software interrupt; an exception.

Volatile memory   Semiconductor memory that loses its stored information when power is removed.

Watchdog timer   A circuit that automatically invokes a reset unless the system being watched sends regular hold-off signals to the watchdog. This function is useful in detecting software bugs.

Word   Two bytes or 16 bits of informatin (Intel definition). Some other companies define 32 bits (or four bytes) as a word.

REFERENCES

1. Kenneth J. Ayala, *The 8051 Microcontroller—Architecture, Programming, & Applications,* 2nd ed. Minneapolis, MN: West Publishing, 1997.

2. Richard H. Barnett, *The 8051 Family of Microcontrollers.* Englewood Cliffs, NJ: Prentice Hall, 1997.

3. Dallas Semiconductor, *High-Speed Microcontroller Data Book.* Dallas, TX: Dallas Semiconductor, 1995.

4. Joseph Di Giacomo, *Digital Bus,* New York, NY: McGraw-Hill, 1990.

5. Han-Way Huang, *MC68HC11—An Introduction.* Minneapolis, MN: West Publishing, 1996.

6. Intel, *MCS 51 Microcontroller Family User's Manual.* Santa Clara, CA: Intel, 1994.

7. Scott Mackenze, *The 8051 Microcontroller.* New York: Merrill, 1992

8. Tom Schultz, *C and the 8051,* 2nd ed. Englewood Cliffs, NJ: Prentice Hall, 1998.

9. Yeraland and Aluwalia, *Programming and Interfacing the 8051 Microcontroller.* Reading, MA: Addison Wesley, 1995.

INDEX